Frommer's®
Montréal &
Québec City
22nd Edition

by Patricia Gajo

WILEY

John Wiley & Sons, Inc.

Published by:
JOHN WILEY & SONS, INC.
111 River St.
Hoboken, NJ 07030-5774

ISBN 978-1-118-10024-0 (paper); 978-1-118-10145-2 (ebk); 978-1-118-10144-5 (ebk); 978-1-118-10146-9 (ebk)

Editor: Gene Shannon
Production Editor: Heather Wilcox
Cartographer: Nick Trotter
Photo Editors: Richard Fox, Cherie Cincilla
Cover Photo Editor: Richard Fox
Design by Vertigo Design
Layout, Graphics & Prepress by Wiley Indianapolis Composition Services

Front cover photo: Restaurant in an old stone building along Rue Saint Paul in Old Montréal, Montréal, Québec, Canada ©Rolf Hicker / All Canada Photos / AGE Fotostock, Inc.
Back cover photo: Snow sculptures at Winter Carnival, Québec City, Canada ©Vespasian / Alamy Images

For information on our other products and services or to obtain technical support, please contact our Customer Care Department within the U.S. at 877/762-2974, outside the U.S. at 317/572-3993 or fax 317/572-4002.

Wiley also publishes its books in a variety of electronic formats. Some content that appears in print may not be available in electronic formats.

Manufactured in China

5 4 3 2 1

CONTENTS

LIST OF MAPS

ABOUT THE AUTHOR

Patricia Gajo is a freelance writer and editor based in Montreal. In addition to this guide, she is also a co-author of *Frommer's Far & Wide*. Her website is www.patriciagajo.com.

ACKNOWLEDGMENTS

This book would not have been possible without Ashley Joseph, Roseanne Lau, Dylan Doyle, Noémie C. Adrien, Lea Monaco, Émilie Guay, Richard Séguin from Québec City Tourism, and my editor, Gene Shannon. A special thank-you to Francine and Guy Côté, Julieta and Jose Leon Gajo, and Miguel Gajo-Côté.

I must also express my gratitude to the previous authors of this book who laid down the framework: Leslie Brokaw, Erin Trahan, and Herbert Bailey Livesey.

Above all, I would like to say *merci beaucoup* to Patrick Côté who knows Montréal like the bottom of his pocket (*wink, wink*). Thank you for holding my hand throughout— and for always giving me the banquette seat in restaurants.

HOW TO CONTACT US

In researching this book, we discovered many wonderful places—hotels, restaurants, shops, and more. We're sure you'll find others. Please tell us about them, so we can share the information with your fellow travelers in upcoming editions. If you were disappointed with a recommendation, we'd love to know that, too. Please write to:

Frommer's Montréal & Québec City, 22nd Edition
John Wiley & Sons, Inc. • 111 River St. • Hoboken, NJ 07030-5774
frommersfeedback@wiley.com

ADVISORY & DISCLAIMER

Travel information can change quickly and unexpectedly, and we strongly advise you to confirm important details locally before traveling, including information on visas, health and safety, traffic and transport, accommodations, shopping, and eating out. We also encourage you to stay alert while traveling and to remain aware of your surroundings. Avoid civil disturbances, and keep a close eye on cameras, purses, wallets, and other valuables.

While we have endeavored to ensure that the information contained within this guide is accurate and up-to-date at the time of publication, we make no representations or warranties with respect to the accuracy or completeness of the contents of this work and specifically disclaim all warranties, including without limitation warranties of fitness for a particular purpose. We accept no responsibility or liability for any inaccuracy or errors or omissions, or for any inconvenience, loss, damage, costs, or expenses of any nature whatsoever incurred or suffered by anyone as a result of any advice or information contained in this guide.

The inclusion of a company, organization, or website in this guide as a service provider and/or potential source of further information does not mean that we endorse them or the information they provide. Be aware that information provided through some websites may be unreliable and can change without notice. Neither the publisher nor author shall be liable for any damages arising herefrom.

FROMMER'S STAR RATINGS, ICONS & ABBREVIATIONS

Every hotel, restaurant, and attraction listing in this guide has been ranked for quality, value, service, amenities, and special features using a **star-rating system.** In country, state, and regional guides, we also rate towns and regions to help you narrow down your choices and budget your time accordingly. Hotels and restaurants are rated on a scale of zero (recommended) to three stars (exceptional). Attractions, shopping, nightlife, towns, and regions are rated according to the following scale: zero stars (recommended), one star (highly recommended), two stars (very highly recommended), and three stars (must-see).

In addition to the star-rating system, we also use **seven feature icons** that point you to the great deals, in-the-know advice, and unique experiences that separate travelers from tourists. Throughout the book, look for:

special finds—those places only insiders know about

fun facts—details that make travelers more informed and their trips more fun

kids—best bets for kids and advice for the whole family

special moments—those experiences that memories are made of

overrated—places or experiences not worth your time or money

insider tips—great ways to save time and money

great values—where to get the best deals

The following abbreviations are used for credit cards:

AE	American Express	**DISC**	Discover	**V**	Visa
DC	Diners Club	**MC**	MasterCard		

TRAVEL RESOURCES AT FROMMERS.COM

Frommer's travel resources don't end with this guide. Frommer's website, **www.frommers.com**, has travel information on more than 4,000 destinations. We update features regularly, giving you access to the most current trip-planning information and the best airfare, lodging, and car-rental bargains. You can also listen to podcasts, connect with other Frommers.com members through our active-reader forums, share your travel photos, read blogs from guidebook editors and fellow travelers, and much more.

THE
BEST OF
MONTRÉAL
& QUÉBEC
CITY

1

f the province of Québec had a tagline, it could be: "Any excuse for a party." An enormous *joie de vivre* pervades the way that Montréal and Québec City go about their business. Their calendars are packed with festivals and events that bring out both locals and guests from around the world year-round.

You'll also find that Montréal is a modern city in every regard. Skyscrapers come in unexpected shapes and noncorporate colors. There's a beautifully preserved historic district. The subway system, called the Métro, is modern and swift. And the city's creative inhabitants provide zest to the ever-changing Plateau Mont-Royal and Mile End, large neighborhoods of artists' lofts, boutiques, and cafes, and miles of restaurants—many of which are unabashedly clever and stylish.

Québec City, more traditional and more French, is replacing its former conservatism with sophistication and playfulness. With an impressive location above the St. Lawrence River and carefully tended 18th- and 19th-century houses, this city is almost impossibly romantic—and unlike any other in North America.

THE most unforgettable
TRAVEL EXPERIENCES
Montréal

o **Enjoy an Afternoon or Evening of Jazz:** In downtown, Vieux-Montréal, and the Plateau, this is a favorite pastime of locals and visitors—especially in July, during the renowned Festival International de Jazz. See "Music & Nightclubs," in chapter 10.

o **Savor Gourmet Meals at Affordable Prices:** Experience all of French cuisine's interpretations—traditional, haute, bistro, Québécois—the way the locals do: by ordering the table d'hôte specials. You'll get to indulge in three or more courses for a fixed price that is only slightly more than the cost of a single main course. Most restaurants offer the option. See p. 85.

o **Explore Vieux-Montréal:** The city's oldest quarter has an overwhelmingly European flavor. Place Jacques-Cartier is the most

Place Jacques-Cartier is Montréal's most popular public square. PREVIOUS PAGE: The cafes along Rue Saint-Denis are the heart of francophone Québec City.

Horse-drawn carriages are part of the romance of Old Québec City.

popular outdoor square, and in any direction, you'll find museums and churches worth savoring. A revitalized waterfront also inspires strolling or biking. A walking tour of the neighborhood is on p. 144.

Québec City

o **Linger at an Outdoor Café:** Tables are set out at Place d'Armes in Upper Town, in the Quartier du Petit-Champlain in Lower Town, and along the Grande-Allée. It's a quality-of-life invention the French and their Québécois brethren have perfected. See chapter 14 for more information.

o **Soak Up Lower Town:** Once all but abandoned to the grubby edges of the shipping industry, the riverside neighborhood of Basse-Ville/Vieux-Port has been reborn. Antiques shops, bistros, and chic boutique hotels now fill rehabilitated 18th- and 19th-century buildings. See p. 304 for a walking tour.

o **Take in a Free Summer Evening Show by Cirque du Soleil:** The internationally known circus company puts on free performances on city streets most summer nights through at least 2013, in a program that got its start as part of Québec City's 400th anniversary celebrations. See p. 286.

Romantic Québec City

Every narrow street, leafy plaza, sidewalk cafe, horse-drawn calèche, pitched roof, and church spire breathes recollections of France's provincial towns. But to get the full Québec City treatment, amble those streets in the evening and find a bench on Terrasse Dufferin, the promenade alongside the Château Frontenac. The river below will be the color of liquid mercury in the moon's glow, and on a clear night, you'll see a sky of stars. Faint music from the *boîtes* in Lower Town is a possibility. Romance is a certainty.

Montréal's W Hotel is known for its lively nightlife.

THE best SPLURGE HOTELS

Montréal

- **Hôtel Le St-James,** 355 rue St-Jacques ouest (© **866/841-3111** or 514/841-3111): This former 19th-century bank in Vieux-Montréal lets no detail escape its attention. From an opulent restaurant to marble-rich bathrooms to an immaculately trained staff, Hôtel Le St-James provides an experience that may well be the highlight of your visit. See p. 72.

- **W Montréal,** 901 Rue de Square-Victoria (© **877/946-8357** or 514/395-3100): Hip, chic, and nightclubby, the W has three bars and lounges, a swank restaurant, and a clientele composed of knockouts of both genders. If you're staying here, it won't hurt if your platinum card is paid up and you don't need much sleep. See p. 72.

Québec City

- **Auberge St-Antoine,** 8 rue St-Antoine (© **888/692-2211** or 418/692-2211): Sure, there's the Château Frontenac, looming on the cliffs above, the very symbol of the city. But for a more intimate visit, stay in Basse-Ville (Lower Town). This romantic luxury hotel has grown into one of Québec's most desirable lodgings, with an arresting lounge and a top restaurant to boot. See p. 254.

The Auberge Saint-Antoine is one of Québec City's most romantic hotels.

- **Hôtel Le Germain-Dominion,** 126 rue St-Pierre (© **888/833-5253** or 418/692-2224): An anchor in the successful redevelopment of the once-dreary Vieux-Port, the Dominion has bedding so cozily enveloping that you may not want to go out. Do, though—for the fireplace, croissants, and café au lait in the lobby, if nothing else. See p. 254.

THE best MODERATELY PRICED HOTELS

Montréal

o **Auberge Bonaparte,** 447 rue St-François-Xavier (*C* **514/ 844-1448**): Even the smallest rooms in this fashionable urban inn are gracefully presented, and taking breakfast in the elegant Bonaparte restaurant (p. 90) is an especially civilized way to start the day. See p. 76.

o **Le Square Phillips Hôtel & Suites,** 1193 Square Phillips (*C* **866/393-1193** or 514/393-1193): Tidy, centrally located, and equipped with full kitchens in every unit. There's even a rooftop pool. See p. 71.

The rooftop pool at Le Square Phillips Hôtel & Spa in Montréal.

Québec City

o **Courtyard Marriott Québec,** 850 Place d'Youville (*C* **866/694-4004** or 418/694-4004): A hot property in recent years due to room renovations, friendly staff, and fair prices. Beds are piled with five pillows and sheet-cover duvets. See p. 256.

o **Hôtel Champlain Vieux-Québec,** 115 rue Ste-Anne (*C* **800/567-2106** or 418/694-0106): Even the smallest rooms boast silk curtains, king or

Québec City's elegant and cozy Hôtel Champlain Vieux-Québec.

queen beds, and 300-thread-count sheets. A self-serve espresso machine by the front desk ensures free cappuccinos at any time of day or night. See p. 249.

THE most unforgettable
DINING EXPERIENCES
Montréal

- **Europea,** 1227 rue de la Montagne (© **514/398-9229**): For the full treatment, order the 10-course *menu degustation*. You'll see why chef Jérôme Ferrer was named Chef of the Year in 2007 by his colleagues and why the accolades keep coming, year after year. See p. 84.

- **Toqué!,** 900 Place Jean-Paul-Riopelle (© **514/499-2084**): Chef/owner Normand Laprise has been thrilling gourmands for years. In dishes of startling innovation, he brings together diverse ingredients that have rarely appeared before on restaurant plates. New menus come out frequently. See p. 88.

Québec City

- **Initiale,** 54 rue St-Pierre (© **418/694-1818**): Gracious, cordial, and subdued, this is one of the best restaurants of the entire province. Dress up and settle in, perhaps with the eight-course seasonal tasting menu. See p. 268.

- **Panache,** 10 rue St-Antoine (© **418/692-1022**): Romance all the way, from the fireplace and velvet couches to the wrought-iron staircase leading to hideaway attic corners. French-Canadian cuisine with a kick, inside the knockout Auberge St-Antoine. See p. 269.

THE best
MUSEUMS
Montréal

- **Musée des Beaux-Arts,** 1339–1380 rue Sherbrooke ouest (© **514/285-2000**): Canada's first museum devoted exclusively to the visual arts opened in 1912. It has expanded over the years, and new for 2011 was the adjacent Erskine and American Church. Temporary exhibits are dazzling

Romantic Panache serves top-quality French-Canadian fare.

and have focused in recent years on musician Miles Davis, fashion designer Jean Paul Gaultier, and China's Terracotta Army. See p. 109.

o **Pointe-à-Callière (Montréal Museum of Archaeology and History),** 350 Place Royale (© **514/ 872-9150**): A first visit to Montréal might best begin here. This strikingly modernistic structure at the edge of Vieux-Montréal marks the spot where the first European settlement put down roots in the city. It stands atop extensive excavations that unearthed not only remains of the French newcomers, but also of the native bands that preceded them. On the self-guided tour, you wind your way through the subterranean complex. See p. 116.

FROM TOP: Montréal's century-old Musée des Beaux-Arts was Canada's first museum devoted exclusively to the visual arts; Québec City's Musée de la Civilisation has extensive exhibits on Québec history.

Québec City

o **Musée de la Civilisation,** 85 rue Dalhousie (© **866/710-8031** or 418/643-2158): Here is that rarity among museums: a collection of cleverly mounted temporary and permanent exhibitions that both children and adults find engrossing, without talking down or metaphysical maunderings. Make time for

"People of Québec . . . Then and Now," a permanent exhibit that is a sprawling examination of Québec history. See p. 276.

o **Musée National des Beaux-Arts du Québec,** Parc des Champs-de-Bataille (© **866/220-2150** or 418/643-2150): Known simply as Musée du Québec, this museum highlights modern art (Jean-Paul Riopelle especially) and has a large, important collection of Inuit art, much produced in the 1980s and 1990s. See p. 281.

THE best
OUTDOOR ACTIVITIES
Montréal

o **Traverse the Lachine Canal:** First constructed in the early 1800s to detour around the rapids of the same name, the canal was reopened for recreational use in 1997 after much renovation. It connects Vieux-Port with Atwater Market. You can explore the canal and its surroundings by guided boat tour, on foot, or on a rented bicycle. See chapter 7.

o **Bike the City:** Montréalers' enthusiasm for bicycling has provided the impetus for the ongoing development of bicycle paths that wind through downtown areas and out to the countryside—more than 560km (348 miles), at last count. Rentals are available from shops and the new BIXI network, which has put thousands of bikes onto the streets for inexpensive borrowing. See p. 140.

Bicycle paths are plentiful and rentals are affordable in Montréal.

Québec City

- **Take a Walking Tour:** Combine immersion in Québec's rich history with a good stretch of the legs among the battlements and along the storied city's cobblestoned streets. Use the walking tours in chapter 16 or go on a group tour. See p. 291.

THE best ACTIVITIES FOR FAMILIES

Montréal

- **Visit the Biodôme de Montréal:** Perhaps the most engaging attraction in the city for younger children. The Biodôme houses replications of four ecosystems: a Laurentian forest; the St. Lawrence marine system; a polar environment; and, most appealingly, a tropical rainforest. See p. 119.

- **Spend a Day at the Centre des Sciences de Montréal:** Running the length of a central pier in Vieux-Port, this ambitious science center has permanent interactive displays, along with special exhibits. One recent exhibit guided kids (big and little) in the archeological adventures of Indiana Jones; there's also a popular IMAX theater. It's designed especially for ages 9 to 14. See p. 116.

Québec City

- **Watch the Changing of the Guard:** La Citadelle is the fortress built by the British to repel an American invasion that never came. It's still an active military post, and the ceremonial Changing of the Guard is colorful and doesn't take too much time. See p. 281.

The ambitious Centre des Sciences de Montréal is specially designed for kids 9 to 14.

○ **Thrill to a Waterfall:** A 15-minute car or bus ride north of the city is Montmorency Falls, a spectacular cascade. You can walk to the base or take a cable car to the top. A footbridge passes directly over the plunging water and is open to anyone brave-hearted enough to walk it. About a half-hour further north, Canyon Ste-Anne also has a waterfall with footbridges that crisscross it and the canyon. See p. 333 and p. 336.

The spectacular Montmorency Falls is a short drive outside of Québec City.

THE best OF MONTRÉAL & QUÉBEC CITY ONLINE

○ **Bonjour Québec** (www.bonjour quebec.com): The official site of the province of Québec is a comprehensive information bank. You'll find details about upcoming events and special package deals.

○ **Midnight Poutine** (www.midnightpoutine.ca) or **the Montréal Buzz** (www. tourisme-montreal.org/blog): These two terrific Montréal blogs provide current insider musings and information.

A NOTE ABOUT english & french IN THIS BOOK

Like the Québecois themselves, this guidebook goes back and forth between using the French names and the English names for areas and attractions.

Most often, we use French. Québec's state-mandated language is French, and most signs, brochures, and maps in the region appear in French. However, we use the English name or translation as well, if that makes the meaning clearer. *Bon voyage!*

2

MONTRÉAL & QUÉBEC CITY IN DEPTH

Montréal and Québec City, the twin cities of the province of Québec, have a stronger European flavor than Canada's other municipalities. Most residents' first language is French, and a strong affiliation with France continues to be a central facet of the region's personality.

The defining dialectics of Canadian life are culture and language, and they're thorny issues that have long threatened to tear the country apart. Many Québécois have long believed that making Québec a separate, independent state is the only way to maintain their rich French culture in the face of the Anglophone (English-speaking) ocean that surrounds them. Québec's role within the Canadian federation has been the most debated and volatile topic of conversation in Canadian politics.

There are reasons for the festering intransigence, of course—about 250 years' worth. After France lost power in Québec to the British in the 18th century, a kind of linguistic exclusionism developed, with wealthy Scottish and English bankers and merchants denying French-Canadians access to upper levels of business and government. This bias continued well into the 20th century.

Many in Québec stayed committed to the French language and culture after British rule was imposed. Even with later waves of other immigrant populations pouring in over the cities, there was still a bedrock loyalty held by many to the province's Gallic roots. France may have relinquished control of Québec to Great Britain in 1763, but France's influence, after its 150 years of rule, remained powerful—and still does. Many Québécois continue to look across the Atlantic for inspiration in fashion, food, and the arts. Culturally and linguistically, it is that tenacious French connection that gives the province its special character.

Two other important cultural phenomena have emerged over the past 12 years. The first is an institutional acceptance of homosexuality. By changing the definition of "spouse" in 39 laws and regulations in 1999, Québec's government eliminated all legal distinctions between same-sex and heterosexual couples and became Canada's first province to recognize the legal status of same-sex civil unions. Gay marriage became legal in all of Canada's provinces and territories in 2005. Montréal, in particular, has transformed into one of North America's most welcoming cities for gay people.

The second phenomenon is an influx of even more immigrants into the province's melting pot. "Québec is at a turning point," declared a 2008 report about the province's angst over the so-called reasonable accommodation of minority religious practices, particularly those of Muslims and Orthodox Jews. "The identity inherited from the French-Canadian past is perfectly legitimate and it must survive," the report said, "but it can no longer occupy alone the Québec identity space." Together with 70,000 aboriginal people from 11 First Nation tribes who live in the province, immigrants help make the region as vibrant and alive as any on the continent.

PREVIOUS PAGE: **The Montréal Jazz Festival is one of the city's biggest events.**

MONTRÉAL & QUÉBEC CITY TODAY

The centuries-old walls that protected Québec City over the centuries are still in place today, and the streets and lanes within their embrace have changed little, preserving for posterity the heart of New France.

Not so in Montréal. It was "wet" when the U.S. was "dry" during U.S. Prohibition from 1920 to 1933. Bootleggers, hard drinkers, and prostitutes flocked to this large city situated so conveniently close to the American border, mixing with rowdy people from the port, much to the distress of many of Montréal's citizenry. For 50 years, the city's image was decidedly racy, but in the 1950s, a cleanup began alongside a boom in high-rise construction, and restoration began in the old port area, which had become a derelict ghost town. In 1967, Montréal welcomed international audiences to Expo 67, the World's Fair.

Today, much of what makes Montréal special is either very old or very new. The city's great gleaming skyscrapers and towering hotels, the superb Métro system, and the highly practical underground city date mostly from the 44 years since the Expo. The renaissance of much of the oldest part of the city, Vieux-Montréal, blossomed in the 1990s.

To understand the province's politics, you need to back up about 50 years. A phenomenon later labeled the Quiet Revolution began bubbling in the 1960s. The movement focused on transforming the largely rural, agricultural province into an urbanized, industrial entity with a pronounced secular outlook. French-Canadians, long denied access to the upper echelons of desirable corporate careers, started to insist on equal opportunity with the powerful Anglophone minority.

In 1968, Pierre Trudeau, a bilingual Québécois, became Canada's prime minister, a post he held for 18 years. More flamboyant, eccentric, and brilliant than any of his predecessors, he devoted much time to trying to placate voters on both sides of the French-English issue.

Montréal's subway system, the Métro, is superb.

Also in 1968, the Parti Québécois was founded by René Lévesque, and a separatist movement began in earnest. Inevitably, there was a radical fringe, and it signaled its intentions by bombing Anglophone businesses. The FLQ (Front de Libération du Québec, or Québec Liberation Front), as it was known, was behind most of the terrorist attacks. Most Québécois separatists, of course, were not violent, but the bombings fueled passions and contributed to a sense that big changes were coming.

For decades, secession remained a dream for many Québécois. In 1995, a referendum on sovereignty lost by a mere 1% of the vote.

During the 1990s, an unsettled mood prevailed in the province. Large businesses left town, anxious that if the province actually did secede, they would find themselves based outside of Canada proper. Economic opportunities were limited.

By 2000, though, things began to change. The Canadian dollar began to strengthen against the U.S. dollar. Unemployment, long in double digits, shrank to less than 6%, the lowest percentage in more than 20 years. Crime in Montréal, which was already one of the continent's safest cities, hit a 20-year low. The presence of skilled workers made Canada a favored destination for Hollywood film and TV production. The rash of FOR RENT and FOR SALE signs that disfigured Montréal in the 1990s was replaced by a welcome shortage of retail and office space.

In 2002, the 28 towns and cities on the island of Montréal merged into one megacity with a population of 1.8 million.

Today, the quest for separatism seems to be fading. Conversations with ordinary Québécois suggest they're weary of the argument. In March 2007, the Liberal Party, headed by Jean Charest, won a minority government, while the new Action Démocratique du Québec party won an out-of-nowhere second-place victory. The separatist Parti Québécois, meanwhile, placed a distant third with just 28% of the vote. The moment marked, many think, the beginning of the end of the campaign for independence.

As significantly, the proportion of foreign-born Québec citizens continues to grow. After the arrival of 1.1 million immigrants to the country between 2001 and 2006, foreign-born nationals made up 20% of Canada's population, with Montréal, Toronto, Vancouver, and Calgary their prime destinations. The province of Québec welcomed over 50,000 permanent residents in 2010, with over 46,000 of them settling in Montréal, and another 2,600 in Québec City. In some areas of Canada, Chinese dialects are outpacing French as the second most commonly spoken language. Visitors to Montréal may notice large pockets of neighborhoods where the primary languages spoken are Mandarin and Cantonese.

LOOKING BACK: MONTRÉAL & QUÉBEC CITY HISTORY

First Immigrants

The first settlers of the region were the Iroquois, who spent time in what's now called Québec long before the Europeans arrived. The Vikings landed in Canada more than 1,000 years ago, probably followed by Irish and Basque fishermen. English explorer John Cabot stepped ashore briefly on the east coast in 1497, but it was the French who managed the first meaningful European toehold.

When Jacques Cartier sailed up the St. Lawrence in 1535, he recognized at once the tremendous strategic potential of Québec City's Cap Diamant (Cape Diamond), the high bluff overlooking the river. But he was exploring, not empire building, and after stopping briefly on land, he continued on his trip.

Montréal, at the time, was home to a fortified Iroquois village called Hochelaga, composed of 50 longhouses. Cartier was on a sea route to China but was halted by the fierce rapids just west of what is now the Island of Montréal. (In a demonstration of mingled optimism and frustration, he dubbed the rapids "La Chine," assuming that China was just beyond them. Today, they're still known as the Lachine.) He visited the Indian settlement in what's now Old Montréal before moving on.

Samuel de Champlain arrived 73 years later, in 1608, motivated by the burgeoning fur trade, obsessed with finding a route to China, and determined to settle Québec. He was perhaps emboldened after the Virginia Company founded its fledgling colony of Jamestown, hundreds of miles to the south, just a year before.

Called Kebec, Champlain's first settlement grew to become Québec City's Basse-Ville, or Lower Town, and spread across the flat riverbank beneath the cliffs of Cap Diamant. In 2008, Québec City hosted major celebrations of the 400th anniversary of this founding.

Champlain would make frequent trips back to France to reassure anxious investors that the project, which he said would eventually "equal the states of greatest kings," was going apace. In truth, the first years were bleak. Food was scarce, and scurvy ravaged many of the settlers. Demanding winters were far colder than in France. And almost from the beginning, there were hostilities, first between the French and the Iroquois, then between the French and the British (and later, the Americans). At issue was control of the lucrative trade of the fur of beavers, raccoons, and bears, and the hides of deer, as the pelts were being shipped off to Paris fashion houses. The commercial battle lasted nearly a century.

To better defend themselves, the settlers in Québec City built a fortress at the top of the cliffs. Gradually, the center of urban life moved to inside the fortress walls.

The French and British struggle for dominance in the new continent focused on their explorations, and in this regard, France outdid England. Far-ranging French fur trappers, navigators, soldiers, and missionaries opened up not only Canada, but also most of what eventually became the United States, moving all the way south to the future New Orleans. At least 35 of the subsequent 50 U.S. states were mapped or settled by Frenchmen, and they left behind thousands of city names to prove it, including Detroit, St. Louis, Duluth, and Des Moines.

Paul de Chomedey, Sieur de Maisonneuve, arrived at what is now the island of Montréal in 1642 to establish a colony and to plant a crucifix atop the rise he called Mont Royal. He and his band of settlers came ashore and founded Ville-Marie, dedicated to the Virgin Mary, at the spot now marked by Place-Royale in the old part of the city. They built a fort, a chapel, stores, and houses. Pointe-à-Callière, the terrific Montréal Museum of Archaeology and History, is built on the site where the original colony was established.

Life was not easy. The Iroquois in Montréal had no intention of giving up land to the Europeans. Fierce battles raged for years. Today, at Place d'Armes,

Montréal was first settled in the 17th century at what is now Place-Royale.

there's a statue of de Maisonneuve marking the spot where the settlers defeated the Iroquois in bloody hand-to-hand fighting.

Still, the settlement prospered. Until the 1800s, Montréal was contained in the area known today as Vieux-Montréal. Its ancient walls no longer stand, but its long and colorful past is preserved in the streets, houses, and churches of the Old City.

England Conquers New France

In the 1750s, the struggle between Britain and France had escalated. The latest episode was known as the French and Indian War (an extension of Europe's Seven Years' War), and strategic Québec became a valued prize. The French appointed Louis Joseph, Marquis de Montcalm, to command their forces in the town. The British sent an expedition of 4,500 men in a fleet under the command of a 32-year-old general, James Wolfe. The British troops surprised the French by coming up and over the cliffs of Cap Diamant, and the ensuing skirmish for Québec, fought on September 13, 1759, became one of the most important battles in North American history: It resulted in a continent that would be under British influence for more than a century.

Fought on the Plains of Abraham, today a beautiful and much-used city park, the battle lasted just 18 to 25 minutes, depending on whose account you read. It resulted in more than a thousand deaths and serious injuries, and both generals died as a result of wounds received. Wolfe lived just long enough to hear that the British had won. Montcalm died a few hours later. Today, a memorial to both men overlooks Terrasse Dufferin in Québec City and uniquely commemorates both victor and vanquished of the same battle. The inscription—in neither French nor English, but Latin—is translated as, simply, "Courage was fatal to them."

The capture of Québec determined the war's course, and the Treaty of Paris in 1763 ceded all of French Canada to England. In a sense, this victory was a bane to Britain: If France had held Canada, the British government might have been more judicious in its treatment of the American colonists. As it was, the British decided to make the colonists pay the costs of the French and Indian War, on the principle that it was their home being defended. Britain slapped so many taxes on all imports that the infuriated U.S. colonists openly rebelled against the crown.

George Washington felt sure that French-Canadians would want to join the American revolt against the British crown, or at least be supportive. He was mistaken on both counts. The Québécois detested their British conquerors, but they were also devout Catholics and saw their contentious American neighbors as godless republicans. Only a handful supported the Americans, and three of Washington's most competent commanders came to grief in attacks against Québec and were forced to retreat.

Thirty-eight years later, during the War of 1812, the U.S. army marched up the banks of the Richelieu River where it flows from Lake Champlain in what's now northern Vermont to the St. Lawrence in Québec. Once again, the French-Canadians stuck by the British and drove back the Americans. The war ended essentially in a draw, but it had at least one encouraging result: Britain and the young United States agreed to demilitarize the Great Lakes and to extend their mutual border along the 49th parallel to the Rockies.

The Rise of Separatism in Québec

In 1867, the British North America Act created the federation of the provinces of Québec, Ontario, Nova Scotia, and New Brunswick. It was a kind of independence for the region from Britain, but was unsettling for many French-Canadians, who wanted full autonomy. In 1883, *"Je me souviens"*—a defiant, proud "I remember"—became the province's official motto. From 1900 to 1910, 325,000 French-Canadians emigrated to the United States, many settling in the northeast states.

In 1968, the Parti Québécois was founded by René Lévesque, and the separatist movement began in earnest. One attempt to smooth ruffled Francophones (French speakers) was made in 1969, when federal legislation stipulated that all services across Canada were henceforth to be offered in both English and French, in effect declaring the nation bilingual.

MARCH OF THE LANGUAGE police
(OR *LA POLICE DE LANGUE*)

When the separatist Parti Québécois took power in the province in 1976, it wasted no time in attempting to make Québec unilingual. Bill 101 made French the provincial government's sole official language and sharply restricted the use of other languages in education and commerce. While the party's fortunes have fallen and risen and fallen, the primacy of Française has remained.

In the early days, agents of L'Office de la Langue Française fanned out across the territory, scouring the landscape for linguistic insults to the state and her people. MERRY CHRISTMAS signs were removed from storefronts, and department stores had to come up with a new name for Harris Tweed.

About 20% of the population spoke English as a primary language, and they instantly felt like second-class citizens.

Francophones responded that it was about time they knew what second-class citizenship felt like.

Affected, too, was the food world. By fiat and threat of punishment, hamburgers became *hambourgeois* and hot dogs were rechristened *chiens chaud*. And Schwartz's Montréal Hebrew Delicatessen, one of the city's fixtures since 1928? It became Chez Schwartz Charcuterie Hébraïque de Montréal.

That didn't assuage militant Québécois, however. They undertook to guarantee the primacy of French in their own province. To prevent dilution by newcomers, the children of immigrants were required to enroll in French-language schools, even if English or a third language was spoken in the home. This is still the case today.

Nevertheless, immigrants made Montréal their own. Ruth Reichl, the editor of the now (sadly) defunct *Gourmet* magazine, wrote in the March 2006 special issue about the city that when she lived there in the 1960s, "[I]t was strangely segregated. The Anglophones I trailed through the staid streets were a proper lot, more English than the English, with their umbrellas and briefcases. They may not have been hurrying home to early tea, but I imagined they were. . . . The Jewish community I found in another part of town was an entirely different experience. The people were boisterous, and their streets were rich with the scent of garlic, cloves, and allspice emanating from the mountains of pickles and deliciously rich smoked meat that I spied each time a restaurant door swung open. The French-Canadians had their own territory, too, and they stuck to themselves, speaking their own robust and expressive language. . . . What struck me most, as a New Yorker accustomed to the hodgepodge piling up of one culture on another, was the barriers between them. They kept themselves strictly separate, each cleaving to their own language, rituals, and food."

In 1977, Bill 101 passed, all but banning the use of English on public signage. The bill funded the establishment of enforcement units, a virtual language police who let no nit go unpicked. The resulting backlash provoked the flight of an estimated 400,000 Anglophones to other parts of Canada.

In 1987, Canadian Prime Minister Brian Mulroney met with the 10 provincial premiers at a retreat at Québec's Meech Lake to cobble together a collection of constitutional reforms. The Meech Lake Accord, as it came to be known, addressed a variety of issues, but most important to the Québécois was that it recognized Québec as a "distinct society" within the federation.

The sign at Montréal's famous Schwartz's Delicatessen.

The Separatist Movement in Brief

○ In 1968, René Lévesque and fellow separatist-movement members found the Parti Québécois (PQ) in an earnest attempt to make Québec independent from the rest of Canada.

○ In 1976, the PQ come to power in Québec and retain leadership until 1985. The PQ regain power again in 1994 and hold it more or less consistently through 2003.

○ Forty years after its founding, the PQ suffers an anemic third-place showing in 2007 provincial elections. This is perceived by many as a crushing defeat for both the party and the separatist movement.

○ The federal election in 2011 saw the decimation of the Bloc Québécois, when it only attained one-third of the 12 seats necessary for official party status.

Manitoba and Newfoundland, however, failed to ratify the accord by the June 23, 1990, deadline. As a result, support for the secessionist cause burgeoned in Québec. An election firmly placed the Parti Québécois in control of the provincial government again. A 1995 referendum on succession from the Canadian union was only narrowly defeated. The issue continued to divide families and dominate political discourse.

The year 2007 may have marked the beginning of the end the issue. In provincial elections, Parti Québécois placed third, with just 28% of the vote. The election was perceived by many as the first step in closing the door on the campaign for independence.

Today, Montréal may well be the most bilingual city in the world. Most residents speak at least a little of both French and English. And Québécois, it must be said, are exceedingly gracious hosts. Most Montréalers switch effortlessly from one language to the other as the situation dictates. Telephone operators go from French to English the instant they hear an English word, as do most store clerks, waiters, and hotel staff. This is less the case in country villages and in Québec City, but for visitors, there is virtually no problem that can't be solved with a few French words, some expressive gestures, and a little goodwill.

Political Power for the First Nations

The French colonialists eventually came to realize that it was only through trade, alliances, and treaties—rather than force—that relations between native peoples and themselves could develop. From early on, formal alliances were part of the texture of their uneasy relationship.

Describing and characterizing the long history of the treatment of native peoples is difficult. Assimilation of natives into European identity, for instance, was once perceived as a positive goal but has since been repudiated by natives, who are collectively known today as First Nations. The 1876 Indian Act established federal Canadian authority over the rights and lands of "Indians" and set in place an assimilation process. Indians who wanted full rights as Canadians had to relinquish their legal Indian status and renounce their Indian identity. Participation in traditional dances, for instance, became punishable by imprisonment.

Those laws changed slowly. It was only in 1985 that the law was modified so that an Indian woman who married a non-Indian would not automatically lose her Indian status. In 2007, the United Nations General Assembly adopted the Declaration on the Rights of Indigenous Peoples, recognizing the right of aboriginals to self-determination.

The interests of native peoples are today represented by the Assembly of the First Nations, which was established in 1985. Economic interests are represented in part by Société Touristique des Autochtones du Québec (STAQ), the aboriginal tourism corporation. STAQ puts out an official tourist guide each year, which is available at tourist offices. It's also posted as a pdf (which is 133 pages long) at www.staq.net.

ART & ARCHITECTURE

Classic European art and architectural influences meet with an urbane, design-heavy aesthetic in Montréal and Québec City. Here are some art highlights.

Frederick Law Olmsted & Parc du Mont-Royal

American landscape architect Frederick Law Olmsted (1822–1903), best known for creating New York City's Central Park, also designed the park that surrounds the "mountain" in the center of Montréal. Parc du Mont-Royal, as it is known, opened in 1876. Olmsted's vision was to make the landscape seem more mountainous by using exaggerated vegetation—shade trees at the bottom of a path that climbs its side, for instance—to create the illusion at the lower elevations of being in a valley. Unfortunately, Montréal suffered a depression in the mid-1870s, and many of the architect's plans were abandoned. The path was built, but not according to the original plan, and the vegetation ideas were abandoned. Still, Parc du Mont-Royal is an urban oasis and is heavily used in all four seasons. For a walking tour of the park, see p. 164.

Bruce Price & His Château Frontenac

It is an American architect, Bruce Price (1845–1903), who is responsible for the most iconic building in the entire province of Québec: Château Frontenac, Québec City's visual center.

"The Château" opened as a hotel in 1893. With its castlelike architecture, soaring turrets, and romantic French-Renaissance mystery, it achieved the goal of becoming the most talked-about accommodation in North America. Today, it's a high-end hotel managed by the Fairmont chain.

The Château was one of many similar-styled hotels commissioned by the bigwigs of the Canadian Pacific Railway in the late 19th century when they were constructing Canada's first transcontinental railway. The company calculated that luxury accommodations would encourage travelers with money to travel by train.

As part of the same Canadian Pacific Railway project, Price also designed Montréal's Windsor Station; the Dalhousie Station in Montréal; the facade of Royal Victoria College in Montréal; and the Gare du Palais train station in Québec City, whose turrets echo those of the Château Frontenac.

Architecture professor Claude Bergeron of Québec City's Univérsité Laval noted that as the leading practitioner of the château style, Price "is sometimes credited with having made it a national Canadian style."

The Château Frontenac is the province's most iconic building.

Avant-Garde Vision

In 1967, Montréal hosted the World's Fair, which it called Expo 67. The event was hugely successful—62 nations participated, more than 50 million people visited, and Montréal became a star overnight. With its avant-garde vision on display, it was viewed as a prototype for a 20th-century city.

One of the most exhilarating buildings developed for the event was Habitat 67, a 158-unit housing complex on the St. Lawrence River. Designed by Montréal architect Moshe Safdie (b. 1938), it looks like a collection of modular concrete blocks all piled together. The vision was to show what community housing could look like. The complex is still full of residents, although it's not open to the public for touring. But it can be seen from the western end of Vieux-Port, and there are photos and information at Safdie's website, www.msafdie.com.

Palais des Congrès (Convention Center), at the northern edge of Vieux-Montréal, is an unlikely design triumph, too. Built between 2000 and 2002 as part of a renovation and extension of the center, the building's transparent glass exterior walls are a crazy quilt of pink, yellow, blue, green, red, and purple rectangles. You get the full effect when you step into the inside hallway—when the sun streams in, it's like being inside a kaleidoscope. It's the vision of Montréal architect Mario Saia.

Design Montréal

Montréal continues to be one of North America's most stylish cities. In 2006, UNESCO (the United Nations Educational, Scientific, and Cultural Organization) designated Montréal a "UNESCO City of Design" for "its ability to inspire synergy between public and private players." With the distinction, Montréal joined Buenos Aires and Berlin, other honorees, as a high-style city worth watching.

Design Montréal (www.designmontreal.com) is an organization devoted to celebrating and networking the city's arts and fashion communities. It holds design and architecture competitions, and its Design Montréal Open House is an annual 2-day event in early May that opens the doors of the city's design-centric agencies and projects.

Much of what constitutes cutting-edge design is creative reuse of older buildings and materials. Among such venues is the industrial Darling Foundry, which houses in its raw, concrete space a contemporary art center and a small restaurant, the **Cluny ArtBar** (p. 94). Fashion also simmers, with an increasing number of innovative locals setting up shop. It all comes to a boil during two events: the Montréal Fashion & Design Festival, which features fashion shows on outdoor stages in the heart of downtown (usually held in summer; the 2011 edition was held Aug 3–6), and Montréal Fashion Week at the Marché Bonsecours (whose date has floated around the calendar; the 2011 event was in Feb, right before New York Fashion Week). Details are at www.sensationmode.com.

The city's aesthetic was well summed up by one fashionista in the *Montréal Gazette* a few years ago: "I'm all about the black, the white, and beige. Fall is about comfort—not that American style of sloppy comfort, but casual style."

Inuit Art

The region's most compelling artwork is indigenous. In Montréal, the Musée McCord has a First Nations room that displays objects from Canada's native population, including meticulous beadwork, baby carriers, and fishing implements. The city's annual First Peoples Festival (© **514/278-4040;** www.nativelynx.qc.ca), held in June and August, highlights Amerindian and

Québec City's Musée National des Beaux-Arts du Québec is home to an important Inuit art collection.

Inuit cultures by way of film, video, visual arts, music, and dance.

In Québec City, the Musée National des Beaux-Arts du Québec is home to an important Inuit art collection assembled over many years by Raymond Brousseau. Also in Québec City, a permanent exhibition at the Musée de la Civilisation, "Nous, les Premières Nations" ("We, the First Nations"), provides a fascinating look at the history and culture of the Abenakis, Algonquins, Atikamekw, Crees, Hurons-Wendat, Inuit, Malecites, Micmacs, Innu, Mohawks, and Naskapis—the 11 First Nation tribes whose combined 70,000 members inhabit Québec today.

Those External Staircases

Montréal's curving outdoor staircases.

Stroll through Montréal's Plateau Mont-Royal and Mile End neighborhoods, and one of the first things you'll notice are the outside staircases on the two- and three-story houses. Many are made of wrought iron, and most have shapely, sensual curves. Some say they were first designed to accommodate immigrant families who wanted their own front doors, even for second-floor apartments. Others say that landlords put the stairs outside to cut down on common interior space that wouldn't count toward rental space.

The Catholic Church, ever a force in the city, was originally all for the stairs because they allowed neighbors to keep an eye on each other. After the aesthetic tide turned, however, brick archways called loggia were built to hide the stairways. But the archway walls created ready-made nooks for teens to linger in, and the church helped push through legislation banning new exterior staircases entirely. That ban was lifted in the 1980s so that citywide efforts to maintain and renovate properties could keep the unique features intact.

MONTRÉAL & QUÉBEC CITY IN POPULAR CULTURE

BOOKS & THEATER The late Jewish Anglophone Mordecai Richler (1931–2001) inveighed against the excesses of Québec's separatists and language zealots in a barrage of books and critical essays in newspapers and magazines. Richler wrote from the perspective of a minority within a minority and set most of his books in the working-class Jewish neighborhood of St. Urbain of the 1940s and 1950s, with protagonists who are poor, streetwise, and intolerant of the prejudices of other Jews, French-Canadians, and WASPs from the city's English-side Westmount neighborhood. His most famous book is *The Apprenticeship of Duddy Kravitz* (Pocket Books, 1959), which in 1974 was made into a movie of the same name starring Richard

Dreyfuss. A film version of Richler's *Barney's Version,* starring Dustin Hoffman and Paul Giamatti (who won a Golden Globe for his role as Barney Panofsky) was released in 2010.

Legendary singer-songwriter Leonard Cohen (b. 1934) wrote two novels set in Montréal. 1963's *The Favorite Game* (Vintage, 2003) and 1966's *Beautiful Losers* (Vintage, 1993).

Playwright Michel Tremblay (b. 1942), an important dramatist, grew up in Montréal's Plateau Mont-Royal neighborhood and uses that setting for much of his work. His *Les Belles-Sœurs (The Sisters-in-Law),* written in 1965, introduced the lives of working-class Francophone Québécois to the world. It was published in English by Talonbooks in 1992.

MUSIC In 2008, the Putumayo World Music record label released a compilation CD called *Québec* in honor of Québec City's 400th anniversary. It's a collection of 11 songs that reflect the province's rich musical diversity, and it provides a great introduction to Québécois music. Highlights include the upbeat, angelic-voiced Chloé Sainte-Marie (b. 1962; "Brûlots"); the pop band DobaCaracol ("Etrange"), which fuses a reggae groove with African rhythms and French-language pop; and the Celtic folk of La Bottine Souriante ("La Brunette Est Là"), the preeminent representatives of traditional Québécois music, which has its roots in French, English, Scottish, and Irish folk traditions. Samples of the songs can be heard at the Putumayo website (www.putumayo.com).

Montréal has a strong showing of innovative musicians who hail from its clubs. Singer-songwriter Leonard Cohen is the best known. He grew up in the Westmount neighborhood and attended McGill University. He was inducted into the U.S. Rock and Roll Hall of Fame in 2008.

Rufus Wainwright (b. 1973), a popular singer-songwriter (and son of folk great, and Montréal native, Kate McGarrigle [1946–2010]) grew up in Montréal and got his start at city clubs. Alternative rock bands Arcade Fire and Wolf Parade are both from the city. (The band Of Montréal, however, is a U.S. band from Athens, Georgia.)

FILM & TELEVISION Many U.S. films are made beyond the northern border for financial reasons, even when their American locales are important parts of the stories (*Brokeback Mountain,* for instance, was filmed in Alberta). Québécois films—made in the province, in French, for Québec audiences—can be difficult to track down outside the region. The Cinémathèque Québécoise (𝄐 **514/842-9763;** www.cinematheque.qc.ca) is a great resource for fun and research. It's located at 335 boul. de Maisonneuve est in Montréal.

Recent Québec-made features worth seeking out include *J'ai tué ma mère (I Killed My Mother),* a breakout hit at Cannes in 2009 by 20-year-old auteur Xavier Dolan (b. 1989). A minicontroversy ensued after Dolan's film, despite international acclaim, was snubbed by the Genie Awards, the Canadian equivalent to the U.S. Academy Awards. The film that swept the 2009 Genies, *Polytechnique,* was the first movie made about the 1989 Montréal Massacre, in which a young man targeted and murdered 14 female engineering students. The event remains a sensitive part of Canadian history. Other noteworthy new Québec-made films include *Atanarjuat: The Fast*

Runner, The Journals of Knud Rasmussen, and *Before Tomorrow,* a mythic trilogy made by a collective of Inuit people.

Alanis Obomsawin (b. 1932) is an important documentarian of the region. A member of the Abenaki Nation who was raised on the Odanak Reserve near Montréal, she began making movies for the National Film Board of Canada (www.nfb.ca) 40 years ago and has produced more than 30 documentaries about the hard edges of the lives of aboriginal people. In 2008, "the first lady of First Nations film"—as the commissioner of the National Film Board termed her—received the Governor General's Performing Arts Award for Lifetime Artistic Achievement. A major retrospective of her work was shown at New York's Museum of Modern Art and Boston's Museum of Fine Art that same year.

Obomsawin has documented police raids of reservation lands, homelessness among natives living in cities, and a wrenching incident in 1990 that pitted native peoples against the government over lands that were slated to be turned into a golf course. That last event, detailed in the 1993 film *Kanehsatake: 270 Years of Resistance,* took place about an hour west of Montréal and included a months-long armed standoff between Mohawks and authorities.

"The land question and Mohawk sovereignty have been issues since the French and English first settled the area," Obomsawin has said. "A lot of promises were made and never kept. What the confrontation of 1990 showed is that this is a generation that is not going to put up with what happened in the past."

In 2007, the CBC television show *Little Mosque on the Prairie* began offering a peek into the religious and cultural issues faced by Canada's large immigrant population. It remains a popular program and is in its fifth season in 2011.

EATING & DRINKING

A generation ago, most Montréal and Québec City restaurants served only French food. A few *temples de cuisine* delivered haute standards of gastronomy, while numerous accomplished bistros served up humbler ingredients in less grand settings and folksy places offered the hearty fare that employed the ingredients long available in New France—game such as caribou, maple syrup, and root vegetables. Everything else was considered "ethnic." Food crazes of the 1980s focusing on Cajun, Tex-Mex, and fusion didn't make much of a dent at the time.

The 1990s recession put many restaurateurs out of business and forced others to reexamine their operation. In Montréal, especially, immigrants brought the cooking styles of the world to the city.

Restaurants are colloquially called "restos," and they range from moderately priced bistros, cafes, and ethnic joints to swank luxury epicurean shrines.

Menu Basics

One thing to always look for are table d'hôte meals. These are fixed-price menus, and with them, three- or four-course meals can be had for little more than the price of an a la carte main course. Even the best restaurants offer them, which

Table d'hôte meals are available at most restaurants and are often the best deal.

Québec cheeses often win awards at international competitions.

means that you'll be able to sample some excellent venues without breaking the bank. Table d'hôte meals are often offered at lunch, when they are even less expensive; having your main meal midday instead of in the evening is the most economical way to sample many of the top establishments.

Remember that for the Québécois, *dîner* (dinner) is the noon meal, and *souper* (supper) is the evening meal. In this book, the word dinner is used in the common American sense—the evening meal. Note, too, that an *entrée* in Québec is an appetizer, while a *plat principal* is a main course. Fancier places may offer a complementary pre-appetizer nibble called an *amuse bouche.*

Many higher-end establishments now offer tasting menus, with many smaller dishes over the course of a meal to show a sampling of the chef's skills. Gaining popularity are surprise menus, also called "chef's whim," where you don't know what you're getting until it's there in front of you. It's becoming more common to find fine restaurants that offer wine pairings with meals, as well, where the sommelier selects a glass (or half glass, if you ask) for each course.

Local Food Highlights

Be sure to try regional specialties. A Québécois favorite is *poutine:* French fries doused with gravy and cheese curds. It's ubiquitous in winter.

Game is popular, including venison, quail, goose, caribou, and wapiti (North American deer). Many menus feature emu and lamb raised north of Québec City in Charlevoix. Mussels and salmon are also standard.

For sandwiches and snacks that cost only a few dollars, try any of the numerous places that go by the generic name *casse-croûte.* Menu items might include soup and *chiens chaud* (hot dogs).

Québec cheeses deserve attention, and many can be sampled only in Canada because they are often unpasteurized—made of *lait cru* (raw milk)—and therefore subject to strict export rules. Better restaurants will offer them as a final course. Of the more than 500 varieties available, you might look for Mimolette Jeune (firm, fragrant, orange), Valbert St-Isidor (similar to Swiss in texture), St-Basil de Port Neuf (buttery), Cru des Erables (soft, ripe), Oka (semisoft, made of cow's milk in a monastery), and Le Chèvre Noire (a sharp goat variety covered in black wax). Québec cheeses pick up armfuls of prizes each year in the American Cheese Society competition, North America's largest.

Cheeses with the *fromages de pays* label are made in Québec with whole milk and no modified milk ingredients. The label represents solidarity among artisanal producers and is supported by Solidarité Rurale du Québec, a group devoted to revitalizing rural communities. It's also supported by Slow Food Québec, which promotes sustainable agriculture and local production. Information is available at www.fromageduquebec.qc.ca.

Beer & Wine

Alcohol is heavily taxed, and imported varieties even more so than domestic versions, so if you're looking to save a little, buy Canadian. That's not difficult when it comes to beer, for there are many regional breweries, from Montréal powerhouse Molson to micro, that produce delicious products. Among the best local options are Belle Gueule and Boréal. The sign BIERES EN FUT means "beers on draft." The Montréal beer festival, the Mondial de la bière (www.festivalmondial biere.qc.ca), is a giddy event. The 18th edition in 2011 was held at Place Bonaventure, where 136 breweries presented their ales, 26 of them representing Québec.

Wine is another matter. It is not produced in significant quantities in Canada due to a climate generally inhospitable to the essential grapes. But you might try bottles from the vineyards of the Cantons-de-l'Est region (just east of Montréal). Sample, too, the sweet "ice wines" and "ice ciders" made from grapes and apples after the first frost. Many decent ones come from vineyards and orchards just an hour from Montréal.

One popular wine is L'Orpailleur, Seyval (www.orpailleur.ca). *L'orpailleur* refers to someone who mines for gold in streams—the idea being that trying to make good wine in Québec's cold climate requires a similar leap of faith in the ability to defy the odds.

WHEN TO GO

High season in the province of Québec is June 24 (Jean-Baptiste Day) through early September (Labour Day). In Québec City, the period from Christmas to New Year's and February weekends during the big winter Carnaval are busy, too. Just north of Montréal, the Laurentian Mountains do big ski business in the cold months. Hotels are most likely to be full and charge their highest rates in these periods.

Low season is during March and April, when few events are scheduled and winter sports start to be iffy. The late-fall months of October and November are also slow due to their all-but-empty social calendars.

Weather

Temperatures are usually a few degrees lower in Québec City than in Montréal. Spring, short but sweet, arrives around the middle of May. Summer (mid-June through mid-Sept) tends to be humid in Montréal, Québec City, and other communities along the St. Lawrence River, and drier at the inland resorts of the Laurentides and the Cantons-de-l'Est. Intense, but usually brief, heat waves mark July and early August, but temperatures rarely remain oppressive in the evenings.

Autumn (Sept–Oct) is as short and changeable as spring, with warm days and cool or chilly nights. It's during this season that Canadian maples blaze with color.

Winter brings dependable snows for skiing in the Laurentides, Cantons-de-l'Est, and, north of Québec City, Charlevoix. Snow and slush are present from November to March. For many, Montréal's underground city is a climate-controlled blessing during this time.

For the current Montréal weather forecast, call ☎ **514/283-3010** or check www.weatheroffice.gc.ca.

Average Monthly Temperatures (°F/°C)

MONTRÉAL

	JAN	FEB	MAR	APR	MAY	JUNE	JULY	AUG	SEPT	OCT	NOV	DEC
HIGH (°F)	21	24	35	51	65	73	79	76	66	54	41	27
HIGH (°C)	−6	−4	1	10	18	22	26	24	18	12	5	−2
LOW (°F)	7	10	21	35	47	56	61	59	50	39	29	13
LOW (°C)	−13	−12	−6	1	8	13	16	15	10	3	−1	−10

QUÉBEC CITY

	JAN	FEB	MAR	APR	MAY	JUNE	JULY	AUG	SEPT	OCT	NOV	DEC
HIGH (°F)	18	21	32	46	62	71	76	74	63	50	37	23
HIGH (°C)	−8	−6	0	7	16	21	24	23	17	10	2	−5
LOW (°F)	2	5	16	31	43	53	58	56	46	36	25	9
LOW (°C)	−16	−15	−8	0	6	11	12	13	7	2	−3	−12

Holidays

Canada's important public holidays are New Year's Day (Jan 1); Good Friday and Easter Monday (Mar or Apr); Victoria Day (the Mon preceding May 25); St-Jean-Baptiste Day, Québec's "national" day (June 24); Canada Day (July 1); Labour Day (first Mon in Sept); Canadian Thanksgiving Day (second Mon in Oct); and Christmas (Dec 25).

Calendar of Events

Year-round, it's nearly impossible to miss a celebration of some sort in Montréal and Québec City. For an exhaustive list of events beyond those listed here, check http://events.frommers.com, where you'll find a searchable, up-to-the-minute roster of what's happening in cities all over the world.

JANUARY

La Fête des Neiges (the Snow Festival), Montréal. Montréal's answer to Québec City's February winter Carnaval (see below) features dog-sled runs, a mock survival camp, street hockey, and tobogganing. It's held during the last 2 weekends in January and the beginning of February. Visit www.parcjeandrapeau.com and search for "Fête des Neiges" or call ☎ **514/872-6120.** January 21 to February 5, 2012.

Carnaval de Québec, Québec City.
Never mind that temperatures in Québec regularly plummet in winter to well below freezing. Québecers are extraordinarily good-natured about the cold and happily pack the family up to come out and play. A snowman called Bonhomme (Good Fellow) shuffles into town to preside over the merriment, and revelers descend upon the city to eddy around a monumental ice palace erected in front of the Parliament Building, to watch a dog-sledding race on Old Town's narrow streets, to play foosball on a human-size scale, to fly over crowds on a zip line, to ride down snowy hills in rubber tubes, and (not least of all) to dance at outdoor concerts.

The party is family-friendly, even considering the wide availability of plastic trumpets and canes filled with a concoction called caribou, the principal ingredients of which are cheap liquor and sweet red wine. Try not to miss the canoe race that has teams rowing, dragging, and stumbling with canoes across the St. Lawrence's treacherous ice floes. It's homage to how the city used to break up the ice to keep a path open to Lévis, the town across the river.

A C$12 pass provides access to most activities over the 17 days. Hotel reservations must be made well in advance. Call ☎ **866/422-7628** or 418/621-5555, or visit www.carnaval.qc.ca for details. January 27 to February 12, 2012.

Festival Montréal en Lumière (Montréal High Lights Festival). At the heart of this winter celebration are culinary competitions and wine tastings. There are also multimedia light shows, classical and pop concerts, and the Montréal All-Nighter that ends with a free breakfast at dawn. Call ☎ **888/477-9955** or 514/288-9955, or visit www.montreal highlights.com, for details. February 16 to 26, 2012.

Bal en Blanc Party Week, Montréal.
Drawing crowds of an estimated 15,000 people, this 5-day rave/dance party is one of the biggest such events in the world. Last year's "White Party Week" was the 16th annual affair and featured house and trance D.J. events at Palais des Congrès and clubs such as Parking. Visit **www.balenblanc.com**. Early or mid-April, over Easter weekend.

Montréal Museums Day. This event is an open house for most of the city's museums, with free admission and free shuttle buses. Visit www.museesmontreal. org or call the tourism office (☎ **877/ 266-5687** or 514/873-2015) for details. Last Sunday in May.

Montréal Bike Fest. For 8 days, tens of thousands of enthusiasts converge on Montréal to participate in cycling competitions that include a nocturnal bike ride (Tour la Nuit) and the grueling Tour de l'Île, a 52km (32-mile) race around the island's rim; it draws 30,000 cyclists, shuts down roads, and attracts more than 100,000 spectators. The nonprofit biking organization Vélo Québec (☎ **800/567-8356** or 514/521-8356) lists details at www.velo.qc.ca. Late May into early June.

Les FrancoFolies de Montréal. Since 1988, this music fest has featured French-language pop, hip-hop, electronic, world beat, and *chanson*. There are 70 indoor shows and twice as many that are outdoors and free. Call ☎ **888/444-9114** or 514/876-8989, or check www.franco folies.com. June 8 to 16, 2012.

Mondial de la Bière, Montréal. Yes, beer fans, this is a 5-day festival devoted to your favorite beverage. Admission is free, and tasting coupons are C$1 each, with most tastings costing one to five coupons for 3-ounce samples. Showcased are world brands and boutique microbreweries, and "courses" lead to a "Diploma in Beer Tasting." For details, call ⓒ **514/722-9640** or check www.festivalmondialbiere.qc.ca. Early June.

Saint-Ambroise Montréal Fringe Festival. For a long time, the main graphic at this event's website was a hand raising its middle finger. That gives you an idea of the attitude behind the Plateau Mont-Royal fest. It's 10 days of out-there theater with acts such as a one-man *Star Wars* stand-up, clowns gone bad, and drunken drag queens. The festival proclaims that there's "No Artistic Direction. Artists are selected by lottery. . . . No Censorship. Artists have complete freedom to present ANYTHING." *Vive le fringe!* Call ⓒ **514/849-3378** or check www.montrealfringe.ca. Mid-June.

Jean-Baptiste Day. Honoring St. John the Baptist, the patron saint of French-Canadians, this day is marked by far more festivities and enthusiasm throughout Québec than is Canada Day on July 1 (listed below). It's Québec's own *fête nationale* with fireworks, bonfires, music in parks, and parades. Call ⓒ **514/527-9891** or visit www.fetenationale.qc.ca for details. June 24.

L'International des Feux Loto-Québec (International Fireworks Competition), Montréal. Pitting the fireworks displays of different countries against each other, this annual competition is a spectacular event. Buy tickets to watch from the open-air theater in La Ronde amusement park on Île Ste-Hélène, or enjoy the pyrotechnics for free from almost anywhere overlooking the river (tickets have the added benefit of admission to the amusement park). *Insider tip:* The Jacques Cartier bridge closes to traffic during the fireworks and offers an unblocked, up-close view. Kids, needless to say, love the whole explosive business. Call ⓒ **514/397-2000** or go to www.internationaldesfeuxloto-quebec.com for details. In 2011, the

country-themed program was held on Wednesdays and Saturdays from late June to the end of July. Check for 2012 dates.

JULY

Canada Day. On July 1, 1867, three British colonies joined together to form the federation of Canada, with further independence from Britain coming in stages in the 1880s. Celebrations of Canada's birthday are biggest in Ottawa, though there are concerts, flag raisings, and family festivities in Montréal and Québec City. July 1.

Festival International de Jazz de Montréal. Since Montréal has a long tradition in jazz, this is one of the monster events on the city's calendar, celebrating America's art form since 1979. The 2011 edition featured performances by guitarist Paco de Lucia, Best New Artist Grammy winner Esperanza Spalding, k. d. lang, Robert Plant, the B-52s, Sade, Prince, Diana Krall, Chick Corea, Youssou N'Dour, and hundreds more. It costs serious money to hear stars of such magnitude, and tickets often sell out months in advance. Fortunately, 450 free outdoor performances also take place during the late-June/early July party, many right on downtown's streets and plazas. Call ⓒ **888/515-0515** or 514/523-3378, or visit www.montrealjazzfest.com. The 33rd edition of the festival will be held from June 28 to July 7, 2012.

Festival Juste pour Rire (Just for Laughs Festival), Montréal. Well-known comics including Bill Cosby, Whoopi Goldberg, and John Cleese have been featured, while smaller-name Francophone and Anglophone groups and stand-ups from around the world come to perform. It's held mostly along rue St-Denis and elsewhere in the Latin Quarter, both indoors and on the street. Call ⓒ **888/244-3155** or 514/845-2322, or check www.hahaha.com, for details. Held July 5 to 24 in 2011; check for 2012 dates.

Festival d'Eté (Summer Festival), Québec City. The world's largest Francophone music festival happens in the heart of Vieux-Québec and, since 2007, in the St-Roch neighborhood. More than 400 performances of rock, jazz, reggae, and classical take place at both indoor and outdoor venues. Elton John and Metallica graced the stage in 2011—although not at the same time. Call ⓒ 888/992-5200 or 418/523-4540, or check www.infofestival.com. Held July 5 to 15, 2012.

Les Grands Feux Loto-Québec, Québec City. Overlapping with Montréal's fireworks competition (see above), Québec's event uses the highly scenic Montmorency Falls 15 minutes north of the city center as its setting. Pyrotechnical teams are invited from countries around the world. Tickets get you admission to the base of the falls: There are 5,500 reserved bleacher seats and 30,000 general-admission tickets. Call ⓒ 888/523-3389 or 418/523-3389, or go to www.quebecfireworks.com, for details. Wednesdays and Saturdays, late July to mid-August. Check for 2012 dates.

Divers/Cité Festival, Montréal. In partnership with government agencies and sponsored by major corporations, Divers/Cité is one of North America's largest parties for gay, lesbian, bisexual, and transgendered people. It's 6 days of dance, drag, art, and music concerts, and nearly everything is outdoors and free. For details, call ⓒ 514/285-4011 or visit www.diverscite.org. Late July.

Festival International de Courses de Bateaux-Dragons de Montréal. The annual dragon boat festival welcomes some 200 teams that pour into the Olympic Basin on Île Notre-Dame. In addition to races, there are drawing contests for children and opportunities to try paddling on the ancient Chinese crafts. Details are at **www.montreal dragonboat.com**. Three days in late July.

Festival des Films du Monde (World Film Festival), Montréal. This festival has been an international film event since 1977. A strong panel of actors, directors, and writers from around the world make up the jury each year, giving the event a weight that many festivals lack. Various movie theaters play host. Call ⓒ 514/848-3883 or check www.ffm-montreal.org for details. Late August to early September.

La Fête des Vendanges. This event gives attendees a chance to discover the scenic wine country and charming streets of Magog and Orford in the Eastern Townships. During the grape harvest season, visitors can partake in dinner cruises along Lac Memphrémagog, street festivals, and restaurant events that bring together chefs and wine producers for special dinner collaborations. Last year's dates were September 3, 4, 5, 10, and 11. Visit **www.fetedes vendanges.com** for updates.

Fall Foliage. Starting midmonth, the maple trees blaze with color, and a walk in the parks of Montréal and Québec City is a refreshing tonic. It's also a perfect time to drive to the Laurentians or Cantons-de-L'Est (both near Montréal) or Île d'Orléans or Charlevoix (both easy drives from Québec City).

Black & Blue Festival, Montréal. One of the biggest gay events on the planet, this party was, a few years ago, named the best international fest by France's Pink TV Awards, beating out even Carnival in Rio. And when we say big, we mean *big:* The main event is an all-night party at Olympic Stadium. There's also a Jock Ball, a Leather Ball, and a Military Ball. Call ⓒ 514/875-7026 or visit www.bbcm.org. Seven days in mid-October.

Festival du Nouveau Cinéma, Montréal. Screenings of new and experimental films ignite controversy, and forums discuss the latest trends in cinema and video. Events take place at halls and cinemas throughout the city. Call ✆ **514/282-0004** or check www. nouveaucinema.ca. Twelve days in mid-October.

DECEMBER

Christmas through New Year's, Québec City. Celebrating the holidays *a la française* is a particular treat here, where the streets are almost certainly banked with snow and nearly every ancient building sports wreaths, decorated fir trees, and glittery white lights.

RESPONSIBLE TRAVEL

Montréal walks the walk when it comes to green living—or, more accurately, it bikes the bike. Its **BIXI system,** a self-service bicycle rental program that debuted in the spring of 2009, began picking up awards even before a single bike hit the streets, including a prestigious Edison Best New Products Award for best product of 2009 in the Energy & Sustainability category.

That was high praise for a service that had yet to satisfy even one customer. But since its launch, BIXI (which is an abbreviation of the words *bicyclette* and *taxi*) has proven popular. Fees and details are listed at www.bixi.com/home or call ✆ **877/820-2453** or 514/789-BIXI (2494). As with programs in Berlin, Paris, and Barcelona, BIXI users pay a small fee to pick up bikes from designated bike stands and drop them off at any other stand. (Helmets are not included.) Modular bike-rack stations are Web-enabled and solar-powered, and are open spring, summer, and fall (Apr–Nov). At the beginning of the 2010 biking season, BIXI had 5,000 bikes on the road and 400 stations in Montréal's central boroughs. Last season, over three million trips were made.

BIXI is most economical for short trips (that's what it's designed for), so visitors who want a bike for a full day or longer will find it cheaper to rent from a shop.

Montréal does make it easy to bike. There is a huge network of bicycle paths throughout the city, with whole sections of roads turned into bike lanes during the warm months. See "Exploring Montréal" on p. 108 and "Exploring Québec City" on p. 275 for information.

These are walking cities, too. In the warm months, Montréal closes off large sections of main streets for pedestrian-only traffic, including rue Ste-Catherine in the Village and, for special events, rue St-Paul in Vieux-Montréal and rue St-Laurent in the Plateau. In 2009, the Plateau neighborhood unveiled a 15-year plan to create more pedestrian-only streets, wider sidewalks, and a tramway line on avenue du Parc, which runs north-south through the eastern side of Parc du Mont-Royal. It's part of a grander effort to reduce traffic and encourage public transport and strolling.

The Hotel Association of Canada (HAC) oversees the **Green Key Eco-Rating Program** (in French, **Clé Verte**), which awards a rating of one to five green keys to hotels that minimize waste and reduce their ecological footprint. The voluntary, self-administered audit assesses five areas within hotel management, including housekeeping and food services. Recipients often display a Green Key/Clé Verte plaque in a prominent location alongside other commendations. While HAC does not currently verify the audits on a national scale, the **Corporation de l'industrie touristique du Québec** (www.citq.info) does so within the province of Québec. To read a description of each award tier and to locate Green Key hotels, visit **www.greenkeyglobal.com**.

Restaurants throughout the region tout locally sourced food on their menus, with much of the region's food grown, raised, or caught within 161km (100 miles). At the high-end **Aix Cuisine du Terroir** (p. 90) in Montréal, for instance, *terroir* refers to soil and the restaurant's allegiance to products grown in the immediate region. You can also find "biodynamic," or organic, wines at many restaurants.

Bring carry bags when you go shopping: BYOB took on a new meaning— Bring Your Own Bag—in early 2009, when the province's Société des alcools du Québec (SAQ) liquor stores stopped using single-use plastic and paper bags. "It's a green action," said a spokesperson. "It's really a big statement for sustainable development." The initiative was easy to push through at the wine and hard-liquor stores because the province has a monopoly on them. The hope is that, by setting the bar high in SAQ stores, other retailers will follow suit. Reusable bags are sold at SAQ stores for C75¢ to C$4.

In addition to the resources listed above, see www.frommers.com/planning for more tips on responsible travel.

TOURS
Academic Trips & Language Classes

If you're itching to dust off your notebooks from high school French class, the **Université du Québec à Montréal** (**UQAM;** ✆ **514/987-3000,** ext. 5621; www.langues.immersion.uqam.ca) offers French immersion courses for 1 to 3 weeks in either July or August. Students can opt for on-campus housing or stay with a host family. One session integrates French instruction with jazz events during the renowned Festival International de Jazz de Montréal. Programs are geared for persons 18 and up, beginners through intermediate.

Adults and teens alike can combine an array of activities with French language immersion in Québec City through **Edu-Inter** (✆ **514/613-0102;** www. learningfrenchinquebec.com). Year-round sessions can quench an *amour pour le français* by combining language programs with skiing, cooking, horseback riding, or sight-seeing.

Adventure & Wellness Trips

Bike touring is wildly popular and well accommodated in Québec. The province inaugurated the **Route Verte (Green Route),** a 4,000km (2,485-mile) bike network, in the summer of 2007. Many inns and restaurants along the route actively work to accommodate the nutritional, safety, and equipment needs of cyclists. See "Biker's Paradise: The 4,000km Route Verte" on p. 207 for details and contact information.

Vélo Québec (✆ **800/567-8356** or 514/521-8356; www.velo.qc.ca) was behind the development of the Route Verte and offers excellent biking information. It also offers guided bike tours throughout the province, coordinating meals, accommodations, and baggage transport.

The gorgeously rural Charlevoix region, an hour north of Québec City, is the perfect place in which to take an eco-tour. Charlevoix was designated a protected UNESCO World Biosphere Reserve in 1988 and is subject to balanced development and cross-disciplinary research into conservation. For tour suggestions, check with **Aventure Ecotourisme Québec** (www.aventure-ecotourisme.qc.ca), an association of tour operators that provides outdoor adventure programs with a focus on environmental care and preservation. It is governed by a commitment policy which member companies promise to respect. It is partner to **Leave No Trace Center for Outdoor Ethics** (www.leavenotrace.ca), which educates operators and tourists about how to minimize the environmental impact of recreation. Aventure Ecotourisme also offers vacation planning.

One association member is **Mer et Monde Ecotours** (✆ 866/637-6663 or 418/232-6779; www.mer-et-monde.qc.ca), which puts on kayak trips in Charlevoix that take clients close to the whales who converge in the region each summer. For more information, see p. 346.

Food & Wine Trips

In Montréal, **Europea** restaurant (p. 84; ✆ 514/398-9229; www.europea.ca) offers 1-hour cooking lessons for C$45 per person (click on "L'Atelier" at the website). Europea knows of which it teaches: The title of Chef of the Year was bestowed on chef Jérôme Ferrer by the Société des Chefs, Cuisiniers et Pâtissiers du Québec in 2007.

Also in Montréal is the **École de cuisine Mezza Luna,** with Italian cooking classes by Elena Faita-Venditelli. She runs the packed-to-the-rafters cookware (and sportswear) shop **Quincaillerie Dante,** 6851 rue St-Dominique (✆ 514/271-2057). In 2008, Faita-Venditelli was named "l'Ordre national," the most prestigious honorary distinction in the province. Call ✆ 514/272-5299 or visit www.ecolemezzaluna.ca to inquire; note that classes are often booked months in advance.

In the Laurentians, about an hour north of Montréal on the way to Mont-Tremblant, guests of **L'Eau à la Bouche** (p. 208) can opt for a weekend package that includes hands-on kitchen training with chef/owner Anne Desjardins. Call ✆ 888/828-2991 or 450/229-2991, or visit www.leaualabouche.com.

In Québec City, the famed restaurant **Laurie Raphaël** (p. 269; ✆ 418/692-4555; www.laurieraphael.com) has a fancy public kitchen on its premises (along with a small boutique of cooking equipment). From September to May, chef/owner Daniel Vézina gives 3- to 4-hour cooking classes here on Saturday afternoons for C$185 per person (cost includes a meal, plus wine). Reservations are required. Also in Québec City, **Les Artistes de la Table** (✆ 418/694-1056; www.lesartistesdelatable.com) offers 4-hour custom cooking classes in the first floor of a gorgeous neoclassical building from 1850. Serious cooks will want to walk by just to peek at the kitchen through the vast windows. Cost is about C$120 per person.

If you have a car, the **Route des Vins (Wine Route),** 103km (64 miles) southeast of Montréal, is a pleasant vineyard tour that goes past **Vignoble de l'Orpailleur** (✆ 450/295-2763; www.orpailleur.ca), **Domaine Pinnacle** (✆ 450/263-5835; www.domainepinnacle.com), and **Le Cep d'Argent** (✆ 877/864-4441 or 819/864-4441; www.cepdargent.com), all within Cantons-de-l'Est (p. 222), the region that specializes in cider and ice wine.

Foodies will also want to take a look at the website for **The Gourmet Route,** www.parcoursgourmand.com. The site promotes "gourmet tourism" and lists some 50 growers, processors, gourmet restaurants, and stores. An interactive map, at www.parcoursgourmand.com/eng/mdl-carte-parcours.asp, is especially useful for seeing what farms are nearest.

SUGGESTED MONTRÉAL & QUÉBEC CITY ITINERARIES

3

Public transportation in Montréal is excellent, and Québec City is compact, so you won't need a car for the itineraries listed here. While some suggestions are best for warm weather, most of the listings are appropriate for all seasons—just remember to bundle up in wintertime.

THE BEST OF MONTRÉAL IN 1 DAY

This exploration of historic Montréal allows time for random exploring, shopping, or lingering in sidewalk cafes. If you're staying only 1 night, book a room in one of Vieux-Montréal's boutique hotels. Visitors find themselves drawn to the plazas and narrow cobblestone streets of this 18th- and 19th-century neighborhood, so you might as well be based there. ***Start:*** *Vieux-Montréal, at Place d'Armes.*

1 Place d'Armes ★★★

The city's oldest building, the Vieux Séminaire de St-Sulpice, can be found at Place d'Armes. PREVIOUS PAGE: The streets of Old Montréal at night.

Begin your day in the heart of **Vieux-Montréal ★★★**, at the site of the city's oldest building, the **Vieux Séminaire de St-Sulpice** (p. 147), erected by priests who arrived in 1657. Next to it is the **Basilique Notre-Dame ★★★** (p. 115), an 1824 church with a stunning interior of intricately gilded rare woods. Its acoustics are so perfect that the late, famed opera star Luciano Pavarotti performed here several times.

Consider taking the walking tour on p. 144, which takes you past every historic structure in Vieux-Montréal and eventually to our next stop. Or, to go to Pointe-à-Callière directly, walk down the slope from the basilica.

2 Pointe-à-Callière ★★★

The **Pointe-à-Callière (Museum of Archaeology and History)** is an engaging and educational museum. Its below-ground tunnels have remnants of Amerindian camps and early French settlements. See p. 116.

3 Olive et Gourmando 🍵

This special cafe is a city highlight—and great for seeing American celebrities who are filming movies in town. Eat in, or take out if the weather's nice for a picnic lunch by the river. The Cuban sandwich is a popular choice. 351 rue St-Paul ouest. ✆ **514/350-1083.** See p. 95.

Unless you're a very ambitious walker, take a cab, the Métro to Guy-Concordia, or a BIXI rental bike to get to:

4 Musée des Beaux-Arts ★★★

This is the city's glorious fine-arts museum. Permanent exhibits are free, and temporary shows are dazzling. See p. 109.

5 Rue Crescent ★

From the museum, walk south on rue Crescent. If you're in a shopping mood, Ste-Catherine, 2 blocks down, is the nexus for

Rue Crescent is close to good shopping and nightlife.

department stores and midpriced shopping (turn left and head east). Rue Crescent itself is downtown's primary nightlife district, albeit a touristy one. If it's warm, grab a seat on a terrace for great people-watching. During the Grand Prix this place is packed.

6 Sir Winston Churchill Pub ☕

Epicenter of the rue Crescent scene for ages, this pub is filled with chatty 20- to 40-somethings. It's a good spot to nurse a pint while taking in the passing parade. 1459 rue Crescent. ✆ **514/288-3814.** See p. 196.

For dinner options downtown or further afield, consult the listings in chapter 6.

THE BEST OF MONTRÉAL IN 2 DAYS

With the absolute essentials of historic Old Montréal and downtown Anglophone cultural institutions under your belt, prepare to take a journey into French Montréal. Just before Montréal hosted the 1976 Olympics, municipal authorities erected some principal venues in the city's eastern, overwhelmingly Francophone precincts, which is where we start. ***Start:*** *Viau Métro station.*

1 Jardin Botanique ★★★

These lush, romantic, year-round botanical gardens comprise 75 hectares (185 acres) of plants and flowers with 10 exhibition greenhouses. The Japanese Garden has an extremely relaxing Zen garden, while the butterfly house (open Feb–Apr) hosts hundreds of live butterflies who flit around and sometimes alight on visitors' shoulders. See p. 120.

The Jardin Botanique is home to a relaxing Zen garden.

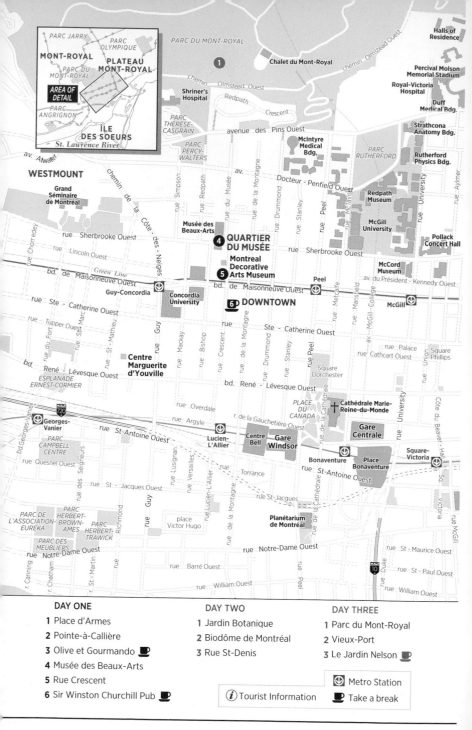

DAY ONE

1. Place d'Armes
2. Pointe-à-Callière
3. Olive et Gourmando ☕
4. Musée des Beaux-Arts
5. Rue Crescent
6. Sir Winston Churchill Pub ☕

DAY TWO

1. Jardin Botanique
2. Biodôme de Montréal
3. Rue St-Denis

DAY THREE

1. Parc du Mont-Royal
2. Vieux-Port
3. Le Jardin Nelson ☕

(i) Tourist Information

🚇 Metro Station
☕ Take a break

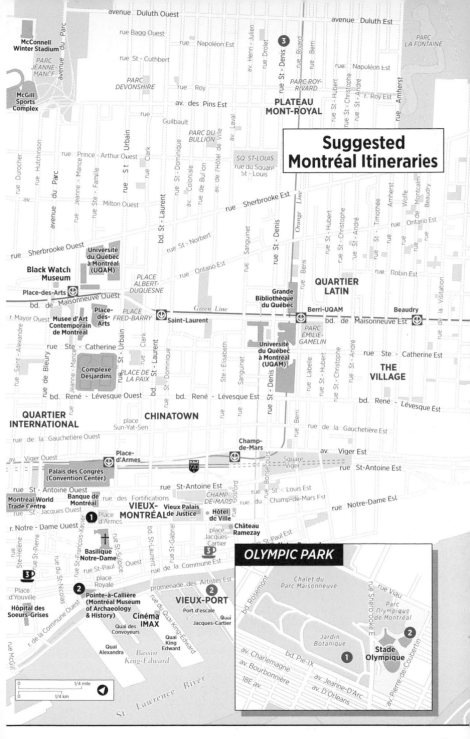

Suggested Montréal Itineraries

OLYMPIC PARK

2 Biodôme de Montréal ★★

Originally a velodrome (cycling track) built for the 1976 Olympics, this unique facility replicates four ecosystems, complete with tropical trees and golden lion tamarin monkeys that swing overhead (p. 119). Just adjacent is **Stade Olympique,** the controversial Olympic Stadium with an inclined tower. It was scorned as the "Big Owe" and then the "Big Woe" due to cost overruns that provoked elevated taxes. It now houses public pools and a funicular to an observation deck. See p. 120.

Take the Métro to Sherbrooke and walk 1 block west to rue St-Denis, turning left (north).

3 Rue St-Denis ★★

Rue St-Denis is the thumping central artery of Francophone Montréal, thick with cafes, bistros, offbeat shops, and lively nightspots. As you head north into the lower precincts of Plateau Mont-Royal, there are no must-see sights, so wander at will and surrender to the heart of French Montréal's color and vitality.

The Plateau Mont-Royal walking tour on p. 159 provides shopping and eating options for once you reach rue Duluth.

THE BEST OF MONTRÉAL IN 3 DAYS

If you've followed the above itineraries, you've already visited Montréal's primary must-see sights. On this third day, take in the great parks and waterways of the city. *Start: Peel Métro station (if you're in the mood for a hike) or a taxi ride to Lac des Castors in Parc du Mont-Royal.*

1 Parc du Mont-Royal

The hill that rises behind downtown is the small mountain, Mont Royal, that gave the city its name. Its rounded crest became a public park somewhat according to plans by architect Frederick Law Olmsted. Throngs of people come for its woods, paths, and meadows in all four seasons. You can join them with a stroll up from Peel station (see p. 164 for a walking tour) or a taxi ride to Lac des Castors (Beaver Lake). See p. 113.

Make your way either by bus and Métro, or by taxi, to the southern end of the city.

2 Vieux-Port ★★

The Old Port at the edge of Vieux-Montréal has been transformed into a broad, vibrant park. Principal among the attractions is the **Centre des Sciences de Montréal** (p. 116), on quai (pier) King Edward. It contains a popular IMAX theater, in addition to interactive exhibits to enthrall most everyone's inner geek.

In the warm months, **Les Sautes-Moutons** (✆ 514/284-9607) depart from the park's east end, near the old clock tower. Also known as Lachine Rapids Tours, the company provides wave-jumper powerboats with which to take on the St. Lawrence River's roiling Lachine Rapids. Other companies provide more sedate river cruises. See p. 137.

The Centre des Sciences de Montréal is one of the Old Town's primary attractions.

You can also rent **bicycles and in-line skates** by the hour or day from here, and then head out to the peaceful **Lachine Canal,** a nearly flat 11km (6.8-mile) bicycle path that's open year-round. See p. 140.

3 Le Jardin Nelson 🍵

Vieux-Montréal has a large number of restaurants. One of the most popular is Le Jardin Nelson, on the main square, Place Jacques-Cartier. It's open in the warm months and has a large terrace where jazz musicians perform during the day and evening. The menu offers a delectable roster of main-course and dessert crepes. 407 Place Jacques-Cartier. ✆ **514/861-5731.**

THE BEST OF QUÉBEC CITY IN 1 DAY

With an ancient wall surrounding the oldest part of the city, Québec City sustains the look of a provincial European village that keeps watch over the powerful St. Lawrence River. For a short visit, book a hotel or B&B within the walls of the Haute-Ville (Upper Town) or in the quieter Basse-Ville (Lower Town). ***Start:*** *Château Frontenac.*

1 Château Frontenac ★★★

As soon as you're done unpacking, head to **Château Frontenac** (p. 248)— its peaked copper roofs are visible from everywhere. Tours of the historic hotel are available (p. 280), and it has a posh bar and pretty cafe. The long promenade alongside the hotel, the **Terrasse Dufferin,** offers panoramic views of the St. Lawrence River and **Basse-Ville (Lower Town)** ★★★ (p. 304). In winter, an old-fashioned toboggan run is set up on the steep staircase at the south end.

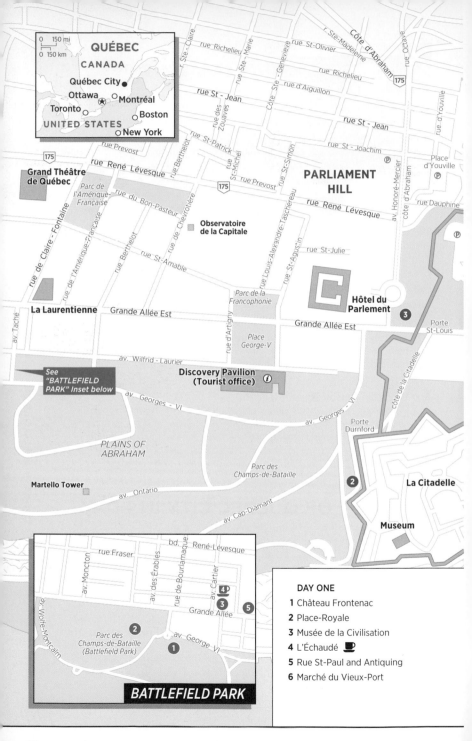

QUÉBEC

CANADA

Québec City
Ottawa ★   ○ Montréal
Toronto ○
○ Boston
UNITED STATES
○ New York

0   150 mi
0   150 km

175

Grand Théâtre
de Québec

Parc de
l'Amérique-
Française

rue René Lévesque

rue Prevost

rue du Bon-Pasteur

rue de Chevrotière

rue Berthelot

rue St-Patrick

rue St-Michel

rue des Zouaves

rue Ste-Claire

rue Richelieu

rue Ste-Marie

Côte Ste-Geneviève

rue St-Olivier

r. Ste-Madeleine

Côte d'Abraham

rue d'Aiguillon

rue Richelieu

rue St - Jean

rue St - Jean

rue St - Joachim

Place
d'Youville

175

rue d'Youville

PARLIAMENT
HILL

rue Prevost

rue René Lévesque

av. Honoré-Mercier

côte d'Abraham

rue Dauphine

Observatoire
de la Capitale

rue St-Simon

rue Louis-Alexandre-Taschereau

rue St-Agustin

rue St-Julie

Hôtel du
Parlement

3

Porte
St-Louis

côte de la Citadelle

La Laurentienne

Grande Allée Est

Grande Allée Est

Parc de la
Francophonie

rue d'Artigny

Place
George-V

av. Wilfrid - Laurier

av. Taché

Discovery Pavilion
(Tourist office) ⓘ

See
"BATTLEFIELD
PARK" Inset below

av. Georges - VI

av. Georges - VI

Porte
Durnford

PLAINS OF
ABRAHAM

Parc des
Champs-de-Bataille

2

La Citadelle

Martello Tower

av. Ontario

av. Cap-Diamant

Museum

rue Fraser

bd. René-Lévesque

av. Moncton

av. des Érables

rue de Boulamaque

av. Cartier

Grande Allée

4
3
5

av. Wolfe-Montcalm

Parc des
Champs-de-Bataille
(Battlefield Park)

2

1

av. George VI

BATTLEFIELD PARK

DAY ONE

1 Château Frontenac
2 Place-Royale
3 Musée de la Civilisation
4 L'Échaudé 🍽
5 Rue St-Paul and Antiquing
6 Marché du Vieux-Port

42

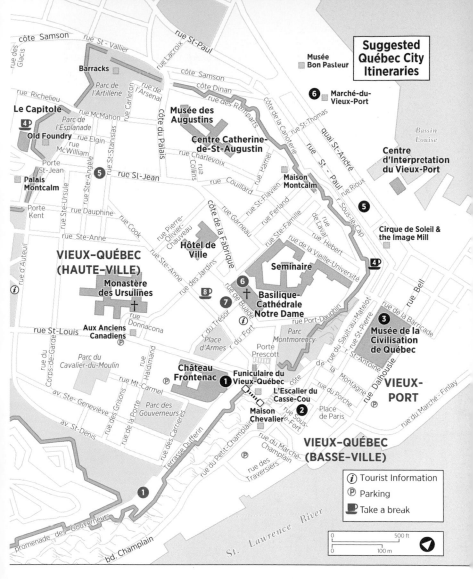

Suggested Québec City Itineraries

côte Samson
rue St-Vallier
rue St-Paul
Barracks
Parc de l'Artillerie
côte Samson
côte Dinan
Musée Bon Pasteur
rue Richelieu
rue de l'Arsenal
rue des Remparts
6 Marché-du-Vieux-Port
Le Capitole
4🄿 Old Foundry
Parc de l'Esplanade
rue McMahon
Musée des Augustins
rue de la Canoterie
côte de la Canoterie
rue St-Thomas
quai St-André
Bassin Louise
rue Elgin
rue McWilliam
Centre Catherine-de-St-Augustin
rue Charlevoix
Maison Montcalm
Centre d'Interprétation du Vieux-Port
Porte St-Jean
5 rue St-Jean
rue Collins
rue Couillard
rue St-Flavien
rue Ferland
Palais Montcalm
Porte Kent
rue Ste-Ursule
rue Dauphine
côte de la Fabrique
rue Garneau
rue Ste-Famille
5
Cirque de Soleil & the Image Mill
rue d'Auteuil
rue Ste-Anne
rue Cook
Hôtel de Ville
rue de la Vieille-Université
4🄿
ⓘ
VIEUX-QUÉBEC (HAUTE-VILLE)
rue Pierre-Olivier-Chauveau
rue Ste-Anne
rue des Jardins
Seminaire
rue Bell
rue de la Barricade
Monastère des Ursulines
8🄿
6 ✝ Basilique-Cathédrale Notre Dame
7
ⓘ
rue St-Louis
Aux Anciens Canadiens
rue Donnacona
Parc Montmorency
3 Musée de la Civilisation de Québec
Parc du Cavalier-du-Moulin
rue Haldimand
Château Frontenac
1
Funiculaire du Vieux-Québec
Porte Prescott
Place d'Armes
rue du Fort
rue Dalhousie
VIEUX-PORT
av. Ste-Geneviève
rue Mt-Carmel
L'Escalier du Casse-Cou
Maison Chevalier
2
Place de Paris
rue du Porche
av. St-Denis
Parc des Gouverneurs
Terrasse Dufferin
VIEUX-QUÉBEC (BASSE-VILLE)
rue du Marché-Champlain
rue des Traversiers
ⓘ Tourist Information
🄿 Parking
☕ Take a break
1
promenade des Gouverneurs
bd. Champlain
St. Lawrence River
0   500 ft
0   100 m

DAY TWO

1 Promenade des Gouverneurs
2 La Citadelle
3 Porte St-Louis and the Walls
4 Ristorante il Teatro ☕
5 Rue St-Jean
6 Basilique Notre-Dame
7 Québec Expérience
8 Le Pain Béni ☕

DAY THREE

1 Musée des Beaux-Arts
  du Québec
2 Parc des Champs-de-Bataille
3 Avenue Cartier
4 Café Krieghoff ☕
5 Grande-Allée

Head down to Basse-Ville either by the *funiculaire,* the glass-encased outdoor eleva-tor, or the staircase called L'escalier du Casse-Cou. They're right next to each other. Both routes end at the top of rue du Petit-Champlain, a touristy pedestrian street of shops and restaurants. Walk down rue Sous-le-Fort and make the first left turn to reach:

2 Place-Royale ★★★

This small but picturesque square was the site of the first European colony in Canada and is surrounded by restored 17th- and 18th-century houses. The **church** on one side was built in 1688. A visit to the **Centre d'Interprétation de Place-Royale** is an option here. See p. 277.

Past the Centre d'Interprétation, at the end of rue Notre-Dame, turn around to view a *trompe l'oeil* mural depicting citizens of the early city. Continue past the mural and turn right to walk toward the river. Turn left on rue Dalhousie and walk to:

3 Musée de la Civilisation ★★★

A city highlight. This ambitious museum, filled with fascinating exhibits, can easily fill 2 or 3 hours. Don't miss the permanent exhibit, "People of Québec . . . Then and Now," which explores the province's roots as a fur-trading colony and gives visitors a rich sense of Québec's daily life over the generations. See p. 276.

Leaving the museum, turn left on rue Dalhousie, left on rue St-Paul, and walk to rue du Sainte-au-Matelot.

The Musée de la Civilisation is one of the highlights of a visit to Québec City.

4 A Bounty of Bistros ☕

Within a block of the corner of rues St-Paul and du Sault-au-Matelot are some of the city's best bistros and casual eating places. Almost any of them will do for a snack or a meal, but our top choice is L'Echaudé ★, 73 rue du Sault-au-Matelot (📞 **418/692-1299**). It offers excellent value for classic French dishes and puts out sidewalk tables in summer. See p. 269.

5 Rue St-Paul & Antiquing ★

The northern end of rue St-Paul is great for browsing for antiques and collectibles. See p. 310 in the walking tour for some highlights.

Turn right at rue St-Thomas and cross rue St-André.

6 Marché du Vieux-Port

This large market is open year-round, and offers produce and other agricultural products for sale. See p. 317.

THE BEST OF QUÉBEC CITY IN 2 DAYS

During repeated conflicts with the British in the 18th century, the residents of New France moved to the top of the cliffs of Cap Diamant. Over the years, they created fortifications with battlements and artillery emplacements that eventually encircled the city. Most of the defensive walls remain, although many have been restored repeatedly. These historic mementos are the centerpiece of today's tour. **Start:** *Terrasse Dufferin.*

1 Promenade des Gouverneurs

Walk south to the end of Terrasse Dufferin. At the end, go up the staircase to the **Promenade des Gouverneurs.** This path was renovated in 2007 and skirts the sheer cliff wall, climbing up and up past Québec's military **Citadelle,** a fort built by the British army between 1820 and 1850 that remains an active military garrison. The promenade/staircase ends at the grassy **Parc des Champs-de-Bataille,** about 15 minutes away.

From here, walk around the rim of the fortress.

2 La Citadelle ★★

The Citadelle has a low profile, dug into the land, instead of rising above it. A ceremonial changing of the guard takes place daily at

The changing of the guard at La Citadelle takes place every morning during the summer.

SUGGESTED MONTRÉAL & QUÉBEC CITY ITINERARIES

The Best of Québec City in 2 Days

10am in summer (June 24 to the first Mon of Sept) and can be viewed from here. See p. 280.

Walk down the hill toward the road. Grande-Allée passes through the city walls at porte (gate) St Louis, our next destination.

3 Porte St-Louis & the Walls

After Grande-Allée passes through **porte St-Louis,** it becomes rue St-Louis, a main road through Old Town. The long greenway on the inside of the walls here is **Parc l'Esplanade.** Stroll along it and down a steep hill to another main gate in the wall, **porte St-Jean** (it is, sad to say, a 20th-century re-creation). Nearby is the **Parc de l'Artillerie,** where you can view an officer's mess and quarters and an old iron foundry. See p. 285.

Walk west on rue St-Jean through the gate. This is Place d'Youville, a plaza with hotels, a concert hall, and restaurants. Many of the city's festivals, in both summer and winter, set up outdoor stages here.

4 Ristorante il Teatro 🍽

A good bet for lunch or dinner, with sidewalk seating in warm weather. Pasta and risotto are specialties. The restaurant is part of Le Capitole, a hotel-theater complex. 972 rue St-Jean. 📞 **418/694-9996.**

Walk back through the gate to browse along:

5 Rue St-Jean

One of the liveliest of Vieux-Québec's streets, rue St-Jean is lined with an ever-updated variety of shops, pubs, and restaurants. Some of the shopping possibilities here are listed in chapter 17.

At the end of rue St-Jean, bear right up Côte de la Fabrique. At the end is:

6 Basilique Notre-Dame ★

What with bombardments, fires, and repeated rebuilding, this home of the oldest Christian parish north of Mexico is nothing if not perseverant. Parts of it, including the bell tower, survive from the original 1647 building, but most of what remains is from a 1771 reconstruction. Step inside to see the blindingly bright gold leaf. See p. 280.

Leaving the church, walk left along rue du Buade and turn right onto the narrow pedestrian alley rue du Trésor. Artists set up here and sell etchings, drawings, and watercolors. Directly on the street at no. 8, go inside for:

7 Québec Expérience

This 3-D show re-creates in vivid detail some of the grim realities of being a settler. Guns and cannons explode at audiences, a simulated bridge crashes down, and walls of water simulate storms at sea. Kids love it. See p. 285.

The Basilique Notre-Dame is the oldest Christian parish in the New World north of Mexico.

Rue du Trésor ends at the central plaza of Upper Town, Place d'Armes. Château Frontenac is directly across the plaza.

8   Outdoor Cafe Dining ☕
If it's warm, snag an outdoor table at any of the restaurants on rue Ste-Anne. One favorite is Le Pain Béni, the restaurant at the Auberge Place d'Armes (p. 265). You can try Québécois classics with modern twists, or more simple pastas. 24 rue Ste-Anne. ☎ **866/333-9485** or 418/694-9485.

THE BEST OF QUÉBEC CITY IN 3 DAYS

While the romance of the capital is largely contained within Vieux-Québec's Lower and Upper towns, there is much to experience outside the Old City. On your third day, try to make time for at least one or two of the following attractions, toward the western end of Parc des Champs-de-Bataille (Battlefields Park). *Start: Musée des Beaux-Arts.*

1   Musée National des Beaux-Arts du Québec ★★★

Inside **Parc des Champs-de-Bataille (Battlefields Park,** which contains the Plains of Abraham) is the capital's most important art museum. It focuses on Inuit sculpture and the works of Québec-born artisans. The original 1933 museum is connected to a newer structure by a glass-roofed pavilion that has a reception area, museum shop, and cafe. See p. 281.

Walk outside into:

2 Parc des Champs-de-Bataille ★★

Get some fresh air with a stroll through the 108 hectares (267 acres) that comprise Canada's first national urban park and the city's playground. Within its rolling hills are two Martello towers, cylindrical stone defensive structures built between 1808 and 1812, as well as cycling and rollerblading paths and picnic grounds. See p. 282.

Head back to the main street, Grand-Allée, and cross over to the perpendicular street:

3 Avenue Cartier

Just a few blocks from the museum, avenue Cartier is part of the laid-back residential Montcalm district. There are intriguing shops and restaurants here.

4 Café Krieghoff ☕

This cheerful cafe has an outdoor terrace a few steps up from the sidewalk. On weekend mornings, it's packed with artsy locals of all ages, whose tables are piled high with bowls of café au lait and huge plates of egg dishes, sweet pastries, or classics like steak *frites*. 1089 av. Cartier. ✆ **418/522-3711.** See p. 272.

5 Grande-Allée

Walk back to Grande-Allée and turn left to get back to the Old City. There's a gentle downhill slope. After about 3 blocks, the shoulder-to-shoulder rows of cafes and clubs begin. One great way to end the day is with a stop at **L'Astral,** the restaurant and bar atop Loews le Concorde Hotel, at the corner of Cours du Général-De Montcalm. The room spins slowly and lets you look back at all the places you've been. See p. 272.

Café Krieghoff has a popular outdoor terrace.

GETTING TO KNOW MONTRÉAL

Somehow **Montréal** knows she's the most eclectic of Canada's cities: The island metropolis hosts international gigs like the Jazz Fest, delights culinary crowds with her French-Canadian cuisine, and struts her Euro-heritage along the historic streets of the newly revitalized **Vieux-Montréal.** Impressively bilingual in English and French, Montréal's global mix is a diverse microplanet of Scottish, Chinese, Haitian, Arabic, Jewish, Italian, Portuguese, Filipino, and Greek immigrants, just to name a few. All this is wrapped up in a vibrant arts and culture scene and energized by an exuberant university community.

Things to Do   Hop on a public BIXI bike and wind your way up **Mont Royal,** the central landmark where Montréal gets her name, then enjoy a leisurely picnic by **Beaver Lake.** If you're smart, you packed a **Schwartz's** smoked-meat sandwich in your basket. Then make your way down to the **Old Port** for some rollerblading along the canal, stopping by a microbrasserie en route to sampling Québec's famous local ales. Unwind with a relaxing body treatment at **Spa Scandinave** or **Bota Bota.**

Shopping   Shopaholics will find much to love here. All the big labels can be found on the city's main drag, **rue Ste-Catherine.** Add a dash of local style by visiting the vintage and antique shops in the bohemian **Plateau, Mile End,** or **Little Burgundy** neighborhoods. For a taste of Francophone living, try the alluring shops and eateries along mainly French **rue St-Denis.** Finally, stroll along the cobblestoned **rue St-Paul** in Vieux-Montréal for avant-garde fashion and art set in a most picturesque corner of Canada.

Restaurants & Dining   Restaurants in the postcard-pretty neighborhood offer authentic old-world ambience and sophisticated European flair. In summer, be the first to snag the seats on the terrace and you'll fit right in. Come winter, beeline it to the fireplace. **Downtown** and **Quartier International** addresses are equally posh with celebrity chefs, such as Normand Laprise at **Toqué!** While Montréal is bursting with award-winning local produce, reinvented French-Canadian classics, and typical Parisian entrées, don't miss the city's beloved fast food, *poutine.*

Nightlife & Entertainment   Once known as the city of 100 churches, Montréal is now the city of 100 festivals. International heavyweights include the **Jazz Fest** and **Just for Laughs,** but there's also an entire four-season calendar of things to celebrate. Of late, the infamous bar scene on **rue Crescent** or **boulevard St-Laurent** has had to make room for the trendy supper-club crowds in Vieux-Montréal. Equal parts restaurant, bar, and nightclub, come dressed to impress.

PREVIOUS PAGE: **Tam Tams is a popular drumming and dancing event that takes place every Sunday during the summer on Mont Royal.**

ORIENTATION
Arriving

For information about arriving in Montréal by plane, train, car, or bus, see "Getting There" (p. 349).

Visitor Information

The main tourist center for visitors in downtown Montréal is the large **Infotouriste Centre,** at 1255 rue Peel (℗ **877/266-5687** or 514/873-2015; Métro: Peel). It's open daily, and the bilingual staff can provide suggestions for accommodations, dining, car rentals, and attractions.

In Vieux-Montréal, there's a teeny **Tourist Welcome Office** at 174 rue Notre-Dame est, at the corner of Place Jacques-Cartier (Métro: Champ-de-Mars). It's open daily from April 1 to November 15, and closed otherwise except for big events such as Nuit Blanche in February. It has brochures, maps, and a helpful staff.

The city of Montréal maintains a terrific website at **www.tourisme-montreal.org**, which also includes an "insider" blog packed with great tips and up-to-the-minute suggestions.

City Layout

MAIN ARTERIES & STREETS   In downtown Montréal, the principal east-west streets include boulevard René-Lévesque, rue Ste-Catherine (*rue* is the French word for "street"), boulevard de Maisonneuve, and rue Sherbrooke. In general, most addresses on the south side of the street are even and those on the north side are odd. The north-south arteries include rue Crescent, rue McGill, rue St-Denis, and boulevard St-Laurent (aka the Main), which serves as the line of demarcation between east and west Montréal. Most of the downtown areas featured in this book lie west of boulevard St-Laurent.

In the Plateau, northeast of the downtown area, major streets are avenue du Mont-Royal and avenue Laurier.

In Vieux-Montréal, the main thoroughfares are rue St-Jacques, rue Notre-Dame, and rue St-Paul. Rue de la Commune is the waterfront road that hugs the promenade bordering the St. Lawrence River.

In addition to the maps in this book, neighborhood street plans are available online at www.tourisme-montreal.org and from the information centers listed above.

FINDING AN ADDRESS   As explained in the sidebar "Montréal: Where the Sun Rises in the South," below, boulevard St-Laurent is the dividing point between east and west (*est* and *ouest*) in Montréal. There's no equivalent division for north and south (*nord* and *sud*)—the numbers start at the river and climb from there, just as the topography does. Make sure you know your east from your west and confirm the cross street for all addresses.

In earlier days, Montréal was split geographically along cultural lines. Those who spoke English lived predominantly west of boulevard St-Laurent, while French speakers were concentrated to the east. Things still do sound more French as you walk east, as street names and Métro stations change from Peel and Atwater to Papineau and Beaudry.

MONTRÉAL: WHERE THE sun RISES IN THE SOUTH

For the duration of your visit to Montréal, you'll need to accept local directional conventions, strange as they may seem. The boomerang- or croissant-shaped island city borders the St. Lawrence River, and as far as locals are concerned, that's south, with the U.S. not far off on the other side. Never mind that the river, in fact, runs almost north and south at this section. For this reason, it has been observed that Montréal is the only city in the world where the sun rises in the south. Don't fight it: Face the river. That's south. Turn around. That's north. All is clear?

The directions given throughout the Montréal chapters conform to this local directional tradition. However, the maps in this book also have the true compass on them. When examining a map of the city, note that prominent thoroughfares, such as rue Ste-Catherine and boulevard René-Lévesque, are said to run "east" or "west." The dividing line is boulevard St-Laurent, which runs "north" and "south." For east-west streets, the numbers start at St-Laurent and then go *in both directions.* They're labeled either *est,* for east, or *ouest,* for west. That means, for instance, that the restaurants Chez l'Épicier, at 311 rue St-Paul est, and Marché de la Villette, at 324 rue St-Paul ouest, are 1km (about a half mile, or 13 short blocks) from each other—not directly across the street. Similarly, 500 rue Sherbrooke est is quite a hike from the same address in the west. Take note—or bring change for *l'autobus* or taxi.

The Neighborhoods in Brief

CENTRE-VILLE/DOWNTOWN   This area contains the Montréal skyline's most dramatic elements and includes most of the city's large luxury and first-class hotels, principal museums, corporate headquarters, main transportation hubs, and department stores.

The district is loosely bounded by rue Sherbrooke to the north, boulevard René-Lévesque to the south, boulevard St-Laurent to the east, and rue Drummond to the west.

Within this neighborhood is the area often called "the Golden Square Mile," an Anglophone (English-speaking) district once characterized by dozens of mansions erected by the wealthy Scottish and English merchants and industrialists who dominated the city's political and social life well into the 20th century. Many of those stately homes were torn down when skyscrapers began to rise here after World War II, but some remain.

At downtown's northern edge is the urban campus of prestigious McGill University, which retains its Anglophone identity.

VIEUX-MONTRÉAL   The city was born here in 1642, down by the river at Pointe-à-Callière. Today, especially in summer, many people converge around Place Jacques-Cartier, where cafe tables line narrow terraces. This is where street performers, strolling locals, and tourists congregate.

The neighborhood is larger than it might seem at first. It's bounded on the north by rue St-Antoine, and its southern boundary is the Vieux-Port

(Old Port), now dominated by a well-used waterfront promenade that provides welcome breathing room for cyclists, in-line skaters, and picnickers. To the east, Vieux-Montréal is bordered by rue Berri, and to the west, by rue McGill.

Several small but intriguing museums are housed in historic buildings here, and the district's architectural heritage has been substantially preserved. Restored 18th- and 19th-century structures have been adapted for use as shops, boutique hotels, studios, galleries, cafes, bars, offices, and apartments. In the evening, many of the finer buildings are beautifully illuminated. In the summer, sections of rue St-Paul and rue Notre-Dame turn into pedestrian-only lanes. The neighborhood's official website is **www. vieux.montreal.qc.ca**. The site usually has a live video feed from a webcam on Place Jacques-Cartier.

PLATEAU MONT-ROYAL "The Plateau" is where many Montréalers feel most at home—away from downtown's chattering pace and the more touristed Vieux-Montréal. It's where locals come to dine, shop, play, and, well, live.

Bounded roughly by rue Sherbrooke to the south, boulevard St-Joseph to the north, avenue Papineau to the east, and rue St-Urbain to the west, the Plateau has a vibrant ethnic atmosphere that fluctuates and shifts with each new immigration surge. Rue St-Denis runs the length of the district from south to north and is the heart of the neighborhood, as central to French-speaking Montréal as boulevard St-Germain is to Paris.

Boulevard St-Laurent, running parallel to rue St-Denis, has a more polyglot flavor. Known as "the Main," St-Laurent was the boulevard first encountered by foreigners tumbling off ships at the waterfront. They simply shouldered their belongings and walked north, peeling off into adjoining streets when they heard familiar tongues or smelled the drifting aromas of food reminiscent of the old country.

Without its gumbo of languages and cultures, St-Laurent would be something of an urban eyesore. It's not pretty in the conventional sense. But its ground-floor windows are filled with glistening golden chickens, collages of shoes and pastries and aluminum cookware, curtains of sausages, and the daringly far-fetched garments of designers on the forward edge of Montréal's active fashion industry.

Many warehouses and former tenements in the Plateau have been converted to house this panoply of shops, bars, and high- and low-cost eateries, their often-garish signs drawing eyes away from the still-dilapidated upper stories. See p. 159 for a walking tour of this fascinating neighborhood.

PARC DU MONT-ROYAL Not many cities have a mountain at their core. Reality insists that Montréal doesn't either, as what it calls a "mountain" would be seen as a very large hill by many other people. Still, Montréal is named for this outcrop—the "Royal Mountain."

The park here is a soothing urban pleasure to drive or walk in. Buses travel through the park, and if you're in moderately good shape you can walk to the top in 1 to 3 hours from downtown, depending on the route taken. See p. 164 for a suggested walking tour.

On its northern slope are two cemeteries, one that used to be Anglophone and Protestant, the other Francophone and Catholic—reminders of the linguistic and religious division that persists in the city.

With its trails for hiking and cross-country skiing, the park is well used by Montréalers, who refer to it simply and affectionately as "the Mountain."

RUE CRESCENT One of Montréal's major dining and nightlife districts lies in the western shadow of the massed phalanxes of downtown skyscrapers. While the northern end of rue Crescent houses luxury boutiques in Victorian brownstones, its southern end holds dozens of restaurants, bars, and clubs of all styles, spilling over onto neighboring streets.

The quarter's Anglophone origins are evident in the street names here: Stanley, Drummond, Crescent, Bishop, and MacKay. The party atmosphere that pervades after dark never quite fades, and it builds to crescendos as weekends approach, especially in warm weather. That's when the area's 20- and 30-something denizens take over sidewalk cafes and balcony terraces.

THE VILLAGE Also known as the Gay Village, Montréal's gay and lesbian enclave is one of North America's largest. This compact but vibrant district is filled with clothing stores, antiques shops, dance clubs, and cafes. It runs along rue Ste-Catherine est from rue St-Hubert to rue Papineau and onto side streets.

In recent years, the city has made the length of rue Ste-Catherine in the Village pedestrian-only for the entire summer. Bars and restaurants build ad-hoc terraces into the street, and a summer-resort atmosphere pervades.

A rainbow, the symbol of the gay community, marks the Beaudry Métro station, which is on rue Ste-Catherine in the heart of the neighborhood.

ST-DENIS Rue St-Denis, which starts almost at the river and runs north into the Plateau Mont-Royal district, is the thumping central artery of Francophone Montréal. It is thick with cafes, bistros, offbeat shops, and lively nightspots.

At its southern end, near the concrete campus of the Université du Québec à Montréal (UQAM) in the Latin Quarter (in French, *Quartier Latin*) neighborhood, the avenue is decidedly student-oriented. Loud indie rock pours out of inexpensive bars, and young adults in jeans and leather swap philosophical insights and telephone numbers. It is rife with the visual messiness that characterizes student and bohemian quarters.

Farther north, above rue Sherbrooke, a raffish quality persists along the rows of three- and four-story Victorian houses, but the average age of residents and visitors nudges past 30. Prices are higher, and some of the city's better restaurants are here. This is the district in which to take in the pulse of Francophone life. There are no museums or important galleries on St-Denis, nor is the architecture notable, which relieves visitors of the chore of obligatory sightseeing. Take in the passing scene—just as the locals do—over bowls of café au lait at any of the numerous terraces that line the avenue.

MILE END Adjoining Plateau Mont-Royal at its northwest corner, this blossoming neighborhood is contained by boulevard St-Joseph on the south, rue Bernard in the north, rue St-Laurent on the east, and avenue du Parc on the west. It's outside of the usual tourist orbit but has a growing number of retail attractions, including designer clothing boutiques, shops specializing in household goods, and many worthwhile restaurants.

Mile End has pockets of many ethnic minineighborhoods, including Italian, Hassidic, Portuguese, and Greek. The area some still call Greektown, for instance, runs along avenue du Parc and is thick with restaurants and taverns.

PARC JEAN-DRAPEAU: ILE STE-HÉLÈNE & ILE NOTRE-DAME St. Helen's Island in the St. Lawrence River was altered extensively to become the site of Expo 67, Montréal's very successful World's Fair in 1967. In the 4 years before the Expo, construction crews doubled its surface area with landfill, and then went on to create an island beside it that hadn't existed before: Ile Notre-Dame. Much of the earth for the island was dredged from the bottom of the St. Lawrence, and 15 million tons of rock were carried in by truck from the excavations for the Métro and the Décarie Expressway.

When the World's Fair was over, the city preserved the site and a few of its exhibition buildings. Parts were used for the 1976 Olympics. Today, Ile Ste-Hélène is home to an amusement park, La Ronde (p. 131), and the popular Casino de Montréal (p. 199).

Connected by two bridges, the islands make up the recently designated **Parc Jean-Drapeau,** which is almost entirely car-free and accessible by Métro. The park has its own website: www.parcjeandrapeau.com.

QUARTIER INTERNATIONAL When Route 720 was constructed in the early 1970s, it left behind a desolate swath of derelict buildings, parking lots, and empty spaces on either side of it, smack-dab between downtown and Vieux-Montréal.

This former no-man's land has been spruced up with new parks, office buildings (notably agencies or businesses with an international focus, hence the name "International Quarter"), and a recently expanded **Palais des Congrès (Convention Center).**

The convention center, in fact, is a design triumph, as unlikely as that seems. Transparent glass exterior walls are a crazy quilt of pink, yellow, blue, green, red, and purple rectangles. You can step into the inside hallway for the full effect—when the sun streams in, it's like being inside a huge kaleidoscope. The walls are the vision of Montréal architect Mario Saia.

A small plaza opposite the convention center's west side is named for Jean-Paul Riopelle (1923–2002), a prominent Québec artist. One of his sculptures stands here. The well-regarded restaurant Toqué! (p. 88) is adjacent to this square, inside the Caisse de depôt building, another architectural gem.

The Quartier incorporates the World Trade Center Montréal, a complex of brokerage houses, law firms, and a selection of fine boutiques on the street level. It is bounded, more or less, by rue St-Jacques on the south, avenue Viger on the north, rue St-Urbain on the east, and rue University on the west.

CHINATOWN Tucked in just north of Vieux-Montréal and centered on the intersection of rue Clark and the pedestrianized section of rue de la Gauchetière, Chinatown is mostly comprised of restaurants and a tiny park. The fancy gates to the area (a gift from the People's Republic of China) on boulevard St-Laurent are guarded by white stone lions. Community spirit is strong and inhabitants remain faithful to their traditions, despite the encroaching modernism all around them.

GETTING TO KNOW MONTRÉAL

The Neighborhoods in Brief

LITTLE BURGUNDY   Not far from the Atwater Market, a small stretch along rue Notre Dame ouest is slowly but surely becoming the hipster haven for its eclectic vintage shops, charming boutiques, eateries, and watering holes. Restaurants Joe Beef and the Burgundy Lion bar are already institutions for savvy insiders.

THE UNDERGROUND CITY   During Montréal's long winters, life slows on the streets of downtown as people escape into *la ville souterraine,* a parallel subterranean universe. Here, in a controlled climate that recalls an eternal spring, it's possible to arrive at the railroad station, check into a hotel, shop for days, and go out for dinner—all without donning an overcoat or putting on snow boots.

The city has begun rebranding it as the "underground pedestrian network," but most people still call it the underground city. It got its start when major downtown developments—such as Place Ville-Marie (the city's first skyscraper), Place Bonaventure, Complexe Desjardins, Palais des Congrès, and Place des Arts—put their below-street-level areas to profitable use, leasing space for shops and other enterprises. Over time—in fits and starts, and with no master plan—these spaces became connected with Métro stations, and then with each other through underground tunnels. It slowly became possible to ride long distances and walk the shorter ones through mazes of corridors, tunnels, and plazas. Today, there are more than 1,000 retailers and eateries in or connected to the network.

The term "underground city" is not 100% accurate because of how some complexes funnel people through their spaces. In Place Bonaventure, for instance, passengers can exit the Métro and find themselves peering out a window several floors above the street.

The city beneath the city has obvious advantages, including no traffic accidents and no winter slush. Natural light is let in wherever possible, which drastically reduces the feeling of claustrophobia that some malls evoke. However, the underground city covers a vast area without the convenience of a logical street grid, and it can be confusing. There are plenty of signs, but it's wise to make careful note of landmarks at key corners along your route if you want to return to where you started. Expect to get lost, but consider it part of the fun of exploring.

GETTING THERE & GETTING AROUND

Montréal is a terrific walking city. One thing to keep in mind when strolling is to cross only at street corners and only when you have a green light or a walk sign. City police began cracking down on jaywalkers in 2007 in an attempt to cut down on the number of accidents involving pedestrians, and newspapers continue to carry stories of fines being issued to people who cross in the middle of the street.

Montréal by Métro

For speed and economy, nothing beats Montréal's **Métro system.** The stations are marked on the street by blue-and-white signs that show a circle enclosing a down-pointing arrow. The Métro is relatively clean, and quiet trains whisk passengers through a decent network. It runs from about 5:30am to 12:30am 6 days

Montréal Métro

MONTMORENCY
De la Concorde
Cartier
Henri-Bourassa
Sauvé
Crémazie
Jarry
JEAN-TALON
De Castelnau
Parc
Acadie
Outremont
CÔTE-VERTU
Du Collège
De La Savane
Namur
Plamondon
Côte-Sainte-Catherine
SNOWDON
Villa-Maria
Vendôme
Place-Saint-Henri
Charlevoix
Jolicoeur
Monk
ANGRIGNON

SAINT-MICHEL
D'Iberville
Fabre
Beaubien
Rosemont
Laurier
Mont-Royal
Sherbrooke
BERRI-UQAM
Saint-Laurent
Place-des-Arts
McGill
Peel
Guy-Concordia
Atwater
Georges-Vanier
LIONEL-GROULX
LaSalle
De L'Église
Verdun

Édouard-Montpetit
Université-de-Montréal
Côte-des-Neiges

HONORÉ-BEAUGRAND
Radisson
Langelier
Cadillac
Assomption
Viau
Pie-IX
Joliette
Préfontaine
Frontenac
Papineau
Beaudry
Champ-de-Mars
Place-d'Armes
Square-Victoria
Bonaventure
Lucien-L'Allier

LONGUEUIL-UNIVERSITÉ-DE-SHERBROOKE
Jean-Drapeau (Île-Ste-Hélène)

St. Laurence

	Line 1
	Line 2
	Line 4
	Line 5

a week, and until about 1am on Saturday night/Sunday morning. Information is available online at **www.stm.info** or by phone at ✆ **514/786-4636.**

Fare prices are by the ride, not by distance. Single rides, exact change only, cost C$3 on the bus. The price is the same with a booth attendant at the Metro station, which is also cash only, but he or she can give you change if you need it. You can buy a set of six tickets for C$14.25, from the booth attendant. Also, there are automatic vending machines that take credit cards. Single- and six-ticket packages are the same price, and there is also the added option of buying a two-trips ticket for C$5.50. Tickets serve as proof of payment, and travelers need to keep the ticket for the duration of the trip—transit police sometimes check at transfer points or as you're exiting the station for proof that you've paid, and if you've thrown out the ticket the fine can run as high as C$214.

One-day and three-day passes are a good deal if you plan to use the Métro more than two times a day. You get unlimited access to the Métro and bus network for 1 day for C$8 or 3 consecutive days for C$16. The front of the card has scratch-off sections like a lottery card—you scratch out the month and day (or 3 consecutive days) on which you're using the card. They're available at select stations; find the list at www.stm.info.

You'll see locals using the plastic OPUS card, on which fares can be loaded from automated machines. The Métro is pushing the use of the new cards, which create less trash and whose purchase can be automated. Using the OPUS card provides reduced fares for seniors, children, and students. Blank OPUS cards must first be purchased for C$6 before any value is loaded onto them, so unless you're a frequent traveler to the city, the paper tickets and 1- or 3-day passes are your best options. To pay, either slip your paper ticket into the slot in the turnstile and take it as it comes out, or show your pass to the booth attendant. A single paper ticket acts as its own transfer ticket; there are 2 hours from the time a ticket is first validated to transfer, and you insert the ticket into the machine of the next bus or metro train.

The system is not immune to transit strikes, and convenient as it is, there can be substantial distances between stations. Accessibility is sometimes difficult for people with mobility restrictions or parents with strollers.

Montréal by Bus

Bus fares are the same as fares for Métro trains, and Métro tickets are good on buses, too. Exact change is required if you want to pay in cash. Although they run throughout the city and give tourists the advantage of traveling aboveground, buses don't run as frequently or as swiftly as the Métro (see "Montréal by Métro," above).

Montréal by Taxi

Cabs come in a variety of colors and styles, so their principal distinguishing feature is the plastic sign on the roof. At night, the sign is illuminated when the cab is available. The initial charge is C$3.30. Each additional kilometer (½ mile) adds C$1.60, and each minute of waiting adds C60¢. A short ride from one point to another downtown usually costs about C$7. Tip about 10% to 15%. Members of hotel and restaurant staffs can call cabs, many of which are dispatched by radio. They line up outside most large hotels or can be hailed on the street.

Montréal taxi drivers range in temperament from unstoppably loquacious to sullen and cranky. Some know their city well; others have sketchy geographical knowledge and poor language skills. It's a good idea to have your destination written down—with the cross street—to show your driver. Also keep in mind that not all drivers accept credit cards, and then, even if they do, preference is given to Visa and MasterCard, while American Express is often rejected. So if you don't have cash on you make sure to double-check with the dispatcher when you call for a taxi, or directly with the driver before you enter the cab.

Montréal by Car

Montréal is an easy city to navigate by car, although traffic during morning and late-afternoon rush hour can be horrendous. As well, current construction in the downtown corridor can be a nightmare. If you'll be doing much driving, pick up the pocket-size atlas published by JDM Géo and MapArt (www.mapart.com), sold for about C$10 at gas stations throughout Canada. The map offers lots of detail, especially in the areas outside the primary tourist orbit. The company also sells good maps for the Laurentians and Cantons-de-l'Est regions discussed in chapter 11.

It can be difficult to park for free on downtown Montréal's heavily trafficked streets, but there are plenty of metered spaces. Traditional meters are set well back from the curb so they won't be buried by plowed snow in winter. Computerized Pay 'N Go stations are in use in many neighborhoods, too. Look for the black metal kiosks, columns about 1.8m (6 ft.) tall with a white "P" in a blue circle. Press the "English" button, enter the letter from the space where you are parked, and then pay with cash or a credit card, following the onscreen instructions. Parking costs C\$3 per hour, and meters are in effect every day until 9pm. Be sure to check for signs noting parking restrictions, usually showing a red circle with a diagonal slash. The words LIVRAISON SEULEMENT mean "delivery only."

Most downtown shopping complexes have underground parking lots, as do the big downtown hotels. Some hotels offer in and out privileges, letting you take your car in and out of the garage without a fee—useful if you plan to do some sightseeing by car.

The limited-access expressways in Québec are called autoroutes, with distances given in kilometers (km) and speed limits given in kilometers per hour (kmph). Because French is the province's official language, most highway signs are only in French, though Montréal's autoroutes and bridges often bear dual-language signs. In Québec, the highway speed limit is 100 kmph (62 mph), and toll roads are rare.

One traffic signal function often confuses newcomers: Should you wish to make a turn and you know that the street runs in the correct direction, you may be surprised to initially see a green arrow pointing straight ahead instead of a green light permitting the turn. The arrow gives pedestrians time to cross the intersection. After a moment, the light will turn from an arrow to a regular green light and you can proceed with your turn.

A blinking green light means that oncoming traffic still has a red light, making it safe to make a left turn. Turning right on a red light is prohibited on the island of Montréal, except where specifically allowed by an additional green arrow. Off the island, it is legal to turn right after stopping at red lights, except where there's a sign specifically prohibiting that move.

As of 2008, drivers using cellphones are required to have hands-free devices. Radar detectors are illegal in Québec. Even if it's off, you can be fined for having one in sight.

While most visitors arriving by plane or train will want to rely on public transportation and cabs, a **rental car** can come in handy for trips outside of town or if you plan to drive to Québec City.

Montréal by Bike

Montréal has an exceptionally great system of bike paths, and bicycling is common not just for recreation, but for transportation, as well.

Since 2009, a self-service bicycle rental program called BIXI (**www.bixi. com**) has become a big presence in the city. A combination of the words *bicyclette* and *taxi*, BIXI is similar to programs in Paris, Barcelona, and Toronto, where users pick up bikes from designated stands throughout the city and drop them off at any other stand, for a small fee. Some 5,000 bikes are in operation and available at 400 stations in Montréal's central boroughs. While 1-year and 30-day subscriptions are available, visitors can buy a 24-hour access pass for C\$5. During those 24 hours, you can borrow bikes as many times as you want, and for each trip, the first 30 minutes are free. Trips longer than 30 minutes incur additional charges, which are added onto the initial C\$5 fee. Depending on your needs, zipping on and off BIXI bikes throughout the day can be both an economical and a fun way to get around. See p. 129 for a personal take on BIXI.

JULY 1: citywide MOVING DAY

Montréal is an island of renters, and close to 100,000 people move from old apartments to new ones every July 1—on that date, and only that date. That's the day all rental leases are required to start, a date chosen in part so that it doesn't fall within the school year. The date also, not coincidentally, coincides with Canada's National Day, ensuring that separatist-minded Francophone Québécois won't have time to celebrate that national holiday.

All but certain to be miserably hot and humid, July 1 is a trial that can, nevertheless, be hilarious to observe. See families struggle to get bedroom sets and large appliances down narrow outdoor staircases! Watch sidewalks become obstacle courses of baby cribs, bicycles, and overflowing cardboard boxes! Listen to the cacophony of horns as streets become clogged with every serviceable van, truck, and SUV! Later in the day, hundreds of people arrive at their new digs and discover gifts of junk no longer desired by their predecessors—busted furniture, pantries of old food, pitiful plants. Unless you're interested in observing the mayhem or taking advantage of the best trash picking of the year, you'll want to avoid strolls or drives in residential areas on that day.

If you want a helmet and lock, which are not included with BIXI, or if you want a bike for a half day or longer, rent from a shop. One of the most centrally located is **Ça Roule/Montréal on Wheels** (✆ **877/866-0633** or 514/866-0633; www.caroulemontreal.com), at 27 rue de la Commune est, the waterfront road in Vieux-Port.

The nonprofit biking organization **Vélo Québec** (✆ **800/567-8356** or 514/521-8356; www.velo.qc.ca) has the most up-to-date information on the state of bike paths and offers guided tours throughout the province (*vélo* means "bicycle" in French).

Passengers can take bicycles on the Métro from 10am to 3pm and after 7pm on weekdays, and all day weekends and holidays. This rule is suspended on special-event days, when trains are too crowded. Board the first car of the train, which can hold a maximum of four bikes (if there are already four bikes on that car, you have to wait for the next train). Details are online at **www.stm.info/ English/metro/a-velo-met.htm**.

Several taxi companies participate in the **Taxi+Vélo** program. You call, specify that you have a bike to transport, and a cab with a specially designed rack arrives. Up to three bikes can be carried for an extra fee of C$3 each. The companies are listed in a PDF file at www.velo.qc.ca (search for *taxi+vélo*). They include **Taxi Diamond** (✆ **514/273-6331**).

WHERE TO STAY IN MONTRÉAL

5

Montréal's boutique hotels are the current super-stars for travelers' accommodations, the highlight being those in the Old Montréal that have transformed historical buildings into chic modern getaways—it's hard to top the ambience of old stone walls while you cozy up in crisp white sheets. So popular are these small and personable spots that they're popping up in the downtown sector alongside the grand establishments. Big hotel chains, many of which arrived in time for Expo 67, may have time against them, but their central location is key (particularly for festival-goers) and recent renovations at several addresses have put them back in the stylish category, with often the added bonus of a pool.

BEST HOTEL BETS

- o **Best Historic Hotels:** While devoid of external artifice (it looks pretty darn plain from the outside), **Fairmont the Queen Elizabeth** marked its 50th anniversary in 2008, reminding the world that it was one of North America's first hotels with escalators, central air-conditioning, and direct-dial phones in each room, as well as the site (room 1742) for John Lennon and Yoko Ono's famous bed-in and recording of "Give Peace a Chance" in 1969. Its reception lobby still impresses. There is also **Hostellerie Pierre du Calvet,** which has historic cut-stone walls, swags of velvet and brocade, and tilting floors that Benjamin Franklin once trod upon. History buffs will also want to check out **Auberge du Vieux-Port.** Many bedrooms offer unobstructed views of the waterfront and the basement boasts an unearthed section of the original ramparts wall dating to 1862. See p. 66 and p. 73 and p. 73.

- o **Best Hotels for a Romantic Getaway:** The sunny atrium, cozy lobby, and luxurious amenities at **Hôtel Nelligan**—not to mention the cobblestoned streets and passing horse-drawn carriages outside—make this Old Montréal spot a choice retreat for couples. See p. 72.

price **CATEGORIES**	
Very Expensive	C$300 and up
Expensive	C$200–C$300
Moderate	C$100–C$200
Inexpensive	Under C$100

PREVIOUS PAGE: **A bedroom at Hôtel Le Germain.**

o **Best Design Hotels: Hôtel St-Paul** softens its austere lines with pale-cream walls, while the **Hôtel Gault** leaves its raw concrete uncovered and incorporates candy-colored furniture. See p. 74 for both.

o **Best Bet for Families:** Rooms in the converted warehouse **Le Square Phillips Hôtel & Suites** provide ample space and everything needed for a home away from home, including en-suite kitchens. A pool and rooftop terrace are nice bonuses. See p. 71.

o **Best B&B-Like Hotel:** In a 1723 structure in Vieux-Montréal, **Auberge Les Passants du Sans Soucy** is more upscale and stylish than most of its peers, and it's near the Old City's top restaurants. See p. 76.

o **Best Value:** The decor at **Auberge Bonaparte** is quintessential Old Montréal, and morning meals are large and served in the elegant Bonaparte restaurant. See p. 76.

o **Best Splurge:** The troops of staff at the wildly luxurious **Hôtel Le St-James** display grace and care when it comes to tending to their guests. See p. 72.

CENTRE-VILLE/DOWNTOWN

Home of all the big chains that grew like weeds just before Expo 67, there is also a sprinkling of boutique hotels throughout the area.

BEST FOR   Travelers here on business or to enjoy any of the festivals that take place around the Quartier des Spectacles. Also, an ideal spot for shoppers since you're in the heart of retail heaven.

DRAWBACKS   Most of the newest bars and restaurants are in the Old Montréal, so if that's your thing, you may find yourself in many a taxi.

Very Expensive

Ritz-Carlton Montréal ★★★   The Ritz and its restaurants were closed for all of 2009 through 2011, and is expected to reopen in January 2012. The C$150-million renovation project will convert some of the property to private condominiums and hopefully retain the grandeur of the hotel accommodations and public spaces, such as the Oval ballroom and "Cinderella staircase." A Tiffany & Co. jewelry store is sure to bring in the chichi clientele, as will legendary chef

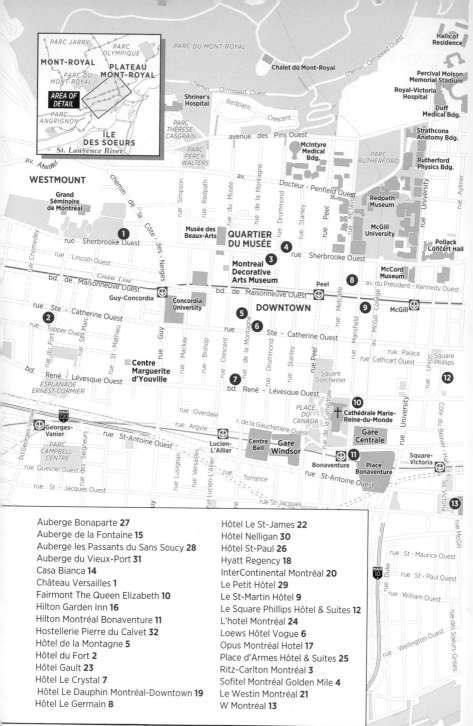

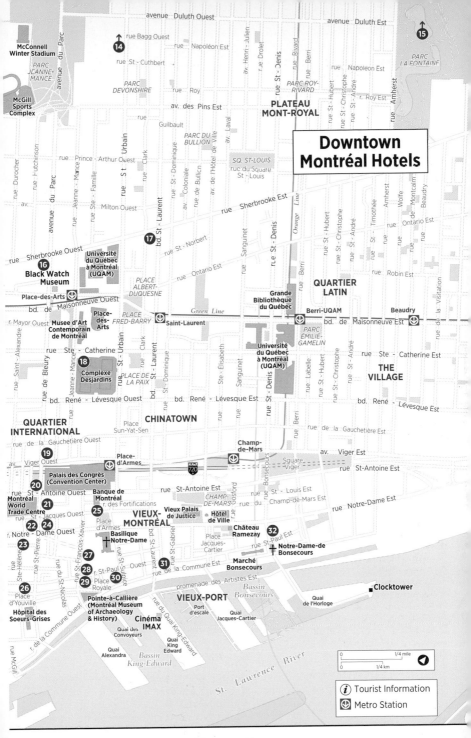

Daniel Boulud who recently signed on to head the new on-site restaurant Maison Boulud. Check the hotel's website for updates and pricing details.

1228 rue Sherbrooke ouest (at rue Drummond), Montréal, PQ H3G 1H6. www.ritzmontreal.com. ✆ **800/363-0366** or 514/842-4212.

Expensive

Château Versailles 🛏 One of the official lodging sites for the **Musée des Beaux-Arts** (p. 109) and McGill University, the Versailles is near the museum but outside most of the tourist orbit. The property, which feted its 100th anniversary in 2011, was once a European-style pension and expanded into adjacent pre-WWI town houses. The most spacious rooms have modern furnishings with Deco and Second Empire touches; 11 rooms have fireplaces. Loyal guests return for just this reason—every room is different. A buffet breakfast is served in the main living room called the "boudoir," where you can sit at a small table or in an easy chair in front of a fireplace. One obstacle: the lack of an elevator by which to deal with the three floors. As well, rooms in the basement level are significantly less cheery. Across the street is sister property **Le Meridien Versailles,** at 1808 rue Sherbrooke ouest (✆ **888/933-8111** or 514/933-8111; www.lemeridienversailles hotel.com).

1659 rue Sherbrooke ouest (at rue St-Mathieu), Montréal, PQ H3H 1E3. www.versailleshotels.com. ✆ **888/933-8111** or 514/933-8111. Fax 514/933-6967. 65 units. C$185–C$375 double; from C$275 suite. Rates include breakfast. Packages available. AE, DC, DISC, MC, V. Valet parking C$26. Métro: Guy-Concordia. Pets accepted (C$20 per day). **Amenities:** Babysitting; concierge; exercise room; room service; sauna. In room: A/C, TV, hair dryer, minibar, Wi-Fi (free).

Fairmont the Queen Elizabeth (Le Reine Elizabeth) ★ Montréal's largest hotel—it has more than 1,000 rooms—stacks its 21 floors atop VIA Rail's Gare Centrale, the main train station, with the Métro and popular shopping areas such as Place Ville-Marie and Place Bonaventure accessible through underground arcades. This desirable location makes "the Queen E" a frequent choice for heads of state and touring celebrities, even though other hotels in town offer more luxurious pampering. The Fairmont Gold 18th and 19th floors are the best choice, but other rooms are satisfactory, with traditional furnishings, easy chairs, ottomans, and bright reading lamps. Most rooms have windows that open, a rarity in this city. May 2009 marked the 40th anniversary of John Lennon and Yoko Ono's weeklong "Bed-in for Peace" in suite no. 1742. The storied Beaver Club restaurant (ask to see the log book) is a masterpiece of local cuisine, including the wine and cheese selections.

900 boul. René-Lévesque ouest (at rue Mansfield), Montréal, PQ H3B 4A5. www.fairmont.com/queenelizabeth. ✆ **866/540-4483** or 514/861-3511. Fax 514/954-2296. 1,037 units. C$189–C$359 double; from C$289 suite. Children 17 and under stay free in parent's room. Packages available. AE, DC, MC, V. Valet parking C$28. Métro: Bonaventure. Pets accepted for fee. **Amenities:** 3 restaurants; 2 bars; babysitting; concierge; executive-level rooms; health club; Jacuzzi; pool (indoor); room service; Wi-Fi (C$14 per day, in lobby). In room: A/C, TV, hair dryer, Internet (C$14 per day), minibar.

Hôtel Le Crystal ★★ The epitome of boutique hotel style, this glimmering downtown address has a sweeping chandelier in the lobby, as well as high-end bathroom fixtures, sleek linens, and contemporary artworks. All rooms are suites, and those with a -08 at the end have impressive corner panoramas of downtown with the Centre Bell in the distance. Eleven suites have fireplaces; some executive suites and all penthouse rooms also have balconies. Celebrity followers should not freak out at the sight of one of the many music, movie, or sports personalities that check into the hotel. The luxurious Izba spa on the 12th floor is a quiet getaway in the middle of the city; it offers guests a saltwater pool and four-season outdoor Jacuzzi—also with stunning views. Ground-floor restaurant **La Coupole** is a corporate-approved lunch spot, as well as magnet at night for pre- or postgame dinner or just drinks.

1100 rue de la Montagne (at boul. René Lévesque), Montréal, PQ H3G 0A1. www.hotellecrystal. com. (*) **877/861-5550** or 514/861-5550. Fax 514/861-5288. 131 units. From C$229 suite. Children 18 and under stay free in parent's room. Packages available. AE, DC, MC, V. Valet parking C$26. Métro: Lucien L'Allier. Pets accepted (C$75 cleaning fee). **Amenities:** Restaurant; bar; cafe; concierge; exercise room; Jacuzzi; pool; room service; spa service. *In room:* A/C, TV, hair dryer, Wi-Fi (free).

Hôtel Le Germain ★★★   Since 1999, this undertaking by the owner of Québec City's equally desirable boutique hotel **Hôtel Le Germain-Dominion** (p. 254) has added a shot of panache to the downtown lodging scene. The hotel vibe is stylish loft, with white Asian minimalist decor accented by candy-pink and lime-green accessories. Bedrooms have supercomfy bedding, marshmallowy-plush reading chairs, ergonomic work areas with eye-level plugs and ports, windows that open, and a useful variety of lighting options. A glass partition between the bed and the shower is standard (the modest can lower a shade). Self-serve breakfasts include perfect croissants and café au lait, and there's a free espresso machine in the lobby. Its in-house **Laurie Raphaël Montréal** is an offshoot of the esteemed Québec City restaurant. Near-constant renovations and sprucing of paint, bedding, and amenities keep Le Germain at the top of its game.

2050 rue Mansfield (at av. du President-Kennedy), Montréal, PQ H3A 1Y9. www.hotelgermain. com. (*) **877/333-2050** or 514/849-2050. Fax 514/849-1437. 101 units. C$230–C$475 double. Rates include breakfast. Packages available. AE, DC, MC, V. Valet parking C$25. Métro: Peel. Pets accepted (C$30 per day). **Amenities:** Restaurant; bar; babysitting; concierge; exercise room; room service. *In room:* A/C, TV, hair dryer, minibar, MP3 docking station, Wi-Fi (free).

Hyatt Regency ☺   In the heart of Quartier des Spectacles, there's no place more central than this during Montréal's summer festivals. If you don't need the chichi factor of a boutique hotel, the Hyatt has recently completed some major renovations that freshened up the entrance, reception hall, bar, and restaurant to keep up with its jet-set clientele—and so it may not be the hotel you once knew if you haven't been there lately. Mind you, lest we forget, the megaterrace overlooking rue Ste-Catherine is still there, as is the ever-popular-with-kids pool (it's indoor, but there are huge windows all around so you'll get lots of nice fresh air). The Hyatt is also conveniently connected to a shopping plaza, as well as the underground city, and just steps away from main drag shopping street Ste-Catherine.

1255 rue Jeanne-Mance (south of rue Ste-Catherine ouest), Montréal, PQ H5B 1E5. www. montreal.hyatt.com. (*) **800/233-1234** or 514/982-1234. Fax 514/285-1243. 605 units. C$169–C$269 double; C$249–C$449 suite. Children 18 and under stay free in parent's room. Packages available. AE, DC, MC, V. Valet parking C$30, self-parking C$19. Métro: Places-des-Arts. Pets not accepted. **Amenities:** Restaurant; lounge; concierge; exercise studio; indoor pool; Jacuzzi; room service; sauna; spa services (massage). *In room:* A/C, TV, hair dryer, Wi-Fi (C$12).

KEEP UP YOUR workout SCHEDULE

If you're staying at a hotel that doesn't have a fitness center or whose exercise room is modest, keep **Club Sportif MAA** in mind (📞 **514/845-2233;** www.club sportifmaa.com). Located centrally downtown at 2070 rue Peel, between rue Sherbrooke and boulevard de Maison-neuve, the luxury facility has a 743-sq.-m (8,000-sq.-ft.) state-of-the-art gym with cardio and strength-training equipment, a lap pool, and a full schedule of classes—everything from spinning to Pilates to Ashtanga yoga. Day passes are available for C$20 for adults and C$10 for children 17 and under.

Loews Hôtel Vogue ★★ ☺ Open since 1990, the Vogue sits at the top tier of the local luxury-hotel pantheon. Confidence and capability resonate from every member of the staff, and luxury permeates the hotel from the lobby to the well-appointed guest rooms. Feather pillows and duvets dress oversize beds, and huge marble bathrooms are fitted with Jacuzzis—double size in suites—and sep-arate shower stalls. Rooms all have consistent decor, so what you see on the website is what you'll get when you arrive. The first floor is also Shabbat-friendly, in that it is only one flight of stairs up (no need to take the elevator) and acces-sible by an old-fashioned key instead of a digitalized card. The hotel's **L'Opéra Bar** is a two-story nook off the lobby with floor-to-ceiling windows and is open until 2am. If you're a regular, you know that "Loews loves kids." They offer free welcome amenity kits, a kiddie room service menu, and rentable playpens.

1425 rue de la Montagne (near rue Ste-Catherine ouest), Montréal, PQ H3G 1Z3. www.loews hotels.com. 📞 **800/465-6654** or 514/285-5555. Fax 514/849-8903. 142 units. C$229–C$329 double; C$429 suite. Children 17 and under stay free in parent's room. Packages available. AE, DC, DISC, MC, V. Valet parking C$32. Métro: Peel. Pets accepted (for fee). **Amenities:** Restaurant; 2 bars; babysitting; children's programs; concierge; exercise room and discounted access to Club Sportif MAA gym and pool; room service. *In room:* A/C, TV/DVD player, CD player, hair dryer, minibar, MP3 docking station, Wi-Fi (C$15 per day).

Opus Montréal Hotel ★ One of Montréal's nightlife epicenters is the Opus's restaurant and bar, **Koko** (p. 198), which boasts the city's most expansive ter-race, and the downstairs lounge called **Suco** (Tues, Fri–Sat). Hotel guests can cut its notoriously long lines and sip neon drinks among the clubbing elite, where heel height regularly exceeds 5 inches. Bedrooms are designed for this crowd: The concrete ceilings and color-coded walls (according to its theme) in red, orange, blue, or taupe look better in evening light, showers are lit from below, and linens are silky soft. Guests often need the earplugs found on every nightstand. The structure began life in 1914 as the first poured concrete building in North America and was a boutique hotel named for its architect, Joseph-Arthur Godin, until the Opus group purchased it in 2007. Though technically downtown, the hotel borders Plateau Mont-Royal, where city dwellers both live and party.

10 rue Sherbrooke ouest (near rue St-Laurent), Montréal, PQ H2X 4C9. www.opushotel.com. 📞 **866/744-6346** or 514/843-6000. Fax 514/843-6810. 136 units. C$199–C$249 double; C$399–C$599 suite. Children 17 and under stay free in parent's room. Packages available. AE, MC, V. Valet parking C$26 (indoor garage). Pets accepted (C$50 per stay). Métro: St-Laurent. **Amenities:** Restaurant; bar; babysitting; concierge; health club; room service; Wi-Fi (free, in lobby). *In room:* A/C, TV, CD player, hair dryer, Internet (C$15 per day), minibar.

Sofitel Montréal Golden Mile ★★ In 2002, the French luxury hotel chain transformed a bland 1970s downtown office tower into this coveted destination for visiting celebrities and the power elite. It wows from the moment of arrival, from the light-filled stone-and-wood lobby to the universally warm welcome visitors get from the staff. The 100 standard rooms (called Superior) have floor-to-ceiling windows, furnishings made from Québec-grown cherry wood, down duvets, and a soothing oatmeal-cream decor. Desks jut out from the wall and are comfortable to use. Bathrooms have rain showers. In-room spa services such as facials and massages were added in 2010, to better compete with hotels with on-site spas. The ambitious **Le Renoir** restaurant is in a bright, airy room and features an upscale bar and elegant terrace. There is no pool, but the exercise room is open 24 hours per day.

1155 rue Sherbrooke ouest (at rue Stanley), Montréal, PQ H3A 2N3. www.sofitel.com. ✆ **514/ 285-9000.** Fax 514/289-1155. 258 units. C$195–C$325 double; from C$295 suite. Packages available. AE, DC, MC, V. Valet parking C$30. Métro: Peel. Pets accepted (no fee). **Amenities:** Restaurant; bar; babysitting; concierge; executive-level rooms; exercise room; room service; sauna; in-room spa services. *In room:* TV, DVD player (by request), CD player (by request), hair dryer, minibar, MP3 docking station, Wi-Fi (C$15 per day).

Moderate

Hilton Montréal Bonaventure ★ ☺ A recent C$12.5-million face-lift gave a hip reno to the entire interior, including the carpets, in-room furniture, and room amenities. Singular in design, guests must take the elevator up to the 16th floor to check in. The entire hotel wraps around a central courtyard (rooms look in or out—and the windows open!), where there is a Zen garden, duck pond, and cozy, chalet-style restaurant **Restaurant-Jardins le Castillon** with terrace. The biggest perk here, however, is the popular outdoor, rooftop pool—a major boon for children—that is even open in Montréal's arctic winters, when it is heated up to 30°C (86°F). Parents should also take note that their kids 18 and under stay in their room for free; keep them occupied with a variety of board games (ask the concierge for details). Strollers are also available free of charge.

900 de la Gauchetière ouest (at rue Mansfield), Montréal, PQ H5A 1E4. www.hiltonmontreal.com. ✆ **800/267-2575** or 514/878-2332. Fax 514/878-3881. 395 units. C$150–C$290 double; from C$219 suite. Packages available. AE, DC, MC, V. Valet parking C$28, self-parking C$19. Métro: Bonaventure. Pets accepted (C$50 nonrefundable fee). **Amenities:** Restaurant; bar; babysitting; concierge; fitness room; lounge; pool; room service. *In room:* A/C, TV, hair dryer, safe, Wi-Fi (free).

Hilton Garden Inn ☺ Everything you expect from this global chain is here, with the added benefit of a rooftop pool and gym that have a breathtaking view of the city. While this multilevel building boasts nothing particularly glamorous or quaint, its enormous size lends it bit of a resort feel. It's also a bit of a hike to Vieux-Montréal and somewhat separated from the downtown core, but the location just next to McGill University makes it an ideal location for visiting parents. The Biodôme, Olympic Stadium, and Botanical Gardens are also just a quick taxi down Sherbrooke—you could probably see all three from the roof.

380 rue Sherbrooke ouest (at rue Hutchison), Montréal, PQ H3A 0B1. www.hiltongardenmontreal. com. ✆ **877/840-0010** or 514/840-0010. Fax 514/840-0180. 221 units. C$169–C$189 double; from C$249 suite. Children 18 and under stay free in parents' room. Packages available. AE, DC, MC, V. Self-parking C$23. Métro: Places-des-Arts. Pets not accepted. **Amenities:** Restaurant; bar; concierge; fitness room; Jacuzzi; pool (rooftop); room service; steam room. *In room:* A/C, TV, hair dryer, Wi-Fi (free).

Hôtel de la Montagne   Eras collide at this hotel, where an Art Deco lobby with giant tusked elephants and a fountain topped by a nude figure with stained-glass butterfly wings opens onto a cabaret lounge (see **Le Cabaret**, p. 195). Just a few steps further and you're in the giant singles watering hole **Thursday's** (p. 196), which has a terrace opening onto lively rue Crescent. In warmer months, patrons from all over the city stand in line for the hotel's rooftop pool and bar (both open till 3am). Factor in the trio of slot machines and the disco, and you could be in Vegas, baby! After that, the relatively serene bedrooms, all with balconies, seem downright bland, but they're clean and include good-size bathrooms and high-end bedding. Some rooms have benefited from a sleek update in the last few years (they cost more). All in all, this family-owned and -operated hotel offers a competent staff and bit of old-fashioned pizzazz.

1430 rue de la Montagne (north of rue Ste-Catherine), Montréal, PQ H3G 1Z5. www.hoteldela montagne.com. ☎ **800/361-6262** or 514/288-5656. Fax 514/288-9658. 142 units. C$169–C$289 double. Packages available. AE, DC, DISC, MC, V. Valet parking C$18, for SUV C$36. Métro: Peel. Pets accepted (for fee). **Amenities:** 2 restaurants; 3 bars; babysitting; concierge; pool (heated; outdoor); room service. *In room:* A/C, TV, hair dryer, minibar, Wi-Fi (free).

Hôtel du Fort ☺   This reliable hotel takes as its primary duty providing lodging to longer-term business travelers, although because all rooms are a good size and many have sofas with hide-a-beds, they're also good for small families or persons who use wheelchairs. Details include a fitness room sufficient enough for a thorough workout, basic kitchenettes with fridges and microwave ovens in every room (the concierge can have groceries delivered), and a wheelchair-accessible underground parking garage. A buffet breakfast is served in the lounge. In a nod toward sustainability, kitchenettes feature energy-efficient appliances with Energy Star designation. The hotel also bills itself as "Shabbat-friendly," offering special accommodation for Jewish guests observing the Sabbath. Kosher breakfasts, manual locks, and a Shabbat elevator service can all be provided upon request.

1390 rue du Fort (at rue Ste-Catherine), Montréal, PQ H3H 2R7. www.hoteldufort.com. ☎ **800/ 565-6333** or 514/938-8333. 124 units. C$159–C$225 double; C$219–C$395 suite. Children 12 and under stay free in parent's room. Packages available. AE, DC, MC, V. Self-parking C$21. Métro: Guy-Concordia. **Amenities:** Babysitting; concierge; exercise room; room service. *In room:* A/C, TV, hair dryer, kitchenette, Wi-Fi (C$11 per day).

Hôtel Le Dauphin Montréal-Downtown ✦   This member of the small Dauphin hotel chain presents a terrific option for travelers on a budget. Room furnishings are simple and clean, if blandly dorm-room functional with new

---

📎 ROOM WITHOUT A view, PLEASE

Some of the more popular areas in the city to stay in, including on or near rue de la Montagne in downtown or on or near rue St-Paul in Vieux-Montréal, have bars and nightlife close by. Bars are open until 3am in this city, so light sleepers might want to ask for rooms that face the back of the hotel or an inside courtyard. They might not have the most scenic views, but they could make the difference between a good night's sleep and a rocky one.

hardwood floors. On the other hand, bathrooms are sleek (black counters, slate floors, and glass-walled shower stalls), beds are comfy, and all units have—get this—a computer terminal and free Internet access. There also are bigger-hotel touches: flatscreen TVs, in-room safes, large refrigerators (unstocked), and morning newspaper delivery. The location, next to the convention center on the northern end of Vieux-Montréal, is central, though the immediate surroundings are nondescript.

1025 rue de Bleury (near av. Viger), Montréal, PQ H2Z 1M7. www.hoteldauphin.ca. *C* **888/784-3888** or 514/788-3888. Fax 514/788-3889. 80 units. C$129–C$195 double. Rates include breakfast. AE, MC, V. Parking C$20 at convention center. Métro: Place d'Armes. **Amenities:** Exercise room. *In room:* A/C, TV/DVD player, fridge, hair dryer, in-room computer w/free Internet, Wi-Fi (free).

Le Square Phillips Hôtel & Suites ★ ☺ ✇ The advantages here are space, livability, and locale. Originally designed as a warehouse by the noted Québec architect Ernest Cormier (1885–1980), the building was converted to its present function in 2003. The vaguely cathedral-like spaces were largely retained (some rooms have columns and arches), and they make for capacious studio bedrooms and suites fully equipped for long stays. Full kitchens in every unit come with all essential appliances—toasters, fridges, stoves, dishwashers, crockery, and pots and pans. Rooms got new mattresses in 2009, and new couches and sofa beds in 2010. There's a rooftop pool with a downtown view and an exercise room, and a laundry room is also available for guest use. The location, at the edge of the downtown shopping district, is central, and an easy walk to Vieux-Montréal and the rue Crescent nightlife district. Because it gets a lot of business travelers, weekends tend to be cheaper than weekdays.

1193 Square Phillips (south of rue Ste-Catherine ouest), Montréal, PQ H3B 3C9. www.squarephillips. com. *C* **866/393-1193** or 514/393-1193. Fax 514/393-1192. 160 units. C$162–C$202 double; C$259–C$358 suite. Rates include breakfast. Discount for stays of 7 or more nights. AE, DC, DISC, MC, V. Valet parking C$22. Métro: McGill. Pets accepted (no fee). **Amenities:** Babysitting; concierge; exercise room; pool (heated, indoor, rooftop). *In room:* A/C, TV, hair dryer, kitchen, Wi-Fi (free).

Le St-Martin Hotel A lone rider on boulevard de Maisonneuve, Le St-Martin is a sophisticated newcomer in the downtown core. A little closer to nightlife-filled Crescent and Peel streets than Le Germain and a little closer to the Museum District than Le Crystal, Le St-Martin rose from the ashes in 2010 on the spot that was once Ben's Deli; the ground floor now boasts chef Jean-François Plante's **L'Aromate** restaurant, which includes a mezzanine overlooking the lobby, and that in summer spreads out an al fresco lounge on the sidewalk. Rooms are uptown classy without being pretentious. Bathrooms also have flatscreen TVs, so you can watch the news while soaking in your tub. Not all the downtown boutique hotels have pools, so the single-lane lap pool here is quite a treat; it also gives a nice view of the city skyline. For a unique stay, ask about the northwest rooms that have unique glass corner windows.

980 boul. de Maisonneuve ouest (at rue Mansfield), Montréal, PQ H3A 0A5. www.lestmartin montreal.com. *C* **877/843-3003** or 514/843-3000. Fax 514/908-3427. 123 units. C$169–$219 double; from C$550 suite. Children 18 and under stay free in parent's room. Packages available. AE, MC, V. Valet parking C$29. Métro: Peel. Pets not accepted. **Amenities:** Restaurant; bar; fitness lounge; pool (heated); room service. *In room:* A/C, TV, hair dryer, MP3 docking station, Wi-Fi (free).

VIEUX-MONTRÉAL (OLD MONTRÉAL)

At the turn of the millennium, a fresh crop of boutique hotels invigorated the once-barren Old Montréal district that was at the time only a place for tourists. Today, it's one of the hottest areas for nightlife and trendy or avant-garde fashion boutiques.

BEST FOR   Jet-setters who need to check into "the Address."

DRAWBACKS   The overabundance of pedestrians (particularly in summer) may be frustrating for some.

Very Expensive

Hôtel Nelligan ★★   Occupying adjoining 1850 buildings, the Nelligan opened in 2002 and expanded in 2007 from 63 to 105 units. More than half of the accommodations are now suites. Many of the bedrooms are dark-wooded, masculine retreats, with puffy duvets, heaps of pillows, and quality mattresses. The staff performs its duties admirably, and the building maintains beautiful public spaces, including Verses Sky Terrace, where drinks and light meals are served until 11pm (p. 197). One distraction is that the hotel's indoor atrium can sometimes pull noise from the downstairs bar up to the rooms. Still, claiming an enveloping lobby chair facing the open front to the street, with a book and a cold drink at hand, is one definition of utter contentment. The hotel is named for the 19th-century Québécois poet Émile Nelligan (1879–1941), whose lines are excerpted on the bedroom walls.

106 rue St-Paul ouest (at rue St-Sulpice), Montréal, PQ H2Y 1Z3. www.hotelnelligan.com. ✆ **877/788-2040** or 514/788-2040. Fax 514/788-2041. 105 units. From C$265 double; from C$315 suite. Rates include breakfast and 1 cocktail per stay. Packages available. AE, DISC, MC, V. Valet parking C$24. Métro: Place d'Armes. **Amenities:** 2 restaurants; bar; babysitting; concierge; exercise room; room service. *In room:* A/C, TV, DVD player (on request), CD player, hair dryer, Wi-Fi (free).

Hôtel Le St-James ★★★   In a word, gorgeous. Montréal's surge of designer hotels spans the spectrum from minimalist to ornate, and Le St-James sits squarely at the ornate end of the range. It began life as a merchant's bank in 1870, and the opulence of that station has been retained. The bronze elevator doors are antiques from New York's Waldorf Astoria hotel, with a second set opening into the massive penthouse with wraparound terrace. The grand hall, with Corinthian columns and balconies with gilded metal balustrades, houses **XO Le Restaurant** (in the former stock exchange space) and a chic bar area. Come for gastronomic cocktails and appetizers or weekend brunch, stay for chef Michele Mercuri's tasting menu. Sumptuous rooms are furnished with antiques and impeccable reproductions. A member of the Leading Small Hotels of the World, Le St-James represents a triumph of design and preservation for visiting royalty—or those who want to be treated like it.

355 rue St-Jacques ouest (near rue St-Pierre), Montréal, PQ H2Y 1N9. www.hotellestjames.com. ✆ **866/841-3111** or 514/841-3111. Fax 514/841-1232. 61 units. From C$400 double; from C$525 suite. Packages available. AE, DC, DISC, MC, V. Valet parking C$35. Métro: Square Victoria. Pets accepted (C$50 per day). **Amenities:** Restaurant; bar; babysitting; concierge; exercise room; room service; spa. *In room:* A/C, TV, CD player, hair dryer, minibar, MP3 docking station, Wi-Fi (free).

W Montréal ★★★   Combining contemporary decor with in-house nightlife and attentive service, the W brand is unique on the hotel landscape, and the

Montréal property follows suit. A dance-club tone greets guests upon entry: neon lights around the doorway, a red glow in the front lobby. The hotel's **Ristorante Otto** attracts a sleek crowd of models, people who date models, and people who wish they were one or the other. So, too, does the intimate **W Bartini** (p. 196), which concocts specialty martinis and is often open until 3am, and the **Wunderbar** (p. 196), which picks up the pace with beat-spinning DJs, also until 3am. Bedrooms follow through, with pillow-top mattresses, goose-down comforters, and 350-count Egyptian cotton sheets. Flatscreen TVs and DVD players are standard in even the basic (called Cozy) rooms. The W is located where Vieux-Montréal meets downtown, both literally and figuratively.

901 Square-Victoria (at rue St-Antoine), Montréal, PQ H2Z 1R1. www.whotels.com/montreal. ✆ **877/W-HOTELS** (946-8357) or 514/395-3100. Fax 514/395-3150. 152 units. C$179–C$720 double. Packages available. AE, DC, DISC, MC, V. Valet parking C$35. Métro: Square Victoria. Pets accepted (C$25 per day, plus C$100 cleaning fee). **Amenities:** Restaurant; 3 bars; concierge; executive-level rooms; exercise room; room service; spa. *In room:* A/C, TV/DVD player, hair dryer, MP3 docking station, Wi-Fi (C$15 per day).

Expensive

Auberge du Vieux-Port ★ Terrifically romantic, this tidy luxury inn is housed in an 1882 building facing the waterfront, and many of the rooms, as well as a rooftop terrace, offer unobstructed views of Vieux-Port—a particular treat on summer nights when there are fireworks on the river or in winter when it's snowing. Exposed brick and stone walls, massive beams, polished hardwood floors, and windows that open define the hideaway bedrooms; no. 403, for instance, has expansive views, space to stretch out, and a king bed. Eighteen new rooms were added in 2011. For each stay, guests receive a complimentary glass of wine in **Narcisse,** the small, sophisticated wine bar off the lobby. In the restaurant's basement floor, you can also see a part of the original ramparts wall.

97 rue de la Commune est (near rue St-Gabriel), Montréal, PQ H2Y 1J1. www.aubergeduvieuxport. com. ✆ **888/660-7678** or 514/876-0081. Fax 514/876-8923. 45 units. C$230–C$285 double. Rates include full breakfast and 1 glass of wine per stay. Children 11 and under stay free in parent's room. AE, MC, V. Valet parking C$25 plus taxes. Métro: Place-d'Armes or Champs-de-Mars. **Amenities:** Bar; babysitting; concierge; exercise room at sister hotel; room service. *In room:* A/C, TV, CD player, CD library, hair dryer, minibar, Wi-Fi (free).

Hostellerie Pierre du Calvet Step from cobblestone streets into an 18th-century home boasting velvet curtains, gold-leafed writing desks, and four-poster beds of teak mahogany. The wildly atmospheric public spaces are furnished with original antiques—not reproductions. Likewise, the voluptuous dining room, **Les Filles du Roy,** suggests a 19th-century hunting lodge (*Masterpiece Theatre* fans, this hotel is for you.), although the menu is likely not up to par for most foodies. Eight of the nine bedrooms sport fireplaces, and rooms 1 and 6 even have stone walls in the shower-tubs. Door locks, which used to look like they could be kicked in by a baby, have been updated. In warm months, a walled-in outdoor courtyard with a small fountain is a hideaway dining terrace. There's also an intimate veranda just outside rooms 8, 9, and 10. Eccentric owner Gaëten Trottier, whose family began the establishment in 1962, has converted a space here into the **Musée du Bronze de Montréal.** It contains his sculptures and is well worth a look.

405 rue Bonsecours (at rue St-Paul), Montréal, PQ H2Y 3C3. www.pierreducalvet.ca. ✆ **866/544-1725** or 514/282-1725. Fax 514/282-0456. 10 units. C$265–C$295 double (about C$100 less in low

LOCAL PLAYERS: THE antonopoulos GROUP

Four of the hotels listed here in the Vieux-Montréal neighborhood—Auberge du Vieux-Port, Hôtel Nelligan, Place d'Armes Hôtel & Suites, and Le Petit Hôtel—are owned by the Antonopoulos Group. Each property has a different personality, but all are consistently well run. The group also owns the restaurants Aix Cuisine de Terroir, Verses, Méchant Beouf, Vieux-Port Steakhouse (p. 93), and Modavie. More information about the local powerhouse and its other bars and restaurants is at www.experienceold montreal.com.

season). Rates include breakfast. Packages available. AE, MC, V. Parking C$15. Métro: Champ-de-Mars. **Amenities:** Restaurant. *In room:* A/C, TV, hair dryer, Wi-Fi (free).

Hôtel Gault ★★   The Gault explores the edges of minimalism; design aficionados will likely love it. Raw, monumental concrete walls and brushed-steel work surfaces have been softened in recent years with a few more rugs and some lollipop-colored mod furniture, cutting down on what used to be a looming sense of austerity. Bedrooms are large, and the color and tone of their design shifts on each floor. Even with just 30 rooms, there are eight styles and shapes. Terra room no. 170, for instance, has brick walls, a snazzy bathtub, and heated floors, while all rooms on the fifth floor have balconies—a rare treat in Montréal. The sleek lobby, where a complimentary breakfast is served, has massive arched windows and comfortable chairs for lounging, and a small library offers a mass of design magazines to browse through next to an intimate fireplace. Painting and photos in public spaces are by local artists and change every 6 months.

449 rue Ste-Hélène (near rue Notre-Dame), Montréal, PQ H2Y 2K9. www.hotelgault.com. © **866/904-1616** or 514/904-1616. Fax 866/904-1717. 30 units. C$187–C$279 double; C$225–C$589 suite. Rates include full breakfast. Packages available. AE, DISC, MC, V. Valet parking $26. Métro: Square Victoria. Pets accepted (C$75 per stay). **Amenities:** Cafe; bar; babysitting; concierge; exercise room; room service; spa. *In room:* A/C, TV/DVD player w/movie library, hair dryer, minibar, MP3 docking station, Wi-Fi (most rooms; free).

Hôtel St-Paul ★★   The St-Paul has been a star to design and architecture aficionados since it opened a decade ago, and it ranks among the most worthwhile of old buildings converted to hotels. Minimalism pervades, with simple lines and muted colors. Hallways are hushed and dark (truth be told, they border on pitch black), and they open into bright rooms with furnishings in grounded tones. This being Canada, pops of texture come from pelt rugs. In the bathroom, marble sinks are square, and clear plastic cubes cover the toiletries. Locally made chocolates are delivered with turndown service. Many rooms face Vieux-Montréal's less touristed, far-western edge, with its mixture of stone and brick buildings (although the rumble of rue McGill's morning buses and commuters may keep you from sleeping in). A splashy restaurant, **Vauvert,** offers locally inspired French cuisine with a Mediterranean flair and attracts the cocktail crowd when the DJ arrives on Thursday and Saturday nights.

355 rue McGill (at rue St-Paul), Montréal, PQ H2Y 2E8. www.hotelstpaul.com. © **866/380-2202** or 514/380-2222. Fax 514/380-2200. 120 units. C$209–C$339 double; C$351–C$439 suite. Children 11 and under stay free in parent's room. Packages available. AE, MC, V. Valet parking

C$23. Métro: Square Victoria. Pets under 30 lb. accepted (C$75 per stay). **Amenities:** Restaurant; bar; babysitting; concierge; exercise room; room service. *In room:* A/C, TV, CD player, hair dryer, minibar, MP3 player, Wi-Fi (C$14).

InterContinental Montréal ★　Across the street from the convention center, the InterContinental completed a floor-to-ceiling renovation in 2009 of its rooms, lobby, bar, restaurant, and reception area, all to better compete with the new Le Westin Montréal (below) and Embassy Suites, both down the block. Guest rooms fall under four confusing categories—Irresistible, Inspiring, Iconic, and Illustrious—but are spacious, quiet, and outfitted with marble bathrooms, low-slung wingback chairs, and comfortable beds. An upscale buffet breakfast in the new Provençal restaurant, **Osco!,** includes plump, ripe fruit and omelets made to order. But what really sets the InterContinental apart is its absinthe bar, the **Sarah B.,** named after actress Sarah Bernhardt (1844–1923), whose spirit is said to roam the adjacent 1888 Nordheimer building. In-hotel posters promise a night of "Pure sexytude, where the green fairy may be met in a suave and relaxed atmosphere." Perhaps what's lost in translation can, after a glass of absinthe, be found.

360 rue St-Antoine ouest (near rue de Bleury), Montréal, PQ H2Y 3X4. www.montreal. intercontinental.com. *©* **800/361-3600** or 514/987-9900. Fax 514/847-8730. 360 units. C$129–C$299 double; from C$277 suite. Children 17 and under stay free in parent's room. Packages available. AE, DC, DISC, MC, V. Valet parking C$29, self-parking C$22. Métro: Square Victoria. Pets accepted (C$35 per stay). **Amenities:** Restaurant; bar; babysitting; concierge; executive-level rooms; health club w/steam rooms; pool (w/whirlpool); room service; sauna. *In room:* A/C, TV, DVD player (on request), hair dryer, minibar, Wi-Fi (C$15 per day).

Le Westin Montréal ★ ☺　Travelers who get points with Westin might not know that the high-end chain opened a massive hotel in Montréal's Quartier International in 2009. Right across from the Palais des Congrès, it's also an easy walk to Old Montréal. Bright rooms with modern touches are centerpieced by the Westin's famous Dream beds. Business travelers are also well taken care of, with abundant desk space, conference rooms, and lots of wining and dining options. In honor of the printing house that the space formally contained, the restaurant is called **Gazette;** it serves French and Italian cuisine in a classy corner dining room. The gym is open 24/7 and offers a good-size pool. Swimmers should take note of the pool's transparent bottom, as it sits above the hotel's main entrance. Those 18 and under stay in their parents' room for free, and get a special "kids' club bag" upon arrival.

270 rue St. Antoine ouest (at rue de Bleury), Montréal, PQ H2Y 0A3. www.westinmontreal.com. *©* **866/837-4262** or 514/380-3333. Fax 514/380-3332. 750 units. C$229–$289 double; from C$309 suite. AE, DC, MC, V. Valet parking C$27. Métro: Place D'Armes. Pets accepted (C$30 per day). **Amenities:** Restaurant; bar; babysitting (by request); concierge; exercise room; pool; room service. *In room:* A/C, TV, music system, hair dryer, Wi-Fi (free).

Place d'Armes Hôtel & Suites ★★　Three adjoining buildings make up this romantic hotel, with their elaborate architectural details of the late 19th and early 20th centuries in abundant evidence. Many bedrooms have richly carved capitals and moldings, high ceilings, or original brick walls, and all are decorated in contemporary fashion: deluxe bedding, slate floors in the bathrooms, spotlight lighting. (That spotlight lighting can be pretty dim in some rooms, especially suites—ask for a bright room if you prefer lots of sun.) Many bathrooms have disc-shaped rain-shower nozzles in the showers. The hushed **Rainspa** has a

5

WHERE TO STAY IN MONTRÉAL

Vieux-Montréal (Old Montréal)

hammam—a traditional Middle-Eastern steam bath—and offers massages and facials. There are two terrific in-house dining options: the hushed and high-end **Aix Cuisine du Terroir** (p. 90), where meals are created around Québec ingredients, and the airy, tall-ceilinged **Suite 701** (p. 197), where guests are served breakfast and the *cinq-à-sept* (5-to-7) after-work crowd gathers to eat and drink.

55 rue St-Jacques ouest, Montréal, PQ H2Y 3X2. www.hotelplacedarmes.com. ℂ **888/450-1887** or 514/842-1887. Fax 514/842-6469. 131 units. C$188–C$255 double; from C$268 suite. Rates include 1 cocktail per stay. Packages available. AE, DISC, MC, V. Valet parking C$25. Métro: Place d'Armes. **Amenities:** 2 restaurants; bar; babysitting; concierge; exercise room; room service. *In room:* A/C, TV, hair dryer, minibar, Wi-Fi (free).

Moderate

Auberge Bonaparte ★ ✐

Even the smallest rooms in this fashionable urban inn are gracefully presented—they're sizeable, with comfortable, firm beds and bright decor. About half feature whirlpool tubs with separate showers. Guests can spend time on the rooftop terrace, which overlooks the Basilique Notre-Dame. **Bonaparte** restaurant (p. 90) on the ground floor—romantic in a Left Bank sort of way—has long been one of our Vieux-Montréal favorites. Generous gourmet breakfasts are included in your rate and served here. Sitting at one of the restaurant's elegant window tables with a newspaper, a croissant, coffee, and an omelet feels like an especially civilized way to start the day.

447 rue St-François-Xavier (just north of rue St-Paul), Montréal, PQ H2Y 2T1. www.bonaparte. com. ℂ **514/844-1448.** Fax 514/844-0272. 30 units. C$180–C$230 double; C$355 suite. Rates include full breakfast. AE, DC, MC, V. Parking C$15 per calendar day. Métro: Place d'Armes. **Amenities:** Restaurant; babysitting; concierge; access to nearby health club; room service. *In room:* A/C, TV, hair dryer, Wi-Fi (free).

Auberge Les Passants du Sans Soucy ★ ✐

This cheery inn in the heart of Vieux-Montréal is a gracefully converted former 1723 fur warehouse where the lobby doubles as an art gallery. The nine romantic rooms feature mortared stone walls, beamed ceilings, lace curtains, buffed wood floors, jet tubs, flatscreen TVs, and electric fireplaces. Renovations in 2008 knocked out some walls and brought in sleeker furnishings to make four smaller rooms larger; new mattresses were also added in 2011. Breakfast is a special selling point: A sky-lit dining nook features communal tables on either side of a fireplace imported from Bordeaux. The substantial morning meals include chocolate croissants and made-to-order omelets. The granite-floored front entry immediately sets a relaxed, urbane tone.

171 rue St-Paul ouest (at rue St-François-Xavier), Montréal, PQ H2Y 1Z5. www.lesanssoucy.com. ℂ **514/842-2634.** Fax 514/842-2912. 9 units. C$160–C$190 double; C$225 suite. Rates include full breakfast. AE, MC, V. Parking C$17 per calendar day. Métro: Place d'Armes. *In room:* A/C, TV, hair dryer, Wi-Fi (free).

Le Petit Hôtel ★

This picturesque section of rue St-Paul in Old Montréal has long housed some favorite small hotels—Auberge Les Passants du Sans Soucy (see above), just across the narrow street, and Auberge Bonaparte (see above) around the corner. Le Petit Hôtel opened in 2009 and is a variation on the same theme: a renovated industrial building from 1885, with original stone and brick walls exposed throughout. Rooms range from extra large (no. 208, with a long stone wall, floor-to-ceiling arched windows overlooking the street, and a flatscreen TV equipped with a Wii workout system) to the medium cozy (no. 306) to the small (no. 303). Continental breakfast features high-end muesli, great croissants,

Vieux-Montréal (Old Montréal)

WHERE TO STAY IN MONTRÉAL

and espresso drinks with soy milk as an option. Front staff is competent and friendly, and the overall vibe is chic. A noisy bar down the block makes rooms on the side or back preferable on warm nights.

168 rue St-Paul ouest (at rue St-François-Xavier), Montréal, PQ H2Y 1Z7. www.petithotelmontreal. com. ☏ **877/530-0360** or 514/940-0360. Fax 514/940-0363. 24 units. C$188–C$268 double. Rates include breakfast. Packages available. AE, MC, V. Valet parking C$24. Métro: Place d'Armes. **Amenities:** Cafe; concierge; access to exercise rooms at sister hotels Hôtel Nelligan and Place d'Armes Hôtel & Suites. *In room:* A/C, TV, DVD rental, hair dryer, minibar, MP3 docking station, Wi-Fi (free).

Lhotel Hotel Montréal 🎁 Formerly Hotel XIXe Siècle, with stately interiors that echoed the building's Second Empire exterior (it began life in 1870 as a bank), the new Lhotel is in the midst of change as new owner Georges Marciano (former fashion designer for Guess!) moves in. One step into the oddly juxtaposed lobby—at once Victorian library, neon bar, and pop-art emporium—and you'll see what we mean. Still, this tidy little hotel is worth seeking out for its central location and spacious, faintly aristocratic guest rooms, with 4.5m (15-ft.) ceilings, large windows, and functional work desks. Rooms facing the nondescript inner courtyard may not be scenic, but they're nearly silent—perfect for light sleepers. And who can complain when original Andy Warhols and Roy Lichtensteins from Marciano's personal collection line the hallways? One of the original LOVE sculptures by Robert Indiana stands sentry next to the front door, across from Botero's "Man on Horse."

262 rue St-Jacques ouest (at rue St-Jean), Montréal, PQ H2Y 1N1. www.lhotelmontreal.com. ☏ **877/553-0019** or 514/985-0019. Fax 514/985-0059. 59 units. C$170–C$190 double; from C$200 suite. Rates include breakfast. Children 12 and under stay free in parent's room. AE, MC, V. Valet parking C$22. Métro: Place d'Armes. **Amenities:** Bar; concierge; exercise room; room service. *In room:* A/C, TV, DVD player (on request), hair dryer, Wi-Fi (free).

PLATEAU MONT-ROYAL

A working-class area with an artsy bohemian feel, this is where many locals live, work, and play.

BEST FOR The culturally curious who live the credo, "When in Montréal, do as the Montréalers do."

DRAWBACKS Not a great selection of hotels, and virtually nothing on par with the design or grandeur of downtown or Vieux-Montréal.

Moderate

Auberge de La Fontaine ★ ✦ Colorful, quirky, and eminently competent, La Fontaine has the feel of a cheerful hostel. It's located directly on the lovely Parc de La Fontaine and one of the city's central bike paths. Bedrooms are done up in bright, funky hues, and beds are comfortable. The downstairs kitchen, in addition to being stocked with free tea, juices, cookies, and cheese, also has a microwave and a refrigerator for guest use. The front desk sells beer and wine. A third-floor terrace faces the park and is open during the day, and one suite has a private park-side patio. For visitors who plan to spend time at the restaurants and bars of Plateau Mont-Royal and who are looking for a casual option, Auberge de La Fontaine can't be beat.

1301 rue Rachel est (at rue Chambord), Montréal, PQ H2J 2K1. www.aubergedelafontaine.com. ☏ **800/597-0597** or 514/597-0166. Fax 514/597-0496. 21 units. May–Oct C$179–C$207 double,

C$235–C$259 suite; Nov–Apr from C$119 double, from C$168 suite. Rates include breakfast. Packages available. AE, DC, MC, V. 3 parking spots; free street parking. Métro: Mont-Royal. **Amenities:** Bikes can be delivered; kitchen. *In room:* A/C, TV, hair dryer, Wi-Fi (free).

Casa Bianca ★ 👜 If you want to know what it feels like to live as a local in Montréal's hip Le Plateau neighborhood, look no further. As the name suggests, this elegant B&B is a white house, and quietly lined up upon a tree-lined residential street. It also runs parallel to boulevard St-Laurent, aka the Main, Montréal's busy thoroughfare for shops, eateries, and great people-watching. Rooms are spacious and many have bear-claw bathtubs that lend a homey feel along with the hand-picked antiques in the room. Most rooms have a clear view of adjacent Parc Jeanne Mance and the mountain just in the distance.

4351 av. de L'Esplanade (at rue Marie-Anne), Montréal, PQ H2W 1T2. www.casabianca.ca. ✆ **866/775-4431** or 514/312-3837. 5 units. C$129–$269 double; from C$229 suite. Rates include breakfast. MC, V. Self-parking C$10. Métro: Mont-Royal. Pets not accepted. **Amenities:** Room service. *In room:* A/C, TV, hair dryer, Wi-Fi (free).

PRACTICAL INFORMATION
The Big Picture

Both Montréal and Québec City have familiar international hotel chains, as well as small B&Bs hosted by locals. In between are the boutique hotels, which combine high-end service with plush room accommodations and decor that ranges from Asian minimalist to country luxury. A good room in one of these smaller hotels could provide the best memories of your trip.

The tourist authorities in the province of Québec apply a six-level rating system (zero to five stars) to seven categories of establishments that host travelers. A shield bearing the assigned rating is posted near the entrance to most hotels and inns. The Québec system is based on quantitative measures such as the range of services and amenities. No star is assigned to properties that meet only the basic minimum standards, while five stars are reserved for establishments deemed exceptional. Most of the recommendations above have gotten at least three stars from the state system. Details are at www.citq.info.

The stars you see in the reviews in this book are based on Frommer's own rating system, which assigns between zero and three stars. The Frommer's ratings are more subjective than the state's, taking into account such considerations as price-to-value ratios, quality of service, ambience, location, helpfulness of staff, and the presence of such facilities as spas and exercise rooms.

All rooms have private bathrooms unless otherwise noted. Most hotels provide complimentary Wi-Fi in either part or all of their facilities, although this continues to be a work in progress for some properties. Ask about the most current Internet options when reserving a room. Some hotels have stopped providing in-room coffeemakers, so ask in advance if this feature is important to you. Most Montréal hotels are entirely nonsmoking. Those that aren't have a limited number of smoking rooms available.

Getting the Best Deal

Most Québec hotels offer online specials and package deals that bundle rooms with meals or sightseeing activities. In many cases, this can result in rates significantly below what's quoted in this book. Always check hotel websites before calling to make a reservation. And check discount sites such as Expedia, which oftentimes offers still more competitive rates.

Because the region is so cold for so many months of the year, tourism here is cyclical. That means that prices drop—often steeply—for many properties much of the September-through-April period. While rooms are less expensive these times of year, some of the essential vibrancy and *joie de vivre* of the region goes into hibernation as well. Hotel rates are highest during the region's busiest times, from May to October, reaching a peak during Grand Prix in June, and remaining relatively high in July and August. Rates also inflate during the virtually nonstop summer of festivals, annual holidays (Canadian *and* American), and winter carnivals in January and February. (Festivals and dates are listed on p. 28.) For those periods, reserve well in advance, especially if you're looking for special prices or packages.

Except for B&Bs, visitors can almost always find discounts and package deals. That's especially the case on weekends, when business clients leave town.

Most goods and services in Canada have a federal tax of 5% (the TPS). On top of that, the province of Québec adds a tax that comes out to 7.88% (the TVQ). An additional accommodations tax of 3.5% is in effect on hotel bills in Montréal. Prices listed in this book do not include taxes.

Reservation Services

Most hotels don't ask for deposits but require that you pay the whole fee upfront, and usually won't reserve your room until your credit card transaction goes through successfully. Most of the larger hotels allow you to cancel rooms, but do check in advance how many days you have to receive all your money back.

Check out time is usually around 11am, but can normally be extended to noon or 1pm if requested. Similarly, check-in time is routinely after 3pm.

Planning and reserving ahead is always a good idea, especially due to the (seemingly) never-ending festival season in Montréal, so arriving with no reservations and the hope of winging it could make you an unhappy camper indeed. In such cases, however, do remember that there is a great selection of hotels near the airport, including a new Marriott adjacent to the arrivals gate at Trudeau International Airport.

BOOKING AGENCIES While there are no "agencies" per se that book hotels for you (other than the discount sites such as Expedia), you may want to look into **Experience Old Montréal** (www.experienceoldmontreal.com), which is run by the Antonopoulos Group (p. 74) and thus concentrates all their hotels and restaurants in one spot. Many, if not all, of their addresses (for spa, food, drinks, and accommodations, as well as seasonal events) are frequented by savvy locals, and so can be an easy go-to site for many of your Old Montréal excursions.

Alternative Accommodations

Bed-and-breakfasts boast cozier settings than many hotels and are often (but not always) lower priced than comparable hotels. They also give visitors the opportunity to get to know a Montréaler or two, since their owners are among the most outgoing and knowledgeable guides one might want. Tourisme Montréal maintains a database of recommended B&Bs at **www.tourisme-montreal.org/accommodations**.

Rules and types of rooms at B&Bs vary significantly. Ask upfront if bathrooms are shared or if children are welcome.

6

WHERE TO EAT IN MONTRÉAL

oie gras, tartare, and charcuterie plates are just a few of the gluttonous, savory items that cause Montréalers to salivate and travelling gastronauts to convene on Montréal's hedonistic, no-mercy culinary scene. Add a penchant for quality, local produce (known as *terroir*), such as duck, pork, award-winning cheeses, and iconic maple syrup, it's no wonder that celebrity chefs are regular visitors or that the city's own kitchen glitterati are international stars as well.

While white-linen restaurants of yore remain a classic culinary art, the heart of Montréal's new foodie culture is found in her bustling, come-as-you-are yet decidedly upscale bistros. Think of the phenomena more as "fine diner" instead of "fine-dining," a happy, hearty concept that makes eating out not only laid-back and accessible but deliciously entertaining.

BEST EATING BETS

o **Best Classic French Bistro:** Plateau Mont-Royal's most Parisian spot, **L'Express** (p. 99), is where you come to see what the Francophone part of this city is all about. From the black-and-white-checkered floor to the grand, high ceilings to the classic cuisine, this is where Old France meets New France. Another good bet is **Leméac** (p. 101) in the chichi Outremont neighborhood.

o **Best Restaurant to Eat So Much Food at You Can't Move:** As the name— "The Pig's Foot"—suggests, **Au Pied de Cochon** is mostly about slabs of meat, especially pork, seafood, and foie gras. The PDC's Cut, weighing in at more than a pound, is emblematic. See p. 96.

o **Best Vegan:** A standard-bearer since 1997, Plateau Mont-Royal's **Aux Vivres** packs in vegans, vegetarians, and the meat eaters who love them. See p. 103.

price CATEGORIES

Very Expensive	C$30 and up
Expensive	C$20–C$30
Moderate	C$10–C$20
Inexpensive	Under C$10

PREVIOUS PAGE: Toqué! is one of Montréal's premier dining experiences.

○ **Best Guilty Treat:** *Poutine* is a plate of French fries (*frites*) drenched with gravy afloat with cheese curds, and it's the bedrock of Québec comfort food, if not the national hangover remedy. **La Banquise,** near Parc La Fontaine's northwest corner, offers upwards of 25 variations and is open 24 hours a day, 7 days a week. See p. 101.

○ **Best Breakfast:** The city has eight outposts of **Eggspectation,** and they all do brisk business serving funky, creative breakfasts with loads of egg options. The menu is extensive, prices are fair, and portions are huge. See p. 94.

○ **Best Smoked Meat:** There are other contenders, but **Chez Schwartz Charcuterie Hébraïque de Montréal,** known simply as Schwartz's, serves up the definitive version of regional brisket. A new takeout-only counter has opened just next door, a practical option after you see the sit-down lineup that snakes its way down the street. See p. 100.

○ **Best Burgers:** If you're looking for tasty burgers, downtown regulars convene at **m:brgr** (p. 86), where the beef is sourced from famed Moishes steakhouse. Connoisseurs, however, should stop by the Quartier Latin's **La Paryse** (p. 105).

○ **Best Bagel:** Even native New Yorkers give it up for Montréal's bagels, which are sweeter and chewier than those produced south of the border. (The secret, they say, is dipping the dough in honey water.) Both **St-Viateur Bagel & Café** (p. 104) and **Fairmont Bagel** (p. 103) are the places to assess the comparison.

○ **Best Restaurant, Period:** Chef Normand Laprise and partner Christine Lamarche keep Vieux-Montréal's **Toqué!** (p. 88) in a league of its own. This dazzlingly postmodern venue is now a deserving member of the gold-standard organization Relais & Châteaux. Laprise fans should also try his more casual spot **Brasserie T** (p. 85) in the Quartier des Spectacles, which in summer boasts a happening patio.

CENTRE-VILLE/DOWNTOWN

In addition to the restaurants listed below, food is also available in downtown Montréal at the jazz clubs **Maison de Jazz** and **Upstairs Jazz Bar & Grill** (p. 191 and 192) and at the pubs **Brutopia, Dominion Square Tavern,** and **Pullman** (all listed in "Bars," p. 195).

Very Expensive

Cavalli ITALIAN   Employing a formula more common in the restaurants over on boulevard St-Laurent than here in the middle of the business district, the owners fill a glamorous space with striking young women in snug black dresses and hunky young men with requisite 4-day-old beards. It's like joining the after-party of a Hollywood premiere. Being seen is top priority, but the food is noteworthy, too. You can make a meal of any of the dozen antipasti, from salmon tartar to pickled veal filet, or opt for one of the eminently worthwhile main events such as the pine nut–crusted filet mignon or rack of lamb with oregano crust and olive *jus*, both of which have been on the menu for ages. Prices are high, assuring a prosperous crowd. The glowing pink bar turns into a heavy scene later in the evening.

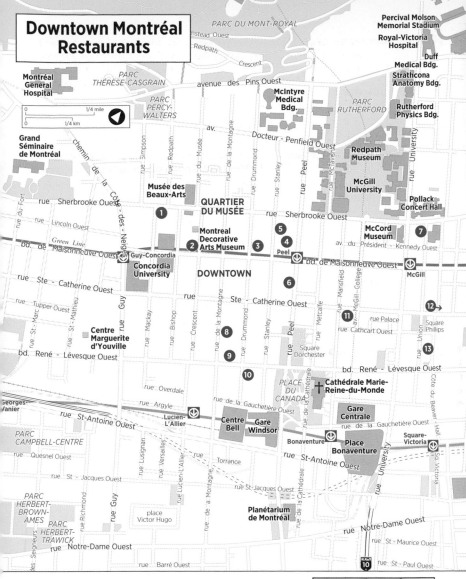

Downtown Montréal Restaurants

Boustan **2**
Brasserie T **12**
Cavalli **4**
Decca 77 **10**
Europea **8**
Ferreira Café **6**
Java U **7**
Julien **13**
La Queue de Cheval **9**
Le Commensal **11**
Le Taj **5**
m:brgr **3**
Nocochi **1**

2042 rue Peel (at boul. de Maisonneuve). ☎ **514/843-5100.** www.ristorantecavalli.com. Reservations recommended. Main courses C$37–C$44; table d'hôte lunch C$29–C$32. AE, DC, MC, V. Mon–Fri noon–2:30pm; Mon–Sat 5:30–11pm (bar open later). Métro: Peel.

Europea ★★★ CONTEMPORARY FRENCH   From the outside, Europea looks like many of the city's low-brow brownstone eateries. But once inside—after either ascending the spiral staircase or tucking into a cozy table in the cellar—you'll see why chef Jérôme Ferrer was named Chef of the Year by the Société des Chefs, Cuisiniers et Pâtissiers du Québec, in 2007, and why *Debeur,* the French-language guidebook for Québec gourmands, named Europea the 2010 Restaurant of the Year. An *amuse* or "teaser" might be a demitasse of lobster-cream cappuccino with truffle shavings. For the main event, consider the scallops served with risotto in béarnaise sauce. Gaps in the procession are short. Be sure to leave room for dessert, which comes in small, delectable servings. For the full treatment, order the 10-course *menu dégustation.* For a bargain, come at lunch, when the table d'hôte starts at C$24.

1227 rue de la Montagne (near rue Ste-Catherine). ☎ **514/398-9229.** www.europea.ca. Reservations strongly recommended. Main courses C$30–C$44; table d'hôte lunch C$24–$30, dinner C$60; 10-course *menu dégustation* C$90. AE, MC, V. Tues–Fri noon–2pm; daily 6–10pm. Métro: Peel.

La Queue de Cheval ★ STEAKHOUSE   Whether it's the lovely hostesses, cigar lounge, the Bell Centre (home of the Montréal Canadiens) across the street, or the 28-ounce porterhouse, dry-aged steaks, it's no wonder that many a bachelor party has unraveled here. Smaller (yet no less extravagant) cuts and varieties of meat are also hanging in the glass meat lockers, offered with nine different sauces and butters. (I recommend the cognac peppercorn or the black truffle, respectively.) Spread over two floors, the centerpiece of the restaurant is the circular grill with a two-story hooded fan and dramatic wrap-around staircase. Start with hefty appetizers such as the Black Tiger jumbo shrimp cocktail, then round out your carnivorous experience with a supersized side order. What about a fluffy cloud of mashed potatoes? You'll be sweating garlic for days.

1221 boul. René-Lévesque ouest (corner of rue Drummond). ☎ **514/390-0090.** www.queuede cheval.com. Reservations strongly recommended. Table d'hôte lunch C$27, lunch à la carte C$30–C$68; main courses C$33–C$70. AE, MC. V. Mon–Fri 11am–2:30pm; Sun–Wed 5:30–10:30pm; Thurs–Sat 5:30–11:30pm. Métro: Bonaventure.

Expensive

Decca 77 ★ CONTEMPORARY FRENCH   The food is stunning, presented with both flair and perfection, yet it's difficult to see past this restaurant's drab setting in the lower corner of an office tower, even with the swaths of raspberry- and cappuccino-colored fabrics and high-design intent. Being steps from the Centre Bell presents a similar conundrum: handy location (with valet parking on hockey game nights—ask when reserving) but not atmospherically rewarding. But darn if the food wasn't divine. Prix-fixe options for both lunch and dinner are good value.

1077 rue Drummond (at boul. René-Lévesque). ☎ **514/934-1077.** www.decca77.com. Reservations recommended. Main courses C$24–C$42; table d'hôte lunch C$25, dinner C$35. AE, DC, MC, V. Mon–Fri 11:30am–2:30pm; Mon–Sat 5:30–10:30pm. Métro: Bonaventure or Lucien L'Allier.

Ferreira Café ★★★ SEAFOOD/PORTUGUESE   You'll feel transported to Portugal at this popular downtown spot. At lunch, customers are mostly dressed in business suits; at night, more festive diners come out to play. One highlight:

Prices listed are for supper unless otherwise indicated (lunch prices are usually lower) and do not include the cost of wine, tip, or the 5% federal tax *and* 8.5% provincial tax that are tacked on the restaurant bill. Montréalers consider 15% of the check (before taxes) to be a fair tip, increased only for exceptional food and service. In all, count on taxes and tip to add another 30% to the bill.

Always look for table d'hôte meals. These fixed-price menus with three or four courses usually cost just a little more than the price of a single à la carte main course. Restaurants at all price ranges offer them, and they represent the best value around. If you want to try many of the top restaurants, schedule some for noon-time meals if they offer table d'hôte menus at lunch. You'll get your best deal that way.

The midday meal is called *dîner* (which is lunch, not dinner) and the evening meal is *souper* (supper). An *entrée* is an appetizer, and a *plat principal* is a main course.

Because parking space is at a premium in most restaurant districts, it's easiest to take the Métro or a taxi. If you're driving, find out whether valet parking is available.

Québec has long had a smoking culture, but smoking in bars and restaurants has been banned since 2006.

Except in a handful of luxury restaurants, dress codes are all but nonexistent. But Montréalers are a fashionable lot and manage to look smart, even in casual clothes. Save the T-shirts and sneakers for another city.

Insider websites featuring reviews and observations about the Montréal dining scene include **www.midnight poutine.ca/food, www.tourisme-montreal.org/blog, www.montrealfor insiders.com**, and **www.endlessbanquet. blogspot.com**. *Montréal Gazette* restaurant critic Lesley Chesterman has a highly regarded blog at **www.lesley chesterman.com** about the city's food scene.

cataplana, which is the name of both a venerated Portuguese recipe and the hinged copper clamshell-style pot in which it is cooked. The dish is a fragrant stew of mussels, clams, potatoes, shrimp, *chouriço* sausage, and chunks of cod and salmon. A smaller late-night menu for C$24 is available from 10pm. As *Montréal Gazette* food critic Lesley Chesterman has noted, "Downtown Montréal may not be the coolest dining destination anymore, but at Ferreira on a sunny Friday night, I can think of few restaurants more impressive."

1446 rue Peel (near boul. de Maisonneuve). (©) **514/848-0988.** www.ferreiracafe.com. Reservations recommended. Main courses C$26–C$42. AE, MC, V. Mon–Fri 11:45am–3pm; Sun–Wed 5:30–11pm; Thurs–Sat 5:30pm–midnight. Closed Sun in winter. Métro: Peel.

Moderate

Brasserie T ★★ BRASSERIE   Snuggled under the wing of the Musée d'Art Contemporain de Montréal is where Montréal's own celebrity chef, Normand Larprise (see **Toqué!,** p. 88), opened restaurant number two. Minus the white linens and elaborate tasting menus he is known for, the more relaxed and intimate setting offers foodies quintessential Montréal comfort food to the highest degree of execution. Everybody starts with a jar of tiny pickles. From the charcuterie selections, the terrine de foie gras is heaven on a wooden board, served with expertly toasted brioche. Beef and salmon tartares are each seasoned to perfection. The *bavette de boeuf* comes with Toqué butter (fresh herbs, lemon and garlic) and revived classic Coquille St-Jacques, potato purée served with scallops in the actual shell. The restaurant is housed in a shoebox-shaped space that has floor-to-ceiling windows and an extremely popular (read: Make reservations in good weather) al fresco dining area for up to 60 people overlooking the Quartier des Spectacles.

1425 rue Jeanne-Mance (near rue Ste-Catherine). ℭ **514/282-0808.** www.brasserie-t.com. Reservations strongly recommended. Main courses C$15–C$24. AE, DISC, MC, V. Sun–Wed 11:30am–10:30pm; Thurs–Sat 11:30am–11:30pm. Métro: Place-des-Arts.

Julien TRADITIONAL FRENCH A quiet downtown block in the financial district has been home to this relaxed Parisian-style bistro for years, hosting businesspeople at lunch and after-work cocktails, and mostly tourists from nearby hotels in the evening. Much of the year, diners have the option of sitting at tables on the heated terrace. The menu offers generous-size portions without any pyrotechnics and features classics such as grilled steak in béarnaise sauce or, in season, mussels with frites. There's always a vegetarian option, too. Service is friendly and attentive.

1191 av. Union (at boul. René-Lévesque). ℭ **514/871-1581.** www.restaurantjulien.com. Reservations recommended. Main courses C$18–C$24. AE, MC, V. Mon–Fri 11:30am–3pm and 5–10pm; Sat 5:30–10pm. Métro: McGill.

m:brgr ★ LIGHT FARE The hype would have it that m:brgr is *the* spot in the city for burgers, when really it's just fine, no better no worse. It's kitschy for sure, with options for what it candidly terms "crazy expensive toppings" such as black-truffle carpaccio. The menu makes a big production about "building your own burger," but choosing cheese and toppings is not revolutionary. The basic burger itself is okay (be sure to specify how you want it cooked), although no threat to best of breed at **La Paryse** (p. 105) or **MeatMarket** (p. 99). The scene is festive and the staff friendly, and there's a big drink menu with mojitos and margaritas. m:brgr comes from solid pedigree: It was started by the family behind **Moishes,** a fancy steak-and-seafood house in Plateau Mont-Royal (p. 95).

2025 rue Drummond. ℭ **514/906-2747.** www.mbrgr.com. Main courses C$8.75–C$39 (most under C$15). AE, MC, V. Mon–Thurs 11:30am–11pm; Fri–Sat 11:30am–midnight; Sun noon–10pm. Métro: Peel.

Le Taj ★ 🍴 INDIAN Still one of downtown's tastiest bargains. The price of the lunch buffet (C$15) has barely changed since the restaurant opened in 1985, and it's a real treat. The kitchen specializes in the Mughlai cuisine of the Indian subcontinent, and seasonings tend more toward the tangy than the incendiary. Dishes are perfumed with turmeric, saffron, ginger, cumin, mango powder, and garam masala (a spice combination that usually includes cloves, cardamom, and cinnamon). Vegetarians have ample choices from the eight-page menu, with the chickpea-based channa masala among the most complex. Evenings are quiet, and lunchtimes are busy but not hectic. On one large wall, a bas-relief mud wall depicts a village scene; that wall was part of the Indian Pavilion at Expo 67.

2077 rue Stanley (near rue Sherbrooke). ℭ **514/845-9015.** www.restaurantletaj.com. Main courses C$14–C$23; lunch buffet C$15; table d'hôte dinner C$36. AE, DC, MC, V. Mon–Fri 11:30am–2:30pm and 5–10:30pm; Sat 5–11pm; Sun 11:30am–2:30pm and 5–11pm. Métro: Peel.

POUTINE, SMOKED MEAT & THE WORLD'S best BAGELS

While you're in Montréal, indulge in at least a couple of Québec staples. Though you'll find them dolled up on some menus, these are generally thought of as the region's basic comfort foods:

- *Poutine:* French fries doused with gravy and cheese curds. Its profile has risen outside of the province in recent years, and a four-page essay in *The New Yorker* magazine in 2009 posited that the "national joke" may be becoming a national dish. It's a perfect symbol, wrote Calvin Trillin, "for a country that prides itself on lumpy multiculturalism—whatever impact it has on another point of pride, the national health-care system."

- **Smoked meat:** A maddeningly tasty sandwich component particular to Montréal whose taste is similar to pastrami and corned beef.

- *Cretons:* A pâté of minced pork, allspice, and parsley.

- *Tourtière:* A meat pie of spiced ground pork, often served with tomato chutney.

- *Queues de Castor:* A deep-fried pastry (the trademark chain originated in Ottawa) the size of a man's footprint served with your choice of sweet or savory toppings. The name means "beaver tails."

- *Tarte au sucre:* Maple-sugar pie, like pecan pie without the pecans. A French-Canadian classic.

- *Bagels:* Crispy on the outside, chewy on the inside, with just a touch of sweetness. Join the national debate and choose your favorite between two longtime bagel rivals, St-Viateur and Fairmont.

Inexpensive

Boustan 🏛 LEBANESE   In the middle of the hubbub among the bars and clubs on rue Crescent, this Lebanese pizza parlor–style eatery, completely non-descript and consistently popular, has a line out the door at 2pm (office workers) and again at 2am (late-night partiers), all jonesing for its famed falafel, *shish taouk,* or *shawarma* sandwiches. Yes, that's former Prime Minister Pierre Trudeau in the photo at the cash register; he was a regular.

2020A rue Crescent (at boul. de Maisonneuve). ℂ **514/843-3576.** Most items cost less than C$10. MC, V. Mon–Sat 11am–4am; Sun 5pm–4am. Métro: Peel.

Java U ☺ LIGHT FARE   This outpost of a small local chain is right across from the McGill campus, ensuring that you'll likely be next to college kids tapping away on MacBooks or looking over music scores. Options are fresh and healthy: sandwiches, quiche, fresh fruit. The atmosphere is on the sophisticated side for what's essentially fast food. It's open daily from at least 8am to at least 8pm.

626 rue Sherbrooke (at av. Union). ℂ **514/286-1991.** www.java-u.com. Most items cost less than C$8. AE, MC, V. Mon–Fri 7am–9pm; Sat–Sun 8am–8pm. Métro: McGill.

Le Commensal ☺ 🍴 VEGETARIAN   Vegetarian fare is presented buffet-style here, and you pay the cashier by the weight of your plate—about C$8 for an ample portion (the restaurant has a "maximum price or less!" policy of C$14 at lunchtime and C$17 in the evening). Dishes include quinoa, garbanzo curry, several types of salads, a large variety of hot dishes, tofu with ginger sauce, and so on. Even avowed meat eaters are likely to not feel deprived. Beer and wine are available, too. A second-floor location overlooking rue Ste-Catherine, this is a satisfying spot to keep in mind when you're downtown. There's another branch at 1720 rue St-Denis (𝄽 **514/845-2627**).

1204 av. McGill College (at rue Ste-Catherine). 𝄽 **514/871-1480.** www.commensal.com. Most meals cost less than C$10. AE, MC, V. Daily 11:30am–10pm. Métro: McGill.

Nocochi BAKERY/LIGHT FARE   At a posh location on the corner of rue Sherbrooke a block west of the Musée des Beaux-Arts, this cute little cafe and patisserie is just the place for salads, sandwiches, or the house specialty pistachio muffin with afternoon tea. After museum browsing or power shopping, the all-white room, decorated with large close-up photos of decadent pastries, is a relief. Sit-down service can be slow, so first try placing an order at the cashier.

2156 rue Mackay (at rue Sherbrooke). 𝄽 **514/989-7514.** Most meals cost less than C$8. MC, V. Sun–Mon 8am–6pm; Tues–Sat 8am–7pm. Métro: Guy-Concordia.

VIEUX-MONTRÉAL (OLD MONTRÉAL)

In addition to the restaurants listed below, food is also available in Vieux-Montréal at **Le Jardin Nelson** (p. 197), which has live jazz and a terrace, and the **Verses Sky Terrace** (p. 197) inside the Hôtel Nelligan.

Very Expensive

Toqué! ★★★ CONTEMPORARY FRENCH   Toqué! is the gem that single-handedly raised the entire city's gastronomic expectations. A meal here has long been obligatory for anyone who admires superb, dazzlingly presented food. "Post-nouvelle" might be an apt description for chef Normand Laprise's creations, featured on a short, ever-changing menu with top-of-the-bin ingredients, some of them rarely seen together—for example, a cauliflower soup with foie gras shavings and milk foam, or smoked suckling pig cheek with maple-water sponge toffee. If you choose the seven-course tasting menu, you can also opt for a wine pairing. The decor is 1960s loungey, with bulbous lamps hanging from the ceiling and low-back chairs. A new 13-person U-shaped bar serves an abbreviated menu, perfect for preshow or pregame meals. Most diners are prosperous looking, so while the stated dress code is casual, you'll want to look sharp, even during busy lunchtime hours. Service is efficient, helpful, and not a bit self-important. In 2011, the patio (open only in good weather) went full force, introducing Italian furniture to accommodate up to 50 diners who like a little fresh air with their haute gastronomy.

900 Place Jean-Paul-Riopelle (at rue St-Antoine). 𝄽 **514/499-2084.** www.restaurant-toque. com. Reservations required. Main courses C$40–C$44; tasting menu C$92 (C$104 with foie gras). AE, DC, MC, V. Tues–Fri 11:30am–2pm; Tues–Sat 5:30–10pm. Métro: Square-Victoria.

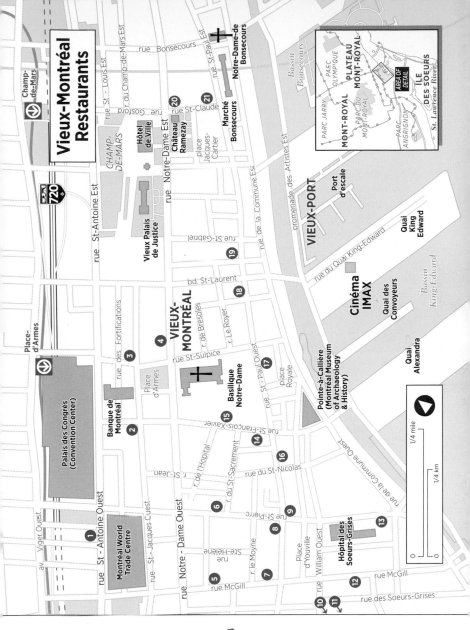

Vieux-Montréal Restaurants

Aix Cuisine du Terroir **3**
Bonaparte **15**
Boris Bistro **5**
Chez l'Épicier **21**
Cluny ArtBar **11**
La Concession **4**
DNA **13**
Eggspectation **2**
Gandhi **16**
Graziella **12**
Holder **7**
Le Club Chasse et Pêche **20**
Le Garde Manger **14**
Le Local **10**
Marché de la Villette **9**
Méchant Boeuf **17**
Modavie **18**
Olive et Gourmando **8**
Titanic **6**
Toqué! **1**
Vieux-Port Steakhouse **19**

Expensive

Aix Cuisine du Terroir ★ CONTEMPORARY QUÉBÉCOIS   Lodged in the high-end **Place d'Armes Hôtel** (p. 75), this resto (just call it "X") is a highlight of Vieux-Montréal dining. *Terroir* refers to soil, and a gastronomical allegiance to products grown in the immediate region dominates, evidenced in dishes like the Medallion de Veau (which features veal medallion and vegetables in a red-wine sauce), might set the course, and portions are generous enough that you could graze on a few appetizers alone. Restful tones, tan banquettes, and flickering gas lamps set an earthy mood. If you just need a snack or a more social atmosphere, head to the snazzy **Suite 701** bar (p. 197), also in the hotel, where young professionals convene after work and into the evening. Food here—like the mini Kobe burgers and Red Bull rabbit "wings" with maple syrup—comes from the same chef.

711 rue St-Jacques ouest (at côte de la Place d'Armes). 🕐 **514/904-1201.** www.aixcuisine.com. Main courses C$29–C$45. AE, DC, DISC, MC, V. Daily 11am–3pm and 5:30–11pm. Métro: Place d'Armes.

Bonaparte ★ TRADITIONAL FRENCH   In a city brimming with accomplished French restaurants, this is a personal favorite. The dining rooms run through the ground floors of two old row houses, with rich decorative details suggestive of the namesake's era. Adroit service is provided by schooled pros who manage to be knowledgeable without being stuffy. The house specialties are Dover sole filet with fresh herbs, and mushroom ravioli seasoned with fresh sage. The seven-course tasting menu, reasonably priced at C$66, lets you try out a large variety of the chef's special creations. Lunches cater to an upscale business crowd, and the restaurant offers an early evening menu for theatergoers. The clean and bright 30-room-and-1-suite **Auberge Bonaparte** (p. 76) is upstairs.

447 rue St-François-Xavier (north of rue St-Paul). 🕐 **514/844-4368.** www.bonaparte.com. Main courses C$23–C$39; table d'hôte lunch C$16–C$23, dinner C$31; 7-course tasting menu C$66. AE, DC, MC, V. Mon–Fri 7–10am and 11:30am–2pm; Sat 7–10:30am; Sun 8–10:30am; daily 5:30–10pm. Métro: Place d'Armes.

Chez l'Épicier CONTEMPORARY QUÉBÉCOIS   The self-assuredness of this bright corner eatery opposite the Marché Bonsecours beckons from the street, where the menu, handwritten on a blackboard (as well as *produits du terroir,* developed by the chef and sold to go), can be glimpsed through large, arched windows. It's not a restaurant you stumble into; it draws you in. You'll find the "surf and turf" of langoustine and sweetbread, miso, butter sauce, caramelized eggplant, and sweet potatoes is as tasty as it is pretty to look at. Global ingredients and techniques are part of the mix, as are witty surprises, like a chocolate club sandwich with pineapple fries for dessert. Dinner is on the steep side, but lunch can be had for under C$30, tip included.

311 rue St-Paul est (at rue St-Claude). 🕐 **514/878-2232.** www.chezlepicier.com. Main courses C$28–C$40; table d'hôte lunch C$20; 7-course tasting menu C$80. AE, MC, V. Thurs–Fri 11:30am–2pm; daily 5:30–10pm. Métro: Champ-de-Mars.

Le Club Chasse et Pêche ★★★ CONTEMPORARY QUÉBÉCOIS   The name Hunting and Fishing Club doesn't suggest fine dining, but here *chasse et pêche* more accurately means "new-school surf and turf." The seasonal menu might include chilled sweet pea soup garnished with fried oysters, or a boar chop drizzled with corn purée. Since its 2005 opening, "Chasse"—as it is known by fashionable insiders—has become the restaurant of choice for romantic tête-à-têtes, chic celebrations, or simply for the enjoyment of judiciously, lovingly, and expertly prepared food. Chef Claude Pelletier, who tends to avoid the limelight, never disappoints with his constantly evolving menu. The restaurant's website includes a quirky blog of reviews, YouTube films, and other stuff the staff likes, and hints at the establishment's loyal, hip following. Interested foodies should also head to the Plateau Mont-Royal, where the same team has opened Le Filet (p. 98), a more casual—but no less stylish—affair.

423 rue St-Claude (btw. rue St-Paul and rue Notre-Dame). ℂ **514/861-1112.** www.leclubchasse etpeche.com. Reservations recommended. Main courses C$29–C$35. AE, MC, V. June–Sept daily 11:30am–2pm (lunch served in garden of nearby Musée du Château Ramezay, p. 125); year-round Tues–Sat 6–10:30pm. Métro: Champ-de-Mars.

DNA ★ CONTEMPORARY QUÉBÉCOIS   Still heating up the Montréal res-taurant scene 3 years after its 2008 opening, DNA suffuses concept dining with affable, expert service. Glass slabs divide the restaurant into nooks that allow the excitement of a packed house to bubble over without sacrificing intimacy or views of the building's architectural elements. Wondering about the origin of the fiddle-heads or nettles? Servers will carry a basket of fresh and locally grown ingredients to your table. This gesture adds charm to an evening out and can prompt gastro-nomic dialogue—so don't hesitate to ask questions. Since the chef buys whole animals, ingredients such as veal-heart tartar mixed with foie gras and pork brain are some of the things you'll see on the menu. The wine list, which earned a 2009 *Wine Spectator* award of excellence, overflows with Canadian options.

355 rue Marguerite D'Youville (at rue St-Pierre). ℂ **514/287-3362.** www.dnarestaurant.com. Main courses C$20–C$44; 5-course tasting menu C$80. AE, MC, V. Tues–Sat 6–10:30pm. Métro: Square-Victoria.

Graziella ITALIAN   Treat yourself to a little oasis for lunch or dinner. Bring your family, your lover, or your business clients (there is free Wi-Fi and even a special conference room with projector access if need be). The windows over-looking the street bring in a beautiful natural light. The interior decor palette of creams, taupes, and honey browns gives the large, tall space an airy spa feeling. Comfort is the key word here when it comes to food, and each oversized plate is presented in a simple, elegant presentation. My only beef here is that if you order the risotto, you have to order it for two, which is no fun if your husband wants to order the *osso buco*. But that's okay; you can share the dark-chocolate tarte that comes with homemade gelato.

116 rue McGill (3 blocks east of rue Notre-Dame ouest). ℂ **514/876-0116.** www.restaurant graziella.ca. Reservations strongly recommended. Main courses C$24–C$42. AE, DC, DISC, MC, V. Mon–Fri noon–2:30pm; Mon–Sat 6–10:30pm. Métro: Square-Victoria.

Le Garde Manger ★★ SEAFOOD   From the dark roadhouse decor to the rowdy slip of a bar, this giddy resto is a smackdown to its gentrified Vieux-Mon-tréal neighbors—if not a trailblazer leading the way for other supper clubs in the area such as L'Orignal and Barroco. On the plus side, the food is pretty good and generously portioned. The menu changes nightly, but options might include spicy jerk snow crab, lobster *poutine*, or beef short ribs over arugula. You'll need a lead stomach to survive a whole portion of the signature dessert, a fried Mars bar, unless deafening rock music helps you digest. There's no sign outside, just a blank, white cube that glows pink when there's action inside—and a burly door-man. If you stop by and the restaurant looks closed, they could be shooting epi-sodes of "Chuck's Day Off" for Canadian Food Network, a reality show starring owner and cook Chuck Hughes, who recently beat out Bobby Flay in an *Iron Chef* showdown.

408 rue St-François-Xavier (north of rue St-Paul). ☎ **514/678-5044.** Reservations recommen-ded. Main courses C$25–C$35. AE, MC, V. Tues–Sun 6–11pm. Bar Tues–Sun 6pm–3am. Métro: Place d'Armes.

Le Local CONTEMPORARY FRENCH   Whereas many of its counterparts have exquisite food but predictably styled atmosphere, or vice versa, Le Local musters originality in both arenas. The kitchen breathes new life into standards like surf and turf, and the brick, wood, and glass interior feels remarkably cur-rent. Chef Charles-Emmanuel Pariseau trained locally before opening these doors in 2008, and sommelier Elyse Lambert has received regional and national recognition for her skills. The *chiogga* beet salad with bacon, tomatoes, and truf-fle oil stands out as a starter; so, too, does the main course of the salmon tartare with truffle oil and lime that's served with fries and/or a salad and blood pudding with pan-seared foie gras. But truly, you can roam anywhere on the menu with great satisfaction. For a more casual night out or to sample highlights without the steep check, check out the bar and its lower-priced offerings.

740 rue William (at rue Prince). ☎ **514/397-7737.** www.resto-lelocal.com. Reservations recom-mended. Main courses C$19–C$35; bar menu C$5–C$14. MC, V. Mon–Fri 11:30am–midnight; Sat 5:30pm–midnight; Sun 5:30–11:30pm. Métro: Square-Victoria.

Moderate

Boris Bistro ★ BISTRO   Boris attracts a smartly dressed crowd of business folk, couples, and groups. It does big volume, but service is fast and efficient. The outdoor space here is especially pretty: In warm months, the restaurant opens its side doors to what feels like an adjacent vacant lot (the facade of a building that once stood here remains at one end), but leafy trees, large umbrellas, and subtle lighting make it an oasis. A standout menu option is the duck risotto with oyster mushrooms, sage, and orange-cream sauce. French fries cooked in duck fat are a signature dish, and there's a choice of about a half-dozen *fromages du terroir,* local cheeses, along with sweet treats, to close a meal. A fun evening option allows you to pick three, four, or five appetizers for a fixed price.

465 rue McGill (1 block south of rue Notre-Dame). ☎ **514/848-9575.** www.borisbistro.com. Main courses C$17–C$25; table d'hôte of 3, 4, or 5 appetizers C$27, C$34, or C$40. AE, MC, V. Summer Mon–Fri 11:30am–11pm, Sat–Sun noon–11pm; winter Mon–Fri 11:30am–2pm, Tues–Fri 5–9pm, Sat 6–9pm. Métro: Square-Victoria.

Gandhi ★ 🍴 INDIAN   Classy but inexpensive enough to accommodate stu-dent and retiree budgets, Gandhi got so busy that the owners expanded into the adjacent building a few years ago, doubling their seating space. The contiguous dining rooms are bright, and service is brisk but polite. Cooking is mostly to order and arrives fresh from the pot, pan, or oven. Biriyani and curry specialties are delicate and subtle, but the kitchen will oblige requests for spicier levels. Tan-doori duck and lamb and chicken *tikka* are popular, and vegetarian dishes fill a large section of the card.

230 rue St-Paul ouest (near rue St-Nicolas). ℂ **514/845-5866.** www.restaurantgandhi.com. Main courses C$12–C$27; table d'hôte lunch C$17–C$21. AE, MC, V. Mon–Fri noon–2:30pm; daily 5:30–10:30pm. Métro: Place d'Armes.

Holder ★ BRASSERIE   While the food isn't always perfect here, the ambience certainly is. A large open space with tall ceilings and matching oversized windows overlooking avenue McGill gives room to the laughter of Montréal's young elite who like to travel in packs—although couples scoop up the smaller tables as well. The bar at the back is the insider's spot for happy hour, as it's decidedly less pretentious than going to a bar or supper club. The tartare should get no complaints, nor should the duck confit or steak and frites. I prefer my foie gras au torchon served with toasted bread, but the thin crackers they serve here do the trick. Service is fast and efficient, if not always friendly, and be wary when asking for wine recommendations. Also, this is an excellent sunny spot for weekend brunch. Tip: Don't come underdressed in yoga gear.

407 rue McGill (corner of rue St. Paul). ℂ **514/849-0333.** www.restaurantholder.com. Reservations recommended on weekends. Main courses C$16–C$25. AE, MC, V. Mon–Fri 11:30am–11pm; Sat–Sun 10am–3pm; Sat 5:30–11pm; Sun 5:30–10pm. Métro: Square-Victoria.

Méchant Boeuf BRASSERIE   When eating out requires some lively ambience, the young and stylish head here, where on some nights there is a DJ to drown out the conversation if your social objective is more visual. Finger foods include nachos, fried calamari, and flights of miniburgers. Many young studs swear by the signature burger (C$17) which comes with AAA+ Angus beef, topped with two kinds of cheese (blue and gruyere), caramelized onions, bacon, and a pile of fries—go all the way and upgrade to a *poutine* for C$6. There are also steaks and an unusual beer-can chicken that's more gimmick than gastro-delight, but interesting and tasty nonetheless. Brick walls that are characteristic of Old Montréal line one side of the restaurant, with a flirty bar on the right and then several small tables that encourage chitchat with neighbors. Come after 11pm (many do) and there's a three-course dinner for C$23 (includes the above burger).

124 rue St-Paul ouest (near rue St-Sulpice). ℂ **514/788-4020.** www.mechantboeuf.com. Reservations strongly recommended on weekends. Main courses C$14–C$40; weekend table d'hôte dinner C$23. AE, DC, MC, V. Sun–Wed 5–11pm; Thurs–Sat 5pm–1am. Métro: Champs-de-Mars.

Vieux-Port Steakhouse ✦ STEAKHOUSE   There are a couple good options for steak clustered on rue St-Paul, including **Le Steak Frites,** at 12 rue St-Paul ouest (ℂ **514/842-0972;** www.steakfrites.ca) and **the Keg Steakhouse & Bar,** 25 St-Paul est (ℂ **514/871-9093;** www.kegsteakhouse.com). But it's hard to go wrong at Vieux-Port Steakhouse. For one thing, you can nearly always get a spot: If all the tables in the pleasant first-floor corner room overlooking St-Paul are full, there are two more floors, plus a 300-seat back terrace in summer, for a capacity of *1,200.* With that kind of space, the restaurant packs in large groups, as well as solo diners. Another draw are the value deals, like the C$13 table d'hôte lunch that offers soup, salad or a "mini croissant with tuna salad," a main course, and coffee (dessert just C$2 extra). The food is executed well, and even with the heavy volume, the atmosphere mixes "proper" and "casual" in good balance.

39 rue St-Paul est (at rue St-Gabriel). ℂ **514/866-3175.** www.vieuxportsteakhouse.com. Main courses C$18–C$39; table d'hôte lunch $13, dinner C$30–C$38. AE, MC, V. Sun–Thurs 11:30am–10pm; Fri–Sat 11:30am–11pm. Métro: Place d'Armes.

Inexpensive

Cluny ArtBar 🍴 LIGHT FARE   Artists and high-tech businesses have repopulated the loft-and-factory district west of avenue McGill, at the edge of Vieux-Montréal, though the streets are still very quiet here. Among the pioneers is the Darling Foundry, an avant-garde exhibition space in a vast, raw, former industrial space. Room is provided for Cluny, which serves coffee, croissants, and lunch, with options such as stuffed leg of lamb, vegetarian antipasto, and macaroni and cheese. Though it's called a bar, it's open only during daylight hours, when the sun streams in through mammoth industrial windows. Still, wine by the glass and other adult beverages are available. Tables are topped with recycled bowling alley floors, just so you know.

257 rue Prince (near rue William). ⓒ **514/866-1213.** www.fonderiedarling.org/louer_e/cluny. html. Main courses C$4–C$19. AE, MC, V. Mon–Fri 8am–5pm. Métro: Square-Victoria.

Eggspectation ☺ BREAKFAST/BRUNCH   Let the punny-funny name deter you and you'll miss a meal that may constitute one of your fondest food memories of Montréal, especially if you're of the breakfast-is-best school of gastronomy. The atmosphere and food here are funky and creative, and prices are fair for the large portions. What's more, the kitchen knows how to deal with volume and turns out good meals in nearly lightning speed, even on packed weekend mornings. There are eight variations of eggs Benedict alone, as well as sandwiches, burgers, and pasta options. Dishes are tagged with names like "Eggiliration" and "Oy Vegg." This is a chain ("constantly eggspanding," as they put it), with eight locations in greater Montréal, three of which are downtown.

201 rue St-Jacques ouest (at rue St-François-Xavier). ⓒ **514/282-0119.** www.eggspectations. com. Most items cost less than C$12. AE, MC, V. Mon–Fri 7am–3pm; Sat–Sun 7am–4pm. Métro: Place d'Armes.

La Concession LIGHT FARE   This sandwich shop started out as a patisserie and chocolatier, and then added some tables and a short menu of daily hot specials. Most customers seem to go for panini, pâtés, and pastries. It's a logical place for a snack or a treat in the midst of a stroll through Vieux-Montréal.

75 rue Notre-Dame ouest (near rue St-Sulpice). ⓒ **514/844-8750.** www.la-concession.com. Most items less than C$12. AE, MC, V. Mon–Fri 7am–7pm; Sat–Sun 9am–5pm. Métro: Place d'Armes.

Marché de la Villette ★ 🔥 BISTRO   If you close your eyes and pretend the dangling plastic ham hocks and artificial ivy clinging to exposed pipes are real, you might convince yourself that there's a quiet French village outside of this simple shop-turned-restaurant. It started life as an atmospheric *boucherie* and charcuterie, and the couple of tables in front multiplied quickly due to demand. Serving breakfast, snacks, and meals throughout the day, Marché de la Villette packs in tourists and office workers, especially between noon and 2pm. The staff is flirty and welcoming (even—especially?—to guests who speak very little French). The several available platters of *merguez* and Toulouse sausages, various cheeses, and smoked meats are beguiling. Quiches, pâtés, and sandwiches are other possibilities. The *cassoulet de maison* is a must-try: It's full of duck confit, pork belly, homemade sausage, and silky smooth cassoulet beans, all topped with crunchy, seasoned bread crumbs.

324 rue St-Paul ouest (at rue St-Pierre). ⓒ **514/807-8084.** Reservations not accepted. Most items cost less than C$15. MC, V. Daily 9am–6pm. Métro: Square-Victoria.

Olive et Gourmando ★ ☺ BAKERY/LIGHT FARE   A neighborhood family favorite, this started out as an earthy bakery, then added table service and transformed itself into a full-fledged healthy-foods cafe with extraordinary kid-approved baked goods. Sample the croissants, scones, biscuits, brioche, or exemplary Morning Glory Muffin (only offered in spring and summer), which features shaved carrot and chunks of pineapple. As for lunch, come early or late—it gets jammed. Interesting sandwich compositions include smoked trout with capers, sun-dried tomatoes, spinach, and herbed cream cheese on grilled bread; or caramelized onions, goat cheese, and homemade ketchup on panini. The only pity is that this eminently appealing spot is not open Sunday, Monday, or evenings.

351 rue St-Paul ouest (at rue St-Pierre). ℭ **514/350-1083.** www.oliveetgourmando.com. Most items cost less than C$15. No credit cards. Tues–Sat 8am–6pm. Métro: Square-Victoria.

Titanic 🎁 LIGHT FARE   Really good sandwiches are getting easier to find in Vieux-Montréal (see Olive et Gourmando, above), but they come to luscious life in Titanic's ramshackle rooms with overhead pipes. Freshly baked baguettes are split and filled with such savory combos as coarse country pâté with green peppercorns, smoked ham, and brie, or roast pork with chutney. There's a short cafeteria line of cold dishes and hot daily specials, or just stop in for a breakfast omelet and use the free Wi-Fi. Note that the restaurant closes by 4pm, sometimes earlier. The owners of Titanic also run the **Cluny ArtBar** (above).

445 rue St-Pierre (1 block south of rue Notre-Dame). ℭ **514/849-0894.** www.titanicmontreal. com. Most sandwiches cost less than C$10. No credit cards. Mon–Fri 8am–4pm. Métro: Square-Victoria/Place d'Armes.

PLATEAU MONT-ROYAL

In addition to the restaurants listed below, other food options in Plateau Mont-Royal include **Casa del Popolo,** which is all-vegetarian; the Spanish **Sala Rosa Restaurant;** and the chichi **Koko,** inside the Opus Hotel (all are reviewed in chapter 10, "Montréal After Dark").

Very Expensive

Moishes ★★ STEAKHOUSE   Those who care to spend serious money for a slab of beef should bring their platinum cards here. Positioned as a home for delicious classics, the constantly evolving menu features T-bones, chopped liver, and herring in cream sauce. A slick renovation that was completed in 2011 freshened up the sophisticated, dimly lit space with wider chairs, tasteful urban art, a stunning 1879 map of St-Laurent Boulevard, new carpet, and shiny tin ceiling—upgrading the longtime gathering place from "family-friendly" to "fashionable family." Patrons include the trim new breed of up-and-coming executives (who are likely to go for the chicken teriyaki or arctic char), the fresh younger crowd who come for the C$25 set menu after 9pm, as well as those members of the older generation who didn't know about triglycerides until it was too late. Owner Lenny Lighter (son of Moishes, and brother to partner Larry) is a refined presence in the dining room and excellent source for wine recommendations.

3961 boul. St-Laurent (north of rue Prince Arthur). ℭ **514/845-3509.** www.moishes.ca. Reservations recommended. Main courses C$28–C$54. AE, DC, MC, V. Mon–Fri 5:30–11pm; Sat–Sun 5–11pm. Métro: Sherbrooke.

Expensive

Au Pied de Cochon ★★ ☺ CONTEMPORARY QUÉBÉCOIS   Packed to the walls 6 nights per week, this laid-back Plateau restaurant is a cult favorite, and I've drunk the Kool-Aid, too. As the name—which means "the pig's foot"—suggests, the menu here is mostly about slabs of meat, especially pork. The PDC's Cut, weighing in at more than a pound, is emblematic. Meats are roasted to the point of falling off the bone in a brick oven, and there's a grand selection of seafood, from oysters to lobster to soft-shell crab. Celebrity chef Martin Picard, who's often spotted hanging out with his own tiny tots in tow, gets particularly clever with one pervasive product: foie gras. It comes in as many as nine combinations, including as a tart, with *poutine,* and in a goofy creation called Duck in a Can which does, indeed, come to the table with a can opener. When you feel like another bite will send you into a cholesterol-induced coma, sugar pie is the only fitting finish.

536 rue Duluth est (near rue St-Hubert). ☎ **514/281-1114.** www.restaurantaupieddecochon.ca. Reservations strongly recommended. Main courses C$14–C$51. AE, MC, V. Tues–Sun 5pm–midnight. Métro: Sherbrooke.

Café Méliès CONTEMPORARY FRENCH   In a section of the Main that bristles with hipness, this low-key, cafe-lounge sports electric-red decor that can best be described as "space-age submarine" (there are portholes throughout). A neighborhood favorite, it can be good for a quick dinner before catching a movie at adjacent **Cinéma Parallèle** (p. 200), but people also drop in for light or bountiful breakfasts on the weekends; a midday meal such as arugula lobster salad with asparagus, artichokes, and lemon vinaigrette; or simply espresso or a glass of wine. Steel, chrome, and glass define the generous space, updating the traditional bistro concept, and it's open nearly round-the-clock on the weekends.

3540 boul. St-Laurent (near av. des Pins). ☎ **514/847-9218.** www.cafemelies.com. Main courses C$20–C$30; table d'hôte lunch C$22. AE, MC, V. Mon–Wed 11am–1am; Thurs–Fri 11am–3am; Sat–Sun 8:30am–3am. Métro: Sherbrooke.

Les Cavistes ★ 🎁 BISTRO   The bright, modern interior of this mainly Francophone restaurant gives out-of-towners a good idea of where local young professionals go to eat and drink well in a casual yet sophisticated ambience. A long banquette on the left is mirrored by a long marble-topped bar at right, with tables for two or four sandwiched in the middle atop a black-and-white-checkered floor. Heralded as Montréal's youngest female chef, Stéphanie Gagnon serves made-to-share platters of charcuterie (cold meats), seafood, cheese and/or oysters. Duck, bison and blood sausage are mainstays on the menu, as is the classic beef tartare. Oenophiles will appreciate the extensive wine options by the glass (caviste is French for "sommelier"), as well as the in-store boutique of carefully selected private import bottles. In good weather, a special outdoor menu is served on the swish, contemporary terrace, a prime spot for people-watching.

4115 rue St-Denis (near rue Rachel est). ☎ **514/903-5089.** www.restaurantlescavistes.com. Reservations recommended. Main courses C$20–C$26. AE, DC, MC, V. Daily 5:30–11pm (open for lunch on terrace in good weather). Métro: Mont-Royal.

Globe ITALIAN   Like the nearby **Buonanotte** (p. 193), Globe is an erotically charged, high-end undertaking that starts with a hostess at the podium who looks like she's stopped by between runway gigs, continues with waitresses who bring

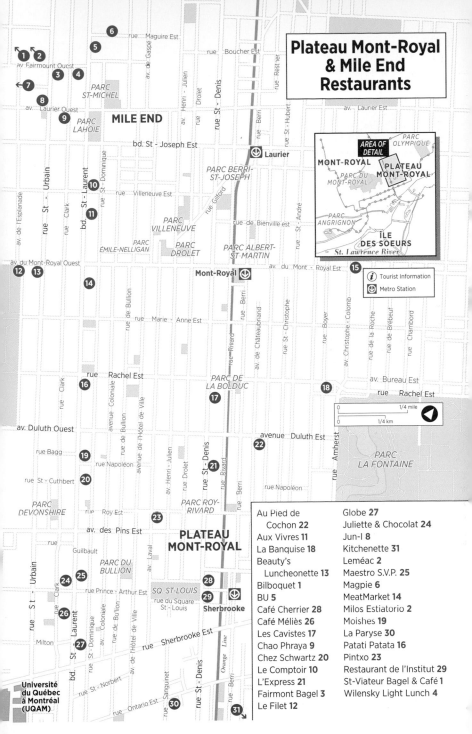

Plateau Mont-Royal & Mile End Restaurants

MILE END

Laurier

Mont-Royal

PLATEAU
MONT-ROYAL

SQ. ST-LOUIS

Sherbrooke

Université
du Québec
à Montréal
(UQAM)

AREA OF DETAIL

MONT-ROYAL

PLATEAU MONT-ROYAL

ÎLE DES SOEURS

St. Lawrence River

i Tourist Information

Ⓜ Metro Station

Au Pied de Cochon **22**	Globe **27**
Aux Vivres **11**	Juliette & Chocolat **24**
La Banquise **18**	Jun-I **8**
Beauty's Luncheonette **13**	Kitchenette **31**
Bilboquet **1**	Leméac **2**
BU **5**	Maestro S.V.P. **25**
Café Cherrier **28**	Magpie **6**
Café Méliès **26**	MeatMarket **14**
Les Cavistes **17**	Milos Estiatorio **2**
Chao Phraya **9**	Moishes **19**
Chez Schwartz **20**	La Paryse **30**
Le Comptoir **10**	Patati Patata **16**
L'Express **21**	Pintxo **23**
Fairmont Bagel **3**	Restaurant de l'Institut **29**
Le Filet **12**	St-Viateur Bagel & Café **1**
	Wilensky Light Lunch **4**

food that's better than it has to be, and ends with lots of hooking up at the bar, where the activity intensifies after 9pm, with DJs who spin Thursday through Saturday. If you're here for the food, starters include trout tartar or foie gras soup. After that, try the lobster risotto. A fun splurge is a *fruits de mer* platter, which starts at C$75 for two. A late-night menu is offered from midnight to 2am Thursday through Saturday.

3455 boul. St-Laurent (north of rue Sherbrooke). ✆ **514/284-3823.** www.restaurantglobe.com. Reservations recommended. Main courses C$24–C$39. AE, DC, MC, V. Sun–Wed 6–11pm; Thurs–Sat 6pm–midnight, but smaller menu available until 2am. Métro: St-Laurent.

Le Filet ★★ TAPAS   The masterminds behind Montréal's beloved **Le Club Chasse et Pêche** restaurant (p. 90) in Old Montréal opened a new venue in early 2011, and it's been packed since day one. The interior is an '80s mishmash of country chairs, metallic walls, and dim lighting. The menu features small and somewhat pricy plates (you'll need to order two or three per person), but refined palettes are sure to be satisfied. Shigoku oysters from B.C. are C$12 for a trio, and the scallop, avocado, orange, and betterave salad is worth every penny. Hot items (in both senses of the word) are the squash ravioli with delicate roasted almond slices; bacon and mushroom tarte, or the snow crab risotto with asparagus. Last-minute reservations at the bar also give you a great view of the open kitchen. A square terrace that kisses the busy sidewalk is currently the spot to see and be seen on hot summer nights.

219 av. du Mont-Royal ouest (near av. du Parc). ✆ **514/360-6060.** www.lefilet.ca. Reservations strongly recommended Thurs–Sat. Main courses C$13–C$20. AE, MC. V. Tues–Sat 5:30pm–midnight. Métro: Mont-Royal.

Maestro S.V.P. SEAFOOD   Smaller and more relaxed than other restaurants in the 2 blocks of the Main north of Sherbrooke, the highlight of this storefront bistro is its oysters—get them raw, baked, or in a vodka shooter. The staff is happy to help you pick a few to taste: The PEI Raspberry Point, for instance, is particularly salty when contrasted with the smooth and creamy BC Kusshi (who knew?). The Maestro Platter, an extravagant medley of clams, mussels, calamari, a half-lobster, *and* king crab, can be shared by the table. A 40-plus-item tapas menu available Tuesday through Thursday from 4 until 11pm makes this a fun spot to kick off an evening or to break for shrimp cocktail and a martini. An all-you-can-eat mussel special is available on Sunday and Monday nights for C$13 per person.

3615 boul. St-Laurent (at rue Prince Arthur). ✆ **514/842-6447.** www.maestrosvp.com. Reservations recommended. Main courses C$16–C$43. AE, DC, MC, V. Sun–Wed 4–10pm; Thurs–Fri 4–11pm; Sat 4pm–midnight. Métro: Sherbrooke.

Restaurant de l'Institut ★ 🌶 CONTEMPORARY FRENCH   The Institut de Tourisme et d'Hôtellerie du Québec is a premiere training ground for city tour guides, hotel managers, front-of-the-room staff—and chefs. It runs two operations of particular interest to visitors: a 42-room training hotel at this prime Plateau location, and a training restaurant where students practice innovative twists on classic dishes under the close eye of their teachers. The C$19 three-course chef's whim lunch is popular and a good value. The dining room is elegant and proper, and service, not surprisingly, is attentive and friendly.

3535 rue St-Denis (1 block north of rue Sherbrooke). ✆ **514/282-5161.** www.ithq.qc.ca. Main courses C$17–C$23; table d'hôte lunch C$19 plus C$4 for dessert. MC, V. Mon–Fri 7–9:30am and noon to late afternoon; Sat–Sun 7:30–10:30am; Tues–Sat 6–9pm. Métro: Sherbrooke.

Moderate

Café Cherrier BREAKFAST/BRUNCH   The tables on the terrace that wraps around this corner building are filled whenever there's even a slim possibility that a heavy sweater and a bowl of café au lait will fend off frostbite. In summer, loyalists stay out until way past midnight, after the kitchen has closed. Brunch is popular even if the food is unexceptional, but do consider this place any time a snack is in order: Croque-monsieur, quiche, black pudding, and Toulouse sausage are all staples. Portions are ample and inexpensive, and an easygoing atmosphere prevails.

3635 rue St-Denis (2 blocks north of Sherbrooke). ℂ **514/843-4308.** Main courses C$10–C$21; table d'hôte dinner C$19–C$23. AE, MC, V. Mon–Fri 7:30am–10pm; Sat–Sun 8:30–11am (sometimes until 1pm). Métro: Sherbrooke.

L'Express ★ BISTRO   No obvious sign announces L'Express, with its name only spelled out discreetly in white tiles in the sidewalk. There's no need to call attention to itself, since *tout* Montréal knows exactly where this most classic of Parisian-style bistros is. Eternally busy and open until 3am, the bistro's atmosphere hits all the right notes, from checkered floor to high ceiling to mirrored walls. Popular dishes include the ravioli *maison* (round pasta pockets filled with a flavorful mixture of beef, pork, and veal), the *soupe de poisson,* and the *croque-monsieur*—and kids will love the crepes. Though reservations are often necessary for tables, single diners and walk-ins can often find a seat at the zinc-topped bar, where full meals also are served. Service is usually good, although be prepared for long waits during brunch hours.

3927 rue St-Denis (just north of rue Roy). ℂ **514/845-5333.** Reservations recommended. Main courses C$14–C$27. AE, DC, MC, V. Mon–Fri 8am–3am; Sat–Sun 10am–3am. Métro: Sherbrooke.

MeatMarket Restaurant Café LIGHT FARE   Neither a butcher shop nor a pickup joint, MeatMarket is actually a stylish sandwich-and-burger cafe. It's on a nondescript block of boulevard St-Laurent well north of the trendier restaurant action. There are vegetarian and salad options, but meats are the main attraction, including burgers and the Cuba Libre sandwich with grilled pork, plantain, Cuban marinade, and mint-and-mango ketchup. Led Zeppelin on the stereo adds exactly the right kick.

4415 boul. St-Laurent (south of av. du Mont-Royal). ℂ **514/223-2292.** www.meatmarketfood.com. Main courses C$8.75–C$29; most items less than C$14. AE, MC, V. Mon noon–3pm; Tues–Thurs noon–10pm; Fri noon–11pm; Sat 5–11pm. Métro: Mont-Royal.

Pintxo ★ SPANISH   Pronounced "peent-choo," the Basque word for tapas, this jovial resto draws from the Spanish Basque tradition, offering exquisitely composed dishes at fair prices in pleasant surroundings. Cooking happens in an open kitchen in a room with antique wood floors and brick walls. Each *pintxo* is true tapa size, only three or four bites, so order recklessly. Some of our favorites include the braised beef cheek, the seared foie gras on a bed of lentils, and the white asparagus with Serrano ham and fried onion cut so fine it looks like tinsel. Dinners aren't confined to meals composed solely of tapas presented on 4-inch tiles or slates, although that isn't a bad way to go. For C$32, the *menu dégustation* provides four chef's-choice *pintxos* and a main dish of your choice, in a considerably larger proportion.

256 rue Roy est (2 blocks west of St-Denis). ℂ **514/844-0222.** www.pintxo.ca. Main courses C$16–C$35; tapas mostly C$7 or less; *menu dégustation* C$32. MC, V. Wed–Fri noon–2pm; Mon–Sat 6–11pm; Sun 6–10pm. Métro: Sherbrooke.

Inexpensive

Beauty's Luncheonette ★★ ☺ LIGHT FARE   A breakfast institution particularly on Saturdays and Sundays, this neighborhood diner has been around since 1942. Owner Hymie Sckolnick, aka Beauty (ask him to tell you the story), is approaching 90 years old, but still mans the weekend traffic at the door, ensuring you never wait too long in line. Banquettes accommodating two to eight people are first come, first serve; lone travelers are wise to ask for counter seats. The mishmash omelet with hot dog, salami, onion, and green pepper or American-style pancakes are popular choices, but classic eggs with bacon or sausage rule. Here, toasted bagels come from nearby St-Viateur bakery, as they have for years; ingredients are fresh, including the squeezed-before-your-eyes OJ, and still mostly hand-picked produce by Beauty himself; and a bright, efficient staff ensures your coffee cup is always full. If you're there for lunch and have a hankering for a gooey mac and cheese, you'll be in heaven.

93 av. du Mont-Royal ouest (corner of rue St-Urbain). ℂ **514/849-8883.** Most items cost less than C$11. AE, DC, DISC, MC, V. Mon–Fri 7am–3pm; Sat 7am–4pm; Sun 8am–4pm. Métro: Mont-Royal.

Chez Schwartz Charcuterie Hébraïque de Montréal ★ ☺ ✦ DELI French-first language laws turned the name of this old-time delicatessen into a linguistic mouthful, but it's still known to its ardent fans simply as Schwartz's, the same name given to a new popular musical written in its honor. Many are convinced it's the only place to indulge in the guilty treat of *viande fumée*—a kind of brisket that's called, simply, smoked meat. Housed in a long, narrow storefront, with a lunch counter, and simple tables and chairs crammed impossibly close to each other, this is as nondescript a culinary landmark as you'll find. Any empty seat is up for grabs. Sandwich plates come heaped with smoked meat and piles of rye bread. Most people also order sides of fries and mammoth garlicky pickles. There are a handful of alternative edibles, but leafy green vegetables aren't among them. Schwartz's has no liquor license, but it's open late. It now has a take-out window, opened in 2008 in honor of its 80th birthday. *Insider tip:* If you can pass up on the ambience of the main restaurant, there are a few seats in the back on the takeout window side.

3895 boul. St-Laurent (just north of rue Roy). ℂ **514/842-4813.** www.schwartzsdeli.com. Sandwiches and meat plates C$5.50–C$17. No credit cards. Daily 8–10:30am takeout only; Sun–Thurs 10:30am–12:30am; Fri 10:30am–1:30am; Sat 10:30am–2:30am. Métro: Sherbrooke.

Juliette et Chocolat ☺ DESSERT   There is a smaller, quieter outpost of this sweet retreat in Outremont at 377 rue Laurier ouest (ℂ **514/510-5651**), but this newer location in the heart of the McGill University ghetto hosts, depending on the time of day or night, a vibrant mix of university students, club kids, various random chocoholics, and the young, energetic staff who never look the slightest bit embarrassed by their kooky floppy hats. Chocolate drinks are listed under "dark or milk vintages," or opt for the Traditional in "Grandma's style," which is over-the-top rich. Next to the cocoa bean, crepes are the specialty here. My fave is with sugar and lemon, as they do in the streets of Paris. Savory versions include the Black Forest, with ham, mushrooms, gruyere, and sour cream. The namesake salad comes with strawberries, pears, and goat cheese on mixed greens, plus— lest we forget where we are—a chocolate-raspberry vinaigrette.

3600 boul. St-Laurent (corner of rue Prince Arthur ouest). ℂ **438/380-1090.** www.julietteet chocolat.com. Reservations available for parties of 6 or more before 9pm. All items under C$15. MC, V. Sun–Thurs 11am–11pm; Fri–Sat 11am–midnight. Métro: Sherbrooke.

La Banquise ★ ☺ 🥄 LIGHT FARE   Open 24 hours a day in the heart of the Plateau on Parc La Fontaine's north end, this friendly, funky, hippie-meets-hipster diner is a city landmark for its *poutine*: La Banquise offers some two dozen variations on the standard French fries with gravy and cheese curds, with add-ons ranging from smoked sausage to hot peppers to smoked meat to bacon. "Regular" size is huge and enough for two. Also on the menu are steamed hot dogs ("steamies") served with hot cabbage coleslaw, as well as burgers, omelets, and club sandwiches. Everything is best washed down with a local brew like Belle Gueule or Boréale. While La Banquise's after-hours clientele is largely club kids and night owls who like loud music (and don't mind crowds or lineups), during the day the colorful diner takes on a quieter atmosphere, making it a cozy hangout for all—what kid doesn't love french fries? In warm weather, there's an outdoor terrace.

994 rue Rachel est (near rue Boyer). ☎ **514/525-2415.** www.restolabanquise.com. *Poutine* plates C$6.50–C$13; most other items less than C$11. No credit cards. Daily 24 hr. Métro: Mont-Royal.

Patati Patata ★ ☺ 🥄 LIGHT FARE   Tiny burgers, tiny prices, tiny space. Saying a harsh word against this beloved diner is nothing short of treason because the staff is *that* friendly. Squeeze yourself onto a stool and watch the chefs sizzle concoctions for carnivores and vegetarians alike—there's even vegetarian *poutine* on this diverse and fairly priced menu. Another plus is the cold draft beer (which must be served with food). Locals often avoid lines by ordering food to go, but visitors will want to wait in the notorious lineup to dine shoulder to shoulder with Montréalers who embrace value over personal space.

4177 boul. St-Laurent (at rue Rachel). ☎ **514/844-0216.** Most items less than C$7. No credit cards. Daily 11am–11pm. Métro: Mont-Royal.

MILE END/OUTREMONT
Expensive

Jun-I ★★ JAPANESE   Many give this the nod for best sushi in town. At first glance, it looks like a standard sushi bar—effusive greetings from the chefs behind the counter, who are preparing traditional-looking *maki* and other bits of fish and rice. But the eponymous chef, Junichi Ikematsu, has ideas that go far beyond what you probably consider typical. You won't soon forget the *unagi* dynamite roll—thick rounds of sticky rice encasing grilled eel, avocado, and Rice Krispies (a signature ingredient that reappears in other rolls). Stick with the sushi and you won't go wrong, although there are options of more conventional, but precisely grilled, meats and fish. The sake martini, with julienned cucumber and a side of ginger, is a refreshing winner.

156 av. Laurier ouest (near rue St-Urbain). ☎ **514/276-5864.** www.juni.ca. Reservations recommended on weekends. Main courses C$28–C$33; sushi C$5–C$14. AE, MC, V. Tues–Fri 11:30am–2pm; Mon–Thurs 6–10pm; Fri–Sat 6–11pm. Métro: Laurier.

Leméac ★★ 🍴 BISTRO   On a recent Saturday night, there was a jovial din among the well-heeled crowd at this bustling, sprightly restaurant on the far western end of the avenue-Laurier scene. With a long, tin-topped bar along one side, well-spaced tables, and a crew of cheerful wait staff, the atmosphere is Parisian elegant. There's a serious wine list, with over 350 options. The food is different—but not startlingly so—and is served in an atmosphere that invites lingering. Weekend brunch is popular, and on a spring morning, a plate of *oeufs pochés, blinis, saumen fumé, et caviar d'Espagne,* served on a street-level terrace, is an affordable slice of decadence. Save room for the homemade donuts, too. Or come late at night: A C$24 appetizer-plus-main menu kicks in at 10pm.

1045 av. Laurier ouest (corner of av. Durocher). ℘ 514/270-0999. www.restaurantlemeac.com. Reservations recommended. Main courses C$19–C$38; late-night menu C$24; weekend brunch C$8–C$16. AE, DC, MC, V. Mon–Fri noon–midnight; Sat–Sun 10am–midnight. Métro: Laurier.

Milos Estiatorio ★★★ SEAFOOD   A stellar meal at Milos best begins with the Milos Special, a plate of paper-thin eggplant and zucchini chips with a side of tzatziki and saganaki cheese, or a plate of sashimi according to the latest delivery. Fresh is the key word here, with deliveries of lobster from Nova Scotia, oysters from Prince Edward Island, and octopus from Morocco on an average day. Anything featuring lobster is worth the hefty price tag, particularly the steamed variation. There's also a salt-encrusted baked cod that's skinned and boned tableside. The service at Milos is as stellar as the seafood. Some waiters have been around for years; if Jerry is there, ask to be seated in his section. Herbs are so fresh that the coriander is snipped right before your eyes. Owner Costas Spiliadis also owns the equally decadent steakhouse Cava, which is just down the street and frequented by the same deep-pocketed crowd.

5357 av. du Parc (near av. St-Viateur). ℘ **514/272-3522.** www.milos.ca. Reservations recommended on weekends. Main courses C$25–C$40. AE, MC, V. Mon–Fri noon–3pm; daily 5:30–11:30pm. Métro: Laurier.

Moderate

BU ITALIAN   Not only has BU won awards for its sleek decor, but it strikes just the right balance between wine and food. A handful of hot dishes are offered nightly, but the purpose of all the food is to complement, not do battle with, the wines. A huge card—500 selections, at last count—eschews the same old bottlings, and even those who regard themselves as connoisseurs make delightful discoveries, guided by the knowledgeable staff. There are more than a dozen wines available by the glass, with several suggested combinations for a trio of 57g (2-oz.) tastings.

5245 boul. St-Laurent (at av. Fairmount). ℘ **514/276-0249.** www.bu-mtl.com. Reservations recommended. Antipasti and main courses C$8–C$24. AE, MC, V. Daily 5–11pm. Métro: Laurier.

Chao Phraya ☺ THAI   Open since 1988 and still a contender for the title of best Thai in town, Chao Phraya has a panache that sets it a few notches above most of its rivals, and it gets packed most evenings (reserve or arrive early). Named for a river in Thailand, Chao Phraya brightens its corner of the fashionable Laurier Avenue with white table linens in an atmosphere that is warm and cozy enough that children don't seem out of place. While the chicken and peanut sauce is heavy duty—it's a tasty combo that includes crispy spinach with tofu— the red curry is a lovely, lighter option. Sides of sticky rice come in small woven baskets. One to three hot-pepper symbols grade hotness, and one or two peppers are fine for milder palates. There is a good selection of vegetarian options on the 12-page menu. (An entire page of the menu is devoted to shrimp.)

50 av. Laurier ouest (1 block west of boul. St-Laurent). ℘ **514/272-5339.** www.chao-phraya. com. Reservations recommended. Main courses C$12–C$21. AE, DC, MC, V. Sun–Wed 5–10pm; Thurs–Sat 5–11pm. Métro: Laurier.

Le Comptoir Charcuteries et Vins ★ 🎁 CONTEMPORARY QUÉBÉCOIS   The hip Mile End neighborhood recently welcomed Le Comptoir ("the Counter"), appropriately named as the 14 stools along the three-sided bar are the best seats in the house. Homemade charcuterie plates are savory palettes of sausages, pâté, and pork porchetta. The good-looking, somewhat artsy crowd (vintage clothing, tattoos, and adults with piercings) represent a friendly mix of English- and French-speaking hipsters who gather here to chill out, enjoy a nice glass of wine, and nibble on little plates—lots of them. Sharing is encouraged; don't be shy to point at another person's food and say, "I'll have that" ("Je vais prendre ça"). As casual as this spot looks, it's serious about its food. Make reservations; even lunch can be busy. There are up to 12 by-the-glass wine selections, and besides a leaning toward French wines, the resto tries to maintain a biodynamic collection.

4807 boul. St-Laurent (1 block south of boul. St-Joseph est). ☎ **514/844-8467.** Reservations strongly recommended. Main courses C$8–C$15. MC, V. Tues–Fri noon–2pm; Tues–Sun 5pm–midnight. Métro: Laurier.

Inexpensive

Aux Vivres ★ ☺ VEGAN   In business since 1997, this bright restaurant with white Formica tables and white walls offers a large menu including bowls of chili with guacamole, and bok choy with grilled tofu and peanut sauce. Other options include salads, sandwiches, desserts, and a daily chef's special. All foods are vegan, all vegetables are organic, and all tofu and tempeh are local and organic. In addition to inside tables, there is a juice bar off to one side and a back terrace.

4631 boul. St-Laurent (north of av. du Mont-Royal). ☎ **514/842-3479.** Most items less than C$12. No credit cards. Daily 11am–11pm. Métro: Mont-Royal.

Bilboquet ☺ DESSERT   Northeast of everything else in this book, in Mile End's ritzy Outremont neighborhood, is this *artisan glacier,* which makes its own splendid ice creams and sorbets. Flavors are rich with caramel, fruit, maple taffy . . . whatever is fresh and strikes the chef's fancy. In warm weather, there's always a line, and there are just a few tables inside, so prepare to stand and then stroll. You don't have to make the trek, though: You can usually find Bilboquet ice cream in **Java U** cafes (p. 87) and at a push cart in the heart of Vieux-Port in warm months.

1311 rue Bernard ouest (at av. Outremont). ☎ **514/276-0414.** Ice cream dishes less than C$8. No credit cards. Daily 11am–9pm. Closed Jan–Mar. Métro: Outremont.

Fairmont Bagel ★ 🍴 BAKERY   Bagels in these parts of North America are thinner, smaller, and crustier than the cottony monsters posing as the real thing outside the province. Here, they're hand-rolled, twist-flipped into circles, and baked in big wood-fired ovens right on the premises. Fairmont was founded in 1919 and now offers 20 types, including trendy options like muesli and (shudder) blueberry, but why opt for oddball tastes when you can get a perfect sesame version? A teeny shop, Fairmont sells its bagels and accoutrements (such as lox and cream cheese) to go only. It's open 24 hours a day, 7 days a week—even on Jewish holidays.

74 av. Fairmont ouest (near rue St-Urbain). ☎ **514/272-0667.** www.fairmountbagel.com. Most bagels less than C$1. No credit cards. Daily 24 hr. Métro: Laurier.

Magpie Pizzeria ☺ 🍴 PIZZA   Twins Boris and Nick Popovic (plus their other brother Peter) run this hangout just off St-Laurent. Boris mans the kitchen—or in this case, the wood-burning high-temp pizza oven. The casual space is elbow to elbow (call ahead for a table) but pleasantly snug—and air-conditioned in the summer. Start your meal with some spicy marinated olives or a fresh romaine salad with anchovies. Then choose from eight kinds of flat-crust pizzas and one weekly special. The classic Margherita reigns supreme in taste and simplicity; meat lovers might go for the *boulettes de viandes aux trois fromages* (meatballs and three cheeses) and veggie types will appreciate the combo of caramelized onions, black olives, and ricotta. Only the finest San Marzano tomatoes are used in the sauce, as well as high-end flour and extra-virgin olive oil. There are a few local ales on tap and a nice selection of wines, all available by the glass for between C$7 and C$10.

16 rue Maguire (near boul. St-Laurent). ℰ **514/507-2900.** www.pizzeriamagpie.com. Reservations recommended. Pizzas C$12–C$18. MC, V. Wed–Fri 11:30am–3pm; Tues–Sun 5:30–10:30pm. Métro: Laurier.

St-Viateur Bagel & Café ★ ☺ LIGHT FARE   The bagel wars flare as hotly as Montréal's eternal smoked-meat battles, but this—an offshoot of the original bakery still at 263 rue St-Viateur ouest in the Mile End neighborhood—is among the top contenders. (We're also partial to **Fairmont Bagel,** above.) You can get bagels to go or to eat in, with sandwiches, soup, or salad. The company notes on its website that it uses the same old-fashioned baking techniques that founder Myer Lewkowicz brought with him from eastern Europe, including hand-rolling the bagels and baking them in a wood-burning oven. Although many varieties are available in the shops, the company's wholesale business keeps with tradition and sells only sesame and poppy seed, the two varieties that existed 40 years ago. Expect a short wait on weekends.

1127 av. du Mont-Royal est (at av. Christophe-Colomb). ℰ **514/528-6361.** www.stviateurbagel. com. Most items less than C$12. No credit cards. Daily 5:30am–11pm. Métro: Mont-Royal.

Wilensky Light Lunch ☺ 🍴 DINER   Wilensky's has been a Montréal tradition since 1932 and has its share of regular pilgrims nostalgic for its grilled-meat sandwiches, low prices, curt service, and utter lack of decor. This is Duddy Kravitz/Mordecai Richler territory, and the ambience can best be described as Early Jewish Immigrant. There are nine counter stools, no tables. The house special is grilled salami and bologna, with mustard, thrown on a bun and squashed on a grill, and never, for whatever reason, cut in two. You can wash it down with an egg cream or cherry soda jerked from the rank of syrups—this place has drinks typical of the old-time soda fountain that it still is. Enter Wilensky's to take a step back in time; we're talking tradition here, not cuisine. The biggest change here in years is that since 2011 the place is now open on Saturdays.

34 rue Fairmount ouest (1 block west of boul. St-Laurent). ℰ **514/271-0247.** All items less than C$5. No credit cards. Mon–Fri 9am–4pm; Sat 10am–3pm. Métro: Laurier.

QUARTIER LATIN/GAY VILLAGE
Expensive

Kitchenette 🍴 BISTRO   Not everybody knows about Kitchenette because it's tucked away across from the Radio Canada building, which means it gets its fair share of local personalities. Texas-born chef Nick Hodge owns and operates this chic corner spot, where the decor is subdued in hush beige tones, with a sleek wooden floor and contemporary furnishings—a perfect backdrop for the playful menu. The southern influence is seen in the gumbo or the po' boy sandwiches. Ever have a Japanese taco? Hodge's version comes with pulled teriyaki beef, wasabi, and daikon slaw. The house burger comes with pimento cheese and bacon. More substantial mains include osso buco, duck confit, or sweet potato gnocchi, all of it done

LATE-NIGHT bites

Most Montréal restaurants serve until 10 or 11pm, but sometimes you need a meal or just a snack a little later. Besides the fact that Chinatown never seems to close, here are some other places to keep in mind:

o **Boustan** (p. 87): In the middle of the late-night hubbub on downtown's rue Crescent, Boustan has lines out the door at 2am of night owls craving a falafel or *shawarma* sandwich. Open until 4am daily.

o **Chez Schwartz** (p. 100): Also in the Plateau, Schwartz's meets the city's smoked-meat needs until 12:30am Sunday to Thursday, 1:30am Friday, and 2:30am Saturday.

o **Globe** (p. 96): An erotically charged restaurant at boulevard St-Laurent near rue Sherbrooke that changes personality after about 10pm to something more akin to a nightclub. Thursday through Saturday, the regular menu is available until midnight, and a smaller menu kicks in from midnight until 2am.

o **La Banquise** (p. 101): Not only is Banquise known citywide for its *poutine,* but it's open 24 hours a day,

7 days a week—that is, whenever the urge strikes to indulge in any of two dozen varieties of french fries with gravy and cheese curds. At the northwest corner of Parc La Fontaine.

o **L'Express** (p. 99): Classic Paris-style food in the heart of rue St-Denis, available until 3am nightly.

o **Leméac** (p. 101): On chichi avenue Laurier in Mile End, Leméac has a special C$24 appetizer-plus-main menu from 10pm to midnight daily.

o **Moishes** (p. 95): Likely the earliest late-night menu in the city, this Plateau institution known for its steaks and A+ service recently began offering C$25 prix fixe menu at 9pm—when the second generation of Moishes devotees come back with their friends instead of their families or business colleagues. Do note closing time at 11pm.

with flair. Fish and chips Friday is a particular crowd pleaser, so call ahead if that's your fancy. At lunchtime, an extra C$5 on your main gets you a starter and coffee.

1353 boul. René-Lévesque est (near rue Beaudry). ☎ **514/527-1016.** www.kitchenetterestaurant. ca. Reservations required Thurs–Sat. Main courses C$18–C$38. AE, MC, V. Tues–Fri 11:30am–3pm and 5:30–10pm; Sat 5:30–11pm. Métro: Beaudry.

Inexpensive

La Paryse ★ 🍴 LIGHT FARE   With about 12 red Formica tables, a handful of counter seats, and a funky, casual vibe, this Quartier Latin standby, in business since 1980, packs in students, professors, young execs, and families. They come for the burgers, the consensus choice for "best in town." Unless you possess a really large appetite and a capacious mouth, you certainly won't need the double burger or the *frites grosse* (big fries). Wines are available by the glass. For vegetarians, there are three options, including a yummy *noix* (nut) burger topped with blue cheese, apple slices, lettuce, and grilled mushrooms.

302 rue Ontario est (west of rue St-Denis). ☎ **514/842-2040.** Most items less than C$9. MC, V. Tues–Sat 11am–11pm. Métro: Berri-UQAM.

LITTLE BURGUNDY
Expensive

Joe Beef ★★ SEAFOOD/STEAK   In 2005, a group of folks who used to run glamorous resto-clubs in downtown Montréal opened this 28-seat steak-and-seafood joint far west of Vieux-Montréal, on a bland street near Atwater Market. The atmosphere is moneyed roadhouse, with diners elbow to elbow. In 2007 and 2008, the owners added two adjacent restaurants—Liverpool House (at no. 2501), a French gastro-pub, and McKiernan (next door), a luncheonette—and suddenly the block was a go-to destination for people serious about food. (McKiernan closed in 2011 and Joe Beef has expanded into that space.) Chef and co-owner David McMillan floats between venues; he's the big guy in the shorts and arm-sleeve tattoos, and takes pride in his efforts "to spend money in the province of Quebec whenever possible" when sourcing his produce, which includes a private vegetable garden just out back. Oysters (from P.E.I.) are customary starters, and mains often include a variety of steaks.

2491 rue Notre-Dame ouest (near rue Vinet). ☏ **514/935-6504.** www.joebeef.ca. Reservations required. Main courses C$21–C$50. MC, V. Tues–Sat 6:30pm–"close." Métro: Lionel-Groulx.

PICNIC FARE

If you're planning a picnic, bike ride, or simply a meal in, pick up supplies in Vieux-Montréal at any of three shops along rue St-Paul. On the street's west end is **Olive et Gourmando** (p. 95) at no. 351 and, just across the street, **Marché de la Villette** (p. 94) at no. 324. Both sell fresh breads, fine cheeses, sandwiches, salads, and pâtés.

Or, make a short excursion by bicycle or Métro (the Lionel-Groulx stop) to **Marché Atwater (Atwater Market),** the farmer's market at 138 av. Atwater. It's open daily. The long interior shed is bordered by stalls stocked with gleaming produce and flowers. The two-story center section is devoted to vintners, butchers, bakeries, and cheese stores. In the *marché,* **Boulangerie Première Moisson** (☏ **514/932-0328**) is filled with the tantalizing aromas of breads and pastries—oh, the pastries!—and has a seating area at which to nibble baguettes or sip a bowl of café au lait. Nearby, **Fromagerie du Marché Atwater** (☏ **514/932-4653**) lays out some 500 cheeses—with hundreds from Québec alone—as well as pâtés and charcuterie. Marché Atwater is on the Lachine Canal, where you can stroll and find a picnic table.

RESTAURANTS BY CUISINE

BAKERY
Fairmount Bagel ★ ($, p. 103)
Nocochi ($, p. 88)
Olive et Gourmando ★ ($, p. 95)

BISTRO
Boris Bistro ★ ($$, p. 92)
Kitchenette ($$$, p. 104)
Leméac ★★ ($$$, p. 101)
Les Cavistes ★ ($$$, p. 96)
L'Express ★ ($$, p. 99)
Marché de la Villette ★ ($, p. 94)

BRASSERIE
Brasserie T ★★ ($$, p. 85)
Holder ★ ($$, p. 93)
Méchant Boeuf ($$, p. 93)

BREAKFAST/BRUNCH
Café Cherrier ($$, p. 99)
Eggspectation ($, p. 94)

CONTEMPORARY FRENCH
Café Méliès ($$$, p. 96)
Decca 77 ★ ($$$, p. 84)

Europea ★★★ ($$$$, p. 84)
Le Local ($$$, p. 92)
Restaurant de l'Institut ★
  ($$$, p. 98)
Toqué! ★★★ ($$$$, p. 88)

CONTEMPORARY QUÉBÉCOIS

Aix Cuisine du Terroir ★ ($$$, p. 90)
Au Pied de Cochon ★★
  ($$$, p. 96)
Chez l'Épicier ($$$, p. 90)
DNA ★ ($$$, p. 91)
Le Club Chasse et Pêche ★★★
  ($$$, p. 90)
Le Comptoir Charcuterie et Vins ★
  ($$, p. 102)

DELI

Chez Schwartz Charcuterie
  Hébraïque de Montréal ★
  ($, p. 100)

DINER

Wilensky Light Lunch ($, p. 104)

DESSERT

Bilboquet ($, p. 103)
Juliette & Chocolat ($, p. 100)

INDIAN

Gandhi ★ ($$, p. 92)
Le Taj ★ ($$, p. 86)

ITALIAN

BU ($$, p. 102)
Cavalli ($$$$, p. 82)
Globe ($$$, p. 96)
Graziella ($$$ p. 91)

JAPANESE

Jun-I ★★ ($$$, p. 101)

LEBANESE

Boustan ($, p. 87)

LIGHT FARE

Beauty's Luncheonette ★★
  ($, p. 100)
Cluny ArtBar ($, p. 94)

Java U ($, p. 87)
La Banquise ★ ($, p. 101)
La Concession ($, p. 94)
La Paryse ★ ($, p. 105)
m:brgr ★ ($$, p. 86)
MeatMarket Restaurant Café
  ($$, p. 99)
Nocochi ($, p. 88)
Olive el Gourmando ★ ($, p. 95)
Patati Patata ★ ($, p. 101)
St-Viateur Bagel ★ ($, p. 104)
Titanic ($, p. 95)

PIZZA

Magpie Pizzeria ($, p. 103)

PORTUGUESE

Ferreira Café ★★★ ($$$, p. 84)

SEAFOOD

Ferreira Café ★★★ ($$$, p. 84)
Joe Beef ★★ ($$$, p. 106)
Le Garde Manger ★★ ($$$, p. 91)
Maestro S.V.P. ($$$, p. 98)
Milos Estiatorio ★★★ ($$$, p. 102)

SPANISH

Pintxo ★ ($$, p. 99)

STEAKHOUSE

Joe Beef ★★ ($$$, p. 106)
La Queue de Cheval ★ ($$$$, p. 84)
Moishes ★★ ($$$$, p. 95)
Vieux-Port Steakhouse ($$, p. 93)

TAPAS

Le Filet ★★ ($$$, p. 98)

THAI

Chao Phraya ($$, p. 102)

TRADITIONAL FRENCH

Bonaparte ★ ($$$, p. 90)
Julien ($$, p. 86)

VEGETARIAN/VEGAN

Aux Vivres ★ ($, p. 103)
Le Commensal ($, p. 88)

KEY TO ABBREVIATIONS:
$$$$ = Very Expensive $$$ = Expensive $$ = Moderate $ = Inexpensive

EXPLORING MONTRÉAL

M ontréal is a feast of choices, able to satisfy the desires of physically active and culturally curious visitors. Hike up the city's mountain, Mont Royal, in the middle of the city; cycle for miles beside 19th-century warehouses and locks on the Lachine Canal; take in artworks and ephemera at more than 30 museums, and as many historic buildings; attend a Canadiens hockey match; party until dawn on rue Crescent, the Main, or in the Old Montréal; or soak up the history of 400 years of conquest and immigration. It's all here for the taking.

Getting from hotels to attractions is easy. Montréal has an efficient Métro system, a logical street grid, and wide boulevards that all aid in the largely uncomplicated movement of people from place to place.

If you're planning to check out several museums, consider buying the Montréal Museums Pass (see the "Money Savers" box on p. 113).

For families, few cities assure children will have as good a time as this one does. There are riverboat rides, Olympic Park and the fascinating Biodôme, summer fireworks at La Ronde Amusement Park, the Centre des Sciences de Montréal by the water, and magical circus performances by the many troupes that come through this circus-centric city. We've flagged attractions that are recommended for children with the "Kids" icon and included an "Especially for Kids" section on p. 130.

Tip: Some museums have good restaurants or cafes. Remember, too, that most museums—though not all—are closed on Mondays.

TOP ATTRACTIONS
Downtown

If this is your first trip to Montréal, consider starting with the downtown walking tour in chapter 8.

Musée des Beaux-Arts ★★★ Montréal's grand Museum of Fine Arts, the city's most prominent museum, was Canada's first structure designed specifically for the visual arts. It's made up of several buildings, including the original neoclassical pavilion on the north side of Sherbrooke, a striking annex built in 1991 directly across the street, and (new in 2011) the adjacent Erskine and American Church, which features the new pavilion of Canadian art behind it. The 1894 church is a designated national historic site and will be a destination in its own right, with a conversion project restoring its Romanesque Revival architecture and interior ornamentation, which includes 20 stained-glass windows created by Louis Comfort Tiffany. The entire complex will be linked through underground galleries.

PREVIOUS PAGE: **The Basilique Notre-Dame at night.**

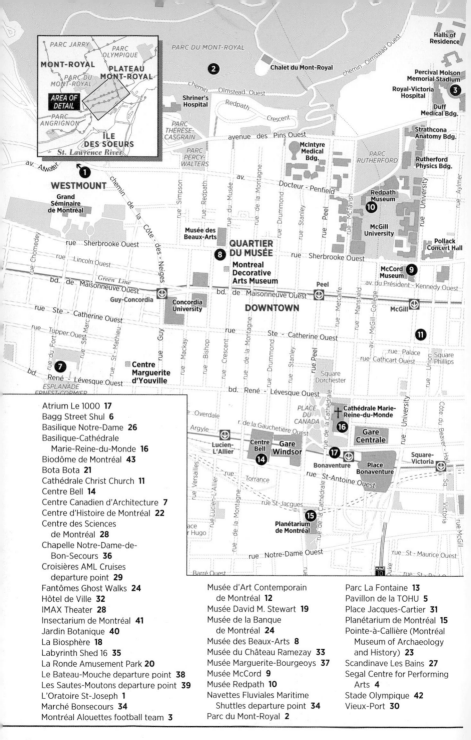

Downtown and Vieux-Montréal Attractions

OLYMPIC PARK

Tourist Information (i)

Metro Station

111

The Musée des Beaux-Arts is the city's most prominent museum.

Art on display is dramatically mounted, carefully lit, and diligently explained in both French and English. In addition to Canadian and international contemporary art created after 1960, the museum features European painting, sculpture, and decorative art from the Middle Ages to the 19th century. Among the collection's gems are paintings by Hogart, Tintoretto, Bruegel, El Greco, and portraitist George Romney—and illustrative, if not world-class, works by Renoir, Monet, Picasso, Cézanne, and Rodin. Temporary exhibitions can be dazzling. Recent shows have focused on the art of Cuba, and the treasures of Catherine the Great, including her spectacular coronation coach, from the Hermitage Museum of Saint Petersburg. Another exhibit imported life-size terra-cotta soldiers of Chinese Emperor Qin, while the summer of 2011 welcomed a multimedia extravaganza highlighting the career of French fashion designer Jean Paul Gaultier. The museum's street-level store on the south side of rue Sherbrooke sells an impressive selection of books, games, and folk art. The museum's quite good restaurant, **Café des Beaux-Arts,** is above the store and has an entrance adjacent to the boutique.

1339–1380 rue Sherbrooke ouest (at rue Crescent). ✆ **514/285-2000.** www.mmfa.qc.ca. Free admission to the permanent collection; donations accepted. Admission to temporary exhibitions C$15 adults, C$12 seniors, C$7.50 students, free for children 12 and under; C$30 families (1 adult and 3 children 16 and under, or 2 adults and 2 children 16 and under); reduced admission Wed 5–9pm C$7.50 adults and seniors, C$15 families. Tues 11am–5pm; Wed–Fri 11am–9pm; Sat–Sun 10am–5pm. Métro: Guy-Corcordia.

Musée McCord ★ The permanent exhibition "Simply Montréal: Glimpses of a Unique History" justifies a trip here all on its own. The show steeps visitors in what city life was like over the centuries, and even includes a substantial section about how Montréal handles the massive amounts of snow and ice it receives each year. Associated with McGill University, McCord showcases the eclectic—and, not infrequently, the eccentric—collections of scores of benefactors from the 19th century through today. More than 16,600 costumes, 65,000 paintings,

and 1.25 million historical photographs documenting Canada's history are rotated in and out of storage to be displayed. A First Nations room has portions of the museum's extensive collection of objects from Canada's native population, including meticulous beadwork, baby carriers, and fishing implements. Exhibits are intelligently mounted, with texts in English and French. There's a small cafe near the front entrance and a shop that sells Canadian arts and crafts, pottery, and more.

The Musée McCord has an extensive collection of First Nations artifacts.

690 rue Sherbrooke ouest (at rue University). ☎ **514/398-7100.** www.mccord-museum.qc.ca. Admission C$13 adults, C$10 seniors, C$7 students, C$5 children 6–12, free for children 5 and under; free admission every Wed 5–9pm. Tues and Thurs–Fri 10am–6pm; Wed 10am–9pm; Sat–Sun 10am–5pm; Mon (Late June through Labour Day and holiday weekends throughout the year) 10am–5pm. Métro: McGill.

Parc du Mont-Royal Montréal is named for this 232m (761-ft.) hill that rises at its heart—the "Royal Mountain." Walkers, joggers, cyclists, dog owners, and in-line skaters all use this largest of the city's green spaces throughout the year.

MONEY savers

○ **Buy the Montréal Museums Pass.** Good for 3 consecutive days, this pass grants entry to 38 museums and attractions, including most of those mentioned in this chapter. The C$65 pass includes unlimited access to public transportation (including the airport shuttle, bus no. 747) along with the museums. The C$60 pass covers just the museums, without the transportation. There are no separate rates for seniors or children. The pass is available at all participating museums, many hotels, the tourist offices at 1255 rue Peel (downtown) and 174 rue Notre-Dame (in Vieux-Montréal), and online at www.montrealmuseums.org.

○ **Visit Vitrine Culturelle de Montréal for last-minute ticket deals.** The discount ticket office for Montréal

cultural events is at 145 rue Ste-Catherine ouest at the Place des Arts (☎ **866/924-5538** or 514/285-4545). The website www.lavitrine.com lists the events on sale.

○ **Flash your AAA card.** Members of the American Automobile Association (AAA) get the same discounts as members of its Canadian sister organization, the CAA. That includes reduced rates at many museums, hotels, and restaurants (and C$2 off the Montréal Museums Pass).

○ **Time your trip to coincide with Montréal Museums Day.** On the last Sunday in May, about 30 museums welcome visitors for free in a citywide open house. Free shuttle buses run between the venues, as well.

Parc du Mont-Royal is the largest green space in the city.

In summer, **Lac des Castors (Beaver Lake)** is surrounded by sunbathers and picnickers (no swimming allowed, however). In winter, cross-country skiers and snowshoers follow miles of paths and trails laid out for their use through the park's 200 hectares (494 acres). Ice-skates, skis, poles, and snowshoes can all be rented for adults and children at the Beaver Lake Pavilion, the glass windowed building with a rippled roof. **Chalet du Mont-Royal** near the crest of the hill is a popular destination, providing a sweeping view of the city from its terrace. A few snack and beverage vending machines are there in case you get hungry or thirsty. Up the hill behind the chalet is the spot where, legend says, Paul de Chomedey, Sieur de Maisonneuve, erected a wooden cross after the colony side-stepped the threat of a flood in 1643. The present incarnation of the steel **Croix du Mont-Royal** was installed in 1924 and is lit at night. It usually glows white, though it was purple in 2005 after the death of Pope John Paul II. See p. 164 for a suggested walking route.

Downtown (entrances include one at rue Peel and av. des Pins). © **514/843-8240** (the Maison Smith information center in the park's center). www.lemontroyal.qc.ca. Métro: Mont-Royal. Bus: 11.

Vieux-Montréal (Old Montréal)

Vieux-Montréal's central plaza is **Place Jacques-Cartier,** the focus of much activity in the warm months. The plaza consists of two repaved streets bracketing a center promenade that slopes down from rue Notre-Dame to Old Port, with venerable stone buildings from the 1700s along both sides. Horse-drawn carriages gather at the plaza's base, and outdoor cafes, street performers, and flower sellers recall a Montréal of a century ago. Locals insist they would never go to a place so overrun by tourists—which makes one wonder why so many of them do, in fact, congregate here. They take the sun and sip sangria on the terraces just as much as visitors do, enjoying the unfolding pageant. If this is your first trip to

Montréal, consider starting with the Vieux-Montréal walking tour in chapter 8. The walk leads past most of the sites listed here and can help you get your bearings.

Basilique Notre-Dame ★★★ Breathtaking in the richness of its interior furnishings and big enough to hold 4,000 worshipers, this magnificent structure was designed in 1824 by James O'Donnell, an Irish-American Protestant architect from New York—who was so profoundly moved by the experience that he converted to Catholicism after its completion. The impact is understandable. Of Montréal's hundreds of churches, Notre-Dame's interior is the most stunning, with a wealth of exquisite details, most of it carved from rare woods that have been delicately gilded and painted. O'Donnell, clearly a proponent of the Gothic Revival style, is the only person honored by burial in the crypt. The main altar was carved from linden wood, the work of Québécois architect Victor Bourgeau. Behind it is the **Chapelle Sacré-Coeur (Sacred Heart Chapel),** much of which was destroyed by an arsonist in 1978; it was rebuilt and rededicated in 1982. The altar displays 32 bronze panels representing birth, life, and death, cast by a Montréal artist named Charles Daudelin. A 10-bell carillon resides in the east tower, while the west tower contains a single massive bell, nicknamed **"Le Gros Bourdon,"** which weighs more than 12 tons and emanates a low, resonant rumble that vibrates right up through your feet. A sound-and-light show called "Et la lumière fut" ("And Then There Was Light") is presented nightly Tuesday through Saturday. Legendary tenor Luciano Pavarotti performed his famous Christmas concert here in 1978, the same place where French-Canadian songstress Céline Dion had her Cinderella wedding some 16 years later.

The stunning interior of the Basilique Notre-Dame.

110 rue Notre-Dame ouest (on Place d'Armes). (**514/842-2925.** www.basiliquenddm.org. Basilica C$5 adults, C$4 children 7–17, free for children 6 and under; includes 20-min. guided tour. Light show C$10 adults, C$9 seniors, C$5 children 17 and younger. Basilica Mon–Fri 8am–4:30pm, Sat 8am–4pm, Sun 12:30–4pm; light show Tues–Thurs 6:30pm, Fri 6:30 and 8:30pm, Sat 7 and 8:30pm. Métro: Place d'Armes.

Centre des Sciences de Montréal ★★ ☺

Running the length of a central pier in Vieux-Port (Old Port), this ambitious complex (in English, the Montréal Science Centre) focuses on science and technology. Its attractions include interactive displays and a popular **IMAX theater** (p. 130), and the extensive use of computers makes it particularly appealing to youngsters (the whole place is designed for 9- to 14-year-olds). One temporary exhibit guided kids in making television news reports using a combination of prerecorded interview clips and video of themselves. Another bold exhibit focused on the human body and sexuality, and addressed in a frank and straightforward way every—and we mean every—question adolescents might have. Admission fees vary according to the combination of exhibits and movie showings you choose. To avoid long lines, preorder tickets for special exhibits. Indoor and outdoor cafes sell sandwiches, salads, and sweets.

Quai King Edward, Vieux-Port. (**877/496-4724** or 514/496-4724. www.montrealsciencecentre. com. Admission for exhibitions C$12 adults, C$11 seniors & children 13–17, C$8.50 children 4–12, free for children 3 and under. Movie ticket prices are extra and are the same amount (you can opt only to go to the IMAX theater). Exhibition and IMAX combination tickets are C$19 adults, C$17 seniors & children 13–17, C$14 children 4–12, free for children 3 and under. Mon–Fri 9am–5pm; Sat 10am–9pm; Sun 10am–6pm. Métro: Place d'Armes or Champ-de-Mars.

Pointe-à-Callière (Montréal Museum of Archaeology and History) ★★★

A first visit to Montréal might best begin here. Built on the very site where the original colony (called Pointe-à-Callière) was established in 1642, this modern museum

The Centre des Sciences de Montréal has many interactive exhibits that appeal to kids.

engages visitors in rare, beguiling ways. The triangular new building echoes the Royal Insurance building (1861) that stood here for many years. Go first to the 16-minute multimedia show in an auditorium that stands above the actual exposed ruins of the earlier city. Music and a playful bilingual narration keep the history slick and painless, if a little chamber-of-commerce upbeat. Children 11 and younger may find it a snooze. Evidence of the area's many inhabitants—from Amerindians to French trappers to Scottish merchants—was unearthed during archaeological digs that took more than a decade. Artifacts are on view in display cases set among the ancient building foundations and burial grounds below street level. Wind your way on the self-guided tour through the subterranean complex until you find yourself in the former customhouse, where there are more exhibits and a well-stocked gift shop. Allow 1½ hours to visit this museum. **L'Arrivage Café** is open daily for lunch and presents a fine view of Vieux-Montréal and Vieux-Port. Food here is terrific.

FROM TOP: **Point-à-Callière is a good place to start your visit to the city; Vieux-Port is a popular summer playground.**

350 Place Royale (at rue de la Commune). ℭ **514/872-9150.** www.pacmuseum.qc.ca. Admission C$15 adults, C$10 seniors, C$8 students, C$6 children 6–12, free for children 5 and under. Late June to early Sept Mon–Fri 10am–6pm, Sat–Sun 11am–6pm; mid-Sept to mid-June Tues–Fri 10am–5pm, Sat–Sun 11am–5pm. L'Arrivage Café Mon 11:30am–2pm, Tues–Sun 11:30am–3pm. Métro: Place d'Armes.

Vieux-Port ★★ ☺ Montréal's Old Port was transformed in 1992 from a dreary commercial wharf area into a 2km-long (1¼-mile), 53-hectare (131-acre) promenade and public park with bicycle paths, exhibition halls, and a variety of family activities, including the **Centre des Sciences de Montréal** (see above). It stretches along the waterfront, parallel to rue de la Commune, from rue McGill to rue Berri.

The area is most active from mid-May through October, when harbor cruises take to the waters and bicycles, in-line skates, and family-friendly quadricycle carts are available to rent. Warm months also bring information booths staffed by bilingual attendants and 45-minute guided tours in the open-sided **La Balade,** a small, motorized tram. **Cirque du Soleil** often sets up its signature blue-and-yellow-striped tents here in spring. In winter, things are quieter, but an outdoor ice-skating rink is a big attraction.

CIRQUE DU SOLEIL: MONTRÉAL'S HOMETOWN circus

The whimsical, talented band of artists that became Cirque du Soleil began as street performers in Baie-St-Paul (p. 340), a river town an hour north of Québec City. These stilt walkers, fire breathers, and musicians had one pure intention: to entertain. The troupe formally founded as Cirque du Soleil (Circus of the Sun) in 1984 and celebrated its 25th year in 2009. It has matured into a spectacle like no other. Using human-size gyroscopes, trampoline beds, trapezes suspended from massive chandeliers, and the like (but no animals), Cirque creates worlds that are spooky, sensual, otherworldly, and beautifully ambiguous. More than 1,000 of the company's acrobats, contortionists, jugglers, clowns, and dancers tour the world. There are resident shows in Las Vegas, Macau, New York, Orlando, and Tokyo. The company's offices are in Montréal in the Saint-Michel district, not far beyond the Mile End neighborhood.

And they're not just offices. Cirque has been developing a small campus of buildings in this industrial zone since 1997. All new artists come here to train for a few weeks to a few months and live in residences on-site. The complex has acrobatic training rooms, a dance studio, workshops in which the elaborate costumes and props are made, and a space large enough to erect a circus tent indoors. Some 1,800 people are employed at the Montréal facility, including more than 400 who work on costumes alone. The company doesn't have regular performances in Montréal, alas. For information about when they're coming to town and where else in the world you can find a show, visit **www.cirquedusoleil.com**.

At the port's far eastern end, in the last of the old warehouses, is a 1922 clock tower, **La Tour de l'Horloge,** with 192 steps leading past the exposed clockworks to observation decks overlooking the St. Lawrence River (admission is free).

Information booth for the Vieux-Port expanse at the Centre des Sciences de Montréal on quai King Edward (King Edward Pier). ℂ **800/971-PORT** (7678). www.quaysoftheoldport.com. La Balade tram June–Sept Fri–Mon 1–8pm. Tickets C$5 adults, C$3.50 seniors (60 and older) and teens (13–17), C$3 children 12 and under. Métro: Champ-de-Mars, Place d'Armes, or Square Victoria.

Elsewhere in the City

A 20-minute drive east on rue Sherbrooke or an easy Métro ride from downtown is **Olympic Park,** located in a neighborhood called Hochelaga-Maisonneuve. It has four attractions: Stade Olympique (Olympic Stadium), Biodôme de Montréal, Jardin Botanique (Botanical Garden), and Insectarium de Montréal. The first three are described below, and the Insectarium is described on p. 130. All are walking distance from each other. You could spend a day touring all four sites, and kids will especially love the Biodôme and Insectarium. Combination ticket packages are available, and the Biodôme, Jardin, and Insectarium are all included in the **Montréal Museum Pass** (see the "Money Savers" box on p. 113). Underground parking at the Olympic Stadium is C$12 per day, with additional parking at the Jardin Botanique and Insectarium.

Biodôme de Montréal ★★ ☺   A terrifically engaging attraction for children of nearly any age, the delightful Biodôme houses replications of four ecosystems: a tropical rainforest, a Laurentian forest, the St. Lawrence marine system, and a polar environment. Visitors walk through each and hear the animals, smell the flora, and (except in the polar region, which is behind glass) feel the changes in temperature. The rainforest area is the most engrossing (the subsequent rooms increasingly less so), so take your time here. It's a kind of "Where's Waldo" challenge to find all the critters, from the capybara (which looks like a large guinea pig) to the golden lion tamarin monkeys that swing on branches only an arm's length away. Only the bats, fish, penguins, and puffins are behind glass. The open-air space features hundreds of shore birds whose shrieks can transport you to the beach. A continual schedule of temporary exhibits and new programs keeps things fresh. The building was originally the velodrome for cycling during the 1976 Olympics. The facility also has a hands-on activity room called Naturalia, a shop, a bistro, and a cafeteria.

4777 av. Pierre-de-Coubertin (next to Stade Olympique). ✆ **514/868-3000.** www.biodome. qc.ca. Admission C$17 adults, C$13 seniors and students, C$8.25 children 5–17, C$2.50 children 2–4. Aug to late June daily 9am–5pm; late June to Aug daily 9am–6pm. Closed most Mon Sept–Dec. Métro: Viau.

The Biodôme de Montréal replicates four entire ecosystems.

Jardin Botanique ★★★   Spread across 75 hectares (185 acres), Montréal's Botanical Garden is a fragrant oasis 12 months a year. Ten large exhibition greenhouses each have a theme: One houses orchids; another has tropical food and spice plants, including coffee, cashews, and vanilla; another features rainforest flora. In a special exhibit each spring, live butterflies flutter among the nectar-bearing plants, occasionally landing on visitors. In September, visitors can watch monarch butterflies being tagged and released for their annual migration to Mexico.

Outdoors, spring is when things really kick in: lilacs in May, lilies in June, and roses from mid-June until the first frost. The **Chinese Garden,** a joint project of Montréal and Shanghai, evokes the 14th- to 17th-century era of the Ming Dynasty and was built according to the landscape principles of yin and yang. It incorporates pavilions, inner courtyards, ponds, and plants indigenous to China. A serene **Japanese Garden** fills 2.5 hectares (6¼ acres) and has a cultural pavilion with an art gallery, a tearoom where ancient ceremonies are performed, a stunning bonsai collection, and a Zen garden. A small train runs through the gardens from mid-May to October and is included in the entrance fee. The grounds are also home to the **Insectarium** (p. 130), which displays some of the world's most beautiful and sinister insects (both mounted and live). Exhibits acquaint young and old with honey bees, cockroaches, beetles, and hundreds of other "misunderstood" creatures.

4101 rue Sherbrooke est (opposite Olympic Stadium). ✆ **514/872-1400.** www.ville.montreal. qc.ca/jardin. Mid-May to Nov C$17 adults, C$13 seniors and students, C$8.25 children 5–17, C$2.50 children 2–4. Nov to mid-May rates drop about 15% and admission to outdoor gardens is free. Admission includes access to the Insectarium. Mid-May to mid-Sept daily 9am–6pm; mid-Sept to Nov daily 9am–9pm; Nov to mid-May Tues–Sun 9am–5pm. No bicycles or dogs. Métro: Pie-IX, Viau (w/free shuttle from Olympic Park).

Stade Olympique   Montréal's space-age and controversial Olympic Stadium, the centerpiece of the 1976 Olympic Games, looks like a giant stapler. It's likely to induce only moderate interest for most visitors. The main event is the 175m

The Jardin Botanique is filled with both indoor and outdoor gardens.

The Stade Olympic was the centerpiece of the 1976 Olympic Games.

(574-ft.) inclined tower, which leans at a 45-degree angle and does duty as an observation deck, with a funicular that whisks passengers to the top in 95 seconds. On a clear day, the deck bestows an expansive view over Montréal and into the neighboring Laurentian mountains. At C$15, however, the admission price is as steep as the tower.

The complex includes a stadium that seats up to 56,000 for sporting events and music concerts (it was home to the Montréal Expos before that baseball team relocated to Washington, D.C., in 2005). The Sports Centre houses seven swimming pools open for public swimming and classes, including one deep enough for scuba diving. Thirty-minute guided tours that describe the 1976 Olympic Games and use of the center today are available daily for C$8. The roof doesn't retract anymore—it never retracted well anyway. That's one reason that what was first known as "the Big O" was scorned as "the Big Woe," then "the Big Owe" after cost overruns led to heavy tax increases.

4141 av. Pierre-de-Coubertin. (*) **877/997-0919** or 514/252-4141. www.rio.gouv.qc.ca. Tower admission C$15 adults, C$11 seniors and students, C$7.50 children 5–17. Public swimming admission C$5.50 adults, C$4.65 students and seniors, C$4.10 children 15 and under. Tower summer daily 9am–7pm, winter daily 9am–5pm. See website for pool hours. Closed mid-Jan to mid-Feb. Métro: Viau.

MORE ATTRACTIONS
Downtown

Basilique-Cathédrale Marie-Reine-du-Monde No one who has seen both will confuse Montréal's "Mary Queen of the World" cathedral with St. Peter's Basilica in Rome, but a scaled-down homage was the intention of Bishop

Ignace Bourget, who oversaw its construction after the first Catholic cathedral here burned to the ground in 1852. Construction lasted from 1875 to 1894, its start delayed by the bishop's desire to place it not in Francophone east Montréal, but in the heart of the Protestant Anglophone west. Most impressive is the 76m-high (249-ft.) dome, about a third of the size of the Italian original. The statues standing on the roofline represent patron saints of the region, providing a local touch. The interior is less rewarding visually than the exterior, but the ceiling and high altar are worth a look. Masses are held three to four times daily.

1085 rue de la Cathédrale (at rue Mansfield). © **514/ 866-1661.** www.cathedralecatholiquedemontreal.org. Free admission; donations accepted. Mon–Fri 7:30am– 6:15pm; Sat–Sun 7:30am–6:15pm. Métro: Bonaventure.

The impressive dome of the Basilique-Cathédrale Marie-Reine-du-Monde.

Cathédrale Christ Church This Anglican cathedral stands in glorious Gothic contrast to the city's downtown skyscrapers. The building was completed in 1859. The original steeple was too heavy for the structure, so a lighter aluminum version replaced it in 1940. It's sometimes called the "floating cathedral" because of the way it was elevated during the construction of malls and corridors in the underground city beneath it. Choirs sing each Sunday at 10am for Sung Eucharist and at 4pm for Choral Evensong, with the Evensong broadcast live at www. radiovm.com. The church also hosts concerts throughout the year.

635 rue Ste-Catherine ouest (at rue University). © **514/843-6577,** ext. 369 (recorded information about music programs). www.montrealcathedral.ca. Free admission; donations accepted. Daily 8am–6pm. Métro: McGill.

Musée d'Art Contemporain de Montréal Montréal's Museum of Contemporary Art is the country's only museum devoted exclusively to the avant-garde. Its focus is works created since 1939, and much of the permanent collection is by Québécois artists such as Jean-Paul Riopelle and Betty Goodwin. Also represented are international artists Richard Serra, Bruce Nauman, Sam Taylor-Wood, and Nan Goldin. No single style prevails, so expect to see installations, video displays, and examples of pop, op, and abstract expressionism. On Friday Nocturnes—the first Friday of most months—the museum stays open until 9pm with live music, bar service, and tours of the exhibition galleries. A mélange of fun videos are online at www.youtube.com/macmvideos. The museum's glass-walled restaurant, **La Rotonde,** was renovated in 2009 and has a summer dining terrace.

185 rue Ste-Catherine ouest. © **514/847-6226.** www.macm.org. Admission C$10 adults, C$8 seniors, C$6 students, free for children 11 and under; free admission Wed 6–9pm. Tues and Thurs-Sun 11am–6pm; Wed and Fri Nocturnes 11am–9pm. Métro: Place des Arts.

Vieux-Montréal (Old Montréal)

Bota Bota ★ Converted from a real boat, Bota Bota's highly modern, all-season spa offers a luxurious water circuit of dry saunas, steam rooms, and three

The Musée d'Art Contemporain de Montréal is the country's only museum devoted exclusively to the avant-garde.

Jacuzzis, two of which are outside and offer stunning northern views of the Old Port. You can also come for relaxing body treatments in one of the many well-appointed private rooms or enjoy a manicure or pedicure in the boat's bow that also gives you lovely views through its panoramic windows. Access to the "boat" starts at C$45 on weekdays (C$50 on weekend and holidays) and gives you 3 hours of play (or relax) time in all the water facilities, lounges, and bistro. The invigorating "Tribal Journey" treatment is C$125 for 90 minutes; it includes body products from four continents and a Tahitian massage.

358 rue de la Commune ouest. (℃) **514/284-0333.** www.botabota.ca. Thurs–Tues 10am–10pm. Métro: Square-Victoria.

Chapelle Notre-Dame-de-Bon-Secours/Musée Marguerite-Bourgeoys

Just to the east of Marché Bonsecours, Notre-Dame-de-Bon-Secours Chapel is called the Sailors' Church because of the special attachment that fishermen and other mariners have to it. Their devotion is manifest in the several ship models hanging from the ceiling inside. There's also an excellent view of the harbor from the church's tower.

The first building, which no longer stands, was the project of an energetic teacher named Marguerite Bourgeoys (1620–1700) and built in 1675. Bourgeoys had come from France to undertake the education of the children of the colonists and, later, the native peoples. She and other teachers founded the Congregation of Notre-Dame, Canada's first nuns' order. The pioneering Bourgeoys was canonized in 1982 as the Canadian church's first female saint, and in 2005, for the chapel's 350th birthday, her remains were brought to the church and interred in the left-side altar.

A restored 18th-century crypt under the chapel houses the museum. Part of it is devoted to relating Bourgeoys's life and work, while another section displays artifacts from an archaeological site here, including ruins and materials from the colony's earliest days. An Amerindian campsite on display dates back more than 2,400 years.

400 rue St-Paul est (at the foot of rue Bonsecours). ☏ **514/282-8670.** www.marguerite-bourgeoys.com. Free admission to chapel. Museum C$8 adults, C$5 seniors and students, C$4 children ages 6–12, free for children 5 and under. Archaeological site with guide and access to museum C$10 for 1, C$18 families. May–Oct Tues–Sun 10am–5:30pm; Nov to mid-Jan, Mar–Apr Tues–Sun 11am–3:30pm. Métro: Champ-de-Mars.

Hôtel de Ville   City Hall, finished in 1878, is relatively young by Vieux-Montréal standards. It's still in use, with the mayor's office on the main floor. The French Second Empire design makes it look as though it was imported, stone by stone, from the mother country: Balconies, turrets, and mansard roofs decorate the exterior. The details are particularly visible when the exterior is illuminated at night. The Hall of Honour is made of green marble from Campan, France, and houses Art Deco lamps from Paris and a bronze-and-glass chandelier, also from France, that weighs a metric ton. It was from the balcony above the awning that, in 1967, an ill-mannered Charles de Gaulle, then president of France, proclaimed, "Vive le Québec Libre!" ("Long live free Québec!")—a gesture that pleased his immediate audience but strained relations with the Canadian government for years.

275 rue Notre-Dame est (at the corner of rue Gosford). ☏ **514/872-0077.** www.ville.montreal. qc.ca. Free admission. Mon–Fri 9am–4pm. 1-hr. guided tours late June to late Aug Mon–Fri 9am–4pm, by reservation only. Métro: Champ-de-Mars.

Marché Bonsecours   Bonsecours Market is an imposing neoclassical building with a long facade, a colonnaded portico, and a silvery dome. It was built in the mid-1800s—the Doric columns of the portico were cast of iron in England—and first used as the Parliament of United Canada, and then as Montréal's City Hall until 1878. The architecture alone makes a brief visit worthwhile. For many years after 1878, it served as the city's central market. Essentially abandoned for much

Hôtel de Ville was built in 1878.

The Marché Bonsecours contains restaurants, art galleries, and boutiques featuring Québécois products.

of the 20th century, it was restored in 1964 to house city government offices. Today, it contains restaurants, art galleries, and high-end but affordable boutiques featuring Québécois products. Twice a year Montréal Fashion Week (Semaine de la Mode) also makes this building its home; visit www.montreal fashionweek.ca for more information.

350 rue St-Paul est (at the foot of rue St-Claude). © **514/872-7730.** www.marchebonsecours. qc.ca. Free admission. Fall–spring daily 10am–6pm; summer daily 10am–9pm. Métro: Champ-de-Mars.

Musée du Château Ramezay ★ ☺ Claude de Ramezay, the colony's 11th governor, built his residence here in 1705. The château became home to the city's royal French governors for almost 4 decades, until Ramezay's heirs sold it to a trading company in 1745. Fifteen years later, British conquerors took it over, and in 1775, an army of American revolutionaries invaded and held Montréal, using the château as their headquarters. For 6 weeks in 1776, Benjamin Franklin spent his days here, trying to persuade the Québécois to rise with the American colonists against British rule (he failed). After the American interlude, the house was used as a courthouse, a government office building, and headquarters for Laval University before being converted into a museum in 1895. Permanent exhibits include "Hochelaga, Ville-Marie, and Montréal," which traces Amerindian history to the early 20th century, and "Life in Montréal in the 18th century," presented among the building's walled vaults.

On school breaks in December and March, the Château invites families to join in on an old-timey bread-making session using its 18th-century hearth. In the summer, there are workshops in the garden that teach how to make soap and dip candles. Dates, details, and additional fees are listed on the website.

Sculpted, formal gardens ringed by a low stone wall evoke 18th-century French *jardins* and provide a soothing respite from the bustle of Place Jacques-Cartier, a few steps away. A cafe, open June through September, overlooks the gardens.

280 rue Notre-Dame est. ✆ **514/861-3708.** www.chateauramezay.qc.ca. Museum admission C$10 adults, C$8 seniors, C$7 students, C$5 children 5–17, free for children 4 and under; C$22 families. Free admission to governor's garden. June to mid-Oct daily 10am–6pm; mid-Oct to May Tues–Sun 10am–4:30pm. Métro: Champ-de-Mars.

Scandinave Les Bains ★ Bath complexes are common throughout Scandinavia, but less so in North America. This center, which opened

Sling-back chairs are scattered throughout Scandinave Les Bains for relaxing between soaks.

in 2009, aims to bring Euro-style relaxation-through-water to Montréal's locals and guests. Visitors check in, change into bathing suits, and then have the run of the complex for the visit. There's a warm bath the size of a small swimming pool with jets and a waterfall, a steam room thick with the scent of eucalyptus oil, and a Finnish-style dry sauna. Peppered throughout the hallways are sling-back chairs, and one room is set aside just for relaxing or having a drink from the juice bar. The recommended routine is to heat your body for about 15 minutes, cool down in one of the icy rinse stations, and relax for 15 minutes—and then repeat the circuit a few times. Call to reserve a spot. Ask for a time when the fewest people are there; the fewer there are, the more relaxing the experience.

71 rue de la Commune ouest. ✆ **514/288-2009.** www.scandinave.com. Admission C$54. Bathrobe rental C$12. Packages available with massage. Must be 16 or older. Daily 10am–10pm. Métro: Champ-de-Mars.

Mont Royal & Plateau Mont-Royal

To explore these areas, take the walking tours in chapter 8.

L'Oratoire St-Joseph ★ This huge Catholic church—dominating Mont-Royal's north slope—is seen by some as inspiring, by others as forbidding. It's Montréal's highest point, with an enormous dome 97m (318 ft.) high. Consecrated as a basilica in 2004, it came into being through the efforts of Brother André, a lay brother in the Holy Cross order who earned a reputation as a healer. By the time he had built a small wooden chapel in 1904 on the mountain, he was said to have performed hundreds of cures. His powers attracted supplicants from great distances, and he performed his work until his death in 1937. His dream of building a shrine to honor St. Joseph, patron saint of Canada, became a reality in 1967. In 1982, he was beatified by the pope—a status one step below sainthood—and on October 17, 2010, he earned the distinction of sainthood, too. A new exhibit is being planned to commemorate this honor.

The church is largely Italian Renaissance in style, its giant copper dome recalling the shape of the Duomo in Florence, but of greater size and lesser grace. Inside is a sanctuary and exhibit that displays Brother André's actual heart in a formalin-filled urn. His original wooden chapel, with its tiny bedroom, is on the grounds and open to the public. Two million pilgrims visit annually, many of whom seek intercession from St. Joseph and Brother André by climbing the middle set of 99 steps on their knees. The 56-bell carillon plays Wednesday to Friday at noon and 3pm, and Saturday and Sunday at 12:15 and 2:30pm. Also on-site is an oratory museum featuring 264 nativity scenes from 111 countries. A modest

L'Oratoire St-Joseph is located at the city's highest point.

14-room hostel on the grounds is called the **Jean XXIII Pavilion.** Single rooms with shared bathroom start at C$50 and include breakfast. Details are at www.saint-joseph.org/en_1060_index.php.

In 2002, the oratory embarked on a 10-year renovation project to improve overall accessibility for the ever-increasing number of visitors, which is likely to be completed in 2012. Most recent completions include an elevator to the basilica and a new vehicle entrance. In coming years, visitors will have unprecedented 360-degree views of Montréal from the basilica's dome.

3800 chemin Queen Mary (on the north slope of Mont-Royal). © **877/672-8647** or 514/733-8211. www.saint-joseph.org. Free admission to most sights, donations requested; oratory museum C$4 adults, C$3 seniors and students, C$2 children 6-17. Crypt and votive chapel daily 6am–9:30pm; basilica and exhibition on Brother André daily 7am–9pm; oratory museum Tues–Sun 10am–4:30pm. C$5 suggested donation for parking. Métro: Côtes-des-Neiges or Snowdon. Bus: 165 or 51.

Half of Parc La Fontaine is landscaped in formal French style, the other in more casual English style.

Parc La Fontaine The European-style park in Plateau Mont-Royal is one of the city's oldest and most popular. Illustrating the traditional dual identities of the city's populace, half the park is landscaped in the formal French manner, the other in the more casual English style. A central lake is used for ice-skating in winter, when snowshoe and cross-country trails wind through trees. In summer, these trails become bike paths, and tennis courts become active. An open amphitheater, the **Théâtre**

de Verdure (p. 190), features free outdoor theater, music, and tango dancing. The northern end of the park is more pleasant than the southern end (along rue Sherbrooke), which attracts a seedier crowd.

Bounded by rue Sherbrooke, rue Rachel, av. Parc LaFontaine, and av. Papineau. ☏ **514/872-3948** for park, 514/872-3626 for tennis reservations. www.ville.montreal.qc.ca. Free admission; C$9 per hr. for use of tennis courts. Park daily 6am–midnight; tennis courts Mon–Fri 9am–11pm, Sat–Sun 9am–9pm. Métro: Sherbrooke.

L'Île Ste-Hélène ★/Parc Jean-Drapeau

The small Île Ste-Hélène and adjacent Île Notre-Dame sit in the St. Lawrence River near Vieux-Port's waterfront. Connected by two bridges, they comprise **Parc Jean-Drapeau,** which is almost entirely car-free and accessible by Métro, bicycle, or foot.

La Biosphère ☺ Not to be confused with the **Biodôme** at Olympic Park (p. 119), this interactive science facility is housed under a geodesic dome designed by Buckminster Fuller to serve as the American Pavilion for Expo 67. A fire destroyed the sphere's acrylic skin in 1976, and for almost 20 years, it served no purpose other than as a harbor landmark. In 1995, Environment Canada (www.ec.gc.ca) joined with the city of Montréal to convert the space. The motivation is unabashedly environmentalist, with exhibition areas, a theater, and an amphitheater devoted to informing visitors about water quality, biodiversity, and climate change. An interactive walking tour, dubbed GeoTour 67, uses GPS (Global Positioning System) devices. "Planète Bucky," a permanent exhibit, highlights Fuller's forward-thinking inventions for sustainable development. There's a preaching-to-the-choir quality, but the displays and exhibits are put together thoughtfully, and engage and enlighten most visitors—at least, for a while.

160 chemin Tour-de-l'Isle (Île Ste-Hélène, Parc Jean-Drapeau). ☏ **514/283-5000.** www.biosphere.ec.gc.ca. Admission C$12 adults, C$8 seniors and students, free for children 17 and under. June–Oct daily 10am–6pm; Nov–May Tues–Sun 10am–6pm. Métro: Jean-Drapeau.

La Biosphère's geodesic dome was designed by American Buckminster Fuller.

📎 DON'T BE shy, GIVE BIXI A TRY

I love the BIXI concept—take a bike, ride it around, drop it anywhere—but I had to wonder: Are those gray-and-red cruisers really for anyone, even little ole non-Montréaler me? The answer: *Mais oui!* A visit to **www.bixi.com** showed the BIXI bike stations closest to my hotel. At the station, I planned my route and drop-off point using the large posted map (and I could take advantage of the bike lanes that are everywhere). I put my bag into BIXI's iron-clad front rack and bungee, which could secure a barrel of daredevils plunging down Niagara Falls. One swipe of a credit card, and off I careened—into, oops, oncoming traffic. One bummer is that BIXI maps don't mark one-way streets. But the city's gridded roadways make it easy to shift course. Soon my curly locks were flowing in the breeze. I was in Montréal, on a bike! Without a helmet! I'm comfortable with urban biking, but I'll admit to wobbling my first few BIXI kilometers. By design, the bikes are unisex and supersturdy, and I am neither. As I watched one neighborhood roll into the next, I realized my feet could barely reach the pedals. Seat height is adjustable, but I could have selected better. I had some of my 30 free minutes left and exchanged bikes at the next station.

The drop-off at the end of my ride turned out to be tricky. A station on rue St-Pierre had one open spot, but when I pushed the frame into the holster, waiting for the dock's green light, nothing. Several attempts, same result. I wheeled towards Vieux-Port. No vacancy at the station there. I realized I could ask for 15 extra minutes, which I used to find a third drop-off. That one worked, but I had a long march back to my hotel. Later I discovered my credit card company had been phone-stalking me to say that BIXI had charged me $250 (a temporary hold that ensures you return the bike). Still, all in all? I wish I could BIXI every day.

—Erin Trahan

Musée David M. Stewart ★ ☺ After a major 18-month renovation, the museum reopened in June 2011. The history of the facility is interesting: After the War of 1812, the British prepared for a possible future American invasion of Montréal by building a moated fortress. The Duke of Wellington ordered the fort's construction as another link in the chain of defenses along the St. Lawrence River, and it was completed in 1824. It was never involved in armed conflict, and the British garrison left in 1870, after the former Canadian colonies confederated. In recent years, the low stone barracks and blockhouses have featured staff in period costume performing firing drills, tending campfires, and attempting to recruit visitors into the king's army. The museum owns maps and scientific instruments that helped Europeans explore the New World, military and naval artifacts, and related paraphernalia from the time of French voyager Jacques Cartier (1491–1557) through the end of the colonial period (1763). The fort typically comes to life in July and August, with reenactments of military parades and retreats by troupes known as La Compagnie Franche de la Marine and the Olde 78th Fraser Highlanders.

Vieux-Fort, Île Ste-Hélène. ℂ **514/861-6701.** www.stewart-museum.org. Admission C$13 adults; C$10 seniors, students, and children; free for children 6 and under. Wed–Sun 11am–5pm. Métro: Parc Jean-Drapeau. By car: Take the Jacques-Cartier Bridge to the Parc Jean-Drapeau exit, then follow the signs.

ESPECIALLY FOR KIDS

In addition to the three Bs—the **Biodôme** (p. 119), **Biosphère** (p. 128), and **boat tours** (p. 136)—here are some venues and programs that cater primarily to the under-18 crowd. Also look for other attractions flagged in this chapter with the "Kids" icon.

Atrium Le 1000   This medium-size indoor ice-skating rink in the heart of downtown offers skating year-round under a glass ceiling. Skate rentals are available, and a food court surrounds the rink. It attracts a full mix of patrons: groups of giggling teenage girls, middle-aged friends chatting and skating side by side, and young children teetering in helmets. Tiny Tot Mornings, typically Saturday and Sunday from 10:30 to noon, are reserved for children 12 and younger, and their parents.

1000 rue de la Gauchetière ouest. ✆ **514/395-0555.** www.le1000.com. Admission C$6.50 adults, C$5.50 seniors and students, C$4.50 children 12 and under. Skate rental C$6. Daily 11:30am–6pm or later. Métro: Bonaventure.

Fantômes Ghost Walks ☺   Evenings at 8:30pm, join with other intrepid souls for a ghost walk of Vieux-Montréal. The 90-minute tour heads down back alleys to places where gruesome events occurred and actors appear as phantoms to tell about the historical crimes of the city. Because their stories include tales of sorcery, hangings, and being burned and tortured, it's probably too scary for children under 10.

360 rue St-François-Xavier. ✆ **800/363-4021** or 514/844-4021. www.fantommontreal.com. Admission C$22 adults, C$19 students, C$13 children 12 and under. July–Oct various evenings at 8:30pm; call or go online for exact days. Métro: Place d'Armes.

IMAX Theater ★   Images and special effects are way larger than life and visually dazzling on this screen in the **Centre des Sciences de Montréal** (p. 116). Recent films have highlighted NASA's Hubble Space Telescope, the art of Vincent Van Gogh, and the deep waters of the South Pacific. Running time is usually less than an hour. One or two screenings per day are in English, and tickets can be ordered online. The movie schedule is available on the website.

Quai King Edward, Vieux-Port. ✆ **877/496-4724** or 514/496-4724. www.montrealsciencecentre. com. Movie tickets C$12 adults, C$11 seniors and children 13–17, C$9 children 4–12, free for children 3 and under. Shows daily 10am–9pm. Métro: Place d'Armes or Champ-de-Mars.

Insectarium de Montréal   Live exhibits featuring scorpions, tarantulas, honeybees, ants, hissing cockroaches, assassin bugs, and other "misunderstood creatures, which are so often wrongly feared and despised," as its website puts it, are displayed in this two-level structure near the rue Sherbrooke gate of the **Jardin Botanique** (**Botanical Garden;** p. 120). Alongside the live creepy critters are thousands of mounted ones, including butterflies, beetles, scarabs, maggots, locusts, and giraffe weevils. The gift shop sells lollipops with mealworm larva inside.

4581 rue Sherbrooke est. ✆ **514/872-1400.** www.ville.montreal.qc.ca/insectarium. Mid-May to Nov C$17 adults, C$13 seniors and students, C$8.25 children 5–17, C$2.50 children 2–4. Nov to mid-May rates drop about 15%. Admission includes access to the Botanical Garden next door. Combination tickets with the Stade Olympique and Biodôme are available. Mid-May to mid-Sept daily 9am–6pm; mid-Sept to Nov daily 9am–9pm; Nov to mid-May Tues–Sun 9am–5pm. Métro: Pie-IX or Viau.

Atrium Le 1000 offers year-round skating under a glass ceiling.

The Insectarium de Montréal has many live exhibits.

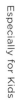

Labyrinth Shed 16 From mid-May to the end of October, this gigantic indoor maze at the far eastern end of Vieux-Port entices children to come and explore a mystery, which changes each year. One year, for instance, the maze was set up like the interior of a castle, with a tale of a priceless black-diamond family treasure; another year, visitors searched throughout the maze for information to open a safe that contained stolen art works. You'll climb through rope bridges, take staircases to secret corridors, wind through walls of enormous oil drums, and slide down chutes, answering math or logic questions along the way. It takes about 90 minutes to get through. A lot of it is dark, and there's some crawling involved, so be prepared.

Quai de l'Horloge, near the Clock Tower. ✆ **514/499-0099.** www.labyrintheduhangar16.com. Admission C$15 adults, C$14 seniors and children 13–17, C$12 children 4–12, free for children 3 and under. Late June to late Aug daily 11am–9pm; mid-May to late June and late Aug to mid-Oct Sat–Sun and holidays 11:30am 5:30pm. Métro: Champs-de-Mars.

La Ronde Amusement Park Montréal's amusement park, opened as part of the Expo 67 World's Fair, was run for its first 34 years by the city. It was sold to the American-owned Six Flags theme-park empire in 2001. New rides have since been added, and like hot sauces, they're categorized by "thrill rating": moderate, mild, or max. There are 13 rides in the "max thrill" category, including Le Vampire, a suspended coaster that has riders experiencing five head-over-heels loops at more than 80kmph (50mph). Other attractions include a Ferris wheel, diving shows, and plenty of places to eat and drink. An antique carousel, Le Galopant, was built by Belgian artisans in 1885 and was part of the Belgian Pavilion at the 1964 to 1965 New York World's Fair. The Minirail is an elevated train that circles the park. Young children also have ample selection, including the Tchou Tchou Train and *tasses magiques,* in which they sit in 1 of 12 giant rotating tea cups. On 10 Saturdays from June to August, La Ronde hosts a huge fireworks competition, **L'International Des Feux Loto-Québec.** Although the pyrotechnics can be enjoyed for free from almost anywhere in the city overlooking the river, tickets

La Ronde Amusement Park has dozens of different rides.

must be purchased to watch from the open-air theater here. Call ℂ **800/361-4595** or go to www.internationaldesfeuxloto-quebec.com for details.

22 chemin. Macdonald, Parc Jean-Drapeau on Île Ste-Hélène. ℂ **514/397-2000.** www.laronde. com. Admission prices (by height) C$40 patrons 1.4m (54 in.) or taller, C$26 patrons under 1.4m (54 in.) and seniors, free for children 2 and under. Special rates available online. Parking C$15–C$25. Summer Sun–Fri 11am–9pm, Sat 11am–11:30pm; spring and fall Sat–Sun 11am–7pm (call or check website to confirm hours). Métro: Papineau, then bus no. 169; Parc Jean-Drapeau, then bus no. 167.

Planétarium de Montréal   A window on the night sky with mythical monsters and magical heroes, the 20m (66-ft.) dome at Montréal's planetarium in the heart of the city dazzles and informs kids at the same time. Multimedia presentations change with the season, exploring time and space travel and collisions of celestial bodies. Up to five different shows are screened daily, alternating between English and French. The website has educational activities, too.

1000 rue St-Jacques ouest (at Peel). ℂ **514/872-4530.** www.planetarium.montreal.qc.ca. Admission C$8 adults, C$6 seniors and students, C$4 children 5–17, free for children 4 and under. Hours vary according to show schedule; call or go online for details. Métro: Bonaventure.

SPECIAL-INTEREST SIGHTSEEING

Bagg Street Shul   Author Mordecai Richler set most of his books in the working-class Jewish neighborhood of St-Urbain of the 1940s and 1950s (his most famous book is *The Apprenticeship of Duddy Kravitz*). The Bagg Street Shul, also called Temple Solomon or Congregation Beth Shloime, is the heart of this neighborhood and one of the last signs of the Plateau's long history as a Jewish enclave. A replica of the old eastern European synagogues of Poland and Ukraine, its interior features robin's-egg-blue walls and paintings of the 12 zodiac signs, labeled in Hebrew, unique for an orthodox shul. It's the city's oldest synagogue in

The Bagg Street Shul is the heart of the St-Urbain neighborhood popularized by local writer Mordecai Richler.

continuous use, and despite financial challenges, it presses on with a volunteer leadership and a small, dedicated membership.

3919 rue Clark (at rue Bagg). ☎ **514/481-9542.** Free admission. Sat mornings (service at 9am followed by kiddush) and holidays. Call or e-mail baggshul@gmail.com in advance for tour. Métro: Sherbrooke.

Centre Canadien d'Architecture

The understated but handsome Canadian Centre for Architecture (CCA) occupies a city block, joining a contemporary structure with an older building, the 1875 Shaughnessy House. Opened in 1989, this museum has received rave reviews from scholars, critics, and serious architecture buffs. CCA functions as both a study center and a museum, with changing exhibits devoted to the art and history of architecture. Exhibits include architects' sketchbooks, elevation drawings, and photography. The collection is international in scope and encompasses architecture, urban planning, and landscape design. Texts are in French and English. The bookstore has a special section about Canadian architecture with an emphasis on Montréal and Québec City. A **sculpture garden** that faces the CCA from boulevard René-Lévesque's south side is part of the museum. Designed by Montréal artist/architect Melvin Charney, it's a quiet retreat in the center of downtown.

1920 rue Baile (at rue du Fort). ☎ **514/939-7026.** www.cca.qc.ca. Admission C$10 adults, C$7 seniors, free for students and children; free admission Thurs after 5:30pm. Wed–Sun 11am–6pm; Thurs 11am–9pm. Métro: Guy-Concordia.

Centre d'Histoire de Montréal Built in 1903 as Montréal's central fire station, this redbrick-and-sandstone building on the edge of Vieux-Montréal is now the CHM, which traces the city's development from when it had its first residents, the Amerindians, to the European settlers who arrived in 1642, to the present day. The permanent exhibit includes memorabilia from the city from 1535 onward, with a growing collection of 20th-century artifacts from everyday life. Each year, the Centre hosts a Montréal-themed photo competition with the winners' images on display. The museum won the 2011 Award of Outstanding Achievement by the Canadian Museums Associations for its project, "You're Part of History!"

335 Place d'Youville (at rue St-Pierre). ☎ **514/872-3207.** www.ville.montreal.qc.ca/chm. Admission C$6 adults, C$5 seniors, C$4 students and children 6–17, free for children 5 and under. Jan–Nov Tues–Sun 10am–5pm. Métro: Square Victoria.

Musée de la Banque de Montréal Facing the **Basilique Notre-Dame** (p. 115) and Place d'Armes, this is Montréal's oldest bank building. Architectural features include a classic facade beneath a graceful dome, a carved pediment, and six Corinthian columns. The outside dimensions and appearance remain largely unchanged since the building's completion in 1847. Pop in for 5 minutes to see the teeny one-room museum just off the front hall. It features a replica of the bank's first office, a display showing how to spot a forged bill, and a collection of 100-year-old mechanical banks. Take a look at the building's sumptuous interior: It was renovated from 1901 through 1905 by the famed U.S. firm McKim, Mead, and White, and features Ionic and Corinthian columns of Vermont granite and walls of pink marble from Tennessee.

129 rue St-Jacques ouest (at Place d'Armes). ℰ **514/877-6810.** Free admission. Mon–Fri 10am–4pm. Métro: Place d'Armes.

Musée Redpath 🍴 This quirky natural history museum, housed in an 1882 building with a grandly proportioned and richly appointed interior, is on the McGill University campus. The main draws—worth a half-hour visit—are the mummies and coffin that are part of Canada's second-largest collection of Egyptian antiquities, and skeletons of whales and prehistoric beasts. If the name seems slightly familiar, it could be because you've seen it on the wrappings of sugar cubes in many Canadian restaurants: John Redpath was a 19th-century industrialist who built Canada's first sugar refinery.

jewish **MONTRÉAL**

At the turn of the 20th century, Montréal was home to more Jewish people than any other Canadian city, attracting an especially large Yiddish-speaking population from eastern Europe. Today, Toronto has nearly twice as many Jewish residents, but vestiges of the community's history and ongoing practices remain in Montréal's Plateau neighborhood, although more so today in the Mile End and Outremont areas. Here, places of worship, celebration of Jewish culture through arts, and the so-called bagel-and-smoked-meat wars smolder on, to the delight of local and visiting connoisseurs. The **Bagg Street Shul** (see above), at the corner of rues Clark and Bagg, began as a two-family residence, was converted to a synagogue in 1920 to 1921, and has been in continuous use ever since. Other synagogues dot the neighborhood but have transitioned as the Jewish community dispersed. Edibles abound. Start the day with a bagel from either **St-Viateur Bagel & Café,** at 1127 av. Mont-Royal est, or **Fairmont Bagel,** at 74 av. Fairmont ouest in Mile End. Get a pressed salami and bologna sandwich while traveling back in time at **Wilensky Light Lunch,** 34 rue Fairmount ouest. For dinner, get an unforgettable smoked meat sandwich at **Schwartz's,** 3895 bd. St-Laurent, or opt for a steak at posh **Moishes,** 3961 bd. St-Laurent. See chapter 7 for restaurant details.

The Snowdon neighborhood in western Montréal is home to the city's contemporary Jewish organizations. The **Jewish Public Library** (ℰ 514/345-2627; www.jewishpubliclibrary.org) boasts the largest circulating collection of Judaica in North America and hosts year-round lectures, readings, and cultural events. Its archive of more than 17,000 photos of Montréal's Jewish history is in the process of being digitized to be put online. The library shares a building, the Cummings House, at 5151 Côte-Ste-Catherine with the **Montréal Holocaust Memorial Centre** (ℰ 514/345-2605; www.mhmc.ca) and a dozen other Jewish community-service agencies. Just across the street, at 5170 Côte-Ste-Catherine, is the **Segal Centre for Performing Arts** (p. 190), which presents plays in Yiddish, offers theater workshops, and has film programs.

The Musée Redpath has a range of natural history exhibits.

859 rue Sherbrooke ouest (rue University). ☏ **514/398-4086.** www.mcgill.ca/redpath. Free admission. Mon–Fri 9am–5pm; Sun noon–5pm. Closed long weekends and public holidays. Métro: McGill.

Pavillon de la TOHU Adjacent to the Cirque du Soleil training complex on reclaimed industrial land, TOHU is many things, most especially a performance facility that brings small circus companies to its intimate in-the-round theater (p. 187). But it's also a model building for green architecture. It's heated by biogas from a landfill next door and uses an ice bunker for cooling in the summer. Both processes produce zero greenhouse-effect gases and are explained in free brochures. For one weekend in August, TOHU hosts an outdoor fair promoting sustainable food practices. For the rest of the year, it's worth a special trip only if you're an environmental architecture fan. Two guided tours are available with advance reservations by phone: One focuses on TOHU's green technologies, the other on the history of the circus arts. If there's a show playing, build a trip around it.

2345 rue Jarry est (corner of rue d'Iberville, at Autoroute 40). ☏ **888/376-8648** or 514/376-8648. www.tohu.ca. Free admission to facility and exhibits. Tour admission C$6 adults; C$4 seniors, students and children 7–11; free for children 6 and under (but not recommended). Tour requires reservations. Mon–Fri 9am–5pm. 8km (5 miles) from downtown; drive up rue St-Denis and east on rue Jarry to where it meets Autoroute 40. Métro: Jarry or Iberville. Bus: 94 nord.

ORGANIZED TOURS

An introductory guided tour is often the best—or, at least, most efficient— way to begin exploring a new city and can certainly give you a good lay of the land and overview of Montréal's history. Tours take you past many of the attractions listed in this chapter and can give you a better sense of which ones to spend time exploring.

For a complete listing of tour options, check under "Guided Tours" in the *Montréal Official Tourist Guide,* available at the downtown **Infotouriste Centre** at 1255 rue Peel (☏ **877/266-5687** or 514/873-2015; Métro: Peel).

Most land tours leave from the (recently relandscaped) Square Dorchester, right at the tourist office. Most boat tours depart from Vieux-Port (Old Port), at the waterfront bordering Vieux-Montréal. There's parking at the dock, or take the Métro to the Champ-de-Mars or Square Victoria Station, and then walk toward the river.

Boat Tours

Among numerous opportunities for experiencing Montréal and environs by water, here are a few of the most popular:

- **Le Bateau-Mouche** (☏ 800/361-9952 or 514/849-9952; www.bateau-mouche.com): an air-conditioned, glass-enclosed vessel reminiscent of those on the Seine in Paris. It plies the St. Lawrence River from mid-May to mid-October. Cruises depart for 60-minute excursions at 11am, 2:30pm, and 4:30pm; for a 90-minute cruise at 12:30pm; and for a 3½-hour dinner cruise at 7pm. The shallow-draft boat takes passengers on a route inaccessible by traditional vessels, passing under several bridges and providing sweeping views of the city, Mont Royal, and the St. Lawrence and its islands. Snacks are available onboard. The 60-minute tours cost C$24 adults, C$22 students and seniors 65 and older, C$12 children 6 to 14, free for children 5 and under. The 90-minute tour costs C$28 adults, C$26 students and seniors, and C$15 children 6 to 14. Dinner cruises, with menus prepared by the kitchen of Fairmont the Queen Elizabeth, cost from C$90, C$128, or C$153 per person, regardless of age, and reservations are essential (prices are higher Sat and the evenings of fireworks). The tours depart from the Jacques-Cartier Pier, opposite Place Jacques-Cartier.

- **Croisières AML Cruises** (☏ 800/563-4643 or 514/842-3871; www.croisieresaml.com): Options include a weekend brunch cruise that departs at 11:30am and lasts 1½ hours for C$48 adults, C$46 students and seniors, C$28 children 6 to 16, and free for children 5 and younger. There are also 60- or 90-minute history trips throughout the day, as well as 4-hour "Love Boat" dinner cruises that depart at 7pm, 4½-hour fireworks and buffet dinner cruises that depart at 7:30pm, and 3-hour "Latin Fiesta" dance parties that board at midnight. Call or check the website for prices and times. Boats depart from the King Edward Pier, in Vieux-Port.

- **Croisière Historique sur le Canal de Lachine** (☏ 514/283-6054; www.pc.gc.ca/canallachine): A leisurely Parks Canada trip up the Lachine Canal, which was inaugurated in 1824 so that ships could

The Bateau-Mouche tours are reminiscent of the tours of the Seine in Paris.

bypass the Lachine Rapids on the way to the Great Lakes. It's lined with 19th-century industrial buildings, many of which are being converted into high-end apartments. The 2-hour guided tours are on a glass-topped *bateau-mouche,* which hold up to 49 passengers. From mid-May to mid-June and early September to mid-October, departures are at 1 and 3:30pm on Saturday, Sunday, and holidays; from late June to early September, departures are daily at 1 and 3:30pm. Phone reservations recommended. Fares are C$18 adults, C$15 children 13 to 17, C$11 children 6 to 12, and free for children 5 and younger. Groups of 18 or more can charter 1- or 2-hour tours. Tours departs from a dock near the Marché Atwater farmer's market (p. 181; Métro: Lionel-Groulx).

○ **Les Descentes sur le St-Laurent** (✆ **800/324-7238** or 514/767-2230; www.raftingmontreal.com): Also provides hydro-jet rides on the white water. This departure point is a little closer to the rapids than the others, so a bit more of an adventure. Rafting and jet-boat options are available for C$41 and C$50 adults, C$35 and C$40 children 13 to 18, and C$24 and C$30 children 12 and under (though kids must be at least 6 years old to go rafting and at least 8 years old to go jet-boating). Reservations are required. Open daily from 9am to 5pm. (Métro: Angrignon. Bus: 110.)

○ **Les Sautes-Moutons** (also known as **Lachine Rapids Tours;** ✆ **514/284-9607;** www.jetboatingmontreal.com): Provides an exciting—and wet—experience. Its wave-jumper powerboats take on the St. Lawrence River's roiling Lachine Rapids. The streamlined jet boat makes the 1-hour trip from May to mid-October daily, with departures every 2 hours from 10am to 6pm. It takes a half-hour to get to and from the rapids, which leaves 30 minutes for storming along the 2.4m to 3.7m (8- to 12-ft.) waves. Reservations are required. Plan to arrive 45 minutes early to obtain and don rain gear and a life jacket. Bring a towel and change of clothes, as you almost certainly will get splashed or even soaked. Fares are C$65 adults, C$55 children 13 to 18, C$45 children 6 to 12. Inquire about children 5 and under. The jet boats depart from the Clock Tower Pier (quai de l'Horlage) in Vieux-Port.

○ **Navettes Fluviales Maritime Shuttles** (✆ **514/281-8000;** www.navettesmaritimes.com): From Jacques-Cartier Pier in Vieux-Montréal to either Ile Ste-Hélène or Longueuil, these are much milder water voyages, but still offer great views. It's one way to begin or end a picnic outing or extend a bike ride beyond Old Montréal. Both ferries operate from mid-May to mid-October, with daily departures every hour in the high season, and cost C$5 per person. Your ticket stub gets you a discount at an array of partners, including the Biosphère (p. 128) and La Ronde amusement park (p. 131).

Land Tours

Gray Line de Montréal (✆ **800/461-1223** or 514/934-1222; www.coachcanada.com) offers commercial guided tours in air-conditioned buses daily year-round. The basic city tour takes 3 hours and costs C$45 for adults, C$41 for seniors and students, C$32 for children 5 to 11, or free for children 4 and under. Tours depart from 1255 rue Peel in downtown.

Amphi-Bus (✆ **514/849-5181;** www.montreal-amphibus-tour.com) is something a little different: It tours Vieux-Montréal much like any other bus—until it waddles into the waters of the harbor for a dramatic finish. Departures are on the hour from 10am until 10pm June through September; and at noon, 2, 4, and

Drivers of Montréal's horse-drawn carriages also serve as guides.

6pm in May and October. Fares are C$32 adults, C$29 seniors, C$25 students, C$18 children 6 to 12, and C$10 children 1 to 5. Reservations are required. The bus departs from the intersection of rue de la Commune and boul. St-Laurent.

Montréal's **calèches** (✆ **514/934-6105;** www.calechesluckyluc.com) are horse-drawn open carriages whose drivers serve as guides. They operate year-round, and in winter, the horse puffs steam clouds in the cold air as the passengers bundle up in lap rugs. Reserved rides for up to four persons can be arranged from downtown for C$150 per hour and from Vieux-Montréal for C$125 per hour. During summer months, visitors can find the carriages waiting at Place Jacques-Cartier and rue de la Commune, and at Place d'Armes opposite Basilique Notre-Dame, where a 30-minute ride costs C$45 and an hour costs C$75. All of the guides speak French and English.

Walking & Cycling Tours

Guidatour (✆ **514/844-4021;** www.guidatour.qc.ca) developed its walking tour of Vieux-Montréal in collaboration with the Centre d'Histoire de Montréal (p. 133). The 90-minute circuit is conducted in English at 11am and 1:30pm daily in summer and costs C$20 for adults, C$18 for seniors and students, or C$11 for children 6 to 12; it's free for children 5 and under. Guidatour also offers a 3-hour bicycling tour in conjunction with **Ça Roule/Montréal on Wheels** that goes from Vieux-Port through the Latin Quarter, to Parc La Fontaine and then west to Parc du Mont-Royal, south through the business district, and back into Vieux-Montréal. The C$55 fee includes rental of a bike, helmet, and lock for the day. Tours are available daily from late June to early September, and Saturday and Sunday mid-May to mid-October. Tours start at 9am at the bike shop at 27 rue de la Commune est in Vieux-Port (also see "Bicycling & In-Line Skating," below). Reservations are required.

SPECTATOR SPORTS

Montréalers are as devoted to ice hockey as other Canadians are, with plenty of enthusiasm left over for soccer, U.S.-style football, and the other distinctive national sport, curling. They liked baseball too, but not enough: In 2005, the

Montréal Expos, plagued by poor attendance, left for Washington, D.C., where they became the Nationals. *Fun fact:* Pioneering black athlete **Jackie Robinson** played for the Montréal Royals in 1946, and there's a sculpture of him outside of Olympic Stadium.

Auto Racing

The **Grand Prix** came back to Montréal in 2010 after a 1-year hiatus (the result of contract negotiations between the city and Formula One, which puts on the race), and the international auto race is slated to return to the city each summer through at least 2014. The event attracts more than 100,000 people to the city's track (and to hotels and restaurants), bringing in as much as C$100 million in tourism dollars and making it the single biggest tourism event of the year. In 2012, it will take place from June 8 to 10. Tickets range from C$45 to C$113 for general admission, C$286 to C$617 for grandstand seats, and C$4,436 for a 1-day pass for the Formula One Paddock Club. Details are at **www.formula1.com**. Auto-race aficionados can also sate their needs with **NASCAR** (www.circuitgillesvilleneuve.ca), which comes to Montréal for 2 days in late August, bringing more than 40 top drivers and race cars. One-day general-admission tickets cost C$30 to C$40, with 2-day tickets ranging from C$55 to C$165.

Football & Soccer

What Americans call soccer most of the rest of the world calls football, and there's a big fan base for *that* kind of football in Montréal—not surprising, given the city's wide and varied immigrant population. The **Montréal Impact** (📞 **514-328-3668;** www.montrealimpact.com) is part of the North American Soccer League and plays at Saputo Stadium, rue 4750 Sherbrooke est, near the Olympic Stadium. Tickets are C$10 to C$30.

Meanwhile, there's also U.S.-style professional football in Canada. The **Montréal Alouettes** (French for "larks") play at McGill University's Percival-Molson Memorial Stadium from June to

November. The "Als," as they're fondly known, enjoy considerable success; they won their seventh Grey Cup in 2010, the Canadian Football League's version of the U.S. Super Bowl. Tickets start at C$25. Details are at 📞 **514/871-2255** and www.montrealalouettes.com.

Hockey

The beloved **Montréal Canadiens** play downtown at the Centre Bell arena. The team has won 24 Stanley Cups (the last one in 1992–93), and the season runs from October to April, with playoff games potentially continuing into June. Tickets are C$25 to C$225. Check wwwcanadiens.com for schedules and ticketing, or call 📞 **877/668-8269** or 514/790-2525.

The storied Montréal Canadiens have won a record 24 Stanley Cups.

Tennis

The **Rogers Cup** tournament (℡ **514/273-1515;** www.rogerscup.com) comes each August to the Uniprix Stadium, which is near the De Castelnau and the Jarry Métro stops, with singles and doubles matches. Men's and women's tournaments are played in two different locations, alternating between Montréal and Toronto. The stadium's Centre Court holds more than 11,000. Tickets cost between C$10 and C$158, with up to four matches included. To make the tournament more green, the stadium provides 175 bike-rack slots, free public transit tickets to all spectators, and a shuttle service.

OUTDOOR ACTIVITIES

After such long winters, locals pour outdoors to get sun and warm air at every possible opportunity (though there's also lots to do when there's snow on the ground). Even if you come to Montréal without your regular outdoor gear, it's easy to join in. A small and typically packed beach at Parc Jean-Drapeau (www.parcjean drapeau.com) is open to the public from mid-June to mid-August. As well, a new "urban beach" in the Old Port is expected to debut in the summer of 2012, complete with sand, sun umbrellas, and lounge chairs. See www.quaysoftheoldport. com for updates and details.

Warm-Weather Activities

BICYCLING & IN-LINE SKATING

Bicycling and rollerblading are hugely popular in Montréal, and the city helps people indulge these passions. It boasts an expanding network of more than 560km (348 miles) of cycling paths and year-round bike lanes. In warm months, car lanes in heavily biked areas are blocked off with concrete barriers, creating protected bike-only lanes.

If you're serious about cycling, get in touch with the nonprofit biking organization **Vélo Québec** (℡ **800/567-8356** or 514/521-8356; www.velo.qc.ca). Vélo (which means bicycle) was behind the development of a 4,000km (2,485-mile) bike network called **Route Verte (Green Route)** that stretches from one end of the province of Québec to the other. The route was officially inaugurated in summer 2007. The Vélo website has the most up-to-date information on the state of the paths, the Montréal Bike Fest, road races, new bike lanes, and more. It also offers guided tours throughout the province. (**Tip:** Several taxi companies provide bike racks and charge C$3 extra for each bike.)

The shop **Ça Roule/Montréal on Wheels** (℡ **877/866-0633** or 514/866-0633; www.caroulemontreal.com) at 27 rue de la Commune est, the waterfront road in Vieux-Port, rents bikes and skates from March to November. Rentals are C$5 to C$9 per hour and C$30 per day on the weekend, with a deposit required. The company now offers high-performance Argon 18 road bikes. Helmets and locks are included. The staff will set you up with a map (also downloadable from their website) and likely point you toward the peaceful **Lachine Canal,** a nearly flat 11km (6¾-mile) bicycle path, open year-round and maintained by Parks Canada from mid-April through October, that travels alongside locks and over small bridges. The canal starts just a few blocks away. See p. 138 for Ça Roule's 3-hour guided bike tours. Also for rent at Vieux-Port in warm months are **quadricycles** (℡ **514/849-9953;** www.quaysoftheoldport.com), or "Q-cycles"—four-wheeled

BIXI bike stands are located throughout the city.

bike-buggies that can hold up to six people. You can ride them only along Vieux-Port, and the rental booth is in the heart of the waterfront area, next to the Pavillian Jacques-Cartier. Rentals are by the half-hour and cost C$20 for a three-seater with spots for two small children, and C$40 for a six-seater.

In the spring of 2009, the city launched a self-service bicycle rental program called BIXI, where users pick up bikes from designated bike stands in the city and drop them off at other stands for a small fee. See "Getting There & Getting Around" in chapter 4 for details.

HIKING

The most popular hike is to the top of **Mont Royal.** There are a web of options for trekking the small mountain, from using the broad and handsome pedestrian-only **chemin Olmsted** (a bridle path named for Frederick Law Olmsted, the park's landscape architect), to following smaller paths and sets of stairs. The park is well marked and small enough that you can wander without getting too lost, but the walking tour on p. 164 suggests one place to start and a number of options once you're inside.

JOGGING

There are many possibilities for running. In addition to the areas described above for biking and hiking, consider heading to the city's most prominent parks: **Parc La Fontaine** in the Plateau Mont-Royal neighborhood (p. 127), or **Parc Maisonneuve** in the city's east side, adjacent to the **Jardin Botanique** and across the street from **Olympic Park** (p. 118). Both parks are formally landscaped and well used for recreation and relaxation.

KAYAKING & ELECTRIC BOATING

It's fun to rent kayaks, large Rabaska canoes, pedal boats, or small eco-friendly electric boats on the quiet **Lachine Canal,** just to the west of Vieux-Port. **H2O Adventures** (© **877/935-2925** or 514/842-1306; www.h2oadventures.com)

The Lachine Canal is a quiet place for kayaking.

won a Grand Prix du tourisme Québécois award for being a standout operation. Their rentals start at C$8 per half-hour. Two-hour introductory kayak lessons, on Wednesday nights and Sunday afternoons, start at C$35. From June to August, the shop is open daily from 9am to 9pm. Cross the footbridge past Marché Atwater (p. 181), where you can also pick up lunch from the inside *boulangerie* and *fromagerie,* adjacent to the canal.

SWIMMING

On Parc Jean-Drapeau, the island park just across the harbor of Vieux-Port, there is an outdoor swimming pool complex and a lakeside beach, the **Plage des Iles** (© **514/872-2323;** www.parcjeandrapeau.com). Admission to the beach is C$6 adults, C$3 children 3 to 13, and free for children 2 and under. Métro: Jean-Drapeau.

Cold-Weather Activities

CROSS-COUNTRY SKIING

Parc du Mont-Royal has an extensive cross-country course, as do many of the other city parks, though skiers have to supply their own equipment. Just an hour from the city, north in the Laurentides and east in the Cantons de l'Est, there are numerous options for skiing and rentals; see chapter 11 for more information.

ICE SKATING

In the winter, outdoor skating rinks are set up in Vieux-Port, Lac des Castors (Beaver Lake), and other spots around the city; check tourist offices for your best options. One of the most agreeable venues for skating any time of the year is **Atrium Le 1000** (p. 130) in the downtown skyscraper at 1000 rue de la Gauchetière ouest. It's indoors and warm, and it's surrounded by cafes at which to relax after twirling around the big rink. And yes, it's even open in the summer.

MONTRÉAL STROLLS

8

Cities best reveal themselves on foot, and Montréal is one of North America's most pedestrian-friendly locales. There's much to see in the concentrated districts—cobblestoned Vieux-Montréal, downtown and its luxurious "Golden Square Mile," bustling Plateau Mont-Royal, and Mont Royal itself—and in this chapter are strolls that will take you to the best of all of them.

Also listed is a destination walk that gets you to Marché Atwater, a large year-round market. The walk takes you past some of the best antiquing in the city and is a way to take in an interesting area the way locals do.

The city's layout is mostly straightforward and simple to navigate, and the extensive Métro system gets you to and from neighborhoods with ease. These strolls will give you a taste of what's best about old and new Montréal, and send you off to discover highlights of your own.

WALKING TOUR 1: **VIEUX-MONTRÉAL**

START:	**Place d' Armes, opposite the Notre-Dame Basilica.**
FINISH:	**Vieux-Port.**
TIME:	**2 hours.**
BEST TIMES:	**Almost any day the weather is decent. Vieux-Montréal is lively and safe, day or night. Note that most museums are closed on Monday. On warm weekends and holidays, Montréalers and visitors turn out in full force, enjoying the plazas, the 18th- and 19th-century architecture, and the ambience of the most picturesque part of their city.**
WORST TIMES:	**Evenings, days that are too cold, and times when museums and historic buildings are closed. Sunny days in winter are known to be particularly cold (as opposed to those when it is snowing and temperatures are notably warmer), but you can take advantage of the bright light. Do as the locals do and wear a warm coat, a toque, mitts, and good boots.**

Vieux-Montréal is where the city was born. Its architectural heritage has been substantially preserved, and restored 18th- and 19th-century structures now house shops, boutique hotels, galleries, cafes, bars, and apartments. This tour gives you a lay of the land, passing many of the neighborhood's highlights and some of its best and most atmospheric dining spots.

If you're coming from outside Vieux-Montréal, take the Métro to the Place d'Armes station, which lets off next to the Palais des Congrès, the convention center. Follow the signs up the short hill 2 blocks toward Vieux-Montréal (Old Montréal) and the Place d'Armes. On the north side of the plaza, at 119 St-Jacques, is the domed, colonnaded:

PREVIOUS PAGE: **A cyclist passes the cross atop Mont Royal.**

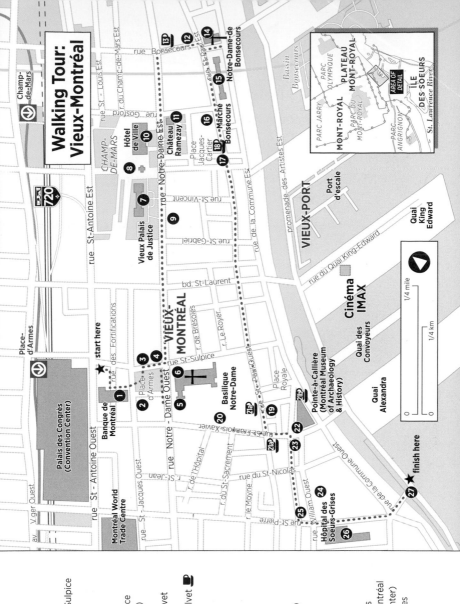

Walking Tour: Vieux-Montréal

1 Banque de Montréal
2 Place d'Armes
3 Édifice New York Life
4 Édifice Aldred
5 Vieux Séminaire de St-Sulpice
6 Basilique Notre-Dame
7 Vieux Palais de Justice
   (Old Courthouse)
8 Place Vauquelin
9 Tourist Information Office
10 Hôtel de Ville (City Hall)
11 Château Ramezay
12 La Maison Pierre du Calvet
   (Calvet House)
13 Hostellerie Pierre du Calvet
14 Chapelle Notre-Dame-
   de-Bon-Secours
15 Marché Bonsecours
   (Bonsecours Market)
16 Hôtel Rasco
17 Place Jacques-Cartier
18 Le Jardin Nelson
19 Vieille Douane
   (Old Customs House)
20 Centaur Theatre
21a Stash Café
21b L'Arrivage Café
22 Pointe-à-Callière
23 Obelisk
24 Youville Stables/Gibby's
25 Centre d'Histoire de Montréal
   (Montréal History Center)
26 Hôpital des Soeurs Grises
   (Grey Nuns Hospital)
27 Vieux-Port (Old Port)

145

The centerpiece of Place d'Armes is a monument to city founder Paul de Chomedey.

1   Banque de Montréal

Montréal's oldest bank building dates from 1847. From 1901 to 1905, American architect Stanford White (1853–1906) extended the original building, and in this enlarged space, he created a vast chamber with green-marble columns topped with golden capitals. The public is welcome to stop in for a look. Besides being lavishly appointed inside and out, the bank also houses a small **banking museum** (p. 133), which illustrates early operations. It's just off the main lobby to the left and admission is free.

Exiting the bank, cross the street to:

2   Place d'Armes

The architecture of the buildings that surround this plaza is representative of Montréal's growth: the Sulpician residence of the 17th century (no. 5, below); the Banque de Montréal and Basilique Notre-Dame (no. 6, below) of the 19th century; and the Art Deco Edifice Aldred (no. 4, below) of the 20th century.

The centerpiece of the square is a monument to city founder Paul de Chomedey, Sieur de Maisonneuve (1612–1676). The five statues that usually are here (on a recent visit, they had been removed for renovation of the park, which is to be completed by May 2012) mark the spot where settlers defeated Iroquois warriors in bloody hand-to-hand fighting, with de Maisonneuve himself locked in combat with the Iroquois chief. De Maisonneuve won and lived here another 23 years. The inscription on the monument reads (in French): YOU ARE THE BUCKWHEAT SEED WHICH WILL GROW AND MULTIPLY AND SPREAD THROUGHOUT THE COUNTRY.

The sculptures at the base of the monument represent other prominent citizens of early Montréal: Charles Lemoyne (1626–1685), a farmer; Jeanne Mance (1606–1673), a woman who founded the city's first hospital; Raphael-Lambert Closse (1618–1662), a soldier and the mayor of Ville-Marie; and an unnamed Iroquois brave. Closse is depicted with his dog, Pilote, whose bark once warned the early settlers of an impending Iroquois attack.

Facing the Notre-Dame Basilica from the square, look over to the left. At the corner of St-Jacques is the:

3 Edifice New York Life

This red-stone Richardson Romanesque building, with a striking wrought-iron door and clock tower, is at 511 Place d'Armes. At all of eight stories, this became Montréal's first skyscraper in 1888, and it was equipped with a technological marvel—an elevator.

Next to it, on the right, stands the 23-story Art Deco:

4 Edifice Aldred

If this building looks somehow familiar, there's a reason: Built in 1931, it clearly resembles New York's Empire State Building, also completed that year. The building's original tenant was Aldred and Co. Ltd., a New York–based finance company with other offices in New York, London, and Paris.

Facing the Notre-Dame Basilica again, just to its right is the:

5 Vieux Séminaire de St-Sulpice

The city's oldest building is surrounded by equally ancient stone walls. This seminary was erected by Sulpician priests who arrived in Ville-Marie in 1657, 15 years after the colony was founded (the Sulpicians are part of an order founded in Paris in 1641). The clock on the facade dates from 1701, and its gears are made almost entirely of wood. It has been under renovation in recent years. The seminary is not open to the public.

After a look through the iron gate, head east on rue Notre-Dame to the magnificent Gothic Revival–style:

6 Basilique Notre-Dame

This brilliantly crafted church was designed in 1824 by James O'Donnell, an Irish Protestant living in New York. Transformed by his experience, he converted to Roman Catholicism and is the only person interred here. The main altar is made from a hand-carved linden tree. Behind it is the Chapel of the Sacred Heart (1982), a perennially popular choice for weddings (Québec-born singer Céline Dion married her manager René Angélil here in 1994). The chapel's altar, 32 bronze panels by Montréal artist Charles Daudelin, represents birth, life, and death. Some 4,000 people can attend at a time, and the bell, one of North America's largest, weighs 12 tons. There's a small museum beside the chapel. Come back at night for a romantic take on the city, when more than a score of buildings in the area, including this one, are illuminated. During the Christmas season, three white angels are suspended at the entrance with ethereal blue lighting. See p. 115 for more about the church.

Exiting the basilica, turn right (east) on rue Notre-Dame. Cross rue St-Sulpice. On the north side of rue Notre-Dame is Claude Postel, a great place for sandwiches and pastries. Walk 4 blocks, passing chintzy souvenir shops, until you reach, on the left side, the grand:

7 Vieux Palais de Justice (Old Courthouse)

Most of this structure was built in 1856. The third floor and dome were added in 1891, and the difference between the original structure and the addition can be easily discerned with a close look. A second city courthouse, designed by Ernest-Cormier, was built in 1925 and is across the street, with a long colonnade. Since 1971, all legal business has been conducted in a third courthouse, the glass-encased building 1 block back, at 1 rue Notre-Dame est. The statue beside the Old Courthouse, called *Homage to Marguerite Bourgeoys,* depicts a teacher and nun and is the work of sculptor Jules LaSalle.

Also on your left, just past the courthouse, is:

8 Place Vauquelin

This small public square, with a splashing fountain and view of the Champ-de-Mars park, was created in 1858. The statue is of Jean Vauquelin (1728–1772), commander of the French fleet in New France; he stares across rue Notre-Dame at his counterpart, the English admiral Horatio Nelson (1758–1805). The two statues are symbols of Montréal's French and British duality.

On the opposite corner is a small but helpful:

9 Tourist Information Office

A bilingual staff stands ready to answer questions and hand out useful brochures and maps. It's open daily from April 1 to November 15 and closed in winter. The famed Silver Dollar Saloon once stood on this site. It got its name from the 350 silver dollars that were embedded in its floor.

Around the corner, on the right, is the Place Jacques-Cartier, a magnet for citizens and visitors year-round, which we will visit later in the stroll. Rising on the other side of rue Notre-Dame, opposite the top of the square, is the impressive, green-capped:

10 Hôtel de Ville (City Hall)

Built between 1872 and 1878 in the florid French Second Empire style, the edifice is seen to particular advantage when it is illuminated at night. In 1922, it barely survived a disastrous fire. Only the exterior walls remained, and after substantial rebuilding and the addition of another floor, it reopened in 1926. Take a minute to look inside at the generous use of French marble, the Art Deco lamps, and the bronze-and-glass chandelier. The sculptures at the entry are *Woman with a Pail* and *The Sower,* both by Québec sculptor Alfred Laliberté. See p. 124 for more details.

Exiting City Hall, you'll see, across rue Notre-Dame, a small, terraced park with orderly ranks of trees. The statue inside the park honors Montréal's controversial longtime mayor, Jean Drapeau (1916–1999). Next to it is:

11 Château Ramezay

Beginning in 1705, this was the home of the city's French governors for 4 decades, starting with Claude de Ramezay, before being taken over and used for the same purpose by the British. In 1775, an army of American rebels invaded and held Montréal, using the house as their headquarters. Benjamin Franklin was sent to try to persuade Montréalers to join the American revolt against British rule, and he stayed in this château. He failed to sway Québec's leaders to join the radical cause. Today, the house shows off furnishings, oil paintings, costumes, and other objects related to the economic and social activities of the 18th century and the first half of the 19th century. In summertime, nearby restaurant **Le Club Chasse et Pêche** (www.leclubchasseetpeche.com) serves an haute cuisine lunch in the garden under a posh white tent. See p. 125 for more about the museum.

Continue in the same direction (east) along rue Notre-Dame. In the far distance, you'll see the Molson beer factory. At rue Bonsecours, turn right. Near the bottom of the street, on the left, is a house with a low maroon roof and an attached stone building on the corner. This is:

12 La Maison Pierre du Calvet (Calvet House)

Built in the 18th century and sumptuously restored between 1964 and 1966, this house was inhabited by a fairly well-to-do family in its first years. Pierre du Calvet, believed to be the original owner, was a French Huguenot who supported the American Revolution. Calvet met with Benjamin Franklin here in 1775 and was imprisoned from 1780 to 1783 for supplying money to the Americans. With a characteristic sloped roof meant to discourage snow buildup and raised end walls that serve as firebreaks, the building is constructed of Montréal gray stone. It is now a **restaurant** and *hostellerie* (p. 73) with an entrance at no. 405. In 2009, eccentric owner/sculptor Gaëtan Trottier opened the Musée du Bronze on-site, as well. Visitors are invited to come in for a look.

13 Hostellerie Pierre du Calvet 🍵

There is a voluptuously appointed dining room inside the Hostellerie Pierre du Calvet, 405 rue Bonsecours, called Les Filles du Roy. The cuisine is nothing to write home about, but in the warm months, lunches, dinners, and Sunday brunches are served in a lovely outdoor courtyard that opened to the public in 2007 (before then, it was privately used by the owner, who still lives on the premises). Take a peek to see the greenhouse and parrots that lead to the stone-walled terrace.

The next street, rue St-Paul, is Montréal's oldest thoroughfare, dating from 1672. The church at this intersection is the small:

14 Chapelle Notre-Dame-de-Bon-Secours

Called the Sailors' Church because so many seamen made pilgrimages here to give thanks for being saved at sea, this chapel was founded by Marguerite Bourgeoys, a nun and teacher who was canonized in 1982. Excavations have unearthed foundations of her original 1675 church—although the building has been much altered, and the present facade was built in the late 18th century. A **museum** (p. 123) tells the story of Bourgeoys's life and incorporates the archaeological site. Climb up to the tower for a view of the port and Old Town.

Head west on rue St-Paul. Just beyond the Sailors' Church is an imposing building with a colonnaded facade and silvery dome, the limestone:

15 Marché Bonsecours (Bonsecours Market)

Completed in 1847, this building was used first as the Parliament of United Canada and then as the City Hall, the central market, a music hall, and then the home of the municipality's housing and planning offices. It was restored in 1992 for the city's 350th birthday celebration to house temporary exhibitions and musical performances. It continues to be used for exhibitions, but it's more of a retail center now, with an eclectic selection of local art shops, clothing boutiques, and sidewalk cafes (p. 124). When Bonsecours Market was first built, the dome could be seen from everywhere in the city and served as a landmark for seafarers sailing into the harbor. Today, it is lit at night.

Continue down rue St-Paul. At no. 281 is the former:

16 Hôtel Rasco

An Italian, Francisco Rasco, came to Canada to manage a hotel for the Molson family (of beer-brewing fame) and later became successful with his own hotel on this spot. The 150-room Rasco was the Ritz-Carlton of its day, hosting Charles Dickens and his wife in 1842, when the author was directing his plays at a theater that used to stand across the street. The hotel lives on in legend, if not in fact, as it's devoid of much of its original architectural detail and no longer hosts overnight guests. Between 1960 and 1981, the space stood empty, but the city took it over and restored it in 1982. It has contained a succession of eateries on the ground floor. The current occupant is L'Autre Version restaurant, whose inner courtyard/al fresco dining space is a hidden gem (www.restoversion.com).

Continue heading west on rue St-Paul, turning right when you reach:

17 Place Jacques-Cartier

Opened as a marketplace in 1804, this is the most appealing of Vieux-Montréal's squares, even with its obviously touristy aspects. The square's cobbled cross streets, gentle downhill slope, and ancient buildings set the mood, while outdoor cafes, street entertainers, itinerant artists, and assorted vendors invite lingering in warm weather. The Ben & Jerry's ice-cream shop doesn't hurt either. Calèches (horse-drawn carriages) depart from both the lower and the upper ends of the square for tours of Vieux-Montréal.

Walk slowly uphill, taking in the old buildings that bracket the plaza (plaques describe some of them in French and English). All these houses were well suited to the rigors of life in the raw young settlement. Their steeply pitched roofs shed the heavy winter snows, rather than collapsing under the burden, and small windows with double casements let in light while keeping out wintry breezes. When shuttered, the windows were almost as effective as the heavy stone walls in deflecting hostile arrows or the antics of trappers fresh from nearby taverns. At the plaza's northern end

Place Jacques-Cartier during a summer evening.

stands a monument to Horatio Nelson, hero of Trafalgar, erected in 1809. This monument preceded London's much larger version by several years. After years of vandalism, presumably by Québec separatists, the statue had to be temporarily removed for restoration. The original Nelson is now back in place at the crown of the column.

18 Le Jardin Nelson ☕

Most of the old buildings in and around the inclined plaza house restaurants and cafes. For a drink or snack during the warm months, try to find a seat in Le Jardin Nelson (no. 407), near the bottom of the hill. It's extremely popular with tourists, and for good reason. The tiered-level courtyard in back often has live jazz, while tables on the terrace overlook the square's activity.

Return to rue St-Paul and continue west. Take time to window-shop the many art galleries that have sprung up alongside the loud souvenir shops on the street. If time permits, enjoy a drink at one of the bars along the way. The street numbers will get lower as you approach boulevard St-Laurent, the north-south thoroughfare that divides Montréal into its east and west halves. Numbers will start to rise again as you move onto St-Paul ouest (west). At 150 rue St-Paul ouest is the neoclassical:

19 Vieille Douane (Old Customs House)

Erected from 1836 to 1838, this building was doubled in size when an extension to the south side was added in 1882; walk around to the building's other side to see how the addition is different. That end of the building faces Place Royale, the first public square in the 17th-century settlement of Ville-Marie. It's where Europeans and Amerindians used to come to trade. The building now houses a **boutique** (p. 184) for the **Pointe-à-Callière museum** (p. 116).

Continue on rue St-Paul to rue St-François-Xavier. Turn right for a short detour; up rue St-François-Xavier, on the right, is the stately:

20 Centaur Theatre

The home of Montréal's principal English-language theater is a former stock-exchange building. The Beaux Arts architecture is interesting in that the two entrances are on either side, rather than in the center, of the facade. American architect George Post, who was also responsible for designing the New York Stock Exchange, designed this building, erected in 1903. It served its original function until 1965, when it was redesigned as a theater with two stages. See p. 190 for theater information.

Return back down rue St-François-Xavier to rue St-Paul.

21 Stash Café & L'Arrivage Café ☕

One possibility for lunch or a pick-me-up is the moderately priced Stash Café at 200 rue St-Paul ouest (at the corner of rue St-François-Xavier). It specializes in Polish fare and opens daily at noon. Another option is the glass-walled, second-floor L'Arrivage Café at the Pointe-à-Callière museum, your next stop. Its lunchtime table d'hôte menu starts at C$11.

Continue on rue St-François-Xavier past St-Paul. At the next corner, the gray wedge-shaped building to the left is the:

22 Pointe-à-Callière

Known in English as the **Museum of Archaeology and History,** Pointe-à-Callière is packed with artifacts unearthed during more than a decade of excavation at the spot, where the settlement of Ville-Marie was founded in 1642. An underground connection also incorporates the **Old Customs House** you just passed. See p. 116 for more about this top-notch museum.

A fort stood here in 1645. Thirty years later, a château was built on the site for Louis-Hector de Callière, the governor of New France, from whom the museum and triangular square that it's on take their names. At that time, the St. Pierre River separated this piece of land from the mainland. It was made a canal in the 19th century and later filled in.

Proceeding west from Pointe-à-Callière, near rue St-François-Xavier, stands an:

23 Obelisk

Commemorating the founding of Ville-Marie on May 18, 1642, the obelisk was erected here in 1893 by the Montréal Historical Society. It bears the names of the city's early pioneers, including French officer Paul Chomedey de Maisonneuve, who landed in Montréal in 1642, and fellow settler Jeanne Mance, who founded North America's first hospital, l'Hôtel-Dieu de Montréal.

Continuing west from the obelisk 2 blocks to 296–316 Place d'Youville, you'll find, on the left, the:

24 Ecuries d'Youville (Youville Stables)

Despite the name, the rooms in the iron-gated compound, built in 1825 on land owned by the Gray Nuns, were used mainly as warehouses, rather than as horse stables (the actual stables, next door, were made of wood and disappeared long ago). Like much of the waterfront area, the U-shaped Youville building was run-down and forgotten until the 1960s, when a group of enterprising businesspeople bought and renovated it. Today, the compound contains offices and a steakhouse, **Gibby's,** 298 Place d'Youville (© **514/ 282-1837**), which is an institution, although not as hip with locals as La Queue de Cheval or Moishes. If the gates are open, go through the passage toward the restaurant door to see the inner courtyard.

Continue another block west to the front door of the brick building on your right, 335 Place d'Youville and the:

25 Centre d'Histoire de Montréal (Montréal History Center)

Built in 1903 as Montréal's central fire station, this building now houses exhibits about life in Montréal, past and present. Visitors learn about traditions of the Amerindians, early exploration, and the evolution of industry, architecture, and professions in the city from 1535 to current day. See p. 133 for details.

Head down rue St-Pierre toward the water. Midway down the block, on the right at no. 138, is the former:

26 Hôpital des Soeurs Grises (Grey Nuns Hospital)

The hospital was founded in 1693 by the Charon Brothers to serve the city's poor and homeless. Bankrupt by 1747, it was taken over by Marguerite d'Youville, founder in 1737 of the Sisters of Charity of Montréal, commonly known as the Grey Nuns. It was expanded several times, but by 1871, the nuns had moved away and portions were demolished to extend rue St-Pierre and make room for commercial buildings. A century later, the Grey Nuns returned to live in their original home. From the sidewalk, visitors can see a very cool contemporary sculpture of inscribed bronze strips that cover the surviving chapel walls. The text on the sculpture comes from a letter signed by Louis XIV in 1694, incorporating the hospital. There are three exhibition rooms open to the public, by appointment only (© **514/842-9411**).

Continue down rue St-Pierre and cross the main street, rue de la Commune, and then the railroad tracks to this tour's final stop:

27 Vieux-Port (Old Port)

Montréal's historic commercial wharves have been reborn as a waterfront park, which, in good weather, is frequented by cyclists, in-line skaters, joggers, walkers, strollers, and lovers. Across the water is the distinctive 158-unit modular housing project **Habitat 67,** built by famed architect Moshe Safdie for the 1967 World's Fair, which Montréal called Expo 67. Safdie's vision was to show what affordable community housing could be. Today, it's a higher-end apartment complex and not open to the public (aerial photos are at Safdie's website, www.msafdie.com); river surfers are known to "hit the waves" in a not-so-publicized spot just in back of this building.

Walk to your right. The triangular building you see is the entrance to **Jardin des Ecluses (Locks Garden),** a canal-side path where the St. Lawrence River's first locks are located. From here, you have several options: If the weather's nice, consider entering the Jardin des Ecluses to stroll the path along **Lachine Canal.** Only open in the summer season, **Café des Eclusiers,** 400 rue de la Commune ouest (© **514/496-0109**), offers a nice, scenic break. In under an hour, you'll arrive at Montréal's colorful **Marché Atwater** (p. 181), which is 3.8km (2¼ miles) down the path. If you walk the other direction, you'll take in the busiest section of the waterfront park and end up back at Place Jacques-Cartier.

To get to the subway, walk north along rue McGill to the Square-Victoria Métro station, the staircase to which is marked by an authentic Art Nouveau portal, designed by Hector Guimard for the Paris subway system. Or return to the small streets parallel to rue St-Paul, where you'll find more boutiques and one of the highest concentrations of art galleries in Canada.

DOWNTOWN

START:	**Bonaventure Métro station.**
FINISH:	**Musée des Beaux-Arts and rue Crescent.**
TIME:	**1½ hours.**
BEST TIMES:	**Weekdays in the morning or after 2pm, when the streets hum with big-city vibrancy but aren't *too* busy.**
WORST TIMES:	**Weekdays from noon to 2pm, when the streets, stores, and restaurants are crowded with businesspeople on lunch-break errands; Monday, when museums are closed; and Sunday, when many stores are closed and the area is nearly deserted.**

After a tour of Vieux-Montréal, a look around the commercial heart of the 21st-century city will highlight the ample contrast between these two areas. To see the city at its contemporary best, take the Métro to the Bonaventure stop to start this tour.

After you've emerged from the Métro station, the dramatic skyscraper immediately to the west (or directly above you, depending on which exit you take) is:

1 1000 rue de la Gauchetière

Also called "Le 1000," this contribution to downtown Montréal is easily identified by its copper-and-blue pyramidal top, which rises to the maximum height permitted by the municipal building code. Inside, past an atrium planted with live trees, is an indoor skating rink (p. 142).

Walk west on rue de la Gauchetière. Ahead is Le Marriott Château Champlain, whose distinctive façade of half-moon windows inspired its nickname "the Cheese Grater." Turn right on rue de la Cathedrale, heading north. At the next corner, you reach:

2 Boulevard René-Lévesque

Formerly Dorchester Boulevard, this primary street was renamed in 1988 following the death of René Lévesque, the Parti Québécois leader who led the movement for Québec independence and use of the French language. Boulevard René-Lévesque is the city's broadest downtown thoroughfare.

Across bd. René-Lévesque is:

3 Square Dorchester

This is one of downtown's central locations. It's a gathering point for tour buses and horse-drawn calèches, and the square's shade trees and benches invite lunchtime brown-baggers. This used to be called Dominion Square, but it was renamed for Baron Dorchester, an early English governor, when the adjacent street, once named for Dorchester, was changed to boulevard René-Lévesque. The square, which was recently spiffed up, was built over an old cemetery for 1832 cholera epidemic victims. Along the square's east side is the **Sun Life Insurance building,** built in three stages between 1914 and 1931, and the tallest building in Québec from 1931 until the skyscraper boom of the post–World War II era.

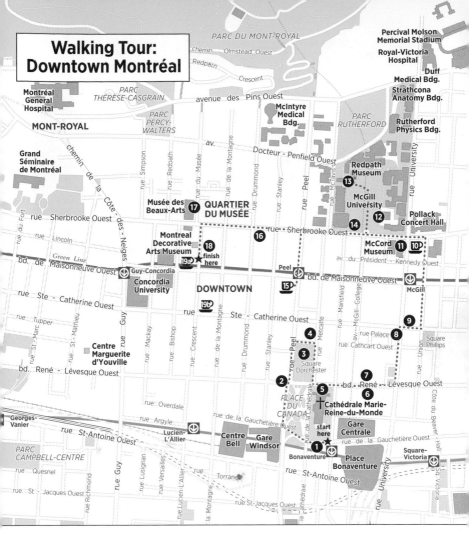

Walking Tour:
Downtown Montréal

1. 1000 rue de la Gauchetière
2. Boulevard René-Lévesque
3. Square Dorchester
4. Montréal's Central Tourist Office
5. Basilique-Cathédrale
   Marie-Reine-du-Monde
6. Fairmont The Queen Elizabeth
   (Le Reine Elizabeth)
7. Place Ville-Marie
8. Rue Ste-Catherine
9. Cathédrale Christ Church
10. Java U ☕
11. Musée McCord
12. McGill University
13. Musée Redpath
14. Site of the Amerindian
    Hochelaga Settlement
15. Café Vasco Da Gama ☕
16. Maison Alcan
17. Musée des Beaux-Arts
    (Museum of Fine Arts)
18. Rue Crescent
19a. Boustan ☕
19b. Sir Winston Churchill Pub ☕

Square Dorchester is a downtown gathering point.

At the north end of the square is:

4 Montréal's Central Tourist Office

The Infotouriste Centre at 1255 rue Peel has maps and brochures, most of them free for the taking. You can also ask questions of the bilingual attendants, purchase tour tickets, make hotel reservations, or rent a car. It's open daily.

On bd. René-Lévesque at the corner of Square Dorchester is the:

5 Basilique-Cathédrale Marie-Reine-du-Monde

Suddenly get the feeling you're in Rome? This cathedral is a copy of St. Peter's Basilica, albeit a fraction of the size. It was built as the headquarters for Montréal's Roman Catholic bishop. The statue in front is of Bishop Ignace Bourget, the force behind the construction. See p. 121.

Continue on bd. René-Lévesque past the cathedral. In the next block, on the right, is:

6 Fairmont the Queen Elizabeth (Le Reine Elizabeth)

Montréal's largest hotel (p. 66) stands above **Gare Centrale,** the main railroad station. The Fairmont is where John Lennon and Yoko Ono had their famous weeklong "Bed-in for Peace" in 1969. Lennon fans should also note there is a garden in his honor in Parc Mont-Royal near the Peel Street entrance.

On the other side of bd. René-Lévesque, directly across from the hotel, is:

7 Place Ville-Marie

One thing to keep in mind is that the French word *place,* or plaza, sometimes means an outdoor square, such as Place Jacques-Cartier in Vieux-Montréal. Other times, it refers to a building or complex that includes stores and offices. Place Ville-Marie is in the latter category. Known as PVM to Montréalers, the glass building was considered a gem of the 1960s urban redevelopment efforts. Its architect? None other than I.M. Pei, who also designed the glass pyramid at the Louvre in Paris. Pei gave the skyscraper a cross-shaped footprint, recalling the cross atop Mont Royal. The complex was completed in 1962.

Continue on bd. René-Lévesque to the end of the block and turn left on rue University. As you walk, look to the top of the skyscraper a few blocks down; this pink, postmodern glass office building is Tour KPMG and was completed in 1987. The two-peaked top is meant to resemble a bishop's miter, or cap, but many see the ears and mask of a certain DC Comics superhero. In 2 blocks, you'll reach:

8 Rue Ste-Catherine

This is one of the city's prime shopping streets, with name brands, local businesses, and department stores. Among them, to the right, is **La Baie**— or "the Bay"—successor to the famous fur-trapping firm Hudson's Bay Co., founded in the 17th century. Also here is **Henry Birks et Fils,** a preeminent jeweler since 1879—the building alone is worth taking in (see "Department Stores," p. 179). Inside the Birks Café is a decidedly posh spot to enjoy lunch, high tea, or buy some take-home chocolates or macaroons.

If you're in the mood to shop, stroll west on this main shopping drag. (Be aware that there are adult shops here, too, most of which are above street level and accessible by stairs.) To continue the tour, return to this corner and the:

9 Cathédrale Christ Church

Built from 1856 to 1859, this neo-Gothic building is the seat of the Anglican bishop of Montréal. The church garden is modeled on a medieval European cloister. In addition to Sunday's 10am Sung Eucharist and 4pm Choral Evensong, the church has services at 8am (7:45am Wed), noon, and 5:15pm on weekdays. See p. 122.

Walk east on rue Ste-Catherine to avenue Union, where the La Baie department store is. Turn left on av. Union and go north 3 blocks, to rue Sherbrooke. You'll be in front of McGill University's Schulich School of Music.

The 19th-century Cathédrale Christ Church.

10 Java U ☕

At the corner of Union and Sherbrooke is an outpost of the cheery Java U (626 rue Sherbrooke), a local coffee chain that got its start in 1996 at Concordia University. It's a buttoned-up venue with friendly, laid-back staff, serving quiches, salads, sandwich wraps, cake, and ice cream from local purveyor Bilboquet (p. 103).

Head left (west) on rue Sherbrooke. This is the city's grand boulevard, and the rest of the tour will take you past the former mansions, ritzy hotels, high-end boutiques, and special museums that give it its personality today. One block down on the left is:

11 Musée McCord

This museum of Canadian history opened in 1921 and was substantially renovated in 1992. Named for its founder, David Ross McCord, the museum maintains an eclectic collection of photographs, paintings, and First Nations folk art. Its special exhibits make it especially worth a visit. Hours and other details are on p. 112.

Continue west. On your right is:

12 McGill University

The gate is usually open to Canada's most prestigious university. It was founded in 1821 after a bequest from a Scottish-born fur trader, James McGill. The central campus mixes modern concrete and glass structures alongside older stone buildings and is the focal point for the school's 34,000 students.

On campus is the:

13 Musée Redpath

Housed in a building dating from 1882, this museum's main draws are the mummies in its Egyptian antiquities collection (p. 134).

Continue on rue Sherbrooke. About 9m (30 ft.) past McGill's front gate, note the large stone on the lawn. This marks the:

14 Site of the Amerindian Hochelaga Settlement

Near this spot was the village of Hochelaga, a community of Iroquois who lived and farmed here before the first Europeans arrived. When French explorer Jacques Cartier stepped from his ship onto the land and visited Hochelaga in 1535, he noted that the village had 50 large homes, each housing several families. When the French returned in 1603, the village was empty.

15 Café Vasco da Gama ☕

Downtown is full of restaurants both fancy and casual. Right in between is Café Vasco Da Gama, 1472 rue Peel (1 block south of rue Sherbrooke), a sleek, high-ceilinged eatery with a Portuguese feel—the owners also run the esteemed Ferreira Café (p. 84) on the same block. It features big breakfasts, pastries, sandwiches, and tapas.

Two blocks farther down on rue Sherbrooke, at no. 1188, just past rue Stanley, is:

16 Maison Alcan

Rue Sherbrooke is the heart of what's known as the "Golden Square Mile." This is where the city's most luxurious residences of the 19th and early 20th centuries were, and where the vast majority of the country's wealthiest citizens lived. (For a period of time, 79 families who lived in this neighborhood controlled 80% of Canada's wealth.) Maison Alcan is an example of a modern office building that has nicely incorporated one of those 19th-century mansions into its late-20th-century facade. Step inside the lobby to see the results over to the right. Also look across the street at Maison Louis-Joseph Forget at no. 1195 and Maison Reid Wilson at no 1201. Both are designated historic monuments.

Continue on rue Sherbrooke, passing on your left the Holt Renfrew department store. At the corner of rue Crescent is the:

17 Musée des Beaux-Arts (Museum of Fine Arts)

This is Canada's oldest museum and Montréal's most prominent. The modern annex on the left side of rue Sherbrooke was added in 1991 and is connected to the original stately Beaux Arts building (1912) on the right side by an underground tunnel that doubles as a gallery. The adjacent church is being converted into an addition to the museum and was set to open in 2011. See p. 109 for details.

There are several options at this point. If you have time to explore the museum, take the opportunity—a visit to the Musée des Beaux-Arts should be part of any trip to Montréal. For high-end boutique shopping, continue on rue Sherbrooke. For drinking or eating, turn left onto:

18 Rue Crescent

Welcome to party central. Rue Crescent and nearby streets are the focal point of the downtown social and dining district. The area is largely yuppie-Anglo in character, if not necessarily in strict demographics. Crescent's first block is stocked with boutiques and jewelers, but the next 2 blocks are a gumbo of terraced bars and dance clubs, inexpensive pizza joints, and upscale restaurants, all drawing enthusiastic consumers looking to party the afternoon and evening away. It's hard to imagine that this was once a run-down slum slated for demolition. Luckily, buyers saw potential in these late-19th-century row houses and brought them back to life.

19 Sir Winston Churchill & Boustan 🍲

Lively spots for food and drink are abundant along rue Crescent. Sir Winston Churchill Pub (no. 1459) is one, if you can find a seat on the balcony.

For a satisfying snack, consider a filling shawarma sandwich from the unassuming Lebanese joint Boustan (no. 2020; p. 87). Yes, that's former Canadian Prime Minister Pierre Trudeau's photo at the register; he was a regular.

WALKING TOUR 3: **PLATEAU MONT-ROYAL**

START:	**The corner of avenue du Mont-Royal and rue St-Denis.**
FINISH:	**Square St-Louis or Parc LaFontaine.**
TIME:	**At least 2 hours, but allow more time if you want to linger in shops, restaurants, or the major park of this intriguing neighborhood.**
BEST TIMES:	**Monday through Saturday during the day, when shops are open. Most of this area is at its liveliest on Saturday. For barhopping, evenings work well.**
WORST TIMES:	**Early mornings, when stores and restaurants are closed.**

This is essentially a browsing-and-grazing tour, designed to provide a sampling of the sea of ethnicities that make up Plateau Mont-Royal, north of downtown Montréal and east of Mont-Royal Park. The largely Francophone neighborhood has seen an unprecedented flourishing of restaurants, cafes, clubs, and shops in recent years. It's bounded on the south by rue Sherbrooke, on the north by boulevard St-Joseph (where the Mile End neighborhood begins), on the west by avenue du Parc, and on the east by avenue Papineau. The residential side streets are filled with row houses that are home to students, young professionals, and immigrants old and new. This walk provides a glance into the lives of both established and freshly minted Montréalers and the ways in which they spend their leisure time. Stores and bistros open and close with considerable frequency in this neighborhood, so be forewarned that some of the highlights listed below may not exist when you visit.

To begin, take the Métro to the Mont-Royal station. Turn left out of the station and walk west on avenue du Mont-Royal to rue St-Denis. Turn left again onto rue St-Denis. The next 4 blocks are filled with some of the best local boutique shopping and Francophone dining in the city. On the left side of the street, at 4481 rue St-Denis, is:

1 Quai des Brumes

This popular gathering spot for electronic, rock, jazz, and blues music—and beer—offers live music on most evenings.

Stroll down rue St-Denis, pausing at shops and cafes that fill the two stories of the small buildings. Toward the end of the block, on the other side of the street, is no. 4380 (but do not cross midstreet; police here give tickets for jaywalking):

2 Renaud-Bray

A large bookstore (p. 175) with mostly French stock, it also carries travel guides and literature in English, as well as CDs, magazines, and newspapers from around the world. Most of the books are upstairs. It's open daily from 9am until 10pm.

Continue south on rue St-Denis. On the next block, at no. 4306, is:

3 Départ en Mer

This small shop with "antiquitiés marines" carries model ships, boating clothes, and shoes.

In the same block, at no. 4268, is:

4 Jacob

With pop music through the speakers and a steady stream of locals, this clothing store is part of the popular Canadian chain where you'll find inexpensive T-shirts, denim jackets, and other casual clothes for the under-30 set.

A little farther, at no. 4246, is:

5 Zone

Zone is a small Montréal-based chain (there are two other stores in Montréal and others in Québec City and Ottawa) that specializes in contemporary housewares, sleekly monochromatic and brightly hued (p. 183).

A little farther still, at no. 4228, is:

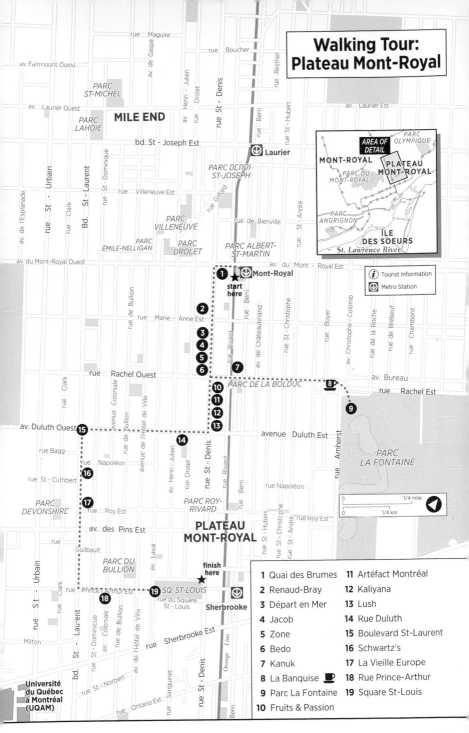

6　Bedo

Another Montréal-based chain, this one has higher-end men's and women's designer sportswear, with colorful blouses in the C$70 range, fun dresses, and well-fitted shirts. This outlet is one of 10 in the city.

At the next intersection, rue Rachel, turn left for a short diversion off of rue St-Denis. On your left at no. 485 is:

7　Kanuk

One of Canada's top manufacturers of winter coats and accessories designs, sews, and sells its wares right here (p. 178). Kanuk first sold its heavy parkas primarily to outdoor enthusiasts. Back then, the company wryly notes on its website, customers had a choice of royal blue or royal blue. Today, jackets come in a multitude of colors and styles. The showroom's fluorescent lighting and mile-high racks do not suggest luxury, but a parka can set you back at least C$600. They're a popular practical necessity—and a status symbol.

Kanuk is one of Canada's top manufacturers of winter coats.

8　La Banquise 🍴

If you haven't yet tried *poutine*, the national comfort food, by all means hop into La Banquise, at 994 rue Rachel est. The restaurant is practically a city landmark, what with its 25 variations on *poutine:* The standard French fries with gravy and cheese curds are offered with add-ons ranging from smoked sausage to hot peppers to smoked meat to bacon. It's open 24 hours a day, every day. See p. 101.

Just beyond the restaurant is the grand:

9　Parc La Fontaine

Strolling this park, particularly on a warm day, is an enormously satisfying way to see Montréal at play. This northwestern end of La Fontaine is well used by people (and puppies) of all ages. In summer, the 2,500-seat **Théâtre de Verdure,** near where rue Duluth runs into the park, becomes an open-air venue for dance, music, theater, and film. In winter, the two ponds are linked and become a skating rink (skate rentals available).

There's a bike-rental shop at this corner just before you enter the park, at 1000 rue Rachel est (www.cyclepop.ca). If you're keen to explore the park or head off for a bike ride, consider this tour done. The Sherbrooke Métro will be closest if you leave the park on its west side. To continue the stroll, retrace your steps to go back to rue St-Denis. Turn left and continue south. Among the boutiques still to explore, at 4159 rue St-Denis, is:

10　Fruits & Passion

This is the newest location in Montréal of the rapidly growing Canadian company that specializes in aromatic lotions, soaps, and products for household and pet care (p. 174).

MONTRÉAL STROLLS　|　Plateau Mont-Royal

8

At 4117 rue St-Denis, is:

11 Artéfact Montréal

Québécois designers sell clothing and paintings at this bright little boutique, where a slip of a summer dress runs about C$250.

After that, find no. 4107:

12 Kaliyana

More women's clothes from a Canadian designer (p. 177): This shop's natural-fiber outfits are flowing, angular, and border on being avant-garde—think Asian-influenced Eileen Fisher. It also stocks contemporary footwear, including Arche from France and Trippen from Germany.

At no. 4067, take a whiff of:

13 Lush

On the ground floor of one of the street's prettiest Queen Anne Victorian row houses, British-import Lush sells soaps presented and wrapped as if they were bubble-gum-colored hunks of cheese.

At the next corner is rue Duluth. Turn right here to get a taste of:

14 Rue Duluth

This street is dotted with an ever-changing collection of Greek, Portuguese, Italian, North African, Malaysian, and Vietnamese eateries. Many of the restaurants state that you can *apportez votre vin* (bring your own wine). There are also several small antiques shops.

Continue along rue Duluth until boulevard St-Laurent, the north-south thoroughfare that divides Montréal into its east and west sides. Turn left.

15 Boulevard St-Laurent

St-Laurent is so prominent in Montréal's cultural history that it's known to Anglophones, Francophones, and Allophones (people whose primary language is neither English nor French) alike simply as "the Main." Traditionally a beachhead for immigrants to the city, St-Laurent has become a street of chic bistros and clubs. The late-night section runs for several miles, roughly from rue Laurier in the north all the way down to rue Sherbrooke in the south. The bistro and club boom was fueled by low rent prices and the large number of industrial lofts in this area, a legacy of St-Laurent's heyday as a garment-manufacturing center. Today, these cavernous spaces are places for the city's hipsters, professionals, artists, and guests to eat and play. Many spots have the life spans of fireflies, but some pound on for years.

At 3895 bd. St-Laurent, you'll find:

16 Schwartz's

The language police insisted on the exterior sign with the French mouthful CHEZ SCHWARTZ CHARCUTERIE HEBRAIQUE DE MONTREAL, but everyone just calls it Schwartz's (p. 100). This narrow, no-frills Jewish deli might appear completely unassuming, but it serves smoked meat against which all other smoked meats must be measured. Don't forget a side of fries, a couple of garlicky pickles, and a cherry soda.

Next, a few steps along at no. 3855, is:

17 La Vieille Europe

An old-European-style deli that sells aromatic coffee beans from around the world, sausages and meats, cheeses, cooking utensils, and other gourmet fare (p. 180). Stock up here if you're thinking of having a picnic in the next day or two.

Continue down bd. St-Laurent 2 more blocks and turn left (east) onto:

18 Rue Prince-Arthur

Named after Queen Victoria's third son, who was governor-general of Canada from 1911 to 1916, this pedestrian street is filled with bars, restaurants, and ice-cream parlors that add more to the area's liveliness than to the city's gastronomic reputation. The older establishments go by such names as La Cabane Grecque, La Caverne Grec, Casa Grecque—no doubt you will discern an emerging theme—but the Greek stalwarts are being challenged by Latino and Asian newcomers. Their owners vie for customers constantly, with such gimmicks as two-for-one drinks and dueling tables d'hôte. Tables and chairs are set out along the sides of the street, and in warm weather, street performers, vendors, and caricaturists also compete for tourist dollars.

Five short blocks later, rue Prince-Arthur ends at:

19 Square St-Louis

This public garden plaza is framed by attractive row houses erected for well-to-do Francophones in the late 19th and early 20th centuries with a fountain in the middle. People stretch out on the grass to take in the sun or sit bundled on benches willing March away. The square ends at rue St-Denis. It should be noted that although this plaza is pretty and has a cute little ice-cream shop on one end, not everyone will appreciate the street-kid crowd that hangs out here.

To pick up the Métro, cross rue St-Denis and walk east on rue des Malines. The Sherbrooke station is just ahead at the corner of rue Berri.

WALKING TOUR 4: **PARC DU MONT-ROYAL**

START:	**At the corner of rue Peel and avenue des Pins.**
FINISH:	**At the cross on top of the mountain (la Croix du Mont-Royal).**
TIME:	**1 hour to ascend to the Chalet du Mont-Royal and its lookout over the city and come back down by the fastest route; 3 hours to take the more leisurely chemin Olmstead route and see all the sites listed below. It's easy to leave out some sites to truncate the walk.**
BEST TIMES:	**Spring, summer, and autumn mornings.**
WORST TIMES:	**During the high heat of midday in summer, or in winter, when snow and slush make a sleigh ride to the top of the mountain much more enticing than a hike.**

Join the locals: Assuming a reasonable measure of physical fitness, the best way to explore the jewel that is Parc du Mont-Royal is simply to walk up it from downtown. It's called a mountain, but is more like a very large hill. A broad

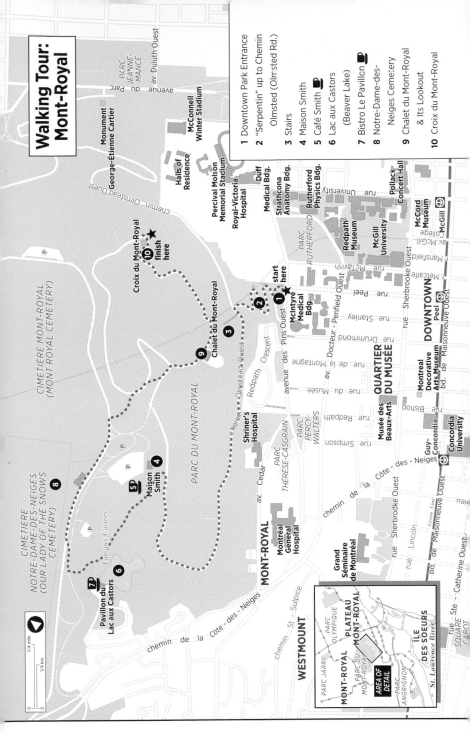

Walking Tour: Mont-Royal

1 Downtown Park Entrance
2 "Serpentin" up to Chemin Olmsted (Olmsted Rd.)
3 Stairs
4 Maison Smith
5 Café Smith
6 Lac aux Castors (Beaver Lake)
7 Bistro Le Pavillon
8 Notre-Dame-des-Neiges Cemetery
9 Chalet du Mont-Royal & Its Lookout
10 Croix du Mont-Royal

CIMETIÈRE MONT-ROYAL
(MONT ROYAL CEMETERY)

CIMETIÈRE NOTRE-DAME-DES-NEIGES
(OUR LADY OF THE SNOWS CEMETERY)

PARC DU MONT-ROYAL

MONT-ROYAL

Lac aux Castors

Pavillon du Lac aux Castors

Maison Smith

Chalet du Mont-Royal

Croix du Mont-Royal
finish here

start here

McIntyre Medical Bdg.

PARC RUTHERFORD

PARC PERCY-WALTERS

PARC THÉRÈSE-CASGRAIN

Shriner's Hospital

Montréal General Hospital

Grand Séminaire de Montréal

chemin de la Côte-des-Neiges

av. Cedar

Redpath Crescent

avenue des Pins Ouest

chemin Olmstead Ouest

Redpath

rue du Musée

av. du Musée

rue de la Montagne

rue Drummond

rue Stanley

rue Peel

rue Metcalfe

rue Mansfield

av. McGill Collège

rue Docteur-Penfield Ouest

rue Sherbrooke Ouest

rue Simpson

rue Redpath

rue Bishop

bd. de Maisonneuve Ouest

rue Lincoln

rue Ste-Catherine Ouest

chemin de la Côte-des-Neiges

chemin St-Sulpice

Shriner's Hospital

Duff Medical Bdg.

Royal-Victoria Hospital

Percival Molson Memorial Stadium

Halls of Residence

McConnell Winter Stadium

Monument George-Étienne Cartier

PARC JEANNE-MANCE

avenue du Parc

av. Duluth Ouest

chemin Olmsted Ouest

Strathcona Anatomy Bdg.

Rutherford Physics Bdg.

Redpath Museum

McGill University

Pollack Concert Hall

rue University

rue McTavish

McCord Museum
McGill

Peel

Guy-Concordia

Concordia University

Montreal Decorative Arts Museum

Musée des Beaux-Arts

QUARTIER DU MUSÉE

DOWNTOWN

Green Line

St. Lawrence River

WESTMOUNT

PLATEAU MONT-ROYAL

ÎLE DES SŒURS

PARC JARRY

PARC OLYMPIQUE

PARC DU MONT-ROYAL

MONT-ROYAL

PARC ANGRIGNON

rue Ste-Catherine Ouest

SQUARE CABOT

AREA OF DETAIL

1/4 mile
1/4 km

N

pedestrian-only road and smaller footpaths form a web of options for strollers, joggers, cyclists, and in-line skaters of all ages. Anyone in search of a little greenery and space heads here in warm weather, while in winter, cross-country skiers follow miles of paths and snowshoers tramp along trails laid out especially for them.

The 200-hectare (494-acre) urban park was created in 1876 by American landscape architect Frederick Law Olmsted, who also designed Central Park in New York City and parks in Philadelphia, Boston, and Chicago (although in the end, relatively little of Olmsted's full design for Mont Royal actually came into being). If you're carrying a PDA or a phone with Internet access, you can pull up a terrific interactive map at **www.lemontroyal.qc.ca**. You can also download podcasts for guided audio-video walks at the same website.

Start at the corner of rue Peel and av. des Pins, at the:

1 Downtown Park Entrance

After years of construction, this entrance is finally a thing of beauty, with new, broad steps and beautiful new plantings. From here, it's possible to reach the top of this small mountain by a variety of routes. Hearty souls can choose the quickest and most strenuous approach—taking the steepest sets of stairs at every opportunity, which go directly to the Chalet du Mont-Royal and its lookout at the top (see no. 9). Those who prefer to take their time and gain altitude slowly can use the switchback bridle path. Or mix and match the options as you go along. Don't be too worried about getting lost; the park is small enough that it's easy to regain your sense of direction no matter which way you head.

Head up the footpath at this entrance. You'll soon reach the broad bridle path:

2 Serpentin & Chemin Olmsted (Olmsted Rd.)

The road zigzags here, giving this short stretch the name "Serpentin." It passes some beautiful stone houses to the left. If you want to bypass some of the switchbacks, use any of a number of paths for a shortcut—but stay only on established trails to prevent erosion. After about the fourth switchback, you'll reach an intersection with the option to go left or right. Turn left. This is chemin Olmsted (Olmsted Rd.), designed by Frederick Law Olmsted. It was built at a gradual grade for horse-drawn carriages, so that horses could pull their loads up the hill at a steady pace, and on the way down would not be pushed from behind by the weight of the carriage. It remains closed to automobiles even today. Following this shaded, pleasant road in the woods will get you to Maison Smith (see no. 4) in about 45 minutes.

Another option is to take the:

3 Stairs

There are numerous sets of stairs through the woods that let you bypass the Serpentin's broad switchbacks. These steps get walkers to the Chalet du Mont-Royal and its lookout (see no. 9) more quickly. *Fair warning:* The last 100 or so steps go almost straight up. On the plus side, you'll get to share sympathetic smiles with strangers. Taking the steps bypasses sites no. 4, 5, and 6.

If you're taking chemin Olmsted, you eventually arrive at:

4 Maison Smith

Built in 1858, this structure has been used as a park rangers' station and park police headquarters. Today, it's a year-round information center with a small exhibit about the park and a gift shop.

5 Café Smith 🍵

Café Smith (☏ 514/843-8240), inside Maison Smith, offers soups, sandwiches, beverages including beer and wine, and sweets. (It boasts about its organic fair-trade hot chocolate, too.) In the summer and fall, there's an outdoor terrace.

From Maison Smith, walk through the field of sculptures, away from the radio tower, until you reach:

6 Lac des Castors (Beaver Lake)

This lake's name refers to the once-profitable fur industry, not to the actual presence of the long-gone animals. In summer, the lake is surrounded by sunbathers and picnickers, and you can rent a paddleboat. In the winter, it becomes an ice skater's paradise and, after the snow, a cross-country ski retreat and tobogganing wonder.

7 Bistro Le Pavillon

Bistro Le Pavillon (☏ 514/849-2002) is a 150-seat French restaurant that looks out on Beaver Lake and features seafood and steak. It's open daily June to September for lunch and dinner, and Wednesday through Sunday the rest of the year for lunch only. Bus no. 11 stops at the restaurant if you're ready to head back into the city from here.

You can rent a paddleboat at Lac des Castors.

Walk across the road behind the pavilion, called chemin de la Remembrance (Remembrance Rd.), to enter:

8 Notre-Dame-des-Neiges Cemetery

This is the city's predominantly Catholic cemetery, and from here, you can visit the adjacent Protestant Mount Royal graveyard. Behind it (to the north), if you're up for a longer walk, is the small adjoining Jewish and Spanish-Portuguese cemetery.

Notre-Dame-des-Neiges Cemetery reveals much about Montréal's ethnic mix: Headstones, some with likenesses in photos or tiles, are engraved with surnames as diverse as Zagorska, Skwyrska, De Ciccio, Sen, Lavoie, O'Neill, Hammerschmid, Fernandez, Müller, Haddad, and Boudreault.

If you've had enough walking, find a no. 11 bus on chemin de la Remembrance that heads east toward the Guy Métro station. To continue the tour, head back to Maison Smith and follow the signs on the main path for:

9 Chalet du Mont-Royal & Its Lookout

The front terrace here offers the most popular panoramic view of the city and the river. The chalet itself was constructed from 1931 to 1932 and has been used over the years for receptions, concerts, and various other events. Inside the chalet, take a look at the 17 paintings hanging just below the ceiling, starting to the right of the door that leads into the snack bar. They relate the region's history and the story of the French explorations of North America. In winter, there's a warming room for skiers.

Facing the chalet from the terrace, locate the path running off to the right, marked by a sign that says CROIX, which means "cross." Follow it for about 10 minutes to the giant:

10 Croix du Mont-Royal

Legend has it that Paul de Chomedey, Sieur de Maisonneuve, erected a wooden cross here in 1643 after the young colony survived a flood threat. The present incarnation of the Croix du Mont-Royal, installed in 1924, is lit at night and visible from all over the city. Beside the cross is a plaque marking where a time capsule was interred in August 1992, during Montréal's 350th-birthday celebration. Some 12,000 children ages 6 to 12 filled the capsule with messages and drawings depicting their visions for the city in the year 2142, when Montréal will be 500 years old and the capsule will be opened.

To return to downtown Montréal, there are a few options. You can go back along the path to the chalet terrace. On the left, just before the terrace, is another path. It leads to the staircase described in no. 3 and descends to where the tour began. The walk down by this route takes about 15 minutes. Or the no. 11 bus runs from the summit to the Mont-Royal Métro. There are bus stops at Beaver Lake and along chemin de la Remembrance.

KALIYANA

9

MONTRÉAL SHOPPING

Y ou can shop in Montréal until your feet swell and your eyes cross. Whether you view shopping as a focus of your travels or simply as a diversion, you won't be disappointed. Among natives, shopping ranks right up there with dining out as a prime activity. Many Montréalers are of French ancestry, after all, and seem to believe that impeccable taste bubbles through the Gallic gene pool. The city has produced a thriving fashion industry, from couture to ready-to-wear, with a history that reaches back to the earliest trade in furs and leather. More than 1,700 shops populate the underground city alone, and many more than that are at street level and above. It is unlikely that any reasonable consumer need— or even outlandish fantasy—cannot be met here.

THE SHOPPING SCENE

When you're making purchases with a credit card, the charges are automatically converted at the going bank rate before appearing on your monthly statement. In most cases, this is the best deal of all for visitors. Visa and MasterCard are the most popular credit cards in this part of Canada. Many shops accept American Express. Discover is accepted less frequently. Most stores are open from 9 or 10am to 6pm Monday through Wednesday, until 9pm on Thursday and Friday, and until at least 5pm on Saturday. Many stores are now also open on Sunday from noon to at least 5pm.

The Best Buys

While not cheap, **Canadian Inuit sculptures** and 19th- to early-20th-century **country furniture** are handsome and authentic. Less expensive crafts than the intensely collected Inuit works are also available, including quilts, drawings, and carvings by Amerindian and other folk artists. The province's daring **high-fashion designers** produce appealing clothing at prices that are often reasonable. And while demand has diminished somewhat, superbly constructed **furs and leather goods** that recall Montréal's long history as part of the fur trade remain high-ticket items.

Ice cider (*cidre de glace*) and **ice wines** made in the province of Québec from apples and grapes left on trees and vines after the first frost are unique products to bring home. They're sold in duty-free shops at the border, in addition to the stores listed at the end of this chapter. A couple choice labels to look for are Domaine Pinnacle and La face cachée de la pomme.

PREVIOUS PAGE: **Merchandise on display at Kaliyana.**

The Best Shopping Areas

In downtown, **rue Sherbrooke** is a major high-end shopping street, with international and domestic designers, luxury shops, art galleries, and the Holt Renfrew department store. Also downtown, **rue Ste-Catherine** is home to the city's top department stores and is the heart of midpriced shopping—it's the central commercial artery. From the cross street rue Aylmer, where the department store **La Baie** is located, Ste-Catherine offers a 12-block stretch of stores heading west that includes jeweler **Henry Birks,** Tommy Hilfiger, **SAQ Signature,** Kiehl's, Banana Republic, **Simons,** Mango, HMV, **Roots,** Guess, H&M, Benetton, **Ogilvy,** Apple, and Steve Madden—to name a sampling (shops in bold are discussed later in this chapter). Streets are crowded here, and the atmosphere is frenetic. Note that Ste-Catherine also has a smattering of adult strip clubs and sex shops right alongside the family-friendly fare (usually on the second floor), with a gigantic neon sign announcing Club Super Sexe, for instance. For better and for worse, the mixed use of the street is a Montréal signature.

Rue Peel, which crosses rue Ste-Catherine in about the middle of the shopping stretch noted above, is known for its men's fashions. In Vieux-Montréal, the western end of **rue St-Paul** has an ever-growing number of art galleries, clothing boutiques, and jewelry shops. In Plateau Mont-Royal, **rue St-Denis** north of Sherbrooke has blocks of shops filled with fun, funky items; see p. 159 for a recommended stroll along St-Denis. **Boulevard St-Laurent** sells everything from budget practicalities to off-the-wall handmade fashions. Further north, **avenue Laurier,** between boulevard St-Laurent and avenue de l'Epée, is where to head for French boutiques, furniture and accessories shops, and products from the ateliers of young Québécois designers. This is a vibrant, upscale street, with a rich selection of restaurants, too.

Shopping Complexes & the Underground City

A unique shopping opportunity in Montréal is the **underground city,** also known, somewhat less dramatically, as the underground pedestrian network, and officially called RÉSO (from *réseau,* which means network in French). It's a warren of passageways connecting more than 1,700 shops in 10 shopping malls that have levels both above and below street level (p. 56). Typical is the **Complexe Desjardins** (© **514/845-4636;** www.complexedesjardins.com), a downtown mall with entrances at street level and underground, bounded by rues Ste-Catherine, St-Urbain, and Jeanne-Mance, and boulevard René-Lévesque. It has waterfalls and fountains, trees and hanging vines, music, and lanes of shops going off in every direction.

Another intriguing hub is **Les Cours Mont-Royal** at 1455 rue Peel (© **514/842-7777;** www.lcmr.ca), which also has entrances both at street level and underground. It feels like a regular mall on the Métro level, where food courts, shoe shines, and scarf kiosks begin to repeat, but upstairs, you'll find shops suitable for outfitting indie rock bands—at least, ones that have sold (many) albums. Here C$300 jeans are *de rigueur* at independently owned boutiques, sunglasses are worn indoors, and a giant chandelier harkens back to the building's former life as the Mont Royal Hotel.

Shoppers are likely to end up at some point in **Place Ville-Marie,** opposite Fairmont the Queen Elizabeth hotel, between boulevard René-Lévesque and Cathcart (© **514/861-9393;** www.placevillemarie.com). This was Montréal's first major post–World War II shopping complex and is known locally as "PVM." It has some 80 boutiques and eateries. A plaque honoring Vincent Ponte, who designed the underground city and died in 2006, is on the PVM esplanade.

The Montréal tourist office's *Official Tourist Guide*, available at tourist offices (p. 51), contains a map of the underground city. It can be difficult (but fun!) to navigate, as maps, signage, and even numbering of levels can differ from one section to the next. To retreat underground, ask for directions to the Métro level, or look for blue signs with a white arrow pointing down. On occasion, you'll see signs marked RESO, which indicate you are headed *souterrain.* Some complexes, including **Eaton Centre** (✆ **514/282-6792;** www.centreeatonde montreal.com), a central artery of the underground, have information desks and printed maps. The main thing to remember is that when you enter a street-level shopping emporium downtown, it's likely that you'll be able to head to a lower level and connect to the tunnels and shopping hallways that lead to another set of stores. It's also likely that the best way to reorient is by surfacing and using actual street signs and a city map.

SHOPPING FROM A TO Z

Antiques

Some of the city's quirkier antiques shops have disappeared in recent years, but there are still tempting shops along **"Antique Alley,"** as it's nicknamed, on rue Notre-Dame west of Vieux-Montréal. They're especially concentrated between rue Guy and avenue Atwater. See p. 144 for directions for an easy stroll to the area.

Antiques can also be found downtown along rue Sherbrooke near the Musée des Beaux-Arts, on the little side streets near the museum, in the Village (the gay neighborhood described on p. 54) on and around rue Amherst, and in the Mile End (Phil'Z 20th Century Design or Style Labo), or along boul. St-Laurent where you can also find many boutiques that sell new furniture and home decor accessories.

Arts, Crafts & Galleries

Some of Montréal's best crafts stores are in museums. See p. 184 for a listing of museum stores.

Atelier Entre-Peaux   This company specializes in lightweight bags made in Québec from recycled billboards—all products, in fact, are produced from 75% to 95% recycled material, earning the business recognition on Recyc-Québec, the official government recycling industry website. The company is officially appointed by the city of Montréal to transform all the banners posted on the city's street lamps. The bags are supercool looking, too. Bike bags run about C$69 and grocery bags about C$17. They can be found at **Galerie Zone Orange** (see below), or the company website (www.entre-peaux-ecodesign.com).

Galerie Le Chariot   Galleries that feature Inuit art are found throughout the city, but few are as accessibly located as Le Chariot, whose showroom is directly on the Place Jacques-Cartier, in the heart of Vieux-Montréal. Here, shoppers can find handmade pieces by Inuk artists from Cape Dorset, Lake Harbour, and Baffin Island—carved bears, seals, owls, and tableaus of mothers and children. Pieces range in price from about C$150 to C$25,000 and are certified by the Canadian

Galerie Zone Orange features the wares of artists from the area.

government. Think of it as a museum where you can buy the art. 446 Place Jacques-Cartier (in the center of the plaza), Vieux-Montréal. ✆ **514/875-4994.**

Galerie Zone Orange   Angry sock monkeys, creative jewelry, and colorful ceramics from regional artists are on display at the small Zone Orange, which also has a teeny espresso bar in its center. Perhaps the coolest products are the lightweight bags made from recycled billboards and street lamp banners by the eco-focused Atelier Entre-Peaux, a Montréal company (see above). There are also sweet dolls for infants made from organic cotton. 410 rue St-Pierre (near rue St-Paul), Vieux-Montréal. ✆ **514/510-5809.** http://shop.galeriezoneorange.com.

Guilde Canadienne des Métiers d'Art ★   In English, it's called the Canadian Guild of Crafts. A small but choice collection of items is displayed in a meticulously arranged gallery setting. Among the objects are blown glass, silk paintings, pewter, tapestries, wooden bowls, and ceramics. The store is particularly strong in avant-garde jewelry and Inuk sculpture. A small carving might be had for C$100 to C$300, while larger, more important pieces go for thousands more. 1460 rue Sherbrooke ouest (near rue Mackay), downtown. ✆ **866/477-6091.** www.canadianguild.com.

L'Affichiste   Artfully displayed in a beautiful Victoria brownstone, this shop offers vintage posters dating from the Belle Epoque to the Art Deco period. 417 rue des Seigneurs (corner of rue Notre Dame ouest). Vieux-Montréal. ✆ **514/656-3301.** www.laffichiste.com.

La Guilde Graphique   Contemporary artists are represented here, working with a variety of media and techniques, but primarily producing works on paper, including drawings, serigraphs, etchings, lithographs, and woodcut prints. 9 rue St-Paul ouest (at boul. St-Laurent), Vieux-Montréal. ✆ **514/844-3438.** www.guildegraphique.com.

Les Artisans du Meuble Québécois   A mix of crafts, jewelry, and other objects makes this an intriguing stop. Among the possibilities are handmade clothing and accessories for women, greeting cards, woven goods, and items for the home. 88 rue St-Paul est (near Place Jacques-Cartier), Vieux-Montréal. ✆ **514/866-1836.**

L'Empreinte   This is a *coopérative artisane* (a craftspersons' collective). The ceramics, textiles, glassware, and other items on sale occupy that vaguely defined territory between art and craft. Quality is uneven but tips toward the high end. 272 rue St-Paul est (next to Marché Bonsecours), Vieux-Montréal. ✆ **514/861-4427.** www.lempreintecoop.com.

Marché Bonsecours   A hotbed for tourists, but still a spot for great finds such as Annie Michaud's blown glass, sold at L'Atelier-Boutique Gogo Glass. 350 rue St-Paul est (near rue St-Denis), Vieux-Montréal. ✆ **514/872-7730.** www.marchebonsecours.qc.ca.

Salon des Métiers d'Art du Québec   Since the 1950s, masses of artisans have gathered into one space for the Christmas season. Today, some 400 exhibitors sell original, handmade, and exclusive creations for the 200,000 gift givers who visit each year. It takes place daily for 3 weeks in December. Place Bonaventure, downtown. ✆ **514/397-4807** (Dec only). www.salondesmetiersdart.com.

Bath & Body

Bella Pella   An apothecary-like display of skincare essentials where hand-made, high-quality soaps are sold like slices of bread. Also look for lotions, scrubs, and bath products. 1201-A av. du Mont-Royal est (near rue la Roche), downtown. © **514/904-1074.** www.bellapella.com.

Fruits & Passion   Started in Candiac, Québec, in 1992, this popular chain features "personal care and ambience products"—fruity lotions, hand soaps, bubble bath, home cleaning agents, and more. There are over 175 Fruits & Passion boutiques throughout the world. 4159 rue St-Denis (at rue Rachel), Plateau Mont-Royal. © **514/840-0778.** www.fruits-passion.ca.

Spa Dr. Hauschka   High-end pampering and getting "in touch with your inner beauty" is the goal of this chichi spa in a rue Sherbrooke brownstone. On-site treatments include facials, lavender baths, volcanic mud baths, and more. You can also buy the Dr. Hauschka products to indulge at home. 1444 rue Sherbrooke ouest (at rue Bishop), downtown. © **514/286-1444.** www.spadrhauschka.com.

Books & Comics

As with arts and crafts, some of Montréal's best bookstores are in the city's museums, p. 184.

Appetite for Books   Addicted to cookbooks? You're not alone. Lose yourself in gastronomic titles on everything from making brunch to Philippine cuisine. In the back of the store there is a kitchen used for classes or cooking demos. 388 av. Victoria (near rue Sherbrooke ouest), Westmount. © **514/369-2002.** www.appetitebooks.ca.

Canadian Centre for Architecture Bookstore   A comprehensive selection of books about architecture, with an emphasis on Montréal in particular and Canada in general. Volumes are also available on landscape and garden history, photography, preservation, conservation, design, and city planning. 1920 rue Baile (at rue du Fort), downtown. © **514/939-7028.** www.cca.qc.ca/bookstore.

Chapters   The flagship store of a chain with many branches is the result of a merger between Smithbooks and Coles booksellers. Thousands of titles are available in French and English. 1171 rue Ste-Catherine ouest (at rue Stanley), downtown. © **514/849-8825.** www.chapters.indigo.ca.

Drawn & Quarterly ★ 🎁   Both a comic store and publishing house, the quirky boutique discovered Daniel Clowes, the graphic novelist who penned *Ghost World*. 211 rue Bernard ouest (near av. de l'Esplanade), Mile End. © **514/279-2224.** www.drawnandquarterly.com.

Librissime   Collectors of high-end books should look no further; only la crème de la crème of art-house publishing makes it onto these shelves. 62 rue St-Paul ouest (near boul. St-Laurent), downtown. © 514/841-0123. www.librissime.com.

Indigo Musique & Café   Occupying a street-level space in the Place Montréal Trust, the very complete sister store to Chapters (see above) sells music, books, magazines, and gifts, and operates a cafe upstairs. 1500 av. McGill College (at rue Ste-Catherine), downtown. © **514/281-5549.** www.chapters.indigo.ca.

Nicholas Hoare   A old-fashioned bookstore with tall, stacked bookshelves, wooden floors and all the newest and classic titles is just waiting for you to pull up a chair and get lost in a book. 1366 av. Greene (near rue Sherbrooke ouest), Westmount. © **514/933-4201.** www.nicholashoare.com.

Paragraphe   This long storefront is popular with students from the McGill campus, which is a block away. The store hosts frequent author readings. 2220 av. McGill College (south of rue Sherbrooke). ☏ **514/845-5811.** www.paragraphbooks.com.

Renaud-Bray ☺   For those who know French or want to brush up, this two-level bookstore with a primarily French-language stock is a valuable resource. It also sells DVDs, CDs, and newspapers and magazines from all over the world. Most English-language books are upstairs. There's a large children's section, too. 4380 rue St-Denis (at rue Marie-Anne), Plateau Mont-Royal. ☏ **514/844-2587.** www.renaud-bray.com.

Ulysses   Pick up travel books of all shapes and sizes in English or French, as well as maps and other *voyageur* accessories. 560 av. President Kennedy (near av. Union), downtown. ☏ **514/843-7222.** www.ulyssesguides.com.

Clothing

FOR MEN

Clusier Habilleur ★   The place for Montréal professionals to get their custom-made suits; also on hand are designer tees by Vicomte and Lacoste, Citizens of Humanity jeans, dandy accessories such as cufflinks, ties, shoes, and hats, and the boutique's own collection of men's shirts. 432 rue McGill (near rue de la Commune), Vieux-Montréal. ☏ **514/842-1717.** www.clusier.com.

Dubuc ★   Edgy and sartorial are two words that come to mind at this Plateau institution. Local resident Philippe Dubuc has been crafting his namesake collection for over a decade to a dedicated—and optimally slender-built—following who come for Dubuc's exquisite suits and shirts. 4451 rue St-Denis, Plateau Mont-Royal. ☏ **514/282-1424.** www.dubucstyle.com.

Duo   One block removed from trendy St-Laurent Boulevard, Duo draws in the dandies with big names such as Lanvin, DSquared, and Burberry, as well as haute accessories such as Tom Ford sunglasses or Paul Smith bracelets and chains. 30 rue Prince Arthur ouest (near rue Clark), Plateau Mont-Royal. ☏ **514/848-0880.** www.boutiqueduo.com.

Eccetera & Co.   Favoring ready-to-wear attire from such higher-end manufacturers as Baldessarini and Canali, this store lays out its stock in a soothing setting with personalized service. Its motto, posted at the front window: GOOD CLOTHES OPEN ALL DOORS. 2021 rue Peel (near boul. de Maisonneuve), downtown. ☏ **514/845-9181.** www.eccetera.ca.

Harry Rosen   For more than 50 years, this well-known retailer of designer suits and accessories has been making men look good in Armani, Dolce & Gabbana, and its own Harry Rosen Made in Italy line. The store's website features a nifty timeline of the shop's evolution from Toronto made-to-measure store to national leader in men's fashion. Les Cours Mont-Royal, 1455 rue Peel (at boul. de Maisonneuve), downtown. ☏ **514/284-3315.** www.harryrosen.com.

L'Uomo Montréal ★   Another top men's clothing boutique on rue Peel, this one was founded in 1980. L'Uomo mostly deals in Italian and other European menswear by such forward-thinking designers as Ermenegildo Zegna, Kiton, Prada, and Borrelli. 1452 rue Peel (near rue Ste-Catherine), downtown. ☏ **514/844-1008.** www.luomo-montreal.com.

Michel Brisson   Montréal's spiffiest men flock to one of these two locations for the latest in contemporary suits, sportswear, and accessories. Some of the heavy-hitter brands are Jil Sander, Eton, and Neil Barrett. 1074 av. Laurier ouest (near rue

Hutchison), Outremont. ☎ **514/270-1012.** 384 rue St-Paul ouest (near rue McGill), Vieux-Montréal. ☎ **514/285-1012.** www.michelbrisson.com.

FOR WOMEN

Montréal Fashion Week happens twice a year, in February/March and August/September. The 2011 event took place at the **Marché Bonsecours** and featured 24 Canadian designers, including Barilà, Marie Saint Pierre, and Rachel F. Photos are at www.montrealfashionweek.ca. The **Montréal Fashion & Design Festival** happens on avenue de McGill College in August. The enormous outdoor catwalk literally stops traffic as it takes over the street, which closes down to pedestrians only; see www.festivalmodedesign.com. If secondhand clothing is your beat, Montréal boasts a heavenly network of vintage boutiques—it's no secret that this is where much of Montréal's artsy style-mavens procure their looks. In the Mile End wander along rue Bernard or St-Viateur (I like Local 23), and in Little Burgundy go to Friperie La Gaillarde or ERA Vintage, a favorite haunt of Jean Paul Gaultier on a 2010 visit. There many other *friperies*, as they're called in French, scattered in the Plateau Mont-Royal, such as Cul de Sac, Roko-konut, and Friperie St-Laurent, all three in a row.

Aime Com Moi If you're heading to the northern end of the Plateau to the hipster bar Bílý Kůň (p. 197), build in time to stroll avenue du Mont-Royal, which is chock-full of new and used clothing. Among the shops is this one, which features original clothing by Québécois designers. 150 av. du Mont-Royal est (3 blocks from boul. St-Laurent), Plateau Mont-Royal. ☎ **514/982-0088.**

Ambre Cocktail dresses and casual wear made of linen, rayon, and cotton are featured in this small shop. Canadian designer Joseph Ribkoff, who was in 2011 the officially designer for Miss America, is well represented. Shoppers might also find bold accessories here, too. 201 rue St-Paul ouest (at rue St-François-Xavier), Vieux-Montréal. ☎ **514/982-0325.**

Bodybag by Jude ★ Hometown trendsetter Judith Desjardins runs her atelier just behind this boutique, which is popular with trendy young ladies for sporty streetwear, hip office apparel, or evening knockouts. 17 rue Bernard ouest (near boul. St-Laurent), Mile End. ☎ **514/274-5242.** www.bodybagbyjude.com.

Collection Méli Mélo 👔 This shop used to feature furniture from sub-Saharan Africa. There's still some of that, but a shift a few years back brought a new concentration: women's fashion by Montréal's chic designers. 205 rue St-Paul ouest (at rue St-François-Xavier), Vieux-Montréal. ☎ **514/285-5585.**

Delano Design For those women looking for eclectic designs you won't find elsewhere, this Vieux-Montréal shop specializes in locally designed clothing, jewelry, accessories, and even artworks. 70 rue St-Paul ouest (near rue St-Sulpice), Vieux-Montréal. ☎ **514/286-5005.** www.delanodesign.com.

Denis Gagnon ★ Canada's own enfant terrible opened up an eponymous boutique in spring 2011. Known for his avant-garde looks, Gagnon's subterranean showroom attracts the elite of this city's fashion crowd. 1170 rue St-Paul ouest (near rue St-Francois Xavier), Vieux-Montréal. ☎ **514/942-8869.** www.denisgagnon.ca.

Espace Pepin Artist Lysanne Pepin uses this bright airy corner location to showcase her ethereal, figurative paintings. Also in store is a finely curated roundup of jewelry, clothing, and accessories, much of it Montréal-made. 350 rue St-Paul ouest (near rue St-Pierre), Vieux-Montréal. ☎ **514/844-0114.** www.pepinart.com.

Fourrures Dubarry Furs Inc. The city's fur-trading past buttresses many wholesale and retail furriers. At the family-run, high-end Dubarry Furs, coats and capes in fur, shearling, cashmere, and leather are on display, along with hats, earmuffs, purses, and scarves. 206 rue St-Paul ouest (at rue St-François-Xavier), Vieux-Montréal. ✆ **514/844-7483.** www.dubarryfurs.com.

Giorgio Femme Ursula B Montréal's malls are peppered with boutiques featuring cutting-edge fashion from around the world, and Ursula B is one of the top options. Among the collections on the racks are Vera Wang, Alexander McQueen, and Giambattista Valli. Les Cours Mont-Royal, 1455 rue Peel (at boul. de Maisonneuve), downtown. ✆ **514/282-0294.** www.ursulab.com.

Harricana ★ One designer taking a unique cue from the city's long history with the fur trade is Mariouche Gagné. Her company recycles old fur into funky patchwork garments and uses the slogan "Made from your mother's old coat." A leader in the ecoluxe movement, Gagné also recycles silk scarves, turning them into tops and skirts. Her workshop-boutique is close to the Marché Atwater (p. 181) and the Lionel-Groulx Métro station. 3000 rue St-Antoine ouest (at av. Atwater), west of Vieux-Montréal. ✆ **877/894-9919** or 514/287-6517, ext 201. www.harricana. qc.ca.

Kaliyana Vaguely Japanese and certainly minimalist, the free-flowing garments sold here are largely asymmetrical separates. Made by a Canadian designer, they come in muted tones of solid colors. Ask for "the kit," and you'll get six of Kaliyana's most popular pieces, apt foundation for a new wardrobe. Simple complementary necklaces and comfy but übercool shoes are available, too. 4107 rue St-Denis (near rue Rachel), Plateau Mont-Royal. ✆ **514/844-0633.** www.kaliyana.com.

Les Createurs Owner and buyer Maria Balla has been bringing Montréalers fashions straight from the runways to her posh boutique for over 30 years, and has pleasing fashionistas with coveted labels like Junya Wanatabe, Rick Owens, and Ann Demeulemeester. 1444 rue Sherbrooke ouest (near rue Redpath), downtown. ✆ **514/284-2102.** www.lescreateurs.ca.

Marie Saint Pierre ★ A veteran on Montréal's fashion scene, Saint Pierre has been catering to power-type females who want to dress a little differently than the masses. She's known for expert tailoring, original silhouettes, and extremely travel-friendly fabrics. 2081 rue de la Montagne (near boul. de Maisonneuve ouest), downtown. ✆ **514/281-5547.** www.mariesaintpierre.com.

Shan ★ Awarded Designer of the Year in the 2011 International Mode City Show in Paris, owner and designer Chantal Levesque brings ladies' (and some men's) swimwear to a new level—if not a hefty price tag. Sister stores in Toronto and Miami only broaden her appeal. 2150 rue Crescent (south of rue Sherbrooke ouest), downtown. ✆ **514/287-7426.** www.shan.ca.

Tag Cuir 🎁 Leather fans have to check this out: suede jeans that are washable! Skotts brand pants (www.skotts.com) are superwarm on icy days. Also on display in this small *cuir* (leather) shop are bomber jackets and other leather items. Sales staff push hard, so gird yourself. 1325 rue Ste-Catherine ouest (at rue Crescent), downtown. ✆ **514/499-1180.**

TNT Two levels of retail therapy, this brand-driven store stocks the shelves with big names such as Isabelle Laurent, Carven, and Missoni. They also recently introduced local hotshots Barilà and Travis Taddeo. 4100 rue Ste-Catherine ouest (near av. Wood), downtown. ✆ **514/935-1588.** www.tntfashion.ca.

Unicorn ★   The black-and-white boudoir setting of Unicorn is home primarily for edgy, local collections such as Valerine Dumaine, Bettina Lou, and Eve Gravel. 5135 boul. St-Laurent (north of boul. St-Joseph), Mile End. ✆ **514/544-2828.** www.boutiqueunicorn.com.

FOR MEN & WOMEN

Club Monaco   Peruse minimalist, largely monochromatic garments for men and women, along with silver jewelry, eyewear, and cosmetics. Think Prada, but more affordable, with a helpful young staff. In Les Cours Mont-Royal shopping complex, 1455 rue Peel (north of rue Ste-Catherine ouest), downtown. ✆ **514/499-0959.** www.clubmonaco.com.

Henri Henri   As the porkpie makes a comeback, so may Henri Henri, a Montréal haberdasher since 1932. Step in and be outfitted with a classic Stetson or any number of styles that come in wool, felt, fur, leather, suede, cotton, or straw. Wondering how you look? Three-way oak mirrors abound, or the gentleman behind the counter will give you his honest assessment. Shop includes a hint of a women's section and accessories like umbrellas with hardwood handles. 189 rue Ste-Catherine est (at Hôtel-de-Ville), downtown. ✆ **888/388-0109** or 514/288-0109. www.henrihenri.ca.

Kanuk   One of the top Canadian manufacturers of high-end winter jackets makes its clothes right in Montréal and has a warehouselike factory store in the heart of Plateau Mont-Royal. Like L.L.Bean in the U.S., Kanuk's first customers for the heavy parkas were outdoor enthusiasts. Today, its clientele includes the general public. The jackets aren't cheap—the heavy-duty ones cost upwards of C$600—but they're extremely popular. The more modestly priced winter caps make nice (and cozy) souvenirs. Look, too, for end-of-season sales. 485 rue Rachel est (near rue Berri), Plateau Mont-Royal. ✆ **514/284-4494.** www.kanuk.com.

Le Château   This megaretailer known across Canada is based right here on the island; this location is a central one downtown. Relied upon for fast fashions on par with H&M and Simons, the brand has recently tried to segue into more refined designs and quality. 706 rue Ste-Catherine ouest (near rue University), downtown. ✆ **514/284-9166.** www.lechateau.com.

MO851 ★★   The simple, timeless designs of this high-quality leather boutique ensure longevity in their jackets, pants, bags, belts, and wallets. Neutral-toned sportswear separates also have a classic appeal. 3526 boul. St-Laurent (near rue Sherbrooke), Plateau Mont-Royal; ✆ **514/849-9759.** 1190 boul. de Maisonneuve ouest (near rue Stanley), downtown; ✆ 514/845-0461. 677 rue Ste-Catherine ouest (near rue University), downtown; ✆ 514/842-2563. www.m0851.com.

Reborn   Owner Brigitte Chartrand scopes Paris and New York—and Montréal—for styles that suit her no-nonsense, avant-garde esthetic, that is original, fashion-forward, and lots of black. On the racks you'll find Rick Owens, Alexander Wang, and hometown hero Rad Hourani. 231 rue St-Paul ouest (near rue St-Nicholas), Vieux-Montréal. ✆ **514/499-8549.** www.reborn.ws.

Roots   This Canadian company with many locations across Canada has churned out stylish casual wear for the masses since 1973. Along with clothing, the store sells leather bags and home accessories. 1025 rue Ste-Catherine ouest (at rue Peel), downtown. ✆ **514/845-7995.** www.roots.com.

S Sense   Three levels of Old Montréal real estate make way for Philip Lim, Opening Ceremony, Alexander McQueen, Marc Jacobs, and more—plus a special floor dedicated to the U.K.-based Top Shop. 90 rue St-Paul ouest (near rue St-Urbain), Vieux-Montréal. ☎ **514/289-1906.** www.ssense.com.

U&I If one-of-a-kind is on top of your want list for clothing, owner Eric Toledano speaks your language. He gravitates toward trendy that's just a little left of center. Prices can be steep, but chances are you'll be the only one in town wearing what you bought. 3650–3652 boul. St-Laurent (near rue Prince-Arthur), Plateau Mont-Royal. ☎ **514/844-8788.** www.boutiqueuandi.com.

Want Apothecary Twin brothers Byron and Dexter Peart opened a chic outpost for their luxe leather collection Want Les Essentiels de la Vie, which has high-end travel bags and accessories. The space will also showcase a selection of other brands including Acne and Nudie Jeans. 4960 rue Sherbrooke ouest (near av. Claremont), downtown. ☎ **514/484-3555.** www.wantapothecary.com.

Department Stores

Montréal's major downtown shopping emporia stretch along rue Ste-Catherine from avenue Union westward to rue Guy. Most of the big department stores here were founded when Scottish, Irish, and English families dominated the city's mercantile class, so most of their names are identifiably English, albeit shorn of their apostrophes. The principal exception is La Baie, French for "the Bay," itself a shortened reference to an earlier name, the Hudson's Bay Company.

Henry Birks et Fils ★★ Across from Christ Church Cathedral at the corner of rue Ste-Catherine stands Henry Birks et Fils, a highly regarded jeweler since 1879. This beautiful old store has marble pillars and an ornamental ceiling, and is a living part of Montréal's Victorian heritage. The expensive products on display go beyond jewelry to encompass pens, desk accessories, watches, belts, glassware, and china. In 2010, the charming Birks Café was added on the mezzanine level. 1240 Phillips Square (at rue Ste-Catherine ouest), downtown. ☎ **514/397-2511.** www.birks.com.

Holt Renfrew ★ One of the best known department stores in the city began as a furrier in 1837 and is now a showcase for the best in international style. A young Montréal clothier recently praised it as hip for "both grandmother and granddaughter." Wares are displayed in miniboutiques and focus on fashion for men and women. Brands, including Armani, Dolce & Gabbana, Eileen Fisher, Michael Kors, and Stella McCartney, are displayed with a tastefulness bordering on solemnity. 1300 rue Sherbrooke ouest (at rue de la Montagne), downtown. ☎ **514/842-5111.** www.holtrenfrew.com.

La Baie has been operating in Canada since 1670.

La Baie ★ No retailer has an older or more celebrated pedigree than the Hudson's Bay Company, whose name was shortened to "the Bay" and then transformed into "La Baie" by Québec language laws that decreed French the *lingua franca*. The company was incorporated in Canada in 1670. Its main store focuses on clothing, but also offers crystal, china, Inuit carvings, and its famous Hudson's Bay "point blanket." The company is the official outfitter of the Canadian Olympic teams in 2012. 585 rue Ste-Catherine ouest (at rue Aylmer), downtown. ✆ **514/281-4422.** www.hbc.com.

Ogilvy ★ The most vibrant of a classy breed of department store that appears to be fading from the scene. Ogilvy was established in 1866 and has been at this location since 1912. A bagpiper still announces the noon hour (a favorite sight for tourists), and special events, glowing chandeliers, and wide aisles enhance the shopping experience. Ogilvy has always had a reputation for quality merchandise and now contains 60 boutiques, including Louis Vuitton, Anne Klein, and Burberry. It's also known for its eagerly awaited Christmas windows. The basement-level **Café Romy** sells quality sandwiches, salads, and desserts. 1307 rue Ste-Catherine ouest (at rue de la Montagne), downtown. ✆ **514/842-7711.** www.ogilvycanada.com.

Simons ★★ This branch was the first expansion for Québec City's long-established family-owned department store. A must-see for teen shoppers and young professionals, Simons takes the labels-within-a-store approach now popular at trendy but affordable chains such as H&M or Forever 21, and throws in a few cutting-edge designers for inspiration. 977 rue Ste-Catherine ouest (at rue Mansfield), downtown. ✆ **514/282-1840.** www.simons.ca.

Edibles

The food markets described in "Picnic Fare" at the end of chapter 6 carry abundant assortments of cheeses, wines, and packaged food products that can serve as gifts or delicious reminders of your visit when you get home.

Canadian Maple Delights ☺ Everything maple-y is presented here by a consortium of Québec producers: pastries, gift baskets, truffles, and every grade of syrup. A wee little cafe serves sweets and gelato; on any day, a cone of maple-raspberry gelato is a good thing. For a taste, the minicone costs just C$1.60. 84 rue St-Paul est (near Place Jacques-Cartier), Vieux-Montréal. ✆ **514/765-3456.** www.maple delights.com.

La Vieille Europe ★ In this compact storehouse of culinary sights and smells, you can choose from wheels of pungent cheeses, garlands of sausages, pâtés, *jamón ibérico* (Iberian ham), cashews, honey, fresh peanut butter, and dried fruits. Coffee beans are roasted in the back, adding to the mixture of maddening aromas. 3855 boul. St-Laurent (north of rue Roy), Plateau Mont-Royal. ✆ **514/842-5773.**

Le Canard Libéré, Espace Gourmand World-famous Lac Brome ducks, found on many of Montréal's finest gastronomic menus, are raised near Lac Brome, just 109km (68 miles) from the city. This shop sells take-home duck products and has a cafe area for eating on the spot, comes with duck-fat French fries. 4396 boul. St-Laurent (near av. du Mont-Royal), Plateau Mont-Royal. ✆ **514/286-1286.** www.canardsdulacbrome.com.

Le Maitre Chocolatier Nada Fares wanted to create a luxury chocolate boutique in the posh Golden Square Mile, and this is exactly what she did. Ask about the Victoria dining room on the second floor where she holds high tea. 1612 rue Sherbrooke ouest (near Chemim de la Côte-des-Neiges), downtown. ✆ **514/544-9475.** www.lemaitrechocolatier.ca.

Les Chocolats de Chloé 🎁 If you approach chocolate the way certain aficionados approach wine or cheese—that is, on the lookout for the best of the best—then the teeny Chocolats de Chloé will bring great delight. Chocolates are made on-site. Try the lemon- or lime-chocolate, a great taste combination. Owner

Chloé Gervais-Fredette moved the shop from rue Roy to the cobblestoned rue Duluth near the restaurant Au Pied de Cochon (p. 96) in 2008. 546 rue Duluth est (near rue St-Hubert), Plateau Mont-Royal. ℂ **514/849-5550.** www.leschocolatsdechloe. com.

Les Glaceurs Day-trippers in Vieux-Montréal may end up making repeated visits to this cheery cafe with pink and lime-green walls, where cupcakes go for C\$2.95 in flavors that include coconut, key lime, strawberry, and *choco-menthe*. The shop also sells sandwiches and ice cream from Montréal favorite Bilboquet (p. 103). 453 rue St-Sulpice (across from Basilique Notre-Dame), Vieux-Montréal. ℂ **514/ 504-1469.** www.lesglaceurs.ca.

Marché Atwater ★ The Atwater market, west of Vieux-Montréal, is an indoor-outdoor farmer's market that's open daily. French in flavor, it features fresh fruits, vegetables, and flowers; *boulangeries* and *fromageries;* and shops with easy-to-travel-with food. There are also specialty boutiques like Chocolats Geneviève Grandbois. You can walk to the market from Vieux-Montréal by heading down rue Notre-Dame, where you'll pass Antique Alley (p. 172), or taking the Métro to Lionel-Groulx. 138 av. Atwater (at rue Notre-Dame ouest), west of Vieux-Montréal. www.marche-atwater.com.

Marché Jean-Talon ★ Gourmands will want to make a pilgrimage to the north part of the city to this market. Many locals prefer it over the Atwater market (above), perhaps because it's surrounded on all sides by the buzz and energy of the city. It's full of fresh fruits and vegetables and a host of gourmet shops. One, for instance, is the spice shop Olives & Épices, which *Food & Wine* magazine named the best of Montréal in 2010, citing its *ras el hanout,* "which contains 24 ingredients, including saffron and three kinds of dried roses." The market isn't near any of the sites, restaurants, or hotels listed in this guidebook, but it's an easy ride on the Métro—just head north to the Jean-Talon stop. 7070 av. Henri-Julien (at rue Jean-Talon est), north of Mile End. ℂ **514/277-1588.** www.marche-jean-talon.com.

Marché Jean-Talon is full of produce vendors and gourmet shops.

Mycoboutique Mushrooms, in every shape and form: fresh, dried, frozen, made into truffle oil, and folded into gelato (really). There are also books and housewares with mushroom motifs. The shop runs mushroom-foraging events, too (in French only). 16 rue Rachel est (at boul. St-Laurent), Plateau Mont-Royal. ✆ 514/223-6977. www.mycoboutique.ca.

Suite 88 Chocolatier More fancy chocolates—not that that's a bad thing. These are displayed in cases like fine jewelry, in flavors that include caramel and sea salt or chili-cayenne. Small bars start at C$3.50. There's a cafe, too, with gelato. And on cold days, be sure to try the hot chocolate—made with cayenne. There's another location at 1225 boul. de Maisonneuve, downtown. 3957 rue St-Denis (near rue Roy), Plateau Mont-Royal. ✆ 514/844-3488. www.suite88.com.

Home Design & Housewares

Also see "Arts, Crafts & Galleries," p. 172, and "Department Stores," p. 179.

Arthur Quentin Doling out household products of quiet taste and discernment for more than 25 years, this St-Denis stalwart sells tableware, kitchen gadgets, and home decor. That means lamps and Limoges china, terrines and tea towels, and cake molds and copper pots. Clay jugs for making vinegar? *Naturellement.* 3960 rue St-Denis (south of av. Duluth), Plateau Mont-Royal. ✆ 514/843-7513. www.arthurquentin.com.

Bouton Jaune ★ Linens, clothing, and the most cuddly of plush toys are ready and waiting for the newest members of your life—shop for newborn babies in a cloud of pastel pink, blue, green, and taupe. 240 av. Laurier ouest (near av. du Parc), Outremont. ✆ 514/526-3400. www.boutonjaune.com.

Bleu Nuit A sister store to Arthur Quentin (above), Bleu Nuit is *the* place to go for natural fiber bedding, supersoft nightwear, and swank soaps. The store does a good job positioning itself as the place for women (and men!) to register to build a classic trousseau of linens for the kitchen and bedroom. 3913 rue St-Denis (south of av. Duluth), Plateau Mont-Royal. ✆ 514/843-5702. www.bleunuit.ca.

Domison ★ Brother-and-sister team Thien and My Le put their design-savvy skills together to create their own line of contemporary beds, desks, sofas, and shelves, most of it at reasonable prices and condo-space sizing. 4117 boul. St-Laurent (near rue Rachel), Plateau Mont-Royal. ✆ 514/563-1268. www.domison.com.

Kitsch 'n Swell From oil paintings on black velvet to leopard print rugs, this reseller of vintage home collectibles takes the pineapple upside-down cake. There are also fur coats and jewelry, and, with two other vintage stores right in the neighborhood, this is definitely worth a trip if you like collectable kitsch. 3968 boul. St-Laurent (near av. Duluth), Plateau Mont-Royal. ✆ 514/845-6789. www.kitschnswell.ca.

La Cornue This outpost of the French company (in business, as its logo notes, since 1908) sells gorgeous kitchen equipment: custom-made ovens and ranges, yes, but tableware, elegant chandeliers, and furniture, too. To stand even from the street gazing in is to see some fabulous magazine photo spread come to glorious life. 371 av. Laurier ouest (near av. du Parc), Outremont. ✆ 514/277-0317. www.maisonlacornue.ca.

L'Émouleur Guillaume De L'Isle sells beautiful, long-lasting knives imported from Japan in this tiny Outremont shop. He'll even show you how to sharpen them the best way, using a stone. 1081 av. Laurier ouest (near av. Querbes), Outremont. ✆ 514/813-3135. www.montrealknife.com.

Les Touilleurs   Kitchenware of the highest order is sold here, meticulously arranged like museum pieces in a minimalist setting (the shop earned design honors shortly after it opened). Stock includes only superior versions of cooking essentials, including small appliances that strike high new standards. It has an on-site kitchen where **cooking classes** are conducted by local chefs. 152 av. Laurier ouest (near rue St-Urbain), Mile End. ✆ **514/278-0008.** www.lestouilleurs.com.

Option D   Option D sells high-end housewares, candy-colored and steel, in the heart of Old Town. Brands include Alessi, Guzzini, Iittala, and Bodum. 50 rue St-Paul ouest (near rue St-Sulpice), Vieux-Montréal. ✆ **514/842-7117.** www.optiond.ca.

Zone   This housewares stores features colorful bowls and plates, clocks and frames, furnishings, and vases at several outposts throughout the province. 4246 rue St-Denis (at rue Rachel est), Plateau Mont-Royal. ✆ **514/845-3530.** www.zone maison.com.

Jewelry & Accessories

Also see "Arts, Crafts & Galleries," p. 172.

Argent Tonic   About as big as an average walk-in closet, the bite-size boutique is overflowing with original silver jewelry from Mexico, as well as one-of-a-kind baubles to please the girly-girl in every woman. 138 av. Laurier ouest (near St-Urbain), Mile End. ✆ **514/274-5668.** www.argenttonic.com.

Château D'Ivoire   When you absolutely, positively have to buy a Rolex *right now,* this upscale shop carries jewelry and watches from that brand, plus other luxury names including Raymond Weil, Omega, and Cartier. 2020 rue de la Montagne (at boul. de Maisonneuve), downtown. ✆ **888/883-8283** or 514/845-4651. www.chateau divoire.com.

Clio Blue, Paris   This little rue Peel shop of the Paris-based international chain features spare displays in a narrow modernist storefront (the store is a design-competition winner). Custom jewelry incorporates Middle Eastern and South Asian motifs, often with carefully spaced semiprecious stones on silver strands and more festively designed bracelets. A sister store, **bleu comme le ciel,** is just up the block at no. 2000 and stocks costume jewelry that's worth a visit for women looking to shake up their image. 1468 rue Peel (near boul. de Maisonneuve), downtown. ✆ **514/281-3112.** www.clioblue.com.

Freitag-Concept   Contemporary stylings for him and her, the earrings, necklaces, bracelets, and cuffs appeal here to brave, urban-minded hipsters. The beautifully displayed selection also includes the shop owner's exclusive designs. 3762 boul. St-Laurent, Plateau Mont-Royal. ✆ **514/845-1788.**

Matt Baily   Not many places sell the statement-making Bell & Ross or U-Boat watches, as seen on many a celebrity, but here they're yours for the taking . . . er, buying. Also on hand are a bevy of glittering baubles imported from Italy. 1472 rue Crescent (near Sainte-Catherine ouest), downtown. ✆ **514/845-8878.** www.mattbaily.ca.

Nicolin Gublin   The main event at this large, sunny shop is the colorful, big prints of big-eyed marine creatures by Swedish-born artist Charlotte Nicolin. But Nicolin has also added the work of lots of other regional artists to the store's mix, and the wide assortment of jewelry is particularly beguiling. 333 Place d'Youville (at rue St-Pierre), Vieux-Montréal. ✆ **514/844-3696.** www.nicolingublin.com.

Museum Stores

Musée d'Art Contemporain Boutique   The contemporary art museum's boutique sells the usual, including poster-size reproductions of paintings and prints, but added to the mix are tasteful design pieces and unusual gifts. 185 rue Ste-Catherine ouest (at rue Jeanne-Mance), downtown. ℂ **514/847-6226.** www.macm.org.

Musée des Beaux-Arts Boutique   An unusually large and impressive shop (which goes by the name M Boutique) that sells everything from folk art to furniture. The expected art-related postcards and prints are at hand, along with ties, watches, scarves, toys, games, jewelry, and Inuit crafts, with special focus on work by Québec artisans. The boutique is also online. 1390 rue Sherbrooke ouest (at rue Crescent), downtown. ℂ **514/285-1600.** www.mbam.qc.ca.

Musée McCord Boutique ★   Part of an expanded museum that relates the province's history, this shop stocks a small, carefully chosen selection of Native and Canadian arts and crafts, china, rustic pottery, books with an emphasis on history, jewelry, and clothing. There's also a nice cafe inside the museum. 690 rue Sherbrooke ouest (at rue Victoria), downtown. ℂ **514/398-7100,** ext. 274. www.mccord-museum.qc.ca.

Pointe-à-Callière Gift Shop   Located in the Old Customs House at the end of the Museum of Archaeology and History's underground tour, this boutique sells collectibles for the home, gift items, souvenirs, toys, and books (in French). Particularly nice are the maple spoons and spatulas made by Québec artist Tom Littledeer. 150 rue St-Paul ouest (at Place Royale), Vieux-Montréal. ℂ **514/872-9149.** www. pacmusee.qc.ca.

Wines & Spirits

The food markets described in "Picnic Fare" at the end of chapter 6 carry a good variety of wines, which are also sold in supermarkets and convenience stores. Beer is also available in these venues.

Liquor and other spirits, on the other hand, can be sold only in stores operated by the provincial **Société des Alcools du Québec (SAQ).** The SAQ website, www.saq.com, provides a wealth of information about Québec wines and area outlets.

One of the largest outlets is the downtown **SAQ Selection** at 440 boul. de Maisonneuve ouest (ℂ 514/873-2274), a veritable supermarket of wines and liquors with thousands of labels. Prices run from less than C$10 to way, way up for Bordeaux vintages. The downtown **SAQ Signature** at 677 rue Ste-Catherine ouest in the Complexe Les Ailes (ℂ 888/454-7007 or 514/282-9445) is one of SAQ's boutique shops, featuring a smaller selection of rarer wines and fine liquors.

Bring your own carry bag when you visit a SAQ store: In 2009, the shops eliminated single-use plastic and paper bags. If you don't have one, you'll have to buy a reusable bag for C75¢ to C$1, depending on the size.

Québec's unique **ice cider (*cidre de glace*),** made from apples left on trees after the first frost, can be purchased in duty-free shops at the border, in addition to the stores listed above. One top producer is **Domaine Pinnacle** (ℂ 450/263-5835; www.domainepinnacle.com), located about an hour and a half east of the city. It's a regular gold medalist in international competitions.

MONTRÉAL AFTER DARK

10

Montréal's reputation for effervescent nightlife reaches back to the Roaring Twenties—specifically, to the 13-year period of Prohibition in the U.S. from 1920 to 1933. Americans streamed into Montréal for relief from alcohol deprivation (while Canadian distillers and brewers made fortunes). Montréal already enjoyed a sophisticated and slightly naughty reputation as the Paris of North America, which added to the allure.

Nearly a century later, packs of Americans still travel across the border to go to the city's bars and strip clubs (as do Canadians from other provinces) for bachelor and bachelorette weekends. Clubbing and barhopping are hugely popular activities, and nightspots stay open until 3am—much later hours than in many U.S. and Canadian cities, which still heed Calvinist notions of propriety and early bedtimes. The legal drinking age is also only 18, a reason perhaps why many McGill University students come from the U.S., where you must be 21 . . . but I'm only speculating.

Nocturnal pursuits are often as cultural as they are social. The city boasts its own outstanding symphony, dozens of French- and English-language theater companies, and the incomparable Cirque du Soleil. It's also on the standard concert circuit that includes Chicago and New York, so internationally known entertainers, music groups, and dance companies pass through frequently. A decidedly French enthusiasm for film, as well as the city's reputation as a movie-production center, ensures support for film festivals and screenings of offbeat and independent movies.

A ticket office for Montréal cultural events is centrally located at the Place des Arts. **Vitrine Culturelle de Montréal (Cultural Window of Montréal;** (*) **866/924-5538** or 514/285-4545; www.vitrine.com) is at 145 rue Ste-Catherine ouest and sells last-minute deals, as well as full-price tickets. In summer, the city is awash in festivals. Many are listed in the "Calendar of Events" in chapter 2.

Coming soon in 2012, the ever-growing, ever-improving Quartier des Spectacles will open **2-22 Ste-Catherine,** an eight-story, LEED-certified building at the southeast corner of boul. St-Laurent and rue Ste-Catherine. It will be built with local materials, and will provide space for local arts and cultural organizations, as well as offer a cafe, bookstore, bar, rooftop terrace—the building will basically be the cultural window on everything happening in the city.

Concentrations of pubs and nightclubs (*les boîtes de nuits*) underscore the city's linguistic dichotomy. While there's much crossover, the parallel blocks of **rue Crescent, rue Bishop,** and **rue de la Montagne** north of rue Ste-Catherine (as well as the up-and-coming Little Burgundy hub) have a pronounced Anglophone (English-speaking) character, while Francophones (French speakers) dominate the area known as the **Quartier Latin,** with college-age patrons most evident along the lower reaches of rue St-Denis. Their elders gravitate to the nightspots of the slightly more uptown blocks of the same street. **Vieux-Montréal,** especially along

PREVIOUS PAGE: **The Cirque du Soleil troupe often comes to town in late spring.**

For details about performances or special events when you're in town, pick up a free copy of *Montréal Scope* (www.montrealscope.com), a monthly ads-and-events booklet usually available in hotel lobbies; the free weekly papers *Mirror* (www.montrealmirror.com) and *Hour* (www.hour.ca), both in English, or *Voir* (www.voir.ca), in French, are available all over town. Also in (mostly) French is the free monthly *Nightlife* magazine (www.nightlifemagazine.ca). *Fugues* (www.fugues.com) provides news and views of gay and lesbian events, clubs, restaurants, and activities. One particularly fun blog about city happenings, and a regular at the top of the *Mirror*'s annual ranking of best blogs, is **Midnight Poutine** (www.midnightpoutine.ca), a self-described "delicious high-fat source of rants, raves and musings." I am also partial to the **Montréal Buzz**, written by a team of local "insiders" (www.tourisme-montreal.org/blog). Extensive listings of mainstream cultural and entertainment events are posted at **www.canada.com** and **www.montrealplus.ca**.

rue St-Paul, has a more universal quality, and many of its bars and clubs showcase live jazz, blues, and folk music. In **Plateau Mont-Royal,** boulevard St-Laurent, parallel to rue St-Denis and known locally as "the Main," has become a miles-long haven of hip restaurants and clubs. It starts roughly from rue Sherbrooke, and goes all the way north into **Mile End** up to rue Laurier. It's a good place to wind up in the wee hours, as there's always someplace with the welcome mat still out, even after the official 3am closings. And if you've still got steam after that, there are always the after-hours clubs in the Gay Village. Most bars and clubs don't charge cover, and when they do, it's rarely more than C$10. Beer is usually C$3 to C$5, while cocktails typically cost C$7 to C$12. Belle Gueule Rousse is a good amber lager made in Montréal by the Les Brasseurs RJ company and on tap in many venues. On Thursdays from 5 to 7pm, nearly every bar and restaurant offers some sort of happy-hour special, locally known as *cinq à sept.*

Smoking has been banned in bars and restaurants since 2006.

THE PERFORMING ARTS
Circus

The extraordinary circus company **Cirque du Soleil** (p. 118) is based in Montréal. Each show is a celebration of pure skill and nothing less than magical, with acrobats, clowns, trapeze artists, and performers costumed to look like creatures not of this world—iguanas crossed with goblins, or peacocks born of trolls. Cirque performs internationally, with as many as 20 shows playing across the globe simultaneously. Although there isn't a permanent show in Montréal, the troupe often comes to town in late spring and sets up its signature blue-and-yellow-striped tents in Vieux-Port. In 2011, the "Totem" show had performances in June and July. The new "Michael Jackson: The Immortal World Tour" also debuted in Montréal at the Centre Bell in Oct. Check **www.cirquedusoleil.com** for the schedule.

Pavillon de la TOHU ♪ Adjacent to Cirque du Soleil's training complex and company offices, TOHU is a performance space devoted to the circus arts. Acrobats and performers from Québec's Productions à Trois Têtes and the Imperial Acrobats of China have performed here, and the annual June shows by students

10

MONTRÉAL AFTER DARK

The Performing Arts

of the National Circus School present many of the top rising stars. TOHU features an intimate in-the-round hall done up like an old-fashioned circus tent, and an exhibit space displays more than 100 circus artifacts. The entire venue was built with recycled pieces of an amusement-park bumper-car ride and wood from a dismantled railroad. The facility is in the lower-income Saint-Michel district well north of downtown, and accessible by Métro and bus, as well as taxi. 2345 rue Jarry est (corner of rue d'Iberville, at Autoroute 40). ℂ 888/376-8648 or 514/376-8648. www.tohu.ca. Free to view facility and exhibits. Tour admission from C$6 adults; C$4 seniors, students, and children 7–11; free for children 6 and under, but not recommended. Tour requires reservations. Mon–Fri 9am–5pm. Performances from C$45 adults, from C$32 children 12 and under. 8km (5 miles) from downtown, up rue St-Denis and east on rue Jarry to where it meets Autoroute 40. Métro: Jarry or Iberville. Bus: 94 nord.

Classical Music & Opera

Many churches have exemplary music programs. At **Cathédrale Christ Church,** 635 rue Ste-Catherine ouest (ℂ **514/843-6577,** ext. 369; www.montrealcathedral.ca), a top-notch choir sings Sundays at 10am and 4pm with programs that often include modernists such as Benjamin Britten and David Lord. See p. 122 for more information.

Opéra de Montréal ★★★   Founded in 1980, this outstanding opera company (it's one of the 15 largest in North America) mounts six productions per year in Montréal, with artists from Québec and abroad participating in such shows as Mozart's *The Magic Flute* and Puccini's *La Bohème.* Video translations are provided from the original languages into French and English. Performances are held from September to June at Place des Arts. Just next door, a new concert hall, **L'Adresse Symphonique,** was scheduled to open in September 2011. Place des Arts, 175 rue Ste-Catherine ouest (main entrance), downtown. ℂ **514/985-2258** for tickets. www.operademontreal.com. Tickets from C$46. Métro: Place des Arts.

Orchestre Métropolitain du Grand Montréal   The orchestra performs during its regular season at Place des Arts. The 2011 schedule included 10 performances, and opened with *Great Classics,* such as Beethoven's Symphony No. 5 and Mozart's Piano Concerto No. 21; an assorted program, *Airs de jeunesse;* and **Mahler's Symphony No. 8.** In summer, it presents free outdoor concerts at Théâtre de Verdure in Parc La Fontaine. Place des Arts, 175 rue Ste-Catherine ouest (main entrance), downtown. ℂ **866/842-2112** or 514/842-2112. www.orchestremetropolitain. com. Tickets from C$30. Métro: Place des Arts.

Orchestre Symphonique de Montréal (OSM) ★★   Kent Nagano, who has been the music director here since 2005, focuses the symphony's repertoire on programs featuring works by Beethoven, Bach, Brahms, Mahler, and Messiaen. The orchestra performs at Place des Arts and occasionally at the Notre-Dame Basilica, and offers a few free concerts in regional parks each summer. Once it opens in September 2011, the **L'Adresse Symphonique** will be Nagano's new home. Place des Arts, 175 rue Ste-Catherine ouest (main entrance), downtown. ℂ **514/842-9951** for tickets. www.osm.ca. Tickets from C$28; discounts available for people under 30. Métro: Place des Arts.

Concert Halls & Auditoriums

Centre Bell   Seating 21,273 for most events, Centre Bell is the home of the Montréal Canadiens hockey team and host to the biggest international rock and pop stars traveling through the city, including Montréal native Céline Dion

The Performing Arts

MONTRÉAL AFTER DARK

(b. 1968), Beyoncé Knowles (b. 1981), and Coldplay, as well as shows like "Disney on Ice." Check the website for information about guided tours and the newly minted 929-sq.-m (10,000-sq.-ft.) Montréal Canadiens Hall of Fame. 1260 rue de la Gauchetière ouest, downtown. ✆ **800/663-6786** or 514/989-2841. www.centrebell.ca. Métro: Bonaventure.

Métropolis   After starting life as a skating rink in 1884, the 2,300-capacity Métropolis is now a prime showplace for traveling rock groups, especially for bands on the way up or retracing their steps down. It has recently hosted Adele, Lauryn Hill, Prince, and Polaris Prize winner Karkwa. There's also a small attached lounge, **Le Savoy.** 59 rue Ste-Catherine est, downtown. ✆ **514/844-3500.** www.montrealmetropolis.ca/metropolis. Métro: St-Laurent or Berri-UQAM.

Place des Arts ★★   Since 1992, Place des Arts has been the city's central entertainment complex, presenting performances of musical concerts, opera, dance, and theater in five halls: **Salle Wilfrid-Pelletier** (2,990 seats), where the Orchestre Symphonique de Montréal (see above) and Les Grands Ballets Canadiens (see below) often perform; **Théâtre Maisonneuve** (1,458 seats), where the Orchestre Métropolitain du Grand Montréal (see above) performs; **Théâtre Jean-Duceppe** (765 seats); **Cinquième Salle** (417 seats); and the small **Studio-Théâtre Stella Artois** (138 seats). Portions of the city's many arts festivals are staged in the halls and outdoor plaza here, as are traveling productions of Broadway shows. *Note:* In 2012, portions of the Place des Arts plaza may be under construction. Consult the website for current parking information and updates about temporary entrances. Place des Arts, 175 rue Ste-Catherine ouest (ticket office), downtown. ✆ **866/842-2112** or 514/842-2112 for information and tickets. www.pda.qc.ca. Métro: Place des Arts.

Pollack Concert Hall   In a landmark building dating from 1899 and fronted by a statue of Queen Victoria, this McGill University venue is in nearly constant use, especially during the school year, with concerts and recitals by university students and music faculty. Recordings of some concerts are available on the university's label, McGill Records. Concerts are also given in the campus's

Place des Arts is the city's central entertainment complex.

smaller **Redpath Hall,** at 861 rue Sherbrooke ouest (✆ **514/398-4547**). On the McGill University campus, 555 rue Sherbrooke ouest, downtown. ✆ **514/398-4547.** www. music.mcgill.ca. Performances are usually free; parking C\$7. Métro: McGill.

Théâtre de Outremont Opened in 1929, the Outremont started a new life in 2001, with a larger stage and terraced seating. Its calendar incorporates all manner of French-language music, comedy, theater, and film, with occasional Anglophone acts. 1248 av. Bernard ouest (at av. Champagneur), Mile End. ✆ **514/495-9944.** www.theatreoutremont.ca. Métro: Outremont.

Théâtre de Verdure 🍴 Tango nights in July are especially popular at the open-air theater nestled in a popular park in Plateau Mont-Royal. Everything is free: music, dance, and theater, often with well-known artists and performers. Many in the audience pack picnics. Performances are held from June to August. Check with the tourism office (p. 51) for days and times. Parc La Fontaine, Plateau Mont-Royal. ✆ **514/872-4041.** Métro: Sherbrooke.

Théâtre St-Denis Refurbished in recent years, this theater complex in the heart of the Latin Quarter hosts a variety of shows by the likes of Norah Jones and Alice Cooper, as well as segments of the Juste pour Rire (Just for Laughs) comedy festival in July. One hall seats 2,218, and the other fits 933. 1594 rue St-Denis (at rue Emery), Quartier Latin. ✆ **514/849-4211.** www.theatrestdenis.com. Métro: Berri-UQAM.

Dance

Montréal hosts frequent appearances by notable dancers and troupes from other parts of Canada and the world—among them Hofesh Shechter Company, National Ballet of Cuba, Balé de Rua, and Toronto's Le Ballet National du Canada—and has accomplished resident companies, too.

Les Grands Ballets Canadiens ★★ The prestigious touring company, performing both a classical and a modern repertoire, has developed a following far beyond national borders in its 50-plus years (it was founded in 1957). In the process, it has brought prominence to many gifted Canadian choreographers and composers. The troupe's production of *The Nutcracker* is always a big event each winter. Performances are held October through May. Place des Arts, 175 rue Ste-Catherine ouest (main entrance), downtown. ✆ **514/842-2112.** www.grandsballets.qc.ca. Tickets from C\$35; discounts available for people under 30. Métro: Place des Arts.

Theater

Centaur Theatre The city's principal English-language theater is housed in a former stock-exchange building (1903). Presented here are a mix of classics, foreign adaptations, and works by Canadian playwrights. It was here that famed playwright Michel Tremblay's *Forever Yours, Marie-Lou* received its first English-language staging in 2008. Slated for the first half of 2012 is *In Absentia* (Jan 31–Mar 4), *The Game of Love and Chance* (Mar 6–Apr 1), *Intimate Apparel* (Mar 27–Apr 29), and *Haunted Hillbilly* (May 8–June 3). 453 rue St-François-Xavier (near rue Notre-Dame), Vieux-Montréal. ✆ **514/288-3161.** www.centaurtheatre.com. Tickets from C\$44. Métro: Place d'Armes.

Segal Centre for Performing Arts From about 1900 to 1930, Yiddish was Montréal's third most common language. That status has since been usurped by any number of languages, but its dominance lives on here. The Centre presents theater performed in both Yiddish and English, and is one of the few North American theaters that still presents plays in Yiddish. Recent productions have included Willy Russell's *Educating Rita* and the Dora Wasserman Yiddish Theatre's production of *Pirates of Penzance*. There is also a performance academy for adults and teens, and a film program. Note that the venue is at a considerable distance from downtown. 5170 Côte-Ste-Catherine (near boul. Décarie), Plateau Mont-Royal. ℭ **514/739-7944.** www.segalcentre.org. Tickets from C$35. Métro: Côte-Ste-Catherine (then bus 129) or Snowdon (then bus 17).

MUSIC & NIGHTCLUBS

Supper clubs are the new nightclubs in Montréal; these are all-in-one venues where you go for drinks, stay for dinner, and then hang around drinking and possibly dancing until closing. If they're listed in our "Where to Eat" chapter, it means the food comes highly recommended; if not, well, you're not a real *Iron Chef* judge, are you? A few trendy supper clubs of late are Barroco, Garde-Manger, Méchant Boeuf, Vauvert, and L'Orignal in Vieux-Montréal; Cavalli and Time in downtown; and Macaroni Bar, Koko, Buonanotte, Med Grill, and Globe in Plateau Mont-Royal. More mature types who are looking to boogie may opt for the more traditional (and less pretentious) dance clubs, such as Funky Town on rue Peel ('70s and '80s disco) or Electric Avenue on rue Crescent, which is '80s music all night long. Get your moonwalk ready.

A note to clubbers: This city is *serious* about partying. Regular bars stay open until 3am, and still others keep the fire burning after hours. Popular clubs can be exclusive—waiting in line is an unfortunate reality, and dress codes are observed. You can increase your chances for entry at the most exclusive spots by making advance reservations or guaranteeing a table by "buying a bottle." Frequent clubbers get cover charge discounts and avoid lines by registering with **www.montrealguestlist.com**. Once on the list, you may have to arrive early or within a small window of time.

A note to walkers: Montréal is one of the safest cities to visit, but the area just north of Vieux-Montréal and the convention center, and south of rue Sherbrooke, has a pocket of streets that are nearly deserted at night. You may want to take a cab or the Métro when traveling through this area after dark.

Downtown

Hurley's Irish Pub   In front is a street-level terrace, and in back are several semi-subterranean rooms. Celtic instrumentalists perform nightly, usually starting around 9:30pm. There are 19 beers on tap and more than 50 single-malt whiskeys to choose from. 1225 rue Crescent (at rue Ste-Catherine), downtown. ℭ **514/861-4111.** www.hurleysirishpub.com. Métro: Guy-Concordia.

Maison de Jazz ★   Right downtown, this New Orleans–style jazz venue has been on the scene for decades. Lovers of barbecued ribs and jazz arrive early to fill the room, which is decorated in mock Art Nouveau style with tiered levels. Live music starts around 8pm most nights and continues until closing time. The ribs are okay, and the jazz is of the swinging mainstream variety, with occasional digressions into more esoteric forms. 2060 rue Aylmer (south of rue Sherbrooke). ℭ **514/842-8656.** www.houseofjazz.ca. Cover C$5. Métro: McGill.

Newtown   A tri-level club in the white-hot center of rue Crescent nightlife, Newtown is a sought-after destination. The square bar in the middle of the main barroom is a friendly place, even if you're on your own. There's a newly reopened nightclub in the basement, **Club Empire,** that plays mainly commercial music

with some house and electro (open Fri and some Sat), a restaurant one floor up (the chef is celebrated Martin Juneau), and most prominently, a rooftop terrace in summer. The bar is open daily, and the restaurant Tuesday through Saturday for dinner. 1476 rue Crescent (at boul. de Maisonneuve), downtown. ✆ **514/284-6555.** www.lenewtown.com. Métro: Peel.

Time Supper Club   Though food is served, it isn't the prime attraction—after dinner, Time's fabulous crowd gets up from the tables and works off the calories to rock, house, and hip-hop, and live acts that thump on until closing at 3am. The waitstaff is startlingly sexy. Dress well, look good, and approach the door with confidence. The club (which is housed in a landmark 1930s Art Deco building), open weekends in winter and 4 nights in summer (on a huge patio), is in a dreary industrial

The Upstairs Jazz Bar & Grill hosts good-quality bands nightly.

neighborhood south of the downtown core, so you might want to arrive by car or taxi. 997 rue St-Jacques ouest (at rue de la Cathédrale), downtown. ✆ **514/392-9292.** www. timesupperclub.com. Métro: Bonaventure.

Upstairs Jazz Bar & Grill ★   The Upstairs Jazz Bar, decidedly *down* a few steps from the street, has been hosting live jazz music nightly for years. Big names are infrequent, but the groups are more than competent. Sets begin as at 8:30pm, and there are three a night, 7 days a week. Decor includes record-album covers and fish tanks. Pretty good food ranges from bar snacks to more substantial meals. Most patrons are edging toward their middle-age years, but as of late a younger jazz-curious crowd has been settling in. 1254 rue Mackay (south of rue Ste-Catherine). ✆ **514/931-6808.** www.upstairsjazz.com. Cover usually C$5–C$30. Métro: Guy-Concordia.

Vieux-Montréal

Le Deux Pierrots ★   This has traditionally been one of the best known of Montréal's *boîtes-à-chansons* (song clubs), but its more visible personality these days is as a sports bar. The sports posters are what you'll mostly see when you walk by, but look for the smaller posters of musicians, too. On Friday and Saturday nights, a French-style cabaret still brings in singers who interact animatedly, and often bilingually, with the crowd. Arrive by 9pm or make a reservation because tables can fill up. 104 rue St-Paul est (west of Place Jacques-Cartier). ✆ **514/861-1270.** www.lespierrots.com. Métro: Place d'Armes.

Modavie   Set aside an evening for dinner with jazz at this popular Vieux-Montréal bistro and wine bar. Music is usually mainstream jazz by duos or trios, and there's no fee for the show. In addition to tables, there are about a dozen seats at a handsome horseshoe-shaped bar just inside the door. There's a long list of scotches, wine, cognacs, grappas, and ports. It's a friendly place, and the food is good, too. 1 rue St-Paul ouest (corner of rue St-Laurent). ✆ **514/287-9582.** www.modavie. com. Métro: Place d'Armes.

Velvet   This cavernous night club has a speakeasy feel, thanks to its virtually nonexistent signage and tunnel entrance through the bar of Auberge St-Gabriel. Some of the bartenders here are models and many of the patrons have deep pockets, so, yes, come dressed to impress. Some nights have been known to have special themes, such as Boudoir Fridays. Music ranges from house, hip-hop to electro, often by top international DJs. 420 rue St-Gabriel (near rue St. Paul est). (?) **514/878-9782.** www.velvetspeakeasy.ca. Metro: Place d'Armes.

Plateau Mont-Royal

Buonanotte It's a high-end, expensive Italian restaurant, but many head to Buonanotte just for a drink, and then a little bit of dancing as the space turns into a makeshift nightclub later into the night. Its reputation comes as much from being a nightspot for the fabulous and the celebrated as anything else, and it attracts people with serious money to spend. It can be crowded, and if you're not a regular, you might get shut out if you show up after 11pm. 3518 boul. St-Laurent (near rue Sherbrooke). (?) **514/848-0644.** www.buonanotte.com. Métro: St-Laurent.

Casa del Popolo ★ The heart of the Montréal indie music scene. Set in a scruffy storefront, Casa del Popolo serves vegetarian food, operates a laid-back bar, and has a small first-floor stage. Across the street is a sister performance space, La Sala Rosa (below). 4873 boul. St-Laurent (near boul. St-Joseph). (?) **514/284-3804.** www.casadelpopolo.com. Cover C$5–C$15. Métro: Laurier.

Club Balattou This club on the Main is a premiere venue for seeing African music and performers from the West Indies and Latin America. An infectious, sensual beat issues from it, a happy variation from the prevailing grunge and dance music of mainstream clubs. 4372 boul. St-Laurent (at rue Marie-Anne). (?) **514/845-5447.** Cover C$5–C$20. www.balattou.com. Métro: Mont-Royal.

La Sala Rosa ★ A bigger venue than its sister performance space Casa del Popolo (see above), La Sala Rosa has a full calendar of interesting rock, experimental, and jazz music, and is probably the premiere indie-rock club in the city. The attached **Sala Rosa Restaurant** serves hearty Spanish food with a big card of tapas and paella—and, every Thursday, live flamenco music with dancing and singing. Reserve your spot a week or more in advance. 4848 boul. St-Laurent (near boul. St-Joseph). (?) **514/844-4227.** www.casadelpopolo.com. Cover C$5–C$30. Métro: Laurier.

Le Divan Orange A laid-back club with a good, hipster vibe, Le Divan Orange has a self-prescribed mission to foster new and experimental musical careers for both English- and French-speaking performers, including indie rock, funk, country, and traditional North African. There are also events best described as performance art. Shows start around 9:30pm every night. 4234 boul. St-Laurent (near rue Rachel). (?) **514/840-9090.** www.ledivanorange.org. Cover C$5–C$10. Métro: Mont-Royal.

Tokyo Bar It's all about the rooftop terrace at this dance club, which draws well-dressed 20-somethings (a high ratio of college students who go to nearby McGill University) and tourists, rain or shine, 10pm to 3am. There's indoor space, too, for live music or DJs, hip-hop to disco. 3709 boul. St-Laurent (near av. des Pins). (?) **514/842-6838.** www.tokyobar.com. Cover C$7–C$10. Métro: Sherbrooke.

The Village & Quartier Latin

Cabaret Mado ★ The glint of the sequins can be blinding! Inspired by 1920s cabaret theater, this determinedly trendy place in the Village has nightly performances and a dance floor, and is considered a premiere venue these days. Friday and Saturday feature festive drag shows, which, on a given night, may honor the likes of "Tina Turner" or "Céline Dion." Look for the pink-haired drag queen on the retro marquee. 1115 rue Ste-Catherine est (near rue Amherst). ✆ **514/525-7566.** www.mado.qc.ca. Cover C$5–C$10. Métro: Beaudry.

Club Soda   The long-established rock club in a seedy part of the Latin Quarter remains one of the prime destinations for performers just below the star level—Queensryche, Mara Tremblay, and Pauly Shore have all come through recently—and also hosts several of the city's comedy festivals and acts for the annual jazz festival. 1225 boul. St-Laurent (at rue Ste-Catherine), Quartier Latin. ✆ **514/286-1010.** www.clubsoda.ca. Tickets from C$17. Métro: St-Laurent.

Gotha Salon Bar Lounge   For a quieter venue in the Village, the cozy Gotha lounge has a fireplace and live piano on Sunday nights, and attracts a mixed gay/straight crowd. Try the honey wine, a digestive that's made in Canada, or the signature Le Gotha martini, with vodka, triple sec, white cranberry juice, and lime. It's at street level below the **Aubergell Bed & Breakfast** (www.aubergell.com) on rue Amherst, a road chockablock with antiques shops sporting vintage and collectible goodies from the 1930s to 1980s. 1641 rue Amherst. ✆ **514/526-1270.** Métro: Beaudry.

Les Foufounes Electriques   From the outside, this Latin Quarter club looks like something out of a *Mad Max* movie, with a spider the size of a Smart Car hanging over the front gate. Inside, it's a multilevel rock club that features hard-core and disco-punk bands and DJs. If you're within 2 blocks, you'll hear it. If you don't sport a tattoo or body piercing, you may want to think twice before entering. It's open daily to 3am. 87 Ste-Catherine est (near boul. St-Laurent). ✆ **514/844-5539.** www.foufounes.qc.ca. Métro: St-Laurent.

Sky Club & Pub ★   A complex that includes drag performances in the cabaret room, a pub serving dinner daily from 4 to 9pm, a hip-hop room, a spacious dance floor that's often set to house music, and a popular roof terrace, Sky is thought by many to be the city's hottest spot for the gay, young, and fabulous. It's got spiffy decor and pounding music. Did we mention there's also a pool? And a spa? 1474 rue Ste-Catherine est (near rue Plessis). ✆ **514/529-6969.** www.complexesky.com. Métro: Beaudry.

Les Foufounes Electriques is a longtime rock and dance club.

Stereo ★   Passionate devotees of this late-night club have been known to tattoo the club's audio-wave logo on their bodies. A 2008 fire crippled and closed the hyper-hip, after-hours club that wouldn't rev up until 3am and then roared until noon, and its 2009 grand reopening was much welcomed by club kids, drag queens, hipsters, and students gay and straight. 858 rue Ste-Catherine est (near rue Berri). ✆ **514/658-2646.** www.stereonightclub.net. Métro: Berri-UQAM.

Outer Districts

Igloofest ★★ 🎁   Little sister to Piknic Electronik (see below), Igloofest is brought to you by the same people. For 3 weekends in January (Fri–Sun), this outdoor music festival attracts hardcore partiers who come to take in electro music and drink under the night sky. Below-zero temperatures demand some serious winter layers. Many enthusiasts come in their best outlandish ski suits. There are al fresco "lounges," ice bars serving vodka and mulled wine, and even marshmallow roasting pits. Jacques-Cartier Quay in the Old Port of Montréal. ✆ **514/904-1247.** www.igloofest.ca. Admission C$10 in advance, C$12 on-site. Weekends in Jan, from 6:30pm-midnight. Métro: Champs-de-Mars or Place d'Armes.

Piknic Electronik ★ 👜 From May to October on sunny Sunday afternoons and into the evenings, a DJ starts spinning or live acts amp up, and the electronica begins at Parc Jean-Drapeau. Hipster kids, families, and dancing queens who just didn't get enough on Saturday night gather and shake it outdoors under the Alexander Calder sculpture, *Man and His World,* located on the Belvedere on the north shore of Ile Sainte-Hélène, facing the river. (The website suggests getting off at the Métro and just following the rhythms!) Music starts by 1 or 2pm and runs until about 8pm, sometimes 10:30pm. From 2010 on, all materials used at the Piknic Electronik site will be recyclable or compostable. Belvedere in Parc Jean-Drapeau (Ile Ste-Hélène). ✆ **514/904-1247.** www.piknicelectronik.com. Admission C$12 adults, free for children 12 and under. May–Oct Sun 2–9pm. Métro: Jean-Drapeau.

BARS

There are four main drags to keep in mind for a night on the town. Downtown's **rue Crescent** hums with activity from late afternoon until far into the evening, especially on summer weekend nights, when the street swarms with people careening from bar to restaurant to club. It's young and noisy—and also considered a tourist trap to locals, although many still tend to end up there to party. In the Plateau Mont-Royal neighborhood, **boulevard St-Laurent**—or the Main, as it's known—has blocks and blocks of bars and clubs, most with a slightly more French personality, as opposed to rue Crescent's Anglo flavor. In Vieux-Montréal, **rue St-Paul** just west of Place Jacques-Cartier falls somewhere in the middle on the Anglophone-Francophone spectrum. And in the Gay Village, **rue Ste-Catherine** est closes in summer to cars and becomes flush with people as the cafes and bars that line the street build temporary terraces that fill in the afternoons and evenings.

Most bars tend to open around 11:30am and stay open until 2 or 3am. Many have *cinq à sept* (happy hour) from as early as 3pm to as late as 9pm.

Downtown

Brutopia ★ This pub pulls endless pints of its own microbrews, which might include maple cream, IPA, or java stout on a given day. With several rooms on three levels, a terrace in back, and a street-side balcony, it draws a mix of ages, students with laptops, and old friends just hanging out. Unlike other spots on rue Crescent, where the sound levels can be deafening, here you can actually have a conversation. The snacking menu spans the globe. Bands perform, too, with an open-mic night on Sunday. 1219 rue Crescent (north of boul. René-Lévesque). ✆ **514/393-9277.** www.brutopia.net. Métro: Lucien L'Allier.

Le Cabaret In Hôtel de la Montagne (p. 70) and within sight of the hotel's trademark lobby fountain, with its nude bronze sprite sporting stained-glass wings, this appealing piano bar draws a crowd of youngish to middle-aged professionals. In summer, the hotel's **Terrasse Magnétic** up on the roof offers meals, drinks, dancing, and use of the outdoor pool until 3am. 1430 rue de la Montagne (north of rue Ste-Catherine). ✆ **514/288-5656.** www.hoteldelamontagne.com. Métro: Guy-Concordia.

Dominion Square Tavern 🎁🍴 Located just steps away from the central tourist office on Square Dorchester (see no. 3 in the Downtown Walking Tour, p. 154, for an explanation of why there are two names for the same square), the tavern got an overhaul in early 2010. It is visually arresting, done up in 1920s grandeur, with original tiles, lead mirrors, and an amber glow. The menu includes *moules et frites* (mussels and french fries) and a Ploughman's Lunch, featuring either meat or fish. Mains run from C$11 to C$23. It's open 11:30am to midnight weekdays and 5pm to midnight Saturday. 1248 Metcalfe (south of rue Ste-Catherine). ℭ **514/564-5056.** www.tavernedominion.com. Métro: Peel.

Pullman ★ 🍴 This sleek wine bar has over 300 different wines and offers either 60mL or 120mL (2- or 4-oz.) pours, so you can sample a number of vintages. In summer, ask the sommelier Gabriel to pour you a Coimbra, a sangria-ish drink with *porto blanco*, tonic, and lime. A competent tapas menu with standards like charcuterie and grilled cheese bedazzled with port are prepared with the precision of a sushi chef. The smartly designed multilevel space creates pockets of ambience, from cozy corners to tables drenched in natural light. It's open daily from 4:30pm to 1am. 3424 av. du Parc (north of Sherbrooke). ℭ **514/288-7779.** www.pullman-mtl.com. Métro: Place des Arts.

Sir Winston Churchill Pub ★ The three levels of bars and cafes here are rue Crescent landmarks, and the New Orleans–style sidewalk and first-floor terraces (open in warm months) make perfect vantage points from which to check out the pedestrian traffic. Inside and down the stairs, the pub, with English ales on tap, attempts to imitate a British public house and gets a mixed crowd of young professionals. It's open daily to 3am, with DJs every day. 1459 rue Crescent (near rue Ste-Catherine). ℭ **514/288-3814.** www.swcpc.com. Métro: Guy-Concordia.

Thursday's A prime watering hole for Montréal's young, professional set. The pubby bar spills out onto a terrace that hangs over the street, and there's a glittery disco in back. It's voted "Best Pick-Up Spot" year after year by the *Montréal Mirror,* which quips that Thursday's "gets more people laid than Craigslist." In L'Hôtel de la Montagne, 1430 rue de la Montagne (north of rue Ste-Catherine). ℭ **514/288-5656.** www.thursdaysbar.com. Métro: Guy-Concordia.

Tour de Ville Memorable and breathtaking. We're talking about the view from Montréal's only revolving restaurant and bar, up on the 30th floor of the Delta Centre-Ville (the bar part doesn't revolve, but you still get a great view). The best time to go is when the sun is setting and the city lights are beginning to blink on. It's open Friday and Saturday from 5:30 to 11pm (and Sunday brunch for two seatings: 10:30am–12:30pm and 1–3pm). In the Delta Centre-Ville Hôtel, 777 rue University (at rue St-Jecques). ℭ **514/879-4777.** www.deltahotels.com. Métro: Square Victoria.

W Hotel With its Plateau Lounge on the mezzanine, W Bartini, and Wunderbar lounge/night club open daily until 3am, W attracts some of the best-looking partiers in town. Located more precisely in the Quartier International, W opens in summer a chic makeshift terrace, which is the spot to be scene, particularly during Grand Prix weekend. 901 Victoria Square (at rue McGill). ℭ **514/395-3100.** www.starwoodhotels.com. Métro: Square-Victoria.

Vieux-Montréal

Garçonnière 🎁🍴 You may miss the doorway if you're not paying attention. This subterranean champagne and oyster bar is as chic as it is small. The menu lists several kinds of bubbly, of which a glass of the rosé variety is free to ladies on

Friday nights. There is also a limited dinner menu should you wish to settle in next to the fireplace for longer. 343 rue St-Paul est (near rue Gosford). ℂ **514/543-8274.** www.bargarconniere.com. Métro: Champ-de-Mars.

Le Jardin Nelson In the summer, the outdoor dining options that line Place Jacques Cartier are tempting but touristy. Le Jardin Nelson has a people-watching porch adjacent to the plaza, but you're better off tucking into its large tree-shaded garden court, which sits behind a stone building dating from 1812. A pleasant hour or two can be spent listening to live jazz, played every afternoon and evening. Food takes second place, but the kitchen does well with its pizzas and crepes, with crepe options both sweet and savory (including lobster). There are heaters outdoors to cut the chill and a few tables indoors, too. When the weather's nice, it's open until 2am. Le Jardin Nelson is closed November through mid-April. 407 Place Jacques-Cartier (at rue St-Paul est). ℂ **514/861-5731.** www.jardin nelson.com. Métro: Place d'Armes or Champ-de-Mars.

Philémon ★ A large racetrack-shaped bar is the center of action here. The look here of the decor is chalet-chic, while the crowd is more urban professional, with a healthy dose of artsy types thrown in for good measure. Order some nibbles with your drinks; the oysters are good and there's a great charcuterie platter. Thursday nights sometimes see lineups at the door, but you probably won't wait for too long. 111 rue St-Paul ouest (at rue St-Urbain). ℂ **514/289-3777.** www.philemonbar. com. Métro: Place d'Armes.

Suite 701 ★★ When Place d'Armes Hôtel (p. 75) converted its lobby and wine bar into this spiffy lounge, young professionals got the word fast. The so-called *cinq-à-sept* (5-to-7pm) after-work crowd fills the space evenings, especially on Thursdays. Upscale bar food comes from the same kitchen as the restaurant's high-end operation, **Aix Cuisine du Terroir** (p. 90), with snacks for C$8 to C$14 and main courses for C$21 to C$25. In good weather, it's also only a short elevator ride to the rooftop terrace. 711 Côte de la Place d'Armes (at rue St-Jacques). ℂ **514/904-1201.** www.suite701.com. Métro: Place d'Armes.

Verses Sky Terrace When the weather is warm enough, ascend to this rooftop restaurant/bar inside the snazzy **Hôtel Nelligan** (p. 72). It's open from 11am to 11pm, with food available all day. 100 rue St-Paul ouest (at rue St-Sulpice). ℂ **514/ 788-4000.** www.versesrestaurant.com. Métro: Place d'Armes.

Plateau Mont-Royal & Mile End

Baldwin Barmacie ★ The split-level space of this all-white bar attracts more of a young professional than starving-artist crowd. Sometimes there's a DJ, sometimes it's just owner Alex Baldwin's iTunes library, consisting of classic rock and old school hip hop. Staff are outfitted in spiffy black and bottles line the walls like they would in an old-fashion pharmacy. On the wall near the front window, a portrait hangs of Alexander Baldwin's grandmother who, indeed, used to work at a pharmacy just around the corner. 115 av. Laurier ouest (at rue St. Urbain). ℂ **514/ 276-4282.** www.baldwinbarmacie.com. Métro: Laurier.

Bílý Kůň ★★ Pronounced "Billy Coon," this popular bar is a bit of Prague right in Montréal, from the avant-garde decor (mounted ostrich heads ring the room) to the full line of Czech beers, local microbrews, and dozen-plus scotches. Martini specials include the Absinthe Aux Pommes. Students and professionals jam in for the relaxed candle-lit atmosphere, which includes twirling ceiling fans and picture windows that open to the street. There's live jazz from 6 to 8pm daily and DJs spinning upbeat pop most nights from 8pm to 3am. Get here early to do a little shopping in the hipster boutiques along the street. 354 av. du Mont-Royal est (near rue St-Denis). *(C)* **514/845-5392.** www.bilykun.com. Métro: Mont-Royal.

Bílý Kůň is popular with students and professionals.

Buvette Chez Simone Simone is only one of a group of friends who own this popular bar. The square-shaped terrace (framed by greenery in summer) is a coveted spot in sunny weather. The stripped-down industrial chic of the interior is dominated by a central, oval-shaped bar. The menu has a satisfying selection of small eats, including cold cut meats and cheese, as well as a decent choice of wines by the glass. 4869 av. du Parc (at boul. St. Joseph ouest). *(C)* **514/750-6577.** www.buvettechez simone.com. Métro: Mont-Royal or Laurier.

Champs Montréalers are no less enthusiastic about sports, especially hockey, than other Canadians, and fans both avid and casual drop by this three-story sports emporium to catch up with their teams and hoist a few. Games from around the world are fed to walls of TVs; more than a dozen athletic events might be showing at any given time. Food is what you'd expect—burgers, steaks, and such. 3956 boul. St-Laurent (near av. Duluth). *(C)* **514/987-6444.** Métro: Sherbrooke.

Dieu Du Ciel ★★ Tucked into a corner building on rue Laurier, this neighborhood artisanal brewpub offers an alternating selection of some dozen beers, including house brews and exotic imports. The place buzzes, even midweek. With good conversation and some friends to sample the array, what more do you need? If it's guidance on where to begin, how about starting with the Première Communion (First Communion), a Scottish ale; moving on to the Rosée d'Hibiscus, which is less sweet than feared; and finishing with the Rigor Mortis ABT. Dieu du Ciel beers are also bottled and sold throughout the province. 29 av. Laurier ouest (near boul. St. Laurent). *(C)* **514/490-9555.** www.dieuduciel.com. Métro: Laurier.

Koko One of *the* chicest bars of the city. Koko is a prime reason to visit, if not stay at, the **Opus Hotel** (p. 68). The bar includes a spectacular terrace and an Asian-influenced menu, and it's open "until late"—1am Sunday through Wednesday and 3am Thursday through Saturday. As befits its positioning as a premier venue for urban glamour, a bouncer often stands watch at the door. Try the C$12 Wilde Child cocktail, with Prosecco and candied wild hibiscus flower. 8 rue Sherbrooke ouest (at boul. St-Laurent). *(C)* **514/657-5656.** www.kokomontreal.com. Métro: Saint-Laurent.

Laïka Amid the plethora of St-Laurent watering stops, this bright little *boîte* offers tasty sandwiches and tapas, and a popular Sunday brunch. DJs spin house, funk, electronica, and whatnot from midevening until 3am for a mostly 18- to 35-year-old crowd. Très cool. 4040 boul. St-Laurent (near av. Duluth). *(C)* **514/842-8088.** www.laikamontreal.com. Métro: Sherbrooke.

Whisky Café If you enjoy scotch, particularly single-malts like Laphraoig and Glenfiddich, then you'll want to visit this spot with more than 150 different labels to sample at this handsome bar. Newbies can try a *degustation* by region or brand, as each of three pours comes with a description of aroma and taste. Side dishes of nuts and cheese are as simple and sophisticated as the decor—wood-framed leather chairs surround handmade tiled tables, or you can grab a cozy booth. Another decorative triumph: The men's urinal has a waterfall acting as the *pissoir*. Attached is a separate cigar lounge with leather armchairs and Cubans. Note that the bar is well north of any of the other bars listed here. 5800 boul. St-Laurent (at rue Bernard). ☎ **514/278-2646.** www.whiskycafe.com. Métro: Laurier.

Little Burgundy

Burgundy Lion ★ This Brit pub is tellingly more Anglophone, as is the area, which is decidedly up and coming. A no-nonsense kind of place with banquettes and taverne-type wooden chairs, the Lion welcomes a slightly younger crowd on weekends than the regulars that come during the week. Television screens and sports team flags ensure that this is a lively spot to take in hockey, footie, baseball, or whatever else is in the news that day. The food menu is also respectable, but try to get a reservation at Joe Beef across the street before coming to enjoy a nightcap here. 2496 rue Notre-Dame ouest (at rue Charlevoix). ☎ **514/934-0888.** www.burgundylion.com. Métro: Lionel-Groulx.

MORE ENTERTAINMENT

Gambling & Cabaret

The **Casino de Montréal** (☎ **800/665-2274** or 514/392-2746; www.casinos duquebec.com), Québec's first, is housed in recycled space: The complex reuses what were the French and Québec pavilions during Expo 67. Asymmetrical and groovy, the buildings provide a dramatic setting for games of chance. Four floors contain more than 120 game tables, including roulette, craps, blackjack, baccarat, and varieties of poker, and there are more than 3,000 slot machines. It has four restaurants, and the elegant **Nuances** is one of the top restaurants in the city. No alcoholic beverages are served in the gambling areas, and patrons must be at least 18 years old and dressed neatly (beachwear and clothing depicting violence are prohibited). The casino is entirely smoke-free, with outside smoking areas. It's open 24 hours a day, 7 days a week, with overnight packages available at nearby hotels. The casino is on Parc Jean-Drapeau. You can drive there, or take the Métro to the Parc Jean-Drapeau stop and then walk or take the casino shuttle bus (no. 167, labeled CASINO). From June through October, a free shuttle bus (*navette*) leaves on the hour from the downtown Infotouriste Centre at 1001 rue du Square Dorchester (it makes other stops downtown, too). Shuttles depart from the Infotouriste Centre starting at 10am and ending at 7pm; the last shuttle leaves the casino for downtown at 7:45pm. Call ☎ **514/392-2746** with questions.

The exterior of the Casino de Montréal.

Cinema

When movie-going in the province of Québec, check what language the films are in and what language they're subtitled. In Montréal, English-language films are usually presented with French subtitles. However, when the initials "VF" (for *version française*) follow the title of a non-Francophone movie, it means that the movie has been dubbed into French. You may or may not find English subtitles on French-language films, so ask at the box office. Admission to films is usually about C$11 for adults, and less for students, seniors, and children. There are usually special afternoon rates for matinees.

Cinéma Parallèle, 3536 boul. St-Laurent near rue Prince Arthur (℃ **514/ 847-9272;** www.cinemaparallele.ca) has showcased independent film since 1967. With an emphasis on new releases—Québécois, Canadian, and international—the cinema frequently hosts filmmakers for postfilm discussions or festivals such as the **Festival du Nouveau Cinéma.** It shares an address with the rebranded and evolving **eXcentris,** known for decades as a film venue but now focused on live performance. The National Film Board (NFB) of Canada operates **CinéRobothèque** at 1564 rue St-Denis (℃ **514/496-6887;** www.nfb.ca). The first floor houses the NFB film library—a high-tech screening center where visitors can browse a multimedia catalog, and then watch a film at a personal viewing station. The second floor features screenings of classic Canadian and international films, or films showing as part of festivals, primarily in English and French. The **Cinémathèque Québécoise** (℃ **514/842-9763;** www.cinema theque.qc.ca) calls itself "Montréal's Museum of the Moving Image." Its mission is to preserve and document film and television heritage, particularly that of Québec and Canada, as well as international animation. In addition to housing archives of films, photographs, and equipment, the Cinémathèque screens exhibits and retrospectives at 335 bd. de Maisonneuve est. Imposing, fantastically huge images confront viewers of the seven-story **IMAX Theatre** screen in the Centre des Sciences de Montréal (p. 130). Many of the films are suitable for the entire family.

Comedy

The once red-hot market for comedy clubs across North America may have cooled off in many places, but it lives on in Montréal, mostly because the city is the home to the highly regarded **Juste pour Rire (Just for Laughs) Festival** (℃ **888/244-3155;** www.hahaha.com) every July. Those who have so far avoided the comedy-club experience should know that profanity, bathroom humor, and ethnic slurs are common fodder. To avoid becoming the object of comedians' barbs, sit well back from the stage. Check whether the show you're interested in is in French or English.

There's a full array of comedy at **Comedyworks,** a long-running club at 1238 rue Bishop (℃ **514/398-9661;** www.comedyworksmontreal.com). Monday is open mic, Tuesday and Wednesday are improv nights (a comedy troupe works off the audience's suggestions), and Thursday through Saturday feature international headliners. No food is served, just drinks. Reservations are recommended, especially on Friday, when it may be necessary to arrive early to secure a seat. Shows are in English and happen nightly at 8:30pm, with additional shows at 11pm on Friday and Saturday. Locals love Montréaler Sugar Sammy, who is a rising star on the international circuit. Check him out if he's in town.

SIDE TRIPS FROM MONTRÉAL

Y ou don't have to travel far from Montréal to reach mountains, parks, or bike trails. In fact, enjoyable touring regions are a mere 30-minute drive from the city. The **Laurentians** (to the north) and the **Cantons-de-l'Est** (aka the Eastern Townships, to the southeast) both are developed with year-round vacation retreats, with skiing in winter, biking and boating in summer, maple sugaring in spring, and vineyard touring and leaf peeping in fall.

The pearl of the Laurentians (also called les Laurentides) is **Mont-Tremblant,** eastern Canada's highest peak and a winter mecca for skiers and snowboarders from all over North America. Development has been particularly heavy in the resort town here.

The region has dozens of other ski centers, too, with scores of trails at every level of difficulty, and many are less than an hour from Montréal. The area loses none of its charm in summer (and in fact gains some with thinned-out traffic). That's when ski resorts turn into attractive, green mountain properties close to biking, fishing, and golfing.

The bucolic Cantons-de-l'Est were known as the Eastern Townships when they were a haven for English Loyalists and their descendants (many still refer to the region by that name today). It has memorable country inns, former homes of early 1900s aristocracy, and the beautiful Lake Massawippi. As with the Laurentians, many of the same trails groomed for winter sports are used for parallel activities in summer. The mountain of **Bromont,** for example, known in the winter for its skiing, has marked paths for mountain biking. Rock climbing, whitewater kayaking, sailing, and fishing are additional options, with equipment readily available for rent.

Because the people of both regions rely heavily on tourism for their livelihoods, knowledge of at least rudimentary English is widespread, even outside hotels and restaurants.

NORTH INTO THE LAURENTIANS (LES LAURENTIDES)

55km–129km (34–80 miles) N of Montréal

Don't expect spiked peaks or high, ragged ridges. The Laurentian Shield's rolling hills and rounded mountains are among the world's oldest, worn down by wind and water over eons. They average between 300m and 520m (984 ft.–1,706 ft.) in height, with the highest being Mont-Tremblant, at 875m (2,871 ft.). In the lower area, closer to Montréal, the terrain resembles a rumpled quilt, its folds and hollows cupping a multitude of lakes, large and small. Farther north, the summits are higher and craggier, with patches of snow persisting well into spring. These are not the Alps or the Rockies, but they're welcoming and embracing.

PREVIOUS PAGE: **Skiers take the gondola at Mont-Tremblant.**

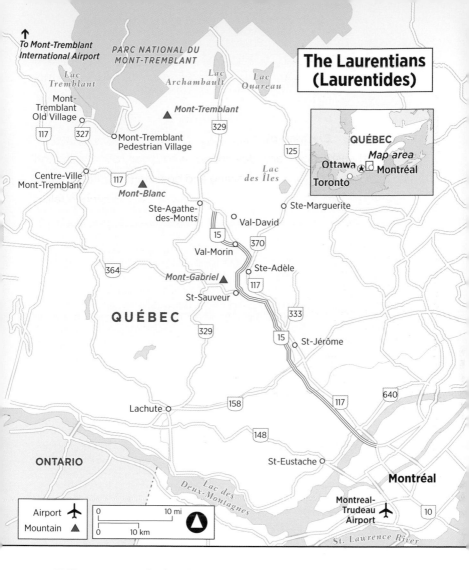

The Laurentians (Laurentides)

Half a century ago, the first ski schools, rope tows, and trails began to appear. Today, there are 13 ski centers within a 64km (40-mile) radius, and cross-country skiing has as enthusiastic a following as downhill. Sprawling resorts and modest lodges and inns are packed in winter with skiers, some of them through April. Trails for those with advanced skills typically have short pitches and challenging moguls, with broad, hard-packed avenues for beginners and the less experienced. Skiers can usually expect reliable snow from early December to late March.

But skiing is only half the story. As transportation improved, people took advantage of the obvious warm-weather opportunities for watersports, golf (courses in the area now total nearly 30), mountain biking, and hiking. Bird-watchers of both intense and casual bent can be fully occupied. Loon lovers, in particular, know that the lakes of the province of Québec's mountains are home to the native waterfowl that gives its name to the dollar coin. Excellent divers and swimmers, the birds' ability to walk on land is limited, which makes nesting a trial. They're identified by a distinctive call that might be described as an extended, mournful giggle.

At any time of year, a visit to any of the villages or resorts in the Laurentians is likely to yield pleasant memories. The busiest times are February and March for skiing, July and August for summer vacation, and during the Christmas-to–New Year's holiday period. In March and April, the maple trees are tapped, and *cabanes à sucre* (sugar shacks) open up everywhere, some selling just maple syrup and candies, others serving full meals and even staging entertainment. May is often characterized by warm days, cool nights, and just enough people that the streets don't seem deserted. September is the same way, and in the last 2 weeks of that month, the leaves put on a stunning show of autumnal color. In May and June, it must be said, the indigenous black flies and mosquitoes can seem as big and as ill-tempered as buzzards, so be prepared. And some of the resorts, inns, and lodges close down for a couple of weeks in spring and fall, so be sure to check ahead if you're traveling during that time.

Prices can be difficult to pin down. Prices listed for hotels in this chapter are the rack rate for double occupancy during the busy skiing and summer-vacation months, unless otherwise noted. At other times of the year, reservations are easier to get and prices for virtually everything are lower. Most hotels offer package deals with meals or activities, so consult their websites for options. Many also offer discounts to AAA members.

Remember that Montréalers fill the highways when they "go up north" on weekends, particularly during the top skiing months, so make reservations early if that's when you'll be traveling, and try to avoid driving on Friday afternoons.

Essentials

GETTING THERE

BY CAR The fast and scenic **Autoroute des Laurentides,** also known as **Autoroute 15,** goes straight from Montréal to the Laurentians. Leaving Montréal, you just follow the signs to St-Jérôme. The exit numbers represent the distance in kilometers that the village lies from Montréal.

Though the pace of development is quickening, flanking the highway with water parks, condos, and chain restaurants, this is still a pretty drive once you're out of the clutches of the tangle of expressways surrounding Montréal and past St-Jérôme. You'll quickly get a sweeping, panoramic introduction to the area, from lower Laurentians' rolling hills and forests to the mountain drama of the upper range.

Those with the time to meander can exit at St-Jérôme and pick up the older, parallel **Route 117,** which plays tag with the autoroute all the way to Ste-Agathe-des-Monts. Many of the region's more appealing towns are along or near this route. (Beware in winter, however, when parts of Rte. 117 can become riddled with potholes large enough to seriously damage your car. The extreme weather does a job on the state of the roads.) North of Ste-Agathe, the autoroute ends and Route 117 becomes the major artery for the region. It continues well past Mont-Tremblant and deep into Québec's north country, finally ending at the Ontario border hundreds of miles from Montréal.

Québec's equivalent of the highway patrol is Sûreté de Québec. While enforcement of speed limits is loose, if you're pulled over, remember that radar detectors are illegal in the province (even if they're not turned on) and can be confiscated.

BY PLANE   Mont-Tremblant International Airport (airport code YTM; ✆ 819/275-9099; www.mtia.ca), 39km (24 miles) northwest of Mont-Tremblant, receives direct flights from Newark, New Jersey, through Continental Airlines in winter months only. It also gets direct flights from Toronto through Porter Airlines (✆ 888/619-8622; www.flyporter.com), which flies to Boston, Chicago, Myrtle Beach, and Newark. Car rentals are available from Hertz and Discount by reservation only. An airport shuttle bus delivers guests directly to 17 hotels in Mont-Tremblant and the ski mountain, and taxis are available. The ride takes about 40 minutes.

Aéroport International Pierre-Elliott-Trudeau de Montréal (airport code YUL; ✆ 800/465-1213 or 514/394-7377; www.admtl.com), known more commonly as **Montréal-Trudeau Airport,** is 30 to 60 minutes from the Laurentians, depending on how far north you're headed. **Skyport** (✆ 800/471-1155 or 514/631-1155; www.skyportinternational.com) runs four daily shuttles to and from Mont-Tremblant in winter and two in summer; check online for schedule and rates. There are also taxis and limousines that will take you to any Laurentian hideaway—for a price. Ask about the best options when making accommodations reservations.

BY BUS   From Montréal, **Galland** buses (✆ 514/333-9555; www.gallandbus.com) depart from **Station Centrale D'autobus,** 505 bd. de Maisonneuve est, stopping in the larger Laurentian towns, including Ste-Sauveur, Ste-Adèle, and Mont-Tremblant. The ride to Mont-Tremblant takes just less than 3 hours.

Another option is the nonprofit **Allo Stop,** an alternative program that coordinates rideshares to help reduce the numbers of cars on the road. Travelers help pay for gas. Call ✆ 514/985-3032 for the Montréal office or visit www.allostopmontreal.com.

VISITOR INFORMATION

Tourist offices are plentiful throughout the Laurentians. Look for the blue "?" signs along the highways or in towns. Closed offices are marked with a sign that reads FERMÉ. For an orientation to the entire region, stop in at the major information center, well marked from the highway, at exit 51 off Autoroute 15. It shares a building with a 24-hour McDonald's, and there's a gas station next door. Called **Tourisme Laurentides** (✆ 800/561-6673 or 450/224-7007; www.laurentides.com), it has racks of brochures and a helpful staff that can, for no charge, make reservations for lodging throughout the Laurentides. It's open daily from 8:30am to 5pm (until 6pm Fri).

St-Sauveur

Only 60km (37 miles) north of Montréal, the village of St-Sauveur (pop. 9,625) can easily be a day trip. The area is flush with outlet malls and the carloads of shoppers they attract, but a few blocks farther north, the older village square is dominated by a handsome church, and the streets around it bustle with a less frenzied activity for much of the year. Be prepared to have difficulty finding a parking place in season (try the large lot behind the church). Dining and snacking on everything from crepes to hot dogs are big activities here, evidenced by the many beckoning cafes. In summer, there's a tourist kiosk on the square.

In summer, **Parc Aquatique du Mont St-Sauveur,** 350 av. St-Denis (*©* **450/227-4671;** www.parcaquatique.com), Canada's largest water park, features rafting, a wave pool, a tidal-wave river, a three-level spa pool, and slides, including one you ride a chairlift to get to the top of and ride down in a tube. Full-day admission is C$32 for adults, C$26 for children 6 to 12, C$16 for children 3 to 5, and free for children 2 and under. Half-day, night, and family admissions are also available.

Ten days in early August are dedicated to St-Sauveur's annual **Festival des Arts** (*©* **450/227-0427;** www.fass.ca), with an emphasis on music and dance, including jazz and chamber concerts, and ballet troupes. The schedule always includes a number of free events.

WHERE TO STAY & EAT

If the idea of a picnic appeals—and in this town of ordinary restaurants, it well might—drive west on the main street, rue Principale, to **Chez Bernard,** 411 rue Principale (*©* **450/240-0000;** www.chezbernard.com). Inside the pretty little house behind the iron fence, you'll find fragrant cheeses, crusty breads, wines, savory tarts, pâtés, sausages, smoked meats, and a variety of prepared meals. Prices range from C$4 to C$17. A patio of tables fills up in the summer, or guests can head to indoor seating on the second floor, where there's also free Wi-Fi. The store opens daily at 9am.

Manoir Saint-Sauveur Just minutes off the autoroute and in the heart of an outlet shopping frenzy, Manoir Saint-Sauveur offers a monster outdoor pool and a comprehensive roster of four-season activities. The crest of Mont Saint-Sauveur is in sight of this hotel, and five other small ski centers are within a short drive. The on-site spa, **Le Spa du Manoir,** specializes in body treatments and massage therapy. Rooms are in one of three complexes and are spacious and comfortable, blandly modern with light-wood furnishings that hint vaguely of 19th-century Gallic inspirations. Options include balconies, fireplaces, and kitchenettes. Like most properties in the region, the front desk adjusts prices up or down according to season and occupancy on any given night, so ask if they have anything less expensive than the advertised rates when booking.

The pool at Manoir Saint-Sauveur.

246 chemin du Lac Millette, St-Sauveur, PQ J0R 1R3. www.manoir-saint-sauveur.com. *©* **800/361-0505** or 450/227-1811. Fax 450/227-8512. 250 units. C$159–C$249 double; C$269–C$369 suite. Children 17 and under stay free in parent's room. Packages available. AE, MC, V. Indoor parking C$10, outdoor parking free. Take exit 60 off Autoroute 15. **Amenities:** Restaurant; bar; babysitting; children's programs; concierge; substantial health club; indoor and outdoor pools; room service; spa; tennis courts. *In room:* A/C, TV, hair dryer, Wi-Fi (C$11 per day).

Ste-Adèle & Mont Gabriel

In winter, the ski mountain of **Mont Gabriel** is a popular destination (for information, see Hôtel Mont Gabriel, below). To get there, follow Autoroute 15 to exit 64

BIKER'S paradise: THE 4,000KM ROUTE VERTE

Québec is bike crazy, and it's got the goods to justify it. In summer 2007, the province officially inaugurated the new **Route Verte (Green Route),** a 4,000km (2,485-mile) bike network that stretches from one end of the province to the other, linking all regions and cities. It's modeled on the Rails-to-Trails program in the U.S. and cycling routes in Denmark, Great Britain, and along the Danube and Rhine rivers, and was initiated by the nonprofit biking organization Vélo Québec with support from the Québec Ministry of Transportation. Route Verte won the prestigious Prix Ulysse, one of the grand prizes given annually by the Québec tourist office, right out of the gate. The National Geographic Society went on to declare it one of the 10 best bicycle routes in the world.

The Route Verte website (**www.route verte.com**) provides maps of all the paths by region, with a "Bienvenue Cyclistes!" link that lists B&Bs, campsites, and hotels that are especially focused on serving bikers. Accredited accommodations display a BIENVENUE CYCLISTES! sticker or sign, and they provide a covered and locked place for overnight bicycle storage, access to high-carb meals with lots of fruits and veggies, a bike pump and tools, and information about where to make repairs nearby. The guidebook *Cycling in Québec: Official Guide to Bicycling on Québec's Route Verte,* published by Route Verte, can be ordered from the site.

Included in the network is the popular **P'tit Train du Nord** bike trail through the Laurentians to Mont-Tremblant and beyond. It's built on a former railway track and passes through the villages of Ste-Adèle, Val David, and Ste-Agathe-des-Monts. Cyclists can hop on for a day trip or a longer tour, and can get food and bike repairs at renovated railway stations along the way. The trail is free to ride on, and maps can be found on the regional tourist office's website (www. laurentians.com/parclineaire). The office also publishes the free *Official Tourist Guide to the Laurentians,* which always has a section on "cyclo-tourism." If you decide to plan a big trip, keep in mind **Transport du Parc Linéaire** (📞 **888/686-1323** or 450/569-5596; www.transport duparclineaire.com), which provides baggage transport from inn to inn.

and turn right at the stop sign. In addition to offering downhill skiing, the mountain is wrapped in cross-country trails that range through the surrounding countryside.

The adjacent village, Ste-Adèle (pop. 11,332), only 67km (42 miles) north of Montréal, is a near-metropolis compared to the other Laurentian villages. What makes it seem big are its services: police, doctors, ambulances, a shopping center, cinemas, art galleries, and a larger collection of places to stay and dine. As rue Morin mounts the hill to Lac Rond, Ste-Adèle's resort lake, it's easy to see why the town is divided into a lower part (*en bas*) and an upper part (*en haut*).

To get to the village, either take Route 117, which swings directly into its main street (boul. Ste-Adèle), or get off Autoroute 15 at exit 67.

EXPLORING STE-ADÈLE

Ste-Adèle's other big street, **rue Valiquette,** is a busy one-way thoroughfare that runs parallel to boulevard Ste-Adèle. It's lined with cafes, galleries, and bakeries.

Lac Rond is the center of summer activities. Canoes, sailboats, and *pédalos* (pedal-powered watercraft)—which can be rented from several docks—glide over the placid surface, while swimmers splash and play near shore-side beaches.

WHERE TO STAY & EAT

Hôtel Mont Gabriel ★ ☺   Perched high atop Mont Gabriel and looking like the rambling log cottages of the turn-of-the-20th-century wealthy, this kid-friendly resort is set on a 480-hectare (1,186-acre) forest estate and features golf and tennis programs in summer and ski and spa packages in winter. The hotel is a ski-in-ski-out facility with more than half the trails open for night-skiing. The spacious rooms in the Tyrol section are the most modern and desirable, and many provide views of the surrounding hills. One luxury suite and two chalets offer the option for more space still, and wheelchair accessible rooms are available. Dog sledding, cross-country skiing, and snowmobiling are possible in winter. The hotel is only 45 minutes from Montréal's Trudeau Airport.

1699 chemin Mont-Gabriel, Ste-Adèle, PQ J8B 1A5. www.montgabriel.com. ✆ **800/668-5253** or 450/229-3547. Fax 450/229-7034. 128 units. C$99–C$199 double. Children 16 and under stay free in parent's room. Packages and meal plans available. AE, MC, V. Free parking. Take exit 64 from Autoroute 15. **Amenities:** Restaurant; bar; babysitting; 18-hole golf course; health club; whirlpools (indoor and outdoor); pools (heated indoor and outdoor); sauna; spa; tennis courts (6 lit, clay) and tennis instruction. *In room:* A/C, TV, hair dryer, Wi-Fi (C$9 per day).

L'Eau à la Bouche ★   The owners leave no doubt as to where their priorities lie. While the hotel, directly on busy Route 117, is entirely satisfactory, the restaurant is their beloved baby. False modesty isn't a factor—*l'eau à la bouche* means "mouthwatering"—and the kitchen uses native ingredients with nouvelle presentations, like a poached half lobster with chanterelles and hand-gathered wild vegetables. Desserts are impressive, and the cheese plate is truly special. Everything is pricey: the C$150 discovery menu that includes wine pairings, the a la carte main courses for C$40 and up, a side of mushrooms for C$17. The hotel also has a spa with massage rooms and pretty outdoor hot and cold pools, which nonguests can visit for C$40. One spa package that includes a gourmet lunch at the smaller **Café-Bistro H2O** makes for a relaxing afternoon, worthy of a day-trip from Montréal.

3003 boul. Ste-Adèle (Rte. 117), Ste-Adèle, PQ J8B 2N6. www.leaualabouche.com. ✆ **888/828-2991** or 450/229-2991. Fax 450/229-7573. 21 units. C$185–C$225 double; C$205–C$325 renovated rooms and suites. Packages and meal plans available. AE, MC, V. Free parking. **Amenities:** Restaurant; cafe; babysitting; pools (outdoor; 1 heated and 1 Nordic cold bath); room service; sauna; spa. *In room:* A/C, TV, hair dryer, Wi-Fi (C$20 per stay).

Val-David

At exit 76 of Autoroute 15 (and also along Rte. 117) is Val-David, the region's faintly bohemian enclave (pop. 4,346). About 80km (50 miles) north of Montréal, it conjures up images of cabin hideaways set among hills rearing above ponds and lakes, and creeks tumbling through fragrant forests.

The **tourist office** is on the main street in the Petite Gare, or old train station, at 2525 rue de l'Église (✆ **888/322-7030**, ext. 235, or 819/322-2900, ext. 235; www.valdavid.com). It's open daily from 9am to 5pm, except for a few weeks in spring and fall. Another possibility for assistance is **Centre d'Exposition de Val-David,** a cultural center that mounts art exhibits in a two-story wooden building at 2495 rue de l'Église (✆ **819/322-7474;** www.culture.val-david.qc.ca).

Note that this far north into the Laurentians, the telephone area code changes to 819.

EXPLORING VAL-DAVID

Val-David is small, so park anywhere and meander at leisure. There are many artist studios, and the village sponsors a huge **ceramic art festival** (© 819/322-6868; www.1001pots.com) from mid-July to mid-August that it claims is "the largest exhibition of ceramics in North America." Sculptors and ceramicists, along with painters, jewelers, pewter smiths, and other craftspeople display their work, and there are concerts and other outdoor activities. There are pottery workshops for children every Saturday and Sunday; reserve a spot online.

Also look for the organic **farmer's market** every Saturday morning from late June to late September on rue de l'Académie (opposite the church).

Val-David is one of the villages along the bike path called **Parc Linéaire le P'Tit Train du Nord,** built on a former railroad track (see "Biker's Paradise: The 4,000km Route Verte," above). Rock-climbing enthusiasts flock to the nearby Dufresne Regional Park to explore its more than 500 rated routes. For a relaxing picnic, get fixings at the **Metro Supermarket** across from the tourist office or around the corner at **Boulangerie La Vagabonde,** 1262 chemin de la Rivière (© **819/322-3953;** www.boulangerielavagabonde.com). From the tourist office, turn left onto the nearby bike path and walk 5 minutes to the North River and the teeny **Parc des Amoureux.** Look for the sign that says SITE PITTORESQUE.

WHERE TO EAT

Au Petit Poucet ★ 🍴 QUEBECOIS If you crave a Québec of hunting cabins and hearty sugar-shack cuisine, look no further than the pig's knuckles, pea soup, and maple-smoked ham at Au Petit Poucet. The restaurant, off Route 117 (south of Val-David), is marked by a sign with a dangling pig and a young boy with giant boots and a knapsack on a stick. A floor-to-ceiling fireplace anchors the interior, rebuilt in 2007 after a devastating fire. Stuffed raccoons keep watchful eyes over diners who fill the room, even on midwinter weekdays. Stave off winter chills with an *érableccino* (espresso, maple syrup, and hot milk topped with a mountain of frothed milk and a sprinkling of maple sugar) or opt for the any-season main course of *tourtière* (meat pie), best sampled with its traditional side of tomato chutney. If there's no time to dine, products can be purchased in the restaurant's shop.

1030 Rte. 117, Val-David. © **888/334-2246** or 819/322-2246. www.aupetitpoucet.com. Main courses C$7–C$17. AE, MC, V. Daily 6:30am–4pm.

Ste-Agathe-Des-Monts

With a population of 9,625, Ste-Agathe-des-Monts, 103km (64 miles) north of Montréal, has as its main thoroughfare **rue Principale,** which is lined with shops, restaurants, and cafes. The town marks the end of Autoroute 15.

Exit from the autoroute and follow the signs for CENTRE-VILLE and then QUAI MUNICIPAL. The town dock on the lake, **Lac des Sables,** and the **waterfront park** make Ste-Agathe a pretty spot to pause in warm months. Bicycles can be rented from **Intersport Jacque Champoux,** 74 rue St-Vincent (© **800/667-3480** or 819/326-3480; www.jacque-champoux.ca), for the 5km (3-mile) ride around the lake. Lake cruises, beaches, and watercraft rentals seduce many visitors into lingering for days.

NAME THAT tremblant!

The abundant use of the name "Tremblant" makes things difficult to keep straight, so here's a primer.

There is Mont-Tremblant, the mountain. At the base of its slope is a growing resort village of hotels, restaurants, and shops that is sometimes called Tremblant, sometimes called Mont-Tremblant Station, and sometimes called the pedestrian village. About 5km (3 miles) northwest of the resort is an area which long ago was the region's center and which is now known as the old village of Mont-Tremblant. A cute commercial district about 12km (7½ miles) south of the mountain used to be known as St-Jovite but is now called Centre-Ville (Downtown) Mont-Tremblant.

Feeding the confusion is the fact that, in 2005, the villages of St-Jovite and Mont-Tremblant and the pedestrian village combined to become a single entity named Ville de Mont-Tremblant. Many maps, hotels, and residents, however, still refer to the areas as distinct "sectors." Also, just adjacent to the pedestrian village is Lac (Lake) Tremblant. And don't forget the large national park: Parc National du Mont-Tremblant.

Clear as mud?

In the heart of the village, casual breakfasts and lunches are available at the sunlit **Au Petit Creux,** 84 rue Principale (℃ **819/326-7055**). Fresh-pressed juices and simple but tasty sandwiches fill any hankering for a snack, just as the restaurant's name suggests: *Avoir un petit creux* is a French idiom that means something like, "I have the munchies." Also be sure to check out desserts made on the premises.

Croisières Alouette (℃ **866/326-3656** or 819/326-3656; www.croisiere alouette.com) offers 50-minute lake cruises that depart from the dock at the foot of rue Principale from late May to late October. A running commentary explains the sights (in English and/or French, with Spanish and Italian available upon request) and provides information about the water-skiing competitions and windsurfing that Ste-Agathe and the Lac des Sables are famous for. The Alouette cruise costs C$16 for adults, C$14 for seniors 60 and older, and C$5 for children 6 to 15, and it's free for children 5 and younger.

Ville de Mont-Tremblant

The Mont-Tremblant area is a kind of Aspen-meets-Disneyland. It's beautiful country, with great skiing and an ever-expanding resort village on the slope—a prime destination in the province in all four seasons.

GETTING THERE

There are four exits to the Mont-Tremblant area from the main roadway, Route 117. The first is exit 113, which takes visitors through Centre-Ville Mont-Tremblant (formerly the village of St-Jovite), a pleasant community with most of the expected services. The main street, rue de St-Jovite, is lined with cafes and shops, including the women's clothing and accessories boutique **Mode Plus,** at no. 813 (℃ **819/425-8969**); the folk-art and Québécois antiques store **Le Coq**

Rouge, no. 821 (© **819/425-3205**); and the restaurant **Antipasto,** no. 855 (p. 220). From the center of town, Route 327 heads to the mountain.

The fourth exit from Route 117 bypasses Centre-Ville and goes directly to the mountain and most of the properties listed here. Take this exit, 119, to Montée Ryan and follow the blue signs for 10km (6¼ miles). Also watch for signs with the resort's logo, which turns the "A" in "Tremblant" into a graphic of a ski mountain.

Mont-Tremblant International Airport (airport code YTM; © **819/275-9099;** www.mtia.ca) is 39km (24 miles) north of the mountain. See p. 205 for more information.

VISITOR INFORMATION

For tourist information, including maps of local ski trails, call © **877/425-2434** or 819/425-2434. There are also two **Visitor Information Centres:** one in Centre-Ville Mont-Tremblant, 48 chemin de Brébeuf (© **819/425-3300**), open daily 9am to 5pm, and another closer to the ski mountain, 5080 Montée Ryan (© **819/425-2434**), open daily 9am to 5pm. You can also check **www.tourismemonttremblant.com**, an official tourism site, and **www.tremblant.ca**, the Mont-Tremblant ski resort's website.

Mont-Tremblant, the mountain, is the highest peak in the Laurentians at 875m (2,871 ft.). In 1894, the provincial government began setting aside land for a government forest preserve, establishing **Parc National du Mont-Tremblant.** The foresight of this early conservation effort has afforded outdoor enjoyment to hikers, skiers, and four-season vacationers ever since. The park is the largest in the province, at 1,510 sq. km (583 sq. miles), and has 400 lakes and six rivers, along with 196 bird species and a forest primarily of sugar maple and yellow birch.

The mountain's name comes from a legend of the area's first inhabitants: Amerindians named the peak after the god Manitou and say that when humans disturbed nature in any way, Manitou became enraged and made the great mountain tremble—*montagne tremblante.*

The hills of Mont-Tremblant.

COLD-WEATHER ACTIVITIES

Downhill Skiing

The **Mont-Tremblant ski resort** (www.tremblant.ca) draws the biggest downhill crowds in the Laurentians and is repeatedly ranked as the top ski resort in eastern North America by *Ski Magazine*. Founded in 1939 by a Philadelphia millionaire named Joe Ryan, it's one of the oldest in North America. It pioneered creating trails on both sides of a mountain and was the second mountain in the world to install a chairlift. The vertical drop is 645m (2,116 ft.).

When the snow is deep, skiers here like to follow the sun around the mountain, making the run down slopes with an eastern exposure in the morning and down the western-facing ones in the afternoon. There are higher mountains with longer runs and steeper pitches, but something about Mont-Tremblant compels people to return time and again. The resort has snowmaking capability to cover almost three-quarters of its skiable terrain (265 hectares/655 acres). Of its 95 downhill runs and trails, half are expert terrain, about a third are intermediate, and the rest beginner. The longest trail, Nansen, is 6km (3¾ miles).

Mont-Tremblant is often ranked as the best ski resort in eastern North America.

Cross-Country Skiing

There is plenty of **cross-country** action in the Mont-Tremblant area. **Parc National du Mont-Tremblant** boasts 10 loops (53km/33 miles) of groomed track in the Diable sector, including 12km (7½ miles) for skate skiing. The Pimbina sector is designated exclusively for snowshoeing and backcountry skiing. Visit www.sepaq.com to locate visitor centers and information kiosks, or to check availability of the sector's five new yurts, which sleep four in any season. Many enthusiasts maintain that some of the best cross-country trails are on the grounds of **Domaine Saint-Bernard,** formerly a congregation of the Brothers of Christian Instruction and now managed by a land trust located at 545 chemin St-Bernard (© **819/425-3588;** www.domainesaintbernard.org). It's also not uncommon for hotels, especially those adjacent to golf courses, to also have trails leading directly from their property.

Additional Snow Sports

Curling, ice climbing, ice fishing, ice skating, dog sledding, tubing, snowmobiling, and **acrobranche**—a series of zip lines that allow you to swing from tree to tree at heights exceeding 22m (72 ft.)—are also available in the Mont-Tremblant region. For a truly unique aerial view, try acrobranche at night; make reservations through the **Tremblant Activity Centre** (© **819/681-4848;** www.tremblantactivities.com).

WARM-WEATHER ACTIVITIES

In warm weather, watersports are almost as popular as the ski slopes are in winter, thanks to the opportunities surrounding the base of Mont-Tremblant. They include Lac Tremblant, a gorgeous stretch of lake, and another dozen lakes, as well as rivers and streams, many of which are accessible through **Parc National du Mont-Tremblant** (www.sepaq.com), along with 82km (51 miles) of hiking trails.

Biking

See p. 209 for information about **Parc Linéaire le P'Tit Train du Nord,** a bike trail on a former rail bed, and p. 207 for "Biker's Paradise: The 4,000km Route Verte." The route runs through the Mont-Tremblant area.

Boating

From June until October, **Croisières Mont-Tremblant,** 2810 chemin du Village (☎ **819/425-1045;** www.croisierestremblant.com), offers a 60-minute narrated cruise of Lac Tremblant, focusing on its history, nature, and legends. Fares are C$18 for adults, C$15 for seniors, C$5 for children ages 6 to 15, and free for children 5 and younger.

Centre Nautique Pierre Plouffe Tremblant, 2900 chemin du Village (☎ **888/681-5634** or 819/681-5634; www.tremblantnautique.com), has a wide array of boats for hire, as well as waterskiing and wakeboarding lessons.

Camping

About 30 campgrounds dot the Laurentians. Some operate through national or regional parks, while some are privately run. **Tourisme Laurentides** (www.laurentians.com) has an online directory with services listed for each campground. Keep in mind the cabins and recently added yurts in the national park, available year-round.

Canoeing & Kayaking

Guided and self-guided trips along the Diable or Rogue rivers can be planned through the **Tremblant Activity Centre** on Place Saint-Bernard in the pedestrian village (☎ **888/736-2526** or 819/681-4848; www.tremblantactivities.com). Reservations are required. Maps and guides are also available through the **Fédération québécoise du canot et du kayak** (☎ **514/252-3001;** www.canot-kayak.qc.ca).

Golf

One could golf a fresh 18 holes every day for a month in this region. Options include the renowned **Le Diable** and **Le Géant** courses, which are operated by the Tremblant ski resort. Le Diable ("the Devil") is the trickier, more challenging course, whereas Le Géant is described *en anglais* as the "gentler giant." Virtual tours and aerial shots can be found at **www.tremblant.ca/golf**.

Horseback Riding

About 10 minutes from the mountain, **Le Ranch de la Rivière Rouge,** 3377 chemin du Moulin, Labelle (☎ **819/686-2280;** www.ranchdelariviererouge.com), leads year-round horseback experiences for persons of all ages and skill levels.

Swimming

You'll be hard-pressed to travel throughout this region without passing by one of more than a dozen public beaches—in fact, it may be difficult not to stop and take a dip! **Crémaillère beach** and **Lac-Provost beach,** in Parc National du Mont-Tremblant (www.sepaq.com), both have lifeguards and bathrooms.

Something Different

Right on the ski mountain at the pedestrian village, there's a downhill dry-land alpine **luge run.** The engineless sleds are gravity-propelled, reaching speeds of up to 48kmph (30mph), if you so choose (it's easy to go down as a slowpoke, too).

WITH apologies TO MONTY PYTHON: "SPA, SPA, SPA, SPA . . . "

Spas are big business around here: They're the most popular new features at hotels, especially in the Mont-Tremblant area, where people are looking for other things to do (and new ways to pamper themselves) beyond dropping a lot of money on skiing.

At some hotels, innkeepers might say they have a "spa" on-site when what they've got is an outdoor hot tub. What we're talking about here, though, is a complex that features therapeutic services—particularly, ones that involve water.

The spa industry has some clear definitions of what constitutes a spa. In the province of Québec, **Spas Relais Santé** (www.spasrelaissante.com) distinguishes between **day spas**, which offer massages and *estétique* services such as facials and pedicures; **destination spas,** which often involve overnight stays and healthy cuisine; and **Nordic spas,** which are built around a natural water source, and include outdoor and indoor spaces.

If you've never experienced a European-style Nordic spa before, set aside 3 hours for a visit to **Le Scandinave Spa,** 4280 Montée Ryan, Mont-Tremblant (*©* **888/537-2263** or 819/425-5524; www.scandinave.com). It's a rustic-chic complex of small buildings among evergreen trees on the Diable River shore. For

C$45, visitors (18 and older only) have run of the facility. Options include outdoor hot tubs designed to look like natural pools (one is set under a man-made waterfall); a Norwegian steam bath thick with eucalyptus; indoor relaxation areas with super-comfortable, low-slung chairs; and the river itself, which the heartiest of folk dip into even on frigid days. (A heat lamp keeps a small square of river open, even through the iciest part of winter.) The idea is to move from hot to cold to hot, which supposedly purges toxins and invigorates your skin. Bathing suits are required, and men and women share all spaces except the changing rooms. Massages and yoga classes are options for extra fees. Couples, mothers and daughters, groups of friends, and people on their own all come to "take the waters." The spa is year-round, and few activities are more relaxing than being in a warm outdoor pool as snow falls, the sun sets, and the temperature plummets. (That stroll back to the locker room is another story.)

Rides are priced by number of descents, starting at C$13 for one ride. The village has other games and attractions, such as dune buggy tours, bungee trampoline, paintball, and outdoor climbing walls that can keep visitors occupied for days.

There are some well-regarded cultural offerings here, too. The **Tremblant International Blues Festival** (www.tremblantblues.com) hosts nearly 150 free shows for 10 days in July with artists such as Tommy Castro, Buckwheat Zydeco, Keb'Mo, Ana Popovic, and Pinetar Perkins. Five stages are set up throughout the pedestrian village.

No matter the season, the lucky (or brave) can hold 'em or fold 'em at **Casino de Mont-Tremblant** (*©* **800/665-2274** or 514/499-5180; www.casinosdu quebec.com/mont-tremblant), which opened its doors in summer 2009. Table games include poker, baccarat, blackjack, craps, and roulette, not to be outdone by 500 slot machines. Admittance is free but restricted to persons over 18. It's open Sunday to Wednesday 11am to 1am and Thursday to Saturday 11am to 3am. Located on the newly developing side of the mountain called Versant Soleil at 300 chemin des Pléiades and connected to the pedestrian village by a gondola, getting there may be half the fun—unless, of course, you win big.

WHERE TO STAY

There are abundant options for housing in the area. In addition to the listings below, **B&Bs** are listed at **www.bbtremblant.com**. For **camping** options within the national park, visit **www.parcsquebec.com** and see "Warm-Weather Activities" on p. 212.

Of the accommodations listed below, the following are in or just adjacent to the pedestrian village: Ermitage du Lac, Fairmont Tremblant, Homewood Suites by Hilton, and Quintessence. Auberge La Porte Rouge and Hôtel Mont-Tremblant are located in the old village, and the following are a short driving distance from both the pedestrian village and the old village: Château Beauvallon, Le Grand Lodge, and Cap Tremblant Mountain Resort.

Note that many mountain-side hotels are booked 9 months in advance for holidays, such as the week between Christmas and New Year's or for school vacation week. Be prepared for and inquire about strict cancellation policies and 2- to 4-night minimum stays. Likewise, some hotels offer discounts for booking and paying in advance.

Past visitors to the area may recall **Gray Rocks,** a 102-year-old Mont-Tremblant resort with its own ski mountain and ski school. In 2009, the resort closed all but its two golf courses, La Belle and La Bête (℅ **800/567-6744** or 819/425-2772; www.golflabelleetlabete.com).

Auberge La Porte Rouge ✦ This unusual motel-inn, run by a third-generation owner, is located in the old village of Mont-Tremblant, on a public beach. Wake to a view of Lake Mercier through your picture window (every unit has one), or take in the vista from a little balcony. Some rooms have both fireplaces and whirlpool tubs. There is a terrace facing the lake and a small cocktail lounge. Rooms accommodate two to three people, while cottages have space for 10. Rowboats, canoes, and pedal boats are all available, and the motel is directly on the regional bike and cross-country ski linear park, Le P'tit Train du Nord.

1874 chemin du Village, Mont-Tremblant, PQ J8E 1K4. www.aubergelaporterouge.com. ℅ **800/665-3505** or 819/425-3505. Fax 819/425-6700. 26 units. C$174–C$224 double. Rates include breakfast and dinner. Packages available. C$30 additional children 6–17; children 5 and under stay free. AE, MC, V. **Amenities:** Restaurant; bike rental; pool (heated outdoor); watersports equipment. *In room:* A/C, TV, hair dryer, Wi-Fi (free).

Cap Tremblant Mountain Resort ★ The Cap Tremblant is a sprawl of handsome condos, both residential and rental, built high into a mountainside with terrific views of Mont-Tremblant, Lake Mercier below, and distances far into the horizon. Rental suites have one to five bedrooms and all the amenities needed for an extended stay: a kitchen, a fireplace, a washer and dryer, a private balcony with a barbecue in summer, and a locker for skis or golf clubs. Outdoor pools include one with a long slide that's popular with kids. The reception office and the resort's restaurant Il Pinnacolo are housed at the very top of the mountain, a steep drive or walk from the condos. There's a shuttle bus to the ski mountain. This is a fine choice if you're looking to be tucked away and left on your own.

400 rue du Mont-Plaisant, Mont-Tremblant, PQ J8E 1L2. www.captremblant.com. ℅ **888/996-3227** or 819/681-8043. Fax 819/681-8086. 170 units. From C$199 suite. Packages available. AE, MC, V. Free parking. Up the hill from the old village of Mont-Tremblant, off chemin du Village.

The outdoor pool at Cap Tremblant Mountain Resort is popular with kids.

Amenities: Restaurant; bar; concierge; exercise room; pools (3 outdoor, 1 heated year-round); spa; 4 tennis courts. *In room:* A/C, TV, CD player, hair dryer, kitchen, Wi-Fi (free).

Château Beauvallon ★★ ☺ 🔑   Since opening in 2005, Château Beauvallon has become the region's premiere property for families who want to stay off the mountain. A member of Small Luxury Hotels of the World, the 70-suite, three-story hotel has positioned itself as an affordable luxury retreat for seasoned travelers, and it delivers with a relaxed elegance. Every suite has two bathrooms, a small bedroom with a plush California-king-size bed, a queen-size Murphy bed, a pullout couch, a balcony, a gas fireplace, a 32-inch high-definition flatscreen TV (with a smaller TV in the bedroom), and an equipped kitchenette. All rooms face the pool or the lake behind the property, which sits between two holes on La Diable golf course. A large central fireplace lounge provides a warm gathering place, and the staff is friendly and competent. Both hotel and restaurant adhere to eco-friendly guidelines set by regional and national associations.

6385 Montée Ryan, Mont-Tremblant, PQ J8E 1S5. www.chateaubeauvallon.com. 𝄐 **888/681-6611** or 819/681-6611. Fax 819/681-1941. 70 units. C$229–C$289 suite. Children 17 and under stay free in parent's room. Packages available. AE, DC, MC, V. Free parking. **Amenities:** Restaurant; bar; babysitting; children's programs (high-season); concierge; golf adjacent; exercise room; hot tub (all-year outdoor); 2 pools (outdoor heated pool w/terrace, indoor heated); room service. *In room:* A/C, TV, DVD player (on request), hair dryer, kitchenette, MP3 docking station, Wi-Fi (free).

Ermitage du Lac ☺   Convenient to the ski mountain and the pedestrian village without being directly upon either, this boutique hotel offers a little more peace and quiet than larger properties closer to the action. It's also agreeably close to Parc Plage, the beach on Lac Tremblant, which makes for an enjoyable summer stay. All units are large studios or one- to three-bedroom suites, with kitchenettes or full kitchens equipped with oven ranges, microwaves, unstocked fridges, and necessary cookware and crockery (not all have dishwashers, though). Most have fireplaces and balconies, too. There is a secure underground parking garage.

150 chemin du Curé-Deslauriers, Mont-Tremblant, PQ J8E 1C9. www.tremblant.ca. 𝄐 **800/461-8711** or 819/681-2222. Fax 819/681-2223. 69 units. C$245 double; from C$335 suite. Rates include breakfast. Packages available. Children 17 and under stay free in parent's room. AE, MC, V. Parking C$10. **Amenities:** Breakfast room; children's activity room; concierge; exercise room; hot tub

(outdoor, year-round); pool (outdoor, in summer). *In room:* A/C, TV, CD player, hair dryer, kitchenette or kitchen, Wi-Fi (C$10 per day).

Fairmont Tremblant ★★ ☺ The high-end resort for families who want to stay directly on the mountain was built in 1996, and a renovation of its slope-side bar and restaurant was completed in 2010. The luxury property stands on a crest above the pedestrian village, as befits its stature among the Tremblant hostelries. Thirteen levels of rooms include the appealing Fairmont View, which overlooks the ski runs and the fairy-tale resort, and Fairmont Gold, which offers access to a private lounge. Families can take advantage of arts-and-crafts programs, year-round outdoor and indoor pools, the 38-person outdoor Jacuzzi, and ski-in-ski-out accessibility to the chairlifts. Couples looking for a quiet break or the attention to detail normally paid at a Fairmont may want to avoid school vacation weeks. An on-site **Amerispa** offers body wraps, facials, and massages. Even vacationers staying elsewhere come for the C$56 surf, turf, and sushi dinner buffet of in-house restaurant **Windigo.**

3045 chemin de la Chapelle, Mont-Tremblant, PQ J8E 1E1. www.fairmont.com/tremblant. ⓒ **800/ 257-7544** or 819/681-7000. Fax 819/681-7099. 314 units. C$249–C$609 double. Children 17 and under stay free in parent's room. Packages available. AE, DC, DISC, MC, V. Valet parking C$20, free self-parking (10-min. walk). Pets accepted (C$25 per pet per day). **Amenities:** Restaurant; bar; cafe (in ski season); babysitting; bike rental; children's programs; concierge; executive-level rooms; exercise room; pools (indoor and heated outdoor); room service; sauna; spa; access to watersports equipment; Wi-Fi (in lobby, C$14 per day). *In room:* A/C, TV, hair dryer, Internet (C$14 per day), minibar.

Homewood Suites by Hilton ★ ✦ Of the hotels that offer ski-in-ski-out access to the mountain's slopes, which are just across the plaza, the Hilton offers the best relative value. Directly on the pedestrian village at Place St-Bernard, a central gathering space, the resort's restaurants, bars, and shops are all within walking distance. An outdoor pool was added in 2008, and in-suite upgrades in 2010 brought in new appliances, granite counters, and new carpeting. The hotel is made up of several buildings decorated on the outside to look like candy-colored row houses, and all accommodations are crisply furnished suites with fireplaces and fully outfitted kitchens—useful when you want to avoid the village's expensive food venues. Suites range in size from studios to two-bedroom units. Laundry facilities and free grocery delivery are added conveniences, and ski lockers are free for guests.

3035 chemin de la Chapelle, Mont-Tremblant, PQ J8E 1E1. www.hiltontremblant.com. ⓒ **888/ 288-2988** or 819/681-0808. Fax 819/681-0331. 103 units. C$200–C$399 suite. Rates include breakfast, afternoon snack, and beverages Mon–Thurs. Children 18 and under stay free in parent's room. Packages available. AE, MC, V. Parking C$10. **Amenities:** Babysitting; hot tub (outdoor year-round); pool (outdoor seasonal); room service; sauna; Wi-Fi (in dining room, free). *In room:* A/C, TV, DVD player (for rent), hair dryer, Internet (free), kitchen.

Hôtel Mont-Tremblant ✦ A modest hotel in the old village of Mont-Tremblant, this 22-room property (founded in 1902) is popular both with skiers who want to avoid the resort village's higher prices (a shuttle bus to the slopes stops just across the street) and, in summer, with cyclists who appreciate the location directly on Le P'tit Train du Nord cycling path (p. 209). Most rooms have twin or double beds, and a few have sitting areas. The inn houses the popular restaurant **Le Bernardin,** which was relocated to the second floor in 2009.

That made room for a new ground-floor Irish pub, which the owners outfitted with antiquities and beer draughts from the mother country. Dinner entrees include French-cut steak with shallots and old-fashioned duck leg with citrus sauce, with main courses priced between C$21 and C$38.

1900 chemin du Village, Mont-Tremblant, PQ J8E 1K4. www.hotelmonttremblant.com. *(℡)* **888/ 887-1111** or 819/425-3232. Fax 819/425-9755. 22 units. C$86–C$209 double. Packages available. Rate includes dinner and breakfast for 2. AE, MC, V. Free parking. **Amenities:** Restaurant; bar; bike storage; Wi-Fi (in restaurant and pub, free). *In room:* A/C, TV, hair dryer.

Le Grand Lodge ★★ ☺ At a quiet distance from the main resort's frequent clamor, this handsome hotel, which consists mostly of suites, is on the shore of Lake Ouimet and draws families, small conventions, and weddings. It was built in 1998 with the palatial log construction of the north country and units leave little to be desired, with full kitchens, gas fireplaces, and balconies. Dog sledding directly from the hotel and snowshoeing flesh out the more obvious winter pursuits (for example, skiing), and in summer, guests partake in tennis, mountain biking, and canoeing and kayaking from a private beach on the lake. There are events for kids every night in the height of the summer and winter ski seasons. A big bar area overlooks the lake, and inside, you'll find what the hotel claims is Mont-Tremblant's largest pool.

2396 rue Labelle (Rte. 327), Mont-Tremblant, PQ J8E 1T8. www.legrandlodge.com. *(℡)* **800/567- 6763** or 819/425-2734. Fax 819/425-9725. 112 units. C$189–C$299 studio or suite. Children 17 and under stay free in parent's room. Packages available. AE, DC, DISC, MC, V. Valet parking C$10, free self-parking. Pets accepted (C$25 per day). **Amenities:** Restaurant; bar; babysitting; bike rental; children's programs; concierge; exercise room; whirlpools (indoor and outdoor); pool (indoor); sauna; spa; 4 tennis courts; watersports equipment. *In room:* A/C, TV, hair dryer, kitchen, Wi-Fi (free).

Quintessence ★★★ The region's most luxurious property. All units have views of Lake Tremblant, and guests have access to a private beach. Go assuming that virtually every service you might find in a larger deluxe hotel will be available to you—then concentrate on the extras. Comfortable beds have thick feather mattress covers. Bathroom floors are heated, showers are of the drenching rainforest variety, and every unit has a wood-burning fireplace and balcony. If it's warm, you can book a ride on the hotel's 1910 mahogany motorboat. There's an outdoor infinity pool and a spa (hotel guests only) that limits the number of visitors to ensure an unhurried atmosphere. Lavish dinners can be taken in the La Quintessence dining room or the intimate Jardin des Saveurs, and there's a 5,000-bottle wine cellar to draw from. Nature fans will want to consider the one rustic cabin, which has a four-poster bed.

3004 chemin de la Chapelle, Mont-Tremblant, PQ J8E 1E1. www.hotel quintessence.com. *(℡)* **866/425-3400**

The luxury hotel Quintessence is on the shore of Lac Tremblant.

MONT-TREMBLANT'S pedestrian VILLAGE

The pedestrian-only resort village on Mont-Tremblant's slope (www.tremblant.ca/village) is the social hub of winter (and, increasingly, summer) tourism in the Laurentians. From the bottom of the village, near the parking lots and bus shuttle, small lanes lead up past clothing shops and more than three dozen restaurants and bars. Along the paths and spread off in all directions are hotels, several of which are described in this chapter.

The village has the prefabricated look of a theme park, but at least planners used the Québécois architectural style of pitched or mansard roofs in bright colors, not ersatz Tyrolean or Bavarian Alpine flourishes. For a sweeping view, take the free gondola from the bottom of the village to the top; it zips over the walkways, candy-colored hotels, and outdoor swimming pools. From there, another free gondola will take you across the side of the mountain, to the casino.

Year-round, the village hosts outdoor concerts, barbecues, and events such as the goofy spring Caribou "Splash" Cup, where skiers dress in Halloween costumes, ski down an alpine trail into a pool of cold water, and then run through the village, stopping for shooters and a full glass of beer. Dude!

Make reservations for lodgings in the resort by contacting the establishments directly, through a central number (✆ **888/738-1777** U.S. and Canada; 514/876-7273; 0800/028-3476 U.K.), or online at www.tremblant.ca. There are options, too, to rent fully equipped condos and single-family residences.

or 819/425-3400. Fax 819/425-3480. 31 units. C$460–C$1,625 suite; C$380–C$545 cabin. Rates include breakfast. Children 5 and under stay free in parent's room. Packages available. AE, MC, V. Free valet parking. **Amenities:** Restaurant; wine bar; babysitting; concierge; health club; hot tub; pool (heated outdoor); room service; sauna; spa; Wi-Fi (free). *In room:* A/C, TV (on request), CD player, hair dryer, minibar.

WHERE TO EAT

Though most Laurentian inns and resorts have their own dining facilities and may require that guests use them (especially in winter), the area does have some good independent dining options for casual lunches or the odd night out. Also keep in mind **La Quintessence** in Quintessence and **Le Bernardin** in Hôtel Mont-Tremblant (see both above).

Right within the pedestrian village, **Au Grain de Café** (✆ **819/681-4567;** www.augraindecafe.com), tucked into a corner of the upper village just off Place St-Bernard, is a favorite for coffee and sandwiches. It's open daily from 7:30am until 11pm during ski season, 8am until 9pm the rest of the year.

Also in the pedestrian village, you can browse for baked goods and specialty chocolates at **La Chouquetterie,** 116 chemin Kandahar (✆ **819/681-4509**). If you're lucky, you'll walk in to the aroma of baking croissants or catch a glimpse of how they're made near the ovens in the cafe area. The desserts are a feast for any adult eye, and children can take home a souvenir chocolate toothbrush.

If you're staying off-mountain and arrive by car or hotel shuttle, get your coffee and croissant fix at **Brûlerie Saint-Denis** (✆ **819/681-2233**), located just left of the main gondola (and the long morning lines that form there) as you face the mountain. It opens daily at 7am. Like most ski mountains, beer is abundant, and there's a worthy reason to trek just beyond the slope-side drink palaces **Le Shack** or **La Forge** to the microbrewery **Microbrasserie La Diable,** housed in a free-standing chalet at 117 chemin Kandahar (see below). Shoulder up to the bar, and the bartender will likely pour a sample or two of the establishment's six home brews.

If you're in the mood for a cocktail, head to **Avalanche Bistro,** 127 chemin Kandahar (☎ **819/681-4727;** www.avalanchebistro.com), just across the path from the microbrewery, where you can choose from more than 35 martinis. There is a small bar that accommodates 10 patrons in winter and outdoor seating in the summer—note that the host may ask for your first and last name upon entering. While more of a place for dining than drinking, the contemporary Japanese menu at **Restaurant Yamada,** 100 chemin Kandahar (☎ **819/681-4141;** www.restaurant yamada.com), offers yet another village option—a wide selection of sake.

Antipasto ITALIAN   Antipasto is housed in an old train station in Centre-Ville Mont-Tremblant. There's the expected railroad memorabilia on the walls, but the owners have resisted the temptation to play up the theme to excess. Captain's chairs are drawn up to big tables with green Formica tops. The César salad (their spelling) is dense and strongly flavored—the half portion is more than enough as a first course. Individual pizzas are cooked in brick ovens with an enormous range of toppings, including scallops and crabmeat, on a choice of regular or whole-wheat crust; pastas are available in even greater variety. There are outdoor tables in summer.

855 rue de St-Jovite (in Centre-Ville Mont-Tremblant). ☎ **819/425-7580.** www.restaurantantipasto. com. Main courses C$13–C$36. AE, MC, V. Daily 11am–10pm.

Aux Truffes ★★ FRENCH CONTEMPORARY The management and kitchen here are more ambitious than just about any on the mountain, evidenced by a wine cellar that sails through Canadian, Californian, Argentine, Australian, Spanish, and many admirable French bottlings (for 9 years running, *Wine Spectator* magazine gave Aux Truffes its award of excellence for its wine list). Put yourself in the hands of the knowledgeable sommelier and go from there. Seared duck foie gras from the region is a steadfast opener. Imaginative mains include a roasted rack of caribou served shepherd's pie style with *chicoutai* berry sauce, and braised veal cheek "profiteroles" with grilled apricot sauce and bleu cheese from Québec. Close with selections from the *plateau* of raw-milk Québec cheeses. The service is impeccable, even on the slowest, snowiest days. The restaurant started serving lunch last winter.

Aux Truffes is known for its stellar wine cellar.

Place Saint-Bernard, 3035 chemin de la Chapelle (in the pedestrian village). ☎ **819/681-4544.** www.auxtruffes.com. Main courses lunch C$15–C$17, dinner C$32–C$47; chef's tasting menu from C$100. AE, MC, V. High season (summer and winter) daily 11:30am–10pm; low season Wed–Sun 6–10pm. Call to confirm hours.

Crêperie Catherine BREAKFAST/BRUNCH   This is the spot for those who long for a hot breakfast and bottomless cup of coffee before venturing onto the ski slopes. In addition to both savory and sweet crepes made before your eyes,

Crêperie Catherine has cultivated something neighboring restaurants can lack—cozy ambience. A collection of chef figurines can be found in every nook of the wood paneled interior, and each comes with a personal story tied to the restaurant's origins. Don't hesitate to smother your crepe with the house specialty, *sucre a la crème* (a concoction of brown sugar and butter). You can order from any part of the menu any time of day.

113 chemin Kandahar (in the pedestrian village). © **819/681-4888.** www.creperiecatherine.ca. Main courses C$12–C$17; dessert crepes from C$4.95. Daily 8am–9pm.

Le Cheval de Jade FRENCH   Chef Oliver Tali is what is known in the culinary world as a *maître canardier,* or master chef in the preparation of duck. Normally, that would mean that there's really only one choice: the house specialty, duckling *à la rouennaise.* But, surprise: The bouillabaisse is also a standout, as is the gracious service. This is a modest-looking roadside restaurant in Centre-Ville Mont-Tremblant with a dozen tables and country decor. If you're interested in having the duck, you have to call in advance to make a special reservation.

688 rue de St-Jovite (in Centre-Ville Mont-Tremblant). © **819/425-5233.** www.chevaldejade. com. Reservations recommended. Main courses C$24–C$36; table d'hôte from C$39; 7-course *menu degustation* for 2 C$174. AE, MC, V. Tues–Sat 5:30–10pm.

Microbrasserie La Diable 🍴 BREW PUB
Though the microbrewery craze has come and gone, it's hard to kill the craving for beer after a day on the slopes (or the links), so why not go local? You're in surprisingly good hands here, for both food and drink. Burgers and ribs are fine options, but we suggest choosing two of four styles of sausage (Smoked Swiss, Ocktoberfest, Toulouse, or Louisiana) with sauerkraut, fries, and side salad for C$14. The six frothy house beers have been brewed on-site since 1995. A pitcher sets you back just C$20, which, after a night or two in this pricey village, feels like a steal. Be warned that it's a bit of a walk down chemin Kandahar from the base of the ski mountain, especially in those clunky boots, but the location makes it easier to find a table.

Microbrasserie La Diable has six house beers brewed on site.

117 chemin Kandahar (in the pedestrian village). © **819/681-4546.** www.microladiable.com. Main courses C$12–C$24. MC, V. Daily 11:30am–2am.

Patrick Bermand ★ CONTEMPORARY FRENCH/SEAFOOD   If you're in the mood for seafood and have been disappointed by the paucity of finned offerings in the pedestrian village, you'll be happy here. The ambience is nonchalant gourmet, reflected in the smartly dressed yet boisterous clientele in their mid-30s through 50s and the log-cabin interior that manages an urban élan. In that spirit, the sparely written menu will need further explanation. The "catch of the day" came as a modestly portioned halibut steak with Parmesan risotto and three asparagus stalks. Appetizers have included garlicky, buttery escargot served in individual ceramic pots, and traditional *soupe à l'oignon* (onion soup). The restaurant is in Mont-Tremblant's old village, a short drive from the base of the ski mountain.

2176 chemin du Village (Rte. 327 in the old village). © **819/425-6333.** www.patrickbermand. com. Main courses C$23–C$39; table d'hôte from C$26. Reservations recommended on weekends. AE, MC, V. June–Aug daily 6–11pm; Sept–May Wed–Sun 6–11pm. Call to confirm hours.

CANTONS-DE-L'EST

20km–160km (12–99 miles) SE of Montréal, toward Sherbrooke

The rolling countryside of Cantons-de-l'Est has long served as the province of Québec's breadbasket. Still referred to by most Anglophones as the **Eastern Townships** (and, less frequently, as Estrie), the region is largely pastoral, marked by billowing hills, small villages, a smattering of vineyards, and the 792m (2,598-ft.) peak of Mont-Orford, the centerpiece of a provincial park. Cantons-de-l'Est's southern edge borders Vermont, New Hampshire, and Maine, and just past the Knowlton exit, at Km 100, there's an especially beguiling vista of the Appalachian Mountains that stretches toward New England, not far over the horizon.

Sherbrooke is the gritty, industrial capital at the center of the region, but the highlights noted below are located before you reach it, in an upside-down triangle approximately bordered by the villages of **Bromont** and **North Hatley** in the north (with 62km/39 miles between them) and **Dunham** in the south.

Serene glacial lakes attract summer swimmers, boaters, and fishers. Bicyclists zip along rural roads, passing day-trippers touring the region's grape and apple orchards (for wine and cider, natch). Except for a few disheartening signs for fast-food stops, the region is largely advertisement-free.

In winter, skiers who don't head north to the Laurentians come this direction; the Ski Bromont center (see below), just 45 minutes from Montréal, offers 67 illuminated trails for night skiing. Fun fact: In 1922, Armand Bombardier, who was born near Sherbrooke, invented the prototype for the Ski-Doo, the first snowmobile, to get through the region's unplowed rural roads.

The Cantons-de-l'Est kick into another gear when spring warmth thaws the ground; crews penetrate every sugar-maple stand to tap the sap and "sugar off." The result? Maple festivals and farms hosting sugaring parties, with guests wolfing down prodigious country repasts capped by traditional maple-syrup desserts. Montréal newspapers and local tourist offices (p. 224) keep up-to-date lists of what's happening and where during the sugaring; most spots are within an hour's drive from the city.

Autumn has its special attractions, too. In addition to the glorious fall foliage (usually best from early Sept to early Oct), the orchards around here sag under the weight of apples of every variety, and cider mills hum day and night to produce Québec's "wine." Particularly special are the ice-cider aperitifs produced by vineyards such as Domaine Pinnacle (see "Cantons-de-l'Est: Wine (& Cidre de Glace) Country," below) from apples that have frosted over. Visitors are invited to help with the harvest and can pay a low price to pick their own baskets of fruit. Cider mills open their doors for tours and tastings.

English town names such as Granby, Sutton, and Sherbrooke are vestiges of the time when Americans loyal to the Crown migrated here during and shortly after the Revolutionary War. Now, however, the population of Cantons-de-l'Est is 90% French speaking, with a name to reflect that demographic. A few words of French and a little sign language are sometimes necessary outside hotels and other tourist facilities, since the area draws fewer Anglophone visitors than do the Laurentides. Most locals speak at least some English. Best of all for tourists,

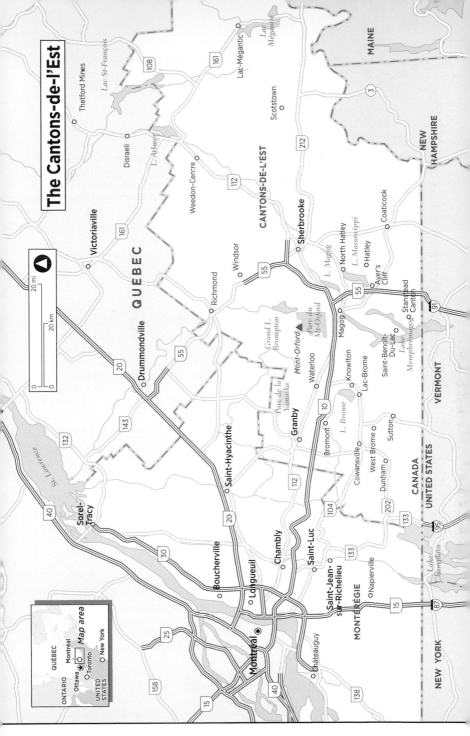

The Cantons-de-l'Est

the Cantons are one of Québec's best-kept secrets: It's mostly Québécois who occupy rental houses here. Follow their lead. For extended stays, consider making your base in one of the several luxury inns along the shores of Lac Massawippi and take day trips from there.

Essentials

GETTING THERE

BY CAR   Leave Montréal by Pont Champlain, a bridge which funnels into arrow-straight Autoroute 10. Go east toward Sherbrooke. Within 20 minutes, you'll be passing fields, clusters of cows, and in summer, meadows strewn with wildflowers. The exit numbers represent the distance in kilometers that the exit is from Montréal.

BY BUS   **Transdey Limocar** (which is actually a bus service) offers about 10 trips a day from Montréal through Cantons-de-l'Est as far north as Sherbrooke. Most of the trips are express, while some make stops at Granby, Bromont, Magog, and other towns. Call ✆ **514/842-2281** for schedules from Montréal or visit www.transdev.ca for a complete schedule and prices.

VISITOR INFORMATION

Tourisme Cantons-de-l'Est (✆ **800/355-5755;** fax 819/566-4445; www.easterntownships.org) provides a slew of information, including updates regarding special packages and promotions.

Driving from Montréal, the first regional **tourist information office** (✆ **866/472-6292** or 450/375-8774; www.granby-bromont.com) is at exit 68 off Autoroute 10. It's open Monday through Friday 8:30am to 4:30pm, and Saturday and Sunday 9am to 5pm (shorter hours in winter).

Telephone area codes in Cantons-de-l'Est are 450 and 819, depending on where you're calling. Towns with a 450 area code are closer to Montréal.

Granby

About an hour out of Montréal, north of Autoroute 10 at exit 68, this largely unassuming city (pop. 60,617) offers a few fun activities for children.

First is the **Zoo de Granby,** 300 boul. David-Bouchard (✆ **877/472-6299** or 450/372-9113; www.zoodegranby.ca). Take exit 68 (or, if you're coming from the east, exit 74) off Autoroute 10 and follow the signs. Two roller coasters were added in 2008, and there is a hippo river, an outside gorilla park, a "Mayan temple" with jaguars and spectacled bears, a lemur's island, and a tiger's habitat, which can be toured by elevated train. There is also a shark petting area (called a "touch tank" and overseen by an educator—don't worry, they're minisharks), bumper cars, and a Ferris wheel. A massive heated wave pool is a highlight of the water park. The zoo is open daily June through early September and weekends early September through mid-October, from 10am to 7pm in peak summer months and until 5pm the rest of the season. Admission is C$33 for adults, C$26 for seniors, C$22 for children 3 to 12, and free for children 2 and younger. The fee includes entry to both the zoo and the water park. Because many families need more than 1 day to visit the entire complex, 2-day passes are also available. Granby is also home to **Parc de la Yamaska** (✆ **800/665-6527** or 450/776-7182; www.sepaq.com/pq/yam/en), which has a popular beachfront and opportunities for such activities as swimming, canoeing, hiking, and biking. This is the northern part of the Appalachian mountain range, and it's lush and verdant in summer.

The Musée du Chocolat has displays of chocolate imported from around the world.

Bromont

Bromont, along with Knowlton and Lac Brome (see below), are all close together on the southern side of Autoroute 10. Medium-size country roads connect them.

Founded in 1964 primarily to accommodate an industrial park and other commercial enterprises, this town of 6,049 at exit 78 is now a popular destination for **Ski Bromont** (© 866/276-6668 or 450/534-2200; www.ski bromont.com). In winter, the mountain offers day and extensive night skiing. In summer, it has mountain biking (rent bikes on-site or at the town's entrance, opposite the tourist office) and the Ski Bromont Water Park. A new wave pool, big enough for 700 people, was added in 2009.

Each May since 2001, Bromont has been home to the **La Fête du Chocolat (Chocolate Festival),** with activities for the whole family, including live music and performances, chocolate body painting, chocolate sculpting, and (of course) tasting upon tasting. For event details, visit www. feteduchocolat.ca or contact the regional tourist office (© **866/472-6292** or 450/375-8774). If you miss the fest, you can stop by the one-room **Musée du Chocolat** (© **450/534-3893;** www.museeduchocolatdebromont.ca), in a red house along in the main stretch of businesses at 679 rue Shefford, opposite the church. Inside, you'll find a display of chocolates both made on the premises and imported from around the world, and a restaurant that serves breakfast and lunch. It's normally open throughout the year Monday through Friday 8:30am to 6pm, and Saturday and Sunday 8am to 5:30pm, with extended hours in the summer. Bromont is also home to the area's largest **flea market (*marché aux puces*),** where anywhere from a couple dozen to several hundred vendors set up in the local drive-in from 9am to 5pm weekends from April to October. It's at 16 rue Lafontaine (© **450/534-0440**).

WHERE TO STAY & EAT

Château Bromont ★ ☺   A landscaped panoramic terrace looks up at the ski mountain across the way, giving this valley hotel a most attractive setting. It sits adjacent to the Château Bromont Golf Club, making this a particularly choice spot for a golf getaway. The hotel coordinates packages with horseback riding or a day at the Granby Zoo (see above), which also appeals to families. For those who just want to relax, an on-site spa features goat's milk baths, a Turkish *hammam,* and a restaurant that serves healthy lunches. If noise is a concern, you may want to inquire about your room's proximity to the courtyard that surrounds the indoor pool. About a quarter of the rooms have fireplaces.

90 rue Stanstead, Bromont, PQ J2L 1K6. www.chateaubromont.com. © **800/304-3433** or 450/534-3433. Fax 450/534-0514. 160 units. C$170–C$220 double. Some dates require 2-night minimum stay. Packages available. AE, MC, V. **Amenities:** 2 restaurants; bar; babysitting; exercise room; 18-hole golf course; indoor/outdoor hot tubs; 2 pools (indoor and summer-only outdoor); spa. *In room:* A/C, TV, hair dryer, minibar, Wi-Fi (free).

Knowlton & Lac Brome

For a good confluence of countryside, cafes, and antiquing, head to the town of Knowlton, at Brome Lake's southeast corner; it's part of the seven-village municipality known as **Lac Brome** (pop. 5,078). From Autoroute 10, take exit 90, heading south on Route 243 toward Lac Brome.

In the summer season, the Lac Brome **tourist kiosk** (also called a *relais d'information touristique*) is open on Route 243 shortly after you've left Autoroute 10. Knowlton is about 8km (5 miles) past the kiosk, and you'll hug the lake's eastern side for most of the trip. (Be careful: Bikers share the road with nary a shoulder to fall back on.) There is a public parking area and a lake beach, **Plage Douglass,** about 5km (3 miles) into the route, just before Knowlton. You can park for C$7 to take a dip or do some easy lakeside walking.

Knowlton is compact, but its two main shopping streets (Lakeside and Knowlton) have about a dozen boutiques and antiques stores that reveal the creeping chic influence of refugees from Montréal. Stores sell toys, gourmet items, quilts, jewelry, pottery, chocolate, and clothing. Knowlton is one of the last towns in the region where a slim majority of the residents keep English as their mother tongue. Paul Holland Knowlton, a Loyalist from Vermont, settled here in the early 1800s, establishing a farm, general store, and sawmill. He was a member of Parliament for Lower Canada from 1830 to 1834.

The major local sight is **Musée Historique du Comté de Brome (Brome County Historical Museum)** at 130 rue Lakeside (Rte. 243; ✆ 450/243-6782). It occupies five historic buildings, including the town's first school. Exhibits focus on various aspects of town life, with re-creations of a general store and courthouse. The Martin Annex (1921) is dominated by a 1917 Fokker single-seat biplane, the foremost German aircraft in World War I. Also on the premises are collections of old radios and 18th- to early-20th-century weapons. Admission is C$5 adults, C$3 seniors, and C$2.50 children. It's open mid-May through mid-September Monday to Saturday 10am to 4:30pm, Sunday 11am to 4:30pm. Allow about an hour.

For a spot of tea, a picnic array of Québec-made cheeses and charcuterie to nibble by the lake, or a mellow sit-down lunch, try **Brie & Cie,** 291 Knowlton Rd. (✆ **450/242-2996;** www.brieetcie.com). If your tastes are broad, the sampling platter includes two pâtés, two cheeses, quiche, salad, and cornichons for C$14. Sandwiches with ham or turkey smoked on-site start at C$10.

On historic Victoria Street is **Barne's General Store,** at no. 39 (✆ **450/243-6840**), where you can buy fancy crackers, tube socks, colored poster board, penny candy, or a spicy red dip made with pomegranate and walnuts called *muhammara*. Mmm!

And how can you leave Knowlton without visiting the **Boutique Gourmet de Canards du Lac Brome?** Though no live ducks are in view, there are more duck products here than the average non-Québécois can fathom. Located at 40 chemin du Centre (✆ **450/242-3825;** www.canardsdulacbrome.com), the store is open Monday to Thursday 8am to 5pm, Friday 8am to 6pm, and Saturday and Sunday 9:30am to 5pm.

WHERE TO STAY & EAT

Auberge & Spa West Brome ★ Out in the country, beyond town limits, this quiet property is made up of a grouping of creamy-yellow buildings amid rolling hills. An 1898 farmhouse at the roadside contains the reception desk and

CANTONS-DE-L'EST: wine (& *CIDRE DE GLACE*) COUNTRY

Canada is known more for its beers and ales than its wines, but that hasn't stopped agriculturists from planting vines and transforming fruit into drinkable clarets, chardonnays, and Sauternes. So far, the most successful efforts have blossomed along southern Ontario's Niagara Frontier and in British Columbia's relatively warmer precincts.

Cantons-de-l'Est enjoys the mildest microclimates in the province, and where apples grow, as they do in these parts, so will other fruits, including grapes. Most vintners and fruit growers are concentrated around **Dunham,** about 103km (64 miles) southeast of Montréal, with several vineyards along Route 202. A stop for a snack or a facility tour makes for a pleasant afternoon. If you're really gung-ho, follow the established **Route des Vins,** which passes 17 vintners (find the map at www.laroutedesvins.ca).

One vineyard on the route is **Vignoble de l'Orpailleur,** at 1086 Rte. 202 in Dunham (© **450/295-2763;** www.orpailleur.ca). It has guided tours every day from June through October for C$5. Its white wines, such as the straw-colored L'Orpailleur, are popular on Montréal restaurant menus.

Ice cider and ice wine are two regional products that may be new to visitors: They're made from apples and grapes, respectively, left on the trees and vines past the first frost, and served ice-cold with cheese or dessert. One top producer is **Domaine Pinnacle,** at 150 Richford Rd. in Frelighsburg (© **450/298-1226;** www.icecider.com), about 13km (8 miles) south of Dunham. Its *cidre de glace* is a regular gold medalist in international competitions: It's delightfully smooth and not cloyingly sweet. The farm's tasting room and boutique are open May through December daily from 10am to 6pm and weekends only January through April 10am to 5pm. Other credible wines come out of **Le Cep d'Argent,** at 1257 chemin de la Rivière in Magog (© **877/864-4441** or 819/864-4441; www.cepdargent.com). Many of its vintages are prizewinners, including the dry white Le Cep d'Argent and the maple-tinged dessert wine L'Archer. There are several tour options, including a "privilege tour" of the champagne cellar that describes the *méthode champenoise* and includes tastings of six wines with regional products. Cost is C$17 for the 90-minute exploration. Reservations are required.

restaurant. About 90m (295 ft.) back are more modern structures, where the bedrooms are. There's also a spa with therapeutic baths, massage rooms, and pedicure chairs. Rooms are in three categories: Classic, on the small side but not cramped; Deluxe, with full kitchens, fireplaces, and decks; and Suite, which can accommodate four. The complex is close to the **Route des Vins** (above), with many of the vineyards near Dunham. The *auberge* recycles all glass, metal, and paper items, 80% of which is composted; uses only recycled-paper products and compact fluorescent light bulbs; and bans fertilizers and pesticides from its gardens and lawns.
128 Rte. 139, West Brome, PQ J0E 2P0. www.awb.ca. © **888/902-7663** or 450/266-7552. Fax 450/266-2040. 26 units. C$160–C$180 double; suites from C$215. Rates include full breakfast. Packages available. 2-night minimum stay during peak summer months. AE, MC, V. Free parking. **Amenities:** Restaurant; babysitting; bikes; exercise room; hot tub (outdoor, year-round); pool (heated indoor); sauna; spa. *In room:* A/C, TV, hair dryer, Wi-Fi (free).

MAPLE heaven IN *CABANES À SUCRE*

For a purely Québec experience that shouldn't be missed, reserve a spot for a meal at a sugar shack. Called *cabanes à sucre* or *érablières* in French, they were once places that merely processed sap from maple trees. When producers realized that they were drawing large audiences, some began offering wider experiences to keep the customers reaching for their wallets, putting in bars and dining rooms where bountiful spreads of simple country food are served at long communal tables. Some even put in dance floors and booked live entertainment. Originally open only during sugaring-off season (roughly Feb–Apr), a few now stay open much longer, even all year. There are hundreds across the province, with small directional signs often positioned at roadsides or on highways. Total cost rarely exceeds C$30 per person, though seats can be hard to come by, so make reservations well in advance. At most shacks, you can see the rendering room, where sap gathered from maple-tree taps is boiled in a trough called an evaporator and then cooked further on a stove. Some sites have interpretative trails that wind through maple groves.

An in-season visit to **Cabane du Pic-Bois,** 1468 Gaspé Rd., off Route 241 south of Bromont (☎ **450/263-6060;** www.cabanedupicbois.com), which offers "typical sugar-party meals" on spring weekends, exceeded every expectation (see photo). Locals packed long rows of tables in an adorable split-wood cabin under maple trees up a muddy road. There isn't a menu—you just sit down, and food starts arriving. In our case, thick pea soup and warm bread arrived, and then we helped ourselves to a buffet of ham, maple-tinged sausages, sweetly spiced baked beans, home fries, and mixed green salad and coleslaw lightly dressed with maple vinegar. Jugs of maple syrup stood at

Auberge Knowlton   Smack in the center of all things Knowlton (which, truth be told, is a four-stop intersection) is Auberge Knowlton, which has been sheltering guests under one moniker or another since 1849. There are 12 rooms of varying sizes and proximity to the bustle of the streets below. Room no. 4 is pretty but small. If high ceilings with exposed wood beams appeal, ask for no. 5. A stay may not be luxurious, but it is historically unique and offers the convenience that it has always offered: a central location. All rooms are on the second and third floors, and require use of stairs. Restaurant Le Relais, open year-round, serves meals on the back deck in summer. The restaurant is a hub for the community and features many locally produced wines.

286 Knowlton Rd., Lac Brome, PQ J0E 1V0. www.aubergeknowlton.ca. ☎ **450/242-6886.** Fax 450/242-1055. 12 units. C$125–C$142 double. Packages available. AE, MC, V. Free parking. Pets accepted (C$20 per stay). At the intersection of routes 243 and 104. **Amenities:** Restaurant; bar. *In room:* A/C, TV, hair dryer, Wi-Fi (free).

Auberge Quilliams   Though small lakes dapple the countryside surrounding Montréal, there are few hotels with lake access, which is what sets this inn apart. Situated between Lac Brome and the Quilliams Wildlife Reserve, a summer afternoon here could consist of crossing the road to the beach, or pushing a canoe (included in your stay) off the downward slope behind the hotel and paddling through miles of marsh. Rooms are up-to-date with crisp white linens and modern amenities. A grand porch wraps around the semicircular dining room,

forms, from syrup to maple candies to spreadable maple butter. Some people, like PicBois's André Pollender, a fourth-generation maple producer, consider the lighter Grade A, from the first run of sap, the best syrup. Others prefer the darker, denser Grade B from later in the season. There's only one way to decide: Taste and see for yourself!

For a more haute sugar shack experience, city folk and fans of celebrity chef Martin Picard (www.restaurant aupieddecochon.ca) head to **Cabane à Sucre Au Pied de Cochon,** mirroring the name of his wildly popular, and engagingly hedonistic, restaurant in Plateau Mont-Royal (p. 96). Only open during sugaring-off season, tables are booked months in advance. If, however, you don't mind going during the week (weekends are packed), chances are you'll nab a table. You can expect prices to be higher than normal.

the ready for an extra dousing. Dessert of *grand-père* dumplings baked in maple syrup, thinly rolled pancakes, and maple taffy lollipops—made by wiggling a line of syrup onto a narrow tray of snow and rolling the taffy onto a popsicle stick—finished off the memorable meal. Signature products are often sold in a variety of sizes and

and a flight of stairs leads down to a wine cellar with more than 250 labels, where tastings can be arranged. Skiers don't tend to think of this hotel, though it's just 5 minutes from Route 10 and 20 minutes from the Ski Bromont resort.

52 chemin Lakeside, Lac Brome, PQ J0E 1R0. www.aubergequilliams.com. © **888/922-0404** or 450/243-0404. Fax 450/243-0770. 38 units. C$169–C$219 double. Packages available. Sat stays in summer require meal package. AE, MC, V. Free parking. Pets accepted (C$10 per day). Exit 90 off Autoroute 10 toward Lac Brome, Route 243 south, hotel on left. **Amenities:** Restaurant; bar; exercise room; indoor whirlpool; pools (1 small indoor and 1 seasonal outdoor); sauna; spa. *In room:* A/C, TV/DVD, CD player, hair dryer, minibar, private balcony, Wi-Fi (free).

WHERE TO EAT

Bistro Beaux Lieux ★ 🎁 FRENCH BISTRO   Chef Christian Beaulieu emigrated from Montréal to Sutton, another jewel of a town in Cantons de l'Est and an easy drive from Knowlton, to start his own enterprise. His crafty, creative bistro is the result, and on one midspring night, in that gray season when the skiers had left and the golfers have yet to arrive, Beaulieu's house was packed. The special, a duck tenderloin with caramelized pears served over red-pepper polenta, was exceptional, and a stack of tofu over quinoa came with crisp vegetables, a welcome reprieve on a weekend otherwise laden with cheese, charcuterie, and croissants. Menus are backed with vintage knitting and pattern book covers, frivolity at its best.

19 rue Principale nord, Sutton. ℭ **450/538-1444.** www.bistrobeauxlieux.com. Main courses C$12–C$20. MC, V. Year-round Thurs–Sat 5–10pm and Sun 5–9pm (also Wed 5–9pm in summer).

Mont Orford

East from Lake Brome, on the north side of Autoroute 10, is one of Québec's most popular national parks. Visitors come to **Parc National du Mont-Orford** (ℭ **800/665-6527** or 819/843-9855; www.sepaq.com/pq/mor/en) in warm weather to hike the 80km (50 miles) of short and long trails; or bike the Route Verte, which passes through the park; or golf at **Mont Orford Golf Club,** which hugs the mountain's lowlands. From mid-September to mid-October, the park blazes with autumnal color, and in winter, people flock to the slopes to ski, snowboard, or traverse the network of cross-country ski and snowshoe trails. From Autoroute 10, take exit 118 north.

The mountain itself, Mont Orford, is a veteran ski area known as **Ski Mont Orford.** It has long provided the preferred slopes for local affluent residents. The resort is composed of three mountains, the contiguous Mont Giroux, Mont Desrochers, and Mont Orford, which is one of the three highest peaks in Québec. Combined, the mountains provide four faces with nine lifts (including a hybrid gondola) and 61 trails. Information for both downhill skiing and golf is at www.orford.com; call ℭ **866/673-6731** or 819/843-6548 for downhill skiing and ℭ **819/843-5688** for golf.

The area's other ski resorts—**Owl's Head** (ℭ **800/363-3342** or 450/292-3318; www.owlshead.com) and **Mont Sutton** (ℭ **866/538-2545** or 450/538-2545; www.montsutton.com)—are more family-oriented and less glitzy. Mont Sutton is particularly known for its "glade skiing," or skiing through the woods. Its trails are regularly the last to thaw each spring.

Orford has another claim to fame in the warm months: **Centre d'Arts Orford,** 3165 chemin du Parc (ℭ **800/567-6155** or 819/843-3981; www.artsorford.org), a world-class music academy set on an 89-hectare (220-acre) estate. From late June to mid-August each year, the **Festival Orford** presents a series of classical and chamber music concerts. Most tickets are C$39 for professional concerts, with student ("rising star") performances for just C$5. Concert and dinner packages are available. The Centre also has an *auberge* with rooms starting at C$68 per person. It's also off exit 118 north from Autoroute 10.

WHERE TO STAY & EAT

The following options are all along Route 141, just minutes north of the town of Magog (see below), toward Parc National du Mont-Orford and Ski Mont Orford.

Auberge Aux 4 Saisons d'Orford   Snugly built at the base of Mont Orford, this eco-friendly chalet is within walking distance of one of the ski resort's chairlifts. With an on-site bistro, burger pub, and spa, you may never feel like leaving, even though Magog and its active downtown are just 12km (7½ miles) south. The *auberge* has a commitment to energy conservation, with geothermal heating that radiates through concrete floors throughout, a design element that ironically gives the rooms a colder ambience. The spare decor is softened by chocolate-colored furniture and fluffy rugs, avocado-green accents, and blown-up photographs of wildflowers, taken on the premises. Cleaning products, shampoos, and soaps are biodegradable. Rooms with private balconies are available.

4940 chemin du Parc (Hwy. 141), Orford, PQ J1X 7N9. www.4saisonsorford.com. ℭ **877/768-1110** or 819/868-1110. Fax 819/868-2220. 28 units. From C$120 double; from C$192 suite. Children 17 and under stay free in parent's room. Packages available. AE, DC, MC, V. Free parking. Pets accepted (C$20 per day). Take exit 118 from Autoroute 10 and follow Rte. 141 north to the hotel, on the left. **Amenities:** Restaurant; bar; exercise room; spa. *In room:* A/C, TV, hair dryer, Wi-Fi (free).

Estrimont Suites & Spa ★ Suites are the key in this easygoing resort that offers fireplaces, kitchenettes, living space, and private terraces as standard fare. Outdoor saltwater baths, a Finnish sauna, and a Nordic shower are fun extras. And at Estrimont, you may also find the friendliest service in the region. Like other resorts in the area, guests are meant to have all the services needed for a complete vacation within a stone's throw of the township's exhaustive outdoor activities. The main dining room's picture windows unreel scenes of Mont Orford and its valleys, while a spacious bistro bar opens to a patio near the pool. Or take a flight of wine and tapas in a cozy room just off the main area. It's worth the extra C$20 for a room with a mountain view.

44 av. de L'auberge, Orford, PQ J1X 6J3. www.estrimont.ca. **℃ 800/567-7320** or 819/843-1616. Fax 819/843-4909. 91 units. C$209–C$259 double. Rates include breakfast. Children 17 and under stay free in parent's room. Packages and meal plans available. AE, MC, V. Free parking. Take exit 118 from Autoroute 10 and follow Rte. 141 north to the hotel, on the right. **Amenities:** Restaurant; 2 bars; babysitting; bikes; exercise room; pools (1 indoor and 1 outdoor); room service; spa; sauna; 2 lit tennis courts. *In room:* A/C, TV/DVD player, hair dryer, kitchenette, Wi-Fi (free).

Manoir des Sables ★★ ☺ This facility is one of the region's most complete resort hotels, and its unofficial motto could be "we have something for everyone." It serves couples, families, golfers, skiers, skaters, fitness enthusiasts, tennis players, kayakers, and business groups. Guests can enjoy on-site snowshoeing, ice skating, and Saturday-night horse-drawn sleigh rides in winter, and canoeing and fishing in the hotel's lake in summer. The spa underwent major renovation in 2009 with the addition of a Turkish *hammam,* a sea salt bath. An 18-hole expert golf course and 9-hole, par-3 executive course are both on-site and become groomed cross-country ski trails in winter. The newer Château section contains 24 upscale suites and its own lounge. A huge number of packages allow guests to pick and choose amenities.

The lobby of Manoir des Sables.

90 av. des Jardins, Orford, PQ J1X 6M6. www.hotelsvillegia.com. **℃ 800/567-3514** or 819/847-4747. Fax 819/847-3519. 141 units. From C$178 double; from C$309 suite. Children 16 and under stay free in parent's room. Packages and meal plans available. AE, DC, MC, V. Free parking. Take exit 118 from Autoroute 10 and follow Rte. 141 north to the hotel, on the right. **Amenities:** Restaurant; 2 bars (1 seasonal); babysitting; bike rental; children's programs; 27-hole golf course; health club; pools (1 indoor and 1 outdoor); room service; outdoor sauna/Nordic baths; spa; 2 tennis courts; water and winter sports equipment rental. *In room:* A/C, TV, hair dryer, Wi-Fi (free).

Magog & Lac Memphrémagog

As with countless other North American town names, Magog (pop. 24,359) came by its handle through corruption of a Native Canadian word. The Abenaki name *Memrobagak* ("great expanse of water") somehow became Memphrémagog, which was eventually shortened to Magog (pronounced *May*-gog).

Confusingly, the town of Magog is not adjacent to Lac Magog, which is about 13km (8 miles) north. Instead, it's positioned at the northernmost end of the large, long Lac Memphrémagog (pronounced Mem-*phree*-may-gog), which spills across the U.S.–Canadian border into Vermont on its southern end.

Bureau d'Information Touristique Memphrémagog (✆ 800/267-2744 or 819/843-2744; www.tourisme-memphremagog.com), at 55 rue Cabana (via Rte. 112), in Magog, is open daily 8:30am to 7pm in summer, 9am to 5pm the rest of the year.

If you're driving and want to take in **Abbaye de Saint-Benoît-du-Lac** (see below), Magog itself, and **Bleu Lavande** (see below), a lavender farm that's stunning in full bloom in July and August, take Route 245 from Autoroute 10 and visit the abbey first. Then head north to Magog and south on Route 247. This drive, along both the west and east sides of Lac Memphrémagog, is wonderfully scenic.

EXPLORING MAGOG & LAC MEMPHRÉMAGOG

The pretty town of Magog has a fully utilized waterfront, and in late July to early August each year, the **Lac Memphrémagog International Swimming Marathon** (✆ 818/847-3007; www.traversee-memphremagog.com) creates a big splash. From 1979 until 2003, competitors started out in Newport, Vermont, at 6am and swam 42km (26 miles) to Magog, arriving in midafternoon. Since 2004, the event has become a 34km (21-mile) race, beginning and ending in Magog.

To experience the lake without such soggy exertion, board a boat. **Croisière Memphrémagog** (✆ 888/842-8068 or 819/843-8068; www.croisiere-memphremagog.com) offers lake cruises; one option is a 2½-hour trip to Abbaye de Saint-Benoît-du-Lac. Boats leave from Point Merry Park, the focal point for many of the town's outdoor activities. Cruises off season depend upon demand; call for times and prices. Several firms rent sailboats, motorboats, kayaks, and windsurfers; **Marina Le Merry Club,** 201 rue Merry sud (✆ 819/843-2728; www.lemerryclub.com), specializes in pontoons, motorboats, and personal watercraft.

Abbaye de Saint-Benoît-du-Lac   There's no mistaking the abbey, with its granite steeple that thrusts into the sky above Lac Memphrémagog's western shore. Although Saint-Benoît-du-Lac dates only from 1912, and the monastery was constructed from 1939 to 1941, its serenity is timeless. Some 45 monks live here largely in silence, keeping the art of Gregorian chant alive in their liturgy. Outsiders are welcome to attend the 45-minute service (sit in back if you want to avoid the otherwise obligatory standing and sitting during the service). A blue cheese known as L'Ermite, among Québec's most famous, is produced here, along with a creamy version and Swiss and cheddar cheeses. They are on sale in a little shop, which also sells honey, books, tapes of religious chants, and a nonalcoholic cider produced from the property's fruit orchard. Visitors that come mid-September to mid-October may want to help pick apples. And be sure to peek into the tiny stone chapel to the left of the property's entrance, opposite the small cemetery.

1 rue Principale, Saint-Benoît-du-Lac, J0B 2M0. ✆ 819/843-4080. www.st-benoit-du-lac.com. Free admission; donations accepted. Abbey daily 5am–9pm; Mass with Gregorian chant daily

at 11am, vespers with Gregorian chant at 5pm (7pm Thurs). No vespers Tues July–Aug. Shop Mon–Sat 9–10:45am and 11:45am–6pm; Sun 10–10:45am and 11.45am–6pm. Exit 106 from Autoroute 10, Rte. 245 south to Bolton center, left on rue Nicolas Austin to village of Austin, right on rue Fisher; follow signs to abbey.

WHERE TO STAY

There are a number of modest B&Bs and small hotels in Magog along the blocks of rue Merry, immediately north and south of its intersection with the main street, rue Principale. **Association des Gîtes Touristiques Magog-Orford** (www.bbmagogorford.com) has a membership of 20 B&Bs accredited by the province. **Tourisme Cantons-de-l'Est** (✆ **800/355-5755**; fax 819/566-4445; www.easterntownships.org) maintains an updated directory of these and other options. Also note that the accommodations listed in the Mont Orford section on p. 230 are within a 10- to 15-minute drive from Magog, while accommodations in the Lake Massawippi section on p. 233 are within a 20-minute drive from Magog. Also consider the hostel at the *auberge* at **Centre d'Arts Orford** (p. 230).

WHERE TO EAT

In addition to the restaurant below, which mainly serves lunch, we recommend strolling Magog's main drag, rue Principale, where there are several family restaurants and some small, more urban cafes. One option is the outpost of the popular regional chain **Piazzetta**, at 399 rue Principale (✆ **819/843-4044**). For a drink with a view, the **Liquor Store Restaurant and Cabaret,** 276 rue Principale (✆ **819/868-4279;** www.liquorstoremagog.com), has an outdoor patio that overlooks the river that runs through town. Live music is performed most summer nights.

Boulangerie Owl's Bread ★ 🍴 FRENCH   This bakery-restaurant is the kind you wish for in every neighborhood. There are mouth-watering pastries for breakfast, sit-down service for lunch every day, house specialties such as *cassoulet toulousain,* and homemade breads that are sold in a shop at the entrance. The "Eastern Township–style" panini with smoked Lake Brome duck breast, blue cheese from nearby Abbaye de Saint-Benoît-du-Lac, Grenoble walnuts, and a touch of maple syrup on a baguette is sandwich making (and eating) at its pinnacle. Service is friendly, and there's a menu in English. Due to the Boulangerie's increasing popularity, hours may be extended in summer months, when you can also eat on a terrace overlooking Rivière Magog. The original Owl's Bread is in Mansonville, on the southwest side of Lac Memphrémagog.

428 rue Principale ouest, Magog, J1X 2A9. ✆ **819/847-1987.** www.owlsbread.com. Most items less than C$13. MC, V. Mon–Fri 8.30am–3pm; Sat–Sun 8am–5pm; winter hours may differ. Shop closes daily at 5:30pm.

North Hatley & Lake Massawippi

Set among rolling hills and fertile farm country, 19km-long (12-mile) Lake Massawippi, with its scalloped shoreline, is easily Cantons-de-l'Est's most desirable resort area. It was settled in the late 19th century by people of wealth and power, including many U.S. Southerners trying to escape their sultry summers (they came up by train and are said to have pulled down their window shades while they crossed through Yankee territory). They built grand estates with verandas and formal gardens on slopes along the lakeshore, with enough bedrooms to house their friends and extended families for months at a time. Several homes have been converted into inns, including the lavish **Auberge Ripplecove & Spa** and **Manoir Hovey** (see both below). For an escape from intensive travel or work, it's difficult to do better than here.

The jewel of Lake Massawippi (which means "deep water" in Abenaki) is the town of **North Hatley** (pop. 742). Only 148km (92 miles) from Montréal and just 34km (21 miles) from the U.S. border, it has a river meandering through it that empties into the lake. See the impressive sunsets over the lake, try the town's very fine restaurants, take advantage of access to 124km (77 miles) of good bike paths, and partake in a summertime program of Sunday-afternoon band concerts. A full listing of activities and a bike map are online at www.northhatley.net.

Horse lovers will want to know about **les Randonnées Jacques Robidas,** 32 chemin McFarland (© 888/677-8767 or 819/563-0166; www.equitation jacquesrobidas.com). Guides lead trail rides through forest and meadow beside the Massawippi in summer, with rates starting at C$65 per person for a 1-hour ride (minimum two people). Buggy and winter sleigh rides are also possibilities. There's a discovery farm and nature school on-site, as well as cabins to rent.

WHERE TO STAY

Note that while the two full-service inns listed below won't refuse children, they do have serious dining rooms that can test youngsters' patience. Other meal arrangements should be made for children 12 and younger.

Auberge Ripplecove & Spa ★★★   The staff extends a warm welcome at this handsome inn, and impeccable housekeeping standards are observed throughout. With 4.8 hectares (12 acres) directly on Lake Massawippi's southern end, the *auberge* is a grand miniresort, with a private beachfront and canoes, kayaks, and pedal boats. In winter, there is cross-country skiing near the property and, on Saturdays, horse-drawn sleigh rides. The core structure dates from 1945, but subsequent expansions have added well-appointed rooms, suites, stand-alone cottages, and in 2003, a spa with a full range of therapies and an outdoor hot tub with a view of the lake. About half the rooms have private balconies and whirlpools. The popular lakeside restaurant fills up in season with diners drawn to the kitchen's reputation for creativity. Members of the same family run **Manoir Hovey,** below.

700 rue Ripplecove, Ayer's Cliff, PQ J0B 1C0. www.ripplecove.com. © **800/668-4296** or 819/838-4296. Fax 819/838-5541. 35 units. Late June to mid-Oct C$316–C$594 double, suites and cottages from C$636; rest of the year from C$266 double, C$520 suites and cottages. Rates include dinner, breakfast, gratuities for 2 and use of most recreational facilities. AE, MC, V. Exit 121 from Autoroute 10, take Autoroute 55 south to exit 21, then Rte. 141 south 5 min. to Ayer's Cliff; follow signs to *auberge.* **Amenities:** Restaurant; pub; bikes; concierge; exercise room; hot tub; pool (heated outdoor); room service; spa; lit tennis court; watersports equipment (some for fee); Wi-Fi (in main building, free). *In room:* A/C, TV, hair dryer, Internet.

Manoir Hovey ★★★   Built in 1898 by the owner of paper manufacturer Georgia Pacific, this lakeside manor house, with its broad veranda and ivy-covered white pillars, was inspired by George Washington's home in Mount Vernon, Virginia. This manor manages to maintain a magical balance of feeling like both a genteel estate for a private getaway and a grand resort for a weekend's pampering; it's a member of the exclusive Relais & Châteaux group. Aristocratic touches include tea and scones in the afternoon, a carefully manicured English garden with fresh herbs (used by cooks in the kitchen), and a massive stone hearth in a

Manoir Hovey was inspired by George Washington's home in Mount Vernon, Virginia.

library lounge with deep chairs and floor-to-ceiling bookshelves. Sumptuously appointed rooms have touches like Italian bathroom tiles and antique sink basins, and all feature high-end bedding and CD players with classical discs. Dinner is included. We still have fond memories of an extraordinary dish of caribou with crystallized foie gras tabbouleh that melted into the meat.

575 chemin Hovey, North Hatley, PQ J0B 2C0. www.manoirhovey.com. © **800/661-2421** or 819/842-2421. Fax 819/842-2248. 41 units. Late June to mid-Oct and Christmas week C$350–C$600 double; rest of the year from C$290 double; from C$690 suite. Rates include 3-course dinner, full breakfast, gratuities, and use of most recreational facilities for 2. Packages available. AE, DC, MC, V. From Autoroute 55 exit 29, take Rte. 108 east, follow signs. **Amenities:** Restaurant; bar; bikes; concierge; exercise room; pool (heated outdoor); room service; tennis court (lit, clay); watersports equipment. *In room:* A/C, TV, CD player, hair dryer, Wi-Fi (free).

WHERE TO EAT

Café Massawippi ★ FRENCH CONTEMPORARY   It was daring to open a restaurant in the same small town as the multistarred inns described above, but chef-owner Dominic Tremblay has pulled it off. Contained in a small roadside house with a plain, unassuming interior, the true art appears on the plate. Think rosemary smoked scallops with parsnip purée, or homemade *ballantine* of duck foie gras with absinthe macaroons and raspberry salsa, or veal sweetbreads with roasted peaches and orange-cardamom tapioca. The chef recommends the table d'hôte for the entire table, served leisurely (plan 2½ hr.), though guests can also order à la carte. There even are unusual options for getting home: For a price, and with advance notice, cafe staff will drive your car while you return via helicopter, limo, vintage auto, or Hummer.

3050 chemin Capelton, North Hatley. © **819/842-4528.** www.cafemassawippi.com. Reservations recommended. Main courses C$42–C$60; table d'hôte dinner C$75. AE, MC, V. Late May to June and Sept to early Oct daily 6–10pm; July–Aug Thurs–Sun 11:30am–3pm, daily 6–10pm; early Oct to late May Wed–Sat 6–10pm.

Pilsen Restaurant & Pub INTERNATIONAL   For food less grand and less expensive than that at the establishments described above, head to Pilsen in the center of North Hatley. Housed in a former 19th-century horse-carriage manu-facturing shop, later a microbrewery, the restaurant has a deck with tables over a narrow river, the better to watch boats setting out or returning. The place fills up quickly on warm days, with patrons enjoying renditions of quesadillas, burgers, pastas, and fried calamari, as well as more adventurous fare, such as the Plough-man's Platter with wild-game terrine, St-Benoît-du-Lac blue cheese pâté, onion confit, and apples. There's an extensive choice of beers, including local brews Massawippi Blonde or Red. Most nights, the bar stays open well past midnight.

55 rue Main, North Hatley. ℗ **819/842-2971.** www.pilsen.ca. Reservations recommended on weekends. Main courses C$10–C$28; table d'hôte C$25–C$39. AE, MC, V. Mid-May to Nov Mon-Sat 11:30am–10:30pm, Sun 9am–10:30pm; Dec to mid-May Thurs–Sat 11:30am–10:30pm, Sun 9am–10:30pm (can close as early as 8pm in winter; may stay open as late as 3am in summer).

Stanstead & Beebe Plain

For a brief detour on the drive south to Vermont, explore the border villages that compose the town of Stanstead, at the end of Route 143.

Stanstead (pop. 3,162) was settled in the 1790s and, as a border town, became a commercial center for the Québec-Boston stagecoach route. Many of the society homes from the late 1800s have been preserved. Canada's largest producer of lavender also happens to be one of the region's most popular destina-tions. **Bleu Lavende** (℗ **888/876-5851** or 819/876-5851; www.bleulavande. ca) is a huge farm, a picnic spot, an agricultural discovery center, and a place to buy chocolate, jelly, home-cleaning products, sprays, and an array of other good-ies all infused with the miraculous properties of *Lavandula*. Hotels in Magog and neighboring towns organize excursions to the farm, which is located at 891 Nar-row Rd., just 4.4km (2¾ miles) from Route 247 in Stanstead. During peak sea-son, when the lavender blooms in July and August, Bleu Lavande can attract more than 2,000 visitors per day. The website offers a complete list of activities, including times for tours, which run daily mid-June through September. Pack-ages with wine sampling or spa services are available. The boutique is open daily during high season and Monday to Friday during low season, and it's closed between Christmas and the first week of January.

Fans of geographical oddities will want to stop by the **Haskell Opera House** (℗ **819/876-2020;** www.haskellopera.org). Dating from 1904, it's literally and logistically half-Canadian and half-American: The stage and performers are in Canada, while the audience watches from the U.S. With recent stiffening of bor-der control, the Opera House has had to make new demands on its audiences: Visi-tors from Canada must park their cars on the Canadian side of the building or report to U.S. Customs; visitors from the U.S. must similarly follow suit. As the website reminds, "It is expected that all visitors will return to their country of ori-gin." **QNEK Productions** is the resident theater company, and it's based in Ver-mont. QNEK ticket information is at ℗ **802/334-2216** and www.qnek.com.

What makes the township of **Beebe Plain** notable is 1km-long (½-mile) **Canusa Street.** The north side is in Canada, the south side in the U.S.—hence the name, CAN-USA. Here, it's long-distance to call a neighbor across the street. While folks are free to walk across for a visit, they are expected, at least techni-cally, to report to the authorities if they drive that same distance.

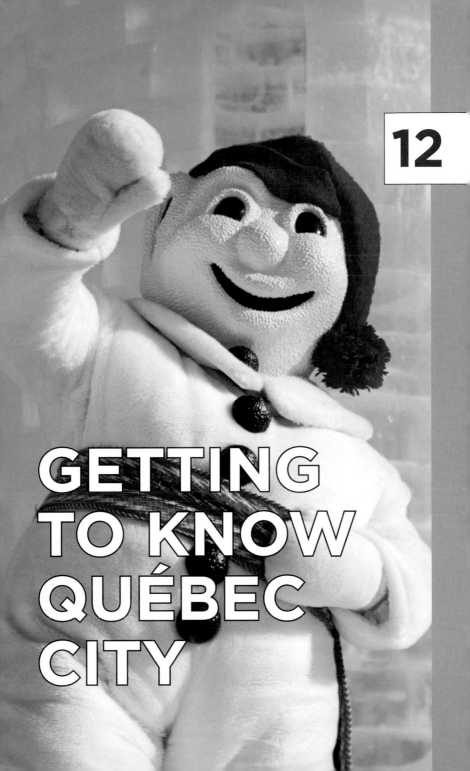

GETTING TO KNOW QUÉBEC CITY

Perched on bluff **Cap Diamant (Diamond Cape)** overlooking the St-Lawrence River, the century-old **Le Fairmont Château Frontenac** marks a dramatic peak in Québec City's skyline. Here, the continent's oldest surviving walled city embraces Canada's first European settlement, christened La Nouvelle France in the 16th century. Over 4 centuries later, the city clings to her French-speaking heritage and Gallic traditions. Steeped in bloody battles and cultured by the fascinating growing pains of the New World, Québec City steps swiftly into the 21st century with one foot rooted proudly in the past.

Things to Do   Stroll along the cobblestoned streets of **Place Royale,** where the famed French explorer **Samuel de Champlain** made his home away from home. Spend the day taking in the war-soaked **Citadel,** the magnificent natural beauty of **La Chute Monmorency,** or the golden interior of the **Notre-Dame de Québec Cathedral,** before your trickle into your charming *auberge* (B&B), enjoy a leisurely walk along the scenic boardwalk, or down a local ale while listening to a *chansonnier* sing his heart out.

Shopping   Peruse the charming antique dealers along **rue St-Paul** or one of the fur shops in **Lower Town.** In **Upper Town,** the winding **Côte de la Fabrique** will take you straight to **La Maison Simons,** the oldest department store in Québec, then head over to **rue de Trésor,** a quaint little alley for local art and city souvenirs. Just a few steps from **Château Frontenac** you'll also find excellent galleries for Native art.

Restaurants & Dining   Enjoy a traditional dinner at **Aux Anciens Canadiens,** the oldest *maison* in Québec, and sample the gastronomy of Canada's ancestors in dishes such as *soupe aux pois* or *tourtière* (pea soup or meat pie). Alternatively, go the other extreme in contemporary dining room of **Initiale** or book a table at one of the many up-and-coming restaurants in the suddenly hip **Nuovo St-Roch** neighborhood. The see-and-be-seen supper club phenomena can also be yours on **rue Parvis.**

Nightlife & Entertainment   No matter the season, it seems there is always a party going on somewhere in Québec City. From the outdoor-activity-filled **Winter Carnaval** to the endless music and theater offerings, including free shows by **Cirque du Soleil,** the city's *joie de vivre* is in the air. While most theater is in French, even non-Francophones can enjoy the artistry of Québécois productions. Nightclubs and bars along **La Grand Allée** or the decidedly more underground hot spots in **Nuovo St-Roch** are keys places for nocturnal pursuits.

PREVIOUS PAGE: **Bonhomme is the famous mascot of Québec City's winter carnival.**

ORIENTATION

Because of its beauty, history, and unique stature as a walled city, Québec City's historic district was named a UNESCO World Heritage Site in 1985. Almost all of a visit to Québec City can be spent on foot in the old Lower Town, which hugs the river below the bluff, and in the old Upper Town, atop Cap Diamant (Cape Diamond). Many accommodations, restaurants, and tourist-oriented services are based in these places.

The colonial city was first built right down by the St. Lawrence River. It was here that the earliest merchants, traders, and boatmen earned their livelihoods. Unfriendly fire from the British and Amerindians in the 1700s moved residents to safer houses atop the cliffs that form the rim of the Cap. The tone and atmosphere of the 17th and 18th centuries still suffuse these areas today.

Basse-Ville (Lower Town) became primarily a district of wharves and warehouses. That trend has been reversed, with small hotels and many attractive bistros and shops bringing life to the area. It maintains the architectural feel of its origins, however, reusing old buildings and maintaining the narrow cobbled streets.

Haute-Ville (Upper Town) turned out to not be immune to cannon fire, as the British General James Wolfe proved in 1759 when he took the city from the French. Nevertheless, the division into Upper and Lower towns persisted for obvious topographical reasons. Upper Town remains enclosed by fortification walls, with a cliff-side elevator (*funiculaire*) and several steep streets connecting it to Lower Town.

Île d'Orléans is an agricultural and residential island within sight of Vieux-Québec. It's less than 20 minutes from downtown by car and makes a pleasant day trip. Consider, too, a drive along the St. Lawrence's northern coast past the shrine of Ste-Anne-de-Beaupré (p. 335), the waterfalls near Mont Ste-Anne (p. 336), and on to pastoral Charlevoix (p. 339) and the Saguenay River, where whales come to play.

Arriving

For information about arriving in Québec City by plane, car, train, or bus, see "Getting There," on p. 349.

Visitor Information

High season in Québec City is from June 24 (Jean-Baptiste Day, a provincial holiday) through Labour Day (the first Mon in Sept, as in the U.S., a national holiday). For those 11 weeks, the city is in highest gear. Tourist offices, museums, and restaurants all expand their operating hours, and hotels charge top dollar. This book notes the changes in hours and prices throughout the year for many venues, but it's best to call and confirm open hours before making a special trip to an attraction or restaurant outside of the high season.

There are several tourist information centers. The most central is in Upper Town, across from the Château Frontenac and directly on Place d'Armes. **Centre Infotouriste de Québec,** 12 rue Ste-Anne (② **877/266-5687;** www. bonjourquebec.com), is run by the province of Québec's tourism department and is open from 9am to 7pm daily from late June through to August and from 9am to 5pm daily the rest of the year. It has brochures, a lodging reservation service, a currency-exchange office, and information about tours by foot, bus, or boat. Also

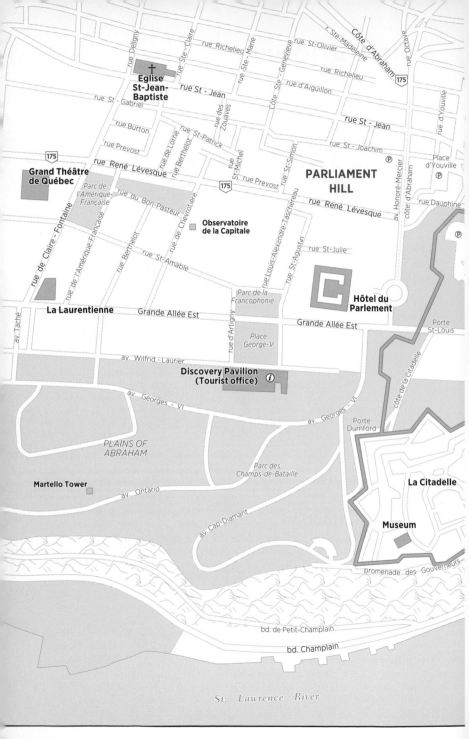

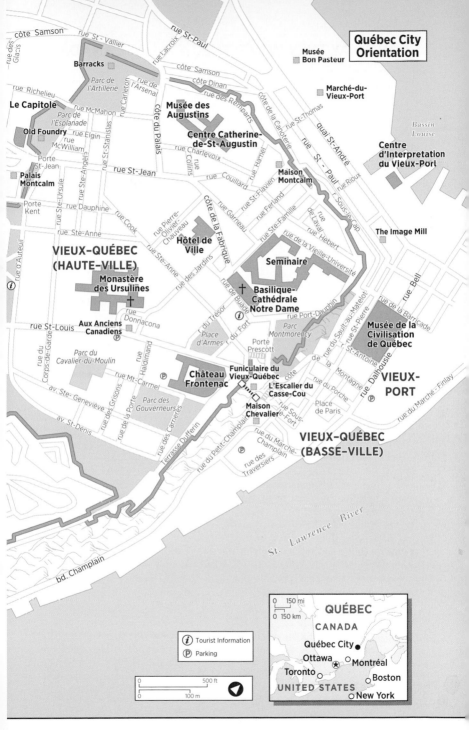

Québec City Orientation

côte Samson
rue St-Vallier
rue St-Paul

rue des Glacis

Barracks

Parc de l'Artillerie

rue Richelieu

Le Capitole

rue McMahon

Parc de l'Esplanade

Old Foundry
rue Elgin
rue McWilliam

Porte St-Jean

Palais Montcalm

Porte Kent

rue St-Jean

côte Samson
côte Dinan

Musée Bon Pasteur

Marché-du-Vieux-Port

Musée des Augustins

Centre Catherine-de-St-Augustin

rue Charlevoix

Maison Montcalm

Centre d'Interpretation du Vieux-Port

Bassin Louise

quai St-André

rue St-André

rue St-Paul

VIEUX-QUÉBEC (HAUTE-VILLE)

Monastère des Ursulines

Hôtel de Ville

Séminaire

The Image Mill

Basilique-Cathédrale Notre Dame

Parc Montmorency

Aux Anciens Canadiens

Place d'Armes

Porte Prescott

Musée de la Civilisation de Québec

rue St-Louis

Parc du Cavalier-du-Moulin

Château Frontenac

Funiculaire du Vieux-Québec

L'Escalier du Casse-Cou

Maison Chevalier

VIEUX-PORT

Parc des Gouverneurs

Place de Paris

Terrasse Dufferin

VIEUX-QUÉBEC (BASSE-VILLE)

bd. Champlain

St. Lawrence River

(i) Tourist Information
(P) Parking

0   150 mi
0   150 km

QUÉBEC

CANADA

Québec City

Ottawa   Montréal

Toronto   Boston

UNITED STATES   New York

0   500 ft
0   100 m

LONG MAY THEY WAVE: THE flags OF CANADA

With a relatively small population spread over a territory larger than the continental U.S., Canadians' loyalties have always tended to be directed to the cities and regions in which they live, rather than to the nation at large. Part of this comes from the semi-colonial relationship the nation retained with England after the British North America Act made it self-governing in 1867 (Queen Elizabeth II is still on all the currency). Part comes from the fact that Canada has two official languages. Canadians didn't even have an official national anthem until "O Canada" was given the honor in 1980.

Local loyalties are reflected in the flags. Québécois began asserting themselves and declaring their regional pride after World War II and officially adopted their national flag, the Fleurdelisé, in 1950. It employs blue-and-white crossbars with four fleurs-de-lis (one in each resulting quadrant) and is flown prominently in Québec City.

In 1965, the red-and-white maple leaf version of the Canadian flag was introduced across all of Canada, replacing a previous ensign that featured a Union Jack in the upper-left corner.

In the face of decades of hurt and outright hostilities between French and English Canada, there must be occasional sighs of longing in some quarters for the diplomatic display of the flag of Montréal. Adopted way back in 1832, it has red crossbars on a white background. The resulting quadrants have depictions of a rose, a fleur-de-lis, a thistle, and a shamrock. They stand, respectively, for the founding groups of the new nation—the English, French, Scots, and Irish.

in front of the Château is the independent **Kiosque Frontenac,** which sells tour tickets and exchanges currency. It's in a small kiosk next to the entrance of the cliff-side elevator to Lower Town.

Just outside the Old City walls on Parc des Champs-de-Bataille's northern edge, **Québec City Tourism** has an information office in the Discovery Pavilion, 835 av. Wilfrid-Laurier (✆ **877/783-1608** or 418/641-6290; www.quebec region.com). You'll find rack after rack of brochures, as well as attendants who can answer questions and make hotel reservations. It's open daily throughout the year, from 8:30am to 7:30pm from June 24 to Labour Day and somewhat shorter hours the rest of the year. The building is marked with a large, blue question mark.

From early June to early September, the city tourist office puts service agents on motor scooters throughout the tourist district. They can answer any questions you have. In French, they're called the *service mobile,* and their blue mopeds bear flags with a large question mark. Just hail them as they approach— they're bilingual.

City Layout

MAIN AVENUES & STREETS Within the walls of Haute-Ville (Upper Town), the principal streets are **St-Louis** (which becomes **Grande-Allée** outside the city walls), **Ste-Anne,** and **St-Jean.** In Basse-Ville (Lower Town), major streets are **St-Pierre, Dalhousie, St-Paul,** and (parallel to St-Paul) **St-André.** Detailed maps of Upper and Lower towns and the metropolitan area are available at the tourist offices.

FINDING AN ADDRESS If it were larger, the historic district's winding and plunging streets might be confusing to negotiate. However, the area is very compact. Most streets are only a few blocks long, making navigation and finding a specific address fairly easy.

The Neighborhoods in Brief

HAUTE-VILLE Old Québec's Upper Town, surrounded by thick ramparts, occupies the crest of Cap Diamant and overlooks the Fleuve St-Laurent (St. Lawrence River). It includes many of the sites for which the city is famous, among them the **Château Frontenac** and the **Basilica of Notre-Dame.** At a still-higher elevation, to the south of the Château and along the river, is the **Citadelle,** a partially star-shaped fortress built by the French in the 18th century and augmented often by the English (after their 1759 capture of the city) well into the 19th century.

With most buildings at least 100 years old and made of granite in similar styles, Haute-Ville is visually harmonious, with few jarring modern intrusions. When they added a new wing to the Château Frontenac, for instance, they modeled it after the original—standing policy here.

Terrasse Dufferin is a pedestrian promenade atop the cliffs that attracts crowds in all seasons for its magnificent views of the river and its water traffic, which includes ferries gliding back and forth, cruise ships, and Great Lakes freighters putting in at the harbor below.

BASSE-VILLE & VIEUX-PORT Old Québec's Lower Town encompasses **Vieux-Port,** the old port district; the impressive **Museum of Civilization,** a highlight of any visit; **Place Royale,** perhaps the most attractive of the city's many small squares; and the pedestrian-only **rue du Petit-Champlain,** which is undeniably touristy, but not unpleasantly so, and has many agreeable cafes and shops. Visitors travel between Lower and Upper towns by the cliff-side elevator *(funiculaire)* at the north end of rue du Petit-Champlain, or by the adjacent stairway.

PARLIAMENT HILL, INCLUDING MONTCALM Once you pass through the walls at St-Louis Gate, you're still in Haute-Ville (Upper Town), but no longer in Vieux-Québec. Rue St-Louis becomes **Grande-Allée,** a wide boulevard that passes the stately Parliament building and runs parallel to the broad expanse of the Plains of Abraham, where one of the most important battles in the history of North America took place between the French and the British for control of the city. This is also where the lively Carnaval de Québec is held each winter. Two blocks after Parliament, Grande-Allée becomes lined on both sides with terraced restaurants and cafes. The city's large modern hotels are in this area, too, and the **Musée National des Beaux-Arts** is a pleasant 20-minute walk up the Allée from the Parliament. Here, the neighborhood becomes more residential and flows into the Montcalm district.

FAUBOURG ST-JEAN This area is the continuation of rue St-Jean after you exit the walled city and go past Place d'Youville. It is definitely a route less travelled by tourists—*quel dommage*—because this vibrant area, which is packed with shops, bars, and restaurants, is where locals work, live, and play.

ST-ROCH Northwest of Parliament Hill and enough of a distance from Vieux-Québec to warrant a cab ride, this newly revitalized neighborhood has some of the city's trendiest restaurants and bars. Along the main strolling street, **rue St-Joseph est,** sidewalks have been widened, new benches added, and artists hired to renovate the interiors and exteriors of industrial buildings. It has all brought a youthful pop and an influx of new technology and media companies to the neighborhood. Information about the neighborhood is online at **www.quartiersaintroch.com**.

Much of St-Roch, including what's referred to as Québec's "downtown" shopping district, remains nondescript and a little grubby. But rue St-Joseph, radiating both directions from rue du Parvis (a nice little street for nightlife), is home to an ever-growing number of top-notch restaurants and cute boutiques. ***Note:*** On older maps, rue du Parvis was called rue de l'Église.

The Neighborhoods in Brief

GETTING TO KNOW QUÉBEC CITY

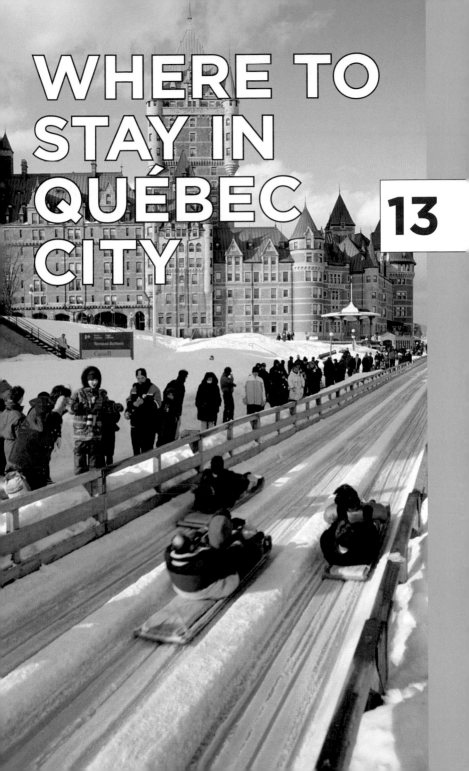

WHERE TO STAY IN QUÉBEC CITY

S taying in one of the small hotels within or below the walls of Vieux-Québec (or at the iconic Château Frontenac) can be one of your trip's most memorable experiences. For the shrewd hotel connoisseur, you'll want to investigate the handful of luxurious boutique properties in the Lower Town that are sure to pass every utopian test. On the other end of the size spectrum, the string of skyscrapers just beyond La Porte St-Jean may lack some of the city's historical charm, but offer high-end facilities and some of the best views of the city.

BEST HOTEL BETS

○ **Best Splurge: Fairmont Le Château Frontenac** is the visual star of the city. It was built more than a century ago as one of the first hotels to serve railroad passengers. Nothing can beat it for proximity to all the sights. In fact, "the Château" *is* one of the sights. Even if you don't stay here, come by for a tour, a meal, or a drink. See p. 248.

○ **Best Service:** The sleek and luxurious **Hôtel Le Germain-Dominion** is a favorite, infusing a pre–World War I building with a cunning modernist flavor. The highly trained staff is at once caring and personable whilst being both professional and respectful. See p. 254.

○ **Best Romantic Hotel: Auberge St-Antoine** features ancient walls and archaeological displays from lobby to bedside, and it's hard to beat curling up with a glass of wine beside the fire in one of the cozy lobby alcoves. See p. 254.

○ **Best Eclectic *Auberge:* Auberge Place d'Armes** is a private B&B where each room is decorated in a different theme. Popular requests are those with a view of the Château Frontenac or the room equipped with a Jacuzzi tub. See p. 249.

price CATEGORIES

Very Expensive	C$300 and up
Expensive	C$200–C$300
Moderate	C$100–C$200
Inexpensive	Under C$100

PREVIOUS PAGE: **Kids enjoy tobogganing at Terrasse Dufferin in the shadows of the Château Frontenac.**

WHAT YOU'LL really PAY

As with the hotel chapter for Montréal, the prices listed here are by no means written in stone, and should be used more as a guideline with comparing prices. Rates provided are typical of Québec City's busy seasons, that is, summer (June–Aug) and winter (around Christmastime to Carnaval), and can be significantly slashed when times are slow.

There are, it seems, more smaller, private B&Bs in and around Old Québec that you'd ever find in Montréal. Sometimes prices can seem high for what you get as demand can very simply inflate prices. Make sure you know what you're getting yourself into.

o **Best Cultural Design:** The **Hôtel-Musée Premières Nations** in Wendake is modeled after a Huron longhouse. A tribute to First Nation's history that dates back hundreds of years, the unique decor is thoroughly modern. See p. 260.

o **Best Location for Peace and Quiet:** The **Parc des Gouverneurs,** next to the Château, is a green space just steps from Upper Town's restaurants and shops. It offers a quiet respite at the end of the day. Many B&Bs and small hotels are on the park or nearby, including **Cap Diamant, Maison du Fort, Manoir Sur-le-Cap,** and **Hôtel Château Bellevue.** See p. 249, 253, 253, and 252.

o **Best Value:** The **Courtyard Marriott Québec** gets consistently high marks for its friendly service, comfy rooms, great location, and solid in-house restaurant. See p. 256.

o **Best Trendy Hotel: Hôtel PUR** is the cool, stylish address of the hip St-Roch neighborhood. It's severe, ultramod, and the kind of place you'll either love or hate. See p. 259.

o **Best Adventure Hotel:** How many chances do you get to sleep in a hotel built completely of ice? On a bed of ice, near a chandelier made of ice, after dancing in a disco made of ice, ice, ice? The **Hôtel de Glace** moved in 2011 (its 11th edition) to a location just 10 minutes from downtown Québec City. It is open from January to late March—or as long as it's cold enough not to melt. See p. 257.

o **Best for Families:** Enjoy fantastic family packages at the **Fairmont Le Château Frontenac** that include admission to various parks and attractions. If you have a little girl, consider the fantastical Fairytale Princess Package that includes staying in the same room where Princess Grace of Monaco stayed in 1969, a princess outfit, a horse-drawn carriage ride, a royal dinner, and more. There are packages for little princes as well, and even one for a king and his queen. See p. 248.

VIEUX-QUÉBEC: HAUTE-VILLE (UPPER TOWN)

Nestled under the wing of the magnificent Château Frontenac, hotels in this area may not compare in size or reputation, but can offer oodles of personal service and historical charm.

BEST FOR   Visitors who want the full visual effect of staying in a wonderland setting.

DRAWBACKS   Because of high demand in this coveted area near the "castle," prices can be expensive for what they offer.

Very Expensive

Fairmont Le Château Frontenac ★★★ ☺   Québec's magical "castle" opened in 1893 and has been wowing guests ever since. Many of the rooms are full-on luxurious, outfitted with elegant château furnishings and marble bathrooms. More than 500 (of 618) rooms were renovated in a 3-year project that finished in 2008 when Québec City feted its 400th anniversary. Prices depend on size, location, and view, with river views garnering top dollar. Lower-priced rooms overlooking the inner courtyard are appealing, too: The gabled roofs they face are quite romantic, and children might imagine Harry Potter swooping by. Anyone can stay on the more princely (and pricey) Fairmont Gold floors, which have a separate concierge and a lounge with an honor bar in the afternoons and breakfast in the mornings. Some of the amenities are a little disappointing (such as the premillennial clock radio, the weight scale that has seen better days, or the Keurig coffee machine instead of a posh Nespresso), but these are minor quibbles. Known locally as "the Château," the hotel was built in phases, following the landline, so the wide halls take crooked paths. The **St-Laurent Bar et Lounge** (p. 324) and Café de la Terrasse both look down on the St. Lawrence River. During summer, an elegant afternoon tea is served on Saturdays from 1:30 to 3pm. If only an indication of the times and the clientele, a Starbucks has now opened on the property.

1 rue des Carrières (at Place d'Armes), Québec City, PQ G1R 4P5. www.fairmont.com/frontenac. ✆ **866/540-4460** or 418/692-3861. Fax 418/692-1751. 618 units. C$259–C$549 double; from C$499 suite. Packages available. AE, DC, DISC, MC, V. Valet parking C$31, self-parking C$26; hybrid vehicles free. Pets accepted (C$30 per day per pet). **Amenities:** 3 restaurants; bar; babysitting; children's programs; concierge; executive-level rooms; health club; pools (1 indoor and 1 kiddie pool w/outdoor terrace); room service; spa; Wi-Fi (public areas, C$19 per day). *In room:* A/C, TV, hair dryer, Internet (C$19 per day), minibar.

Expensive

Hôtel Manoir Victoria ★   With an air of a grand old-timer, Manoir Victoria is formal and proper, from a lobby that features elegant old-world decor to an elaborate formal dining room. Over half the comfortable bedrooms were renovated in 2009, with everything from new mattresses to rugs and curtains to flatscreen TVs, and some now feature gas fireplaces and deep soaking, whirlpool tubs. The hotel has some special touches not normally found in midsize properties: a small indoor pool (albeit underground), a full-service spa that offers massages and Canadian specials such as maple body scrubs, and a pub/bistro in addition to the main restaurant. It's located around the corner from the busy rue St-Jean restaurant-and-bar scene. Note that there's a steep staircase from the front door to the lobby that can't be avoided, although elevators make the trip to most guest rooms.

44 Côte du Palais (at rue St-Jean), Québec City, PQ G1R 4H8. www.manoir-victoria.com. ✆ **800/463-6283** or 418/692-1030. Fax 418/692-3822. 156 units. High season C$175–C$400 double; low season C$129–C$300 double. Packages available. AE, DC, MC, V. Valet parking C$20. **Amenities:** 2 restaurants; bar; babysitting; concierge; exercise room; pool (indoor); sauna; room service; spa. *In room:* A/C, TV, hair dryer, minibar, Wi-Fi (free).

Moderate

Auberge Place d'Armes ★ Renovated with care in 2008, this high-end *auberge* offers 21 sumptuous rooms with stone walls that date from 1640 and handmade artisanal furniture—at surprisingly moderate prices. The *auberge* swallowed up a museum that had been here previously, and the most eye-popping unit, the Marie Antoinette suite, has actual 17th-century furnishings from Versailles. A portion of the rooms are done up in blue-and-white French decor, with the others have red-and-white British touches. Rooms have high-end flourishes, such as heated bathroom floors, flatscreen TVs, and massage showers. Installation of an elevator is in the works for fall 2011. Breakfasts are served in the very good in-house restaurant **Le Pain Béni** (p. 265).

24 rue Ste-Anne (at Place d'Armes), Québec City, PQ G1R 3X3. www.aubergeplacedarmes.com. ✆ **866/333-9485** or 418/694-9485. Fax 418/694-9899. 21 units. Summer C$159–C$219 double; fall–spring from C$90 double. Rates include continental breakfast. Packages available. AE, MC, V. Pets accepted (C$25 per day). **Amenities:** Restaurant; babysitting; concierge; room service. *In room:* A/C, CD player, fridge, hair dryer, MP3 docking station, Wi-Fi (free).

Cap Diamant There are lots of B&Bs in the quiet, pretty corner of Vieux-Québec behind the Château Frontenac. Owner Florence Guillot has turned this 1826 home into a Victoriana showpiece, with antiques and old photos richly decorating common areas and bedrooms. The whole thing is quite grand and romantic. Many rooms feature ornate fireplaces, mantles, heavy gold-edged mirrors, oriental rugs, and glass lamps. There's a small all-season back porch where breakfast is served (it recently got a sleek update), and a summer garden. Although it's a B&B, all rooms have private baths. Ask to see the industrial-size dumb waiter that descends from a secret trap door ceiling to carry luggage up to the top floors—the controls are behind a painting in the front hall, like something out of a James Bond movie.

39 av. Ste-Geneviève (at rue Ste-Ursule), Québec City, PQ G1R 4B3. www.hotelcapdiamant.com. ✆ **888/694-0303** or 418/694-0303. 9 units. Mid-May to mid-Oct C$164–C$174 double; mid-Oct to mid-May from C$114 double. Rates include continental breakfast. Packages available. AE, MC, V. Parking C$15. *In room:* A/C, TV, fridge, hair dryer, Wi-Fi (free).

Hôtel Champlain Vieux-Québec ★ 🔥 Don't be alarmed when you arrive and see the bleh 1960s facade; it doesn't reflect the pizzazz inside. A total overhaul by new owners in 2006 made this an elegant, cozy, modern new option. All rooms have king or queen beds, 300-count cotton sheets, flatscreen TVs, and silk curtains, and most units are quite roomy. A midpriced room, no. 13, has views of stone buildings across the street and feels very French, while guests in no. 47 can see the Château Frontenac from their bed. A self-serve espresso machine by the

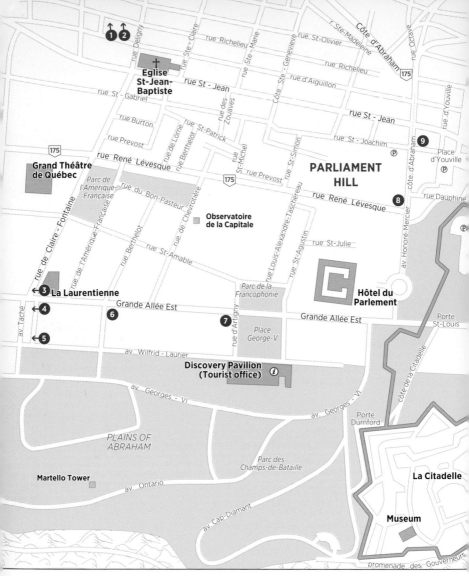

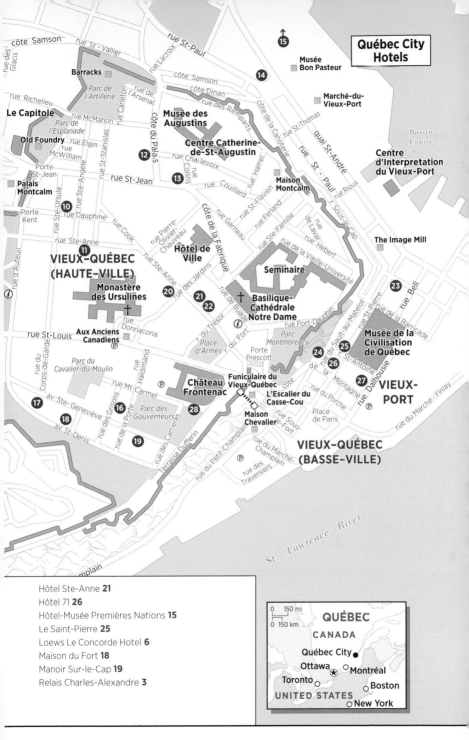

Québec City Hotels

Hôtel Ste-Anne **21**
Hôtel 71 **26**
Hôtel-Musée Premières Nations **15**
Le Saint-Pierre **25**
Loews Le Concorde Hotel **6**
Maison du Fort **18**
Manoir Sur-le-Cap **19**
Relais Charles-Alexandre **3**

front desk provides free cappuccinos any time of day or night. A new unit called "La vieille maison," which is only accessible by stairs, has four rooms with kitchenettes. The hotel is centrally located but not on a main thoroughfare, so it's quiet at night.

115 rue Ste-Anne (near rue Ste-Ursule), Québec City, PQ G1R 3X6. www.champlainhotel.com. ✆ **800/567-2106** or 418/694-0106. Fax 418/692-1959. 52 units. Summer C$169–C$259 double; fall–spring C$129–C$219 double. Rates include continental breakfast. AE, DISC, MC, V. Limited on-site parking C$15. **Amenities:** Concierge. *In room:* A/C, TV/DVD player, fridge, hair dryer, MP3 docking station, Wi-Fi (free).

Hôtel Château Bellevue   Occupying several row houses at the top of the Jardin des Gouverneurs in one of Vieux-Québec's prettiest areas, this 48-room hotel has a helpful staff, as well as some of the creature comforts typical of larger facilities. Renovations knocked out walls and combined rooms to make fewer, bigger units. Higher-priced rooms overlook the park, and all rooms are quiet and bright. The lobby features an unusual wine machine that dispenses selections by the glass. A sister hotel, **Château Laurier** (p. 258), is outside the walls on Parliament Hill.

16 rue de la Porte (at av. Ste-Geneviève), Québec City, PQ G1R 4M9. www.hotelchateaubellevue. com. ✆ **800/463-2617** or 418/692-2573. Fax 418/692-4876. 48 units. July–Oct C$139–C$245 double; Nov–June from C$89 double. Rates include continental breakfast for reservations made directly through the hotel. Packages available. AE, DC, DISC, MC, V. Valet parking C$15. **Amenities:** Exercise room. *In room:* A/C, TV, hair dryer, Wi-Fi (free).

Hôtel Clarendon ★   In operation since 1870, the Clarendon has the rank and the feel of a grand old-timer. Public spaces and bedrooms have high ceilings and dignified decor, and the handsome bar hosts live jazz on Friday and Saturday. Rooms are decorated with heavy drapery, patterned bedspreads, and dark furniture. School groups are among the clientele during the academic year; they're generally booked on the first and second floors, so consider asking for a room on any of the other five floors. There is a tunnel from the hotel to the city parking lot, which is especially convenient in winter.

57 rue Ste-Anne (at rue des Jardins), Québec City, PQ G1R 3X4. www.hotelclarendon.com. ✆ **888/222-3304** or 418/692-2480. Fax 418/692-4652. 143 units. C$94–C$179 double. Packages available. AE, MC, V. Valet parking C$25. **Amenities:** Restaurant; bar; exercise room; room service. *In room:* A/C, TV, CD player, hair dryer, Wi-Fi (free).

Hôtel du Vieux-Québec ☺   This century-old brick hotel is centrally located and has been renovated with care. The most recent updates were completed in 2011. Furnishings are local mahogany or maple from the province, with reproductions of paintings by Québec artists on the walls. There's a lounge with board games, and many rooms have two queen beds, making the hotel understandably popular with families. In addition to the French bistro, **Les Frères de la Côte** (✆ **418/692-5445**) on the ground floor, many moderately priced restaurants and nightspots are nearby. In July and August, the hotel offers a complimentary orientation walk at 9:30am. A page on the website describes the hotel's many green activities. Children will no doubt be distracted by the hustle and bustle of rue St-Jean just outside the door, or the chaletlike salon with cushy couches, fireplace, library, and board games.

1190 rue St-Jean (at rue de l'Hôtel Dieu), Québec City, PQ G1R 1S6. www.hvq.com. ✆ **800/361-7787** or 418/692-1850. Fax 418/692-5637. 45 units. May to late Oct C$157–C$227 double; late Oct to Apr from C$116 double. Rates include continental breakfast for rooms booked directly with hotel. Packages available. AE, MC, V. Pets accepted (C$25 per day). **Amenities:** Restaurant; fitness room. *In room:* A/C, TV/DVD player, DVD library, hair dryer, Wi-Fi (free).

Hôtel Ste-Anne ★   Modern European style is on offer in this 19th-century row house that fronts a pedestrian block in Upper Town's historic district. Exposed stone and brick walls are common, and most of the rooms have a free-standing cabinet housing a TV, an unstocked fridge, and a closet. The effect is spare but clean, and unusual lighting fixtures add drama. Swank, high-design bathrooms feature satisfyingly drenching showers. There's no lobby to speak of, and in the off-season the in-house restaurant **Le Grill** is open only for breakfast, so there are no areas besides the bedrooms to relax. But that's hardly a deal breaker, with so many other restaurants and the grand Château Frontenac just steps away.

32 rue Ste-Anne (near rue des Jardins), Québec City, PQ G1R 3X3. www.hotelste-anne.com. ℰ **877/222-9422** or 418/694-1455. Fax 418/692-4096. 28 units. C$189–C$229 double. AE, DC, MC, V. **Amenities:** Restaurant (breakfast year-round, dinner mid-May to Oct). *In room:* A/C, TV, fridge, hair dryer, Wi-Fi (free).

Maison du Fort   One of the cheeriest B&Bs near Parc des Gouverneurs. The owner, who lives on the property, is friendly, and even the smallest rooms, such as no. 2 on the first floor, are pleasant, with yellow-and–lime green decor. Tea and muffins are served in the morning. The home was built in 1851 and has a tasteful manner to match its pedigree, as well as a new AC. There are two resident cats. (Just down the block at no. 25, look for the plaque for the Têtu House, which was home to Antoine de St-Exupéry, author of *Le Petit Prince*.)

21 av. Ste-Geneviève (near rue de la Porte), Québec City, PQ G1R 4B1. www.hotelmaisondufort. com. ℰ **888/203-4375** or 418/692-4375. Fax 418/692-5257. 9 units. C$129–C$219 double. Rates include breakfast. MC, V. *In room:* TV (some units), hair dryer, Wi-Fi (free).

Manoir Sur-le-Cap   Continual sprucing keeps this inn on Parc des Gouverneurs, opposite the Château Frontenac, looking spiffy. Many guest rooms feature exposed stone or brick walls. If you require air-conditioning, be sure to request one of the six units that have it. Room no. 8 is one of the least expensive units but has a small balcony, while room no. 10 has a king bed, claw-foot tub, and large windows with a view of the Château. Photos of each room are online.

9 av. Ste-Geneviève (near rue de la Porte), Québec City, PQ G1R 4A7. www.manoir-sur-le-cap. com. ℰ **866/694-1987** or 418/694-1987. Fax 418/692-3062. 14 units. C$105–C$175 double. AE, MC, V. *In room:* A/C (some units), TV, hair dryer, Wi-Fi (free).

Inexpensive

Auberge Internationale de Québec   Most of the 277 beds in this centrally located hostel are in dorms standard to Hostelling International, but there are also 25 modest rooms for one to five people, with either shared or private bathrooms. Sheets and blankets are provided (sleeping bags, in fact, are not permitted). The facility is open 24 hours and has a four-star hostel rating for its comfort, range of services, and overall quality. Reservations are necessary in summer.

19 rue. Ste-Ursule (near rue Ste-Anne), Québec City, PQ G1R 4E1. www.aubergeinternationalde quebec.com. ℰ **866/694-0950** or 418/694-0755. Fax 418/694-2278. 25 private rooms, 277 beds. C$76–C$92 private room for 2; C$30 per person for shared dorm room. Discount available for H.I. members. Rates for private rooms include breakfast. AE, DC, MC, V. **Amenities:** Restaurant; bar; self-service kitchen; Wi-Fi (in lobby, free).

VIEUX-QUÉBEC: BASSE-VILLE (LOWER TOWN)/VIEUX-PORT

Lower town is more or less an extension of the Upper Town, separated by a photogenic bluff that divides the two areas. A *funiculaire* conveniently connects the two areas, or you can take the stairs at L'éscalier casse-cou (Breakneck Steps), which is not as scary or steep as it may sound.

BEST FOR   Discerning travelers who gravitate toward small hotels that are big on luxury.

DRAWBACKS   Certain areas during off season can seem empty and lonely.

Expensive

Auberge St-Antoine ★★★   This hotel is a knockout. A stay here is sure to be memorable, especially for enthusiasts of historic preservation. The *auberge* began life as an 1830 maritime warehouse. It kept the soaring ceilings, dark beams, and stone floors, and is now one of the city's landmark luxury boutique hotels (and a member of the prestigious Relais & Châteaux luxury group). Bedrooms are modern and sleek with luxury linens, plush robes, Bose sound systems, heated bathroom floors, and bathing nooks with rain-shower nozzles directly overhead. Many rooms have balconies, terraces, fireplaces, or kitchenettes; ask when booking if you want to ensure having any of these features in your room. The striking Café Artéfact lounge with cathedral-like windows serves lunch, snacks, and drinks, and its high-end restaurant, **Panache** (p. 269), where breakfast is served, has become one of the best in town.

8 rue St-Antoine (next to the Musée de la Civilisation), Québec City, PQ G1K 4C9. www.saint-antoine.com. ℰ **888/692-2211** or 418/692-2211. Fax 418/692-1177. 95 units. C$149–C$299 double; from C$299 suite. Packages available. AE, DC, MC, V. Valet parking C$25. Pets accepted (C$150 per visit). **Amenities:** Restaurant; bar; babysitting; concierge; exercise room; room service. *In room:* TV, espresso maker, hair dryer, minibar, Wi-Fi (free).

Hôtel des Coutellier ★   In a quiet nook across from the city's market and down the block from the train station, Coutellier does lots of small things right, so it's no wonder it was recently upgraded to four stars. As a result, it boasts of having one of the highest occupancy rates in the city. It gets lots of repeat business travelers, but also caters to vacationers who appreciate the personal touch that can come with a 24-room operation. Breakfasts of croissant, yogurt, and orange juice are delivered each morning in a basket that hangs from the front doorknob. For bicyclists, the hotel offers free indoor bike storage. Charmingly, a *pétanque* pit (similar to boule or bocce) in front of the hotel brings out local players in the afternoons. All rooms require use of stairs. The hotel recently upgraded two suites: a "romantic" that's ideal for couples and the other for families (it has a lunch counter); both have double whirlpools.

253 rue St-Paul (at Quai St-André), Québec City, PQ G1K 3W5. www.hoteldescoutellier.com. ℰ **888/523-9696** or 418/692-9696. Fax 418/692-4050. 24 units. C$185–C$275 double. AE, MC, V. Parking C$9. **Amenities:** Room service (from adjacent restaurant Môss). *In room:* A/C, TV, hair dryer, minibar, MP3 docking station, Wi-Fi (free).

Hôtel Le Germain-Dominion ★★★   Old Québec meets new in one of the city's most romantic boutique hotels. The owners stripped the 1912 building down to the studs in 1997 and started over, keeping the angular lines and adding soft touches. Forty rooms got a complete overhaul in 2010 and each now features a huge black-and-white photo of the building's curlicue cornices as a headboard, white walls, and charcoal-black ceilings and trim. The urban modernism is tempered by a comfortable reading chair and lamp. Beds remain exceptionally comfortable. About two-thirds of rooms have both tubs and showers, and bathrooms are well lit and elegant. A hearty continental breakfast featuring local products is set out near the fireplace in the handsome lobby, and a machine that dispenses free espresso is available round the clock. In summer there is a lovely terrace in the back and they lend out vintage bicycles to guests. All in all, intimate and chic.

126 rue St-Pierre (at rue St-Paul), Québec City, PQ G1K 4A8. www.germaindominion.com. ✆ 888/833-5253 or 418/692-2224. Fax 418/692-4403. 60 units. C$179–C$325 double. Rates include breakfast. AE, DC, MC, V. Parking C$19. Pets accepted (C$35 per day). **Amenities:** Espresso bar; babysitting; concierge; exercise room; room service. *In room:* A/C, TV, CD player, espresso machine, fridge, hair dryer, Wi-Fi (free).

Hôtel 71 ★★   Owned by the same people as the adjacent **Le St-Pierre** (see below), the two properties share **Il Matto** (p. 269), a new (and happening) Italian restaurant on the first floor, but Hôtel 71 is slicker and ultracontemporary. Room no. 620 is typical, with 4.5m-high (15-ft.) cream-colored walls and curtains that extend nearly floor to ceiling, warmed up with deep-red velveteen chairs and cloth panels that serve as closet doors. Bathrooms are in the open style common to the area's boutique hotels. Many rooms feature bird's-eye views of the tops of the 19th-century buildings of Old Québec, the St. Lawrence River, or the ramparts of the fortress wall.

71 rue St-Pierre (near rue St-Antoine), Québec City, PQ G1K 4A4. www.hotel71.ca. ✆ 888/692-1171 or 418/692-1171. Fax 418/692-0669. 60 units. C$199–C$290 double. Packages available. AE, DC, MC, V. Valet parking C$20. **Amenities:** Restaurant; bar; babysitting; concierge; espresso machine; exercise room; room service. *In room:* A/C, TV/DVD player, CD player, hair dryer, Wi-Fi (free),

Hôtel Le Priori ★   A playful Art Deco interior sets the mood for this renovated 1726 house—you'll find conical stainless-steel sinks in the bedrooms and, in four units, claw-foot tubs beside brightly patterned duvet bed covers. Several units, including no. 10, are quite masculine, with brown walls, animal-skin rugs, and fur throws. Others have designer sofas. Suites (in a separate building) include sitting rooms with wood-burning fireplaces, and Jacuzzis. Once only accessible by stairs, in fall 2011 an elevator was installed to access the suites, which is good news for some, but those who enjoyed cooking in a full kitchen in the past will now only have a microwave and a minifridge. Rooms face either the small street out front or a leafy, pretty inner courtyard. The inventive in-house restaurant **Toast!** (p. 270) moves into the courtyard on summer nights.

15 rue Sault-au-Matelot (at rue St-Antoine), Québec City, PQ G1K 3Y7. www.hotellepriori.com. ✆ 800/351-3992 or 418/692-3992. Fax 418/692-0883. 26 units. Summer C$199–C$259 double, winter C$129–C$199 double; year-round from C$279 suites. Rates include breakfast. Packages available. AE, MC, V. **Amenities:** Restaurant; bar; babysitting; concierge; room service. *In room:* A/C, TV/DVD player, CD player, hair dryer, Wi-Fi (free).

Moderate

Le St-Pierre ★   One of the city's country-cozy *auberge* options—though recent renovations have sleeked up the hotel. Most rooms are surprisingly spacious, and the even more commodious suites are a luxury on a longer visit, especially since they have modest kitchen facilities. The made-to-order furnishings suggest traditional Québec style, and units have wood floors and original brick or stone walls. All rooms are on the first to fourth floors, and some have a river view. Most rooms also have whirlpool baths. The full breakfasts, included, are cooked to order. Italian restaurant **Il Matto** (p. 269) is also on-site.

79 rue St-Pierre (behind the Musée de la Civilisation), Québec City, PQ G1K 4A3. www.le-saint-pierre.ca. *(C)* **888/268-1017** or 418/694-7981. Fax 418/694-0406. 41 units. C$149–C$219 double; C$195–C$299 suite. Rates include full breakfast. Packages available. AE, DC, MC, V. Valet parking C$20. **Amenities:** Restaurant; bar; babysitting; concierge. *In room:* A/C, TV, hair dryer, Wi-Fi (free).

PARLIAMENT HILL (ON OR NEAR GRANDE-ALLÉE)

A flat land that extends away from Vieux-Québec, the area includes green spaces Battlefield Park and the Plains of Abraham, as well as the Musée National des Beaux-Arts du Québec near the posh Mont Calm residential neighborhood.

BEST FOR   Travelers who have rented a car, or those attending events in the area.

DRAWBACKS   The lack of variety. Accommodations in the area may have more of a generic feel than the character options in Vieux-Québec.

Expensive

Courtyard Marriott Québec ★★ 🍴   The Courtyard Marriott has become a hot property in recent years, due in part to across-the-board raves on online posting boards for its friendly staff, comfortable rooms, and fair prices. Someone here is paying attention to the right details. Beds have been given the deluxe treatment and are piled with five pillows and sheet-cover duvets. All rooms have either a sofa bed or an oversized chair that pulls out into a single bed, and all feature ergonomic chairs at the desks. The in-house restaurant, **Que Sera Sera,** is well regarded. Note that the hotel is right on the central Place d'Youville, where there's a small ice rink in winter, but can be noisy in any season. Ask for a room higher up or towards the back if that's a concern.

850 Place d'Youville (near rue St-Jean), Québec City, PQ G1R 3P6. www.marriott-quebec.com. *(C)* **866/694-4004** or 418/694-4004. Fax 418/694-4007. 111 units. C$129–C$299 double. Packages available. AE, DC, MC, V. Valet parking C$20, self-parking C$17. **Amenities:** Restaurant; bar; exercise room; whirlpool; room service. *In room:* A/C, TV, fridge, hair dryer, Internet (free).

Hilton Québec ★ ☺   Recently renovated rooms feature luxe bedding, big desks, ergonomic work chairs, and sand-colored walls. The idea: less clutter, more Zen. Views facing the St. Lawrence River and Vieux-Québec are spectacular and provide views of sunrise over the Citadelle. The busy boulevard René-Lévesque provides a steady hum of cars but, in higher rooms, is only particularly noticeable during morning rush hour. On weekdays, business lunches can take the high road to the 23rd floor and enjoy "Le 23," which includes a buffet lunch, a glass of wine, and free parking for 2 hours for C$23; reservations are required. The hotel is connected to the Place Québec convention center; it is also just steps away from le Faubourg St-Jean, a vibrant street with shops, boutiques, bars, and restaurants that is still (largely) undiscovered by tourists.

QUÉBEC'S ICE HOTEL: THE coldest RECEPTION IN TOWN

Québec's **Ice Hotel** (☎ **877/505-0423**; www.icehotel-canada.com), which is reincarnated each winter in a new design; it was formerly located a half-hour outside of Québec City, but as of 2011 they have moved to a spot just 10 minutes from downtown (9530 rue de la Faune). In 2010 they celebrated their 10th anniversary. For C$17 you can visit, but for C$259 per person (and up), you can have dinner and spend the night. Tempted?

The *Hôtel de Glace* is crafted each year from 500 tons of ice, and nearly everything is ice, from the ice chandelier in the 5.4m (18-ft.) vaulted main hall, to the thick-ice shot glasses in which vodka is served, to the pillars and arches and furniture. That includes the frozen slabs they call beds; and high-tech sleeping bags provide insulation (there's even a highly recommended how-to class on how to zip yourself up correctly).

Nighttime guests get their rooms at 9pm, after the last tour ends, and have to clear out by 9am, before the next day's arrivals. Rooms are vaguely grand and some are designed according to the yearly theme: One year there was a Chess Room featuring solid-ice chess pieces the size of small children at each corner of the bed. Other rooms bring the words "monastic" or "cell block" to mind.

Bear in mind that, except for in the hot tub (a good soak is also highly recommended to bring your body heat up), temperatures everywhere hover between 23° and 27°F (–5° and –3°C). Refrigerators are used not to keep sodas cold, but to *keep them from freezing.* And to whoever dreamed up the luxury suite with a real fireplace that somehow emits no heat: There is a special circle in hell for you.

The hotel has 36 rooms and suites, a wedding chapel (any Dr. Zhivago fans out there?), and a nightclub with DJ for guests to shake the chill from their booties. Open each January, it takes guests until late March—after that, it's destroyed.

1100 boul. René-Lévesque est, Québec City, PQ G1R 4P3. www.hiltonquebec.com. ☎ **800/447-2411** or 418/647-2411. Fax 418/647-6488. 571 units. C$175–C$400 double. Packages available. AE, DC, DISC, MC, V. Valet parking C$25, self-parking C$23. Pets allowed (C$25 per visit). **Amenities:** Restaurant; bar; babysitting; concierge; executive-level floors; exercise room; pool (outdoor, heated, year-round); room service; sauna. *In room:* A/C, TV, hair dryer, Internet (C$12 per day).

Loews Le Concorde Hotel ★ ☺ The skyscraper that houses this hotel rises discordantly from a neighborhood of late-Victorian town houses. But for guests, no matter: With all rooms on the fifth floor and above, the hotel offers spectacular views of the river and the Old City, and some rooms even have outdoor terraces. It's also adjacent to the Grande-Allée restaurant and party scene on one side and the pristine Joan of Arc garden in Parc des Champs-de-Bataille on the other. **L'Astral** (p. 272), the hotel's revolving rooftop restaurant with a bar and live piano music on weekends, is definitely worth a stop. For kids, there's a lending library of toys. There's a fee for pets, but they get the royal treatment.

1225 Cours du Général de Montcalm (at Grande-Allée), Québec City, PQ G1R 4W6. www.loewsle concorde.com. ☎ **800/463-5256** or 418/647-2222. Fax 418/647-4710. 406 units. C$229–C$369 double. Packages available. AE, DC, DISC, MC, V. Valet parking C$28, self-parking C$23. Pets accepted (C$25 per stay). **Amenities:** Restaurant; bar; babysitting; concierge; health club; pool (outdoor heated); room service; sauna. *In room:* A/C, TV, hair dryer, minibar, Wi-Fi (C$12 per day).

Moderate

Hôtel Château Laurier Québec ★ Sprawling along a broad strip of the action-packed Grande-Allée on one side and the quiet Plains of Abraham on the other, the Château Laurier is the largest nonchain hotel in the city. It takes pride in both its "eco-responsibility" and its "Franco-responsibility," with artwork and music of French and Québécois artists featured in hallways. Keep in mind when booking that the hotel has five categories of rooms of varying age, style, and price. "Prestige" rooms in the new section are the most stylish and enveloping, with king-size beds and goose-down duvets. Prestige floors are accessible only by room key, and they feature a nifty wine-by-the-glass vending machine. "Deluxe" rooms have a therapeutic bath and a fireplace. Rooms in the older section are way plainer, although some on the higher floors have views of the Citadelle and the St. Lawrence River. A courtyard has an igloo in winter and barbecue in the summer.

1220 Place Georges-V ouest (at Grande-Allée), Québec City, PQ G1R 5B8. www.hotelchateau laurier.com. ⓒ **877/522-8108** or 418/522-8108. Fax 418/524-8768. 291 units. C$109–C$409 double. Packages available. AE, DC, MC, V. Parking C$19. **Amenities:** Restaurant; bar; concierge; executive-level floors; exercise room; Jacuzzis (1 indoor and 2 outdoor); pool (indoor, saltwater); room service; Finnish sauna; spa. *In room:* A/C, TV, hair dryer, Wi-Fi (free).

Inexpensive

Relais Charles-Alexandre 🦪 This little hotel is close to the Musée National des Beaux-Arts du Québec and the pleasant area for shops and eateries along avenue Cartier. The first floor houses a mini art gallery, while its proximity to the Plains of Abraham makes it a good choice, if you're visiting for one of the festivals held there. Rooms are very basic but crisply maintained. Spend the extra C$10 for one of the superior units, which are bigger and/or have better views. Call to inquire before bringing children.

91 Grande-Allée est (2 blocks east of av. Cartier), Québec City, PQ G1R 2H5. www.relaischarles alexandre.com ⓒ **418/523-1220.** Fax 418/523-9556. 23 units. May–Oct and Carnaval C$134–C$144 double; Nov–Apr C$89–C$99 double. Rates include breakfast. MC, V. Parking C$9. **Amenities:** Breakfast room. *In room:* A/C, TV, hair dryer, Wi-Fi (free).

ST-ROCH

Until 10 years ago, there were few reasons for travelers to include Québec's St-Roch neighborhood in their plans, but that's changing. Young restaurateurs, artists, media techies, and fashionistas have settled in and dubbed the area "Le Nouvo St-Roch" (proper spelling would be too traditional). Pronunciation, however, is simple: "Saint-Rock." Another up-and-coming area is Limoilou (after Jacques Cartier's manor in France), but let's revisit this area in another 5 years. Urban locals down with style convene in this up-and-coming neighborhood that is growing with new boutiques and restaurants even as we speak.

BEST FOR Fashion or media society who can't bother scouting hotel options when they know this is where they need to be.

DRAWBACKS While close to Vieux-Québec by car, St-Roch is slightly removed from the main attractions—unless, of course, St-Roch is central to your itinerary.

Expensive

Auberge Le Vincent ★ 🗡 Tucked in among the restaurants, bistros, tech companies, skateboard punks, and well-heeled hipsters of the St-Roch neighborhood is the Van Gogh–inspired Le Vincent. Housed in a renovated 100-year-old building, the sophisticated accommodations represent a terrific value, considering all the luxe features: goose duvets, 400-thread-count sheets, custom-made dark cherry-wood furniture, generous lighting options, and local art. Breakfast, which is included, is served in a brick-walled seating area off the lobby. Bike storage is available. Rooms are up either one or two flights of stairs. A significant upgrade to the windows has reduced ambient noise from the streets below.

295 rue St-Vallier est (corner of rue Dorchester), Québec City, PQ G1K 3P5. www.aubergelevincent. com. 📞 **888/523-5005** or 418/523-5000. Fax 418/523-5999. 10 units. C$199–C$279 double. Rates include full breakfast. Packages available. AE, MC, V. Parking C$15. *In room:* A/C, TV/DVD player, CD player, fridge, hair dryer, Wi-Fi (free).

Hôtel PUR ★★ Step into the severely white lobby of this ultramod hôtel tower, and you'll either love it or hate it. Either way, it'll snap you to attention. The rooms above are cubicle but cozy, with top-of-the-line linens, plush robes, spalike bathrooms, and a desk area for getting some work done. From room no. 1807, the views overlooking the curved steps of Église St-Roch down below are stunning (a new lightshow at Christmas time, however, might encourage you to book another perspective). Along with one of the nicest fitness rooms in the area, PUR also claims to have the largest indoor pool in Québec City. The owners converted a Holiday Inn into this boutique accommodation and accompanying ground-floor restaurant, **Table,** which was recently renovated and now open for lunch and dinner—one more example of the St-Roch neighborhood's gentrification. Though nothing in Québec City is too far apart, the hotel is a good walk from the more touristy Vieux-Québec.

395 rue de la Couronne (at rue St-Joseph), Québec City, PQ G1K 7X4. www.hotelpur.com. 📞 **800/267-2002** or 418/647-2611. Fax 418/640-0666. 242 units. C$199–C$249 double. Packages available. AE, DC, DISC, MC, V. Pets accepted (free with restrictions). Valet parking C$19. **Amenities:** Restaurant; fitness center; pool (indoor, heated); sauna. *In room:* A/C, TV, hair dryer, minibar, MP3 docking station, Wi-Fi (free).

JUST OUTSIDE THE CITY

Sometimes, yes, it happens that visitors to Québec City are not here for the century-old sights in the historic center. These hotels offer great accommodations for those with other activities on their travel agenda.

BEST FOR Travelers who are interested in golf, shopping, or First Nations culture.

DRAWBACKS Obviously it can be a bit of a trek if your interests lie in Québec City.

Moderate

Château Bonne Entente ★★ ☺ You can choose to golf at the 18-hole, 200-acre **La Tempête** club; paddle around the large, three-season heated outdoor pool; or get a warm aromatic-oil massage at this elegant spa property 20 minutes from the city. Bushels of dollars have elevated it from its former folksy-country feel to something more sophisticated. To attract design aficionados who head to the boutique hotels of Vieux-Québec, it built a wing called Urbania, a hotel-within-a-hotel that has loft suites and a private lounge with afternoon cocktails. Equally new and modern are the Terzo rooms. Older guestrooms come in three personalities: business (streamlined), cocooning (feminine), and distinctive. An on-site **AmeriSpa** serves up massages, scrubs, facials, and pedicures.

3400 Chemin Ste-Foy, Québec, PQ G1X 1S6. www.chateaubonneentente.com. ✆ **800/463-4390** or 418/653-5221. Fax 418/653-3098. 165 units. C$159–C$219 double; from C$245 suite. Packages available. AE, DC, DISC, MC, V. Free parking. From Rte. 40 west, take exit 305 south onto Autoroute Duplessis (540), then exit 5 and turn right onto Chemin Ste-Foy. **Amenities:** 2 restaurants (1 extra in summer); bar; babysitting; concierge; golf course; exercise room; 2 Jacuzzis; pool (heated, outdoor); room service; sauna; spa. *In room:* A/C, TV, CD player, hair dryer, minibar, Wi-Fi (free).

Hôtel Alt ★   Brought to you by the same folks who graced Lower Town with **Hôtel Le Germain-Dominion** (p. 254), this business-friendly tower is decidedly more budget-friendly, but no less warm and professional. Guests are welcomed by a bright and airy reception hall. It's kind of a drag to have to go back down to the lobby to buy your coffee pouch (no, it's not included) the next morning, so buy it when you check in. In fact, any minibar contents must be picked up at the front desk, but there's no scrimping on other amenities here: crisp linens, ultramodern bathroom with impressive showerhead power, flatscreen TV, and comfortable work station. There are a few rooms that offer more space and a bathtub for only C$40 more per night. The adjacent resto **Bistango** is where breakfast is served. Shoppers, in particular, should note that the hotel is directly across a row of malls. A taxi ride to the Old City is about 20 minutes and C$30.

1200 av. Germain des Prés, Québec, PQ, G1V 3M7. www.quebec.althotels.ca. ✆ **800/463-5253** or 418/658-1224. Fax 418/658-8846. 126 units. C$135 for a standard room with 1 queen bed; C$175 for a larger room with tub. Packages available. AE, MC, V. Free parking. From Rte. 40, take exit 540 for boul. Laurier, and turn left at the 3rd traffic light. **Amenities:** Restaurant. *In room:* A/C, TV, fridge, hair dryer, Wi-Fi (free).

Hôtel-Musée Premières Nations ★   Fifteen minutes from Québec City by car is a First Nations reservation called Wendake. It's here that a beautifully airy, earthy hotel that shows off native furnishings opened in early 2008. The hotel is surrounded by a grove of maple trees along the shores of the Akiawenrahk River, and each room overlooks the river and has a small balcony with seating. The lounge just off the lobby is particularly stunning, with hand-carved furnishings and fur accents, opening onto a lovely terrace. Throughout the hotel there are also beautiful paintings and sculptures, all created by First Nations artists. A high-end restaurant features First Nations–inspired cuisine such as elk, bison, and smoked mackerel, and includes a four-course table d'hôte for C$40. The menu changes every season: The last time I was there they were serving kangaroo and seal. An on-site museum celebrates Huron-Wendat culture, and there are shops and a few restaurants in Wendake for guests to poke around.

5 Place de la Rencontre, Wendake, Québec, PQ G0A 4V0. www.hotelpremieresnations.ca. ✆ **866/551-9222** or 418/847-2222. Fax 418/847-2903. 55 units. C$129–C$249 double. Packages available. AE, MC, V. Free parking. From Rte. 175 north, take exit 154 for rue de la Faune, enter Wendake reservation and follow signs. **Amenities:** Restaurant; bar; babysitting; bike rental. *In room:* A/C, TV, fridge, hair dryer, Wi-Fi (free).

PRACTICAL INFORMATION

The Big Picture

Both Montréal and Québec City have familiar international hotel chains, as well as small B&Bs hosted by locals. In between are the boutique hotels, which combine high-end service with plush room accommodations and decor that ranges from Asian minimalist to country luxury. Unless otherwise noted, all rooms in the lodgings listed above have private bathrooms—*en suite,* as they say in Canada. Most of the accommodations listed here are completely nonsmoking.

Getting the Best Deal

Most Québec hotels offer online specials and package deals that bundle rooms with meals or sightseeing activities. In many cases, this can result in rates significantly below what's quoted in this book. Always check hotel websites before calling to make a reservation.

Because the region is so cold for so many months of the year, tourism here is cyclical. That means that prices drop—often steeply—for many properties much of the September-through-May period, with the exception of the Christmas holiday and winter carnival in February. While rooms are less expensive these times of year, some of the essential vibrancy and *joie de vivre* of the region goes into hibernation as well.

Note: Prices listed here are rack rates for a double-occupancy room in high season (which includes the warm months, Christmastime, and Carnaval), unless otherwise noted. See p. 78 for information about the Frommer's star-rating system, price rankings, categories, and taxes.

Reservation Services

Most established hotels take credit card payments online or over the phone. Full payments are often required upfront. If you think there's a possibility you may need to cancel, do take note of refund policies and deadlines to do so.

Smaller properties typically have their own way of doing business. When calling to make arrangements at a B&B, be very clear about your needs and requirements; in some cases you may be speaking directly to the owner. A deposit is often required, as are minimum stays of 2 nights. Credit cards may not be accepted.

Alternative Accommodations

Vieux-Québec has about a dozen B&Bs. With rates mostly in the C$90-to-C$140 range, they don't represent substantial savings over the small hotels but do give you the opportunity to get to know some of the city dwellers. Many will post signs that say COMPLET, meaning full, or VACANT, which means that rooms are available. The *Official Accommodation Guide* put out by Québec City Tourism lists every member of the Greater Québec Area Tourism and Convention Bureau, from B&Bs to five-star hotels, with details about the number of rooms, the prices, and the facilities. It's available at tourist offices (p. 239). There's also a handy search feature for B&Bs at www.quebecregion.com.

14

WHERE TO EAT IN QUÉBEC CITY

With a little research, it's possible to eat extraordinarily well in Québec City. It used to be that this gloriously scenic town had no *temples de cuisine* comparable to those of Montréal. That has changed. There are now restaurants equal in every way to the most honored establishments of any North American city, with surprising numbers of creative, ambitious young chefs and restaurateurs bidding to achieve similar status.

BEST EATING BETS

o **Best Restaurants for a Special Evening: Panache** may be the most romantic restaurant in the city. **Initiale** is hushed and elegant. **Laurie Raphaël** is endlessly eclectic, with a nightclubby atmosphere in the evening. These stellar restaurants are just blocks from each other in Lower Town. See p. 269, 268, and 269.

o **Best Bistros:** In a city that specializes in the informal bistro tradition, **L'Echaudé** is a star. The classic dishes are all in place, and the tone is casual sophistication. **Le Clocher Penché Bistrot** offers a cozy atmosphere and a reason to explore the trendy St-Roch neighborhood. See p. 269 and 273.

o **Best Bargains:** A main course at **Aux Anciens Canadiens** can set you back C$60 or more, but from noon until 5:30pm from Friday to Sunday, the purveyor of classic Québécois fare offers a three-course meal with wine or beer for C$20. The modest **Mistral Gagnant** has terrific food and a table d'hôte lunch for just C$11 to C$16, while ritzy **Laurie Raphaël** also has a lunchtime deal of three courses for about C$23. See p. 264, 271, or 269.

o **Best Big View:** Revolving rooftop restaurants rarely dish out food as elevated as their lofty venues, but **L'Astral** in the Hôtel Loews le Concorde is an exception. The food is above average and the view one of a kind. Lunchtime offers the best value. See p. 272.

price CATEGORIES

Very Expensive	C$30 and up
Expensive	C$20–C$30
Moderate	C$10–C$20
Inexpensive	Under C$10

PREVIOUS PAGE: **A dish from elegant Initiale.**

There are blatantly touristy restaurants along rue St-Louis in Upper Town and around the Place d'Armes, many of them with hawkers outside. They can produce decent meals and are entirely satisfactory for lunch.

At the better places, reservations are essential during holidays and festivals. Other times, it's necessary to book ahead only for weekend evenings. Dress codes are rarely stipulated, but "dressy casual" works almost everywhere.

The evening meal tends to be served earlier in Québec City than in Montréal, at 7pm rather than 8pm. In the winter months, when tourist traffic slows, restaurants can close early or cut down on their days, so confirm before heading out. The best dining deals in Québec City are table d'hôte, fixed-priced meals. Nearly all full-service restaurants offer them. Generally, these meals include at least soup or salad, a main course, and a dessert. Some places add an extra appetizer and/or a beverage. The total price ends up being approximately what you'd pay for the main course alone. At lunchtime, table d'hôte meals are even cheaper (and you have more time to walk off the big meal).

- **Best Idyllic Terrace:** The crimson-red main room *is* sexy, but try to have a dinner on the leafy enclosed back terrace of Lower Town's **Toast!** See p. 270.

- **Best for Families:** Large (it seats 180) and jovial, **Le Café du Monde** manages the nearly impossible: classic French food *and* fast service without a compromise in quality, even on crowded holiday weekends. See p. 270.

- **Best Breakfast with Locals:** In the residential neighborhood of Montcalm, not far from the Musée des Beaux-Arts du Québec, **Café Krieghoff** gets a mix of families, singles, and artsy folks of all ages. See p. 272.

- **Best "Name Your Price" Dinner:** The recently expanded **Le Cercle** draws adult hipsters to its St. Roch location with killer food and quirks such as a name-your-price "tapas mania." See p. 274.

- **Best Sugar Pie:** We have to go with **Aux Anciens Canadiens** for this category as well. Québec's favorite dessert reaches its apogee at this admittedly tourist-heavy venue in central Upper Town. Think maple syrup with a crust, or pecan pie without the pecans. See below.

VIEUX-QUÉBEC: HAUTE-VILLE (UPPER TOWN)

In addition to the options listed below, food is also available in Upper Town at the jazz club **Charles Baillairgé** and the **Pub St-Patrick, Pub St-Alexandre** (p. 324), and **St-Laurent Bar et Lounge** (p. 324).

Very Expensive

Aux Anciens Canadiens ★ TRADITIONAL QUEBECOIS   Inundated by travelers during peak months, this venerable restaurant with costumed servers is in what's probably the city's oldest house (1677); its front windows are small because their original glass came over from France, packed in barrels of molasses. Surprisingly, it's one of the best places in La Belle Province at which to sample cooking that has its roots in New France's earliest years. Traditional Québécois recipes are done well here, and servings are large enough to ward off hunger for a week. Caribou figures into many of the dishes, as does maple syrup, which goes into, for example, the duckling, goat-cheese salad, and luscious sugar pie. Prices are high except for the restaurant's afternoon special, from 4 to 5:30pm on Monday to Thursday and noon to 5:30pm on Friday to Sunday, which is a terrific bargain: soup, a main course, a dessert, and a glass of beer or wine for C$20.

34 rue St-Louis (at rue des Jardins). ℰ **418/692-1627.** www.auxancienscanadiens.qc.ca. Reservations recommended. Main courses C$29–C$64; table d'hôte lunch C$20, dinner C$37–C$75. AE, DC, MC, V. Mon–Thurs 4–9pm; Fri–Sun noon–9pm.

Le St-Amour ★★ CONTEMPORARY QUEBECOIS   Perhaps the most talked-about restaurant in the city, in terms of gastronomic dining. The otherwise formal wait-staff heartily boasts of visits from rock stars Paul McCartney (see "Eating Vegetarian in a Land That's Definitely Not," below) and Sting. Foie gras aficionados will be in heaven here, for it is served as a terrine, seared, or "fantasy," an artfully present plate of the sinful liver in seven ways. The atmosphere has a dated feel, yet the staff here pulls it off in the same way that a fashionista can pull off stirrup pants. Both young and mature couples celebrate milestone anniversaries here, particularly in the indoor garden under an airy atrium. Oenophiles will enjoy the extensive wine menu organized by regions in France. Curious carnivores will not be disappointed with the red deer plate served in a poivrade sauce with a reduction of wild blueberry juice, but the house specialty not to be missed is the sweetbreads smartly accompanied by morel mushrooms and Samos Muscat creamy sauce.

48 Rue Sainte-Ursule (near rue St-Louis). ℰ **418/694-0667.** www.saint-amour.com. Reservations recommended. Main courses C$40–C$53; table d'hôte lunch C$15–C$28; discovery dinner C$115. AE, DC, MC, V. Mon–Fri 11:30am–2pm; daily 6–10:30pm.

Expensive

Ristorante Il Teatro ★ 🍴 ITALIAN   There's so much to like about this convivial Italian restaurant. There's the huge menu (24 types of pasta, for instance) and the generous portions, which can make up for the hefty prices of the main courses (most are around C$25). There's the large sidewalk cafe, directly on the hopping Place d'Youville. And there's the general ambiance: friendly, bustling, and never snooty. Actors, musical performers, and theater staff from the adjoining **Le Capitole** theater (p. 321) and other nearby arts venues often stop in after their shows.

972 rue St-Jean (at Place d'Youville). ℰ **418/694-9996.** www.lecapitole.com/en/restaurant.php. Main courses C$15–C$36; table d'hôte C$28–C$35. AE, DC, MC, V. Daily 7am–midnight or later.

Moderate

Le Pain Béni ★ CONTEMPORARY QUEBECOIS   Reopened in 2010 after a fire, this popular restaurant in the touristic heart of Upper Town now boasts a stylishly renovated space with a few more private nooks than before. The vibe remains warm and casually romantic, with stone and brick walls from the 1600s. The menu is wildly innovative—hello, shiitake ice cream and shrimp with *ras el hanout* spices—and the lamb ravioli is a must. There are pizza options for the less adventurous. Le Pain Béni is in the **Auberge Place d'Armes** (p. 249).

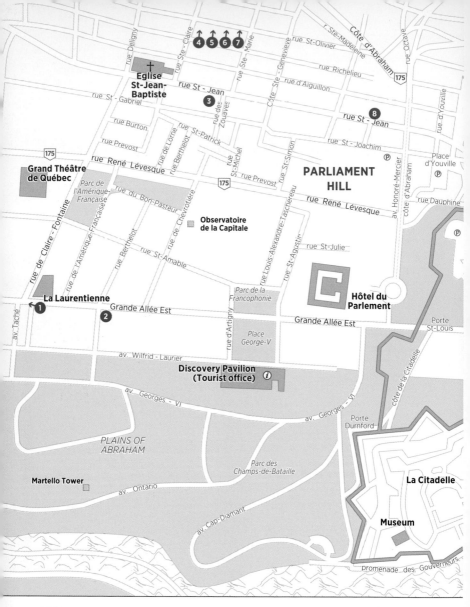

Québec City
Restaurants

Musée
Bon Pasteur

Marché-du-
Vieux-Port

Barracks

Le Capitole

9

Old Foundry

Palais
Montcalm

Porte
St-Jean

Porte
Kent

Musée des
Augustins

Centre Catherine-
de-St-Augustin

Maison
Montcalm

20

Centre
d'Interpretation
du Vieux-Port

Bassin
Louise

The Image Mill

19

24

VIEUX-QUÉBEC
10 (HAUTE-VILLE)

Monastère
des Ursulines

Hôtel de
Ville

11

12

Seminaire

Basilique-
Cathédrale
Notre Dame

14

18

17

16

Musée de la
Civilisation
de Québec

23

Aux Anciens
Canadiens 13

Parc du
Cavalier-du-Moulin

rue St-Louis

Château
Frontenac

Funiculaire du
Vieux-Québec

L'Escalier du
Casse-Cou

21

22

VIEUX-
PORT

15

Maison
Chevalier

Parc des
Gouverneurs

Place
de Paris

VIEUX-QUÉBEC
(BASSE-VILLE)

St. Lawrence River

bd. Champlain

ⓘ Tourist Information

Ⓟ Parking

0   500 ft
0   100 m

QUÉBEC

CANADA

Québec City

Ottawa

Montréal

Toronto

Boston

UNITED STATES

New York

0   150 mi
0   150 km

267

24 rue Ste-Anne (at rue du Trésor). ☎ **866/333-9485** or 418/694-9485. www.aubergeplace
darmes.com. Main courses C$16–C$38; table d'hôte cost of main plus C$10, or C$20 for a more
elaborate version. AE, MC, V. May–Oct daily 11:30am–10:30pm; Nov–Apr daily 11:30am–2:30pm
and 5:30–10:30pm.

Inexpensive

In addition to **Paillard,** below, children may like **Casse-Crêpe Breton,** 1136
rue St-Jean (☎ **418/692-0438;** www.cassecrepebreton.com). Its savory and
sweet crepes run C$6 to C$9. Centrally located in the heart of Upper Town, it's
usually packed at lunch. Go a little early or a little late if you don't want to wait.

Chez Temporel LIGHT FARE   Nestled on an Upper Town side street just off
course of tourist traffic, this tiny *"crème des cafés,"* as it calls itself, has been serving locals of all stripes since 1974, and with good reason. Reliable, made-from-
scratch basics such as quiche Lorraine are served quickly and within budget for
nearby students, professors, and hospital workers. Parties of four or more will
want to peek in to decide if it's possible to fit at one of nine tables. Beer and wine
are available.

25 rue Couillard (near rue Christie). ☎ **418/694-1813.** Most items less than C$10. V. Mon–Sat
7am–11pm; Sun 8am–11pm.

Paillard LIGHT FARE ☺   Keep this bright sandwich shop in mind when
you're looking for healthy, fast food to eat in or take out. Soups, along with hot
and cold sandwiches on hearty ciabatta, baguettes, or croissants, are the main
event, and natural sodas, satisfying espresso drinks, and a yummy selection of
pastries and gelato fill out the menu. There are small tables, as well as communal
seating at large tables.

1097 rue St-Jean (near rue St-Stanislas). ☎ **418/692-1221.** www.paillard.ca. All items less than
C$10. MC, V. Winter Sun–Thurs 7:30am–6pm, Fri–Sat 7:30am–7pm; summer daily 7:30am–10pm.

VIEUX-QUÉBEC: BASSE-VILLE (LOWER TOWN)/VIEUX-PORT

In addition to the options listed below, food is also available in Lower Town at the
bars **Aviatic Club** and **SSS,** which are listed on p. 323 and 324, and the wine
bar/music room **Le Pape-Georges,** listed on p. 321.

Very Expensive

Initiale ★★ CONTEMPORARY QUEBECOIS   Initiale is not only one of the
elite restaurants of Québec City, but one of the best in the entire province. The
somewhat austere setting of tall windows, columns, and a deeply recessed ceiling
sets a gracious tone in a calm neutral palette of beige, and the welcome is both
cordial and correct. Lighting is subdued and the buzz barely above a murmur.
This is a good place to cast economy to the winds and go with one of the prix-fixe
menus. Dinner might start with a buckwheat crepe folded around an artichoke,
a round of crabmeat with a creamy purée of onions, and a flash-fried leaf of baby
spinach all arrayed on the plate as on an artist's palette. It might continue with
grilled tuna supported by sweet garlic, salsify, and lemon marmalade, and a swirl
of pasta with marguerite leaves. Québec cheeses are an impressive topper. Men
should wear jackets, and women can pull out the stops.

54 rue St-Pierre (corner of Côte de la Montagne). ☎ **418/694-1818.** www.restaurantinitiale.com. Reservations recommended on weekends. Table d'hôte dinners C$59–C$72; tasting menu C$129. AE, DC, MC, V. Thurs–Fri 11:30am–2pm; Tues–Sat 6–9pm.

Laurie Raphaël ★ CONTEMPORARY QUEBECOIS   The owners of this creative restaurant, long one of the city's most accomplished, tinker relentlessly with their handiwork. If the prices scare you off, come at lunch, when cream of butternut squash soup is topped with vanilla oil, and the skirt steak comes with red-wine *jus,* parsnip purée, mushrooms, and roasted root vegetables, all for C$23. Service is friendly and correct, and the meal's pace spot on. Sophisticated decor is tempered by dashes of eye-popping red and electric purple. For their 20th anniversary they added a brand-new terrace in black and glass, lit in an awesome blue hue at night. A second locale opened in Montréal inside the **Hôtel Le Germain** (p. 67) in 2007, but only at the Québec location does chef/owner Daniel Vézina give cooking classes (p. 34).

117 rue Dalhousie (at rue St-André). ☎ **418/692-4555.** www.laurieraphael.com. Reservations recommended. Main courses C$36–C$50; 3-course chef's inspiration lunch C$23, dinner C$60; gourmet dinner C$96. AE, DC, DISC, MC, V. Tues–Fri 11:30am–2pm; Tues–Sat 5:30–10pm.

Panache ★★★ CONTEMPORARY QUEBECOIS   The restaurant of the superb **Auberge St-Antoine** (p. 254) is housed in a former 19th-century warehouse delineated by massive wood beams and rough stone walls. A wrought-iron staircase winds up to a second dining level, where tables feel like they're tucked into the eaves of a secret attic. A central glass fireplace, velvet couches, generous space between tables, and good acoustics enhance the inherent romantic aura, and service is flawless. Aiming to serve *cuisine québécoise revisitée*—French-Canadian cuisine with a twist—the frequently changing menu is heavy on locally sourced game, duck, fish, and vegetables. A slip of a bar seats about a dozen. **Café Artéfact,** a separate lounge just off the hotel's main lobby, provides a casual and cozy premeal meeting spot. If the steep dinner prices put you off, try Panache at lunch, when main courses start at C$14.

10 rue St-Antoine (in Auberge St-Antoine). ☎ **418/692-1022.** www.saint-antoine.com. Reservations recommended. Main courses lunch C$14, dinner C$36–C$49; 7-course signature menu C$95. AE, DC, MC, V. Mon–Fri 6:30–10:30am; Sat–Sun 7–11am; Wed–Fri noon–2pm; daily 6–10pm.

Expensive

Il Matto ITALIAN   A trendy, contemporary setting that serves Italian classics just like Mama makes them is a recipe that's proving to work well amongst the young and aspirational crowd of Québec City. Any meal preceded by a limoncello martini seems to start off on the right step. Try the aubergine Parmesan and bruschetta, then choose from no-fail classics like lasagna, manicotti, four kinds of pizza, and more. The owner of the resto is young Rocco Cortina, the son of Nicolas Cortina, who owns the highly regarded Ristorante Michelangelo in Ste-Foy (worth the taxi ride if you're craving haute Italian).

71 rue St-Pierre (near rue St-Antoine). ☎ **418/266-9444.** www.ilmatto.ca. Reservations strongly recommended on weekends. Main courses C$15–C$38. AE, DC, DISC, MC, V. Daily 11:30am–2:30pm and 5:30pm–close.

L'Echaudé ★ BISTRO   The most polished of the necklace of restaurants adorning this Vieux-Port corner, L'Echaudé is like a well-worn cashmere sweater—it goes well with both silk trousers and your favorite pair of jeans.

z

14

WHERE TO EAT IN QUÉBEC CITY

Vieux-Québec: Basse-Ville/Vieux-Port

269

Grilled meats and fishes, and the seafood stews, are an excellent value. Among classics on the menu are steak *frites,* duck confit, and salmon *tartare.* Less expected are the calf sweetbreads served with ginger, celery root, and shrimp. The owner keeps an important cellar with hundreds of wines, with the full list posted online. The bistro is frequented mostly by locals of almost all ages (although the very young are rarely seen), and visitors are attended to by a highly efficient staff. In summer, the small street in front of the patio becomes pedestrian only.

73 rue Sault-au-Matelot (near rue St-Paul). ✆ **418/692-1299.** www.echaude.com. Reservations suggested on weekends. Main courses C$18–C$42; table d'hôte dinner cost of main course, plus C$12. AE, DC, MC, V. Mon–Sat 11:30am–2:30pm; Sun 10:30am–2:30pm; daily 5:30–10pm.

Le Marie-Clarisse SEAFOOD   This spot, at the bottom of the **Breakneck Stairs** (**L'Escalier du Casse-Cou;** p. 287) and perched overlooking the pedestrian-only rue du Petit-Champlain, sits where the streets are awash with day-trippers and shutterbugs. Location is key: On a summer afternoon, a more pleasant hour cannot be passed anywhere in Québec City than on the terrace here, over a platter of shrimp or pâtés. The menu changes daily, so look closely at the specials posted on chalkboards. The inside rooms are formed of rafters, brick, and stone walls that are more than 360 years old, evoking the feel of a small country inn. In winter, sit beside the stone fireplace and indulge in the dense bouillabaisse.

12 rue du Petit-Champlain (at the *funiculaire*). ✆ **418/692-0857.** www.marieclarisse.qc.ca. Table d'hôte from C$53. AE, MC, V. Summer Mon–Fri 11:30am–2:30pm; year-round daily 6–10pm.

Moderate

Toast! ★ CONTEMPORARY QUEBECOIS   The kitchen for the zesty Toast! has its base in the French idiom but takes off in many directions. There's a poached quail egg with a truffled poultry emulsion, and goose breast served over spaghetti squash treated like risotto. For dessert, maybe hot-and-cold apple with cheese from nearby L'Île-aux-Grues? Dishes on the ever-changing menu are like that: sprightly, with joined tastes and textures, often from local sources. Outdoor dining, on a secluded terrace in back of the restaurant with big leafy trees overhead, is an oasis. In 2009, the owners opened the dialed-down but volume-up **SSS** around the corner (p. 324), where small plates can be nibbled in a dining room, or under blue lights and the thumping beat of the lounge.

17 rue Sault-au-Matelot (at rue St-Antoine). ✆ **418/692-1334.** www.restauranttoast.com. Reservations recommended on weekends. All entrees C$15. AE, MC, V. Sun–Wed 6–10:30pm; Thurs–Sat 6–11pm.

Moderate

Le Café du Monde ★ ☺ ✦ TRADITIONAL FRENCH   A longtime and entirely convivial eating venue, Café du Monde is a large, Parisian-style space, seating more than 100 inside and nearly that number on a terrace overlooking the St. Lawrence River. At night, the glass walls on the northern side look out on Robert Lepage's light installation, which bathes a huge stand of grain silos in an ever-changing wash of color (p. 286). The staff is amiable, and the food creative but still within bistro conventions. The long menu features classic French preparations of pâtés, duck confit, onion soup, smoked salmon *tartare,* and mussels

EATING vegetarian IN A LAND THAT'S DEFINITIVELY NOT

Satirist Fran Lebowitz once joked, "If you're going to America, bring your own food." That's definitely not necessary in Québec City, a destination with a rich regional cuisine, where calf brains are a delicacy and pies are made of meat.

But what if you're vegetarian? How do you get the most from the region if you prefer stalk over steak? To go totally veg, look no further than **Le Commensal** (p. 273), where everything is vegetarian. Many restaurants offer a standing veggie option, such as the green- and yellow-squash spaghetti with an aroma of truffle oil at **Toast!** (p. 270). Others will tweak an entrée if you call ahead and ask. Of course, making special requests is easier for someone like Paul McCartney, who rang **Le St-Amour** (p. 265) a few days ahead of his free concert in 2008 and then enjoyed a meatless gastronomic extravaganza with his entire entourage. Though meat-free dishes are by no means the house specialty, a recent visit confirmed this kitchen's veget-abilities for the common folk.

If you eat dairy products, a cheese plate traditionally served as a last course could become your main dish, although you'll have to ignore the raised eyebrows. You'll have limitless options, though, with the innovations of the province, which include Pied-de-Vent, Le Riopelle de l'Ile, and Le Migneron de Charlevoix. Those three cheeses, plus 150 more in summer, can be found at **La Fromagère du Marché** (✆ **418/692-2517,** ext. 238), in the **Marché du Vieux-Port.** While you're there, you'll find a generous selection of seasonally fresh fruits and vegetables, and freshly baked baguettes.

One final tip: If the French language isn't your strong suit, assume that most dishes have meat and learn to recognize a few terms. Sorry to say, *saucisse* is sausage, not sauce, and *fruits de mer* do not grow on trees.

---

with *frites.* The signature house salad features duck three ways: confit (duck leg), foie gras, and shaved duck breast.

84 rue Dalhousie (next to the cruise terminal). ✆ **418/692-4455.** www.lecafedumonde.com. Reservations recommended. Main courses C$14–C$28; table d'hôte C$36–C$40. AE, DC, MC, V. Mon–Fri 11:30am–11pm; Sat–Sun and holidays 9am–11pm. First 2 hours of parking are free.

Mistral Gagnant ★ 🍴 BISTRO   This "restaurant Provençal" channels the spirit of a modest village cafe in France, in both its sunny decor and its friendly atmosphere. Better yet, the food is fairly priced and tasty. The Bouillabaisse à la Provençale is a rich broth with big chunks of salmon, flakey white fish, mussels, scallop, and shrimp, served with rounds of bread and a porcelain spoon with tangy *rouille.* Lunch here, with soup to start and a dessert such as sublime lemon pie, can be had for less than C$16 and is the best bargain in the area. "Le Mistral" attracts many locals and regulars.

160 rue St. Paul (near rue Rioux). ✆ **418/692-4260.** www.mistralgagnant.ca. Main courses C$15–C$31; table d'hôte dinner C$18–C$36; lunch and 3-course early-bird special (5:30–6:30pm) C$12–C$17. AE, MC, V. Summer Mon–Sat 11:30am–2pm and 5:30–9pm; winter Tues–Sat 11:30am–2pm and 5:30–9pm. Closed Jan.

PARLIAMENT HILL (ON OR NEAR GRANDE-ALLÉE)

In addition to the options listed below, food is also available on Grande-Allée at the bar/restaurant **Savini,** listed on p. 324.

Expensive

L'Astral TRADITIONAL QUEBECOIS   On the 29th floor of the **Loews Le Concorde Hotel** (p. 257), L'Astral is a round, slowly revolving restaurant. All tables hug the windows, and over the course of a meal, visitors get a phenomenal 360-degree view of the city and river below. Dinner is pricey, but lunchtime table d'hôte is as low as C$14. For dessert, ask if they have their delectable version of the classic French-Canadian *pudding chômeur,* a pound cake soaked with maple syrup and brown sugar. Or order up a selection of regional cheeses, such as the nutty semisoft Migneron de Charlevoix or Le Cendrillon, a Québec-made goat cheese that was named best in the world in 2009. Although not an obvious choice for families, they do have a children's menu, and kids will be enthralled by the view.

1225 Cours du Général de Montcalm (at Grande-Allée). ℂ **800/463-5256** or 418/780-3602. www.lastral.ca. Reservations recommended on weekends. Main courses C$20–C$42; table d'hôte lunch C$14–C$20, dinner C$35. AE, DC, DISC, M, V. Mon–Sat 6:30–10:30am and noon–3pm; Sun 9am–3pm; Sun–Fri 6–10:45pm; Sat: 5:45-10:45pm.

Moderate

Le Moine Échanson ★ 🎁 CONTEMPORARY QUEBECOIS   In this tiny smidge of a restaurant, the daily menu is written on a chalkboard exclusively in French, taking up an entire wall. (Don't worry, the staff, if not locals seated next to you, will help with translations.) The wine list is adventurous, with rotating regions as focal points—Loire, Alsace, and Jura on a recent visit. A turnip salad with fresh dill and tarragon came sliced microscopically thin, while the small crock of potatoes au gratin bubbled long after the friendly waiter arranged it on the table. There's no shying from butter, bacon, or intense cheeses; at least two out of three are likely to show up in every hearty dish, served shabby-chic on slabs of slate or wood, or in mason jars.

585 rue St-Jean (at rue Ste-Marie). ℂ **418/524-7832.** www.lemoineechanson.com. Reservations recommended. Main courses C$16–C$24. AE, DC, V. Tues–Sun 5-11pm.

Inexpensive

For a quick snack, **Al Wadi,** 615 Grande-Allée est (ℂ **418/649-8345**), is in the heart of the Grande-Allée party district and open 24 hours a day, 7 days a week. Gyros, *shawarma,* falafel, and other veggie options are on tap.

Café Krieghoff ★ 🎁 LIGHT FARE   Walk down Grande-Allée about 10 minutes from the Parliament building and turn right on avenue Cartier. The 5-block street is the heart of the Montcalm residential neighborhood, with bakeries, boutiques, and a minimall of food shops. In the middle of the hubbub is the cheerful Krieghoff, which features an outdoor terrace a few steps up from the sidewalk. On weekend mornings, it's packed with artsy locals of all ages, whose tables get piled high with bowls of café au lait and huge plates of egg dishes, sweet pastries, or steak *frites.* Service is efficient and good natured.

1089 av. Cartier (north of Grande Allée). ☎ **418/522-3711.** www.cafekrieghoff.qc.ca. Most items less than C$14. MC, V. Daily 8am–10pm.

Le Commensal 🌱 VEGETARIAN   Like its sister outpost in Montréal (p. 88), Commensal is a vegetarian buffet, where you pay for your food by weight. Options include stir-fries, Chinese *seitan,* hazelnut cake, and sugar pie.

860 rue St-Jean (at av. Honoré-Mercier). ☎ **418/647-3733.** www.commensal.com. Pay by weight; most meals less than C$10. AE, MC, V. Sun–Wed 11am–9pm; Thurs–Sat 11am–10pm.

ST-ROCH
Expensive
Le Clocher Penché Bistrot ★★ BISTRO   Open since 2000, the development of this unpretentious neighborhood bistro parallels the polishing up of the overall neighborhood during the same period. With its caramel-toned woods, tall ceilings, and walls serving as gallery space for local artists, Clocher Penché has a laid-back European sophistication. There's a huge wine list, with the majority of the bottles organic or "biodynamic." The short menu changes regularly and can include duck confit or a terrific blood sausage *(boudin noir),* which we had with a delicate pastry, caramelized onions, and yellow beets. The menu touts that nearly everything is sourced locally. Service reflects the food—amiable and without flourishes.

203 rue St-Joseph est (at rue Caron). ☎ **418/640-0597.** www.clocherpenche.ca. Reservations recommended. Main courses C$19–C$26; table d'hôte lunch and weekend brunch C$16. MC, V. Tues–Fri 11:30am–2pm; Sat–Sun 9am–2pm; Tues–Sat 5–10pm.

Moderate
Bistro Les Bossus ★ BISTRO   Both menu and atmosphere are urban and simple at this newer addition to the St. Roch neighborhood. One tall booth lines an exposed brick wall opposite the long bar, and a center row of square tables completes the symmetry. Typical bistro options include *quiche du moment* with a flaky crust and creamy but firm filling. With fries and salad for C$11, it's a value. There's also French onion soup, mussels and fries, and salad with grilled vegetables and goat cheese, dressed with the lightest touch. Wear jeans or spruce yourself up; the vibe here will accommodate. The large windows open when the weather warms.

620 rue St-Joseph est (near rue de la Chappelle). ☎ **418/522-5501.** www.lesbossus.com. Main courses lunch C$10–C$23, dinner C$13–C$26. AE, MC, V. Mon–Fri 11am–10pm; Sat–Sun 9am–10pm.

L'Affaire est Ketchup 🍴 BISTRO   This is likely the closest you'll get to eating at a friend's house in Québec City—that is, if your friend is like Jamie Oliver. A short string of tables runs parallel to a wall of banquette seating, with an additional few tables to fill out the small shabby-hip space. If you're solo or with a single companion, sit at the bar at the back, which gives you front-row seating to the open kitchen, basically a happy mess of appliances, of the very young chef François Jobin. His menu is written on a chalkboard wall and changes weekly, or according to his whim. The *velouté de champignons* served in a jar normally used for conserves is delightfully tasty. Follow that with a savory rack of lamb served with star anise, orange *gastrique,* perfectly pan-seared asparagus, and heavenly potato mash. For dessert, the chocolate and pistachio brownie should put a smile on your face.

46 rue St-Joseph est (near boul. Langelier). ☎ **418/529-9020.** www.laffaireestketchup.net. Main courses C$14–C$20; table d'hôte lunch C$15 (plus dessert). MC, V. Tues–Sat 11am–9pm.

Le Cercle ★ FUSION   Le Cercle started as a modish tapas and wine bar with live music and art happenings, kid sister to an adjacent restaurant, the esteemed Utopie. When Utopie shut down in 2009, Le Cercle started edging into its space, and now it has performance on one side, and food and drink on the other. The fun chef's whim "tapas mania" can be ordered at whatever price you name. Wine pairing is a separate journey, best left in the capable hands of co-owner and sommelier Fréderic Gauthier. The spirit here is to bring great wine and food to anyone who wanders in. Food is served until midnight daily, with a weekend brunch.

226½ rue St-Joseph est (near rue Caron). ✆ **418/948-8648.** www.le-cercle.ca. Reservations recommended on weekends. Tapas C$3–C$9; main courses C$15–C$34; table d'hôte cost of main course plus C$7. AE, MC, V. Mon–Fri 11:30am–3am; Sat–Sun 10am–3am.

Inexpensive

Brûlerie St-Roch LIGHT FARE   Get your caffeine fix the way hipster locals do, at this coffee bar in the heart of the St-Roch neighborhood. A wall of coffee-bean bins lines one wall, a coffee roaster works its magic in a corner, and folks chat or work on glowing laptops at tables and tall chairs along a front window. There are two other locations around the city: Brûlerie Limoilou (in the up-and-coming Limoilou area) and Brûlerie St-Jean (a couple blocks outside of La porte St-Jean).

375 rue St-Joseph est (near rue Dorchester), St-Roch. ✆ **418/529-1559.** www.brulerie-st-roch. com. All pastry items less than $5. MC, V. Sun–Wed 6:30am–11pm; Thurs-Sat 6:30am–midnight.

RESTAURANTS BY CUISINE

BISTRO
Bistro Les Bossus ★ ($$, p. 273)
L'Affaire est Ketchup ($$, p. 273)
Le Clocher Penché Bistrot ★★ ($$$, p. 273)
L'Echaudé ★ ($$$, p. 269)
Mistral Gagnant ★ ($$, p. 271)

CONTEMPORARY QUÉBÉCOIS
Initiale ★★ ($$$$, p. 268)
Laurie Raphaël ★ ($$$$, p. 269)
Le Moine Échanson ★ ($$, p. 272)
Le Pain Béni ★ ($$, p. 265)
Le St-Amour ★★ ($$$$, p. 265)
Panache ★★★ ($$$$, p. 269)
Toast! ★ ($$, p. 270)

FUSION
Le Cercle ★ ($$, p. 274)

ITALIAN
Il Matto ($$$, p. 269)
Ristorante Il Teatro ★ ($$$, p. 265)

LIGHT FARE
Brûlerie St-Roch ($, p. 274)
Café Krieghoff ★ ($, p. 272)
Chez Temporel ($, p. 268)
Paillard ($, p. 268)

SEAFOOD
Le Marie-Clarisse ($$$, p. 270)

TRADITIONAL FRENCH
Le Café du Monde ★ ($$, p. 270)

TRADITIONAL QUÉBÉCOIS
Aux Anciens Canadiens ★ ($$$$, p. 264)
L'Astral ($$$, p. 272)

VEGETARIAN
Le Commensal ($, p. 273)

KEY TO ABBREVIATIONS:
$$$$ = Very Expensive $$$ = Expensive $$ = Moderate $ = Inexpensive

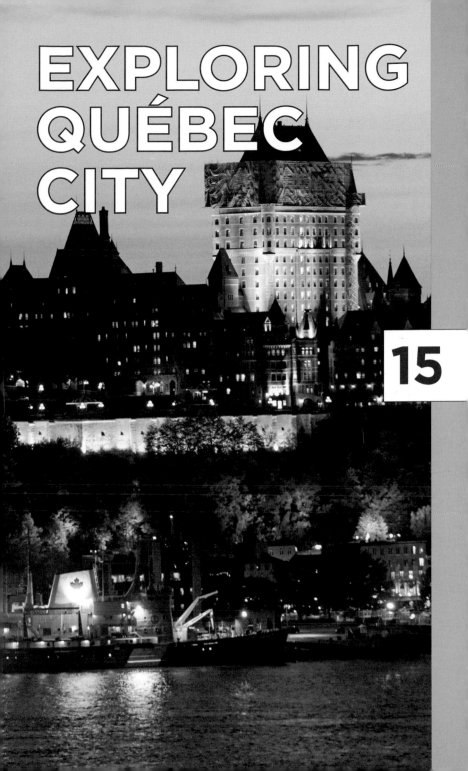

EXPLORING QUÉBEC CITY

15

Wandering the streets of Vieux-Québec is a singular pleasure, comparable to exploring a provincial capital in Europe. You might happen upon an ancient convent, gabled houses with steeply pitched roofs, a battery of 18th-century cannons in a leafy park, or a bistro with a blazing fireplace on a wintry day.

The Old City, Upper and Lower, is so compact that it's hardly necessary to plan precise sightseeing itineraries. Start at Terrasse Dufferin alongside the Château Frontenac and go off on a whim, down Breakneck Stairs (L'Escalier du Casse-Cou) to the Quartier du Petit-Champlain and Place-Royale, or out of the walls to the military fortress of the Citadelle that overlooks the mighty St. Lawrence River and onto the Plains of Abraham, where generals James Wolfe of Britain and Louis-Joseph, marquis de Montcalm of France, fought to their mutual deaths in a 20-minute battle that changed the continent's destiny.

Most of the historic sights are within the city walls of Vieux-Québec's Haute-Ville (Upper Town) and Basse-Ville (Lower Town). While Upper Town is hilly, with sloping streets, it's nothing like, say, San Francisco, and only people with physical limitations are likely to experience difficulty. Other sights are outside Upper Town's walls, along or just off the boulevard called Grande-Allée. If rain or ice discourages exploration on foot, tour buses and horse-drawn calashes are options.

THE TOP ATTRACTIONS
Vieux-Québec: Basse-Ville (Lower Town)

Musée de la Civilisation ★★★ ☺   Try to set aside at least 2 hours for a visit to this terrifically engrossing museum. Open since 1988, it's an innovative presence on the waterfront of historic Basse-Ville. Its precise mission has never been entirely clear: Recent temporary exhibits, for example, have focused on extraterrestrials (the 10-ft. Alien Queen from the movie *Aliens* greeted visitors) and the concept of free time. No matter. Through imaginative display techniques, hands-on devices, and holograms, curators ensure that visitors will be so enthralled by the experience that they won't pause to question its intent. A dramatic atrium-lobby sets the tone with a representation of the St. Lawrence River with an ancient ship beached on the shore. If nothing else, definitely take in *"People of Québec . . . Then and Now,"* a permanent exhibit that is a sprawling examination of Québec history, moving from the province's roots as a fur-trading colony to the turbulent movement for independence from the 1960s to the present, providing visitors with a rich sense of Québec's daily life over the generations. Another permanent exhibition, "Encounter with the First Nations," examines the culture of the aboriginal tribes that inhabited the region before the Europeans arrived and who still live in Québec today. Exhibit texts are in French and English. There's a

PREVIOUS PAGE: **A view of Vieux-Québec from across the St. Lawrence River.**

Displays at the innovative Musée de la Civilisation.

Place-Royale is considered by Québécois to be the birthplace of French America.

bright cafe and a small museum shop, the latter which is located in an attached house that dates from 1752.

85 rue Dalhousie (at rue St-Antoine). ℂ **866/710-8031** or 418/643-2158. www.mcq.org. Admission C$13 adults, C$12 seniors, C$9 students, C$4 children 12–16, free for children 11 and under; free to all Nov–May Tues and Jan–Feb Sat 10am–noon. Late June to mid-Oct daily 9:30am–6:30pm; mid-Oct to late June Tues–Sun 10am–5pm.

Place-Royale ★★★ This small but picturesque plaza is considered by Québécois to be the literal and spiritual heart of Basse-Ville—in grander terms, the birthplace of French America. There's a **bust of Louis XIV** in the center. In the 17th and 18th centuries, Place-Royal, or "Royal Square," was the town marketplace, and the center of business and industry. **Eglise Notre-Dame-des-Victoires** dominates the plaza. It's Québec's oldest stone church, built in 1688 after a massive fire in Lower Town destroyed 55 homes in 1682. The church was restored in 1763 and again in 1969. Its paintings, altar, and large model boat suspended from the ceiling were votive offerings brought by early settlers to ensure safe voyages. The church is open daily to visitors May through September, and admission is free. Sunday Masses are held at 10:30am and noon. During one visit there was a wedding that had just ended, and the whole square was there to greet the new couple as they exited their church.

Commercial activity here began to stagnate around 1860, and by 1950, this was a poor, rundown district. Rehabilitation began in 1960, and all the buildings on the square have now been restored, though only some of the walls are original.

For years, there was an empty lot behind the stone facade on the west side. Today, there is a whole building housing the **Centre d'Interprétation de Place-Royale** on the ground floor. A 20-minute multimedia show and other exhibitions detail the city's 400-year history. When you exit, turn left and, at the end of the block, turn around to view a *trompe l'oeil* mural depicting citizens of the early city.

Centre d'Interprétation de Place-Royale, 27 rue Notre-Dame. ℂ **866/710-8031** or 418/646-3167. www.mcq.org. Centre admission C$7 adults, C$6 seniors, C$5 students, C$2 children 12–16, free for children 11 and under; free to all Nov–May Tues. Free admission to the Place-Royale and Eglise Notre-Dame-des-Victoires. Late June to early Sept daily 9:30am–5pm; early Sept to late June Tues–Sun 10am–5pm.

15

EXPLORING QUÉBEC CITY

The Top Attractions

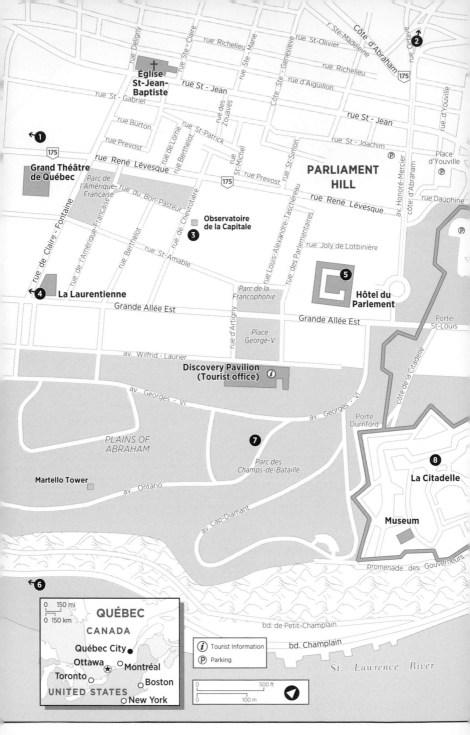

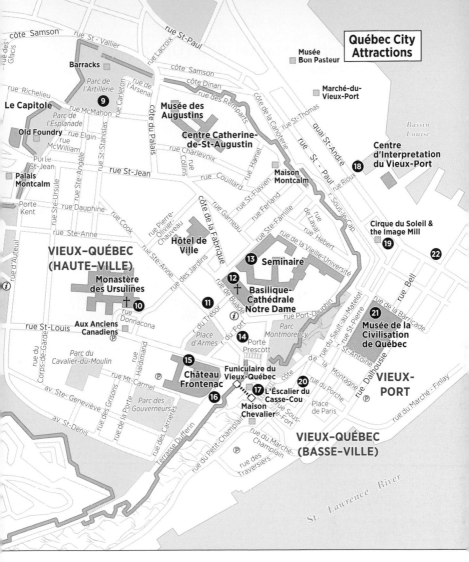

Vieux-Québec: Haute-Ville (Upper Town)

Basilique Cathédrale Notre-Dame de Québec ★ Notre-Dame Basilica, representing the oldest Christian parish north of Mexico, has weathered a tumultuous history of bombardment, reconstruction, and restoration. Parts of the existing basilica date from the original 1647 structure, including the bell tower and portions of the walls, but most of today's exterior is from the reconstruction completed in 1771. The interior, a re-creation undertaken after a fire in 1922, is flamboyantly neo-baroque, with glinting yellow gold leaf and shadows wavering by the fluttering light of votive candles. It's beautifully maintained, with pews buffed to a shine. Paintings and ecclesiastical treasures still remain from the time of the French regime, including a chancel lamp given by Louis XIV. More than 900 people are buried in the crypt, including four governors of New France.

Parts of Basilique Cathédrale Notre-Dame de Québec date from the original 1647 structure.

20 rue Buade (at Côte de la Fabrique). ✆ **418/694-0665.** www.patrimoine-religieux.com. Free admission for worshippers; donations encouraged. Crypt tour C$2 adults, C$1 children 16 and under. Cathedral Sept to April daily 8am–4pm; May to Labour Day daily 8am–9pm. Guided tours are available May–Oct daily; check website or ask in person for details.

Château Frontenac ★★ ☺ Visitors curious about the interior of Québec City's emblem, its Eiffel Tower, can take a 50-minute guided tour. Tours are led by 19th-century-costumed guides—maybe a "chambermaid," maybe a "wealthy guest." Designed as a version of a Loire Valley palace, the hotel opened in 1893 to house railroad passengers and encourage tourism. It's visible from almost every quarter of the city, commanding its majestic position atop Cap Diamant, the rock bluff that once provided military defense. Reservations required. See p. 248 for hotel information.

1 rue des Carrières, at Place d'Armes. ✆ **418/691-2166.** www.tourschateau.ca. Tours C$8.50 adults, C$8 seniors, C$6 children 6–16, free for children 5 and under. Tours start on the hour; reservations required. May to mid-Oct daily 10am–6pm; mid-Oct to Apr Sat–Sun noon–5pm.

La Citadelle ★★ The duke of Wellington had this partially star-shaped fortress built at the south end of the city walls in anticipation of renewed American attacks after the War of 1812. Some remnants of earlier French military structures were incorporated into the Citadelle, including a 1750 magazine. Dug into the Plains of Abraham high above Cap Diamant (Cape Diamond), the rock bluff adjacent to the St. Lawrence River, the fort has a low profile that keeps it all but invisible until walkers are actually upon it. The facility has never actually exchanged fire with an invader but still continues its vigil for the state. It's now a national historic site and, since 1950, has been home to Québec's **Royal 22e**

Régiment, the only fully Francophone unit in Canada's armed forces. That makes it North America's largest fortified group of buildings still occupied by troops. You can enter only by guided tour, which provides access to the Citadelle and its 25 buildings, including the small regimental museums in the former powder house and prison. The hour-long walk is likely to test the patience of younger visitors and the legs of many older people, though. For them, it might be better simply to attend the 45-minute choreographed ceremony of the **Changing of the Guard,** which runs from June 24 until the first Monday of September. It's an elaborate ritual inspired by the Changing of the Royal Guard in London and is included in the regular admission fee. Note that it can be cancelled if the weather's bad.

Guards from Québec's Royal 22e Régiment at La Citadelle.

1 Côte de la Citadelle (at rue St-Louis). ✆ **418/694-2815.** www.lacitadelle.qc.ca. Admission C$10 adults, C$9 seniors and students, C$5.50 children 8–17, free for children 7 and under; families C$22. Apr daily 10am–4pm; May–Sept daily 9am–5pm; Oct daily 10am–3pm; Nov–Mar 1 bilingual tour a day at 1:30pm.

Parliament Hill (near Grande-Allée)

Musée National des Beaux-Arts du Québec ★★★   Toward the southwestern end of Parc des Champs-de-Bataille (Battlefields Park) and a half-hour walk from Upper Town is the city's major art museum. Musée du Québec, as it's known, occupies a former prison and includes a soaring glass-roofed Grand Hall. A central reason to visit is to see the Inuit art assembled over the years by Québécois Raymond Brousseau and acquired by the museum in 2005. Much of the 2,635-piece collection was produced in the 1980s and 1990s, and some 285 works are on display. Look for the small, whimsical statue called *Woman Pulling out Grey Hairs.* The 1933 **Gérard-Morisset Pavilion** houses much of the rest of the museum's permanent collection, North America's largest aggregation of Québécois art. The museum tilts toward the modern, as well as the indigenous, with a permanent exhibition of works by famed Québec abstract expressionist and surrealist Jean-Paul Riopelle (1923–2002). Included is his *L'Hommage à Rosa Luxemburg,* a triptych made up of 30 individual paintings that is quite a vision.

The museum hosts some splashy temporary exhibitions, such as 2010's eye-popping show on haute couture of Paris and London from 1947 to 1957, and 2011's tribute to Marc-Aurèle Fortin. An 1867 section of the museum is a former prison (one cellblock has been left intact as an exhibit). The watchtower room at the top of the pavilion is worth making your way to: It's accessible only by spiral staircase, and the petite space holds a massive wooden sculpture of a body in motion by Irish artist David Moore. There are also expansive views of the city in every direction from here.

Parc des Champs-de-Bataille (near where av. Wolfe-Montcalm meets Grande Allée). ℭ **866/ 220-2150** or 418/643-2150. www.mnba.qc.ca. Free admission to permanent collection; admission for special exhibitions C$15 adults, C$12 seniors, C$7 students, C$4 children 12–17, free for children 11 and under. June to Labour Day Thurs-Tues 10am–6pm, Wed 10am–9pm; day after Labour Day to May Tues and Thurs–Sun 10am–5pm, Wed 10am–9pm. Bus: 11.

Parc des Champs-de-Bataille ★★ ☺ Covering 108 hectares (267 acres) of grassy hills, sunken gardens, monuments, fountains, and trees, Québec's Battlefields Park was Canada's first national urban park. A section called the **Plains of Abraham** is where Britain's General James Wolfe and France's Louis-Joseph, marquis de Montcalm, engaged in their short but crucial battle in 1759, which resulted in the British defeat of the French troops. It's also where the national anthem, "O Canada,"

The Musée Nationale des Beaux-Arts du Québec tilts toward the modern, as well as indigenous art.

was first performed. Today, the park is a favorite place for Québécois when they want sunshine or a bit of exercise. From spring through fall, visit the **Jardin Jeanne d'Arc (Joan of Arc Garden),** just off avenue Wilfrid-Laurier, near the Loews le Concorde Hotel. This spectacular garden combines French classical design with British-style flower beds. In the rest of the park, nearly 6,000 trees of more than 80 species blanket the fields and include the sugar maple, Norway maple, American elm, and American ash. Also in the park are two Martello towers, cylindrical stone defensive structures built between 1808 and 1812 when Québec feared an American invasion.

On the eastern end of the park, the **Discovery Pavilion of the Plains of Abraham,** at 835 av. Wilfrid-Laurier (ℭ **418/648-4071**), has a tourist office and a multimedia exhibit called "Odyssey: A Journey Through History on the Plains of Abraham." It's presented in English, French, Spanish, and Japanese.

Parc des Champs-de-Bataille. www.ccbn-nbc.gc.ca. Odyssey show C$10 adults, C$8 seniors and children 13–17, C$3 children 12 and under; discount prices mid-Sept to late Mar. Pavilion open late June to mid-Sept daily 8:30am–5:30pm; mid-Sept to late June Mon–Fri 8:30am–5pm, Sat 9am–5pm, Sun 10am–5pm.

MORE ATTRACTIONS

Vieux-Québec: Haute-Ville (Upper Town)

La Promenade Samuel-De Champlain ★★ ☺ 👪 When Québec celebrated its 300th anniversary, the government of Québec gave the people **Parc des Champs-de-Bataille** (see above). For the 400th anniversary (in 2008) they created La Promenade Samuel-De Champlain, a scenic path approximately 2.5 km long (1½ miles) along the St-Laurent river between Quai des Cageux and

Parc des Champs-de-Bataille was Canada's first national urban park.

Côte de Sillery. The space required shifted the road inland so that the public could bike, roller-blade, or walk along the water's edge all year long. With Pont de Québec and Pont Pierre Laporte framing the picturesque setting in the Ste-Foy-Sillery-Cap-Rouge *arrondissement,* Québec City has a beautiful new space, which involved planting 1,500 trees and outdoor contemporary art. There is a sports zone for activities such as soccer, quaint picnic nooks, lights at night for evening strolls, and at the Quai des Cageux there is modular 25m-high (82-ft.) observation tower next to a small cafe where you can enjoy over-the-counter foods like paninis, wraps, hot dogs, ice cream, and beverages.

2795 boul. Champlain. ℰ **877/783-1608.** www.quebecregion.com. Free admission and parking. Cafe daily 9am–8pm, depending on weather.

Musée de l'Amérique Française ★   Located on the site of the Québec Seminary, which dates from 1663, the Museum of French America highlights the evolution of French culture in Canada and the U.S. It reopened in October 2008 after a round of renovation, and exhibits are a touch more high-tech, accompanied by clever photo montages, atmospheric lighting, and a few interactive displays. The complex includes the chapel of the seminary, which has beautiful *trompe l'oeil* ornamentation, and an exhibition pavilion a short walk away. Shows there have focused on the Huguenots (French Protestants) of New France and the settling of French Americans in New England, and there's a permanent exhibit on the heritage of the seminary and its founding of Laval University in 1852. Even if you don't plan to visit the museum, walk down the driveway to the right of the entrance to see the inner courtyard of the complex. It's a wash of all-white walls, four stories high. It's a quiet, peaceful spot and one of the most photographed nooks in the city.

2 Côte de la Fabrique (next to Basilique Notre-Dame). ℰ **866/710-8031** or 418/692-2843. www. mcq.org. Admission C$8 adults, C$7 seniors, C$5.50 students, C$2 children 12–16, free for children 11 and under; free to all Nov–May Tues. Late June to early Sept daily 9:30am–5pm; early Sept to late June Tues–Sun 10am–5pm.

Musée des Ursulines/Chapelle Marie de l'Incarnation arrived in Québec City in 1639, and her Ursuline convent, originally built as a girls' school in 1642, is North America's oldest. The chapel is significant for the wooden sculptures in its pulpit and two richly decorated altarpieces, created by Pierre-Noël Levasseur between 1726 and 1736. Although the present building dates only from 1902, much of the interior decoration is nearly 200 years older. Marie de l'Incarnation's tomb is to the right of the entry. She was beatified by Pope John Paul II in 1980. The museum tells the story of the nuns, who were also pioneers and artists. The museum reopened in March 2011 after being closed much of the previous year with two new exhibits. The first one (a permanent exhibit) pertains to girls' education by the Ursulines, called "L'Académie des Demoiselles," and the second one pertains to the Ursulines' embroideries and will run for two years. They also added an elevator in the annex building that allows people with reduced mobility to have access to all three floors of the museum.

12 rue Donnacona (at rue des Jardins). ☎ **418/694-0694.** www.museedesursulines.com. Free admission to chapel. C$8 for adults, C$6 for seniors and students, C$4 for students 13–17, free for children 11 and under. Call or check the museum website for open hours.

Musée du Fort ☺ Built by a history teacher in the 1960s and updated some in the 1980s, this floor-sized diorama depicts the French, British, and U.S. battles for control of Québec. As a voice-over tells the tales, teeny boats rock, wee red lights blink to depict firefights, and wisps of smoke replicate burning buildings. In December 2010, they restored the whole kit and caboodle, and added cinema-style seats. The new and improved show and soundtrack is now approximately 30 minutes. It's charmingly old-fashioned and especially fun for history buffs, but the show is not likely to seem like a good value to most other visitors. The gift shop has a good selection of Québec maps from the 17th through 19th centuries.

10 rue Ste-Anne (at Place d'Armes). ☎ **418/692-2175.** www.museedufort.com. Admission C$8 adults, C$6 seniors, C$5 students. Apr–Oct daily 10am–5pm; Feb–Mar and Nov Thurs–Sun 11am–4pm.

The Musée de l'Amérique Française highlights the evolution of French culture in Canada and the U.S.

The Musée du Fort contains a diorama that depicts the French, British, and U.S. battles for control of Québec.

Observatoire de la Capitale ★ ☺

Take the elevator to the 31st floor and enjoy a spectacular view of the city from the highest point possible. A video hostess also takes you back in time to see how Québec City's skyline has evolved over the years with some accompanying visuals in 3-D. There are lots of interactive and educational exhibits for the kiddies—and their parents.

Edifice Marie-Guyart 1037, rue De La Chevrotière, Parliament Hill. ☎ 888/497-4322 or 418/644-9841. www.observatoire-capitale.com. Admission C$10 adults, C$8.65 students, C$8 seniors, free for children 11 and under. Mid-Oct to Jan Tues–Sun 10am–5pm; Feb to mid-Oct daily 10am–5pm.

Parc de l'Artillerie

A complex of defensive buildings erected by the French in the 17th and 18th centuries make up Artillery Park. They include an ammunition factory that was functional until 1964. An iron foundry, officers' mess and quarters, and a scale model of the city created in 1806 are on view. It may be a blow to romantics and history buffs to learn that the nearby St-Jean Gate in the city wall was built in 1940, the fourth in a series that began with the original 1693 entrance, which was replaced in 1747, and then replaced again in 1867.

2 rue d'Auteuil (near Porte St-Jean). ☎ 888/773-8888 or 418/648-7016. www.pc.gc.ca/artillerie. Admission C$3.90 adults, C$3.40 seniors, C$1.90 children 6–16, free for children 5 and under, C$9.80 for groups and families. Additional fees for audio guide, tea ceremony, and special activities. Early May to early Sept daily 10am–6pm; early Sept to early Oct daily 10am–5pm.

Québec Expérience ☺

A 3-D show that re-creates the grand, but more often grim, realities of the evolution of the city—the difficult weather conditions endured by the European explorers in the 17th century, the disease and fire that plagued immigrant workers in Old Port in the 18th century, the wars between French and British troops in the 19th century, and modern construction disasters in the 20th century. Guns and cannons point at audiences, a simulated bridge comes crashing down, and faux flames and screams fill the hall. All in all, it's quite vivid. Take a padded bench seat at least halfway back to get the full experience, and prepare to leave expecting an anvil or piano to land on your head. It lasts about 30 minutes.

8 rue du Trésor. ☎ 418/694-4000. www.quebecexperience.com. Admission C$9.50 adults, C$7 seniors and students, free for children 5 and under, C$26 family. Mid-May to Sept daily 10am–10pm; Oct to mid-May daily 10am–5pm. English- and French-language shows alternate throughout the day.

(Excavation under) Terrasse Dufferin

Excavation alongside the Château Frontenac took place from 2005 to 2009 as part of a project to perform maintenance work on the promenade and the fortification wall beneath it. Remnants of forts and other buildings dating back to 1620 were unearthed, and visitors can now stroll through the site in warm weather on self-directed walks, with signs explaining the significance of each item. Parks Canada staff is on-site to answer questions.

Cirque du Soleil puts on free performances every Tuesday through Saturday evening from June 24 to Labour Day.

Terrasse Dufferin. www.pc.gc.ca/lhn-nhs/qc/fortifications/ne/index_E.asp. Free admission. May to mid-Oct daily 11am–6pm.

Vieux-Québec: Basse-Ville (Lower Town)

Cirque du Soleil ★★★ ☺ The ever-innovative Cirque du Soleil, which got its start just north of Québec City and now is an internationally known circus company, puts on free—yes, free—performances every Tuesday through Saturday evening from June 24 to Labour Day. The show takes place in a no-mans-land-turned-theater under a highway where Vieux-Québec meets St-Roch. It's all very cool and an extraordinary coup for the city. The program got started in 2008 as part of Québec City's 400th anniversary celebrations and will be continuing each summer through at least 2013. Check the city tourist office for details about start times for the 1-hour event. Be prepared to be standing throughout. C$15 gives you access to a small set of bleachers—still standing room but with better views; advance tickets are available at www.billetech.com.

Espace 400e At the site of what used to be an old-fashioned interpretation center, this all-new waterfront pavilion opened in the summer of 2008 as the central location for Québec's 400th-anniversary celebrations. Purposely raw-looking, it's a vast glass, metal, and concrete space. It's now being used for temporary exhibitions by Festival d'été international de Québec. In 2010, there was a show about the Titanic, followed by *Hockey dans la peau* ("Hockey, it's in our DNA") in 2011. Check the provincial tourist office (© **877/BONJOUR** or 514/873-2015; www.bonjourquebec.com) for current information.

100 quai St-André (at rue Rioux).

"Image Mill" and "Aurora Borealis" Light Installation ★★★ This is something entirely unique to Québec City. In 2008, as part of the city's 400th anniversary celebrations, installation artist Robert LePage created a massive outdoor multimedia show of photos of city history called "Image Mill." It was projected in Vieux-Port along 600m (over a third of a mile) of industrial grain silos and produced an outdoor community event, akin to nightly fireworks displays. Like the free Cirque du Soleil show (above), the project was a highlight of the 2008 festivities and is being extended through 2013. The content for 2012 has been almost completely updated and will also be available in 3-D. The 50-minute show takes place

Tuesday through Saturday evenings from June 24 to Labour Day, with music broadcast from speakers by the water. During the other evening hours from dusk to 11:30pm, the silos are bathed in a light show called "Aurora Borealis," inspired by the Technicolor of the Northern Lights. For a taste of the whole thing, check out photos at LePage's website, www.lacaserne.net/index2.php/other_projects.

L'Escalier du Casse-Cou ★   These stairs connect Terrasse Dufferin at the top of the cliff with rue Sous-le-Fort at the base. The name translates to "Breakneck Stairs," and they lead—very steeply, although hardly neck-break-inducing anymore—from Haute-Ville to the Quartier du Petit-Champlain in Basse-Ville. A stairway has existed here since the settlement began. Nestled along the northern side of the steps (right side if going downward) are quaint bistros and even a chocolate shop. In 1698, the town council had to explicitly forbid citizens from taking their animals up or down the stairway, and those who didn't comply were punished with a fine.

Musée Naval de Québec   After being closed for years for renovation, this museum of naval history reopened in the summer of 2010 in time to celebrate the Canadian Navy's centennial birthday. A permanent exhibition called "Meanders" looks at the history of the St. Lawrence River as a battlefield. A virtual exhibition online (www.privateers.ca) uses an interactive comic book to explore the difference between pirates and "privateers." In the warm months, you can board a scenic river cruise here.

170 rue Dalhousie (near boul. Champlain). ℭ **418/694-5387.** www.navalmuseumofquebec. com. Free admission. June–Sept daily 10am–6pm; call for hours Oct–May.

Parliament Hill (near Grande-Allée)

Hôtel du Parlement   Since 1968, what the Québécois call their "National Assembly" has occupied this imposing Second Empire château constructed in 1886. Twenty-two bronze statues of some of the most prominent figures in the province's tumultuous history grace the facade. Inside, highlights include the

L'Escalier du Casse-Cou lead from Haute-Ville to the Quartier du Petit-Champlain in Basse-Ville.

The chateau-style Hôtel du Parlement is the home of the provincial parliament.

Assembly Chamber and the Legislative Council Chamber, where parliamentary committees meet. Throughout the building, representations of the fleur-de-lis and the initials VR (for Victoria Regina) remind visitors of Québec's dual heritage. Thirty-minute guided tours are available weekdays year-round, and weekends in summer. Tours start at the Parliament building visitor center; enter at door no. 3. Note that during summer hours, tours of the gardens are also available.

The grand Beaux Arts–style restaurant **Le Parlementaire** (© **418/643-6640**) is open to the public, as well as parliamentarians and visiting dignitaries. Featuring Québec products and cuisine, it serves breakfast and lunch (C$14–C$26) from 8am to 2:30pm Monday through Friday most of the year (it is closed starting the second week of Dec until the second week of Jan). The massive fountain in front of the building, **La Fontaine de Tourny,** was commissioned by the mayor of Bordeaux, France, in 1857. It was installed in 2007 as a gift from the Simons department store to the city for its 400th anniversary. Also outdoors, to the right of the main entrance as you're facing it, is a large **Inukshuk** statue.

Entrance at corner of Grande-Allée est and av. Honoré-Mercier. © **866/337-8837** or 418/643-7239. www.assnat.qc.ca. Free admission. Guided tours late June to Labour Day Mon–Fri 9am–4:30pm, Sat–Sun and holidays 10am–4:30pm; rest of the year Mon–Fri 9am–4:30pm. Reservations recommended.

Izba ★ 🍃   With its sister location in Montréal, this is the original Izba spa. The signature Izba body treatment incorporates a traditional Russian banya (steam bath) where branches of oak leaves are brushed over the skin, after which a honey rub draws out toxins and softens the skin. Choose from a menu of soothing massages, all performed by experienced masseuses. You can then relax in the Jacuzzi, chill in your white fluffy robe in the Romanesque lounge, or get a mani-pedi in the sunny atrium in the back.

36 boul. René-Lévesque est (near av. de Salaberry). © **418/522-4922.** www.izbaspa.qc.ca. Tues and Fri–Sat 10am–5pm; Wed–Thurs 9am–9:30pm.

ESPECIALLY FOR KIDS

Children who have responded to Arthurian tales of fortresses and castles or to Harry Potter's adventures will delight in walking around this storybook city and the **Château Frontenac,** which offers tours (p. 280). Start at **Terrasse Dufferin** in Upper Town, where there are coin-operated telescopes, street entertainers, and ice-cream stands. Halfway down **Breakneck Stairs (L'Escalier du Casse-Cou;** see above) are giant **cannons** ranged along the battlements. The gun carriages are impervious to the assaults of small humans, so kids can scramble all over them at will.

If military sites might be appealing, take them to see the colorful Changing of the Guard ceremony at **La Citadelle** (p. 280). Or just head for the **Parc des Champs-de-Bataille (Battlefields Park,** also called the **Plains of Abraham;** p. 282) adjacent to the La Citadelle if young ones need to run off excess energy. Acres of grassy lawn provide room to roam and are perfect for a family picnic. **Québec Expérience** (p. 285) is a flashy way to introduce some history of the region to kids, although it might be too vivid for younger children. In Lower Town, the **Musée de la Civilisation** (p. 276) presents exhibits for families and, given that it's free for children 11 and younger, it's great value.

When in doubt, head to the water. **Montmorency Falls** (p. 333) makes a terrific day trip for children of all ages during any season (in winter it's an icy

Kids will enjoy the street entertainers at Terrasse Dufferin.

wonderland). It's just 10 minutes north of the city by car, and there are bus tours to the site, as well. It costs to park, but walking around near the water is free. On Wednesdays and Saturdays from late July to mid-August, the falls are host to a grand fireworks competition, **Les Grands Feux Loto-Québec** (p. 31). It pits international pyrotechnical teams against each other in a contest for who can make the biggest and brightest presentation.

Canyon Ste-Anne (p. 336) is a 45-minute drive northeast and offers thrilling bridge walks over a rushing waterfall. It's particularly spectacular in spring when the snow begins to melt. **Village Vacances Valcartier** (© **888/384-5524;** www.valcartier.com) in St-Gabriel-de-Valcartier, about a half-hour northwest of the city, is a major man-made water park. In summer, it boasts 35 slides, a gigantic wave pool, a huge pirate ship, and a faux Amazon River to go tubing down. In winter, the same facilities are put to use for "snow rafting" on inner tubes and skating. In the summer of 2010, it introduced a fingerprint-reading technology called Money at My Fingertip. Instead of carrying cash or credit cards in their bathing suits, visitors can register their credit cards and then pay for food and other services simply by pressing a finger to a screen.

Québec City is close to where whales come out to play each summer. For a **whale-watching cruise,** travel northeast about 200km (125 miles) along the St. Lawrence River into the Charlevoix region. Boats leave from the towns of Baie Ste-Catherine and Tadoussac, and typically spend 2½ hours out with the giants. Buses from the city can take you up and back in a (long) day (see below). Or, if you have a car, consider booking an overnight stay at Hôtel Tadoussac (p. 347) and get a package that includes a cruise. See p. 346 for more information.

ORGANIZED TOURS

Québec City is small enough that you can get around with a good map and a guidebook, but a tour is tremendously helpful for getting background information about the city's history and culture, for grasping the lay of the land, and in the

Horse-drawn carriage tours are a romantic way to see the city.

case of bus tours, for seeing those attractions that are a bit of a hike or require wheels to reach.

Below are some agencies and organizations that have proved to be reliable. Arrange tours by calling the companies directly or by stopping by the large tourist center at the Place d'Armes in Upper Town.

Bus Tours

Buses are convenient if extensive walking is difficult, especially in hilly Upper Town. Among the established tour operators, **Dupont,** which also goes by the name **Old Québec Tours** (© 800/267-8687 or 418/664-0460; www.tour dupont.com), offers English-only tours (preferable to bilingual tours since you get twice as much information in the same amount of time). The company's city tours are in small coaches, while day trips out of the city are in full-size buses. They also offer a **whale-watching excursion** hours north into the Charlevoix region. The 10-hour day includes a 3-hour cruise among the belugas.

Horse-Drawn Carriage Tours

A romantic, if somewhat expensive, way to see the city at a genial pace is in a horse-drawn carriage, called a calash. Carriages will pick you up or can be hired from locations throughout the city, including at Place d'Armes. A 40- to 45-minute ride costs C$80, plus tip, for four people maximum. Carriages operate year-round, rain or shine. Companies include **Calèches du Vieux-Québec** (© **418/683-9222;** www.calecheduvieuxquebec.com) and **Calèches de la Nouvelle-France** (© **418/692-0068;** www.calechesquebec.com).

River Cruises

Croisières AML (© **800/563-4643** or 418/692-1159 in late-spring to mid-fall season; www.croisieresaml.com) offers a variety of cruises. Its *Louis Jolliet* is a three-decked, 1930s ferry boat–turned–excursion vessel, which carries 1,000 passengers and is stocked with bilingual guides, full dining facilities, and a bar. The company offers brunch and dinner cruises, as well as jaunts that take in the fireworks or the "Image Mill" presentation. The boats dock at quai Chouinard, at 10 rue Dalhousie, in Vieux-Port.

Similar cruises are offered by **Groupe Dufour** (© **800/463-5250** or 418/692-0222; www.dufour.ca), which also runs the Hôtel Le Clarendon. They are well known for their whale-watching tours.

Walking Tours

Times and points of departure for walking tours change, so get up-to-date information at any tourist office (addresses are listed on p. 239). Many tours leave from the Place d'Armes in Upper Town, just in front of the **Château Frontenac.**

Tours Voir Québec (© **866/694-2001** or 418/694-2001; www.toursvoir quebec.com) specializes in English-only guided tours of the Old City. "The Grand Tour," which is available year-round, is a 2-hour stroll that covers the architecture, events, and cultural history of the city. Tours are limited to 15 people. Cost is C$23 adults, C$20 students (ISIC card required), C$11 children 6 to 12, and free for children 5 and under. The company also offers private tours. Foodies will want to note "the Food Tour," which stops at about seven different places, sampling local goodies such as cheese, ice cider, pâté, and chocolate. Cost is C$38 per adult.

One way to split the difference between being out on your own and being on a guided tour is to use **Map Old Québec** (www.oldquebecmap.com), a website that offers a beautifully designed map and MP3 files. After you purchase the map and audio files, you can download a tour onto your MP3 player and go at your own pace.

SPECTATOR SPORTS

In March the **Red Bull Crashed Ice World Championship** event takes over Vieux-Québec. The newly invented sport brings athletes from all over the world. Dressed in hockey gear, four brave souls skate downhill in a rough and tumble roller derby–esque race with lots of leaps, drops, and sharp turns. The starting line is drawn in Upper Town and the finish line in Lower Town's Place Royale. It is immensely exhilarating to watch—and free. See www.redbull.ca for details.

Québec has not had a team in any of the major professional leagues since the NHL Nordiques left in 1995. (The city, however, is currently abuzz over a possible Nordiques revival, which looks promising with the highly anticipated opening of a new arena in fall 2015.) Since 1999, though, it has been represented by **Les Capitales de Québec** (www.capitalesdequebec.com), a baseball club in the Can-Am League. Home games take place at Stade Municipal (Municipal Stadium), 100 rue du Cardinal Maurice-Roy (© **877/521-2244** or 418/521-2255), not far beyond the St-Roch neighborhood. Tickets cost C$8 to C$16.

There's also a local fan base for Québec City's junior hockey team (with players 16 to 20 years old), **Les Remparts de Québec** (www.remparts.ca). They play at the Colisée Pepsi from September to March. Tickets are C$6 to C$13.

If you're going to **Carnaval** (p. 29; www.carnaval.qc.ca), you shouldn't miss the canoe races, where teams push, pull, or paddle (depending on the state of the river) from one end to another. The best place to view the competition is from the Terrasse Dufferin or from the lookout on the opposite bank in Lévis. Following that, hockey enthusiasts will enjoy the **Tournoi International de Hockey Pee-Wee de Québec** (www.tournoipee-wee.qc.ca) held in February, where many hockey greats have been known to start their careers. Around the same time is the **Snowboard Jamboree** (www.snowjamboree.com), a trendy festival that even includes a fashion show.

OUTDOOR ACTIVITIES

Inside the city, **Parc des Champs-de-Bataille** (**Battlefields Park;** p. 282) is the most popular park for bicycling and strolling.

Parc de la Jacques-Cartier is less than an hour from the city.

Outside the city, lakes and hills provide countless opportunities for outdoor recreation, including swimming, rafting, fishing, skiing, snowmobiling, and sleigh riding. There are three centers in particular to keep in mind, all within a 45-minute drive from the capital. The provincial **Parc de la Jacques-Cartier** (© 800/665-6527; www.sepaq.com/pq/jac/en) is off Route 175 north; **Station touristique Duchesnay** (© 877/511-5885; www.sepaq.com/duchesnay) is a resort in the town of Ste-Catherine-de-la-Jacques-Cartier; and **Parc du Mont Ste-Anne** is northeast of the city toward the Charlevoix region (p. 337). All three centers are mentioned in the listings below.

From mid-November through March, the **Taxi Coop Québec** shuttle service (© **418/525-5191;** www.taxicoop-quebec.com) picks up passengers at Québec City hotels in the morning to take them to alpine and cross-country ski runs, and to snowmobile trails, with return trips in the late afternoon.

Warm-Weather Activities

BIKING

There's lots of good biking in the city, either along the river or up in Parliament Hill in Parc des Champs-de-Bataille. A marked path for cyclists (and in-line skaters) along the waterfront follows the second half of the route described in "Walking Tour 2: Lower Town (Vieux-Québec: Basse-Ville & Vieux-Port)" on p. 304. The path was new in 2008 and is well maintained. It extends both directions alongside the river and heading out of the city. Tourist information centers provide bicycle-trail maps and can point out a variety of routes.

Mountain bikers head to **Mont Ste-Anne** (www.mont-sainte-anne.com), which has the most well-known mountain bike network in eastern Canada. It was host to the 2010 Mountain Bike and Trial World Championships, and every year to **Vélirium** (www.velirium.com), the International Mountain Bike Festival and World Cup. It's 42km (26 miles) northeast of Québec City. See p. 338 for more information.

CAMPING

The greater Québec City area has 23 campgrounds. Most have toilets and showers. For a list of sites and their specs, go to **www.quebecregion.com** and search for "camping."

CANOEING

The lakes and rivers of **Parc de la Jacques-Cartier** are easy to reach, yet still seem to be in the midst of wilderness. You can rent canoes in the park. The **Station touristique Duchesnay** resort is on the shores of Lac Saint-Joseph and rents out canoes, kayaks, and pedal boats. See the intro above for contact information.

FISHING

The river that flows through **Parc de la Jacques-Cartier** is home to trout and salmon, and fishing of the former is allowed. Permits are required and can be purchased at many sporting-goods stores. Check with the park for details; see the intro above for contact information.

GOLF

An 18-hole course, **Golf de la Faune** (© 866/627-8008 or 418/627-1576; www.golfdelafaune.com), opened in June 2008, 10 minutes from downtown, at the **Four Points by Sheraton Québec** (© 418/627-8008; www.fourpoints. com/quebec). The course has eight water hazards and 45 sand traps. Green fees start at C$40.

Golf de la Faune is an 18-hole course a short distance from downtown.

About 40 minutes north of the city at Parc Mont Ste-Anne, **Le Grand Vallon** (© 888/827-4579 or 418/827-4653; www. legrandvallon.com) is an 18-hole, par-72 course with tree-lined stretches, 4 lakes, and 40 sand traps. Rates start at C$42 and include a golf cart, access to the driving range, and practice balls. Also a short drive west of Québec City, **Golf Le Grand Portneuf** (www.le grandportneuf.com) offers 36 challenging holes in a peaceful, scenic environment.

SWIMMING

Those who want to splash around during their visit should plan to stay at one of the hotels with pools. Fairmont Le Château Frontenac has one, as do Hôtel Manoir Victoria, Hilton Québec, Loews Le Concorde, Hôtel Château Laurier, Hôtel PUR, and Château Bonne Entente. They're all listed in chapter 13.

Cold-Weather Activities

CROSS-COUNTRY SKIING

Parc des Champs-de-Bataille, where Carnaval de Québec establishes its winter playground during February, has a network of groomed cross-country trails in winter. Equipment can be rented at the **Discovery Pavilion** (p. 282), near the Citadelle. Thirty minutes outside the city, **Station touristique Duchesnay** (p. 292) offers extensive trails and ski rentals. This is where the **Ice Hotel** (p. 257) is built each winter. The resort also has a spa, other hotel accommodations, and a bistro. The **Association of Cross-Country Ski Centers of Québec Area** (www.skidefondraquette.com) maintains a website with venue listings and maps.

DOG SLEDDING

Aventure Inukshuk (© 418/875-0770; www.aventureinukshuk.qc.ca) is located in Station touristique Duchesnay, in the town of Ste-Catherine-de-la-Jacques-Cartier. Guides show you how to lead a sled pulled by six dogs. A 1-hour trip takes you deep into a hushed world of snow and thick woods, past rows of Christmas trees, and over a beaver pond. The dogs live in a field of individual pens and houses under evergreen trees. Guides train and care for their teams themselves. Overnight camping trips are available. The 1-hour trip, which includes an additional half-hour of training, costs C$95 in December, January, and March, and C$104 in February. Children 6 to 12 are half price, and children 2 to 5 go free (children 1 and younger aren't allowed). It's expensive, especially for families, but the memory stays with you.

ICE SKATING

From the end of October to mid-March, a mini outdoor rink is set up in Place d'Youville just outside the Upper Town walls. Admission is free, and skates can be rented.

SKIING

Foremost among the nearby downhill centers is **Mont Ste-Anne,** which offers eastern Canada's largest total skiing surface, with 66 trails (17 are lit for night skiing). See p. 337 for more information.

SNOWMOBILING

Snowmobiles, known here as "ski-doos," are hugely popular. It's said, in fact, that there are more trails for snowmobiling than there is asphalt in Québec City. In addition to options for day trips, many restaurants and hotels outside the city accommodate snowmobile touring, making it possible to travel from locale to locale. Check the tourist office for current options.

TOBOGGANING

An old-fashioned toboggan run called **Les Glissades de la Terrasse** (© 418/829-9898) is set up on the steep wooden staircase at Terrasse Dufferin's south end in winter. The slide extends almost to the Château Frontenac. Next to the ticket booth, a little sugar shack sells sweet treats. Cost is C$2.50 per person.

Kids enjoy Les Glissades de la Terrasse toboggan run.

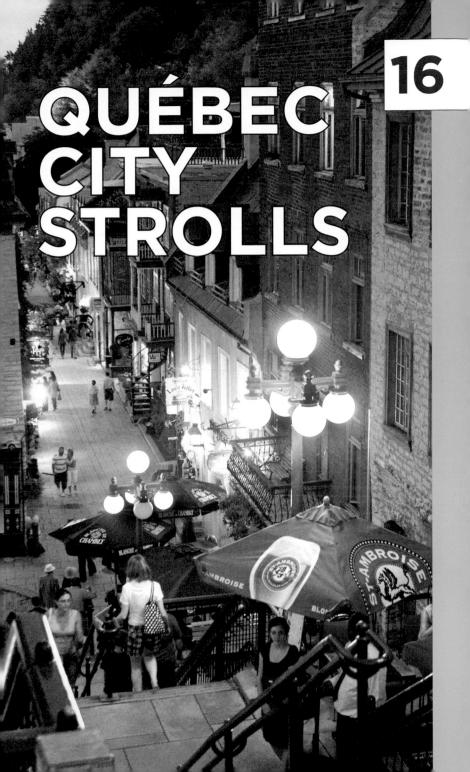

QUÉBEC CITY STROLLS

The many pleasures of walking in picturesque French Québec are easily comparable to walking in similar *quartiers* in northern European cities. Stone houses rub shoulders with each other, carriage wheels creak behind muscular horses, sunlight filters through leafy canopies, drinkers and diners lounge in sidewalk cafes, childish shrieks of laughter echo down cobblestone streets. Not common to other cities, however, is the bewitching vista of river and mountains that the higher elevations bestow.

In winter especially, Vieux-Québec takes on a Dickensian quality, with a lamp glow flickering behind curtains of falling snow. The man who should know—Charles Dickens himself—described the city as having "splendid views which burst upon the eye at every turn."

WALKING TOUR 1: UPPER TOWN (VIEUX-QUÉBEC: HAUTE-VILLE)

START:	**Château Frontenac, the castlelike hotel that dominates the city.**
FINISH:	**Hôtel du Parlement, on Grande-Allée, just outside the walls.**
TIME:	**2 to 3 hours, depending on whether you take all the optional diversions.**
BEST TIMES:	**Anytime, although early morning when the streets are emptier is most atmospheric, and the best time to take unobstructed photographs.**
WORST TIMES:	**None.**

The Upper Town (Haute-Ville) of Old Québec (Vieux-Québec) is surrounded by fortress walls. This section of the city overlooks the St. Lawrence River and includes much of what makes Québec so beloved. Buildings and compounds along this tour have been carefully preserved, and most are at least a century old. We start at the grand Château Frontenac, the visual heart of the city.

1 Château Frontenac

Reportedly the most photographed hotel in the world, and it's not hard to see why. A copper roof only needs replacing every 100 years, and, it seems, the time is now for Québec City's "castle." A major, multimillion-dollar renovation project presently underway is projected to be completed by the end of 2012. This means that between now and then, over 36 tonnes (about 80,000 lbs.) of new chocolate-brown metal will begin to dominate the skyline—that is, until it oxidizes into its eventual green patina. The original

PREVIOUS PAGE: **L'Escalier du Casse-Cou takes you between Upper and Lower Town.**

section of the famous edifice that defines the Québec City skyline was built as a hotel from 1892 to 1893 by the Canadian Pacific Railway Company. Known locally as "the Château," the hotel today has 618 rooms (p. 248). Guided tours are available (p. 280).

Walk around to the river side of the Château, where there is a grand boardwalk called:

2 Terrasse Dufferin

With its green-and-white-topped gazebos in warm months, this boardwalk promenade looks much as it did 100 years ago, when ladies with parasols and gentlemen with top hats strolled along it on sunny afternoons. It offers vistas of river, watercraft, and distant mountains, and is particularly romantic at sunset.

Walk south on Terrasse Dufferin, past the Château. If you're in the mood for some exercise, go to the end of the boardwalk and continue up the stairs—there are 310 of them—walking south along the:

3 Promenade des Gouverneurs

This path was renovated in 2007 and skirts the sheer cliff wall, climbing up and up past Québec's military Citadelle, a fort built by the British army between 1820 and 1850 that remains an active military garrison. The promenade/staircase ends at the grassy **Parc des Champs-de-Bataille,** about 15 minutes away. If you go to the end, return back to Terrasse Dufferin to continue the stroll.

Walk back on the terrace as far as the battery of old (but not original) cannons on the left, which are set up as they were in the old days. Climb the stairs toward the obelisk into the:

4 Parc des Gouverneurs

Just southwest of the Château Frontenac, this park stands on the site of the mansion built to house the French governors of Québec. The mansion burned in 1834, and the ruins lie buried under the great bulk of the Château. B&Bs and small hotels now border the park on two sides.

The **obelisk monument** is dedicated to both generals in the momentous battle of September 13, 1759, when Britain's General James Wolfe and France's Louis-Joseph, marquis de Montcalm, fought for what would be the ultimate destiny of Québec (and, quite possibly, all of North America). The French were defeated, and both generals died. Wolfe, wounded in the fighting, lived only long enough to hear of England's victory. Montcalm died a few hours after Wolfe. Told that he was mortally wounded, Montcalm replied, "All the better. I will not see the English in Québec."

Walk up rue Mont-Carmel, which runs between the park and Château Frontenac. Turn right onto rue Haldimand. At the next corner, rue St-Louis, stands a white house with blue trim. This is:

5 Maison Kent

Built in 1648, this might be Québec's oldest building. It's most famous for being the building in which France signed the capitulation to the British forces. Its name comes from the duke of Kent, Queen Victoria's father. He lived here for a few years at the end of the 18th century, just before he married Victoria's mother in an arranged liaison. His true love, it is said, was with him in Maison Kent. Today, the building houses France's consulate general.

To the left and diagonally across from Maison Kent, at rue St-Louis and rue des Jardins, is:

6 Maison Jacquet

This small, white dwelling with crimson roof and trim dates from 1677 and now houses a popular restaurant called **Aux Anciens Canadiens** (p. 264). Among the oldest houses in the province, it has sheltered some prominent Québécois, including Philippe Aubert de Gaspé, the author of *Aux Anciens Canadiens,* which recounts Québec's history and folklore. He lived here from 1815 to 1824.

7 Aux Anciens Canadiens ☕

Try Québécois home cooking right here at the restaurant named for de Gaspé's book, *Aux Anciens Canadiens,* 34 rue St-Louis. Consider caribou in blueberry-wine sauce or Québec meat pie, and don't pass up the maple sugar pie with cream. See p. 264.

Leaving the restaurant, turn back toward Maison Kent (toward the river) and walk along rue St-Louis to no. 17:

8 Maison Maillou

This house's foundations date from 1736, though the house was enlarged in 1799 and restored in 1959. It's best seen from the opposite side of the street. Maison Maillou was built as an elegant luxury home and later served as headquarters of militias and armies. Note the metal shutters used to thwart weather and unfriendly fire.

Continue on rue St-Louis to arrive at the central plaza called:

Aux Anciens Canadiens is a good place to try traditional Québécois cuisine.

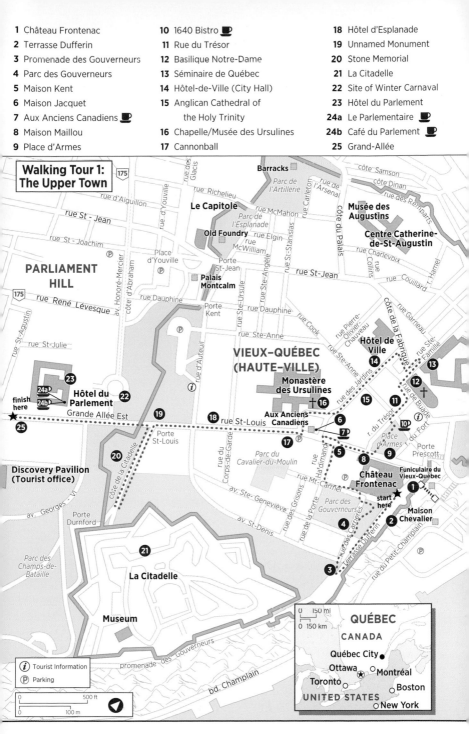

1 Château Frontenac
2 Terrasse Dufferin
3 Promenade des Gouverneurs
4 Parc des Gouverneurs
5 Maison Kent
6 Maison Jacquet
7 Aux Anciens Canadiens ☕
8 Maison Maillou
9 Place d'Armes
10 1640 Bistro ☕
11 Rue du Trésor
12 Basilique Notre-Dame
13 Séminaire de Québec
14 Hôtel-de-Ville (City Hall)
15 Anglican Cathedral of
   the Holy Trinity
16 Chapelle/Musée des Ursulines
17 Cannonball
18 Hôtel d'Esplanade
19 Unnamed Monument
20 Stone Memorial
21 La Citadelle
22 Site of Winter Carnaval
23 Hôtel du Parlement
24a Le Parlementaire ☕
24b Café du Parlement ☕
25 Grand-Allée

9 ## Place d'Armes

This plaza was once the military parade ground outside the governors' mansion (which no longer exists). In the small park at the center is the fountain **Monument to the Faith,** which recalls the arrival of the Recollet monks from France in 1615. France's king granted them a large plot of land in 1681 on which to build their church and monastery.

Place d'Armes contains several monuments to Québec history.

Facing the square is the **monument to Samuel de Champlain**, who founded Québec in 1608. Created by French artist Paul Chevré and architect Paul Le Cardonnel, the statue has stood here since 1898. Its pedestal is made from stone that was also used in the Arc de Triomphe and Sacré-Coeur Basilica in Paris.

Near the Champlain statue is the diamond-shaped **UNESCO monument** designating Québec City as a World Heritage Site, a rare distinction. Installed in 1986, the monument is made of bronze, granite, and glass.

The city's major **tourist information center** faces the plaza, at 12 rue Ste-Anne.

10 ## 1640 Bistro 🍴

This part of town is a great place to sit and watch the world go by. Grab a sidewalk table and enjoy something to drink or eat. One option is 1640 Bistro, in the red-roofed Auberge du Trésor with a mock-Tudor facade at 16 rue Ste-Anne.

Just adjacent to 1640 Bistro is the narrow pedestrian lane called:

11 ## Rue du Trésor

Artists (or their representatives) hang their prints and paintings of Québec scenes on both sides of the walkway. In decent weather, it's busy with browsers and sellers. Most prices are within the means of the average visitor, but don't be shy to bargain for a better deal.

Follow rue du Trésor down to rue Buade and turn left. On the right, at the corner of rue Ste-Famille is the:

12 ## Basilique Notre-Dame

The basilica's golden interior is ornate and its air rich with the scent of burning candles. Many artworks remain from the time of the French regime. The chancel lamp was a gift from Louis XIV, and the crypt is the final resting place for most of Québec's bishops. The basilica dates back to 1647 and has suffered a tumultuous history of bombardment and reconstruction; see p. 280 for more information.

As you exit the basilica, turn a sharp right to enter the grounds and, a few steps in, the all-white inner courtyard of the historic:

13 Séminaire de Québec

Founded in 1663 by North America's first bishop, Bishop Laval, this seminary had grown into Laval University by 1852. During summer, visitors can take a 1-hour tour of the old seminary's grounds and some of its buildings, which reveal lavish decorations of stone, tile, brass, and gilt-framed oil paintings. The tours are conducted by the **Musée de l'Amérique Française** (© **418/692-2843;** www.mcq.org), based inside the seminary grounds. In the summer, there are five tours a day with the language of the tour (French or English) determined by the first registered visitor. Off-season, tours are available on the weekends.

Head back to the basilica. Directly across the small park from the church is:

14 Hôtel-de-Ville (City Hall)

The park next to City Hall is often converted into an outdoor show area in summer, especially during the **Festival d'Eté (Summer Festival),** with concerts and other staged programs.

As you face City Hall, the tall building to the left is **Edifice Price,** Old City's tallest building at 18 stories. It was built in 1929 in Art Deco style with geometric motifs and a steepled copper roof. When it was built, it inadvertently gave a bird's-eye view into the adjacent Ursuline Convent, and a "view tax" had to be paid to the nuns to appease them. It is dramatically lit at night.

Facing the front of Hôtel-de-Ville, walk left on rue des Jardins toward Édifice Price. On your left, you'll pass a small statue celebrating the city's connections to *le cirque* and its performers. Cross over rue Ste-Anne. On the left are the spires of the:

15 Anglican Cathedral of the Holy Trinity

Modeled after London's St-Martin-in-the-Fields, this building dates from 1804 and was the first Anglican cathedral to be built outside the British Isles. The interior is simple, but spacious and bright, with pews of solid English oak from the Royal Windsor forest and a latticed ceiling with a gilded-chain motif. Lucky visitors may happen upon an organ recital or choral rehearsal.

One block up rue des Jardins, turn right at the small square (triangle shaped, actually) and go a few more steps to 12 rue Donnacona, the:

16 Chapelle/Musée des Ursulines

Handiwork by Ursuline nuns from the 17th, 18th, and 19th centuries is on display here, along with Amerindian crafts and a cape that was made for Marie de l'Incarnation, a founder of the convent, when she left for New France in 1639.

Peek into the restored chapel if it's open. The tomb of Marie de l'Incarnation is here. The altar, created by sculptor Pierre-Noël Levasseur between 1726 and 1736, is worth a look. See p. 284 for more details.

From the museum, turn right on rue Donnacona to walk past the **Ursuline Convent,** originally built in 1642. The present complex is actually a succession of different buildings added and repaired at various times until 1836, as frequent fires took their toll. A statue of Marie is outside. The convent is now a private girls' school and not open to the public.

Continue left up the hill along rue du Parloir to rue St-Louis. Turn right. At the next block, rue du Corps-de-Garde, note the tree on the left side of the street with a:

17 Cannonball

Lodged at the base of the trunk, one story says that the cannonball landed here during the Battle of Québec in 1759 and, over the years, became firmly embraced by the tree. Another story says that it was placed here on purpose to keep the wheels of horse-drawn carriages from bumping the tree when making tight turns.

Continue along rue St-Louis another 2 blocks to rue d'Auteuil. The house on the right corner is:

18 Hôtel d'Esplanade

Notice that many of the windows in the facade facing rue St-Louis are blocked by stone. This is because houses were once taxed by the number of windows they had, and the frugal homeowner who lived here found this way to get around the law—even though it cut down on his view.

Continue straight on rue St-Louis toward the Porte St-Louis, a gate in the walls. Before the gate on the right is the Esplanade powder magazine, part of the old fortifications. Just before the gate is an:

19 Unnamed Monument

This monument commemorates the 1943 meeting in Québec of U.S. President Franklin D. Roosevelt and British Prime Minister Winston Churchill. It remains a soft-pedaled reminder to French Québécois that it was the English-speaking nations that rid France of the Nazis.

Just across the street from the monument is a small road, Côte de la Citadelle, that leads to La Citadelle. Walk up that road. On the right are headquarters and barracks of a militia district, arranged around an inner court. Near its entrance is a:

20 Stone Memorial

This marks the resting place of 13 soldiers of General Richard Montgomery's American army, felled in the unsuccessful assault on Québec in 1775. Obviously, the conflicts that swirled for centuries around who would ultimately rule Québec didn't end with the British victory after its 1759 battle with French troops.

Continue up the hill to:

21 La Citadelle

The impressive star-shaped fortress just beyond view keeps watch from a commanding position on a grassy plateau 108m (354 ft.) above the banks of the St. Lawrence. It took 30 years to complete, by which time it had become obsolete. Since 1920, the Citadelle has been the home of the French-speaking **Royal 22e Régiment,** which fought in both world wars and in Korea. With good timing and weather, it's possible to watch a **Changing of the Guard** ceremony, or (as it's called) "beating the retreat." See p. 280 for more details.

Return to rue St-Louis and turn left to pass through Porte St-Louis, which was built in 1873 on the site of a gate dating from 1692. Here, the street broadens to become Grande-Allée. To the right is a park that runs alongside the city walls.

22 Site of Winter Carnaval

One of the most captivating events on the Canadian calendar, the 17-day **Carnaval de Québec** happens every February and includes outdoor games, snow tubing, dogsled races, canoe races along the St. Lawrence River, night parades,

and more. A palace of snow and ice rises on this spot just outside the city walls, with ice sculptures throughout the field. Colorfully clad Québécois come to admire the palace and dance the nights away at outdoor parties. On the left side of Grande-Allée, a carnival park of games, food, and music is set up on Parc des Champs-de-Bataille. For an instant pick-me-up during the cold winter festival, try to find the Carnaval's signature drink, the caribou, which is an elixir of wine and hard liquors. See p. 29 for more about the festivities.

Snow tubing is just one of many events at the February Carnaval de Québec.

Across the street from the park, on your right, stands the province of Québec's stately:

23 Hôtel du Parlement

Constructed in 1884, this government building houses what Québécois call their "National Assembly" (note the use of the word "national" and not "provincial").

The massive fountain in front of the building, **La Fontaine de Tourny,** was commissioned by the mayor of Bordeaux, France, in 1857. Sculptor Mathurin Moreau created the dreamlike figures on the fountain's base. It was installed as a gift from the Simons department store to the city for its 400th anniversary in 2008.

In the sumptuous Parliament chambers, the fleur-de-lis symbol and the initials VR (for Victoria Regina) are reminders of Québec's dual heritage. If the crown on top is lit, Parliament is in session. Along the exterior facade are 22 bronze statues of prominent figures in Québec's tumultuous history.

Guided tours are available weekdays year-round from 9am to 4:30pm, and weekends in summer from 10am to 4:30pm. See p. 287 for more information.

24 Le Parlementaire & Café du Parlement ☕

Le Parlementaire restaurant (✆ 418/643-6640), in the Hôtel du Parlement (p. 287) at 1045 rue des Parlementaires, is done up in regal Beaux Arts decor and open to the public (as well as parliamentarians and visiting dignitaries) for breakfast and lunch Monday through Friday most of the year. The more casual Café du Parlement (✆ 418/643-5529) has eat-in or takeout options in biodegradable containers, and is located on the ground floor. Or mosey on down Grande-Allée to find plenty of other options.

Continue down:

25 Grand-Allée

Just past Hôtel du Parlement is a park called Place George-V, and behind the park are the charred remains of the **1885 Armory.** A major visual icon and home to the country's oldest French-Canadian regiment, the Armory was all but destroyed in an April 2008 fire. The stone facade still stands. The destruction was a huge blow to the city, and discussions over what kind of rebuilding to do are still continuing.

To the left of the armory is a building that houses **a tourist information office** and the **Discovery Pavilion** (p. 282), where a multimedia exhibit called "Odyssey: A Journey through History on the Plains of Abraham" is presented.

After the park, the street becomes lined with cafes, restaurants, and bars on both sides. This strip really gets jumping at night, particularly in the complex that includes **VooDoo Grill** and **Maurice Night Club** (p. 323), at no. 575.

One food possibility is **Chez Ashton,** at 640 Grande-Allée est. The Québec fast-food restaurant makes what many consider the town's best *poutine*—French fries with cheese curds and brown gravy.

A great way to end the stroll is with a stop at **L'Astral,** the restaurant and bar atop Loews le Concorde Hotel, at the corner of Grande-Allée est and Cours du Général-De Montcalm. The room spins slowly (it takes about 1½ hours for a full rotation) and lets you look back at all the places you've been and all the places still to go. See p. 272 for information.

The city bus along Grande-Allée can return you to the Old City, or turn left at Loews and enter the **Parc des Champs-de-Bataille** (**Battlefields Park;** p. 282) at the Joan of Arc Garden. If you turn left in the park and continue along its boulevards and footpaths, you'll end up at the Citadelle. If you turn right, you'll reach the **Musée National des Beaux-Arts du Québec** (p. 281).

WALKING TOUR 2: LOWER TOWN (VIEUX-QUÉBEC: BASSE-VILLE & VIEUX-PORT)

START:	**Either in Upper Town at Terrasse Dufferin, the boardwalk in front of Château Frontenac, or if you're already in Lower Town, at the *funiculaire* (the cable car that connects the upper and lower parts of the Old City).**
FINISH:	**Place-Royale, the restored central square of Lower Town.**
TIME:	**1½ hours.**
BEST TIMES:	**Anytime during the day. Early morning lets you soak up the visual history, though shops won't be open.**
WORST TIMES:	**Very late at night.**

The Lower Town (Basse-Ville) part of Old Québec (Vieux-Québec) encompasses the city's oldest residential area—now flush with boutique hotels, high-end restaurants, and touristy shops—and Vieux-Port, the old port district. The impressive Museum of Civilization is here, and if you have time, you may want to pause from the tour for a visit. We start at the cliff-side elevator (*funiculaire*) that connects Upper and Lower towns.

If you're in Upper Town, descend to Lower Town by one of two options:

1 Funiculaire (Option A)

This cable car's upper terminus is on Terrasse Dufferin near the Château Frontenac. As the car descends the steep slope, its glass front provides a broad view of Basse-Ville (Lower Town).

Or, if you prefer a more active means of descent, use the stairs to the left of the *funiculaire,* the:

2 L'Éscalier du Casse-Cou (Option B)

"Breakneck Stairs" is the self-explanatory name given to this stairway (although truth be told, they're not *that* harrowing any-

The Funiculaire can take you from Upper Town to Lower Town.

more). Stairs have been in place here since the settlement began. In 1698, the town council had to forbid citizens from taking their animals up and down the stairway.

Both Breakneck Stairs and the *funiculaire* arrive at the intersection of rues Petit-Champlain and Sous-le-Fort. Look at the building from which the *funiculaire* passengers exit:

3 Maison Louis Jolliet

This building is now the *funiculaire*'s lower terminus and full of tourist trinkets and gewgaws, but it has an auspicious pedigree. It was built in 1683 and was home to Louis Jolliet, the Québec-born explorer who, along with a priest, Jacques Marquette, was the first person of European parentage to explore the Mississippi River's upper reaches.

Walk down the pretty little street here:

4 Rue du Petit-Champlain

Allegedly North America's oldest street, this pedestrian-only lane swarms with restaurantgoers, cafe sitters, strolling couples, and gaggles of schoolchildren in the warm months. Many of the shops listed in Chapter 17 are here. In winter, it's a snowy wonderland, with ice statues and twinkling white lights.

5 Le Lapin Sauté 🍵

Though it's early in the stroll, there are so many eating and shopping options here that you might want to pause for a while. Look for the sign with the flying rabbits for Le Lapin Sauté, at 52 rue du Petit-Champlain, a country-cozy bistro with hearty food in generous portions. A lovely terrace overlooks a small garden and, in the warm months, street musicians serenade diners.

At the end of Petit-Champlain, turn left onto boulevard Champlain. A lighthouse from the Gaspé Peninsula used to stand across the street, but it has been returned to its original home, leaving just an anchor and cannons to stand guard (rather forlornly) over the river.

Follow the street's curve; this block offers pleasant boutiques and cafes. At the corner is the crimson-roofed:

6 Maison Chevalier

Dating from 1752, this was once the home of merchant Jean-Baptiste Chevalier. Note the wealth of windows, more than 30 in front-facing sections alone. In 1763, the house was sold at auction to ship owner Jean-Louis Frémont, the grandfather of Virginia-born John Charles Frémont. John Charles went on to become an American explorer, soldier, and politician who mapped some 10 Western and Midwestern territories.

The Chevalier House was sold in 1806 to an Englishman, who in turn rented it to a hotelier, who transformed it into an inn. In 1960, the Québec government restored the house, and it became a museum about 5 years later. It's overseen by the Musée de la Civilisation, which mounts temporary exhibitions. Entrance is free.

Just past the maison's front door, turn left and walk up the short block of rue Notre-Dame, a carefully restored street of stone and brick buildings. There's a fun shop, Vert Tuyau Coop, featuring all-Québec products, just around the corner at 6 rue Cul-De-Sac. Otherwise, turn right at Sous-le-Fort and walk 1 block to the:

7 Royal Battery

Fortifications were erected here by the French in 1691 and the cannons added in 1712 to defend Lower Town from the British. The cannons got their chance in 1759, but the English victory silenced them, and eventually, they were left to rust. Sunken foundations were all that remained by the turn of the 20th century, and when the time came for restorations, it had to be rebuilt from the ground up.

From the Royal Battery, walk back up rue Sous-le-Fort. This is a good photo opportunity, with the imposing Château Frontenac on the cliff above framed between ancient houses.

Turn right on rue Notre-Dame. Half a block up the grade is the heart of Basse-Ville, the small:

8 Place-Royale

Occupying the center of New France's first permanent colony, this small and still very much European-feeling enclosed square served as the town marketplace. It went into decline around 1860 and, by 1950, had become a derelict, run-down part of town. Today, it has been restored to very nearly recapture its historic appearance. The prominent bust is of Louis XIV, the Sun King, a gift from the city of Paris in 1928. The striking 17th- and 18th-century houses once belonged to wealthy merchants. Note the ladders on some of the steep roofs, used to fight fire and remove snow. See p. 277 for more information about the square.

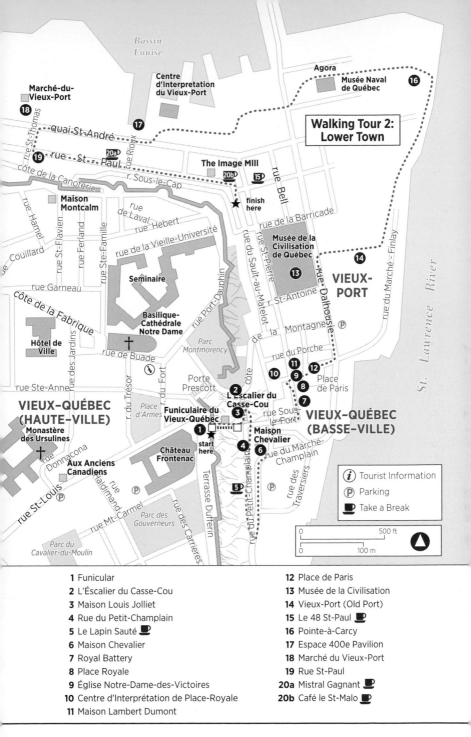

1 Funicular
2 L'Éscalier du Casse-Cou
3 Maison Louis Jolliet
4 Rue du Petit-Champlain
5 Le Lapin Sauté
6 Maison Chevalier
7 Royal Battery
8 Place Royale
9 Église Notre-Dame-des-Victoires
10 Centre d'Interprétation de Place-Royale
11 Maison Lambert Dumont

12 Place de Paris
13 Musée de la Civilisation
14 Vieux-Port (Old Port)
15 Le 48 St-Paul
16 Pointe-à-Carcy
17 Espace 400e Pavilion
18 Marché du Vieux-Port
19 Rue St-Paul
20a Mistral Gagnant
20b Café le St-Malo

Facing directly onto the square is:

9 Église Notre-Dame-des-Victoires

Named for French naval victories over the British in 1690 and 1711, Québec's oldest stone church was built in 1688 after a massive Lower Town fire destroyed 55 homes in 1682. The church was restored in 1763 after its partial destruction by the British in the 1759 siege. The white-and-gold interior has a few murky paintings and a large model boat suspended from the ceiling, a votive offering brought by early settlers to ensure safe voyages. On the walls, small prints depict the stages of the Passion. The church is open to visitors daily 10am to 4pm from May through September. See p. 277 for more information.

Walk straight across the plaza, passing the:

10 Centre d'Interprétation de Place-Royale

For decades, this space was nothing but a propped-up facade with an empty lot behind it, but it has been rebuilt to serve as an interpretation center with shows and exhibitions about this district's history; it's good for kids, as well as adults (p. 277).

At the corner on the right is the:

11 Maison Lambert Dumont

This building now houses Geomania, a store selling rocks and crystals. In earlier years, though, it was home to the Dumont family and one of several residences in the square. To the right as you're facing it once stood a hotel where U.S. President William Taft would stay as he headed north to vacation in the picturesque Charlevoix region.

Walk about 15m (49 ft.) past the last building on your left and turn around; the entire end of that building is a *trompe l'oeil* mural of streets and houses, and depictions of citizens from the earliest colonial days to the present, an amusing splash of fool-the-eye trickery. Have your photo taken here—nearly everyone does!

Return to Place-Royale and head left toward the water, down two small sets of stairs to the:

12 Place de Paris

This plaza contains a discordantly bland white sculpture that resembles three stacked Rubik's Cubes. It's called *Dialogue avec L'Histoire* and was a gift from the city of Paris in 1987.

Continue ahead to rue Dalhousie, a main street for cars, and turn left. A few short blocks up and on the left is the:

13 Musée de la Civilisation

This wonderful museum, which opened in 1988, may be housed in a lackluster gray-block building, but there is nothing plain about it once you enter.

The Musée de la Civilisation has many ingeniously arranged exhibits.

Spacious and airy, with ingeniously arranged multidimensional exhibits, it's one of Canada's most innovative museums. If there is no time now, put it at the top of your must-see list for later. See p. 276.

Across the street from the museum is:

14 Vieux-Port (Old Port)

In the 17th century, this 29-hectare (72-acre) riverfront area was the port of call for European ships bringing supplies and settlers to the new colony. With the decline of shipping by the early 20th century, the port fell into precipitous decline. But since the mid-1980s, it has experienced a rebirth, becoming the summer destination for international cruise ships. It got additional sprucing up for Québec's 400th anniversary in 2008.

15 Le 48 St-Paul ☕

If you're doing this stroll in the colder months, you might want to head indoors at this point. Le 48 St-Paul, named after its address, is just steps from the corner of rues Dalhousie and St-Paul, 1 block past the museum. It's sleek and affordable, with creative burgers and pizzas, most under C$10. To continue the tour, head back to rue Dalhousie and cross over toward Terminal de Croisières to the waterfront.

From the museum, head across the parking lot to the river and turn left at the water's edge. After Terminal de Croisières, the cruise terminal, you'll pass the Agora, an outdoor theater, and behind it, the city's Customs House, built between 1830 and 1839.

Continue along the river's promenade, past the Agora, to the small landscaped:

16 Pointe-à-Carcy

The bronze statue of a sailor here is a memorial to Canadian merchant seamen who lost their lives in World War II. From the point, you can look out across Louise Basin to the Bunge of Canada grain elevator, which stores wheat, barley, corn, and soybean crops that are produced in western Canada before they are shipped to Europe. These silos make up the massive "screen" upon which the nightly show **"Image Mill"** is projected on summer nights (p. 286).

Follow the walkway left from Pointe-à-Carcy along the Louise Basin. You'll pass the **Musée Naval de Québec,** which was closed for years of renovation and reopened in the summer of 2010, in time to celebrate the navy's centennial birthday. See p. 287. In the warm months, you can board a scenic river cruise here.

At the end of the basin, take a short jog left, and then right to stay along the water's edge. Up ahead is a modern glass building, the:

17 Espace 400e Pavilion

This new building was the central location for Québec's 400th-anniversary celebrations in 2008. It was scheduled to open as a state-run Discovery Center in 2010, but that project was cancelled. For now it hosts temporary exhibitions, usually in summer (p. 286).

From the pavilion, continue 1 block to:

18 Marché du Vieux-Port

This colorful market at 160 quai St-André has jaunty teal-blue roofs and, in summer, rows and rows of booths heaped with fresh fruits and vegetables, regional wines and ciders, soaps, pâtés, jams, handicrafts, cheeses, chocolates, fresh fish, and meat. Cafes and kiosks offer options for a meal or sweet treat.

As you approach, you'll see, down the street, the city's grand train station, designed in 1916 by New York architect Bruce Price. He designed the Château Frontenac in 1893 and used his signature copper-turned-green spires here, too.

You can find all kinds of different foods at the Marché du Vieux-Port.

Leaving the market, cross rue St-André at the light and walk a short block to:

19 Rue St-Paul

Turn left onto this street, home to galleries, craft shops, and about a dozen antiques stores. They include **Maison Dambourgès,** at no. 155, which sells folk art and pine furniture, and **l'Héritage Antiquité,** at no. 109, which has old postcards, bits of china sets, and the like. Rue St-Paul manages to maintain a sense of unspoiled neighborhood.

20 Mistral Gagnant and Café le St-Malo ☕

Mistral Gagnant (p. 271), at 160 rue St-Paul, is a sunny Provençal restaurant that features hearty food such as omelets, escargot, bouillabaisse, and outrageously good lemon pie. Café le St-Malo, at 75 rue St-Paul, has low ceilings, rough stone walls, and storefront windows that draw patrons in.

From here, return to the heart of Lower Town—Place-Royale and the *funiculaire*—by turning right off rue St-Paul onto either rue du Sault-au-Matelot or the parallel rue St-Pierre. Both are quiet streets with galleries and restaurants.

QUÉBEC CITY SHOPPING

Vieux-Québec's compact size, with its upper and lower sections (to conserve your energy, take the *funiculaire* to transfer between the two), makes it especially convenient for browsing and shopping. Unlike Montréal, which carries a lot of familiar American or international brands, Québec City seems to lean toward more local merchandise, making it a unique experience with many interesting retail opportunities.

THE SHOPPING SCENE

Vieux-Québec's Lower Town, particularly the area known as **Quartier du Petit-Champlain,** offers many possibilities—clothing, souvenirs, gifts, household items, collectibles—and is avoiding the trashiness that can afflict heavily touristed neighborhoods with an upswell of shops that feature locally made products. The area is just around the corner from the *funiculaire* entrance.

In Upper Town, wander along **rue St-Jean,** both within and outside the city walls, and on **rue Garneau** and **Côte de la Fabrique,** which branch off the east end of St-Jean. For T-shirts, postcards, and other souvenirs, check out the myriad shops that line **rue St-Louis.** If you're heading to St-Roch to eat, build in a little time to stroll **rue St-Joseph,** which, for a few blocks, has new boutiques alongside cafes and restaurants.

Outside the walls, just beyond the strip of eateries and nightspots that line Grande-Allée, **avenue Cartier** has shops and restaurants of some variety, from clothing and ceramics to housewares and gourmet foods. The 5 blocks attract crowds of youngish and middle-aged locals. The area remains outside the tourist orbit, but it's an easy walk: Head up wide, tree-lined Grande-Allée and turn right onto Cartier. To continue past some of the city's finest culinary shops, take another right on chemin Ste-Foy, which leads to the western edge of rue St-Jean, where you'll find grocers, butchers, and bakers galore.

Most stores are open Monday through Wednesday from 9 or 10am to 6pm, Thursday and Friday until 9pm, and Saturday from 10am to 5pm. Many stores are now also open on Sunday from noon to 5pm. Call and confirm store hours before making a special trip.

The Best Buys

Indigenous crafts, handmade sweaters, and **Inuit art** are among the desirable items specific to Québec. An official igloo trademark identifies authentic Inuit (Eskimo) art, though the differences between the real thing and the manufactured variety become apparent with a little careful study. Inuit artwork, which is usually in the form of carvings in stone or bone, is an excellent purchase not for its low price, but for its high quality. Expect to pay hundreds of dollars for even a relatively small piece.

PREVIOUS PAGE: **Québec cheeses are one of the province's most distinctive products.**

Inuit art is a popular gift item.

You're bound to see a lot of the **Inukshuk** figurine, which looks like a human figure made of stacked rocks. It was the centerpiece of the logo of the 2010 Winter Olympics, which took place in Vancouver in February and March 2010. **Maple syrup** products make sweet gifts, as do **regional wines** and **jams.** Look for Québec **cheeses, chocolate,** and products made from local crops such as **cranberries** or **black currants.** New shop **Le Touriste Gourmand** (p. 317) was opened with visitors like you in mind. Be sure to double-check Customs policies (p. 353) before crossing the border with perishables.

Apart from a handful of boutiques, Québec City does not offer the high-profile designer clothing showcased in Montréal, although Montréal-based fashion icon Philippe **Dubuc** (p. 315) recently opened a second boutique in the hip St-Roch neighborhood in the Lower Town area, west of Old Québec. That said, more and more Québec City artisans are making intriguing clothes and accessories from recycled wool and fur.

SHOPPING FROM A TO Z

Listed with the address for each shop below is its neighborhood: Lower Town or Upper Town in Vieux-Québec; Montcalm, the residential neighborhood just west of Parliament Hill; Faubourg St-Jean, just past Porte St-Jean in Upper Town; and Nouvo St-Roch in Lower Town, a little west of Old Québec.

Antiques Row

About a dozen antiques shops line rue St-Paul in Lower Town. They're filled with knickknacks, Québec country furniture, candlesticks, old clocks, Victoriana, Art Deco and Art Moderne objects, and the increasingly sought-after kitsch and housewares of the early–World War II period. **Machin Chouette,** 225 rue St-Paul (**℃ 418/525-9898;** www.machinchouette.com), hand selects antiques for homes with a modern flair and also makes custom storage units out of album covers, vinyl records, and wood butter boxes. At **Les Antiquités Bolduc,** 89 rue St-Paul (**℃ 418/694-9558;** www.lesantiquitesbolduc.com), brother-and-sister duo Stéphanie and Frédéric Bolduc sell vintage knickknacks, such as antique sconces and grandfather clocks.

Arts & Crafts

Boutique des Métiers d'Art   In a stone building at the corner of Place-Royale, this carefully arranged store displays works by scores of Québécois craftspeople, at least some of which are likely to appeal to almost any customer. Among these objects are wooden boxes, jewelry, graphics, and a variety of gifts. When departing, be sure to turn left, walk past the end of the building, and turn around—it's a surprise! 29 rue Notre-Dame, Lower Town. ☏ **418/694-0267.** www.metiers-d-art.qc.ca.

Dugal One of the owners works in wood, carving sinuous and remarkably comfortable rocking chairs, while the other creates jewelry featuring black pearls set in gold and silver. 15 rue Notre-Dame, Lower Town. ☏ **418/692-1564.**

Galerie Brousseau et Brousseau In 2005, the important Inuit art collection assembled over 50 years by Québécois Raymond Brousseau was acquired by the Musée des Beaux-Arts du Québec, and 285 works from the 2,635-piece collection are on display at that museum. Here, you can buy Native Canadian carvings selected by the same family to take home. This is the most prominent of the city's art dealers, and it offers certificates of authenticity. Prices are high but competitive for merchandise of similar quality. The shop is set up like a gallery, so feel free just to browse. 35 rue St-Louis (at rue des Jardins), Upper Town. ☏ **418/694-1828.** www.sculpture.artinuit.ca.

Galerie d'Art du Petit-Champlain The superbly detailed carvings of Roger Desjardins, who applies his skills to meticulous renderings of waterfowl, are featured here. The inventory also includes lithographs, paintings, and canvas transfers. A complete list of artists can be found online. 88 rue du Petit-Champlain (near boul. Champlain), Lower Town. ☏ **418/692-5647.** www.gapc.ca.

Rose Bouton The buttons Grandma collected take on new life in the hands of Marie-Noëlle Bellegarde, whose playful shop turns all kinds of something-old into new earrings, necklaces, bracelets, and more. 387 rue St-Jean (near rue de Claire-Fontaine), just outside Upper Town. ☏ **418/614-9507.** www.boutiquerose.blogspot.com.

Rue du Trésor Outdoor Gallery Sooner or later, everyone passes this outdoor alley near the Place d'Armes. Artists gather along here much of the year to exhibit and sell their work. Most of the prints on view are of Québec scenes and can make attractive souvenirs. The artists seem to enjoy chatting with interested passersby. Rue du Trésor (between rue Ste-Anne & rue Buade), Upper Town. www.ruedutresor.qc.ca.

Sachem Fur hats, baby moccasins, carvings, music, and jewelry are all packed into this compact boutique, which specializes in *"art amérindien."* Included are a variety of miniature Inukshuk human figurines, which look like they've been made of stacked rocks. 17 rue des Jardins (near Hôtel-de-Ville), Upper Town. ☏ **418/692-3056.**

Vert Tuyau Coop The fused glass jewelry, earring made of vinyl records, turned-wood bowls, and felted wool or organic cotton garments on offer here are all 100% Québec-made. Everything is created by one of this artist collective's members, which was founded to offer tourists an alternative to T-shirts and trinkets manufactured then shipped from the other side of the globe. 6 rue Cul-de-Sac, Lower Town. ☏ **418/692-1111.** www.verttuyau.com.

Bath & Body

Fruits & Passion Outposts of this Québec-based chain are found throughout the region. They all carry soaps, lotions, candles, foods, and even men's and baby lines. The Fruits & Passion Cucina hand-care line uses olive-leaf extract with scents ranging from fig to lime zest. 75 rue du Petit-Champlain, Lower Town. ☏ **418/692-2859.** www.fruits-passion.ca.

Clothing

Atelier La Pomme Just steps from the funicular in Lower Town, this cute boutique of women's clothes specializes in chic dresses by Québécois designers and *vêtements de cuir*, or leather clothing, including hats and handbags. 47 Sous-Le-Fort (near rue du Petit-Champlain), Lower Town. ℂ **418/692-2875.**

Code Vert A very cool boutique. The work of 35 *"éco-désigners"* is on display, including jewelry made from recycled fur, fitted T-shirts, mittens knit from patches of old sweaters, yoga clothes, and so on. The store's tagline is "Mode.Éthique.Urbaine"—ethical, urban clothing, with a focus on sustainability. 586 B rue St-Jean (near rue Ste-Marie), Faubourg St-Jean. ℂ **418/524-4004.** www.codevert.ca.

Dubuc ★ Get your Euro-look up to par with Canadian darling and Montréal-based fashion designer Philippe Dubuc's avant-garde menswear in urban shades of cement, steel, and charcoal. While most of the edgy suit styles compliment the slimmer male, there are also more universal shirts—always, however, with impeccable tailoring. 537 rue St-Joseph est (near rue du Parvis). ℂ **418/614-5761.** www.dubucstyle.com.

Fourrures du Vieux-Port The fur trade underwrote the development and exploration of Québec and the vast lands west, and continues to be important to the region to this day. This Lower Town merchant has as good a selection as any, including knit furs and shearlings, along with designer coats by Christia and Olivieri. The store was recently renovated and now boasts three floors. 55 rue St-Pierre (at Côte de la Montagne), Lower Town. ℂ **866/692-6688** or 418/692-6686. www.quebecfourrure.com.

Harricana ★ Montréal designer Mariouche Gagné, who was born on Île d'Orléans in 1971, is a leader of the so-called eco-luxe movement. Her company recycles old fur, silk scarves, and even wedding dresses to create new coats, winter hats, tops, and skirts. One favorite on a recent visit: a white aviator hat of recycled fur and scraps of a lace wedding gown, for C$250. 44 Côte de la Fabrique, Upper Town. ℂ **418/204-5340.** www.harricana.qc.ca.

Code Vert displays the work of 35 "éco-désigners."

LOGO Sport ☺   The top spot for sports jerseys and hats: hockey, of course, but soccer, baseball, and basketball as well. 1028 rue St-Jean (at rue Ste-Ursule), 1047 rue St-Jean (at rue Ste-Angèle), Upper Town. ☎ **418/692-1351.** www.logosport.ca.

La Maison Darlington   The popular emporium in this historic house (it was built in 1775) comes on strong with both tony and traditional clothing for men and women produced by such makers as Dale of Norway and Geiger. Inventory includes high-quality and tasteful men's and women's hats, scarves, and sweaters, especially in cashmere and other wools. As appealing are the hand-smocked, locally made dresses for little girls. 7 rue de Buade (near Place d'Armes), Upper Town. ☎ **418/692-2268.**

Marie Dooley   This Québec-born designer boasts two adjacent shops: Signature, a teeny boutique featuring chic, youthful women's clothing, and Le Salon, a corner salon of formal gowns. 1005 rue Salaberry (1 block northeast of av. Cartier at boul. René-Lévesque), Montcalm. ☎ **418/522-7597.** www.mariedooley.com.

Michael   Fashionable women's clothing for work or for play, featuring the chic Animale, Sandwich, and Desigual labels. A store by the same name for men is next door, at no. 1060. 106 rue St-Jean (near rue Ste-Angèle), Upper Town. ☎ **418/692-2766.**

Murmure   Off the tourist track on avenue Cartier, this small boutique has casual dresses, jackets, and skirts, primarily for 30- to 50-something women. For designer jeans and skimpy jackets for younger women, visit **Urbain,** directly across the street. 989 av. Cartier (at boul. René-Lévesque), Montcalm. ☎ **418/522-1016.**

Simons ★ ☺   Vieux-Québec's only department store opened here in 1840. Small by modern standards, Simons has two floors for men's and women's clothing, emphasizing sportswear for adults and teens. Most of it is pretty basic, but trendy and generally inexpensive. 20 Côte de la Fabrique (near the Hôtel-de-Ville), Upper Town. ☎ **418/692-3630.** www.simons.ca.

Zazou   This boutique focuses primarily on casual and dressy fashions from Québécois designers, including wool sweaters with nature motifs and silk scarves. 31 Petit-Champlain (near the funicular), Lower Town. ☎ **418/694-9990.** www.quartier petitchamplain.com/zazou.

Food

Canadian Maple Delights ☺   This maple syrup foods boutique stocks everything from maple chocolate and maple crystals to gift bottles of syrup and freshly made pastries and cookies. Maple-sweetened gelatos come in flavors such as passion fruit, mango-pineapple, and raspberry. This is one of the few shops where you'll find the English translation of the name getting as much prominence in signage as the French translation, Les Délices de l'Erable. 1044 rue St-Jean (near rue Ste-Angèle), Upper Town. ☎ **418/692-3245.** www.mapledelights.com.

Choco-Musée Érico ☺   Gourmet chocolates in an old-timey shop that includes a small room with historical information about how chocolate is made. Flavors include Szechuan, jasmine, chai cardamom, and hibiscus sorbet. You can also buy ice cream here for just over C$1. 634 rue St-Jean (5 blocks outside Upper Town walls), Faubourg St-Jean. ☎ **418/524-2122.** www.chocomusee.com.

Épicerie J.A. Moisan ★   A true food emporium—there must be close to 30 olive oils to choose from, for instance, making this *épicerie* a special spot. For one thing, it's a step back in time, dating to 1871 (it claims to be the oldest grocery store in North America). As engagingly, it maintains an international selection of foods whose expanse is usually found only in shops 20 times its size. 699 rue St-Jean (4 blocks outside Upper Town walls), Faubourg St-Jean. ☎ **418/522-0685.** www.jamoisan.com.

Épicerie J.A. Moisan claims to be the oldest grocery store in North America.

Marché du Vieux-Port By the water near the train station, this market is a year-round operation that blossoms in spring and summer with farmers' bounty from Île d'Orléans and beyond. In addition to fresh fruits and vegetables, you'll find relishes, jams, honey, wines, meats, cheeses, and handicrafts. 160 Quai St-André (near the train station), Lower Town. ✆ **418/692-2517.** www.marchevieux port.com.

La Petite Cabane à Sucre ☺ Canada is the biggest producer of maple syrup in the world, and Québec is the source of 90% of Canada's share. "The little sugar shack," as this store's name translates into English, sells ice cream, honey, maple syrup, maple candy, and related products, including tin log cabins that pour syrup from their chimneys. 94 rue du Petit-Champlain (near boul. Champlain), Lower Town. ✆ **418/692-5875.** www.petitecabaneasucre.com.

Le Touriste Gourmand ★ Owner Richard Verret stocks his shelves with food products from across Québec (*saveurs du terroir*), which are all thoughtfully (and beautifully) displayed by region. Shoppers can stock up on over 600 different items, including wild strawberry jam or fiddleheads marinated in wine vinegar from Gaspésie, emu pâté from Charlevoix (a very lean meat from a bird smaller than an ostrich), and black currant products such as crème de cassis from **Monna et Filles** on Île d'Orléans (p. 333). Popular items are the predictable (but nevertheless tasty) maple products and apple butter, as well as the unusual caribou pâtés (three peppers and cognac, or blueberry and maple wine) that are only available when hunted by the Inuit. 54 boul. Champlain (near rue des Traversiers), Lower Town. ✆ **418/977-3999.** www.letouristegourmand.com.

Housewares

Boutique Ketto ☺ From the impish imaginations of two Québécois graphic designers come the motifs on Boutique Ketto's pottery, ceramic jewelry, and stationery made in Québec. It's in the residential area of Montcalm, within walking distance of Upper Town. 951 av. Cartier (at Crémazie), Montcalm. ✆ **418/522-3337.** www.kettodesign.com.

Zone Just down the block from Boutique Ketto (above), Zone is a nifty housewares store featuring colorful bowls and plates, clocks and frames, furnishings, and mod pendant lamps and vases. Zone has several outposts throughout the

Archambault is a good place to pick up local books and music.

province. 999 av. Cartier (at the corner of boul. René-Lévesque), Montcalm. ℂ**418/522-7373.** www.zonemaison.com.

Music

Archambault ☺ Part of a Canadian chain, Archambault has two floors with CDs, DVDs, books, magazines, and some toys for children. 1095 rue St-Jean, Upper Town. ℂ **418/694-2088.** www.archambault.ca.

Newspapers & Magazines

Maison de la Presse Internationale As its name implies, this store in the midst of the St-Jean shopping-and-nightlife bustle offers up racks and racks of magazines and a good assortment of newspapers from around the world, in many languages. It's open Monday to Saturday from 7am until 11pm, and Sunday 8am to 11pm. 1050 rue St-Jean (at the corner of rue Ste-Angèle), Upper Town. ℂ **418/694-1511.**

Shopping Complexes

Shopping malls on a grand scale aren't found in or near the Old Town. For that, it's necessary to travel to the neighboring municipality of **Ste-Foy.** The malls there differ little from their cousins throughout North America in terms of layout and available products. With 350 shops, **Laurier Québec,** 2700 boul. Laurier, in Sainte-Foy (ℂ **800/322-1828;** www.laurierquebec.com), is the biggest, and it claims some 13 million shoppers each year. Two smaller complexes, **Place de la Cité** (ℂ **418/657-6920;** www.placedelacite.com) and **Place Ste-Foy** (ℂ **418/653-4184;** www.placestefoy.com) are within walking distance of Laurier, which offers a shuttle bus from several hotel stops in Québec City from mid-May through mid-October; call ℂ **418/664-0460** for schedule information. Families with their own cars can drive about 10 minutes northwest of Vieux-Québec to the indoor amusement park, ice rink, IMAX, movie screens, and 280 shops at **Galeries de la Capitale** (ℂ **418/627-5800;** www.galeriesdelacapitale.com), located at 5401 boul. des Galeries. If after you've shopped, you need to drop, the achingly chic **Alt Hotel** (www.quebec.althotels.ca) is just across the street.

Wines & Spirits

Société des Alcools du Québec Liquor and other spirits can be sold only in stores operated by this provincial agency. SAQ outlets are supermarkets of wines and spirits, with thousands of bottles in stock. Most feature large sections with Québec products, including the unique ice cider (*cidre de glace*), made from apples left on trees after the first frost, for around C$25. 1 rue des Carrières, in the Château Frontenac, Upper Town. ℂ **418/692-1712.** www.saq.com.

QUÉBEC CITY AFTER DARK

18

T hough Québec City has fewer nighttime diversions than exuberant Montréal, there are more than enough to occupy visitors' evenings. Apart from theatrical productions, which are usually in French, knowledge of the language is rarely needed to enjoy the entertainment.

There are two terrifically innovative events to plan summer evenings around: free outdoor performances by **Cirque du Soleil** and, later at night, the **"Image Mill" Light Installation.** See p. 286 for details.

The neighborhood for each venue below is listed with the address: Lower Town and Upper Town in Vieux-Québec; Vieux-Port, adjacent to Lower Town; Parliament Hill; Montcalm, the neighborhood just west of Parliament Hill; and St-Roch.

THE PERFORMING ARTS
Classical Music, Opera & Dance

The region's premier classical groups are **Orchestre Symphonique de Québec** (*©* **877/643-8486** or 418/643-8486; www.osq.org), Canada's oldest symphony, which performs at the Grand Théâtre de Québec (see below), and **Les Violons du Roy** (*©* **418/692-3026;** www.violonsduroy.com), a string orchestra that recently celebrated its 25th year. It features musicians in the early stages of their careers and performs at the centrally located Palais Montcalm (see below).

Concert Halls & Performance Venues

Many of the city's churches host sacred and secular music concerts, as well as special Christmas festivities. Look for posters on outdoor kiosks around the city and check with the tourist office (p. 239) for listings.

Colisée Pepsi This 16,500-seat arena is home to the Remparts, a popular junior hockey team. The stadium also hosts events such as monster truck extravaganzas, boxing matches, and occasional rock shows. It's a 10-minute drive northwest of Parliament Hill. 250 boul. Wilfrid-Hamel (ExpoCité), north of St-Roch. *©* **418/691-7110.** www.expocite.com/www/colisee-pepsi.php.

The Orchestre Symphonique de Québec performs at the Grand Théâtre; PREVIOUS PAGE: Québec City's Festival d'Été bills itself as Canada's largest outdoor arts festival.

Grand Théâtre de Québec ★★★ Classical music concerts, opera, dance, jazz, klezmer, and theatrical productions are presented in two halls. Visiting conductors, orchestras, and dance companies perform here, in addition to resident companies such as the Orchestre Symphonique de Québec. 269 boul. René-Lévesque est (near av. Turnbull), Parliament Hill. ✆ **877/643-8131** or 418/643-8131. www.grandtheatre.qc.ca.

Le Capitole Big musical productions such as *The Beatles Story* and *Cats,* along with live musical performances, keep this historic 1,262-seat theater on Place d'Youville buzzing along (productions are in French). More intimate shows, such as up-and-coming star Nadja, are put on in the attached Le Cabaret du Capitole. 972 rue St-Jean (at Place d'Youville), Parliament Hill. ✆ **800/261-9903** or 418/694-4444. www.lecapitole.com.

Palais Montcalm ★ Recent renovations made this venue bigger and more modern, and it's now a hub of the city's cultural community. The main performance space seats 979 and presents a mix of dance programs, plays, and classical music concerts. More intimate recitals happen in a 125-seat cafe-theater. 995 Place d'Youville (near Porte Saint-Jean), Parliament Hill. ✆ **877/641-6040** or 418/641-6040. www.palaismontcalm.ca.

THE CLUB & MUSIC SCENE

If you want to stroll around and take in the nightlife options, there are three principal streets to choose from: **rue St-Jean** inside and outside the walls, **Grande-Allée** outside the walls, and **avenue Cartier** in the Montcalm neighborhood.

Québec City's **Festival d'Eté (Summer Festival)** bills itself as Canada's largest outdoor arts festival. It's held in Vieux-Québec for 11 days each July. Highlights include the free jazz and folk combos who perform in an open-air theater next to City Hall. The festival hosts more than 400 shows with performers from Africa, Asia, Europe, and North America showcasing theater, music, and dance. For details, call ✆ **888/992-5200** or check www.infofestival.com.

Boites à Chansons & Other Music Clubs

Boîtes à chansons (literally, "boxes with songs") are small clubs for a casual evening of music from singer-songwriters. They're popular throughout Québec.

Largo Resto-Club An attractive restaurant and jazz club, Largo is one of a growing number of businesses sprucing up a blocks-long strip of rue St-Joseph in the St-Roch district. High ceilings and chandeliers give it old-time class, while blond-wood floors, clean angles, and contemporary art make it modern. There's jazz on Fridays and Saturdays, usually free for diners. Main courses range from C$16 to C$25. 643 rue St-Joseph est, St-Roch. ✆ **418/529-3111.** www.largorestoclub.ca.

Le Cercle A unique gallery-bar-resto-concert venue, this multiroom, multilevel address is the spot in St-Roch to go to for drinks, tapas, and good music—especially if you've tired of the see-and-be-seen vibe on nearby rue du Parvis. A hubbub of creative minds, they even have their own magazine that you can download online (click on the link at the top of their website). 228 rue St-Joseph est (near rue Caron). ✆ **418/948-8648.** www.le-cercle.ca. Bus: 801 or 802 takes you to nearby corner of rue St-Joseph est and rue de la Couronne.

Le Pape-Georges 🎁 A cozy wine bar in a 345-year-old stone-and-beamed room that features *chanson* (a French-cabaret singing style), along with other music, Friday through Sunday at 10pm (and Thurs in summer). Light fare is available, along with up to 15 choices of wine by the glass (the bar's motto: "Save water; drink wine!"). 8 rue Cul-de-Sac (near boul. Champlain), Lower Town. ℂ **418/692-1320.** www.papegeorges.com.

Théâtre Petit-Champlain   Québécois and French singers alternate with jazz and blues groups in this roomy cafe and theater in Lower Town. Performances take place most Wednesdays through Saturdays at 8pm. Tickets run about C$20 to C$40. There's a pretty outdoor patio for preshow drinks. 68 rue du Petit-Champlain (near the funiculaire), Lower Town. ℂ **418/692-2631.** www.theatrepetitchamplain.com.

Dance Clubs

Boudoir Lounge ★   The hottest club in St-Roch, Boudoir opens at noon from Monday to Friday and 4pm on Saturday and Sunday, and closes each night at 3am. DJs work the sound systems from 10pm on Thursday, Friday, and Saturday. Live music is featured every Sunday at 10pm. In warm weather, there's a terrace on the pedestrian street in front. The seasonal cocktail menu keeps up with trends from herbal infusions to locally inspired mix-ins of ice wine or maple syrup. Local hipsters generally hop between here, **Versa** across the street at no. 432 (www.versarestaurant.com), and **Yuzu** Sushi-Bar (www.yuzu.ca) at no. 438; the latter reopened in spring 2011 after a million-dollar reno and expansion. 441 rue du Parvis (at boul. Charest est), St-Roch. ℂ **418/524-2777.** www.boudoirlounge.com.

Dagobert Night-Club   An imposing mansionlike structure, the Dagobert is a Québec City institution, and, seemingly, a rite of passage for many young locals. "Le Dag" imports DJs from Montréal, the U.K., and beyond and lets you live it up like a VIP with everything from private tables to limousines available to book on their website. Dance under lights of every color, until the big one in the sky rises and sends you on your way. While Dagobert is considered by some locals an embarrassing place to be seen at night, its 1,000-person patio is packed with them during happy hour. I guess the two-for-one drinks don't hurt. 600 Grande-Allée est (at rue de la Chevrotière), Parliament Hill. ℂ **418/522-0393.** www.dagobert.ca.

Le Drague Cabaret Club   Catering mostly to gay and lesbian clientele, "the Drag" has been around since 1983 and features two dance rooms and a cabaret

The cozy Le Pape-Georges is inside a building nearly 350 years old.

Maurice Night Club is inside a converted mansion on the Grand-Allée.

with drag shows on Thursday, Friday, and Sunday nights. Other nights bring live shows, karaoke, and country-music dancing. 815 rue St-Augustin (just off rue St-Jean), Faubourg St-Jean. ☎ **418/649-7212.** www.ledrague.com.

Maurice Night Club   Find this club in the converted mansion at the thumping heart of the Grande-Allée scene. It includes a surprisingly good restaurant (**Voo-Doo Grill**), a couple of bars (an older crowd gravitates toward **Charlotte Lounge,** where there is usually live acts), and music that tilts heavily toward Latin. In winter, it has been known to set up a sidewalk-level "Icecothèque" with a bar made completely of ice, ice sculptures, and roaring music. Theme nights are frequent, and large crowds are not unusual. 575 Grande-Allée est, Parliament Hill. ☎ **418/647-2000.** www.mauricenightclub.com.

BARS

If you're young and looking for fun, keep in mind the **Grande-Allée** strip just past Place George-V, where a beery collegiate atmosphere can sometimes rule as the evening wears on. The bars listed here are removed from Grande-Allée's mêlée. Note that smoking has been banned in bars throughout the province since 2006.

L'Astral ★   Spinning slowly above the city, this restaurant and bar atop the **Hôtel Loews Le Concorde** (p. 257) unveils a breathtaking 360-degree panorama. L'Astral is mainly regarded as a restaurant (p. 272), but you can also come just for drinks and the sunset view. 1225 Cours du Général de Montcalm (at Grande-Allée), Parliament Hill. ☎ **800/463-256** or 418/780-3602. www.lastral.ca.

Aviatic Club   A good locale when you're coming or going by train, as it's right inside the station. Food ranges from Asian to vaguely Tex-Mex. 450 de la Gare-du-Palais (near rue St-Paul), Lower Town. ☎ **418/522-3555.** www.aviatic-club.com.

Fou Bar   No matter what your age, you'll feel welcome and comfortable sipping on a draught pulled at Fou Bar. Old stone walls, an abandoned fireplace, and walls with local art make the place feel homey. It's a great predinner warm-up. Or stay to catch a night of reggae, jazz, bluegrass, or acoustic live performance. It opens Monday to Friday at 2:30pm, and Saturday and Sunday at noon, until 3am. 525 rue St-Jean (near rue Ste-Claire), Faubourg St-Jean. ☎ **418/522-1987.** www.foubar.ca.

La Ninkasi du Faubourg   A relaxed go-to spot if you're young and gay, or just happy to be livin' la vida loca. With a tagline *"bières et culture,"* the Ninkasi features 200 Québécois microbrews. In warm months, it sometimes lays sod grass over the asphalt on the outdoor terrace. It's open daily from 2pm. 811 rue St-Jean (1 block west of av. Honoré-Mercier), Faubourg St-Jean. ☎ **418/529-8538.** www.ninkasi.ca.

The Pub St-Alexandre is one of the best-looking bars in the city.

Pub St-Alexandre ★   Roomy and sophisticated, this is one of the best-looking bars in town. It's done in British-pub style: polished mahogany, exposed brick, and a working fireplace that's particularly comforting during the 8 cold months of the year. Bartenders serve more than 40 single-malt scotches and 250 beers, along with hearty bar food (croque-monsieur, steak-and-kidney pie, fish and chips). Check the schedule for the occasional live music—rock, blues, jazz, or Irish. 1087 rue St-Jean (near rue St-Stanislas), Upper Town. ✆ **418/694-0015.** www.pubstalexandre.com.

Ristorante Il Teatro ★   This friendly Italian restaurant (p. 265) directly on the Place d'Youville is open from 7am to at least 2am every day. It's part of a complex that includes **Le Capitole** theater (p. 321), and actors, musical performers, and theater staff often come in for a drink or a meal after shows. 972 rue St-Jean (at Place d'Youville), Upper Town. ✆ **418/694-9996.** www.lecapitole.com/en/restaurant.php.

Savini   Only a few months old when we stopped by, the self-dubbed *"vinothèque"* had the trappings of a red-hot addition to Québec: a 2-hour wait for dinner, booming sound system, hostesses in teeny dresses, and nightly DJs. A big menu offers a variety of Italian food options, and a short menu of pizza and salad is available until 1am, too. 680 Grande-Allée (near rue D'Artigny), Parliament Hill. ✆ **418/647-4747.** www.savini.ca.

SSS   SSS may be the only lounge and restaurant in Vieux-Québec that adopts the sleek, bigger-city approach of sounding its techno beats onto the sidewalk to lure cocktail seekers. The most recent experiment of chefs Christian Lemelin and Stéphane D'Anjou, co-owners of the highly regarded restaurant **Toast!** (p. 270), brings French flair to American comfort foods—ribs, hot dogs, onion rings. Best example: *beignet de morue,* or cod donuts, with lemon aioli. Guests can opt for entrees or apps, dining room or bar. On busy nights, a snack menu kicks in after 10:30pm (and on busy afternoons between 2 and 5pm). 71 rue St-Paul (near rue Sault-au-Matelot), Lower Town. ✆ **418/692-1991.** www.restaurantsss.com.

St-Laurent Bar et Lounge   A swank little room inside Québec's magical castle, the Château Frontenac. Dark wood and marble lend an air of elegance, and a bank of windows overlooks the river. The crowd is older and well heeled, reflected in the drink options: 19 types of single malt; 15 wines by the glass; and 30 mixed drinks, including the signature St-Laurent Club, with muddled blueberries, Tanqueray #10 Gin, and lemon juice. There's a small food menu. Château Frontenac, 1 rue des Carrières, Upper Town. ✆ **418/692-3861.** www.fairmont.com/frontenac/guestservices/restaurants/lesaint-laurent.

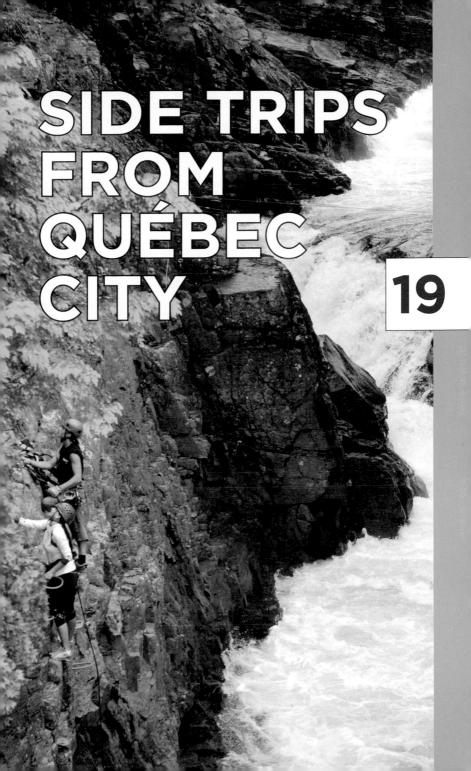

SIDE TRIPS FROM QUÉBEC CITY

19

The first four excursions described in this chapter can be combined into a day trip. Admittedly, it will be a morning-to-night undertaking, but the farthest of the four destinations is only 42km (26 miles) from Québec City. Bucolic **Île d'Orléans,** just over a bridge outside the city, is an unspoiled mini-oasis with farms, orchards, maple groves, and 18th- and 19th-century houses—another whole day, or weekend, if you wish. The waterfalls of **Montmorency** and **Canyon Ste-Anne** both make for dazzling fun, especially in the spring, when winter thaws make them thunder. The fourth destination, **Ste-Anne-de-Beaupré,** is home to one of Canada's most visited basilicas.

Further up the northern shore of the St. Lawrence River is the **Charlevoix region,** where the stunning expanse of the river, high-end inns, and a wide variety of outdoor activities, including whale-watching in summer and fall, invite an overnight stay.

Although it's preferable to drive in this region, there are tour-bus options to visit Montmorency Falls and the shrine of Ste-Anne-de-Beaupré, to circle Île d'Orléans, or to make the trek all the way up to **Tadoussac** for whale-watching cruises.

For more information, visit the Québec City website at **www.quebec region.com**. Prices listed for hotels in this chapter are the rack rate for double occupancy during the busy skiing and summer-vacation months, unless otherwise noted.

ÎLE D'ORLÉANS

16km (10 miles) NE of Québec City

Île d'Orléans was first inhabited by native people, and then settled by the French as one of their initial outposts of New France in the 17th century. Jacques Cartier had landed here in 1535 and first named the island Bacchus, in celebration of its many grapevines, but renamed it later to honor the duke of Orléans. Long isolated from the mainland, the island's 7,000 or so current residents firmly resist development, so far preventing the potential of becoming just another sprawling bedroom community. Many of the island's oldest houses are intact, and it remains a largely rural farming area. Notable are the many red-roofed homes.

Until 1935, the only way to get to Île d'Orléans was by boat (in summer) or over the ice in sleighs (in winter). The highway bridge built that year has allowed the island's fertile fields to become Québec City's primary market garden. During harvest periods, fruits and vegetables are picked fresh on the farms and trucked into the city daily.

In mid-July, hand-painted signs posted by the main road announce FRAISES: CUEILLIR VOUS-MÉME (STRAWBERRIES: YOU PICK 'EM). The same invitation to pick

PREVIOUS PAGE: **Climbers scale Canyon Ste-Anne.**

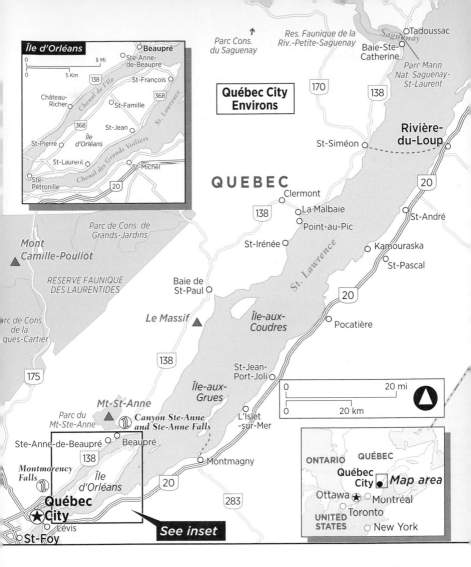

Île d'Orléans

0 ___ 5 Mi
0 ___ 5 Km

Beaupré
Ste-Anne-de-Beaupré
St-François
138
Château-Richer
St-Famille
368
St-Jean
368
St-Pierre
Île d'Orléans
Chenal de l'Île
St. Lawrence
Chenal des Grands Voiliers
St-Laurent
St-Michel
Ste-Pétronille
20

Québec City Environs

Parc Cons. du Saguenay
Res. Faunique de la Riv.-Petite-Saguenay
Saguenay
Tadoussac
Baie-Ste-Catherine
Parc Marin Nat. Saguenay-St-Laurent
170
138
Rivière-du-Loup
St-Siméon
20

QUEBEC

Clermont
138
La Malbaie
Point-au-Pic
St-André
St-Irénée
Kamouraska
St-Pascal
St. Lawrence
Parc de Cons. de Grands-Jardins
Baie de St-Paul
20
Mont Camille-Pouliot
RÉSERVE FAUNIQUE DES LAURENTIDES
Le Massif
Île-aux-Coudres
Pocatière
rc de Cons. de la ques-Cartier
138
St-Jean-Port-Joli
175
Île-aux-Grues
20 mi
0 ___ 20 km
Mt-St-Anne
Parc du Mt-Ste-Anne
Canyon Ste-Anne and Ste-Anne Falls
L'Islet-sur-Mer
Ste-Anne-de-Beaupré
Beaupré
138
Montmagny
Montmorency Falls
Île d'Orléans
20
Québec City
283
See inset
Lévis
St-Foy

ONTARIO
QUÉBEC
Québec City
Map area
Ottawa
Montréal
Toronto
UNITED STATES
New York

your own is made during apple season, August through October. Farmers hand out baskets and quote the price, and you pay when the basket's full. Bring along a bag or box to carry away the bounty. Other seasonal highlights include the visit of thousands of migrating snow geese, ducks, and Canada geese in April and May and again in late October. It's a spectacular sight when they launch in flapping hordes so thick that they almost blot out the sun. Late May also brings the blooming of the many apple trees on the island. Look for the cookbook *Farmers in Chef Hats* (www.farmersinchefhats.com), which in 2008 received a Gourmand World Cookbook award for "Best in the World" in the local-growers category. Featuring 50 products from Île d'Orléans, the bilingual cookbook has 50 recipes, as well as an agro-tourism map.

Essentials

GETTING THERE

BY CAR   The drive from Québec City to the island is short. Get on Autoroute 440 east, in the direction of Ste-Anne-de-Beaupré. In about 15 minutes, the Île d'Orléans bridge will be on your right. Take exit 325. If you'd like to hire a guide, **Maple Leaf Guide Services** (© 877/622-3677 or 418/622-3677; www.mapleleafservices.com) can provide one in your car or theirs. Biking over the bridge is not recommended, given the bridge's narrow and precarious pedestrian sidewalk. Cyclists who arrive with their bikes on the back of their cars can park at the tourist office for a small fee, or in any of the parking lots of the island's churches for free.

BY BUS   **Dupont,** which also goes by the name **Old Québec Tours** (© 800/267-8687 or 418/664-0460; www.tourdupont.com), offers a 4½-hour "countryside" tour that besides Île d'Orléans includes a visit to the Montmorency Falls, a "sugar shack" bakery (with maple-based products), Basilica of Sainte-Anne-de-Beaupré, and the Albert Gilles Copper Art Boutique and Museum—he's the artist who created the doors of the Basilica.

VISITOR INFORMATION

After arriving on the island, follow the "?" signs and turn right on Route 368 east toward Ste-Pétronille. The **Bureau d'Accueil Touristique,** or Tourist Information Center (© 866/941-9411 or 418/828-9411; www.iledorleans.com), is in the house on the right corner. Pick up the useful map that has most of the restaurants, farms, and accommodations marked. The bureau is open daily from about 9am to 5pm, with longer hours in the peak summer months and somewhat shorter hours in winter. Note that there are a limited number of restrooms on the island.

The tourist office offers a 2-hour English- or French-language audio tour on CD for sale (C$20), and has English-language brochures that detail a "Gourmet Route" driving tour, "Artists and Artisans" tour, and "Historic and Cultural Sites" tour. PDFs of the tours are available at the tourism website. A coast-hugging road—Route 368, also called chemin Royal and, in a few stretches, chemin de Bout-de-l'Île—circles the island, which is 34km (21 miles) long and 8km (5 miles) wide. Another couple of roads bisect the island. Farms and picturesque houses dot its east side, and abundant apple orchards enliven the west side.

The island has six tiny villages, originally established as parishes, and each has a church as its focal point. Some are stone churches that date from the days of the French regime, and with fewer than a dozen such churches left in all of the province of Québec, this is a particular point of pride for the islanders. It's possible to make a circuit of Île d'Orléans in a half-day, but you can justify a full day if you eat a good meal, visit a sugar shack, do a little gallery hopping, or just skip stones at the edge of the river. If you're strapped for time, loop around as far as St-Jean, and then drive across the island on route du Mitan ("Middle Road"). You'll get back to the bridge by turning left onto Route 368. Many of the attractions on the island are closed or have limited hours from October through May. This includes the historical venues, as well as the agricultural ones. Check before making a special trip for any one place. There are about 18 restaurants on the island, and as with the attractions, many have limited off-season hours.

Lodgings include *auberges,* with full-service restaurants open to nonguests, as well as B&Bs, also known as *gîtes* (homes with a few rooms available to travelers). You can see brief details about many of these offerings on the tourist office's

📎 AN IMPORTANT navigational NOTE

Street numbers on the ring road called chemin Royal start anew in each village. That means you could pass a no. 1000 chemin Royal in one stretch and then another no. 1000 chemin Royal a few minutes later. Be sure that you know not just the number of your destination, but also which village it's in.

website, **www.iledorleans.com**. Many lodgings also provide leaflets to the tourist office.

For much of the year, you can meander the roads of the island at 40kmph (25mph), pulling over only occasionally to let a car pass. There is no bike path, which means that bikers share the narrow rural roads. Both drivers and cyclists need to move with care in the busy summer months.

Ste-Pétronille

The first village reached on the recommended counterclockwise tour is Ste-Pétronille, only 3km (1¾ miles) from the bridge (take a right turn off the bridge). Note that in this village, Route 368, which is called chemin Royal on most of the rest of the island, is called chemin du Bout-de-l'Île.

When the British occupied the island in 1759, General James Wolfe had his headquarters here before launching his successful attack on Québec City. At the end of the 19th century, this parish was a top vacation destination for the Québécois. The village is now best known for its Victorian inn, **La Goéliche** (see below), and also claims North America's northernmost stand of **red oaks,** which dazzle in autumn. The houses were the summer homes of wealthy English in the 1800s, and the church dates from 1871. Many of the homes sport red roofs, which made for better visibility from the river, especially when traveling through rain or snow. Drive down to the water's edge to take in the view back to Québec City. One option is to turn right onto the small rue Horatio-Walker. The road goes past the former workshop of its namesake, a successful painter who spent his summers in Ste-Pétronille from the late 1800s to his death in 1938. Another option is to turn off at the sign for La Goéliche, the inn listed below. Adjacent to the property is a small public area with benches and views of Québec City.

For a light snack, the **Chocolaterie de l'Île d'Orléans,** 148 chemin du Bout-de-l'Île (© **418/828-2252**), sells soups, sandwiches, and pizzalike *tartes flambées;* the *saumon fumé* (smoked salmon) is good, along with homemade chocolates and ice cream. It's open daily May through early October; call for exact hours.

WHERE TO STAY & EAT

La Goéliche ★ On a rocky point of land at the southern tip of Île d'Orléans stands this romantic country inn and restaurant with a wraparound porch. The building is a replica of the 1880 Victorian house that stood here until a 1996 fire, which burned it to the ground. The new building re-creates the period flavor with tufted chairs, Tiffany-style lamps, and antiques. All rooms face the water, and first-floor units have small terraces. There are two apartments suitable for groups or longer stays. The river slaps at the foundation of the glass-enclosed terrace dining room, which is a grand observation point from which to watch cruise ships and Great Lakes freighters steaming past. Nonguests can come for breakfast, lunch, or dinner. A *goéliche,* by the way, is a small schooner; until the mid-1900s, they transferred goods from the river's shore to larger boats. 22 chemin du quai, Ste-Pétronille, PQ G0A 4C0. www.goeliche.ca. ☎ **888/511-2248** or 418/828-2248. Fax 418/828-2745. 16 units. C$188–C$333 double. Rates include breakfast. Packages available. AE, DC, MC, V. Free parking. **Amenities:** Restaurant; bar; babysitting; pool (unheated, outdoor). *In room:* Hair dryer, minibar (some rooms), Wi-Fi (free).

La Goéliche is a replica of the 1880 Victorian house.

St-Laurent

From Ste-Pétronille, continue on Route 368, which continues to be called chemin du Bout-de-l'Île in this village. There are a few restaurants and art galleries in this stretch, and bicycle rentals at **Ecolocyclo,** 1979 chemin Royal (☎ **418/828-0370;** www.ecolocyclo.net). After 7km (4¼ miles), you'll arrive at St-Laurent, founded in 1679, once a boat-building center turning out ships that could carry up to 5,300 tons for Glasgow ship owners. To learn about the town's maritime history, visit **Le Parc Maritime de St-Laurent** (☎ **418/828-9672;** www.parcmaritime.ca), an active boatyard from 1908 to 1967. Before the bridge was built, islanders journeyed across the river to Québec City by boat from here. The park offers demonstrations of the art of building flat-bottomed schooners. It's open daily from 10am to 5pm mid-June through mid-October. Admission is C$4 adults, free for children 12 and under.

WHERE TO STAY & EAT

Le Moulin de St-Laurent ★   A former flour mill that was in operation from 1720 to 1928, it's now one of the island's most romantic restaurants. Rubble-stone walls and hand-wrought beams form the interior with candlelight glinting off the hanging copper and brass pots. On a warm day, try for a table on the

---

📎 ÉCONOMUSEUMS: A LOCAL (TOURISM) tradition

The province of Québec is enamored of minimuseums, especially museums of food products. Called *économusées* or interpretation centers, they're often simply a room or two attached to a store. Usually, they display tools used in production and feature photographs and explanatory text in French and (usually) English. Examples include, on Île d'Orléans, Chocolaterie de l'Île d'Orléans in Ste-Pétronille (see above) and Cassis Monna et Filles in St-Pierre (see below); and in Québec City, Canadian Maple Delights and Choco-Musée Érico (both on p. 316). Designed both to educate and provide tourist oomph, they're rarely worth a visit on their own but usually provide a few minutes of interesting reading if you've stopped to shop. Many are listed at www.economusee.com.

shaded terrace beside a small waterfall. Lunch, which is served daily from 11:30am to 2:30pm, might be a quiche or a plate of assorted cheeses. Main courses at dinner range from C$16 to C$29. The menu changes every 3 or 4 weeks, but typically offers maple sirloin and a braised lamb shank. The restaurant is closed from November to April, but the owners rent six cottage chalets during the winter and 10 from spring to fall. Each has a fully equipped kitchen, and some have a fireplace and a washing machine.

754 chemin Royal (Rte. 368), St-Laurent, PQ G0A 3Z0. www.moulinstlaurent.qc.ca. (888/629-3888 or 418/829-3888. Fax 418/829-3716. 10 units. C$190–C$270 double. Rates include breakfast and dinner. In winter the lowest rate is C$100, in summer the highest rate for a unit, which can hold up to 12 people, is C$380, not including supper. Packages available. AE, DC, MC, V. Free parking. Pets allowed in some units for no additional charge. **Amenities:** Restaurant; pool (small outdoor heated pool in summer). *In room:* TV, kitchen.

Le Moulin de St-Laurent is one of Île d'Orléans most romantic restaurants.

St-Jean

St-Jean, 6km (3¾ miles) from St-Laurent, was home to sea captains—that might be why the houses in the village appear more luxurious than others on the island. The creamy-yellow "Scottish brick" in the facades of several of the homes was ballast in boats that came over from Europe and was considered a sign of luxury and wealth. The village **church** was built in 1734, and the walled **cemetery** is the final resting place of many fishermen and seafarers.

On the left as you enter St Jean is **Manoir Mauvide-Genest,** 1451 chemin Royal ((**418/829-2630;** www.manoirmauvidegenest.com). It was the manor home of a French surgeon who settled here in 1720 and went on to acquire much of the western part of the island, becoming one of New France's leading figures in the process. Jean Mauvide built this small estate in 1752, and the building is unlike any other on the island. It's filled with authentic and reproduction furnishings from Mauvide's era and is classified as a historic monument. It's open daily 10am to 5pm from mid-May to mid-October. Admission is C$6 for adults and C$2 for children 6 to 12, with an additional C$2 per person for a guided tour. Recently, an exhibit was added showcasing furniture related to the era of this monument, as well as a garden called Jardin Nouvelle France, which highlights the particularities of the manorial regime. You can get the MP3 audio tour for C$7. A gorgeous bed-and-breakfast option is **Dans les bras de Morphée,** 225 chemin Royal ((**418/829-3792;** www.danslesbrasdemorphee.com). The five-star B&B was awarded Grand Prize in 2009 in its category by the provincial tourist board. With just four rooms, it is a stunning country cottage in splendid style, at C$153 to C$162 for double occupancy. In low season the price can go down to C$120, but still includes breakfast.

If you're pressed for time, cross the island here to Ste-Famille, back near the bridge. Route du Mitan is marked (barely) with a small sign on the left just past the church in St-Jean. Even if you're continuing the full island loop, you might want to make a short detour to see the inland farmland and forest. To continue the tour, return to St-Jean and proceed east on Route 368.

St-François

St-François is at the island's most northeastern tip. Potatoes and leeks are grown on this part of the island, which lead some to dub this "the village of vichyssoise." The 9km (5½-mile) drive from St-Jean to St-François exposes vistas of the Laurentian Mountains on the other side of the river. **Mont Ste-Anne** can be seen on the opposite side of the river in the distance, its slopes scored by ski trails.

The St. Lawrence River is 10 times wider here than when it flows past Québec City and can be viewed especially well from the town's **observation tower,** which you'll pass on your right. You can park here and climb for a view. The town's original church from 1734 burned in 1988. It was replaced in 1992.

After you've looped around the island's northern edge, the road stops being Route 368 east and becomes Route 368 west.

Ste-Famille

Founded in 1661, Ste-Famille is the island's oldest parish. It's 8km (5 miles) from St-François. Across the road from its triple-spired church (1743) is the convent of **Notre-Dame Congregation,** founded in 1685 by Marguerite Bourgeoys, one of Montréal's prominent early citizens (for more about her, see p. 123).

Maison de Nos Aïeux, 3907 chemin Royal (✆ **418/829-0330;** www. fondationfrancoislamy.org), is a genealogy center with short films about some of the island's oldest families and information about its history. The adjacent **Parc des Ancêtres** is a riverside green space with picnic tables. Sharing the same parking lot is **Pub le Mitan,** 3887 chemin Royal (✆ **418/829-0408**), a microbrewery with a deck that overlooks the river. Other potential Ste-Famille stopping points in warm months are **Les Fromages de l'Îsle d'Orléans,** 4696 chemin Royal (✆ **418/829-0177**), an artisanal dairy that makes a 17th-century-style cheese called Paillasson, and the adjacent **Maison Drouin,** 4700 chemin Royal (✆ **418/829-0330;** www.fondationfrancoislamy. org), a beautifully preserved home from the 1730s that has never been modernized. It is the oldest house on the island open to visitors.

St-Pierre

When you reach St-Pierre, you're nearly back to where you started. If you haven't stopped at any orchards yet, consider popping into **Bilodeau,** 2200 chemin Royal (✆ **418/828-9316;** www.cidreriebilodeau.qc.ca). It's open

Bilodeau produces ciders and sweet wines.

daily 9am to 6pm year-round. It produces some of Île d'Orléans's regular ciders and *cidre de glace,* a sweet wine made from apples left on the trees until after the first frost. Visitors can sample products such as the yummy hazelnut-and-apple-syrup mustard, and guided tours are available. Apple picking is an option mid-August to mid-October.

Another wine option is the appealing **Cassis Monna et Filles,** 721 chemin Royal (📞 **418/828-2525;** www.cassismonna.com). Black currants, or *gadelle noire,* are grown here, and a chic shop features a display on how the berries are harvested and transformed into Crème de Cassis, the key element to a Kir cocktail. A variety of wines are available for tasting or purchase, next to the *économuseum.* It's open daily May to November 10am to 6pm (and until 7pm Saturdays and Sundays in June and every day from July through Nov). In season there is a charming cafe with a terrace where you can enjoy a light lunch. Sisters Catherine and Anne (les Filles) are usually around, if not in the adjacent fields.

St-Pierre's central attraction is its original church, the island's oldest (1717). Services are no longer held here, but there's a large **handicraft shop** in the back, behind the altar. This room (nondescript today) dates to 1695, making it even older than the church. Look for the stone church on your right (followed immediately by a larger, newer church) and a small blue-and-white sign for CORPORATION DES ARTISANS at 1249 chemin Royal. Although the church's front doors are locked, you can get inside for a viewing from an entrance at the shop. The shop is open most days May to October.

MONTMORENCY FALLS

11km (6¾ miles) NE of Québec City

Back on the mainland, the impressive **Montmorency Falls** are visible from Autoroute 440. At 83m (272 ft.) tall, they're 30m (98 ft.) higher than Niagara Falls—a boast no visitor is spared. These falls, however, are far narrower. They were named by Samuel de Champlain for his patron, the duke of Montmorency,

Cable cars provide views of Montmorency Falls.

to whom he dedicated his voyage of 1603. On summer nights, the plunging water is illuminated. Wednesdays and Saturdays from late July to mid-August, an international fireworks competition, **Les Grands Feux Loto-Québec,** is held at the falls (p. 31). In winter, there's a particularly impressive sight: The freezing spray sent up by crashing water builds a mountain of white ice at the base, nicknamed *pain de sucre* (sugarloaf). It grows as high as 30m (98 ft.) and attracts ice climbers, or you can simply come to observe. The yellow cast of the falls comes from the high iron content of the riverbed.

Essentials

GETTING THERE

BY BUS **Dupont,** which also goes by the name **Old Québec Tours** (✆ 800/267-8687 or 418/664-0460; www.tourdupont.com), offers tours to the falls.

BY CAR Take Autoroute 440 east out of Québec City. After 10 minutes, watch for exit 325 for the falls and the parking lot. If you miss the exit, you'll see the falls on your left and will be able to make a legal U-turn.

Viewing the Falls

The falls are surrounded by the provincial **Parc de la Chute-Montmorency** (✆ 800/665-6527 or 418/663-3330; www.sepaq.com/montmorency), where visitors can take in the view and have a picnic. The grounds are accessible year-round.

Montmorency Falls ★ ☺ There are a couple ways to see the 83m (272-ft.) falls. A path from the lower parking area leads to the base of the falls, where the water comes crashing down. The view is spectacular from here in all seasons. Stairs ascend from here to the top, with viewing platforms along the way. At the top, a footbridge spans the water where it flows over the cliff. If you don't want to walk, a cable car runs from the parking lot to a terminal alongside the falls, with a pathway that leads close the water's edge. At that top terminal is **Manoir Montmorency,** a villa that contains an interpretation center, a cafe, and a restaurant. The dining room and porch have a side view of the falls; reservations are suggested. Parking is available at the top of the falls by the villa, too.

2490 av. Royale, Beauport. ✆ **800/665-6527** or 418/663-3330. www.sepaq.com/montmorency. Free admission to the falls. Round-trip fare on the cable car C$9.99 adults, C$4.61 children 6–17, free for children 5 and under. Parking C$9.50. Cable car operates mid-Apr to Oct and late Dec to early Jan daily, Feb to mid Apr weekends.

STE-ANNE-DE-BEAUPRÉ

33km (21 miles) NE of Québec City; 22km (14 miles) NE of Montmorency Falls

The village of Ste-Anne-de-Beaupré is a religious destination, centered around a two-spired basilica that is one of Canada's most famous shrines. Some 1.5 million people make the pilgrimage each year to the complex.

Legend has it that French mariners were sailing up the St. Lawrence River in the 1650s when they ran into a terrifying storm. They prayed to their patroness, St. Anne, to save them, and when they survived, they dedicated a wooden chapel to her on the north shore of the St. Lawrence, near the site of their perils. Not long afterward, a chapel laborer was said to have been cured of lumbago, the first of many documented miracles. Since that time, believers have made their

A million-and-a-half people make the pilgrimage each year to Ste-Anne-de-Beaupré basilica.

way here to pay their respects to St. Anne, mother of the Virgin Mary and grandmother of Jesus.

Route 138 travels along the river, which is tidal. At low tide, the beach can become speckled with hundreds of birds, such as purple sandpipers, pecking for food. Look for them behind the houses, gas stations, and garages that pepper the road.

Essentials

GETTING THERE

BY BUS **Dupont,** also called **Old Québec Tours** (☎ **800/267-8687** or 418/664-0460; www.tourdupont.com), offers a country tour that includes a visit to Ste-Anne-de-Beaupré.

BY CAR Autoroute 440 turns into Autoroute 40 at Montmorency Falls and then becomes Route 138 almost immediately. Continue on Route 138 to Ste-Anne-de-Beaupré. The church and exit are visible from the road.

A Religious Tour

Basilica and Shrine of Ste-Anne-de-Beaupré ★ The towering basilica that dominates this small village is the most recent building raised here in St. Anne's honor. After the French sailors' first modest wooden chapel (1658) was swept away by a flood, another chapel was built on higher ground. Floods, fires, and the ravages of time dispatched later buildings, until a larger structure was erected in 1887. In 1926, it, too, lay in ruins, gutted by fire. The present basilica is constructed in stone, following an essentially neo-Romanesque scheme, and was consecrated on July 4, 1976.

Inside the front doors, look for the two columns dressed with racks of canes—presumably from people cured of their ailments and no longer in need of assistance—that go 9m (30 ft.) high. There are several Masses per day, and in the summer, daily outdoor candlelight processions at 8:15pm.

Other parts of the shrine complex include the **Scala Santa Chapel** (1891); the **Memorial Chapel** (1878), with a bell tower and altar from the late 17th and early 18th centuries, respectively; and the **Way of the Cross,** which is lined with life-size bronze figures depicting Christ's life. There's also a church store and the **Musée Sainte-Anne,** a small facility housing paintings and sculptures. The church runs the **Auberge de La Basilique** for visiting pilgrims. Double-occupancy rooms cost C$60.

The basilica and town are particularly busy on Ste-Anne's Novena (July 17–25) and Ste-Anne's Feast Day (July 26), days of saintly significance.

10018 av. Royale, Ste-Anne-de-Beaupré. ☎ **418/827-3781.** www.ssadb.qc.ca. Free admission to basilica and chapels; admission to museum C$3 adults, free for children 5 and under. May to mid-Oct daily basilica 7am–8pm, museum 9:30am–4:30pm (open only to groups by reservation mid-Oct to May).

CANYON STE-ANNE, STE-ANNE FALLS & PARC DU MONT STE-ANNE

42km (26 miles) NE of Québec City; about 9km (5½ miles) NE of Ste-Anne-de-Beaupré

After Ste-Anne-de-Beaupré, the road enters into thick evergreen woods, and the frenetic pace of urban life begins to slip away. A short drive off Route 138 is Canyon Ste-Anne, a deep gorge and powerful waterfall created by the Ste-Anne-du-Nord River. Unseen from the main road, the canyon and its falls are an exhilarating attraction. A bit inland is the Parc du Mont Ste-Anne, which surrounds an 800m-high (2,625-ft.) peak. In winter, it's the area's busiest ski mountain, while summertime invites camping, hiking, and biking.

Birders will want to visit the **Cap Tourmente National Wildlife Area** (℃ **418/827-4591**; www.followthegeese.com), on the coast of the St. Lawrence River. Over 300 species of birds have been seen here, but it's the great snow geese who are the stars. During migration season, usually late April to mid-May and early October into mid-November, tens of thousands of geese stop at the cape, making it an important ornithological site. Naturalists lead walks through the marshes. It's open daily mid-April through October and January to mid-March. Watch for the sign on Route 138.

Essentials

GETTING THERE

BY BUS From mid-November until late April, the **Taxi Coop Québec** (℃ **418/525-5191**; www.taxicoop-quebec.com) shuttle service picks up passengers at Québec City hotels in the morning to take them to Parc Mont Ste-Anne, returning them to Québec City in the late afternoon.

BY CAR Continue along Route 138 from Ste-Anne-de-Beaupré. To get to the waterfalls and other destinations in this chapter, stay on Route 138. A marked entrance to the falls will be on your left. To get to the park and ski mountain, exit onto Route 360 east. Château Mont Sainte-Anne (see below) will be on your left, with the entrance to the park directly after it.

Outdoor Fun

Canyon Ste-Anne Waterfalls ★★★ ☺ These falls don't get the attention that the Montmorency Falls do. Perhaps it's because they're a little further out and tucked into the woods, but it's a shame—they're spectacular and kitsch-free. Follow the narrow driveway from Route 138 to a parking lot, picnic grounds, and a building containing a cafeteria, a gift shop, and the ticket booth. The falls are a 10-minute walk from the entrance, although an open-sided shuttle bus also drives visitors to the top of the falls. Trails go down both sides to the bottom. Part of the excitement comes from the approach: You hear the falls before you see them, and you step out of the woods practically beside them. Three (optional) footbridges go directly across the water. The first crosses the narrow river just before the water starts to drop. The second, and most thrilling, crosses right over the canyon, from the top of the rock walls that drop straight down. Being so close to the thundering, unending force crashing over massive rocks is likely to induce vertigo in even the most stable of nerves. The final suspension bridge is at the gorge's base, just 9m (30 ft.) or so above the water where the river flattens out

again. The very, very brave hearted can ride a zip line or walk a rope bridge across the canyon harnessed onto a cable wire.

The falls are 74m (243 ft.) high and at their most awe-inspiring in the spring, when melt-off of winter snows bloats the rivers above and sends 100,000 liters (more than 26,000 gal.) of water over *per second.* (The volume drops to 10,000L/2,600 gal. per second in Aug–Sept.) So voluminous is the mist coming from the fall that it creates another wall of miniwaterfalls on the side of the gorge. From 1904 to 1965, the river was used to float logs from lumbering operations, and part of the dramatic gorge was created by dynamiting in 1917, to reduce the amount of literal logjams.

Footbridges cross the river above the Canyon Ste-Anne Waterfalls.

Along the trails are platforms that jut over the water and well-written information plaques. Management has wisely avoided commercial intrusions along the trails, letting the powerful natural beauty speak for itself. Those who have difficulty walking can see the falls without going too far from the bus. Those with a fear of heights can stay on the side trails, strolling amid the poplar trees and away from the bridges altogether. A visit takes about 1½ hours.

206 Rte. 138 East, Beaupré. ✆ **418/827-4057.** www.canyonsa.qc.ca. Admission C$12 adults, C$8.50 children 13–17, C$5.50 children 6–12, free children 5 and under. May to late Oct daily 9am–4:30pm (until 5:30pm June 24 to Labour Day). Hours subject to change due to weather, so call to confirm.

Parc du Mont Ste-Anne ★ ☺ The area's premier wilderness resort surrounds an 800m-high (2,625-ft.) peak and is an outdoor-enthusiast's dream. In winter, **downhill skiing** on Mont Ste-Anne is terrifically popular. Just 40 minutes from Québec City, this is the region's largest and busiest mountain. There are 66 trails on three sides, and about a third of the resort is expert terrain. At night, 17 trails are lit. During low season (before Christmas Eve and after first week of Jan), 1-day lift tickets for adults are C$64, seniors C$54, children 13 to 17 C$51, and children 7 to 12 C$34. During high season (Christmas holiday season), adult prices are C$69, seniors C$57, children 13 to 17 C$55, and children 7 to 12 C$37.

Also in the winter, the park offers Canada's largest network of **cross-country skiing** trails—208km (129 miles) of them. A day ticket is C$23 adults, C$18 seniors, C$17 children 13 to 17, C$12 children 7 to 12, and free for children 6 and under. There are seven heated shelters along trails, including three for overnights. Other winter options include **snowshoeing, dog sledding, ice canyoning,** and **winter paragliding.** From mid-November to late April, **Autobus Les Tours de Vieux-Québec Inc./Tours Dupont** (✆ **418/664-0640;** www.tours vieuxquebec.com/en/page/city-and-country-tours) provides daily shuttle service from Québec City.

Parc du Mont Ste-Anne has 66 trails for skiers.

In summer and early fall, Mont Ste-Anne is especially well known for its huge network of trails for both hard-core **mountain biking** and milder day-tripping (bikes can be rented). It has grown to be the most prominent network of mountain bike trails in eastern Canada, and in 2010, it hosted the UCI Mountain Bike and Trials World Championships. The park also offers **camping, hiking,** and **golfing** in summer. A panoramic **gondola** operates daily from late June to early September, weather permitting. Details about these activities are listed on the Mont Ste-Anne website.

2000 boul. Beau-Pré, Beaupré. ℭ **888/827-4579** or 418/827-4561. www.mont-sainte-anne. com. Admission C$5.27 adults, C$3.51 children 7–17; C$11 families (in car). Gondola tickets C$18 adults, C$17 seniors, C$15 children 7–17, free for children 6 and under; a variety of family rates.

WHERE TO STAY & EAT

Auberge La Camarine ★ Quirky bedrooms full of personality and bathed in sunny, Provençal yellows and blues are uniformly roomy. More than half have wood-burning fireplaces. Normally, units facing the St-Lawrence River would have the most appeal, but given the inn's locale just above busy Route 138, backside rooms such as nos. 43 and 49, which face quiet fields, are more relaxing. The kitchen is solid, providing options for three-, five-, and seven-course dinners. In summer, an outdoor terrace is available for all three meals a day for guests and nonguests.

10947 boul. Ste-Anne (Rte. 138), Beaupré, PQ GOA 1E0. www.camarine.com. ℭ **800/567-3939** or 418/827-5703. Fax 418/827-5430. 31 units. C$99–C$139 double. Packages available. AE, DC, MC, V. Free parking. **Amenities:** Restaurant. *In room:* A/C (some rooms), TV, hair dryer, Wi-Fi (free).

There are plenty of ways to relax at Château Mont Sainte-Anne.

Château Mont Sainte-Anne ★ ☺ Set into the base of its namesake mountain and Parc du Mont Ste-Anne, this resort provides the closest lodging for all mountain activities. In the winter, it has ski-in-ski-out accessibility at the base of the gondola lift. In summer, the mountain's internationally regarded network of mountain biking trails and 18-hole, par 72 golf course bring brisk business. Units have either kitchenettes or full kitchens. The older units are called "Standard," while the newer, sleek ones go by the name "Nordik."

500 boul. Beau-Pré, Beaupré, PQ G0A 1E0. www.chateaumsa.ca. ☎ **800/463-4467** or 418/827-5211. Fax 418/827-5072. 237 units. C$119–C$219 double. Packages available. AE, DC, DISC, MC, V. Free parking. Pets accepted (in some units). **Amenities:** Restaurant; bar; exercise room; golf courses; Jacuzzis; pools (large outdoor, small indoor); sauna. *In room:* A/C, TV, hair dryer, kitchenette, Wi-Fi (free).

CENTRAL CHARLEVOIX: BAIE-ST-PAUL, ST-IRÉNÉE & LA MALBAIE

Baie-St-Paul: 93km (58 miles) NE of Québec City; St-Irénée: 125km (78 miles) NE of Québec City; La Malbaie: 140km (87 miles) NE of Québec City

The Laurentian mountains move closer to the shore of the St. Lawrence River as they approach the mouth of the intersecting Malbaie River. U.S. President William Howard Taft, who had a summer residence in the area, said that the air here was "as intoxicating as champagne, but without the morning-after headache." Taft was among the political and financial elite of Canada and the eastern U.S. who made Murray Bay, or La Malbaie, a wildly popular vacation destination in the early and mid-19th century. The Charlevoix region (**www.tourisme-charlevoix.com**) first blossomed under the British regime in the 18th century. In 1762, Scottish officers in the British Army, John Nairne and Malcolm Fraser, built sawmills and flour mills here. They attracted French-speaking Catholics, making the region a combination of Old France and Old Scotland.

Grand vistas over the St. Lawrence abound, and there are many farms in the area. Moose sightings are not uncommon, and the rolling, dark green mountains with their white ski slope scars offer numerous places to hike and bike in the warm months and ski when there's snow. (It's not unheard of for it to snow in May.) In 1988, Charlevoix was named a UNESCO World Biosphere Reserve, which means that it's a protected area for cross-disciplinary conservation-oriented research, with development balanced against environmental concerns. It was one of the first populated areas to get the designation.

Because of the area's raw, undeveloped beauty, a group of entrepreneurs has been developing big plans to build an "anti-resort" in the area, a year-round destination that could hold large international events and become what they've termed "a type of Davos of sustainable tourism development." Called the Massif de Charlevoix project, it's led by Daniel Gauthier, a co-founder of Cirque du Soleil and owner since 2002 of the ski resort **Le Massif** (p. 341).

Essentials

GETTING THERE

BY CAR   Take Route 138 to Baie-St-Paul. Turn onto Route 362 to go into downtown Baie-St-Paul. To continue northeast, you have the option of taking either Route 138 or the smaller, more scenic Route 362, which travels closer to the water and lets you visit St-Irénée on the way to La Malbaie.

VISITOR INFORMATION

Baie-St-Paul has a year-round **tourist office** directly on Route 138 (✆ **800/667-2276** or 418/665-4454) that's open daily from 9am to 4pm, and until 7pm in the summer. It's on a dramatic hill approaching the village and is well marked from the highway. (Beware, though: It's an extremely sharp turnoff.) Stop here for one of the grandest vistas of the river and town below.

There are two other tourism offices: in downtown Baie-St-Paul at 6 rue St-Jean-Baptiste, and in La Malbaie on the water at 495 boul. de Comporté, Route 362. Regional information is also available at **www.tourisme-charlevoix.com**.

Baie-St-Paul

The main town in Charlevoix is Baie-St-Paul, an attractive, funky community of 7,317 that continues to earn its century-old reputation as an artists' retreat. Some two dozen boutiques and galleries, and a couple of small museums, show the works of local painters and artisans. Given the setting, it isn't surprising that many of the artists are landscapists, but other styles and subjects are represented, too. Work runs the gamut from hobbyist to highly professional. Options include the **Maison de René Richard,** 58 rue St-Jean-Baptiste (✆ **418/435-5571**), which celebrates the Swiss-born artist who made Baie-St-Paul his home until his 1982 death. Richard painted many of his well-regarded semiabstract landscapes here.

During July and August, downtown can get thick with tourists, filling the main street with bumper-to-bumper traffic. Try to avoid driving in midday. Or pop off the mainland entirely to the small island of Isle-aux-Coudres ("Island of Hazelnuts") for some **bicycling.** The island is accessible by free 15-minute car ferry. Popular paths offer a 23km (14-mile) island loop. From May to October, single bikes, tandems, and quadricycles for up to six adults and two small children can be rented from **Vélo-Coudres** (✆ 418/438-2118; www.charlevoix. qc.ca/velocoudres). The island also has a smattering of boutiques and hotels. The

Baie-St-Paul's outdoor scenery makes it popular with landscape painters.

ferry leaves from the town of St. Joseph-de-la-Rive, along Route 362 just east of Baie-St-Paul.

In winter, the area's largest ski mountain is **Le Massif** (© **877/536-2774** or 418/632-5876; www.lemassif.com). Located in Petite-Rivière-St-François, about 23km (14 miles) south of Baie-St-Paul, it's a growing powerhouse. Its fans wax rhapsodic over its Zen qualities, including quiet ski lifts and runs that give the illusion of heading directly into the adjacent St. Lawrence river, and healthy food options. It has 52 runs, including one that's 4.8km (3 miles). A day ticket is C$64 adults, C$53 seniors, C$48 children 13 to 17, C$35 children 7 to 12, and free for children 6 and under. There's a daily shuttle bus from Québec City to the mountain.

Cirque du Soleil co-founder Daniel Gauthier owns Le Massif and has been working for years to develop both the ski operations and the outlying area. Marketing materials for his Groupe Le Massif call it the largest tourism project in the province. The plan is to build a 150-room hotel; another 400 rooms in a combination of condos, inns, and even yurts at the base of the mountain (and potentially another 50 at the summit); a 500-seat multipurpose venue; a train station in Baie-St-Paul; and finally to build and refurbish an existing railroad track to connect Baie-St-Paul to Petite-Rivière to Québec City. The budget for the project is C$230 million. Trains started carrying passengers September 2011 (return trips from Québec City to La Malbaie cost C$249 for adults, C$199 children 6 to 17 years old, free for kids 5 and under). A lunch is served on the way to the resort, and a four-course dinner on the return journey. The full project is expected to be in place in 2013; go to www.lemassif.com for more info.

Gauthier calls the region "a place where tranquility and energy coexist in perfect harmony." That's true. He also says that the project is necessary for the long-term survival of his mountain. That may be true, too. Whether he'll achieve the second without soiling the first is the essential question. Locals are watching with great interest and more than a little nervousness.

WHERE TO STAY

La Maison Otis   Right in the heart of Baie-St-Paul, with a long porch that fronts the colorful main street, Otis is a rambling collection of connecting buildings with rooms that offer fireplaces, whirlpools, and four-poster beds. In the hotel is Mon Ami Alex, a bistro that serves regional fare. Attached to the hotel is a **spa** with a large offering of massage services and facials, **Café des Artistes** (see below), and a **cabaret** (www.lecafedesartistes.com/cabaret.htm) open some Fridays and Saturdays.

23 rue St-Jean-Baptiste, Baie-St-Paul, PQ G3Z 1M2. www.maisonotis.com. © **800/267-2254** or 418/435-2255. Fax 418/435-2464. 36 units. C$122–C$207 double; C$237–C$262 suite. Packages available. MC, V. Free parking. **Amenities:** 2 restaurants; bar; pool (small, indoor); spa. *In room:* A/C, TV/DVD player, hair dryer, MP3 docking station, Wi-Fi (free).

WHERE TO EAT

Foodies should consider visits to some of the region's unique food producers. **La Ferme Basque de Charlevoix,** 813 rue St-Edouard in St-Urbain, just west of Baie-St-Paul (© **418/639-2246;** www.lafermebasque.ca), is a small-scale family farm that raises ducks and makes foie gras sold throughout the province. Tours are C$4 adults. **La Maison d'Affinage Maurice Dufour,** 1339 boul. Mgr-de-Lavel/Rte. 138, Baie-St-Paul (© **418/435-5692;** www.fromagefin.com), is a *fromagerie* that makes Le Ciel de Charlevoix, an artisanal cheese that is a highlight of the region (and 2009 champion in the *Grand prix des fromages Canadiens,* or Canadian Cheese Grand Prix).

Café des Artistes   The hotel La Maison Otis runs this appealing bistro. Pizzas with wafer-thin crusts are exceptional, and there are 15 types to choose from. Other options include the pâté du jour, Hot-Dogs Français, and paninis. The cafe does good business with locals and artist types. Because it's small and features a bar, patrons must be at least 18 years old.

25 rue St-Jean-Baptiste, Baie-St-Paul. ℂ **418/435-5585.** www.lecafedesartistes.com. Main courses C$8–C$14. MC, V. Daily 11:30am–10pm.

Le St-Pub   A casual restaurant that's part of the town's *microbrasserie,* or micro-breweries. There's always a selection of over a dozen brews made on-site, and visitors sometimes get to try test beverages. The kitchen serves up solid renditions of bar food, Québécois-style, and specialties include barbecue chicken and concoctions cooked with beer (beer-and-onion soup, lamb burger marinated in beer, chocolate-and-stout pudding, sugar pie with beer). There's a patio in summer.

2 rue Racine, Baie-St-Paul. ℂ **418/240-2332.** Main courses C$11–C$25; table d'hôte C$23–C$30. MC, V. Daily 11:30am–8pm.

St-Irénée

From Baie-St-Paul, take Route 362 northeast toward La Malbaie. The air is scented by sea salt and rent by the shrieks of gulls, and the road roller-coasters over bluffs above the river, with wooded hills and well-kept villages. This stretch, from Baie-St-Paul to La Malbaie, is one of the most scenic in the entire region and is dubbed the **Route du Fleuve,** or "River Route." It can be treacherous in icy weather, though, so in colder months, opt for the flatter Rte. 138.

In 32km (about 20 miles) is St-Irénée, a cliff-top hamlet of just 704 year-round residents. Apart from the setting, the best reason for dawdling here is the 60-hectare (148-acre) property and estate of **Domaine Forget** (ℂ **888/336-7438** or 418/452-3535; www.domaineforget.com). The facility is a performing-arts center for music and dance, and offers an **International Festival** from mid-June through early September. Concerts are staged in a 604-seat concert hall, with **Sunday musical brunches** on an outdoor terrace that has spectacular views of the river. The program emphasizes classical music with solo instrumentalists and chamber groups, but is peppered with jazz and dance. Most tickets are C$22 to C$42. From September to May, Domaine **rents its student dorms** to the general public. They're clean and well-appointed studios, with cooking areas and beds for two to five people. They start at C$65 for double occupancy, with discounts for longer stays.

Kayaking eco-tours from a half-day to 5 days can be arranged through several companies in the area. **Katabatik** (ℂ **800/453-4850** or 418/665-2332; www.katabatik.ca), based in La Malbaie, offers trips that combine kayaking with education about the bays of the St. Lawrence estuary. A half-day tour costs C$55 adults, C$44 children 12 to 15, and C$36 children 5 to 11. Tours start at various spots along the coast and are in operation from March to October.

La Malbaie

From St-Irénée, Route 362 starts to bend west after 10km (6¼ miles), as the mouth of the Malbaie River starts to form. La Malbaie (or Murray Bay, as it was called by the wealthy Anglophones who made this their resort of choice from the Gilded Age through the 1950s) is the collective name of five former municipalities: Pointe-au-Pic, Cap-à-l'Aigle, Rivière-Malbaie, Ste-Agnès, and St-Fidèle. At its center is a small, scenic bay. The 8,930 inhabitants of the region justifiably wax poetic about their wildlife and hills and trees, the place where the sea meets the sky.

A CASINO & A MUSEUM

Casino de Charlevoix   Established in 1994, the casino's cherry-wood paneling and granite floors enclose about 950 slot machines and two dozen tables, including Texas Hold 'Em, blackjack, and baccarat. Poker tournaments are held regularly. A 200-seat bar has live pop music on Friday and Saturday nights. Visitors must 18 years old. The casino is just steps from the **Fairmont Le Manoir Richelieu** hotel (see below).

183 av. Richelieu (follow the many signs). ℭ **800/665-2274** or 418/665-5300. www.casino-de-charlevoix.com. Free admission (18 and over only). Daily 11am–midnight (extended hours in summer and on weekends).

Musée de Charlevoix ★   A terrific little museum. One of the three gallery spaces is devoted to a marvelous permanent exhibition called "Appartenances" ("Belonging") about the history and culture of Charlevoix. Included are photographs from the 1930s of beluga whale-hunting and frontierswomen skinning eels, artifacts from the Manoir Richelieu before its major fire in 1928, and folk art from the 1930s and 1940s. Descriptive text in English and French is engaging and thorough.

10 chemin du Havre (at the corner of Rte. 362). ℭ **418/665-4411.** www.museedecharlevoix.qc.ca. Admission C$7 adults, C$5 seniors and students, free for children 11 and under. June to mid-Oct daily 9am–5pm; mid-Oct to May Mon–Fri 10am–5pm, Sat–Sun 1–5pm.

WHERE TO STAY & EAT

Fairmont Le Manoir Richelieu ★★★ ☺   The region's grand resort. Since 1899, there has been a hotel at the river's edge here, first serving those who summered in this aristocratic haven with spectacular views of the St. Lawrence River. After waves of renovations, the decor of the hotel long dubbed the "Castle on the Cliff" is reminiscent of its posh heritage, and many rooms meet deluxe standards. The golf course is a glorious 27-hole expanse overlooking the river on one side and Charlevoix's hills and mountains on the other. In winter, snowmobile rentals are available to use on the area's extensive network of trails. Guests run the gamut, from young couples and families to gamers from the casino next door and older folks who have been coming here forever.

181 rue Richelieu, La Malbaie, PQ G5A 1X7. www.fairmont.com/richelieu. ℭ **866/540-4464** or 418/665-3703. Fax 418/665-8131. 405 units. June–Oct from C$179 double, Nov–May from

The Fairmont Le Manoir Richelieu offers traditional opulence.

C$159 double; year-round from C$379 suite. Packages available. AE, DC, DISC, MC, V. Valet parking C$22, free self-parking. Pets accepted (C$25 per pet per day). **Amenities:** 3 restaurants (confirm in off season); 2 bars; babysitting; children's programs; concierge; executive-level rooms; golf club; health club; 2 pools (indoor and outdoor); room service; spa; watersports equipment. *In room:* A/C, TV, hair dryer, minibar, Wi-Fi (C$15 per day).

La Pinsonnière ★★★   Romance with a princely touch are on offer at this understated, intimate hideaway. The six deluxe rooms of this Relais & Châteaux inn are the most spectacular, with stunning vistas of the St. Lawrence River. They deliver a serious "wow" factor and offer the most transporting visit, with private terraces and bathrooms with oversized whirlpools, private saunas, and/or steam showers. These new rooms have a contemporary, clean decor. Older rooms are classic Queen Anne and face gardens and the front driveway. An indoor pool, unspoiled river beach at the base of the property, small on-site spa, and attentive service make this tiny resort a regional star. Dinners featuring local products are extravagant, with a la carte options and three discovery menus. Wines are a particular point of pride, with 750 labels in the 12,000-bottle cellar.

124 rue St-Raphaël, La Malbaie, PQ G5A 1X9. www.lapinsonniere.com. ⓒ **800/387-4431** or 418/665-4431. Fax 418/665-7156. 18 units. May–Oct and holiday season C$345–C$495 double; rest of year C$295–C$445 double. Packages available. Minimum 2-night stay on weekends, 3 nights on holiday weekends. AE, MC, V. Free parking. **Amenities:** Restaurant; bar; babysitting; concierge; health club nearby; pool (heated, indoor); room service; spa. *In room:* A/C, TV, fireplace in select rooms, hair dryer, minibar, Wi-Fi (free).

UPPER CHARLEVOIX: ST-SIMÉON, BAIE STE-CATHERINE & TADOUSSAC

St-Siméon: 173km (107 miles) NE of Québec City; Baie Ste-Catherine: 207km (128 miles) NE of Québec City; Tadoussac: 214km (133 miles) NE of Québec City

After visiting La Malbaie, you have several options. You can return back to Québec City the same way you came—it's only 140km (87 miles) along the river's north shore. Or you can continue up Route 138 for 33km (21 miles) to St-Siméon and cross the St. Lawrence by ferry, landing at Rivière-du-Loup on the opposite shore a little over an hour later to return to Québec City along the river's south shore.

But if it's summer or early fall, and you have more time—a full afternoon or an extra day to stay overnight—consider continuing on to Baie Ste-Catherine and Tadoussac. Here, at the northern end of Charlevoix, is one of the world's richest areas for **whale-watching.** The confluence of the St. Lawrence and Saguenay rivers attracts 10 to 12 species each summer—as many as 1,500 minke, humpback, finback, and blue whales, who join the 1,000 or so sweet-faced beluga (or white) whales who are here year-round. Add to that the harbor porpoises who visit, and there can be 5,000 creatures diving and playing in the waters. Many can be seen from land mid-June through late October, and up close by boat or kayak.

Springtime comes to this area in May and June—yellow forsythia in May, lilacs in June. *Note:* In winter and spring, when the whales are gone and the temperatures are lower, most of the very few establishments between

The northern end of Charlevoix is one of the world's richest areas for whale-watching.

St-Siméon and Tadoussac are closed. If you're driving, pack some snacks and water, take bathroom breaks when they're available, and make sure you've got enough gasoline.

Essentials

GETTING THERE

BY CAR Route 138 leads to both the ferry at St-Siméon and to the northern end of Charlevoix, at Baie Ste-Catherine. The highway dead-ends at the dramatic Saguenay River, with the town of Tadoussac just across the river. There is a free car ferry for the 10-minute passage.

VISITOR INFORMATION

St-Siméon maintains a **seasonal tourist office** at 494 rue St-Laurent, open daily from 10am to 6pm between mid-June and Labour Day. More information about the area is online at **www.tourisme-charlevoix.com**.

St-Siméon

St-Siméon is where you can pick up the ferry that crosses the St. Lawrence to return to Québec City along the river's south shore. *Note:* The ferry is out of service through mid-June 2011. After mid-June, confirm the schedule at www.traverserdl.com or ✆ **418/638-2856.** Ferry capacity is 100 cars, and boarding is on a first-come, first-served basis. One-way fares are C$40 for a car, C$16 adults, C$14 seniors, C$11 children 5 to 11, and free for children 4 and under. Voyages take about 1 hour. Even though this isn't a whale-watching cruise, you may enjoy a sighting from late June to September, when whales are active.

Baie Ste-Catherine & Tadoussac

Teeny Baie Ste-Catherine (pop. 211) sits at the meeting point of the St. Lawrence River and the Saguenay River, which comes down from the northwest. It is at the northern end of the Charlevoix region. Tadoussac (pop. 850), just across the Saguenay, is the southernmost point of the Manicouagan region. Tadoussac is known as "the Cradle of New France." Established in the 1600s, it's the oldest permanent European settlement north of Florida and became a stop on the fur-trading route. Missionaries stayed until the middle of the 19th century. The hamlet might have vanished soon after had a resort hotel, now called **Hôtel Tadoussac** (see below), not been built in 1864. In those days, a steamship line brought wealthy vacationers from Montréal and points west, and deposited them here for stays that often lasted all summer. Apart from the hotel, there's not much in Tadoussac besides a whaling educational center (see below), a boardwalk, and some small motels. This is raw country, where the sight of a beaver waddling up the hill from the ferry terminal is met with only mild interest.

Route 138 dead-ends at the Saguenay River and picks up again on the other side. Passage is courtesy of a free 10-minute car ferry (© **418/235-4395;** www. traversiers.gouv.qc.ca). In summer, there are departures every 13 minutes between 8am and 8pm, and every 20, 40, or 60 minutes the other 12 hours and in low season. The ferry is the reason that trucks travel in convoys on the highway—they pour out in groups after each ferry crossing.

The vista on the crossing is dramatic and nearly worth a trip to Tadoussac on its own. Palisades with evergreens poking out of rock walls rise sharply from both shores. So extreme is the natural architecture that the area is often referred to as a fjord.

WHALE-WATCHING

From mid-May to mid-October, there are many options to see whales or cruise the majestic Saguenay River. Companies use different sizes and types of watercraft, from stately catamarans and cruisers that carry up to 500 to powered inflatables called Zodiacs that carry 10 to 25 passengers. The larger boats have snack bars and naturalists onboard to describe the action, and options to sit at tables inside or ride the observation bowsprit, high above the waves. Zodiacs are more maneuverable, darting about at each sighting to get closer to the rolling and breaching behemoths. Zodiac passengers are issued life jackets and waterproof overalls, but expect to get wet. It's cold out there, so layers and gloves are a good idea.

Two of the biggest companies are **Croisières AML** (© **866/856-6668;** www.croisieresaml.com) and **Group Dufour** (© **800/463-5250;** www.dufour. ca). Both offer departures from wharves in both Baie Ste-Catherine and Tadoussac (other companies send tours out of St-Siméon, to the south). In high season, each offers about three daily whale-watching trips. Fares are comparable: 3-hour tours on the larger boats cost about C$69 adults, C$64 seniors and students, C$32 children 6 to 12, and free for children 5 and under. Two-hour Zodiac trips cost C$59 adults, C$54 seniors and students, and C$44 children 8 to 12; children younger than 8 and/or shorter than 1.4m (4½ feet) are not permitted. For Zodiac tours enquire within. Check with each company for exact times, prices, and trip options. Children may also like the interactive online Blue Museum, at www.museebleu.ca/en.

Kayak trips that search out whales are available from **Mer et Monde Ecotours** (© **866/637-6663** or 418/232-6779; www.mer-et-monde.qc.ca). Visitors report that they *felt* the whales before they saw them—imagine being out from the shore and feeling a vibration under the kayak hull! The company is based in Les Bergeronnes, a coastal town 20km (12 miles) north of Tadoussac, and offers tours in summer that start at the bay of Tadoussac just beyond Hôtel Tadoussac's lawn. A 3-hour trip costs C$53 adults, C$40 children 15 and under.

Although the St. Lawrence is, of course, a river, it's tidal and often called the "sea" (you'll see references to "sea kayaking"). The waters here are in a marine park, which was designated as a conservation area to protect the whales and their habitat.

Centre d'Interprétation des Mammifères Marins (CIMM) ☺ Start here to learn why Tadoussac is such a paradise for whale researchers. At this interpretation center directly on the Saguenay River's edge, there's a small exhibition room, an exhilarating 15-minute video about the whales who visit each summer, and a bilingual expert who answers questions and explains what the scientific research team who works upstairs—as many as 50 people in summer—are up to. There's also a shop with books, cuddly toys, and clothing. There is also a new exhibit called "Jardin du GREMM" which showcases five actual-size beluga sculptures, as well as an addition to their collection of jaws from a blue whale.

108 rue de la Cale Sèche (on the waterfront), Tadoussac. ☎ **418/235-4701.** www.gremm.org. Admission C$12 adults, C$11 seniors, children 17 and under free. Daily summer 9am–8pm; spring and fall noon–5pm. Closed in winter.

WHERE TO STAY

Hôtel Tadoussac Established in 1864 and now in a building from 1942, this handsome old-time hotel is king of the hill that is Tadoussac. Public spaces and bedrooms have a shambling, country-cottage appearance—there's zero pretense of luxury. Pay the premium for a river-view room. Rooms are simple and recently refreshed with new paint, linens and curtains, and polished floors, with overhead fans and no air-conditioning. Meals are resort-pricey (C$38 for buffet dinner, for instance) and are okay, though short of impressive. A large front lawn overlooks the river, which is wide enough here to feel like an ocean. If you're planning to whale-watch or kayak, consider a package deal.

165 rue Bord de l'Eau, Tadoussac, PQ G0T 2A0. www.hoteltadoussac.com. ☎ **800/561-0718** or 418/235-4421. Fax 418/235-4607. 149 units. C$155–C$249 double. Packages available. AE, DC, MC, V. Free parking. Closed mid-Oct to early May. **Amenities:** 3 restaurants when busy (otherwise, 2 open); bar; babysitting; children's programs (in peak months); pool (heated, outdoor); spa; Wi-Fi (in lobby, free). *In room:* Overhead fan, TV, hair dryer.

WHERE TO EAT

Café Bohème Just a few steps from Hôtel Tadoussac is a cheery 1892 house with a white picket fence and mansard roof. It's a dependable stop for healthy food, homemade ice cream (*mmm* chocolate-cardamom), and groovy world music.

239 rue des Pionniers, Tadoussac. ☎ **418/235-1180.** Main courses C$7.50–C$15; table d'hôte C$15–C$22. MC, V. Mid-May to mid-Oct daily 8am–10pm.

PLANNING YOUR TRIP TO MONTRÉAL & QUÉBEC CITY

20

Ţhe province of Québec is immense: It's physically the largest province in the second-largest country in the world (after Russia); covers an area more than three times the size of France; and stretches from the northern borders of New York, Vermont, and New Hampshire up almost to the Arctic Circle.

That said, most of the region's population lives in the stretch just immediately north of the U.S. border. Its major cities and towns, including Montréal and Québec City, are in this band of land, with the greater Montréal metropolitan area home to nearly half of the province's population. Québec City lies just 263km (163 miles) northeast of Montréal, commanding a stunning location on the rim of a promontory overlooking the St. Lawrence River, which is at its narrowest here. Most of the province's developed resort and scenic areas lie within a 3-hour drive of either city.

GETTING THERE

Served by highways, transcontinental trains and buses, and several airports, Montréal and Québec City are easily accessible from within Canada, the U.S., or overseas.

For information on navigating each city once you've arrived, see the "Getting There & Getting Around" sections in chapters 4 and 12.

By Plane

Most of the world's major airlines fly into the **Aéroport International Pierre-Elliott-Trudeau de Montréal** (airport code YUL; ℂ **800/465-1213** or 514/394-7377; www.admtl.com), more commonly known as Montréal-Trudeau Airport. It used to be called Montréal-Dorval, which you'll find on older maps.

In Québec City, the teeny **Jean Lesage International Airport** (airport code YQB; ℂ **418/640-2600;** www.aeroportdequebec.com) is served by a number of major airlines. Most air traffic comes by way of Montréal, although there are some direct flights from Canadian and U.S. cities, including Toronto; Ottawa; Chicago; Washington, D.C.; Philadelphia; New York; and Detroit. Some direct flights are seasonal only.

Tip: Save time and hassle by arranging your flights so that your Customs entry takes place at your final Canadian destination. For instance, if you are flying from the U.S. and have to make one or more stops en route to Canada, make the transfer in the U.S. Otherwise, when you land in Canada you'll have to collect your bags, pass through Customs, and then check your bags again before continuing on to your final destination.

To find out which airlines travel to Québec City, please see "Airline Websites," p. 362.

PREVIOUS PAGE: **Roads are closed to traffic in June during Montréal's Tour de L'Île bike event.**

GETTING INTO TOWN FROM THE AIRPORT

Montréal-Trudeau is served by **Express Bus 747,** which debuted in March 2010. It operates 24 hours a day, 7 days a week, and runs between the airport and the Berri-UQAM Métro station (the city's main bus terminal). It has about half a dozen designated stops along boulevard René-Lévesque. A trip takes about 35 minutes, and buses leave every 20 to 30 minutes. One-way tickets are sold for C$8 at the currency exchange (ICE) location on the airport's international arrivals level, and downtown at the Berri-UQAM station and the Infotourist Centre, 1255 rue Peel (℃ **877/266-5687** or 514/873-2015; Métro: Peel). Details are at www.stm.info/info/747.htm. Hotels that offer shuttles are listed on the airport's website under "Access and Parking."

A taxi trip to downtown Montréal costs a flat fare of C$38, plus tip. Call ℃ **514/394-7377** for more information.

From Québec City's airport, a taxi to downtown is a fixed-rate C$33. There is a public bus, no. 78, but it runs only to the Les Saules bus terminal, at the corner of boulevard Massona and rue Michelet, which is well outside the tourist area. You'll need to transfer from there. The bus runs Monday through Friday and costs C$2.60, exact change only. Ask at the airport for the best route; you can also call ℃ **418/627-2511** or visit www.rtcquebec.ca.

RENTING A CAR ON ARRIVAL

Terms, cars, and prices for car rentals are similar to those in the rest of North America and Europe, and all the major companies operate in Québec. Basic rates are about the same from company to company, although a little comparison shopping can unearth modest savings. A charge is usually levied when you return a car in a location other than the one in which it was rented.

Québec is the first Canadian province to mandate that residents have radial snow tires on their cars in winter. The law, which went into effect in late 2008, runs from mid-December until March 15. Rental-car agencies are required to provide snow tires on car rentals during that period, and many charge an extra, nonnegotiable fee.

The minimum driving age is 16 in Québec, but some car-rental companies will not rent to people under 25. Others charge higher rates for drivers under the age of 21. Renters under 25 may be asked for a major credit card in the same name as their driver's license.

By Bus

Montréal's central bus station, called **Station Centrale d'Autobus** (℃ **514/842-2281**), is at 505 boul. de Maisonneuve est. It has a restaurant and an information booth. Beneath the terminal is **Berri-UQAM Station,** the junction of several Métro lines. (UQAM—pronounced "*Oo*-kahm"—stands for Université de Québec à Montréal.) Alternatively, **taxis** usually line up outside the terminal building.

Québec City's bus terminal, at 320 rue Abraham-Martin (℃ **418/525-3000**), is just beside the train station. As from the train station, it's an uphill climb or short cab ride to Upper Town or other parts of Lower Town.

By Car

All international drivers must carry a **valid driver's license** from their country of residence. A U.S. license is sufficient as long as you are a visitor and actually are a U.S. resident. A U.K. license is sufficient, as well. If the driver's license is in a language other than French or English, an additional **International Driver's Permit** is required.

From Toronto to Montréal, the drive is about 5 hours. Most of your route is along the 401 highway (Macdonald-Cartier Hwy.), which you'll take until you reach "the 20" (Autoroute du Souvenir) at the Ontario-Québec border. From there it's about an hour to downtown Montréal.

Driving north to Montréal from the U.S., the entire journey is on expressways. From New York City, all but about the last 64km (40 miles) of the 603km (375-mile) trip are within New York state on Interstate 87. I-87 links up with Canada's Autoroute 15 at the border, which goes straight to Montréal.

From Boston, I-93 goes up through New Hampshire's White Mountains and merges into I-91 to cross the tip of Vermont. At the border, I-91 becomes Autoroute 55. Signs lead to Autoroute 10 west, which goes into Montréal. Boston to Montréal is 518km (322 miles).

Québec City is 867km (539 miles) from New York City and 644km (400 miles) from Boston. From New York, follow the directions to Montréal, and then pick up Autoroute 20 to Québec City. From Boston, follow the directions to Montréal, but at Autoroute 10, go east instead of west to stay on Autoroute 55. Get on Autoroute 20 to Québec City and follow signs for the Pont Pierre-Laporte, the major bridge into the city. Turn right onto Boulevard Wilfrid-Laurier (Rte. 175) shortly after crossing the bridge. It changes names first to Boulevard Laurier and then to Grande-Allée, a main boulevard that leads directly into the central Parliament Hill area and the Old City. Once the street passes through the ancient walls that ring the Old City, it becomes rue St-Louis, which leads straight to the famed Château Frontenac on the cliff above the St. Lawrence River.

Another appealing option when you're approaching Québec City from the south is to follow Route 132 along the river's southern side to the town of Lévis. A car ferry there, **Traverse Québec-Lévis** (© **877/787-7483** or 418/643-2019; www.traversiers.gouv.qc.ca), provides a 10-minute ride across the river and a dramatic way to see the city, especially for the first time. Though the schedule varies substantially through the year, the ferry leaves at least every hour from 6am to 2am. One-way costs C$6.75 for the car and driver, C$3 for each additional adult, and C$12 for a car with up to six passengers.

When driving between Québec City from Montréal, there are two options: Autoroute 40, which runs along the St. Lawrence's north shore, and Autoroute 20, on the south side (although not hugging the water at all). The trip takes about 3 hours.

In Canada, highway distances and speed limits are given in kilometers (km). The speed limit on the autoroutes is 100kmph (62 mph). There's a stiff penalty for neglecting to wear your seatbelt, and all passengers must be buckled up.

Note on radar detectors: Radar detectors are prohibited in the province of Québec. They can be confiscated, even if they're not being used.

It is illegal to turn right on a red light on the island of Montréal. It is permitted in the rest of Québec and Canada.

Cellphone use is restricted to hands-free only while driving.

In 2008, Québec became the first province to mandate that residents have **radial snow tires** on their cars in winter. Visitors and their cars are exempt, but the law does give an indication of how seriously rough the winter driving can be. Consider using snow tires when traveling in the region from December through March. Members of the American Automobile Association (AAA) are covered by

Fill Up Before Crossing Over

Gasoline in Canada is expensive by American standards. Gas is sold by the liter, and 3.78 liters equals 1 gallon. Recent prices of about C$1.40 per liter are equivalent to about US$4.35 per gallon. If you're driving from the U.S., fill up before crossing the border.

the Canadian Automobile Association (CAA) while driving in Canada. See "Fast Facts: Montréal & Québec City," below.

By Train

If you're coming from Toronto, you'll board the train at Union Station, which is downtown and accessible by subway. Montréal is a major terminus on Canada's **VIA Rail** network (✆ **888/842-7245** or 514/989-2626; www.viarail.ca). Its station, **Gare Centrale,** at 895 rue de la Gauchetière ouest (✆ **514/989-2626**), is centrally located downtown. The station is connected to the Métro subway system at **Bonaventure Station.** (Gare Windsor, which you might see on some maps, is the city's former train station. It's a castlelike building now used for offices.)

Québec City's train station, **Gare du Palais,** is in Lower Town at 450 rue de la Gare-du-Palais. Many of the hotels listed in this book are up an incline from the station, so a short cab ride might be necessary.

VIA Rail trains are comfortable—all major routes have Wi-Fi, and some trains are equipped with dining cars and sleeping cars.

The U.S. train system, **Amtrak** (✆ **800/872-7245;** www.amtrak.com), has one train per day to Montréal from New York that makes intermediate stops. Called the *Adirondack,* it's very slow, but its scenic route passes along the Hudson River's eastern shore and west of Lake Champlain. It takes 11 hours from New York if all goes well, although delays aren't unusual.

The train ride between Montréal and Québec City takes about 3 hours.

By Boat

Both Montréal and Québec City are stops for cruise ships that travel along the St. Lawrence River (in French, Fleuve Saint-Laurent). The Port of Montréal, where ships dock, is part of the lively Vieux-Port neighborhood and walking distance from restaurants and shops.

Similarly, in Québec City, ships also dock in a neighborhood called Vieux-Port. As in Montréal, there is an abundance of restaurants and shops in walking distance.

[FastFACTS] MONTRÉAL & QUÉBEC CITY

American Automobile Association (AAA)   Members of **AAA** are covered by the **Canadian Automobile Association (CAA)** while traveling in Canada. Bring your membership card and proof of insurance. The 24-hour hot line for emergency road service is ✆ **800/222-4357.** The AAA card also provides discounts at a wide variety of hotels and restaurants in the province of Québec. Visit **www.caaquebec.com** for more information.

Area Codes   The Montréal area codes are **514** and **438,** and the Québec City code is **418.** Outside of Montréal, the area code for the southern Laurentides is **450,** and the northern Laurentides (from Val-David up) uses **819.** The Cantons de l'Est are the same: **450** or **819,** depending on how close you are to Montréal. In August 2010, new telephone numbers in the **450** region were given the area code **579.** Outside Québec City, the area code for Ile d'Orléans and north into Charlevoix is **418,** the same as in the city. You always need to dial the three-digit area code, in addition to the seven-digit number. Numbers that begin with **800, 866, 877, 888,** or **855** are free to call from both Canada and the U.S.

Business Hours   Most stores in the province are open from 9 or 10am until 5 or 6pm Monday through Wednesday, 9 or 10am to 9pm on Thursday and Friday, 9 or 10am to 5 or 6pm on Saturday, and Sunday from noon to 5pm. **Banks** are usually open Monday through Friday from 8 or 9am to 4pm and are closed for the entire weekend. More and more, however, banks in Montréal are open on Saturdays; since February 2011 TD Canada Trust has 16 branches open on Sundays. Bankers' hours in Québec City are shorter, from 10am to 3pm. **Post office** hours vary wildly by location, but are generally open from 9:30am to 5:30pm on weekdays. Some are open 9:30am to 5pm on Saturdays, and most are closed on Sundays. While many **restaurants** are open all day between meals, some shut down between lunch and dinner. Most restaurants serve until 9:30 or 10pm. **Bars** normally stay open until 3am, while some "after-hours" clubs open when other clubs are closing and keep people dancing until noon.

Car Rental   See "Getting There: Renting a Car on Arrival," earlier in this chapter.

Cellphones   See "Mobile Phones," later in this section.

Crime   See "Safety," later in this section.

Customs   International visitors can expect at least a probing question or two at the border or airport. Normal baggage and personal possessions should be no problem, but plants, animals, and weapons are among the items that may be prohibited or require additional documents before they're allowed in. For specific information about Canadian rules, check with the **Canada Border Services Agency** (✆ **506/636-5064** from outside the country or 800/461-9999 within Canada; www.cbsa-asfc.gc.ca). Search for "bsf5082" to get a full list of visitor information.

Tobacco and alcoholic beverages face strict import restrictions: Individuals 18 years or older are allowed to bring in 200 cigarettes, 50 cigars, or 200 grams of tobacco; and only one of the following amounts of alcohol: 1.14 liters of liquor, 1.5 liters of wine, or 24 cans or bottles of beer. Additional amounts face hefty taxes. Possession of a car radar detector is prohibited, whether or not it is connected. Police officers can confiscate it and fines may run as high as C$1,000. A car driven into Canada can stay for the duration allowed the visitor, which is up to 6 months unless the visitor has arranged permission for a longer stay. Visitors can temporarily bring recreational vehicles, such as snowmobiles, boats, and trailers, as well as outboard motors, for personal use. If you do not declare goods or falsely declare them, they can be seized *along with the vehicle in which you brought them.*

For information on what you're allowed to bring home, contact one of the following agencies:

U.S. Citizens: U.S. Customs & Border Protection (CBP), 1300 Pennsylvania Ave., NW, Washington, DC 20229 (✆ **877/287-8667;** www.cbp.gov).

U.K. Citizens: HM Revenue & Customs, Crownhill Court, Tailyour Road, Plymouth, PL6 5BZ (✆ **0845/010-9000,** or 020/8929-0152 from outside the U.K.; www.hmrc.gov.uk).

Australian Citizens: Australian Customs Service, Customs House, 5 Constitution Avenue, Canberra City, ACT 2601 (✆ **1300/363-263,** or 612/6275-6666 from outside Australia; www.customs.gov.au).

New Zealand Citizens: New Zealand Customs, the Customhouse, 17–21 Whitmore St., Box 2218, Wellington, 6140 (☏ **0800/428-786** or 04/473-6099; www.customs.govt.nz). If you're traveling with expensive items, such as laptops or musical equipment, consider registering them before you leave your country to avoid challenges at the border on your return.

Disabled Travelers   Québec regulations regarding wheelchair accessibility are similar to those in the U.S. and the rest of Canada, including requirements for curb cuts, entrance ramps, designated parking spaces, and specially equipped bathrooms. While the more modern parts of the cities are fully wheelchair accessible, access to the restaurants and inns housed in 18th- and 19th-century buildings, especially in Québec City, is often difficult or impossible.

Advice is provided in the French-language guide *Le Québec Accessible,* which lists more than 1,000 hotels, restaurants, theaters, and museums. It costs C$20 and is available from **Kéroul** (☏ **514/252-3104;** www.keroul.qc.ca). Kéroul also publishes an English-language brochure called *The Accessible Road,* which has information about everything from how to get a handicapped parking sticker to which top attractions are most accessible. It's available as a free download at www.keroul.qc.ca. Québec's provincial tourism organization maintains an online, **searchable database of accessible establishments** and tourist sites at www.bonjourquebec.com. Also look for the **Tourist and Leisure Companion Sticker (T.L.C.S.)** at tourist sites. It designates that companions of travelers with disabilities can enter for free. A list of participating enterprises is online at www.vatl-tlcs.org.

Doctors   See "Hospitals," later in this section.

Drinking Laws   The legal drinking age in the province is 18. All hard liquor and spirits in Québec are sold through official government stores operated by the Québec Société des Alcools (look for maroon signs with the acronym SAQ). Wine and beer are available in grocery stores and convenience stores, called *dépanneurs.* Bars can pour drinks as late as 3am, but often stay open later.

Penalties for drunk driving in Canada are heavy. Provisions instituted in 2008 include higher mandatory penalties, such as a minimum fine of C$1,000 and 1 year driving prohibition for a convicted first offense, and for a second offense, a minimum of 14 days in jail and 2 to 5 years probation. Drivers caught under the influence face a maximum life sentence if they cause death, and a maximum 10-year sentence and possible lifetime ban on driving if they cause bodily harm. Learn more at **www.saaq.gouv.qc.ca/en**.

Driving Rules   See "Getting There," earlier in this chapter.

Electricity   Like the U.S., Canada uses 110 to 120 volts AC (60 cycles), compared to the 220 to 240 volts AC (50 cycles) used in most of Europe, Australia, and New Zealand. If your small appliances use 220 to 240 volts, you'll need a 110-volt transformer and a plug adapter with two flat parallel pins to operate them in Canada. They can be difficult to find in Canada, so bring one with you.

Embassies & Consulates   Embassies are located in Ottawa, Canada's capital. There are consulate offices throughout the Canadian provinces, including Québec. The U.S. Embassy information line ☏ **888/840-0032** costs C$1.59 per minute. The U.S. has a consulate in Montréal at 1155 rue St-Alexandre (☏ **514/398-9695**), where nonemergency American citizen services are provided by appointment only. There is also a U.S. consulate in Québec City, on Jardin des Gouverneurs at 2 rue de la Terrasse-Dufferin (☏ **418/692-2095**).

The U.K. consulate in Montréal is at 1000 rue de la Gauchetière ouest, Ste. 4200 (☏ **514/866-5863**). The U.K. consulate in Québec City is in the St-Amable Complex, 1150 Claire-Fontaine, Ste. 700 (☏ **418/521-3000**).

For contact information for other embassies and consulates, search for "foreign representatives in Canada" at www.international.gc.ca.

Emergencies Dial ✆ **911** for police, firefighters, or an ambulance.

Family Travel Montréal and Québec City offer an abundance of family-oriented activities. Many of them are outdoors, even in winter. Watersports, river cruises, fort climbing, and fireworks displays are among summer's many attractions, with dog sledding and skiing the top choices in snowy months. Québec City's walls and fortifications are fodder for imagining the days of knights and princesses. In both cities, many museums make special efforts to address children's interests and enthusiasms.

For accommodations, restaurants, and attractions that are particularly kid-friendly, look for the "Kids" icon throughout this guide. Also, see "Especially for Kids" in chapter 7 on p. 130 and in chapter 15 on p. 288. Children who speak French or are learning French might like a guidebook of their own. The fun **Mon Premier Guide de Voyage au Québec** (Ulysse) has 96 pages of photos, miniessays, and activities for kids age 6 to 12. You can find it in provincial bookshops.

For a list of more family-friendly travel resources, visit www.frommers.com/planning.

Gasoline Gasoline in Canada is sold by the liter; 3.78 liters equals 1 gallon. At press time, a liter cost approximately C$1.40, the equivalent of about US$4.35 per gallon.

Health Canada has a state-run health system, and Québec hospitals are modern and decently equipped, with well-trained staffs. You are unlikely to get sick from Canada's food or water.

In general, Canadians who reside outside the province of Québec are covered by an interprovincial agreement, which allows them to present their own province's health card (e.g., OHIP card in Ontario) and have their health services covered by direct billing. In some cases, however, services must be paid for upfront and patients must seek reimbursement from their home province.

Medical treatment in Canada isn't free for foreigners, and doctors and hospitals will make you pay at the time of service. See "Insurance" below for suggestions about medical insurance.

Familiar over-the-counter medicines are widely available in Canada. If there is a possibility that you will run out of prescribed medicines during your visit, take along a prescription from your doctor. Have the generic name of prescription medicines in case a local pharmacist is unfamiliar with the brand name. Pack medications in your carry-on luggage and have them in their original containers with pharmacy labels—otherwise, they may not make it through airport security. If you're entering Canada with syringes used for medical reasons, bring a medical certificate that shows they are for medical use and be sure to declare them to Canadian Customs officials.

If you suffer from a chronic illness, consult your doctor before departure.

Hospitals In Montréal, hospitals with emergency rooms include **Hôpital Général de Montréal,** 1650 rue Cedar (✆ **514/934-1934**), and **Hôpital Royal Victoria,** 687 av. des Pins ouest (✆ **514/934-1934**). **Hôpital de Montréal pour Enfants,** 2300 rue Tupper (✆ **514/412-4400**), is a children's hospital. All three are associated with McGill University.

In Québec City, go to the **Centre Hospitalier Hôtel-Dieu de Québec,** 11 Côte du Palais (✆ **418/525-4444**). The hospital is in Upper Town inside the city walls.

Insurance Even though Canada is just a short drive or flight away for many Americans, U.S. health plans (including Medicare and Medicaid) do not provide coverage here, and the ones that do often require you to pay for services upfront and reimburse you only after you return home. As a safety net, you may want to buy travel medical insurance. Travelers from the U.K. should carry their European Health Insurance Card (EHIC), which replaced the E111 form as proof of entitlement to free/reduced cost medical treatment abroad (☏ **0845/606-2030;** www.ehic.org.uk). Note, however, that the EHIC covers only "necessary medical treatment," and for repatriation costs, lost money, baggage, or cancellation, travel insurance from a reputable company should always be sought (www.travelinsuranceweb.com).

For information on traveler's insurance, trip cancellation insurance, and medical insurance while traveling, please visit **www.frommers.com/planning**.

Internet & Wi-Fi   Most hotels and *auberges,* as well as many cafes, now offer Wi-Fi. Some hotels still offer high-speed Internet access through cable connections. Except at the larger hotels, Wi-Fi usually is free. For travelers in Montréal, Ile Sans Fil (www.ilesansfil.org) lists free Wi-Fi spots in the city. The listing is available as a free iPhone app, too. For travelers in Québec City, ZAP Québec (www.zapquebec.org) lists free Wi-Fi spots.

Most hotels maintain business centers with computers for use by guests or outsiders, or at least have one computer available for guest use. Again, except at the larger hotels, this access often is free. Cybercafes are not common. In Vieux-Montréal, Café-Bistro Van Houtte, 165 rue St-Paul ouest (☏ **514/288-9387**), has a bank of computers and prepaid Internet access cards for C$5 per hour. In Québec City, the Centre Info-touriste de Québec, 12 rue Ste-Anne (☏ **877/266-5687;** www.bonjourquebec.com), has a bank of computers for visitor use. The cost is C$2.50 for 20 minutes.

Language   Canada is officially bilingual, but the province of Québec has laws that make French mandatory in signage. About 65% of Montréal's population has French as its first language (and about 95% of Québec City's population does). An estimated four out of five Francophones (French speakers) speak at least some English. Hotel desk staff, sales clerks, and telephone operators nearly always greet people initially in French, but usually switch to English quickly, if necessary. Outside of Montréal, visitors are more likely to encounter residents who don't speak English. If smiles and sign language don't work, look around for a young person—most of them study English in school.

Legal Aid   If you are arrested, your country's embassy or consulate can provide the names of lawyers who speak English. See "Embassies & Consulates" above for more information.

LGBT Travelers   The province of Québec is a destination for international gay travelers. Gay life here is generally open and accepted (gay marriage is legal throughout the province), and gay travelers are heavily marketed to. Travelers will find the rainbow flag prominently displayed on the doors and websites of many hotels and restaurants in all the city's neighborhoods.

The **Tourisme Montréal** website, www.tourisme-montreal.org, has a "Gay and Lesbian" link under "Tourist" that lists gay-friendly accommodations, events, websites for queer meet-ups, and more. Of several local queer publications, the most thorough is *Fugues* (www.fugues.com), which lists events, as well as gay-friendly lodgings, clubs, saunas, and other resources. Free copies are available at tourist offices and in racks around the city. **Gay Line** (☏ **888/505-1010** or 514/866-5090; www.gayline.qc.ca) is a help line offering advice on over 550 accommodations, events, and services. In Montréal, many gay and lesbian travelers head straight to **the Village** (also known as "the Gay Village"), a neighborhood east of downtown located primarily along rue Ste-Catherine est between rue St-Hubert and rue Papineau. Here, there are antiques shops, bars, B&Bs, and clubs, clubs, clubs (see p. 193 in "Montréal After Dark" for a listing). The Beaudry Métro station is at the heart of the neighborhood and is marked by the rainbow flag. As the Tourisme Montréal website says, "Rainbow columns on a subway station entrance? I've got a feeling we're not in Kansas anymore!" The Village is action central on any night, but it especially picks up during the weeklong celebration of sexual diversity known as **Divers/Cité** (www.diverscite.org) in late July and early August and the **Black & Blue Festival** (www.bbcm.org), an October event that's one of the world's largest circuit parties, with a week of entertainment and club dancing. Both events are listed in the calendar on p. 28. In 2006, Montréal added a pink feather to its cap by hosting the first World Outgames, attracting more than 16,000 athletes. When you're visiting the neighborhood, stop in at the **Village Tourism Information Centre** at 1307 rue Ste-Catherine est (☏ **888/595-8110** or 514/522-1885), open June to August from noon to 6pm (days vary; call in advance). There's information about everything from wine bars to yoga classes. It's operated by the **Québec Gay Chamber of Commerce** (www.ccgq.ca).

In Québec City, the community is much smaller. Geographically, it's centered in Upper Town just outside the city walls, on rue St-Jean and the parallel rue d'Aiguillon, starting from where they cross rue St-Augustin and heading west. **Le Drague Cabaret Club** at 815 rue St-Augustin (☏ **418/649-7212;** www.ledrague.com), or "the Drag," is a central gathering place with a cabaret and two dance rooms (p. 322).

In early September, Québec City hosts a 3-day gay-pride fest, **Fête Arc-en-Ciel** (www. glbtquebec.org), which attracts thousands of people to Place d'Youville.

Mail   All mail sent through **Canada Post** (☏ **866/607-6301** or 416/979-8822; www. canadapost.ca) must bear Canadian stamps. That might seem painfully obvious, but apparently a large number of U.S. visitors use U.S. stamps. A letter or postcard to the U.S. costs C$1.03. A letter or postcard to anywhere else outside of Canada costs C$1.75. A letter to a Canadian address costs C59¢. **FedEx** (☏ **800/463-3339;** www. fedex.com/ca) offers service from Canada and lists locations at its website.

Medical Requirements   Also see "Health." Unless you're arriving from an area known to be suffering from an epidemic (particularly cholera or yellow fever), inoculations or vaccinations are not required for entry into Canada.

Mobile Phones   Cellphone service is good in Québec cities and sometimes spotty in areas beyond city borders. Cellphone service is widely available throughout the regions mentioned in this book.

Visitors from the U.S. should be able to get roaming service that allows them to use their cellphones in Canada. Some wireless companies let customers adjust their plans to get cheaper rates while traveling. Sprint, for instance, has a "Canadian roaming" option for US$3 per month that reduces the per-minute rate. Ask your provider for options. Europeans and most Australians are on the GSM (Global System for Mobile Communications) network with removable plastic SIM cards in their phones. Call your wireless provider for information about traveling. You may be able to purchase pay-as-you-go SIM cards in Canada with local providers such as Rogers (www.rogers.com). American travelers may find that their SIM card is locked by their carrier, but consumers are legally allowed to unlock their phones, although it takes some ingenuity to do so. If you go this route, plan enough time to request an approval code from your carrier. Cellphone rentals are not common in Canada, so if you end up traveling without a phone or with a phone that doesn't get reception, **prepaid phone services** are a good option. With **OneSuite.com** (☏ **866/417-8483;** www.onesuite.com), for instance, you prepay an online account for as little as US$10. You can then dial a toll-free or local access number from a hotel phone, enter your PIN, and then dial the number you're calling. Calls from Canada to mainland U.S. cost just US2.5¢ to US3.5¢ per minute. Some hotels charge for local and even toll-free calls, so check before dialing.

Cheaper still are phone calls conducted over the Web. **Skype** (www.skype.com) allows you to make international calls from your laptop or a mobile app on your smartphone. Calls to people who also have the program on their computers are free. You can call people who don't have the service, although modest fees apply.

Money & Costs   Frommer's lists exact prices in the local currency. The currency conversions provided were correct at press time. However, rates fluctuate, so before departing consult a currency exchange website such as **www.oanda.com/currency/converter** to check up-to-the-minute rates.

One of the perks of a holiday in Montréal is that it's noticeably less expensive than other major world cities such as New York, London, and Tokyo.

ATMs *(guichet automatique)* are practically everywhere, in shopping centers, bars, variety stores, gas stations, etc. Bank machines don't typically charge user fees if that is your banking institution back home, but call ahead to make sure. Elsewhere, ATMs are notorious for charging extremely high flat rates to withdraw cash, often about C$5 even on a minimum withdrawal of C$20. Many institutions (and some taxis) now also accept payment by bank card, and credit card microchip usage with PIN instead of signing. Most machines only allow a four-digit PIN, so check with your bank beforehand should you have a five- or six-digit PIN.

Beware of hidden credit card fees while traveling. Check with your credit or debit card issuer to see what fees, if any, will be charged for overseas transactions. Check with your bank before departing to avoid any surprise charges on your statement.

For help with currency conversions, tip calculations, and more, download Frommer's convenient Travel Tools app for your mobile device. Go to www.frommers.com/go/mobile and click on the Travel Tools icon.

THE VALUE OF CANADIAN DOLLAR VS. OTHER POPULAR CURRENCIES

Can$	Aus$	Euro (€)	NZ$	UK£	US$
C$1	A$1.08	€ 0.75	NZ$1.33	£0.63	$1

Newspapers & Magazines   The *Globe and Mail* (www.theglobeandmail.com) is the national English-language paper. *La Presse* (www.cyberpresse.ca/actualites/regional/montreal) is the leading French-language newspaper. A sister publication, *Le Soleil* (www.cyberpresse.ca/le-soleil), is published in Québec City. Montréal's primary English-language newspaper is the *Montréal Gazette* (www.montrealgazette.com). The most extensive list of arts and entertainment happenings appears in print on Friday (the Sun paper, by the way, is web only). Visit www.montrealgazette.com/arts. Most large newsstands and shops in larger hotels carry the *New York Times, Wall Street Journal,* and *International Herald Tribune.*

Packing   Both Montréal and Québec City have four distinct seasons. It goes without saying to pack light, breathable fabrics in warmers months, and warm layers in colder ones. For more helpful information on packing for your trip, download our convenient Travel Tools app for your mobile device. Go to www.frommers.com/go/mobile and click on the Travel Tools icon.

WHAT THINGS COST IN MONTRÉAL & QUÉBEC CITY	C$
Taxi from the airport to downtown Montréal	38.00
Taxi from the airport to downtown Québec City	33.00
Double room, moderate	from 160.00
Double room, inexpensive	from 100.00
Three-course dinner for one without wine, moderate	20.00–25.00
Bottle of beer	2.00–4.00
Cup of coffee	1.00–2.00
1 liter of premium gas	1.42
Admission to most museums	10.00–17.00
Admission to most national parks	Free

Passports   See p. 361 for general information about passports, visas, and other documents that may be necessary for entrance into Canada.

For country-specific passport information, contact the following agencies:

For Residents of Australia   Contact the Australian **Passport Information Service** at ✆ **131-232** or visit www.passports.gov.au.

For Residents of Canada   Contact the central **Passport Office,** Department of Foreign Affairs and International Trade, Ottawa, ON K1A 0G3 (✆ **800/567-6868;** www.ppt.gc.ca).

For Residents of Ireland   Contact the **Passport Office,** Setanta Centre, Molesworth Street, Dublin 2 (✆ **01/671-1633;** www.foreignaffairs.gov.ie).

For Residents of New Zealand   Contact the **Passports Office,** Department of Internal Affairs, 47 Boulcott Street, Wellington, 6011 (✆ **0800/225-050** in New Zealand or 04/474-8100; www.passports.govt.nz).

For Residents of the United Kingdom   Visit your nearest passport office, major post office, or travel agency, or contact the **Identity and Passport Service (IPS),** 89 Eccleston Square, London, SW1V 1PN (✆ **0300/222-0000;** www.ips.gov.uk).

For Residents of the United States   To find your regional passport office, check the **U.S. State Department website** (http://travel.state.gov/passport) or call the **National Passport Information Center** (✆ **877/487-2778**) for automated information.

Petrol   Please see "Gasoline," earlier in this chapter.

Police   Dial ✆ **911** for police, firefighters, or an ambulance.

Safety   Montréal and Québec City are extremely safe cities, and far safer than their U.S. or European counterparts of similar size. Montréal in 2008, for instance, had 29 homicides for the entire year, the lowest number since police began collecting statistics. Street gang wars, which plague many cities, are nearly nonexistent here.

Still, common sense insists that visitors stay alert and observe the usual urban precautions. It's best to stay out of parks at night and to take a taxi when returning from a late dinner or nightclub.

PLANNING YOUR TRIP

Safety

Québec is one of Canada's more liberal provinces. Mass demonstrations are rare and political violence is unusual. Tolerance of others is a Canadian characteristic, and it's highly unlikely that visitors of ethnic, religious, or racial minorities will encounter even mild forms of discrimination. That applies to sexual orientation, as well, especially in Montréal, which has one of the largest and most visible gay communities in North America.

Senior Travel   Mention the fact that you're a senior citizen when you make your travel reservations. Many Québec hotels offer discounts for older travelers. Throughout the province, theaters, museums, and other attractions offer reduced admission to people as young as 60.

Many reliable agencies and organizations target the 50-plus market. **Elderhostel** (© **800/454-5768;** www.elderhostel.org) arranges worldwide study programs for those aged 55 and older, and offers a variety of trips to Québec City and Montréal. The best-selling paperback *Unbelievably Good Deals and Great Adventures That You Absolutely Can't Get Unless You're Over 50* (McGraw-Hill), by Joann Rattner Heilman, includes information about Canadian travel.

Smoking   Smoking was banned in the province's bars, restaurants, clubs, casinos, and some other public spaces in 2006. Most small inns and many larger hotels have become entirely smoke-free over the past few years as well. Check before you book if you're looking for a room in which you can smoke.

Taxes   Most goods and services in Canada are taxed 5% by the federal government (the GST/TPS) and 8.5% by the province of Québec (the TVQ). Confusingly—and, once you figure it out, maddeningly—the provincial tax comes out to 8.92% because the federal tax is added to the cost of the good or service *before* the provincial tax is calculated. In Montréal, hotel bills have an additional 3.5% accommodations tax. Nonresident visitors used to be able to apply for a tax rebate, but that practice was eliminated in 2007. A Foreign Convention and Tour Incentive Program provides limited rebates on the GST for services used during foreign conventions held in Canada, for nonresident exhibitors, and for the short-term accommodations portion of tour packages for nonresident individuals and tour operators. Details are at **www.cra-arc.gc.ca/visitors**.

Telephones   The Canadian telephone system, operated by Bell Canada, closely resembles the U.S. model. All **operators speak English and French,** and they respond in the appropriate language as soon as callers speak to them. In Canada, dial © **0** to reach an operator. When making a **local call** within the province of Québec, you must dial the area code before the seven-digit number.

Phone numbers that begin with 800, 888, 877, and 866 are **toll-free.** That means they're free to call within Canada and from the U.S. You need to dial 1 first. Remember that both local and long-distance calls usually cost more from hotels—sometimes a lot more, so check before dialing. Some hotels charge for all calls, including toll-free ones.

To call the province of Québec from the U.S.: Simply dial 1, then the three-digit area code, then the seven-digit number. *Example:* To call the Infotouriste Centre in Montréal, dial 1-514-873-2015.

To call Québec from the U.K./Ireland/Australia/New Zealand: Dial the international access code 00 (from Australia, 0011), then the Canadian country code 1, then the area code, and then the seven-digit number. *Example:* To call the Infotouriste Centre in Montréal, dial 00-1-514-873-2015.

St. Thomas Public Library

Monday - Friday: 9am-8:30pm
Saturday: 9am-5pm
www.stthomaspubliclibrary.ca

(519) 631-6050

*Make Sparks at STPL - Join the monthly
donor society!*

www.stthomaspubliclibrary.ca/donate

Date Due Receipt

Today's date: July 13, 2022

Items checked out to: 6036

TITLE   Amsterdam.

BARCODE   36278009413592

DUE DATE   **Aug   03 2022**

TITLE   Frommer's Montreal and

BARCODE   36278006900302

DUE DATE   **Aug   03 2022**

To call the U.S. from Québec: Simply dial 1, then the three-digit area code and seven-digit number. *Example:* To call the U.S. Passport Agency from the province of Québec, dial 1-202-647-0518.

To call the U.K./Ireland/Australia/New Zealand from Québec: Dial 011, then the country code (U.K. 44, Ireland 353, Australia 61, New Zealand 64), then the number.

A local call at a **pay phone** in the province of Québec costs C50¢. **Directory information** calls (dial ✆ **411**) are free of charge from pay phones.

For help with time translations, and more, download our convenient Travel Tools app for your mobile device. Go to www.frommers.com/go/mobile and click on the Travel Tools icon.

Time   Montréal and Québec City are in the Eastern Standard Time (EST) zone, that is, 5 hours behind Greenwich Mean Time (GMT). Canada has six primary time zones: For example, when it's 9am in Vancouver, British Columbia (Pacific Time), it's 10am in Calgary, Alberta (Mountain Time), 11am in Winnipeg, Manitoba (Central Time), noon in Montréal and Québec City, Québec (Eastern Time), 1pm in Halifax, Nova Scotia (Atlantic Time), 1:30pm in St. John's, Newfoundland (Newfoundland Time), 5pm in London, U.K. (GMT), and 2am the next day in Sydney, Australia.

Daylight saving time (summer time) is in effect from the second Sunday in March to the first Sunday in November. Daylight saving time moves the clock 1 hour ahead of standard time.

For help with time translations, and more, download our convenient Travel Tools app for your mobile device. Go to www.frommers.com/go/mobile and click on the Travel Tools icon.

Tipping   Tipping practices in the province are similar to those in large Western cities. In hotels, tip bellhops C$1 per bag and tip the chamber staff C$3 to C$5 per day, which seems to go a long way if you enjoy getting extra chocolates or candies on your pillow. Tip the doorman or concierge a few dollars only if he or she has provided you with some specific service (for example, calling a cab for you or obtaining difficult-to-get theater tickets). Tip the valet-parking attendant C$2 to C$3 every time you get your car. In restaurants, bars, and nightclubs, tip waiters 15% to 20% of the check, tip checkroom attendants C$1 per garment, and tip valet-parking attendants C$1 per vehicle. Other service personnel: Tip taxi drivers 15% of the fare, tip skycaps at airports C$1 per bag, and tip hairdressers, barbers, and estheticans 15% to 20%.

For help with tip calculations, currency conversions, and more, download our convenient Travel Tools app for your mobile device. Go to www.frommers.com/go/mobile and click on the Travel Tools icon.

Toilets   You won't find public toilets on the streets in Montréal or Québec City, but they can be found in tourist offices, museums, railway and bus stations, service stations, and large shopping complexes. Restaurants and bars in heavily visited areas often reserve their restrooms for patrons.

Visas   For citizens of many countries, including the U.S., U.K., Ireland, Australia, and New Zealand, only a passport is required to visit Canada for up to 90 days; no visas or proof of vaccinations are necessary. For the most up-to-date list of visitor visa exemptions, visit **Citizenship and Immigration Canada** at **www.cic.gc.ca**.

Visitor Information   The terrific website **www.tourisme-montreal.org** offers a broad range of information for Montréal visitors, while **www.quebecregion.com** serves Québec City travelers. The equally good **www.bonjourquebec.com** is run by the province of Québec's tourism department and covers the entire province.

In Montréal, the main tourist center in downtown is the large **Infotouriste Centre,** 1255 rue Peel (✆ **877/266-5687** or 514/873-2015; Métro: Peel). It's open daily, and the bilingual staff can provide suggestions for accommodations, dining, car rentals, and attractions. In Vieux-Montréal, there's a small **Tourist Information Office** at 174 rue Notre-Dame est, at the corner of Place Jacques-Cartier (Métro: Champ-de-Mars). It's open April to May 10am to 6pm daily, June to September 9am to 7pm, and October to mid-November 9am to 5pm; it's closed in winter, but open during Montréal High Lights Festival in February.

In Québec City, there's a tourist office in Upper Town, across from the Château Frontenac and directly on Place d'Armes. It's full French name is **Centre Infotouriste de Québec,** 12 rue Ste-Anne (✆ **877/266-5687;** www.bonjourquebec.com), and it's open daily from mid-June to mid-August 9am to 7pm, and from 9am to 5pm the rest of the year. It has brochures, a lodging reservation service, a currency-exchange office, and information about tours by foot, bus, or boat.

The travel blog **A Key in the Door** (www.akeyinthedoor.com) offers an insider's perspective on international travel and is written by Herbert Bailey Livesey, who authored *Frommer's Montréal & Québec City* for over a decade.

Water   Tap water is safe to drink. See "Health," earlier in this section.

Wi-Fi   See "Internet & Wi-Fi," earlier in this section.

Women Travelers   Montréal and Québec City are generally safe cities for female adults. Do exercise caution, however, especially when walking alone at night.

AIRLINE WEBSITES

Air Canada
www.aircanada.ca
www.aircanada.com

Air France
www.airfrance.com

American Airlines
www.aa.com

British Airways
www.british-airways.com
www.britishairways.com

Continental Airlines
www.continental.com

Delta Air Lines
www.delta.com

Lufthansa
www.lufthansa.com

Olympic Airlines
www.olympicairlines.com
www.olympicair.com

Porter Airlines
www.flyporter.com

Swiss Air
www.swiss.com

United Airlines
www.united.com

US Airways
www.usairways.com

WestJet
www.westjet.com

Index

See also Accommodations and Restaurant indexes, below.

General Index

A

AAA (American Automobile Association), 113, 352
Abbaye de Saint-Benoît-du-Lac, 232–233
Academic trips, 33
Accommodations. *See also* Accommodations Index
Baie-St-Paul, 341
best, 4–6
Knowlton and Lac Brome, 226–229
La Malbaie, 343–344
Magog, 233
Montréal, 62–79
best, 62–63
Centre-Ville/Downtown, 63–71
practical information, 78–79
Vieux-Montréal (Old Montréal), 72–77
Mont-Tremblant area, 215–219
North Hatley, 234–235
Orford, 230–231
Québec City, 246–261
Basse-Ville (Lower Town)/Vieux-Port, 254–256
best, 246–247
Haute-Ville (Upper Town), 248–253
just outside the city, 259–260
Parliament Hill (on or near Grande-Allée), 256–258
practical information, 261
prices, 246, 247
St-Roch, 258–259
Ste-Adèle, 208
Tadoussac, 347
Addresses, finding
Montréal, 51–52
Québec City, 243
Adventure and wellness trips, 33–34
Aime Com Moi (Montréal), 176
Airline websites, 362
Air travel, 349–350
Alt Hotel (Québec City), 318
Ambre (Montréal), 176
American Automobile Association (AAA), 113, 352
Amerindian Hochelaga Settlement, Site of the, 158
Amphi-Bus (Montréal), 137–138
Amtrak, 352

Anglican Cathedral of the Holy Trinity (Québec City), 301
Antiques
Montréal, 172
Québec City, 313
Antonopoulos Group, 74
Appetite for Books (Montréal), 174
Archambault (Québec City), 318
Area codes, 352–353
Argent Tonic (Montréal), 183
Armory (Québec City), 304
Art and architecture, 20–23
Artéfact Montréal (Montréal), 163
Arthur Quentin (Montréal), 182
Artisans du Meuble Québécois (Montréal), 173
Arts, crafts, and galleries
Montréal, 172–173
Québec City, 313–314
Atelier Entre-Peaux (Montréal), 172
Atelier La Pomme (Québec City), 315
Atrium Le 1000 (Montréal), 130
Atwater Market (Marché Atwater; Montréal), 106
Aurora Borealis (Québec City), 287
Autoroute des Laurentides (Autoroute 15), 204
Aventure Ecotourisme Québec, 33–34
Aventure Inukshuk (Ste-Catherine-de-la-Jacques-Cartier), 294
Aviatic Club (Québec City), 323

B

Bagg Street Shul (Montréal), 132–133
Baie Ste-Catherine, 345–347
Baie-St-Paul, 339–342
Baldwin Barmacie (Montréal), 197
Bal en Blanc Party Week (Montréal), 29
Banque de Montréal, 146
Barne's General Store (Knowlton), 226
Bars
Montréal, 195–199
Québec City, 323–324
Basilica and Shrine of Ste-Anne-de-Beaupré, 335
Basilique-Cathédrale Marie-Reine-du-Monde (Montréal), 121–122, 156
Basilique Cathédrale Notre-Dame de Québec (Québec City), 280
Basilique Notre-Dame
Montréal, 115–116, 147
Québec City, 300

Basse-Ville (Lower Town; Québec City), 239, 243
accommodations, 254–256
restaurants, 268–271
sights and attractions, 276–282, 286–287
Bath and body products
Montréal, 174
Québec City, 314
Battlefields Park (Québec City), 282, 291, 293, 297
Beaver Lake (Lac des Castors; Montréal), 114, 167
Bed-and-breakfasts
Montréal, 79
Québec City, 261
Bedo (Montréal), 162
Beebe Plain, 236
Beer, 27, 29–30
Bella Pella (Montréal), 174
Biking and mountain biking, 29
Baie-St-Paul, 340
Montréal, 59–60, 140–141
tours, 138
Mont Ste-Anne, 338
Mont-Tremblant, 213
Québec City, 292
Ste-Agathe-des-Monts, 209
St-Laurent, 330
tours, 33
Bilodeau (St-Pierre), 332–333
Bíly K** (Montréal), 197–198
Biodôme de Montréal, 119
BIXI system (Montréal), 32, 59, 129
Black & Blue Festival (Montréal), 31
Bleu comme le ciel (Montréal), 183
Bleu Lavende (Stanstead), 232, 236
Bleu Nuit (Montréal), 182
Boating (boat rentals). *See also* Canoeing; Kayaking
Lac Memphrémagog, 232
Montréal, 141–142
Boat tours and cruises
Lac Memphrémagog, 232
Lac Tremblant, 213
Montréal, 136–137
Québec City, 290
Ste-Agathe-des-Monts, 210
Bodybag by Jude (Montréal), 176
Bonsecours Market (Montréal), 124–125, 149–150
Books, recommended, 23–24
Books and comics, Montréal, 174–175
Bota Bota (Montréal), 122–123
Boudoir Lounge (Québec City), 322
Boulangerie La Vagabonde (Val-David), 209

Photo Credits